THE
WORKS OF
SCHOPENHAUER

ABRIDGED EDITION

Edited by Will Durant

With an
Introduction by
THOMAS MANN

FREDERICK UNGAR PUBLISHING CO.
NEW YORK

PRINTED IN THE UNITED STATES OF AMERICA

Library of Congress Catalog Card No. 61-13633

INTRODUCTION

BY THOMAS MANN

The pleasure we take in a metaphysical system, the gratification purveyed by the intellectual organization of the world into a closely reasoned, complete and balanced structure of thought, is always of a pre-eminently aesthetic kind. It flows from the same source as the satisfaction, the high and ever happy satisfaction we get from art, with its power to shape and order its material, to sort out life's manifold confusions so as to give us a clear and general view.

Truth and beauty must always be referred the one to the other. Each by itself, without the support given by the other, remains a very fluctuating value. Beauty which has not truth on its side and cannot have reference to it, does not live in it and through it, would be an empty chimaera — and "What is truth?" Our conceptions, created out of the phenomenal world, out of a highly conditioned point of view, are, as a critical and discriminating philosophy admits, applicable in an immanent, not in a transcendental sense — that is, they deal with knowledge vouchsafed to us in time, space and causality, and are conditioned by these, instead of being obtained by applying reason upon itself. The subject matter of our thinking, and indeed the judgments we build up on it, are inadequate as a means of grasping the essence of things in themselves, the true essence of the world and of life. Even the most convinced and convincing, the most deeply experienced definition of that which underlies the manifestation, does not avail to get at the root of things and draw it to the light. What alone encourages the spirit of man in his persistent effort to do this is the necessary assumption that our own very being, the deepest thing in us, has the same universal basis, that it must of necessity root therein; and that accordingly we may be able

iii

to draw from it some data wherewith to clarify the relation of the world of phenomena with the true essence of things.

The history of Schopenhauerean thought goes back to the sources of the life of thought in our western world, whence issue European science and European art, and in which the two are still one. It goes back to Plato. The Greek philosopher taught that the things of this world have no real existence; they are always becoming, they never *are*. They are of no avail as objects of actual knowledge, for that can subsist only of what is in and of itself and always in the same way; whereas they, in their multiplicity and their purely relative, borrowed existence, which might as well be called nonexistence, are never anything but the subject of an opinion based on sense experience. They are shadows. The only things that have real existence, that always are and never pass away, are the actual originals of those shadows, the eternal ideas, the primeval forms of all things. These are not multiple, being by their very nature each unique, each the archetype, the shadows of imitations of which are merely like-named, ephemeral, individual things of the same kind. Ideas do not, like these, come up and die away; they are timeless and true existent, not becoming and passing like their perishable imitations. Of them alone then can there be actual knowledge, as of that which always and in every respect *is*.

Obviously, it is the scientific spirit and training which teach us to subordinate to the idea the multiplicity of phenomena; which attribute truth and genuine reality to it alone and adhere to the contemplative abstraction and spiritualization of knowledge. Because of this discriminating distinction between the phenomenon and the idea, between the empiric and the intellectual, between the world of truth and the world of appearance, between the temporal and the eternal, the life of Plato was a very great event in the history of the human spirit; and first of all it was a scientific and a moral event. Everyone feels that something profoundly moral attaches to this elevation of the ideal as the only actual, above the ephemeralness and multiplicity of the phenomenal, this devaluation of the senses to the advantage of the spirit, of the temporal to the advantage of the eternal — quite in the spirit of the Christianity which came after it. For in a way the transitory phenomenon, and the sensual attaching to it, are put thereby into a state of sin: he alone finds truth and salvation who turns his face to the eternal. From this point of view Plato's philosophy exhibits the connection between science and ascetic morality.

But it exhibits another relationship: that with the world of art. According to such a philosophy time itself is merely the partial and piecemeal view which an individual holds of ideas — the latter, being outside time, are thus eternal. "Time" — so runs a beautiful phrase of Plato — "is the moving image of eternity." And so this pre-Christian, already Christian doctrine, with all its ascetic wisdom, possesses on the other hand extraordinary charm of a sensuous and creative kind; for a conception of the world as a colorful and moving phantasmagoria of pictures, which are transparencies for the ideal and the spiritual, eminently savors of the world of art, and through it the artist first comes into his own. He it is who may owe his bond to the world of images and appearances — be sensually, voluptuously, sinfully bound to them, yet be aware at the same time that he belongs no less to the world of the idea and the spirit, as the magician who makes the appearance transparent that the idea and spirit may shine through. Here is exhibited the artist's mediating task, his hermetic and magical rôle as broker between the upper and the lower world, between idea and phenomenon, spirit and sense. Here, in fact, we have what I may call the cosmic position of art; her unique mission in the world, the high dignity — which flings dignity away — of her functioning, can be defined or explained in no other way.

Plato as artist. I hold that a philosophy is valid not only — sometimes least of all — by reason of its ethical teaching, by the doctrine which it links to its interpretation of the world and its experience of it; but also and especially through this very experience itself. This indeed — not the spiritual and ethical concomitant of its doctrine of truth and salvation — is the essential, primary and personal part of a philosophy. If one divorce from a philosopher his philosophy there is much left; and it would be a pity if there were not. Nietzsche, the intellectually apostate pupil of Schopenhauer, wrote of his master:

> "What he *taught* is put aside;
> What he *lived,* that will abide —
> Behold a man!
> Subject he was to none."

The philosophy of Schopenhauer which I am about to discuss, its validity and dynamic power, proved as liable to abuse as the ascetic, scientific and creatively fruitful message of Plato. I refer here to the exploitation which Schopenhauer suffered at the hands of a colossally gifted artist, Richard Wagner — of this perhaps more at another time. But whosesoever the blame, it certainly does not lie at the door of Schopenhauer's other teacher and inspirer, who contributed to the structure of his system. I mean, of course, Kant. Kant's bent was exclusively and positively on the side of mind — very much aloof from art but by so much the closer to critique.

Immanuel Kant, the critic of pure knowledge, rescued philosophy from the speculation into which it had retreated and brought it back into the realm of the human intellect; made this his field and delimited the reason. At Königsberg in Prussia, in the second half of the eighteenth century, he was teaching something very like the premises laid down two thousand years before by the Athenian thinker. Our whole experience of the world, he declared, is subject to three laws and conditions, the inviolable forms in which all our knowledge is effectuated. These are time, space and causality. But they are not definitions of the world as it may be in and for itself, of *Das Ding an sich,* independently of our apperception of it; rather they belong only to its appearance, in that they are nothing but the forms of our knowledge. All variation, all becoming and passing away is only possible through these three. Thus they depend only on appearance and we can know nothing through them of the "thing in itself" to which they are in no way applicable. This fact applies even to our own ego: we apprehend it only as manifestation, not as anything which it may be in itself. In other words, time, space and causality are mechanisms of the intellect, and as I have said above, we call immanent the conception of things which is vouchsafed to us in their image and conditioned by them; while that is transcendent which we might gain by applying reason upon itself, by critique of the reason, and by dint of seeing through these three devices as mere forms of knowledge.

This is Kant's fundamental concept; and as we can see, it is closely related to Plato's. Both explain the visible world as phenomenal, in other words as idle seeming, which gains significance and some measure of reality only by virtue of that which shines through it. For both Plato and Kant, the true reality lies above, behind, in short "beyond" the phenomenon. Whether it was called "idea" or *"Das Ding an sich"* is relatively unimportant.

Both these concepts penetrated deeply into Schopenhauer's thought. He early elected the exhaustive study of Plato and Kant (Göttingen, 1809-11) and placed above all others these two philosophers so widely separated in time and space. He took from them what he could use, and it gratified his craving for the traditional that he could so well use it; although due to his entirely different constitution — so much more "modern," storm-tossed and suffering — he made out of it something else altogether.

What he took was the "idea" and the *"Ding an sich."* But with the latter he did something very bold, even scarcely permissible, though at the same time with deeply felt, almost compulsive conviction: he defined the *Ding an sich,* he called it by name, he asserted — though from Kant himself you would never have known — that he knew what it was. It was the Will. The will was the ultimate, irreducible, primeval principle of being, the source of all phenomena, the begetter present and active in every single one of them, the impelling force producing the whole visible world and all life — for it was the will to live. It was this through and through; so that whoever said "will" was speaking of the will to live, and if you used the longer term you were guilty of a pleonasm. The will always willed one thing: life. And why? Because it found it priceless? Because it afforded the experience of any objective knowledge of life? Ah, no. All knowledge alike was foreign to the will; it was something independent of knowledge, it was entirely original and absolute, a blind urge, a fundamental, uncaused, utterly unmotivated impulse; so far from depending on any evaluation of life, the converse was the case, and all judgments were dependent upon the strength of the will to live.

The will, then, this "in-itself-ness" of things, existing outside of time, space and causality, blind and causeless, greedily, wildly, ruthlessly demanded life, demanded *objectivation;* and this objectivation occurred in such a way that its original unity became a multiplicity — a process which received the appropriate name of the *principium individuationis* (the principle of individuality). The will, avid of life, to wreak its desire objectivated itself in accordance with the

principium, thus dispersing itself into the myriad parts of the phenomenal world existing in time and space; but at the same time
it remained in full strength in each single and smallest of those
parts. The world, then, was the product and the expression of the
will, the objectivation of the will in space and time. But it was at
the same time something else besides: it was the *idea,* my idea and
yours, the idea of each one and each one's idea about himself — by
virtue, that is, of the discerning mind, which the will created to be
a light to it in the higher stages of its objectivation. Note that it was
not the intellect which brought forth the will; the converse was the
case, the will brought forth the intellect. It was not intellect, mind,
knowledge, that was the primary and dominant factor; it was the
will, and the intellect served it. And how could it have been otherwise, since after all enough knowledge even for the objectivation of
will belonged to a later stage and without will simply had no chance
to appear? In a world entirely the work of will, of absolute, unmotivated, causeless and unvaluated life-urge, intellect had of course only
second place. Sensibility, nerves, brain, were — just like the other
parts of the organism and quite specifically like the sex organs, the
opposite pole of the discerning brain — an expression of the will at
a given phase of its objectivation. And the idea, coming into being
through the will, was just as much intended to serve it and just as
little an end in itself, as were those other parts. This relation between mind and will, this premise of Schopenhauer that the first is
only the tool of the second, has about it much that is humiliating
and deplorable, much that is even comic. It puts in a nutshell the
whole tendency and capacity of mankind to delude itself and imagine that its will receives its direction and content from its mind,
whereas our philosopher asserts the direct opposite, and relegates the
intellect — aside from its duty of shedding a little light on the immediate surroundings of the will and aiding it to achieve the higher
stages of its struggle for life — to a position as mere mouthpiece of
the will: to justify it, to provide it with "moral" motivations and in
short to rationalize our instincts.

It was a remarkably pessimistic valuation. Indeed, all the text-
books tell us that Schopenhauer is first the philosopher of the will
and second the philosopher of pessimism. But actually there is no
first and second, for they are one and the same, and he was the

second because and by virtue of his being the first; he was necessarily pessimist because he was the philosopher and psychologist of the will. Will, as the opposite pole of inactive satisfaction, is naturally a fundamental unhappiness, it is unrest, a striving for *something* — it is want, craving, avidity, demand, suffering; and a world of will can be nothing else but a world of suffering. The will, objectivating itself in all existing things, quite literally wreaks on the physical its metaphysical craving; satisfies that craving in the most frightful way in the world and through the world which it has brought forth, and which, born of greed and compulsion, turns out to be a thing to shudder at. In other words, will becoming world according to the *principium individuationis*, and being dispersed into a multiplicity of parts, forgets its orginal unity and, although in all its divisions it remains essentially one, it becomes will a million times divided against itself. Thus it strives against itself, seeking its own well-being in each of the millions of its manifestations, its place in the sun at the expense of another, yes, at the expense of all others, and so constantly sets its teeth in its own flesh, like that dweller in Tartarus who avidly devoured his own members. This is meant in a literal sense. Plato's "ideas" have in Schopenhauer become incurably gluttonous. As various stages of the objectivation of the will, space, time and matter fall upon each other. The plant world has to serve as nourishment for the animal, each animal for another as prey and food, and thus the will to live gnaws forever at itself. And lastly man sees the whole created for his use but in his turn makes frightfully explicit the horror of the struggle of all against all, the division of the will against itself. We express all this in the phrase *homo homini lupus.*

Everywhere that Schopenhauer takes occasion to talk of the anguish of the world and the rage for life of the will's multiple incarnations (and he talks much and explicitly about them) his extraordinary native eloquence, his genius as a writer, reach their utmost height of icy brilliance. He speaks with a cutting vehemence, in accents of experience and all-embracing knowledge that horrify and bewitch us by their power and veracity. Certain pages display a fierce and caustic mockery of life, uttered as it were with flashing eyes and compressed lips, and in a shower of Greek and Latin quotations: a pitiful-pitiless coruscation of statement, citation and proof of the utter misery of the world. All this is far from being so depressing as one would expect from the pitch of acuity and sinister eloquence it arrives at. Actually it fills the reader with strange, deep satisfaction, whose source is the spiritual rebellion speaking in the words, the human indignation betrayed in what seems like a suppressed quiver of the voice. Everyone feels this satisfaction; everyone realizes that when this great writer and commanding spirit speaks of the suffering of the world, he speaks of yours and mine; all of us feel what amounts almost to triumph at being thus avenged by the heroic word.

Poverty, need, concern for the mere preservation of life — these come first. Then, when they are painfully allayed, come sexual urge, the sufferings of love, jealousy, envy, hatred, fear, ambition, avarice, illness — and so on and so on, without end. All the evils whose source is the inner conflict of the will come out of Pandora's box. And what is left at the bottom? Hope? Ah, no. Satiety, tedium. For between pain and satiety every human being is tossed to and fro. The pain is postive, the pleasure merely the absence of pain — a negative, passing over at once into boredom, just as the tonic to which the melodic labyrinth leads back, just as the harmony in which disharmony issues, would bore us intolerably if they went on and on. Are there real satisfactions? They exist. But compared with the long tortue of our desires, the endlessness of our requirements, they are short and scant, and to one gratified desire there are at least ten which remain unstilled. Moreover the appeasement itself is only apparent, for the fulfilled desire soon makes a new vacancy — the first is now a known error, the second still unknown. No achieved object of desire can give lasting satisfaction. It is like alms thrown to a beggar, which merely linger out from day to day his miserable life. Happiness? It would be in repose. But precisely this is impossible for him who feels desire. To flee, to pursue, to fear disaster, to covet pleasure — it is all one: preoccupation with the will's incessant demands fills and animates the consciousness without cease, and thus the subject of the willing lies ever on Ixion's turning wheel, takes up water in the sieve of the Danaides and plays the ever-toiling Tantalus.

But yet: there *is* release from miseries and mistakes, from the errors and penalties of this life. This gift is laid in the hand of the human being, the highest and most developed objectivation of the will and accordingly the most richly capable of suffering. Would you think the gift might be death? Not at all. Death belongs utterly and entirely to the sphere of the phenomenal, the empirical, the sphere of change. It has no contact with transcendent and true actuality. What is mortal in us is merely the individuation; the core of our being, the will, which is the will to live, remains entirely unassailed, and can, if it continue to affirm itself, find out fresh avenues of approach to life. Herein, may I say in passing, resides the folly and immortality of suicide: in its futility. For the individual denies and destroys only his individuation, not the original error, the will to live, which in suicide is only seeking a route to more complete realization. So, then, not death. Redemption bears quite another name and has quite a different conditioning. One does not suspect the mediator to be thanked for this blessing when it comes. It is the intellect.

But the intellect — is it not the creature of the will, its instrument, its light in the darkness, destined only for its service? It is, and so remains. And yet — not always, not in all cases. Under peculiar, happy — ah, verily, under blissful — conditions; in exceptional circumstances, then, the servant and poor tool may become the master of his master and creator, may get the better of him, emancipate himself, achieve his own independence, and, at least at times, assert his single sovereignty, his mild, serene and all-embracing rule. Then the will, put aside and shorn of power, falls into a bland and peaceful decline. There is a state, where the miracle comes to pass, that knowledge wrenches itself free from will, the subject ceases to be merely individual and becomes the pure, will-less subject of knowledge. We may call it the aesthetic state. This is one of the greatest and profoundest of Schopenhauer's perceptions. And however frightful the accents he commands in describing the tortures of the will and the domination of the will, in equal degree his prose discovers seraphic tones, his gratitude speaks with surpassing exuberance, when abundantly and exhaustively he discourses of the blessings of art. The intellectual formulation and interpretation of this, perhaps Schopenhauer's most personal experience, he owes to his teachers, Plato and Kant. "Beautiful," Kant had declared, "is what happens without *interest*." Without interest. That, for Schopenhauer, and

rightly, meant without reference to the will. The aesthetic gratification was pure, disinterested, free from will; it was clear, unclouded,
profoundly satisfied contemplation. And why was it that? Here Plato
came in, with the latent aestheticism of his philosophy of ideas.
Ideas. They it was, for which, in the aesthetic state, phenomena, the
mere images of eternity, became transparent. The eyes opened upon
ideas — and here was the great, pure, sunny, objective contemplation,
by which alone the genius — and even he only in his creative hours
and moments — and with him his audience, was justified of his
aesthetic achievement.

Apollo, god of the muses, "he who shoots his arrows from afar,"
is a god of distance, of space, not of pathos and pathology or involve-
ment with the painful. He is an objective god, the god of irony. In
irony, then, as Schopenhauer saw it, in creative objectivity, knowledge was freed from its bondage to will, and the attention was no
longer blurred by any purpose. We reached a state of selfless resignation, where reference was had to things as sheer ideas, no longer as
purposes; and a peace heretofore unknown was all at once vouchsafed us. "It is," says our author, "wholly well with us. It is the
painless state praised by Epicurus as the highest good and the state
of the gods; we are, for that moment, released from the base urge of
the will, we celebrate the sabbath of our toil in the prison-house
of will, the wheel of Ixion stands still."

Famous, oft-quoted words, lured from this bitter and tormented
soul by the vision of the beautiful and the peace it purveyed? Are
they true? But what is truth? An experience that finds such words
to describe itself must be true, must be justified by the power of its
feeling. Or should we believe that these words of sheer and boundless gratitude were coined to describe a relative, at bottom a merely
negative, happiness? For happiness anyhow is negative, it is the
surcease of torment; and even in all our glad objective contemplation of aesthetic ideas it cannot be other than the same. Schopenhauer, in the choice of the images he is inspired to use, unequiv-
ocally reveals the fact. This happiness too is temporal, transitory.
The creative state, so he found, the sojourn among images irradiated
by the idea — these would not bring the final redemption. The
aesthetic state was but the prior stage to a perfected one, in which
the will, not permanently satisfied in the aesthetic, would be once for

all outshone by knowledge, would void the field and be annihilated. The consummation of the artist would be the saint.

What, after all, is ethic? It is the philosophy of the actions of human beings, the teaching of good and evil. The teaching? Then was the will, blind, causeless and senseless as it was, teachable? Certainly not. Certainly virtue was not a thing to be learned; no more than was art. Just as a man could not become an artist by having explained to him the essence of the creative state, so he could not shun evil and ensue good by instruction in the nature of the one and the other. No prescriptions could be issued to the will. It was free, absolute, all-powerful. Freedom, indeed, dwelt in the will alone, thus it existed wholly in transcendence, never in the empiric world, which was the objectivation of the world subsisting in time, space and causality. Here everything was strictly causal, bound and determined by cause and effect. Freedom, like the will, was beyond and on the other side of the phenomenal, but there it was present and dominant, and therein lay the freedom of the will. As so often, the situation respecting freedom was just contrary to that conceived by ordinary common sense. It lay not in doing but in being, not in *operari* but in *esse*. In *doing*, indeed, then, inevitably necessity and determinacy reigned; while *being* was originally and metaphysically free. The human being who performed a culpable action had indeed so *acted* of necessity, as a being existing in the realm of the empiric, and under the influence of definite motives. But he could have *been* different; and his fear, his pangs of conscience, also had reference to his being, not his doing.

A harsh, cruel thought — arrogant, offensive, ruthless. To accept it runs contrary to our feelings — and yet it is precisely our feelings which are challenged by its mysticism. For it has at the bottom of it a mystic truth, by virtue of which the twin conceptions of merit and demerit, far from being invalidated, become even more profound and awe-inspiring. They are, of course, divorced thereby from the moral sphere as such. But aristocratic intellects, not much concerned with considerations of "justice," have always been inclined to favor this divorce. Goethe liked to talk of "inborn merits," an absurd phrase from any logical or ethical point of view. For "merit" is entirely and by definition an ethical concept; whereas what is inborn — be it beauty, talent, wit, refinement, or, in the sphere of outward destiny, good fortune — can thus not logically be merits. In order to speak of merit in this sense it must be the issue of choice, the expression of a will antecedent to the phenomenon. And this is just what Schopenhauer asserts when he harshly and haughtily declares that each of us, blest or unblest, gets exactly what he deserves.

But this aristocratic complaisance at injustice and the varied lot of morals is soon enough resolved in the most peremptory and democratic equality; simply because the variations — and even the differentiation itself — are shown to be an illusion. Schopenhauer calls this illusion by a name drawn from Hindu metaphysics, which he greatly admires because of its pessimistic harmony with his own account of the world: he calls it the "veil of Maya." But much earlier he had, as occidental scholars do, clothed it in Latin, thus: he says that the great illusion of inequality and injustice in the character, situation and fate of individuals rests on the *principium individuationis*. Variation, inequality, are only attributes of multiplicity in time and space. That is to say, they are mere appearance, the notion which we, as individuals, thanks to the organization of the intellect, have of a world which in reality is the objectivation of the will to live, in the general and in the particular, in you and in me. But the individual, with his strong sense of being separate and set apart from the universe, does not recognize this — how could he, when the conditioning of his knowledge, the "veil of Maya," enfolding his vision and the outlying world, prevents him from getting sight of the truth? The individual does not see the essence of things, which is one, but its manifestations, which he beholds as separate and differing, yes, even opposed: pleasure and pain, the tormentor and the tormented, the joyous life of one and the other's wretched lot. You affirm, that is, for yourself, the one, and deny, with special reference to yourself, the other. The will, which is your origin and essence, makes you demand good fortune and the enjoyment of existence. You stretch out your hands for them, you press them to you, and it escapes your notice that when you thus affirm these as goods you affirm at the same time all the evils, all the torments in the world and press them no less to your heart. The evil that you do thereby, the evil that you inflict; on the other hand your indignation at the world's injustice, your envy, yearning and desire,

your cosmic craving — all these come from the delusion of multiplicity, the false belief that you are not the world and the world is not
you. All this comes from the illusion of Maya, from the illusory
distinction between the I and the you.

Thence, likewise, comes your fear of death. Death is only the
setting right of an error, a confusion — for every individual is a confusion. Death is nothing but the disappearance of an imaginary
partition-wall shutting off the I you are enclosed in from the rest
of the world. You believe that when you die this rest of the world
will go on existing, while you, horrible to say, will be no more.
But I say to you, this world, which is your idea, will no longer be;
whereas you, precisely that in you which, because it is the will to
live, fears death and rejects it, *you* will remain, will live. For the
will, out of which you have your being, will always know how to
find the gate of life. To it all eternity belongs; and together with
life, which it recognizes as time, though actually it is perpetual
present, time too will be vouchsafed you again. Your will, so long
as it wills, is always sure of life, with all its torments and blisses.
Better it were for you if it were not.

Meanwhile you live, as he who you are. You see and love, you
look and long, you covet the unknown image of your desire — ah, so
strange and different from yourself! — you suffer for it, you long to
draw it to your heart, to draw it into you, to *be* it. But to be a thing
is something quite different, and incomparably more grievous and
onerous than to see it. The longing set up by the idea is all a delusion. You yourself are given to yourself, your body is given to you,
as idea, as all the rest of the world is. But at the same time it is given
to you as will — the only thing in the world which is given to you
at the same time as will. Everything else is for you only idea.
The universe is, so to speak, a play, a ballet; all your natural, instinctive convictions tell you that it has nothing like the same
reality as you, the spectator, have; that it is not to be taken with
anything like the same seriousness as you yourself are. Trapped in
the *principium individuationis,* shrouded in the veil of Maya, the
ego sees all other forms of life as masks and phantoms, and is simply
incapable of ascribing anything like the same importance or seriousness to them as to itself. Are not you the only actually existent thing,
are you not all that matters? You are the navel of the world; if it be

well with you, if the afflictions of this life be kept as far from you as possible, its blisses as near, that is the one vital thing. What happens to others is nothing by comparison. It does you neither good nor harm.

Such is the conviction of native, unbroken and quite unenlightened egotism: absolute prepossession with the *principium individuationis*. To see through this principle, to divine its illusory, truth-shrouding character; to begin to perceive that the I and the you are indistinguishable the one from the other; to have the emotional intuition that the will is the same in the one and the all: such is the beginning and the essence of ethics. Evil is that man who, so soon as no other outer power prevents him, inflicts evil. I mean a man who, not content with affirming the will to life as manifested in his own body, also denies the will manifest in other individuals and seeks to destroy their existence as soon as it is in the way of his own efforts. A wild, untamed will, one not content with the affirmation of his own body, speaks in the bad character. But there is above all so profound a prejudice in favor of the manifestation and the *principium individuationis* that it clings with iron grip to the distinctions fixed by the *principium* between its own person and all others. And accordingly it considers the existence of others wholly foreign to its own, severed from it by a deep abyss. It regards them as empty shells, and cherishes a profound conviction that reality is an attribute of itself alone.

Goodness is positive. It performs the service of love. Its motive is profoundly emotional: were it not to do so, it would seem to itself like a man who starves today in order tomorrow to have more than he can eat. Just so it would seem to the good man, to let others famish while he lived in abundance. For such a one the veil of Maya has become transparent, he has lost the great illusion whereby will, in its multiple manifestation, here starves and suffers, there enjoys, because it is after all the same will, and the same torture, which he thus both invokes and suffers. Love and goodness are *sympathy* — in recognition of the *"Tat twam asi,"* the *"*This thou art," when the veil of Maya is lifted. Spinoza said: *"Benevolentia nihil aliud est, quam cupiditas ex commiseratione orta"* (Goodness is nothing else than love born of sympathy). But from this it is clear that as justice can rise to heights of goodness, so goodness in its turn can rise to greater heights: not only to most disinterested love and most magnanimous self-sacrifice, but verily to saintliness. For a man with such knowledge of love will regard the suffering of everything living as his own suffering, and make his own the pain of all the world. He sees the whole: sees life as an internal conflict; and continual pain, suffering humanity, suffering animal world and the knowledge of the essence of things in themselves combine to lay a quieting hand upon his will. In him will turns away from life. Obliged, in his sympathetic understanding, to deny life, how then can he affirm even in himself the will to live, life being but the work, mirror and expression of will? Thus to recognize, thus to resolve, means renunciation, means the ultimate quietism. And so it comes about that virtue passes over into *ascesis;* and this is a paradox, truly a high and great one: an individuation of the will here rejects the essence manifesting and expressing itself in its very own body. Its acts give the lie to its manifestation, they openly controvert it. The ascetic rejects the satisfactions of sex. His chastity is the sign that with the life of the body likewise the life of the will abrogates itself. What is the mark of the saint? That he does nothing of all that he would like to do, and does all that he does not like to do. If ascetic chastity were to become a general practice, it would bring about the end of the human race. And since all manifestations of the will are one, with man, the highest of these, would also fall away his feebler copy, the animal kingdom. All knowledge would fail, and since without subject there is no object all the rest of the visible world would dissolve and melt way. Man is the potential redeemer of nature. The mystic Angelus Silesius says:

> "O man, all living love thee; they press about thee,
> They run to thee that they may reach their god."

Schopenhauer — all his misanthropy notwithstanding and all that he says about the corrupt condition of life in general and the distortions of the spirit of man in particular; notwithstanding his despair over the wretched social state one is born into as a human being — Schopenhauer is humanly full of pride and reverence as he contemplates the "crown of creation." To him the words mean, just as they did to the author of Genesis, man, the highest and most developed

objectivation of the will. This most significant form of Schopenhauer's humanism perfectly — if by implication — accords with his
political skepticism, his anti-revolutionarism. Man, according to him,
is to be reverenced because he is the *knowing* creature. All knowing,
of course, is fundamentally subject to the will out of which it sprang
just as the head springs from the trunk. In the animal kingdom,
indeed, this subjection of the intellect is never overcome. But look at
the difference between man and beast in this relation between head
and trunk. In the lower animal kingdom they are completely grown
together, and in all animals the head is inclined to the earth, where
lie the objects of the will; yes, even in the higher animals head and
trunk are much more one than in man, whose head (Schopenhauer
here uses the German word *Haupt*, to make the distinction clear)
appears to be independently set on the shoulders, and uses the body
to carry it, instead of being subject to it. This human advantage
is shown pre-eminently in the Apollo Belvedere. The god of the
muses carries his mobile, wide-eyed head so easily on his shoulders
that it seems to have escaped from the body and to need to take no
further interest in it.

What association of ideas could be more humanistic than this?
Not for nothing does Schopenhauer choose the statue of the god
of the muses as the image of human dignity. Art, knowledge and
the dignity of human suffering are here envisaged as one — a profound and significant perception of our pessimistic humanist. And
since humanism in general is prone to rhetoric and the wearing of
rose-tinted spectacles, we have here something quite new, and, I
venture to assert, something in the realm of ideas considerably in
advance of its time. In the human being, the highest objectivation
of the will, the latter is most brightly irradiated by knowledge. But
in equal measure as knowledge arrives at clarity, the consciousness is
heightened, the suffering increases, and thus in man it reaches its
highest point. Even in individuals it varies in degree. "The degree
of suffering," says Nietzsche, "is determined by the position in the
hierarchy." Here Nietzsche betrays his ultimate dependence upon
Schopenhauer's aristocratic theory of man's noble vocation to suffer.
And in particular the highest type of man, the genius. It is this vocation that gives rise to the two great possibilities which Schopenhauer's humanism envisages for man. They are: art, and consecra-

tion. Only the human being possesses the possibility of the aesthetic state, as "disinterested" contemplation of the idea, to humanity alone is it given to achieve the final redemption, the renunciation of the will to live, as the artist mounts to the still loftier stage of ascetic saintliness. To man is vouchsafed the opportunity to right the wrong, to reverse the great error and mistake of being; to get the supreme insight which teaches him to make the suffering of the whole world his own and can lead him to renunciation and the conversion of the will. And so man is the secret hope of the world and of all creatures; towards whom as it were all creation trustfully turns as to its hoped-for redeemer and savior.

This is a conception of great mystical beauty. It expresses a humane reverence for the mission of man, such as outweighs all misanthropy and supplies the corrective to all Schopenhauer's loathing of humanity. To me the importance of it lies in this union of pessimism and humanism, revealed to us by the philosopher: the assertion that the one in no wise excludes the other, and that in order to be a humanist one does not need to be a rhetorical flatterer of humanity.

But we should be careful not to take too literally or seriously Schopenhauer's humanistic attitude or his classical, apollonian pronouncements. In his case, as in many others, we must distinguish between the person and the opinion, the human being and his judgments. What warns us is Schopenhauer's extremist position, a grotesque and dualistic antithesis in his nature, a romanticism (in the most colorful sense of the word) which removed him further from the Goethean sphere than he would ever have let himself even dream of.

Seldom has a book had a more expressive, more exhaustive title than Schopenhauer's chief work, his only work, in truth, developing his own original train of thought. All else that he wrote in a lifetime of seventy-two years only forms an assiduously collected accompaniment and reinforcement to it. *The World as Will and Idea.* That is not only the theme, in its most compendious formulation: it is the man, the human being, his personality, his life, his suffering. The compulsive force of this man, and in particular his sexual urge, must have been enormous — cruel and tortuous as are the mythological figures he employs to describe the bondage to the will. It must have opposed with such equal power the compulsive force of his urge for knowledge, his lucid and mighty intellectuality, as to produce a frightfully radical duality and conflict, with a correspondingly profound craving for release; and to issue in the intellectual denial of life itself, the impeachment of his own essence as evil, erroneous and culpable. Rightly, if in an elevated sense, one may call this tortuous and grotesque. Sex is to Schopenhauer the focal point of the will; in its physical objectivation the opposite pole of the brain, which represents knowledge. Obviously, his capacity in both spheres went far beyond the average; though that in itself would only speak for the intensity and range of his nature. What makes him a pessimist; a *denier* of the world, is just the contradictory and hostile, exclusive and anguishing relation of the two spheres to each other. We need not, though it would be easy to do so, fail to understand his pessimism as the intellectual product of that very richness and power. Here is a bi-polar nature, full of contrasts and conflicts, tortured and violent; after its own pattern it must experience the world: as instinct and spirit, passion and knowledge, "will" and "idea." But suppose he had learned to reconcile them in his genius, in his creative life. Suppose he had understood that genius does not at all consist in sensuality put out of action and will unhinged, that art is not mere objectivation of spirit, but the fruitful union and interpenetration of both spheres, immensely heightening to life and more fascinating than either can be by itself! That the essence of the creative artist is nothing else — and in Schopenhauer himself was nothing else — than sensuality spiritualized, than spirit informed and made creative by sex! Goethe's interpretation and experience differed from the pessimist's; it was happier, healthier, more blithely "classic," less pathologic (I use the word in its rarer, unclinical sense) — less romantic, shall I say? For Goethe, sex and spirit (mind) were the highest, most provocative charms in life. He wrote: *"Denn das Leben ist die Liebe, und des Lebens Leben — Geist"* (For life is love, and spirit the life of life). But in Schopenhauer genius intensified both spheres until they took refuge in the ascetic. To him, sex is of the devil, a diabolic distraction from pure contemplation; knowledge is that denial of sex which says: "If thine eye offend thee, pluck it out." Knowledge as "peace of the soul," art as a sedative and liberating condition of pure contemplation unmarred by will; the artist as a halfway stage to sainthood, divorced from the will to live: that is Schopenhauer. And again, in so far as this conception of mind and art is objective, it approaches Goethe's, it has a classic cast. But being exaggerated and ascetic, it is definitely romantic, in one sense of the word, and that would not have appealed to Goethe — as witness his attitude to Heinrich von Kleist.

But after all, terms and antitheses like classic and romantic do not apply to Schopenhauer. Neither the one nor the other is adequate to describe a mentality later in time than those for whom they once played their rôle. He stands nearer to us than do the minds who in their day were occupied with such distinctions and ranged themselves accordingly. Schopenhauer's mental life, the dualistic, overstrained irritability and fever of his genius is less romantic than it is modern. I should like to enlarge this distinction, but content myself with making it refer in general to a state of mind the increasing strain of which became only too marked in our western world in the century between Goethe and Nietzsche. In this respect Schopenhauer stands between the two, he makes a bridge between them: more "modern," more suffering and difficult than Goethe, but much more "classic," robust and healthy than Nietzsche. From which it is clear that optimism and pessimism, the affirmation or denial of life, have nothing to do with health and illness. Illness and health, accordingly, have to be used with great caution as criteria or valuations. They are biological conceptions whereas the nature of man is not exhausted in the biological.

Schopenhauer, as psychologist of the will, is the father of all modern psychology. From him the line runs, by way of the psychological radicalism of Nietzsche, straight to Freud and the men who built up his psychology of the unconscious and applied it to the mental sciences. Nietzsche's anti-socratism and hostility to mind are nothing but the philosophic affirmation and glorification of Schopenhauer's discovery of the primacy of the will, his pessimistic insight into the secondary and subservient relation of mind to will. He makes the statement, certainly not humane in the classical sense, that the intellect is there to do the pleasure of the will, to justify it, to provide it with motivations which are often very shallow and self-deluding, in fine to rationalize the instincts. It is a skeptical and pessimistic psychology, an analysis of relentless penetration. And it not only prepared the way for what we call psycho-analysis, it was already just that. At bottom all psychology is the unmasking, the acute, ironic, naturalistic perception of the riddling relation that obtains between the reason and the instincts. A little dialogue in the *Wahlverwandt-schaften* well illustrates this underhand game our natures play. Eduard, already in love after his first meeting with Ottilie, is made by Goethe to say: "She is a highly intelligent person." To which his wife replies: "Intelligent? She never opened her mouth." Schopenhauer must certainly have enjoyed this passage. It is a pleasant, blithely classic illustration of his own thesis, that one does not want a thing because it is good, but finds it good because one wants it.

This essay is an attempt to evoke today a figure little known to the present generation; and to reconsider and recapitulate his concepts. Its object is to reassert the idea of the connection between pessimism and humanism. I should like to hand on, to a world where human feeling is today finding itself in sore straits, the knowledge of this combined melancholy and pride in the human race which make up Schopenhauer's philosophy. His pessimism — that is his humanity. His interpretation of the world by the concept of the will, his insight into the overweening power of instinct and the derogation of the one-time godlike reason, mind and intellect to a mere tool with which to achieve security — all this is anti-classic and in its essence inhumane. But it is precisely in the pessimistic hue of his philosophy that his humanity and spirituality lie; in the fact that this great artist, practised in suffering and wielding the prose of a great humane cultural epoch in our history, lifts man out of the biological sphere of nature, makes his own feeling and understanding soul the theatre where the will meets its reverse, and sees in the human being the savior of all creation.

The twentieth century has in its first third taken up a position of reaction against classic rationalism and intellectualism. It has surrendered to admiration of the unconscious, to a glorification of instinct, which it thinks is overdue to life. And the bad instincts have accordingly been enjoying a heyday. We have seen instead of pessimistic conviction deliberate malice. Intellectual recognition of bitter truth turns into hatred and contempt for mind itself. Man has greedily flung himself on the side of "life" — that is, on the side of the stronger — for there is no disputing the fact that life has nothing

to fear from mind, that not life but knowledge, or rather, mind, is
the weaker part and the one needing protection on this earth. Yet
the anti-humanity of our day is a humane experiment too in its way.
It is a one-sided answer to the eternal question as to the nature and
destiny of man. We palpably need a corrective to restore the balance,
and I think the philosophy I here evoke can do good service. I spoke
of Schopenhauer as modern. I might have called him futurist. The
chiaroscuro harmonies of his human traits, the mixture in him of
Voltaire and Jacob Böhme;* the paradox of his classic, pellucid
prose, employed to lighten the darkest and lowest purlieus of being;
his proud misanthropy, which never belies his reverence for the idea
of the human being; in short, what I called his pessimistic humanity,
seems to me to herald the temper of a future time. Once he was
fashionable and famous, then half-forgotten. But his philosophy may
still exert a ripe and humanizing influence upon our age. His intellectual sensitivity, his teaching, which was life, that knowledge,
thought and philosophy are not matters of the head alone but of the
whole man, heart and sense, body and soul; in other words, his
existence as an artist may help to bring to birth a new humanity of
which we stand in need, and to which they are akin: a humanity
above dry reason on the one hand and idolatry of instinct on the
other. For art, accompanying man on his painful journey to self-
realization, has always been before him at the goal.

* Jacob Böhme, German mystic, 1575–1624.

TABLE OF CONTENTS

INTRODUCTION

I

WHAT we like in Schopenhauer is his honesty. How refreshing it is to turn to him from philosophers who dig their heads into the sand at the sight or the mention of evil! Every man knows, and every woman too, that the years bring a rich assortment of pains and sorrows to every soul; and that life is still a precious thing only because the joys it gives are deep enough to be worth all the price we pay. But if one were to believe the more respectable of modern philosophers, evil is almost as negative and questionable a thing as in Aquinas's theology. Philosophers tend to look upon themselves as apologists for the cosmos, press-agents for the Deity; the smell of theology is still strong upon them, and they are never quite content until they have justified all the ways of God to man.

By the side of this whistling in the dark, Schopenhauer's rugged pessimism is almost cheerful in its bravery. We wish to believe in life, but with both eyes open; and Schopenhauer opens both eyes without pity and without fear. Let the truth be spoken mercilessly; let nature's law of career open to every talon, and man's law of insatiable acquisition and periodical war, be revealed to us; let the disillusionment of love be told, and the thousand illnesses that punctuate our lives, and the breaking of hearts and families in the strife of the young with the old; let death be brought upon the stage as brutally as in Elizabethan days, and let us acknowledge its sovereignty over every organism and every mind. Let Jacques intone, in the midst of Rosalind's merry love, his ruthless summary of life:

> And so from hour to hour we ripe and ripe,
> And then from hour to hour we rot and rot,
> And thereby hangs a tale. (*As You Like It*, ii, 7)

Let Timon take to the woods, "where he shall find the unkindest beasts more kinder than mankind"; let him say to his dearest friend, "I do wish thou wert a dog, that I might love thee something"; let him offer mankind a halter and a tree as the best remedy for this "long sickness of health and living." Let loyal Kent turn back the hands that would restore dying Lear to life:

> Vex not his ghost: Oh, let him pass! He hates him
> That would upon the rack of this rough world
> Stretch him out longer! (*King Lear*, v. 3)

And let Macbeth phrase angrily his creator's pessimism, far deeper than Schopenhauer's:

> Out, out, brief candle!
> Life's but a walking shadow; a poor player,
> That struts and frets his hour upon the stage,
> And then is heard no more; it is a tale
> Told by an idiot, full of sound and fury,
> Signifying nothing. (*Macbeth*, v. 6)

We wish to know the worst, and armor ourselves with knowledge against the slings and arrows of our fortune. To know the worst and yet to love the best: this is the gift which strong souls can find even in Schopenhauer.

We live in an age strangely like that of this great scorner of the earth. We too, like him, have lived in the midst of alarms (cf. the kindred pessimism of the harassed Lucretius and Hobbes), and have known the horrors of a war that fertilized the soil with human hecatombs each day for many years. We too have seen reaction triumph, have seen might laugh Mephistopheleanly in the face of right; we too have drunk the cup of our democratic hopes to as bitter dregs as revolutionary Europe did; we too have had our rebellions, massacres, terrors, and restorations; and is not Spengler our Cassandra-Schopenhauer?

Perhaps we can take a leaf from Spengler, and foresee the future through the analogies of the past. Could desolation be greater than that which covered Europe when Schopenhauer wrote *The World as Will and Idea?* Could cynicism be more fashionable now in the midst of wealth than it was in the nadir of poverty and universal desolation, than it was in the days when Byron cursed life, and Heine cursed love, and Shelley welcomed death? And yet within a generation after Waterloo, Europe was again alive with energy and creation; Balzac was rivalling the myriad-mindedness of Shakespeare, Hugo was winning the battle of *Ernani,* and youth was in the saddle once more.

It will be no different with ourselves. We shrug our shoulders pessimistically to-day, but to-morrow we shall hope again. We are the remnants of an exhausted generation; our children will not know our memories, and will not tremble at our fears; the great transition that has torn us into a chaos of mind and morals will have passed into a new order and stability; youth will push forward gaily to new victories, and plant the flag of man a little farther in the war for liberation and enlightenment. Time sides with the young.

And so we can listen calmly to the worst that Schopenhauer can say. Let him call life names; we suspect that secretly he loved it none the less. We shall smile as we pass through his *Inferno,* knowing that every sunrise redeems the earth, and that every birth renews the victory of life. We shall be made stronger and braver by this fruit of the tree of the knowledge of good and evil; and if we are doomed by that knowledge to forfeit our childhood Paradise, we shall go out willingly to make, with the toil of our hands and the sweat of our brow, a man's Eden of our own.[1]

[1] The reader will find a biographical and analytical chapter on Schopenhauer in *The Story of Philosophy* (page 326).

WILL DURANT

PREFACE TO THE FIRST EDITION

I PROPOSE to point out here how this book must be read in order
to be thoroughly understood. By means of it I only intend to impart a single thought. Yet, notwithstanding all my endeavours, I
could find no shorter way of imparting it than this whole book.
I hold this thought to be that which has very long been sought for
under the name of philosophy, and the discovery of which is therefore regarded by those who are familiar with history as quite as
impossible as the discovery of the philosopher's stone, although it
was already said by Pliny: *Quam multa fieri non posse, priusquam
sint facta, judicantur?* (Hist. nat. 7, 1.) [1]

According as we consider the different aspects of this one
thought which I am about to impart, it exhibits itself as that
which we call metaphysics, that which we call ethics, and that
which we call æsthetics; and certainly it must be all this if it is
what I have already acknowledged it to be.

A *system of thought* must always have an architectonic connection or coherence; that is, a connection in which one part always
supports the other, though the latter does not support the former,
in which ultimately the foundation supports all the rest without
being supported by it, and the apex is supported without supporting. On the other hand, a *single thought,* however comprehensive
it may be, must preserve the most perfect unity. If it admits of
being broken up into parts to facilitate its communication, the
connection of these parts must yet be organic, *i. e.,* it must be a
connection in which every part supports the whole just as much as
it is supported by it, a connection in which there is no first and no
last, in which the whole thought gains distinctness through every
part, and even the smallest part cannot be completely understood

---

[1] "How many things are judged impossible, before they are accomplished!"

unless the whole has already been grasped. A book, however, must always have a first and a last line, and in this respect will always remain very unlike an organism, however like one its content may be: thus form and matter are here in contradiction.

It is self-evident that under these circumstances no other advice can be given as to how one may enter into the thought explained in this work than *to read the book twice,* and the first time with great patience, a patience which is only to be derived from the belief, voluntarily accorded, that the beginning presupposes the end almost as much as the end presupposes the beginning, and that all the earlier parts presuppose the later almost as much as the later presuppose the earlier. . . .

How can I venture to present a book to the public under conditions and demands which are presumptuous and altogether immodest, and this at a time when there is such a general wealth of special ideas, that in Germany alone they are made common property through the press, in three thousand valuable, original, and absolutely indispensable works every year, besides innumerable periodicals, and even daily papers; at a time when especially there is not the least deficiency of entirely original and profound philosophers, but in Germany alone there are more of them alive at the same time, than several centuries could formerly boast of in succession to each other? How is one ever to come to the end, asks the indignant reader, if one must set to work upon a book in such a fashion?

As I have absolutely nothing to advance against these reproaches, I only hope for some small thanks from such readers for having warned them in time, so that they may not lose an hour over a book which it would be useless to read without complying with the demands that have been made, and which should therefore be left alone, particularly as apart from this we might wager a great deal that it can say nothing to them, but rather that it will always be only *paucorum hominum,*[1] and must therefore quietly and modestly wait for the few whose unusual mode of thought may find it enjoyable. For apart from the difficulties and the effort which it requires from the reader, what cultured man of this age, whose knowledge has almost reached the august point at which the paradoxical and the false are all

[1] "Of few men."

one to it, could bear to meet thoughts almost on every page that
directly contradict that which he has yet himself established once
for all as true and undeniable? And then, how disagreeably disappointed will many a one be if he finds no mention here of what
he believes it is precisely here he ought to look for, because his
method of speculation agrees with that of a great living philosopher,[2] who has certainly written pathetic books, and who only
has the trifling weakness that he takes all he learned and approved
before his fifteenth year for inborn ideas of the human mind.
Who could stand all this? Therefore my advice is simply to lay
down the book.

But I fear I shall not escape even thus. The reader who has
got as far as the preface and been stopped by it, has bought the
book for cash, and asks how he is to be indemnified. My last refuge
is now to remind him that he knows how to make use of a book in
several ways, without exactly reading it. It may fill a gap in his
library as well as many another, where, neatly bound, it will
certainly look well. Or he can lay it on the toilet-table or the
tea-table of some learned lady friend. Or, finally, what certainly
is best of all, and I specially advise it, he can review it.

And now that I have allowed myself the jest to which in this
two-sided life hardly any page can be too serious to grant a place,
I part with the book with deep seriousness, in the sure hope that
sooner or later it will reach those to whom alone it can be addressed; and for the rest, patiently resigned that the same fate
should, in full measure, befall it, that in all ages has, to some
extent, befallen all knowledge, and especially the weightiest
knowledge of the truth, to which only a brief triumph is allotted
between the two long periods in which it is condemned as paradoxical or disparaged as trivial. The former fate is also wont to befall
its author. But life is short, and truth works far and lives long:
let us speak the truth.

ARTHUR SCHOPENHAUER

Written at Dresden in August 1818.

[2] F. H. Jacobi.

PREFACE TO THE SECOND EDITION

NOT to my contemporaries, not to my compatriots—to mankind I commit my now completed work in the confidence that it will not be without value for them, even if this should be late recognised, as is commonly the lot of what is good. For it cannot have been for the passing generation, engrossed with the delusion of the moment, that my mind, almost against my will, has uninterruptedly stuck to its work through the course of a long life. And while the lapse of time has not been able to make me doubt the worth of my work, neither has the lack of sympathy; for I constantly saw the false and the bad, and finally the absurd and senseless,[1] stand in universal admiration and honour; and I bethought myself that if it were not the case that those who are capable of recognising the genuine and right are so rare that we may look for them in vain for some twenty years, then those who are capable of producing it could not be so few that their works afterwards form an exception to the perishableness of earthly things; and thus would be lost the reviving prospect of posterity which every one who sets before himself a high aim requires to strengthen him. . . .

While philosophy has long been obliged to serve entirely as a means to public ends on the one side and private ends on the other, I have pursued the course of my thought, undisturbed by them, for more than thirty years, and simply because I was obliged to do so and could not help myself, from an instinctive impulse, which was, however, supported by the confidence that anything true one may have thought, and anything obscure one may have thrown light upon, will appeal to any thinking mind, no matter when it comprehends it, and will rejoice and comfort it. To such an one we speak as those who are like us have spoken to us, and

[1] The Hegelian Philosophy.

have so become our comfort in the wilderness of this life. Meanwhile the object is pursued on its own account and for its own sake. Now it happens curiously enough with philosophical meditations, that precisely that which one has thought out and investigated for oneself, is afterwards of benefit to others; not that, however, which was originally intended for others. The former is confessedly nearest in character to perfect honesty; for a man does not seek to deceive himself, nor does he offer himself empty husks; so that all sophistication and all mere talk is omitted, and consequently every sentence that is written at once repays the trouble of reading it. Thus my writings bear the stamp of honesty and openness so distinctly on the face of them, that by this alone they are a glaring contrast to those of three celebrated sophists of the post-Kantian period. I am always to be found at the standpoint of *reflection, i. e.,* rational deliberation and honest statement, never at that of *inspiration,* called intellectual intuition, or absolute thought; though, if it received its proper name, it would be called empty bombast and charlatanism. Working then in this spirit, and always seeing the false and bad in universal acceptance, yea, bombast [2] and charlatanism [3] in the highest honour, I have long renounced the approbation of my contemporaries. It is impossible that an age which for twenty years has applauded a Hegel, that intellectual Caliban, as the greatest of the philosophers, so loudly that it echoes through the whole of Europe, could make him who has looked on at that desirous of its approbation. It has no more crowns of honour to bestow; its applause is prostituted, and its censure has no significance.

One word more for the professors of philosophy. I have always been compelled to admire not merely the sagacity, the true and fine tact with which, immediately on its appearance, they recognised my philosophy as something altogether different from and indeed dangerous to their own attempts, or, in popular language, something that would not suit their turn; but also the sure and astute policy by virtue of which they at once discovered the proper procedure with regard to it, the complete harmony with which they applied it, and the persistency with which they have re-

[2] Fichte and Schelling.
[3] Hegel.

mained faithful to it. This procedure, which further commended itself by the great ease of carrying it out, consists, as is well known, in altogether ignoring and thus in secreting—according to Goethe's malicious phrase, which just means the appropriating of what is of weight and significance. The efficiency of this quiet means is increased by the corybantic shouts with which those who are at one reciprocally greet the birth of their own spiritual children—shouts which compel the public to look and note the air of importance with which they congratulate themselves on the event. Who can mistake the object of such proceedings? Is there then nothing to oppose to the maxim, *primum vivere, deinde philosophari?* [4] These gentlemen desire to live, and indeed to live by philosophy. To philosophy they are assigned with their wives and children, and in spite of Petrarch's *povera e nuda vai filosofia,* [5] they have staked everything upon it. Now my philosophy is by no means so constituted that any one can live by it. It lacks the first indispensable requisite of a well-paid professional philosophy, a speculative theology, which—in spite of the troublesome Kant with his Critique of Reason—should and must, it is supposed, be the chief theme of all philosophy, even if it thus takes on itself the tack of talking straight on of that of which it can know absolutely nothing.

Thus the ignoring and silent system may hold out a good while, at least the span of time I may have yet to live, whereby much is already won. And if, in the meantime, here and there an indiscreet voice has let itself be heard, it is soon drowned by the loud talking of the professors, who, with important airs, know how to entertain the public with very different things. I advise, however, that the unanimity of procedure should be somewhat more strictly observed, and especially that the young men should be looked after, for they are sometimes so fearfully indiscreet. For even so I cannot guarantee that the commended procedure will last for ever, and cannot answer for the final issue. It is a nice question as to the steering of the public, which, on the whole, is good and tractable. Although we nearly at all times see the Gorgiases and the Hippiases uppermost, although the absurd, as a rule, predominates, and it seems impossible that the voice of the

---

[4] First one must live; then one can philosophize.
[5] Philosophy goes poor and nude.

individual can ever penetrate through the chorus of the befooling and the befooled, there yet remains to the genuine works of every age a quite peculiar, silent, slow, and powerful influence; and, as if by a miracle, we see them rise at last out of the turmoil like a balloon that floats up out of the thick atmosphere of this globe into purer regions, where, having once arrived, it remains at rest, and no one can draw it down again.

ARTHUR SCHOPENHAUER

Written at Frankfort-on-the-Maine
in February 1844.

FIRST BOOK

THE WORLD AS IDEA

First Aspect

THE IDEA SUBORDINATED TO THE PRINCIPLE OF SUFFICIENT REASON: THE OBJECT OF EXPERIENCE AND SCIENCE

Sors de l'enfance, ami réveille toi!
—*Jean Jacques Rousseau.*
"Come out of your infancy, my friend; awake!"

I.

§ 1

"THE world is my idea":—this is a truth which holds good for everything that lives and knows, though man alone can bring it into reflective and abstract consciousness. If he really does this, he has attained to philosophical wisdom. It then becomes clear and certain to him what he knows is not a sun and an earth, but only an eye that sees a sun, a hand that feels an earth; that the world which surrounds him is there only as an idea, *i. e.,* only in relation to something else, the consciousness, which is himself. If any truth can be asserted *a priori,* it is this: for it is the expression of the most general form of all possible and thinkable experience: a form which is more general than time, or space, or causality, for they all presuppose it; and each of these . . . is valid only for a particular class of ideas; whereas the antithesis of object and subject is the common form of all these classes, is that form under which alone any idea of whatever kind it may be, abstract or intuitive, pure or empirical, is possible and thinkable. No truth therefore is more certain, more independent of all others, and less in need of proof than this, that all that exists for knowledge, and therefore this whole world, is only object in relation to subject, perception of a perceiver, in a word, idea. This is obviously true of the past and the future, as well as of the present, of what is farthest off, as of what is near; for it is true of time and space themselves, in which alone these distinctions arise. All that in any way belongs or can belong to the world is inevitably thus conditioned through the subject, and exists only for the subject. The world is idea. . . .

§ 5

So far as we have considered the question of the reality of the outer world, it arises from a confusion which amounts even to a misunderstanding of reason itself, and therefore thus far, the question could be answered only by explaining its meaning. After examination of the relation of subject and object, and the special conditions of sense perception, the question itself disappeared because it had no longer any meaning. There is, however, one other possible origin of this question, quite different from the purely speculative one which we have considered, a specially empirical origin, though the question is always raised from a speculative point of view, and in this form it has a much more comprehensible meaning than it had in the first. We have dreams; may not our whole life be a dream? or more exactly: is there a sure criterion of the distinction between dreams and reality? between phantasms and real objects? The assertion that what is dreamt is less vivid and distinct than what we actually perceive is not to the point, because no one has ever been able to make a fair comparison of the two; for we can compare only the recollection of a dream with the present reality. . . .

The only sure criterion by which to distinguish them is in fact the entirely empirical one of awaking, through which at any rate the causal connection between dreamed events and those of waking life, is distinctly and sensibly broken off. This is strongly supported by the remark of Hobbes in the second chapter of *Leviathan,* that we easily mistake dreams for reality if we have unintentionally fallen asleep without taking off our clothes, and much more so when it also happens that some undertaking or design fills all our thoughts, and occupies our dreams as well as our waking moments. We then observe the awaking just as little as the falling asleep, dream and reality run together and become confounded. In such a case there is nothing for it but the application of Kant's criterion; but if, as often happens, we fail to establish by means of this criterion, either the existence of causal connection with the present, or the absence of such connection, then it must for ever remain uncertain whether an event was dreamt or really happened. Here, in fact, the intimate relationship between life and dreams is brought out very clearly, and we need not be ashamed to confess it, as it has been recognized and spoken of by many great men. The Vedas and Puranas have no better simile than a dream for the whole knowledge of the actual world, which they call the web of Mâyâ, and they use none more frequently. Plato often says that men live only in a dream; the philosopher alone strives to awake himself. Pindar says (ii., η. 135): σκιας οναρ ανθρωπος [1] and Sophocles:—

Ορω γαρ ημας ουδεν οντας αλλο, πλην
Σιδωλ' οσοιπερ ζωμεν, η κουφην σκιαν.—Ajax, 125.[2]

Beside which most worthily stands Shakespeare:—

"We are such stuff
As dreams are made on, and our little life
Is rounded with a sleep."—Tempest, Act iv., Sc. I.

Lastly, Calderon was so deeply impressed with this view of life that he sought to embody it in a kind of metaphysical drama—"Life a Dream."

After these numerous quotations from the poets, perhaps I also may be allowed to express myself by a metaphor. Life and dreams are leaves of the same book. The systematic reading of this book is real life, but when the reading hours (that is, the day) are over, we often continue idly to turn over the leaves, and read a page here and there without method or connection: often one we have read before, sometimes one that is new to us, but always in the same book. Such an isolated page is indeed out of connection with the systematic study of the book, but it does not seem so very different when we remember that the whole continuous perusal begins and ends just as abruptly, and may therefore be regarded as merely a larger single page.

Thus although individual dreams are distinguished from real life by the fact that they do not fit into that continuity which runs through the whole of experience, and the act of awaking brings this into consciousness, yet that very continuity of experience belongs to real life as its form, and the dream on its part can point to a similar continuity in itself. If, therefore, we consider the question from a point of view external to both, there is no distinct difference in their nature, and we are forced to concede to the poets that life is a long dream.

[1] Man is like a shadow.
[2] For I perceive that we, whoever we are, are only images and thin shadows.

Let us turn back now from this quite independent empirical origin of the question of the reality of the outer world, to its speculative origin. . . . I think that the true expression of the inmost meaning of the question is this:—What is this world of perception besides being my idea? Is that of which I am conscious only as idea, exactly like my own body, of which I am doubly conscious, in one aspect as *idea,* in another aspect as *will?* The fuller explanation of this question and its answer in the affirmative, will form the content of the second book, and its consequences will occupy the remaining portion of this work. . . .

§ 7

With reference to our exposition up to this point, it must be observed that we did not start either from the object or the subject, but from the idea, which contains and presupposes them both; for the antithesis of object and subject is its primary, universal and essential form. . . .

This procedure distinguishes our philosophical method from that of all former systems. For they all start either from the object or from the subject, and therefore seek to explain the one from the other. . . .

The systems starting from the object had always the whole world of perception and its constitution as their problem; yet the object which they take as their starting-point is not always this whole world of perception, nor its fundamental element, matter. On the contrary, a division of these systems may be made, based on the four classes of possible objects set forth in the introductory essay. Thus Thales and the Ionic school, Democritus, Epicurus, Giordano Bruno, and the French materialists, may be said to have started from the first class of objects, the real world: Spinoza (on account of his conception of substance, which is purely abstract, and exists only in his definition) and, earlier, the Eleatics, from the second class, the abstract conception: the Pythagoreans and Chinese philosophy in Y-King, from the third class, time, and consequently number: and, lastly, the schoolmen, who teach a creation out of nothing by the act of will of an extra-mundane personal being, started from the fourth class of objects, the act of will directed by knowledge.

Of all systems of philosophy which start from the object, the most consistent, and that which may be carried furthest, is simple materialism. It regards matter, and with it time and space, as existing absolutely, and ignores the relation to the subject in which alone all this really exists. It then lays hold of the law of causality as a guiding principle or clue, regarding it as a self-existent order (or arrangement) of things, and so fails to take account of the understanding, in which and for which alone causality is. It seeks the primary and most simple state of matter, and then tries to develop all the others from it; ascending from mere mechanism, to chemism, to polarity, to the vegetable and to the animal kingdom. And if we suppose this to have been done, the last link in the chain would be animal sensibility—that is, knowledge—which would consequently now appear as a mere modification or state of matter produced by causality. Now if we had followed materialism thus far with clear ideas, when we reached its highest point we would suddenly be seized with a fit of the inextinguishable laughter of the Olympians. As if waking from a dream, we would all at once become aware that its final result—knowledge, which it reached so laboriously, was presupposed as the indispensable condition of its very starting-point, mere matter; and when we imagined that we thought matter, we really thought only the subject that perceives matter; the eye that sees it, the hand that feels it, the understanding that knows it. Thus the tremendous *petitio principii* [3] reveals itself unexpectedly; for suddenly the last link is seen to be the starting-point, the chain a circle, and the materialist is like Baron Münchausen who, when swimming in water on horseback, drew the horse into the air with his legs, and himself also by his cue. The fundamental absurdity of materialism is that it starts from the *objective,* and takes as the ultimate ground of explanation something *objective,* whether it be matter in the abstract, simply as it is *thought,* or, after it has taken form, is empirically given—that is to say, is *substance,* the chemical element with its primary relations. Some such thing it takes, as existing

[3] Begging of the question.

absolutely and in itself, in order that it may evolve organic nature and finally the knowing subject from it, and explain them adequately by means of it; whereas in truth all that is objective is already determined as such in manifold ways by the knowing subject through its forms of knowing, and presupposes them; and consequently it entirely disappears if we think the subject away. Thus materialism is the attempt to explain what is immediately given us by what is given us indirectly. All that is objective, extended, active—that is to say, all that is material—is regarded by materialism as affording so solid a basis for its explanation, that a reduction of everything to this can leave nothing to be desired (especially if in ultimate analysis this reduction should resolve itself into action and reaction). But we have shown that all this is given indirectly and in the highest degree determined, and is therefore merely a relatively present object, for it has passed through the machinery and manufactory of the brain, and has thus come under the forms of space, time and causality, by means of which it is first presented to us as extended in space and ever active in time. From such an indirectly given object, materialism seeks to explain what is immediately given, the idea (in which alone the object that materialism starts with exists), and finally even the will from which all those fundamental forces, that manifest themselves, under the guidance of causes, and therefore according to law, are in truth to be explained. To the assertion that thought is a modification of matter we may always, with equal right, oppose the contrary assertion that all matter is merely the modification of the knowing subject, as its idea. Yet the aim and ideal of all natural science is at bottom a consistent materialism. The recognition here of the obvious impossibility of such a system establishes another truth which will appear in the course of our exposition, the truth that all science properly so called, by which I understand systematic knowledge under the guidance of the principle of sufficient reason, can never reach its final goal, nor give a complete and adequate explanation: for it is not concerned with the inmost nature of the world, it cannot get beyond the idea; indeed, it really teaches nothing more than the relation of one idea to another.

Every science must start from two principal data. One of these is always the principle of sufficient reason in some form or another, as organon; the other is its special object as problem. Thus, for example, geometry has space as problem, and the ground of existence in space as organon. Arithmetic has time as problem, and the ground of existence in time as organon. Logic has the combination of concepts as such as problem, and the ground of knowledge as organon. History has the past acts of men treated as a whole as problem, and the law of human motives as organon. Natural science has matter as problem, and the law of causality as organon. Its end and aim is therefore, by the guidance of causality, to refer all possible states of matter to other states, and ultimately to one single state; and again to deduce these states from each other, and ultimately from one single state. Thus two states of matter stand over against each other in natural science as extremes: that state in which matter is furthest from being the immediate object of the subject, and that state in which it is most completely such an immediate object, *i. e.,* the most dead and crude matter, the primary element, as the one extreme, and the human organism as the other. Natural science as chemistry seeks for the first, as physiology for the second. But as yet neither extreme has been reached, and it is only in the intermediate ground that something has been won. The prospect is indeed somewhat hopeless. The chemists, under the presupposition that the qualitative division of matter is not, like quantitative division, an endless process, are always trying to decrease the number of the elements, of which there are still about sixty; and if they were to succeed in reducing them to two, they would still try to find the common root of these. For, on the one hand, the law of homogeneity leads to the assumption of a primary chemical state of matter, which alone belongs to matter as such, and precedes all others which are not essentially matter as such, but merely contingent forms and qualities. On the other hand, we cannot understand how this one state could ever experience a chemical change, if there did not exist a second state to affect it. Thus the same difficulty appears in chemistry which Epicurus met with in mechanics. For he had to show how the first atom departed from the original direction of its motion. Indeed this contradiction, which develops entirely of itself and can neither be escaped nor solved, might quite properly be set up as a chemical *antinomy*. Thus an antinomy appears in the one extreme of natural science, and a corresponding one will appear in the other. There is just as little hope of reaching this opposite extreme of natural science, for we see ever more clearly that what is chemical can never be referred to what is mechanical, nor what is organic to what is chemical or electrical. Those who in our own day are entering anew on this old, misleading path, will soon slink back silent and ashamed, as all their predecessors have done before them. We shall consider this more fully in the second book. Natural science encounters the difficulties which we have cursorily mentioned, in its own province. Regarded as philosophy, it would further be materialism; but this, as we have seen, even at its birth, has death in its heart, because it ignores the subject and the forms of knowledge, which are presupposed, just as much in the case of the crudest matter, from which it desires to start, as in that of the organism, at which it desires to arrive. For, "no object without a subject," is the principle which renders all materialism forever impossible. Suns and planets without an eye that sees them and an understanding that knows them, may indeed be spoken of in words, but for the idea, these words are absolutely meaningless. On the other hand, the law of causality and the treatment and investigation of nature which is based upon it, lead us necessarily to the conclusion that, in time, each more highly organized state of matter has succeeded a cruder state: so that the lower animals existed before men, fishes before land animals, plants before fishes, and the unorganized before all that is organized; that, consequently, the original mass had to pass through a long series of changes before the first eye could be opened. And yet, the existence of this whole world remains ever dependent upon the first eye that opened, even if it were that of an insect. For such an eye is a necessary condition of the possibility of knowledge, and the whole world exists only in and for knowledge, and without it is not even thinkable. The world is entirely idea, and as such demands the knowing subject as the supporter of its existence. This long course of time itself, filled with innumerable changes, through which matter rose from form to form till at last the first percipient creature appeared,— this whole time itself is only thinkable in the identity of a consciousness whose succession of ideas, whose form of knowing it is, and apart from which, it loses all meaning and is nothing at all. Thus we see, on the one hand, the existence of the whole world necessarily dependent upon the first conscious being, however undeveloped it may be; on the other hand, this conscious being just as necessarily entirely dependent upon a long chain of causes and effects which have preceded it, and in which it itself appears as a small link. These two contradictory points of view, to each of which we are led with the same necessity, we might again call an *antinomy* in our faculty of knowledge, and set it up as the counterpart of that which we found in the first extreme of natural science. The fourfold antinomy of Kant will be shown, in the criticism of his philosophy appended to this volume, to be a groundless delusion. But the necessary contradiction which at last presents itself to us here, finds its solution in the fact that, to use Kant's phraseology, time, space, and causality do not belong to the thing-in-itself, but only to its phenomena, of which they are the form; which in my language means this: The objective world, the world as idea, is not the only side of the world, but merely its outward side; and it has an entirely different side—the side of its inmost nature—its kernel—the thing-in-itself. This we shall consider in the second book, calling it after the most immediate of its objective manifestations—will. But the world as idea, with which alone we are here concerned, only appears with the opening of the first eye. Without this medium of knowledge it cannot be, and therefore it was not before it. But without that eye, that is to say, outside of knowledge, there was also no before, no time. Thus time has no beginning, but all beginning is in time. Since, however, it is the most universal form of the knowable, in which all phenomena are united together through causality, time, with its infinity of past and future, is present in the beginning of knowledge. The phenomenon which fills the first present must at once be known as causally bound up with and dependent upon a sequence of phenomena which stretches infinitely into the past, and this past itself is just as truly conditioned by this first present, as conversely the present is by the past. Accordingly the past out of which the first present arises, is, like it, dependent upon the knowing subject, without which it is nothing. It necessarily happens, however, that this first present does not manifest itself as the first, that is, as having no past for its parent, but as being the beginning of time. It manifests itself rather as the consequence of the past, according to the principle of existence in time. In the same way, the phenomena which fill this first present appear as the effects of earlier phenomena which filled the past, in accordance with the law of casuality. Those who like mythological interpretations may take the birth of Kronos ($\chi\rho\text{ovos}$), the youngest of the Titans, as a symbol of the moment here referred to at which time appears, though, indeed it has no beginning; for with him, since he ate his father, the crude productions of heaven and earth cease, and the races of gods and men appear upon the scene.

This explanation at which we have arrived by following the most consistent of the philosophical systems which start from the object, materialism, has brought out clearly the inseparable and reciprocal dependence of subject and object, and at the same time the inevitable antithesis between them. And this knowledge leads us to seek for the inner nature of the world, the thing-in-itself, not in either of the two elements of the idea, but in something quite distinct from it, and which is not encumbered with such a fundamental and insoluble antithesis.

Opposed to the system we have explained, which starts from the object in order to derive the subject from it, is the system which starts from the subject and tries to derive the object from it. The first of these has been of frequent and common occurrence throughout the history of philosophy, but of the second we find only one example, and that a very recent one; the "philosophy of appearance" of J. G. Fichte. In this respect, therefore, it must be considered; little real worth or inner meaning as the doctrine itself had. It was indeed for the most part merely a delusion, but it was delivered with an air of the deepest earnestness, with sustained loftiness of tone and zealous ardour, and was defended with eloquent polemic against weak opponents, so that it was able to present a brilliant exterior and seemed to be something. But the genuine earnestness which keeps truth always steadfastly before it as its goal, and is unaffected by any external influences, was entirely wanting to Fichte, as it is to all philosophers who, like him, concern themselves with questions of the day. In his case,

indeed, it could not have been otherwise. A man becomes a
philosopher by reason of a certain perplexity, from which he seeks
to free himself. This is Plato's θαυμαξειν,[4] which he calls a μαλα
ΦιλοσοΦικον παθος.[5] But what distinguishes the false philosopher
from the true is this: the perplexity of the latter arises from the
contemplation of the world itself, while that of the former results
from some book, some system of philosophy which is before him.
Now Fichte belongs to the class of the false philosophers. He was
made a philosopher by Kant's doctrine of the thing-in-itself, and
if it had not been for this he would probably have pursued entirely
different ends, with far better results, for he certainly possessed
remarkable rhetorical talent. If he had only penetrated somewhat
deeply into the meaning of the book that made him a philosopher,
"The Critique of Pure Reason," he would have understood that
its principal teaching about mind is this. The principle of sufficient
reason [6] is not, as all scholastic philosophy maintains, a *veritas
aeterna*—that is to say, it does not possess an unconditioned validity before, outside of, and above the world. It is relative and conditioned, and valid only in the sphere of phenomena, and thus
it may appear as the necessary nexus of space and time, or as the
law of causality, or as the law of the ground of knowledge. The
inner nature of the world, the thing-in-itself can never be found
by the guidance of this principle, for all that it leads to will be
found to be dependent and relative and merely phenomenal, not
the thing-in-itself. Further, it does not concern the subject, but
is only the form of objects, which are therefore not things-in-
themselves. The subject must exist along with the object, and the
object along with the subject, so that it is impossible that subject
and object can stand to each other in a relation of reason and
consequent. . . .

§ 16

After this full consideration of reason as a special faculty of
knowledge belonging to man alone, and the results and phenomena

[4] Wonder.
[5] A black philosophical disease.
[6] *I. e.*, the principle of causation.

peculiar to human nature brought about by it, it still remains for me to speak of reason, so far as it is the guide of human action, and in this respect may be called *practical*. But what there is to say upon this point has found its place elsewhere in the appendix to this work, where I controvert the existence of the so-called practical reason of Kant, which he (certainly very conveniently) explained as the immediate source of virtue, and as the seat of an absolute (*i. e.,* fallen from heaven) imperative. . . .

At the commencement of our treatment of reason we remarked, in general terms, how much the action and behaviour of men differs from that of brutes, and that this difference is to be regarded as entirely due to the presence of abstract concepts in consciousness. The influence of these upon our whole existence is so penetrating and significant that, on account of them, we are related to the lower animals very much as those animals that see are related to those that have no eyes (certain larva, worms, and zoophytes). Animals without eyes know only by touch what is immediately present to them in space, what comes into contact with them; those which see, on the contrary, know a wide circle of near and distant objects. In the same way the absence of reason confines the lower animals to the ideas of perception, *i. e.,* the real objects which are immediately present to them in time; we, on the contrary, on account of knowledge in the abstract, comprehend not only the narrow actual present, but also the whole past and future, and the wide sphere of the possible; we view life freely on all its sides, and go far beyond the present and the actual. Thus what the eye is in space and for sensuous knowledge, reason is, to a certain extent, in time and for inner knowledge. But as the visibility of objects has its worth and meaning only in the fact that it informs us of their tangibility, so the whole worth of abstract knowledge always consists in its relation to what is perceived. Therefore men naturally attach far more worth to immediate and perceived knowledge than to abstract concepts, to that which is merely thought; they place empirical knowledge before logical. But this is not the opinion of men who live more in words than in deeds, who have seen more on paper and in books than in actual life, and who in their greatest degeneracy become pedants and lovers of the mere letter. . . .

The many-sided view of life as a whole which man, as distinguished from the lower animals, possesses through reason, may
be compared to a geometrical, colourless, abstract, reduced plan
of his actual life. He, therefore, stands to the lower animals as
the navigator who, by means of chart, compass, and quadrant,
knows accurately his course and his position at any time upon
the sea, stands to the uneducated sailors who see only the waves
and the heavens. Thus it is worth noticing, and indeed wonderful,
how, besides his life in the concrete, man always lives another
life in the abstract. In the former he is given as a prey to all the
storms of actual life, and to the influence of the present; he must
struggle, suffer, and die like the brute. But his life in the abstract, as it lies before his rational consciousness, is the still reflection of the former, and of the world in which he lives; it is
just that reduced chart or plan to which we have referred. Here
in the sphere of quiet deliberation, what completely possessed
him and moved him intensely before, appears to him cold, colourless, and for the moment external to him; he is merely the spectator, the observer. In respect of this withdrawal into reflection
he may be compared to an actor who has played his part in one
scene, and who takes his place among the audience till it is time
for him to go upon the stage again, and quietly looks on at whatever may happen, even though it be the preparation for his own
death (in the piece), but afterwards he again goes on the stage
and acts and suffers as he must. From this double life proceeds
that quietness peculiar to human beings, so very different from
the thoughtlessness of the brutes, and with which, in accordance
with previous reflection, or a formed determination, or a recognized necessity, a man suffers or accomplishes in cold blood, what
is of the utmost and often terrible importance to him; suicide,
execution, the duel, enterprises of every kind fraught with danger
to life, and, in general, things against which his whole animal
nature rebels. Under such circumstances we see to what an extent
reason has mastered the animal nature, and we say to the strong:
οιδηρειον νυ τοι ἦτορ! (*ferreum certe tibi cor.* Il., 24, 521).[7] Here
we can say truly that reason manifests itself practically, and thus
wherever action is guided by reason, where the motives are ab-

---

[7] Surely your heart is of iron.

stract concepts, wherever we are not determined by particular ideas of perception, nor by the impression of the moment which guides the brutes, there *practical reason* shows itself. But I have fully explained in the Appendix, and illustrated by examples, that this is entirely different from and unrelated to the ethical worth of actions; that rational action and virtuous action are two entirely different things; that reason may just as well find itself in connection with great evil as with great good, and by its assistance may give great power to the one as well as to the other; that it is equally ready and valuable for the methodical and consistent carrying out of the noble and of the bad intention, of the wise as of the foolish maxim; which all results from the constitution of its nature, which is feminine, receptive, retentive, and not spontaneous. . . .

The ideal explained in the *Stoical philosophy* is the most complete development of *practical reason* in the true and genuine sense of the word; it is the highest summit to which man can attain by the mere use of his reason, and in it his difference from the brutes shows itself most distinctly. For the ethics of Stoicism are originally and essentially, not a doctrine of virtue, but merely a guide to a rational life, the end and aim of which is happiness through peace of mind. Virtuous conduct appears in it as it were merely by accident, as the means, not as the end. Therefore the ethical theory of Stoicism is in its whole nature and point of view fundamentally different from the ethical systems which lay stress directly upon virtue, such as the doctrines of the Vedas, of Plato, of Christianity, and of Kant. The aim of Stoical ethics is happiness. Yet the ethics of Stoicism teach that happiness can only be attained with certainty through inward peace and quietness of spirit (αταραξια), and that this again can only be reached through virtue; this is the whole meaning of the saying that virtue is the highest good. But if indeed by degrees the end is lost sight of in the means, and virtue is inculcated in a way which discloses an interest entirely different from that of one's own happiness, for it contradicts this too distinctly; this is just one of those inconsistencies by means of which, in every system, the immediately known, or, as it is called, felt truth leads us back to the right way in defiance of syllogistic reasoning; as, for exam-

ple, we see clearly in the ethical teaching of Spinoza, which deduces a pure doctrine of virtue from the egoistical *suum utile
quærere* [8] by means of palpable sophisms. According to this, as I
conceive the spirit of the Stoical ethics, their source lies in the
question whether the great prerogative of man, reason, which, by
means of planned action and its results, relieves life and its burdens
so much, might not also be capable of freeing him at once, directly,
i. e., through mere knowledge, completely, or nearly so, of the
sorrows and miseries of every kind of which his life is full. They
held that it was not in keeping with the prerogative of reason
that the nature given with it, which by means of it comprehends
and contemplates an infinity of things and circumstances, should
yet, through the present, and the accidents that can be contained
in the few years of a life that is short, fleeting, and uncertain,
be exposed to such intense pain, to such great anxiety and suffering,
as arise from the tempestuous strain of the desires and the antip-
athies; and they believed that the due application of reason must
raise men above them, and can make them invulnerable. Therefore Antisthenes says: Δει κτασθαι νουν, η βροχον (*aut mentem
parandam, aut laqueum.*[9] Plut. de stoic. repugn., c. 14), *i. e.,* life
is so full of troubles and vexations, that one must either rise above
it by means of corrected thoughts, or leave it. It was seen that want
and suffering did not directly and of necessity spring from not
having, but from desiring to have and not having; that therefore
this desire to have is the necessary condition under which alone it
becomes a privation not to have and begets pain. Ου πενια λυπην
εργαζεται, αλλα επιθυμια (*non paupertas dolorem efficit, sed cupiditas*), Epict., fragm. 25.[10] Men learned also from experience that
it is only the hope of what is claimed that begets and nourishes
the wish; therefore neither the many unavoidable evils which are
common to all, nor unattainable blessings, disquiet or trouble us,
but only the trifling more or less of those things which we can
avoid or attain; indeed, not only what is absolutely unavoidable
or unattainable, but also what is merely relatively so, leaves us
quite undisturbed; therefore the ills that have once become joined

[8] To seek one's own good.
[9] Either a prepared mind, or death.
[10] It is not poverty but desire that brings unhappiness.

to our individuality, or the good things that must of necessity always be denied us, are treated with indifference, in accordance with the peculiarity of human nature that every wish soon dies and can no more beget pain if it is not nourished by hope. It followed from all this that happiness always depends upon the proportion between our claims and what we receive. It is all one whether the quantities thus related be great or small, and the proportion can be established just as well by diminishing the amount of the first as by increasing the amount of the second; and in the same way it also follows that all suffering proceeds from the want of proportion between what we demand and expect and what we get. Now this want of proportion obviously lies only in knowledge, and it could be entirely abolished through fuller insight. Therefore Chrysippus says: δει ζην κατ’ εμπειριαν των φυσει συμβαινοντων (Stob. Ecl., L. ii., c. 7, p. 134), that is, one ought to live with a due knowledge of the transitory nature of the things of the world. For as often as a man loses self-command, or is struck down by a misfortune, or grows angry, or becomes faint-hearted, he shows that he finds things different from what he expected, consequently that he was caught in error, and did not know the world and life, did not know that the will of the individual is crossed at every step by the chance of inanimate nature and the antagonism of aims and the wickedness of other individuals: he has therefore either not made use of his reason in order to arrive at a general knowledge of this characteristic of life, or he lacks judgment, in that he does not recognize in the particular what he knows in general, and is therefore surprised by it and loses his self-command. Thus also every keen pleasure is an error and an illusion, for no attained wish can give lasting satisfaction; and moreover, every possession and every happiness is but lent by chance for an uncertain time, and may therefore be demanded back the next hour. All pain rests on the passing away of such an illusion; thus both arise from defective knowledge; the wise man therefore holds himself equally aloof from joy and sorrow, and no event disturbs his αταραξια.

In accordance with this spirit and aim of the Stoa, Epictetus began and ended with the doctrine as the kernel of his philosophy, that we should consider well and distinguish what depends upon

us and what does not, and therefore entirely avoid counting upon
the latter, whereby we shall certainly remain free from all pain,
sorrow, and anxiety. But that which alone is dependent upon us
is the will; and here a transition gradually takes place to a doctrine of virtue, for it is observed that as the outer world, which
is independent of us, determines good and bad fortune, so inner
contentment with ourselves, or the absence of it, proceeds from the
will. But it was then asked whether we ought to apply the words
bonum and *malùm* to the two former or to the two latter? This
was indeed arbitrary and a matter of choice, and did not make
any real difference, but yet the Stoics disputed everlastingly with
the Peripatetics and Epicureans about it, and amused themselves
with the inadmissible comparison of two entirely incommensurable
quantities, and the antithetical, paradoxical judgments which proceeded from them, and which they flung at each other. The
Paradoxa of Cicero afford us an interesting collection of these
from the Stoical side.

Zeno, the founder, seems originally to have followed a somewhat different path. The starting-point with him was that for
the attainment of the highest good, *i. e.,* blessedness and spiritual
peace, one must live in harmony with oneself. Now this was
only possible for a man if he determined himself entirely rationally,
according to concepts, not according to changing impressions and
moods; since, however, only the maxims of our conduct, not the
consequences nor the outward circumstances, are in our power,
in order to be always consistent we must set before us as our aim
only the maxims and not the consequences and circumstances, and
thus again a doctrine of virtue is introduced.

But the ethical principle of Zeno—to live in harmony with
oneself—appeared even to his immediate successors to be too formal
and empty. They therefore gave it material content by the addition—"to live in harmony with nature" (ὁμολογουμενως τῃ φυσει
ζῃν), which, as Stobæus mentions in another place, was
first added by Kleanthes, and extended the matter very much on
account of the wide sphere of the concept and the vagueness of
the expression. For Kleanthes meant the whole of nature in general, while Chrysippus meant human nature in particular (Diog.
Laert., 7, 89). It followed that what alone was adapted to the

latter was virtue, just as the satisfaction of animal desires was adapted to animal natures; and thus ethics had again to be forcibly united to a doctrine of virtue, and in some way or other established through physics. For the Stoics always aimed at unity of principle, as for them God and the world were not dissevered.

The ethical system of Stoicism, regarded as a whole, is in fact a very valuable and estimable attempt to use the great prerogative of man, reason, for an important and salutary end; to raise him above the suffering and pain to which all life is exposed, by means of a maxim—

> *"Qua ratione queas traducere leniter ævum:*
> *Ne te semper inops agitet vexetque cupido,*
> *Ne pavor et rerum mediocriter utilium spes,"* [11]

and thus to make him partake, in the highest degree, of the dignity which belongs to him as a rational being, as distinguished from the brutes; a dignity of which, in this sense at any rate, we can speak, though not in any other. It is a consequence of my view of the ethical system of Stoicism that it must be explained at the part of my work at which I consider what reason is and what it can do. But although it may to a certain extent be possible to attain that end through the application of reason, and through a purely rational system of ethics, and although experience shows that the happiest men are those purely rational characters commonly called practical philosophers,—and rightly so, because just as the true, that is, the theoretical philosopher carries life into the concept, they carry the concept into life,—yet it is far from the case that perfection can be attained in this way, and that the reason, rightly used, can really free us from the burden and sorrow of life, and lead us to happiness. Rather, there lies an absolute contradiction in wishing to live without suffering, and this contradiction is also implied in the commonly used expression, "blessed life." This will become perfectly clear to whoever comprehends the whole of the following exposition. In this purely rational system of ethics the contradiction reveals itself thus, the Stoic is obliged in his

[11] "Would you learn how to pass your years quietly?
Do not let greedy desire always vex and agitate you,
Nor fear or hope of mediocre wealth."

doctrine of the way to the blessed life (for that is what his ethical system always remains) to insert a recommendation of suicide (as among the magnificent ornaments and apparel of Eastern despots there is always a costly vial of poison) for the case in which the sufferings of the body, which cannot be philosophized away by any principles or syllogistic reasonings, are paramount and incurable; thus its one aim, blessedness, is rendered vain, and nothing remains as a mode of escape from suffering except death; in such a case then death must be voluntarily accepted, just as we would take any other medicine. Here then a marked antagonism is brought out between the ethical system of Stoicism and all those systems referred to above which make virtue in itself directly, and accompanied by the most grievous sorrows, their aim, and will not allow a man to end his life in order to escape from suffering. Not one of them, however, was able to give the true reason for the rejection of suicide, but they laboriously collected illusory explanations from all sides: the true reason will appear in the Fourth Book in the course of the development of our system. But the antagonism referred to reveals and establishes the essential difference in fundamental principle between Stoicism, which is just a special form of endæmonism, and those doctrines we have mentioned, although both are often at one in their results, and are apparently related. And the inner contradiction referred to above, with which the ethical system of Stoicism is affected even in its fundamental thought, shows itself further in the circumstance that its ideal, the Stoic philosopher, as the system itself represents him, could never obtain life or inner poetic truth, but remains a wooden, stiff lay-figure of which nothing can be made. He cannot himself make use of his wisdom, and his perfect peace, contentment, and blessedness directly contradict the nature of man, and preclude us from forming any concrete idea of him. When compared with him, how entirely different appear the overcomers of the world, and voluntary hermits that Indian philosophy presents to us, and has actually produced; or indeed, the Holy Man of Christianity, that excellent form full of deep life, of the greatest poetic truth, and the highest significance, which stands before us in perfect virtue, holiness, and sublimity, yet in a state of supreme suffering.

SECOND BOOK

THE WORLD AS WILL

First Aspect

THE OBJECTIFICATION OF THE WILL

Nos habitat, non tartara, sed nec sidera coeli:
Spiritus, in nobis qui viget, illa facit.

A spirit dwells in us, but not in the depths or the stars;
It made them, and gives us life.

II

§ 17

IN the first book we considered the idea merely as such, that is, only according to its general form. . . .

But what now impels us to inquiry is just that we are not satisfied with knowing that we have ideas, that they are such and such, and that they are connected according to certain laws, the general expression of which is the principle of sufficient reason. We wish to know the significance of these ideas; we ask whether this world is merely idea; in which case it would pass by us like an empty dream or a baseless vision, not worth our notice; or whether it is also something else, something more than idea, and if so, what. . . .

Thus we see already that we can never arrive at the real nature of things from without. However much we investigate, we can never reach anything but images and names. We are like a man who goes round a castle seeking in vain for an entrance, and sometimes sketching the façades. And yet this is the method that has been followed by all philosophers before me.

§ 18

In fact, the meaning for which we seek of that world which is present to us only as our idea, or the transition from the world as mere idea of the knowing subject to whatever it may be besides this, would never be found if the investigator himself were nothing more than the pure knowing subject (a winged cherub without a body). But he is himself rooted in that world; he finds himself in it as an *individual,* that is to say, his knowledge, which is the necessary supporter of the whole world as idea, is yet always given through the medium of a body, whose affections are, as we have shown, the starting-point for the understanding in the perception of that world. . . . The answer to the riddle is given to the subject of knowledge who appears as an individual, and the answer is *will*. This and this alone gives him the key to his own existence, reveals to him the significance, shows him the inner mechanism of his being, of his action, of his movements. The body is given in two entirely different ways to the subject of knowledge, who becomes an individual only through his identity with it. It is given as an idea in intelligent perception, as an object among objects and subject to the laws of objects. And it is also given in quite a different way as that which is immediately known to every one, and is signified by the word *will*. Every true act of his will is also at once and without exception a movement of his body. The act of will and the movement of the body are not two different things objectively known, which the bond of causality unites; they do not stand in the relation of cause and effect; they are one and the same, but they are given in entirely different ways,— immediately, and again in perception for the understanding. The action of the body is nothing but the act of the will objectified, *i. e.*, passed into perception. It will appear later that this is true of every movement of the body, not merely those which follow upon motives, but also involuntary movements which follow upon mere stimuli, and, indeed, that the whole body is nothing but objectified will, *i. e.*, will become idea. All this will be proved and made quite clear in the course of this work. In one respect, therefore, I shall call the body the *objectivity of will;* as in the previous book, and in the essay on the principle of sufficient reason, in accordance with the one-sided point of view intentionally adopted there (that of the idea), I called it *the immediate object*. Thus in a certain sense we may also say that will is the knowledge *a priori* of the body, and the body is the knowledge *a posteriori* of the will. Resolutions of the will which relate to the future are merely deliberations of the reason about what we shall will at a particular time, not real acts of will. Only the carrying out of the resolve stamps it as will, for till then it is never more than an intention that may be changed, and that exists only in the reason *in abstracto*. It is only in reflection that to will and to act are different; in reality they are one. Every true, genuine, immediate act of will is also, at once and immediately, a visible act of the body. And, corresponding to this, every impression upon the body is also, on the other hand, at once and immediately an impression upon the will. As such it is called pain when it is opposed to the will; gratification or pleasure when it is in accordance with it. The degrees of both are widely different. It is quite wrong, however, to call pain and pleasure ideas, for they are by no means ideas, but immediate affections of the will in its manifestation, the body; compulsory, instantaneous willing or not-willing of the impression which the body sustains. There are only a few impressions of the body which do not touch the will, and it is through these alone that the body is an immediate object of knowledge, for, as perceived by the understanding, it is already an indirect object like all others. These impressions are, therefore, to be treated directly as mere ideas, and excepted from what has been said. The impressions we refer to are the affections of the purely objective senses of sight, hearing, and touch, though only so far as these organs are affected in the way which is specially peculiar to their specific nature. This affection of them is so excessively weak an excitement of the heightened and specifically modified sensibility of these parts that it does not affect the will, but only furnishes the understanding with the data out of which the perception arises, undisturbed by any excitement of the will. But every stronger or different kind of affection of these organs of sense is painful, that is to say, against the will, and thus they also belong to its objectivity. Weakness of the nerves shows itself in this, that the impressions which have only such a degree of strength as would usually be sufficient to make them data for the understanding reach the higher degree at which they influence the will, that is to say, give pain or pleasure, though more often pain, which is, however, to some extent deadened and inarticulate, so that not only particular tones and strong light are painful to us, but there ensues a generally unhealthy and hypochondriacal disposition which is not distinctly understood. The identity of the body and the will shows itself further, among other ways, in the circumstance that every vehement and excessive movement of the will, *i. e.,* every emotion, agitates the body and its inner constitution directly, and disturbs the course of its vital functions. . . .

Lastly, the knowledge which I have of my will, though it is immediate, cannot be separated from that which I have of my body. I know my will, not as a whole, not as a unity, not completely, according to its nature, but I know it only in its particular acts, and therefore in time, which is the form of the phenomenal aspect of my body, as of every object. Therefore the body is a condition of the knowledge of my will. Thus, I cannot really imagine this will apart from my body. . . .

We can turn the expression of this truth in different ways and say: My body and my will are one;—or, What as an idea of perception I call my body, I call my will, so far as I am conscious of it, in an entirely different way which cannot be compared to any other;—or, My body is the *objectivity* of my will. . . .

§ 19

In the first book we were reluctantly driven to explain the human body as merely idea of the subject which knows it, like all the other objects in this world of perception. But it has now become clear that what enables us consciously to distinguish our own body from all other objects which in other respects are precisely the same, is that our body appears in consciousness in quite another way *toto genere* different in idea, and this we denote by the word *will;* and that it is just this double knowledge which we have of our own body that affords us information about it, about its action and movement following on motives, and also about what it experiences by means of external impressions; in a word, about what it is, not as idea, but as more than idea; that is to say, what it is *in itself*. None of this information have we got directly with regard to the nature, action, and experience of other real objects.

It is just because of this special relation to one body that the knowing subject is an individual. For regarded apart from this relation, his body is for him only an idea like all other ideas. But the relation through which the knowing subject is an *individual,* is just on that account a relation which subsists only between him and one particular idea of all those which he has. Therefore he is conscious of this one idea, not merely as an idea, but in quite a different way as a will. If, however, he abstracts from that special relation, from that twofold and completely hetero-geneous knowledge of what is one and the same, then that *one,* the body, is an idea like all other ideas. Therefore, in order to understand the matter, the individual who knows must either as-sume that what distinguishes that one idea from others is merely the fact that his knowledge stands in this double relation to it alone; that insight in two ways at the same time is open to him only in the case of this one object of perception, and that this is to be explained not by the difference of this object from all others, but only by the difference between the relation of his knowledge to this one object, and its relation to all other objects. Or else he must assume that this object is essentially different from all others; that it alone of all objects is at once both will and idea, while the rest are only ideas, *i. e.,* only phantoms. Thus he must assume that his body is the only real individual in the world, *i. e.,* the only phenomenon of will and the only immediate object of the subject. That other objects, considered merely as *ideas,* are like his body, that is, like it, fill space (which itself can only be present as idea), and also, like it, are causally active in space, is indeed demonstrably certain from the law of causality which is *a priori* valid for ideas, and which admits of no effect without a cause; but apart from the fact that we can only reason from an effect to a cause generally, and not to a similar cause, we are still in the sphere of mere ideas, in which alone the law of causality is valid, and beyond which it can never take us. But whether the objects known to the individual only as ideas are yet, like his own body, manifestations of a will, is, as was said in the First Book, the proper meaning of the question as to the reality of the external world. To deny this is *theoretical egoism,* which on that account regards all phenomena that are outside its own will as phantoms, just as in a practical reference exactly the same thing is done by practical egoism. For in it a man regards and treats himself alone as a person, and all other persons as mere phantoms. Theoretical egoism can never be demonstrably refuted, yet in philosophy it has never been used otherwise than as a sceptical sophism, *i. e.,* a pretense. As a serious conviction, on the other hand, it could only be found in a madhouse, and as such it stands in need of a cure rather than a refutation. We do not therefore combat it any further in this regard, but treat it as merely the last stronghold of scepticism, which is always polemical. Thus our knowledge, which is always bound to individuality and is limited by this circumstance, brings with it the necessity that each of us can only *be one,* while, on the other hand, each of us can *know all;* and it is this limitation that creates the need for philosophy. We, therefore, who, for this very reason, are striving to extend the limits of our knowledge through philosophy, will treat this sceptical argument of theoretical egoism which meets us, as an army would treat a small frontier fortress. The fortress cannot indeed be taken, but the garrison can never sally forth from it, and therefore we pass it by without danger, and are not afraid to have it in our rear.

The double knowledge which each of us has of the nature and activity of his own body, and which is given in two completely different ways, has now been clearly brought out. We shall accordingly make further use of it as a key to the nature of every phenomenon in nature, and shall judge of all objects which are not our own bodies, and are consequently not given to our consciousness in a double way but only as ideas, according to the analogy of our own bodies, and shall therefore assume that as in one aspect they are idea, just like our bodies, and in this respect are analogous to them, so in another aspect, what remains of objects when we set aside their existence as idea of the subject, must in its inner nature be the same as that in us which we call *will.* For what other kind of existence or reality should we attribute to the rest of the material world? Whence should we take the elements out of which we construct such a world? Besides will and idea nothing is known to us or thinkable. If we wish to attribute the greatest known reality to the material world which exists immediately only in our idea, we give it the reality which our own body has for each of us; for that is the most real thing for every one. But if we now analyse the reality of this body and its actions, beyond the fact that it is idea, we find nothing in it except the will; with this its reality is exhausted. Therefore we can nowhere find another kind of reality which we can attribute to the material world. Thus if we hold that the material world is something more than merely our idea, we must say that besides being idea, that is, in itself and according to its inmost nature, it is that which we find immediately in ourselves as *will*. I say according to its inmost nature; but we must first come to know more accurately this real nature of the will, in order that we may be able to distinguish from it what does not belong to itself, but to its manifestation, which has many grades. Such, for example, is the circumstance of its being accompanied by knowledge, and the determination by motives which is conditioned by this knowledge. As we shall see farther on, this does not belong to the real nature of will, but merely to its distinct manifestation as an animal or a human being. If, therefore, I say,—the force which attracts a stone to the earth is according to its nature, in itself, and apart from all idea, will, I shall not be supposed to express in this proposition the insane opinion that the stone moves itself in accordance with a known motive, merely because this is the way in which will appears in man. We shall now proceed more clearly and in detail to prove, establish, and develop to its full extent what as yet has been only provisionally and generally explained. . . .

§ 20

If now every action of my body is the manifestation of an act of will in which my will itself in general, and as a whole, thus my character, expresses itself under given motives, manifestation of the will must be the inevitable condition and presupposition of every action. For the fact of its manifestation cannot depend upon something which does not exist directly and only through it, which consequently is for it merely accidental, and through which its manifestation itself would be merely accidental. Now that condition is just the whole body itself. Thus the body itself must be manifestation of the will, and it must be related to my will as a whole, that is, to my intelligible character, whose phenomenal appearance in time is my empirical character, as the particular action of the body is related to the particular act of the will. The whole body, then, must be simply my will become visible, must be my will itself, so far as this is object of perception, an idea of the first class. It has already been advanced in confirmation of this that every impression upon my body also affects my will at once and immediately, and in this respect is called pain or pleasure, or, in its lower degrees, agreeable or disagreeable sensation; and also, conversely, that every violent movement of the will, every emotion or passion, convulses the body and disturbs the course of its functions. Indeed we can also give an etiological account, though a very incomplete one, of the origin of my body, and a somewhat better account of its development and conservation, and this is the substance of physiology. But physiology merely explains its theme in precisely the same way as motives explain action. Thus the physiological explanation of the functions of the body detracts just as little from the philosophical truth that the whole existence of this body and the sum total of its functions are merely the objectification of that will which appears in its outward actions in accordance with a motive, as the establishment of the individual action through the motive and the necessary sequence of the action from the motive conflicts with the fact that action in general, and according to its nature, is only the manifestation of a will which itself has no ground. If, however, physiology tries to refer even these outward actions, the immediate voluntary movements, to causes in the organism,—for example, if it explains the movement of the muscles as resulting from the presence of fluids ("like the contraction of a cord when it is wet," says Reil), even supposing it really could give a thorough explanation of this kind, yet this would never invalidate the immediately certain truth that every voluntary motion is the manifestation of an act of will. Now, just as little can the physiological explanation of vegetative life, however far it may advance, ever invalidate the truth that the whole animal life which thus develops itself is the manifestation of will. In general, then, as we have shown above, no etiological explanation can ever give us more than the necessarily determined position in time and space of a particular manifestation, its necessary appearance there, according to a fixed law; but the inner nature of everything that appears in this way remains wholly inexplicable, and is presupposed by every etiological explanation, and merely indicated by the names, force, or law of nature, or, if we are speaking of action, character or will. Thus, although every particular action, under the presupposition of the definite character, necesarily follows from the given motive, and although growth, the process of nourishment, and all the changes of the animal body take place according to necessarily acting causes (stimuli), yet the whole series of actions, and consequently every individual act, and also its condition, the whole body itself which accomplishes it, and therefore also the process through which and in which it exists, are nothing but the manifestation of the will, the becoming visible, *the objectification of the will.* Upon this rests the perfect suitableness of the human and animal body to the human and animal will in general, resembling, though far surpassing, the correspondence between an instrument made for a purpose and the will of the maker, and on this account appearing as design, *i. e.,* the teleological explanation of the body. The parts of the body must, therefore, completely correspond to the principal desires through which the will manifests itself; they must be the visible expression of these desires. Teeth, throat, and bowels are objectified hunger; the organs of generation are objectified sexual desire; the grasping hand, the hurrying feet, correspond to the more indirect desires of the will which they express. As the human form corresponds to the human will generally, so the individual bodily structure corresponds to the individually modified will, the character of the individual, and therefore it is throughout and in all its parts characteristic and full of expression. . . .

§ 21

Whoever has now gained from all these expositions a knowledge *in abstracto,* and therefore clear and certain, of what every one knows directly in *concreto, i. e.,* as feeling, a knowledge that his will is the real inner nature of his phenomenal being, which manifests itself to him as idea, both in his actions and in their permanent substratum, his body, and that his will is that which is most immediate in his consciousness, though it has not as such completely passed into the form of idea in which object and subject stand over against each other, but makes itself known to him in a direct manner, in which he does not quite clearly distinguish subject and object, yet is not known as a whole to the individual himself, but only in its particular acts,—whoever, I say, has with me gained this conviction will find that of itself it affords him the key to the knowledge of the inmost being of the whole of nature; for he now transfers it to all those phenomena which are not given to him, like his own phenomenal existence, both in direct and indirect knowledge, but only in the latter, thus merely onesidedly an *idea* alone. He will recognize this will of which we are speaking not only in those phenomenal existences which exactly resemble his own, in men and animals as their inmost nature, but the course of reflection will lead him to recognize the force which germinates and vegetates in the plant, and indeed the force through which the crystal is formed, that by which the magnet turns to the north pole, the force whose shock he experiences from the contact of two different kinds of metals, the force which appears in the elective affinities of matter as repulsion and attraction, decomposition and combination, and, lastly, even gravitation, which acts so powerfully throughout matter, draws the stone to the earth and the earth to the sun,—all these, I say, he will recognize as different only in their phenomenal existence, but in their inner nature as identical, as that which is directly known to him so intimately and so much better than anything else, and which in its most distinct manifestation is called *will*. It is this application of reflection alone that prevents us from remaining any longer at the phenomenon, and leads us to the *thing in itself*. Phenomenal existence is idea and nothing more. All idea, of whatever kind it may be, all *object,* is *phenomenal* existence, but the *will* alone is a *thing in itself*. As such, it is throughout not idea, but *toto genere* different from it; it is that of which all idea, all object, is the phenomenal appearance, the visibility, the objectification. It is the inmost nature, the kernel, of every particular thing, and also of the whole. It appears in every blind force of nature and also in the preconsidered action of man; and the great difference between these two is merely in the degree of the manifestation, not in the nature of what manifests itself. . . .

§ 22

I should be misunderstood by any one who should think that it is all the same in the end whether we denote this inner nature of all phenomena by the word *will* or by any other. This would be the case if the thing-in-itself were something whose existence we merely *inferred,* and thus knew indirectly and only in the abstract. Then, indeed, we might call it what we pleased; the name would stand merely as the symbol of an unknown quantity. But the word *will,* which, like a magic spell, discloses to us the inmost being of everything in nature, is by no means an unknown quantity, something arrived at only by inference, but is fully and immediately comprehended, and is so familiar to us that we know and understand that will is far better than anything else whatever. The concept of will has hitherto commonly been subordinated to that of force, but I reverse the matter entirely, and desire that every force in nature should be thought of as will. It must not be supposed that this is mere verbal quibbling or of no consequence; rather, it is of the greatest significance and importance. For at the foundation of the concept of force, as of all other concepts, there ultimately lies the knowledge in sense-perception of the objective world, that is to say, the phenomenon, the idea; and the concept is constructed out of this. It is an abstraction from the province in which cause and effect reign, *i. e.,* from ideas of perception, and means just the causal nature of causes at the point at which this causal nature is no further etiologically explicable, but is the necessary presupposition of all etiological explanation. The concept will, on the other hand, is of all possible concepts the only one which has its source *not* in the phenomenal, *not* in the mere idea of perception, but comes from within, and proceeds from the most immediate consciousness of each of us, in which each of us knows his own individuality, according to its nature, immediately, apart from all form, even that of subject and object, and which at the same time is this individuality, for here the subject and the object of knowledge are one. If, therefore, we refer the concept of *force* to that of *will,* we have in fact referred the less known to what is infinitely better known; indeed, to the one thing that is really immediately and fully known to us, and have very greatly extended our knowledge. If, on the contrary, we subsume the concept of will under that of force, as has hitherto always been done, we renounce the only immediate knowledge which we have of the inner nature of the world, for we allow it to disappear in a concept which is abstracted from the phenomenal, and with which we can therefore never go beyond the phenomenal.

§ 23

The *will* as a thing in itself is quite different from its phenomenal appearance, and entirely free from all the forms of the phenomenal, into which it first passes when it manifests itself, and which therefore only concern its *objectivity,* and are foreign to the will itself. Even the most universal form of all idea, that of being object of a subject, does not concern it; still less the forms which are subordinate to this and which collectively have their common expression in the principle of sufficient reason, to which we know that time and space belong, and consequently multiplicity also, which exists and is possible only through these. In this last regard I shall call time and space the *principium individuationis,*[1] borrowing an expression from the old schoolmen, and I beg to draw attention to this, once for all. For it is only through the medium of time and space that what is one and the same, both according to its nature and to its concept, yet appears as different, as a multiplicity of co-existent and successive phenomena. Thus time and space are the *principium individuationis,* the subject of so many subtleties and disputes among the schoolmen, which may be found collected in Suarez (Disp. 5, Sect. 3). According to what has been said, the will as a thing-in-itself lies outside the province of the principle of sufficient reason in all its forms, and is consequently completely groundless, although all its manifestations are entirely subordinated to the principle of sufficient reason. Further, it is free from all *multiplicity,* although its manifestations in time and space are innumerable. It is itself one, though not in the sense in which an object is one, for the unity

[1] *I. e.,* the principle of individuation, the means of distinguishing one individual from another.

of an object can only be known in opposition to a possible multiplicity; or yet in the sense in which a concept is one, for the unity of a concept originates only in abstraction from a multiplicity; but it is one as that which lies outside time and space, the *principium individuationis, i. e.,* the possibility of multiplicity. Only when all this has become quite clear to us through the subsequent examination of the phenomena and different manifestations of the will, shall we fully understand the meaning of the Kantian doctrine that time, space and causality do not belong to the thing-in-itself, but are only forms of knowing.

The uncaused nature of will has been actually recognized, where it manifests itself most distinctly, as the will of man, and this has been called free, independent. But on account of the uncaused nature of the will itself, the necessity to which its manifestations is everywhere subjected has been overlooked, and actions are treated as free, which they are not. For every individual action follows with strict necessity from the effect of the motive upon the character. All necessity is, as we have already said, the relation of the consequent to the reason, and nothing more. The principle of sufficient reason is the universal form of all phenomena, and man in his action must be subordinated to it like every other phenomenon. But because in self-consciousness the will is known directly and in itself, in this consciousness lies also the consciousness of freedom. The fact is, however, overlooked that the individual, the person, is not will as a thing-in-itself, but is a *phenomenon* of will, is already determined as such, and has come under the form of the phenomenal, the principle of sufficient reason. Hence arises the strange fact that every one believes himself *a priori* to be perfectly free, even in his individual actions, and thinks that at every moment he can commence another manner of life, which just means that he can become another person. But *a posteriori,* through experience, he finds to his astonishment that he is not free, but subjected to necessity; that in spite of all his resolutions and reflections he does not change his conduct, and that from the beginning of his life to the end of it, he must carry out the very character which he himself condemns, and as it were play the part he has undertaken to the end. I cannot pursue this subject further at present, for it belongs, as ethical, to another part of this work. In the meantime, I only wish to point out here that the *phenomenon* of the will which in itself is uncaused, is yet as such subordinated to the law of necessity, that is, the principle of sufficient reason, so that in the necessity with which the phenomena of nature follow each other, we may find nothing to hinder us from recognizing in them the manifestations of will.

Only those changes which have no other ground than a motive, *i. e.,* an idea, have hitherto been regarded as manifestations of will. Therefore in nature a will has been attributed only to man, or at the most to animals; for knowledge, the idea, is of course, as I have said elsewhere, the true and exclusive characteristic of animal life. But that the will is also active where no knowledge guides it, we see at once in the instinct and the mechanical skill of animals. That they have ideas and knowledge is here not to the point, for the end towards which they strive as definitely as if it were a known motive, is yet entirely unknown to them. Therefore in such cases their action takes place without motive, is not guided by the idea, and shows us first and most distinctly how the will may be active entirely without knowledge. The bird of a year old has no idea of the eggs for which it builds a nest; the young spider has no idea of the prey for which it spins a web; nor has the ant-lion any idea of the ants for which he digs a trench for the first time. The larva of the stag-beetle makes the hole in the wood, in which it is to await its metamorphosis, twice as big if it is going to be a male beetle as if it is going to be a female, so that if it is a male there may be room for the horns, of which, however, it has no idea. In such action of these creatures the will is clearly operative as in their other actions, but it is in blind activity, which is indeed accompanied by knowledge but not guided by it. If now we have once gained insight into the fact, that idea as motive is not a necessary and essential condition of the activity of the will, we shall more easily recognize the activity of will where it is less apparent. For example, we shall see that the house of the snail is no more made by a will which is foreign to the snail itself, than the house which we build is produced through another will than our own; but we shall recognize in both houses the work of a will which objectifies itself in both the phenomena—a will which works in us according to motives, but in the snail still blindly as formative impulse directed outwards. In us also the same will is in many ways only blindly active: in all the functions of our body which are not guided by knowledge, in all its vital and vegetative processes, digestion, circulation, secretion, growth, reproduction. Not only the actions of the body, but the whole body itself is, as we have shown above, phenomenon of the will, objectified will, concrete will. All that goes on in it must therefore proceed through will, although here this will is not guided by knowledge, but acts blindly according to causes, which in this case are called *stimuli*.

I call a *cause,* in the narrowest sense of the word, that state of matter, which, while it introduces another state with necessity, yet suffers just as great a change itself as that which it causes; which is expressed in the rule, "action and reaction are equal." Further, in the case of what is properly speaking a cause, the effect increases directly in proportion to the cause, and therefore also the reaction. So that, if once the mode of operation be known, the degree of the effect may be measured and calculated from the degree of the intensity of the cause; and conversely the degree of the intensity of the cause may be calculated from the degree of the effect. Such causes, properly so called, operate in all the phenomena of mechanics, chemistry, and so forth; in short, in all the changes of unorganized bodies. On the other hand, I call a *stimulus,* such a cause as sustains no reaction porportional to its effect, and the intensity of which does not vary directly in proportion to the intensity of its effect, so that the effect cannot be measured by it. On the contrary, a small increase of the stimulus may cause a very great increase of the effect, or conversely, it may eliminate the previous effect altogether, and so forth. All effects upon organized bodies as such are of this kind. All properly organic and vegetative changes of the animal body must therefore be referred to stimuli, not to mere causes. But the stimulus, like every cause and motive generally, never determines more than the point of time and space at which the manifestation of every force is to take place, and does not determine the inner nature of the force itself which is manifested. This inner nature we know, from our previous investigation, is will, to which therefore we ascribe both the unconscious and the conscious changes of the body. The stimulus holds the mean, forms the transition between the motive, which is causality accompanied throughout by knowledge, and the cause in the narrowest sense. In particular cases it is sometimes nearer a motive, sometimes nearer a cause, but yet it can always be distinguished from both. Thus, for example, the rising of the sap in a plant follows upon stimuli, and cannot be explained from mere causes, according to the laws of hydraulics or capillary attraction; yet it is certainly assisted by these, and altogether approaches very near to a purely causal change. On the other hand, the movements of the *Hedysarum gyrans* and the *Mimosa pudica,* although still following upon mere stimuli, are yet very like movements which follow upon motives, and seem almost to wish to make the transition. The contraction of the pupils of the eyes as the light is increased is due to stimuli, but it passes into movement which is due to motive; for it takes place, because too strong light would affect the retina painfully, and to avoid this we contract the pupils. The occasion of an erection is a motive, because it is an idea, yet it operates with the necessity of a stimulus, *i. e.,* it cannot be resisted, but we must put the idea away in order to make it cease to affect us. This is also the case with disgusting things, which excite the desire to vomit. Thus we have treated the instinct of animals as an actual link, of quite a distinct kind, between movement following upon stimuli, and action following upon a known motive. Now we might be asked to regard breathing as another link of this kind. It has been disputed whether it belongs to the voluntary or the involuntary movements, that is to say, whether it follows upon motive or stimulus, and perhaps it may be explained as something which is between the two. Marshall Hall ("On the Diseases of the Nervous System," § 293 sq.) explains it as a mixed function, for it is partly under the influence of the cerebral (voluntary), and partly under that of the spinal (non-voluntary) nerves. However, we are finally obliged to number it with the expressions of will which result from motives. For other motives, *i. e.,* mere ideas, can determine the will to check it or accelerate it, and, as is the case with every other voluntary action, it seems to us that we could give up breathing altogether and voluntarily suffocate. And in fact we could do so if any other motive influenced the will sufficiently strongly to overcome the pressing desire for air. According to some accounts Diogenes actually put an end to his life in this way (Diog. Laert. VI. 76). Certain negroes also are said to have done this (F. B. Osiander "On Suicide" [1813] pp. 170–180). If this be true, it affords us a good example of the influence of abstract motives, *i. e.,* of the victory of distinctively rational over merely animal will. For, that breathing is at least partially conditioned by cerebral activity is shown by the fact that the primary cause of death from prussic acid is that it paralyses the brain, and so, indirectly, restricts the breathing; but if the breathing be artificially maintained till the stupefaction of the brain has passed away, death will not ensue. We may also observe in passing that breathing affords us the most obvious example of the fact that motives act with just as much necessity as stimuli, or as causes in the narrowest sense of the word, and their operation can only be neutralized by antagonistic motives, as action is neutralized by re-action. For, in the case of breathing, the illusion that we can stop when we like is much weaker than in the case of other movements which follow upon motives; because in breathing the motive is very powerful, very near to us, and its satisfaction is very easy, for the muscles which accomplish it are never tired, nothing, as a rule, obstructs it, and the whole process is supported by the most inveterate habit of the individual. And yet all motives act with the same necessity. The knowledge that necessity is common to movements following upon motives, and those following upon stimuli, makes it easier for us to understand that that also which takes place in our bodily organism in accordance with stimuli and in obedience to law, is yet, according to its inner nature—will, which in all its manifestations, though never in itself, is subordinated to the principle of sufficient reason, that is, to necessity. Accordingly, we shall not rest content with recognizing that animals, both in their actions and also in their whole existence, bodily structure and organization, are manifestations of will; but we shall extend to plants also this immediate knowledge of the essential nature of things which is given to us alone. Now all the movements of plants follow upon stimuli; for the absence of knowledge, and the movement following upon motives which is conditioned by knowledge, constitutes the only essential difference between animals and plants.

Therefore, what appears for the idea as plant life, as mere vegetation, as blindly impelling force, we shall claim, according to its inner nature, for will, and recognise it as just that which constitutes the basis of our own phenomenal being, as it expresses itself in our actions, and also in the whole existence of our body itself.

It remains for us to take only the final step, the extension of our way of looking at things to all those forces which act in nature in accordance with universal, unchangeable laws, in conformity with which the movements of all those bodies take place, which are wholly without organs, and have therefore no susceptibility for stimuli, and have no knowledge, which is the necessary condition of motives. Thus we must also apply the key to the understanding of the inner nature of things, which the immediate knowledge of our own existence alone can give us, to those phenomena of the unorganized world which are most remote from us. And if we consider them attentively, if we observe the strong and unceasing impulse with which the waters hurry to the ocean, the persistency with which the magnet turns ever to the north pole, the readiness with which iron flies to the magnet, the eagerness with which the electric poles seek to be re-united, and which, just like human desire, is increased by obstacles; if we see the crystal quickly and suddenly take form with such wonderful regularity of construction, which is clearly only a perfectly definite and accurately determined impulse in different directions, seized and retained by crystallization; if we observe the choice with which bodies repel and attract each other, combine and separate, when they are set free in a fluid state, and emancipated from the bonds of rigidness; lastly, if we feel directly how a burden which hampers our body by its gravitation towards the earth, unceasingly presses and strains upon it in pursuit of its one tendency; if we observe all this, I say, it will require no great effort of the imagination to recognize, even at so great a distance, our own nature. That which in us pursues its end by the light of knowledge; but here, in the weakest of its manifestations, only strives blindly and dumbly in a one-sided and unchangeable manner, must yet in both cases come under the name of will, as it is everywhere one and the same—just as the first dim light of dawn must share the name of sunlight with the rays of the full mid-day. For the name *will* denotes that which is the inner nature of everything in the world, and the one kernel of every phenomenon.

Yet the remoteness, and indeed the appearance of absolute difference between the phenomena of unorganized nature and the will which we know as the inner reality of our own being, arise chiefly from the contrast between the completely determined conformity to law of the one species of phenomena, and the apparently unfettered freedom of the other. For in man, individuality makes itself powerfully felt. Every one has a character of his own; and therefore the same motive has not the same influence over all, and a thousand circumstances which exist in the wide sphere of the knowledge of the individual, but are unknown to others, modify its effect. Therefore action cannot be predetermined from the motive alone, for the other factor is wanting, the accurate acquaintance with the individual character, and with the knowledge which accompanies it. On the other hand, the phenomena of the forces of nature illustrate the opposite extreme. They act according to universal laws, without variation, without individuality in accordance with openly manifest circumstances, subject to the most exact predetermination; and the same force of nature appears in its million phenomena in precisely the same way. In order to explain this point and prove the identity of the *one* indivisible will in all its different phenomena, in the weakest as in the strongest, we must first of all consider the relation of the will as thing-in-itself to its phenomena, that is, the relation of the world as will to the world as idea; for this will open to us the best way to a more thorough investigation of the whole subject we are considering in this second book. . . .

§ 24

Whatever the thing-in-itself may be, Kant is right in his conclusion that time, space, and causality (which we afterwards found to be forms of the principle of sufficient reason, the general expression of the forms of the phenomenon) are not its properties, but come to it only after, and so far as, it has become idea. That is, they belong only to its phenomenal existence, not to itself. For since the subject fully understands and constructs them out of itself, independently of all object, they must be dependent upon *existence as idea* as such, not upon that which becomes idea. They must be the form of the idea as such; but not qualities of that which has assumed this form. They must be already given with the mere antithesis of subject and object (not as concepts but as facts), and consequently they must be only the more exact determination of the form of knowledge in general, whose most universal determination is that antithesis itself. Now, that in the phenomenon, in the object, which is in its turn conditioned by time, space and causality, inasmuch as it can only become idea by means of them, namely *multiplicity,* through co-existence and succession, *change* and *permanence* through the law of causality, *matter* which can only become idea under the presupposition of causality, and lastly, all that becomes idea only by means of these,—all this, I say, as a whole, does not in reality belong to that which appears, to that which has passed into the form of idea, but belongs merely to this form itself. And conversely, that in the phenomenon which is not conditioned through time, space and causality, and which cannot be referred to them, nor explained in accordance with them, is precisely that in which the thing manifested, the thing-in-itself, directly reveals itself. It follows from this that the most complete capacity for being known, that is to say, the greatest clearness, distinctness, and susceptibility of exhaustive explanation, will necessarily belong to that which pertains to knowledge *as such,* and thus to the *form* of knowledge; but not to that which in itself is not idea, not object, but which has become knowledge only through entering these forms; in other words, has become idea, object. Thus only that which depends entirely upon being an object of knowledge, upon existing as idea in general and *as such* (not upon that which *becomes* known, and has only *become* idea), which therefore belongs without distinction to everything that is known, and which, on that account, is found just as well if we start from the subject as if we start from the object,—this alone can afford us without reserve a sufficient, exhaustive knowledge, a knowledge which is clear to the very foundation. But this consists of nothing but those forms of all phenomena of which we are conscious *a priori,* and which may be generally expressed as the principle of sufficient reason. Now, the forms of this principle which occur in knowledge of perception (with which alone we are here concerned) are time, space, and causality. The whole of pure mathematics and pure natural science *a priori* is based entirely upon these. Therefore it is only in these sciences that knowledge finds no obscurity, does not rest upon what is incomprehensible (groundless, *i. e.,* will), upon what cannot be further deduced. It is on this account that Kant wanted, as we have said, to apply the name science specially and even exclusively to these branches of knowledge together with logic. But, on the other hand, these branches of knowledge show us nothing more than mere connections, relations of one idea to another, form devoid of all content. All content which they receive, every phenomenon which fills these forms, contains something which is no longer completely knowable in its whole nature, something which can no longer be entirely explained through something else, something then which is groundless, through which consequently the knowledge loses its evidence and ceases to be completely lucid. This that withholds itself from investigation, however, is the thing-in-itself, is that which is essentially not idea, not object of knowledge, but has only become knowable by entering that form. The form is originally foreign to it, and the thing-in-itself can never become entirely one with it, can never be referred to mere form, and, since this form is the principle of sufficient reason, can never be completely explained. If therefore all mathematics affords us an exhaustive knowledge of that which in the phenomena is quantity, position, number, in a word, spatial and temporal relations; if all etiology gives us a complete account of the regular conditions under which phenomena, with all their determinations, appear in time and space, but, with it all, teaches us nothing more than why in each case this particular phenomenon must appear just at this time here, and at this place now; it is clear that with their assistance we can never penetrate to the inner nature of things. There always remains something which no explanation can venture to attack, but which it always presupposes; the forces of nature, the definite mode of operation of things, the quality and character of every phenomenon, that which is without ground, that which does not depend upon the form of the phenomenal, the principle of sufficient reason, but is something to which this form in itself is foreign, something which has yet entered this form, and now appears according to its law, a law, however, which only determines the appearance, not that which appears, only the how, not the what, only the form, not the content. Mechanics, physics, and chemistry teach the rules and laws according to which the forces of impenetrability, gravitation, rigidity, fluidity, cohesion, elasticity, heat, light, affinity, magnetism, electricity, etc., operate; that is to say, the law, the rule which these forces observe whenever they enter time and space. But do what we will, the forces themselves remain *qualitates occultæ*.[2] For it is just the thing-in-itself, which, because it is manifested, exhibits these phenomena, which are entirely different from itself. In its manifestation, indeed, it is completely subordinated to the principle of sufficient reason as the form of the idea, but it can never itself be referred to this form, and therefore cannot be fully explained etiologically, can never be completely fathomed. It is certainly perfectly comprehensible so far as it has assumed that form, that is, so far as it is phenomenon, but its inner nature is not in the least explained by the fact that it can thus be comprehended. Therefore the more necessity any knowledge carries with it, the more there is in it of that which cannot be otherwise thought or presented in perception—as, for example, space-relations—the clearer and more sufficing then it is, the less pure objective content it has, or the less reality, properly so called, is given in it. And conversely, the more there is in it which must be conceived as mere chance, and the more it impresses us as given merely empirically, the more proper objectivity and true reality is there in such knowledge, and at the same time, the more that is inexplicable, that is, that cannot be deduced from anything else.

It is true that at all times an etiology, unmindful of its real aim, has striven to reduce all organized life to chemism or electricity; all chemism, that is to say quality, again to mechanism (action determined by the shape of the atom), this again sometimes to the object of phoronomy, *i. e.,* the combination of time and space, which makes motion possible, sometimes to the object

[2] Occult qualities.

of mere geometry, *i. e.,* position in space (much in the same way as we rightly deduce the diminution of an effect from the square of the distance, and the theory of the lever in a purely geometrical manner) : geometry may finally be reduced to arithmetic, which, on account of its one dimension, is of all the forms of the principle of sufficient reason, the most intelligible, comprehensible, and completely susceptible of investigation. As instances of the method generally indicated here, we may refer to the atoms of Democritus, the vortex of Descartes, the mechanical physics of Lesage, which towards the end of last century tried to explain both chemical affinities and gravitation mechanically by impact and pressure, as may be seen in detail in *"Lucrèce Neutonien";* Reil's form and combination as the cause of animal life, also tends in this direction. Finally, the crude materialism which even now in the middle of the nineteenth century has been served up again under the ignorant delusion that it is original, belongs distinctly to this class. It stupidly denies vital force, and first of all tries to explain the phenomena of life from physical and chemical forces, and those again from the mechanical effects of the matter, position, form, and motion of imagined atoms, and thus seeks to reduce all the forces of nature to action and reaction as its thing-in-itself. According to this teaching, light is the mechanical vibration or undulation of an imaginary ether, postulated for this end. This ether, if it reaches the eye, beats rapidly upon the retina, and gives us the knowledge of colour. Thus, for example, four hundred and eighty-three billion beats in a second give red, and seven hundred and twenty-seven billion beats in a second give violet. Upon this theory, persons who are colour-blind must be those who are unable to count the beats, must they not? Such crass, mechanical, clumsy, and certainly knotty theories, which remind one of Democritus, are quite worthy of those who, fifty years after the appearance of Goethe's doctrine of colour, still believe in Newton's homogeneous light, and are not ashamed to say so. They will find that what is overlooked in the child (Democritus) will not be forgiven in the man. They might indeed, some day, come to an ignominious end; but then every one would slink away and pretend that he never had anything to do with them. We shall soon have to speak again of this false reduction of the forces of nature to each other; so much for the present. Supposing this theory were possible, all would certainly be explained and established and finally reduced to an arithmetical problem, which would then be the holiest thing in the temple of wisdom, to which the principle of sufficient reason would at last have happily conducted us. But all content of the phenomenon would have disappeared, and the mere form would remain. The "what appears" would be referred to the "how it appears," and this "how" would be what is *a priori* knowable, therefore entirely dependent on the subject, therefore only for the subject, therefore, lastly, mere phantom, idea and form of idea, through and through: no thing-in-itself could be demanded. Supposing, then, that this were possible, the whole world would be derived from the subject, and, in fact, that would be accomplished which Fichte wanted to *seem* to accomplish by his empty bombast. But it is not possible: phantasies, sophisms, castles in the air, have been constructed in this way, but science never. The many and multifarious phenomena in nature have been successfully referred to particular original forces, and as often as this has been done, a real advance has been made. Several forces and qualities, which were at first regarded as different, have been derived from each other, and thus their number has been curtailed. (For example, magnetism from electricity.) Etiology will have reached its goal when it has recognized and exhibited as such all the original forces of nature, and established their mode of operation, *i. e.,* the law according to which, under the guidance of causality, their phenomena appear in time and space, and determine their position with regard to each other. But certain original forces will always remain over; there will always remain as an insoluble residuum a content of phenomena which cannot be referred to their form, and thus cannot be explained from something else in accordance with the principle of sufficient reason. For in everything in nature there is something of which no ground can ever be assigned, of which no explanation is possible, and no ulterior cause is to be sought. This is the specific nature of its action, *i. e.,* the nature of its existence, its being. Of each particular effect of the thing a cause may be certainly indicated, from which it follows that it must act just at this time and in this place; but no cause can ever be found from which it follows

that a thing acts in general, and precisely in the way it does. If
it has no other qualities, if it is merely a mote in a sunbeam, it yet
exhibits this unfathomable something, at least as weight and impenetrability. But this, I say, is to the mote what.his will is to a
man; and, like the human will, it is, according to its inner nature,
not subject to explanation; nay, more—it is in itself identical with
this will. It is true that a motive may be given for every manifestation of will, for every act of will at a particular time and in
a particular place, upon which it must necessarily follow, under
the presupposition of the character of the man. But no reason
can ever be given that the man has this character; that he wills
at all; that, of several motives, just this one and no other, or indeed that any motive at all, moves his will. That which in the case
of man is the unfathomable character which is presupposed in
every explanation of his actions from motives is, in the case of
every unorganized body, its definitive quality—the mode of its action, the manifestations of which are occasioned by impressions
from without, while it itself, on the contrary, is determined by
nothing outside itself, and thus is also inexplicable. Its particular
manifestations, through which alone it becomes visible, are subordinated to the principle of sufficient reason; it itself is groundless. This was in substance rightly understood by the schoolmen,
who called it *forma substantialis*.[3] (Cf. Suarez, Disput. Metaph.,
disp. xv. sect. i.)

It is a greater and a commoner error that the phenomena which
we best understand are those which are of most frequent occurrence, and which are most universal and simple; for, on the contrary, these are just the phenomena that we are most accustomed
to see about us, and to be ignorant of. It is just as inexplicable to
us that a stone should fall to the earth as that an animal should
move itself. It has been supposed, as we have remarked above,
that, starting from the most universal forces of nature (gravitation, cohesion, impenetrability), it was possible to explain from
them the rarer forces, which operate only under a combination of
circumstances (for example, chemical quality, electricity, magnetism), and, lastly, from these to understand the organisms and
the life of animals, and even the nature of human knowing and

[3] Substantial form,—*i. e.*, the underlying cause.

willing. Men resigned themselves without a word to starting from
mere *qualitates occultæ,* the elucidation of which was entirely
given up, for they intended to build upon them, not to investigate
them. Such an intention cannot, as we have already said, be carried
out. But apart from this, such structures would always stand in
the air. What is the use of explanations which ultimately refer
us to something which is quite as unknown as the problem with
which we started? Do we in the end understand more of the
inner nature of these universal natural forces than of the inner
nature of an animal? Is not the one as much a sealed book to us
as the other? Unfathomable because it is without ground, because
it is the content, that which the phenomenon is, and which can
never be referred to the form, to the how, to the principle of
sufficient reason. But we, who have in view not etiology but
philosophy, that is, not relative but unconditioned knowledge
of the real nature of the world, take the opposite course, and
start from that which is immediately and most completely known
to us, and fully and entirely trusted by us—that which lies nearest to us, in order to understand that which is known to us only
at a distance, one-sidedly and indirectly. From the most powerful,
most significant, and most distinct phenomenon we seek to arrive
at an understanding of those that are less complete and weaker.
With the exception of my own body, all things are known to me
only on *one* side, that of the idea. Their inner nature remains
hidden from me and a profound secret, even if I know all the
causes from which their changes follow. Only by comparison with
that which goes on in me if my body performs an action when I
am influenced by a motive—only by comparison, I say, with what
is the inner nature of my own changes determined by external
reasons, can I obtain insight into the way in which these lifeless
bodies change under the influence of causes, and so understand
what is their inner nature. For the knowledge of the causes of
the manifestation of this inner nature affords me merely the rule
of its appearance in time and space, and nothing more. I can make
this comparison because my body is the only object of which I know
not merely the *one* side, that of the idea, but also the other side
which is called will. Thus, instead of believing that I would better

understand my own organization, and then my own knowing and willing, and my movements following upon motives, if I could only refer them to movements due to electrical, chemical, and mechanical causes, I must, seeing that I seek philosophy and not etiology, learn to understand from my own movements following upon motives the inner nature of the simplest and commonest movements of an unorganized body which I see following upon causes. I must recognize the inscrutable forces which manifest themselves in all natural bodies as identical in kind with that which in me is the will, and as differing from it only in degree. That is to say, the fourth class of ideas given in the Essay on the Principle of Sufficient Reason must be the key to the knowledge of the inner nature of the first class, and by means of the law of motivation I must come to understand the inner meaning of the law of causation.

Spinoza (Epist. 62) says that if a stone which has been projected through the air had consciousness, it would believe that it was moving of its own will. I add to this only that the stone would be right. The impulse given it is for the stone what the motive is for me, and what in the case of the stone appears as cohesion, gravitation, rigidity, is in its inner nature the same as that which I recognize in myself as will, and what the stone also, if knowledge were given to it, would recognize as will. In the passage referred to, Spinoza had in view the necessity with which the stone flies, and he rightly desires to transfer this necessity to that of the particular act of will of a person. I, on the other hand, consider the inner being, which alone imparts meaning and validity to all real necessity (*i. e.,* effect following upon a cause) as its presupposition. In the case of men this is called character; in the case of a stone it is called quality, but it is the same in both. When it is immediately known it is called will. In the stone it has the weakest, and in man the strongest degree of visibility, of objectivity. . . .

The multiplicity of things in space and time, which collectively constitute the objectification of will, does not affect the will itself, which remains indivisible notwithstanding it. It is not the case that, in some way or other, a smaller part of will is in the stone and a larger part in the man, for the relation of part and whole belongs exclusively to space, and has no longer any meaning when we go beyond his form of intuition or perception. The more and the less have application only to the phenomenon of will, that is, its visibility, its objectification. Of this there is a higher grade in the plant than in the stone; in the animal a higher grade than in the plant: indeed, the passage of will into visibility, its objectification, has grades as innumerable as exist between the dimmest twilight and the brightest sunshine, the loudest sound and the faintest echo. . . .

The subject which will therefore be fully considered in the next book, and which has, doubtless, already presented itself to the mind of every student of Plato, is, that these different grades of the objectification of will which are manifested in innumerable individuals, and exist as their unattained types or as the eternal forms of things, not entering themselves into time and space, which are the medium of individual things, but remaining fixed, subject to no change, always being, never becoming, while the particular things arise and pass away, always become and never are,—that these *grades of the objectification of will* are, I say, simply *Plato's Ideas*. I make this passing reference to the matter here in order that I may be able in future to use the word *Idea* in this sense. In my writings, therefore, the word is always to be understood in its true and original meaning given to it by Plato, and has absolutely no reference to those abstract productions of dogmatising scholastic reason, which Kant has inaptly and illegitimately used this word to denote, though Plato had already appropriated and used it most fitly. By idea, then, I understand every definite and fixed grade of the objectification of will, so far as it is thing-in-itself, and therefore has no multiplicity. These grades are related to individual things as their eternal forms or prototypes. The shortest and most concise statement of this famous Platonic doctrine is given us by Diogenes Laertes (iii. 12): "ὁ Πλατων φησι, εν τη φυσει τας ιδεας ἑσταναι, καθαπερ παραδειγματα, τα δ'αλλα ταυταις εοικεναι, τουτων ὁμοιωμάτα καθεστωτα." [4] . . .

---

[4] "Plato said that Ideas exist in nature as models; that other things were like these, fashioned after their image."

§ 26

The lowest grades of the objectification of will are to be found in those most universal forces of nature which partly appear in all matter without exception, as gravity and impenetrability, and partly have shared the given matter among them, so that certain of them reign in one species of matter and others in another species, constituting its specific difference, as rigidity, fluidity, elasticity, electricity, magnetism, chemical properties and qualities of every kind. They are in themselves immediate manifestations of will, just as much as human action; and as such they are groundless, like human character. Only their particular manifestations are subordinated to the principle of sufficient reason, like the particular actions of men. They themselves, on the other hand, can never be called either effect or cause, but are the prior and presupposed conditions of all causes and effects through which their real nature unfolds and reveals itself. It is therefore senseless to demand a cause of gravity or electricity, for they are original forces. Their expressions, indeed, take place in accordance with the law of cause and effect, so that every one of their particular manifestations has a cause, which is itself again just a similar particular manifestation which determines that this force must express itself here, must appear in space and time; but the force itself is by no means the effect of a cause, nor the cause of an effect. It is therefore a mistake to say "gravity is the cause of a stone falling"; for the cause in this case is rather the nearness of the earth, because it attracts the stone. Take the earth away and the stone will not fall, although gravity remains. The force itself lies quite outside the chain of causes and effects, which presupposes time, because it has only meaning in relation to it; but the force lies outside time. The individual change always has for its cause another change just as individual as itself, and not the force of which it is the expression. For that which always gives its efficiency to a cause, however many times it may appear, is a force of nature. As such, it is groundless, i. e., it lies outside the chain of causes and outside the province of the principle of sufficient reason in general, and is philosophically known as the immediate objectivity of will, which is the "in-itself" of the whole of nature; but in etiology, which in this reference is physics, it is set down as an original force, *i. e.,* a *qualitas occulta.*

In the higher grades of the objectivity of will we see individuality occupy a prominent position, especially in the case of man, where it appears as the great difference of individual characters, *i. e.,* as complete personality, outwardly expressed in strongly marked individual physiognomy, which influences the whole bodily form. None of the brutes have this individuality in anything like so high a degree, though the higher species of them have a trace of it; but the character of the species completely predominates over it, and therefore they have little individual physiognomy. The farther down we go, the more completely is every trace of the individual character lost in the common character of the species, and the physiognomy of the species alone remains. We know the physiological character of the species, and from that we know exactly what is to be expected from the individual; while, on the contrary, in the human species every individual has to be studied and fathomed for himself, which, if we wish to forecast his action with some degree of certainty, is, on account of the possibility of concealment that first appears with reason, a matter of the greatest difficulty. It is probably connected with this difference of the human species from all others, that the folds and convolutions of the brain, which are entirely wanting in birds, and very weakly marked in rodents, are even in the case of the higher animals far more symmetrical on both sides, and more constantly the same in each individual, than in the case of human beings. It is further to be regarded as a phenomenon of this peculiar individual character which distinguishes men from all the lower animals, that in the case of the brutes the sexual instinct seeks its satisfaction without observable choice of objects, while in the case of man this choice is, in a purely instinctive manner and independent of all reflection, carried so far that it rises into a powerful passion. While then every man is to be regarded as a specially determined and characterized phenomenon of will, and indeed to a certain extent as a special Idea, in the case of the brutes this individual character as a whole is wanting, because only the species has a special significance. And the farther we go from man, the fainter becomes the trace of this individual character, so that plants have no individual qualities left, except such as may be fully explained from the favourable or unfavourable external influences of soil, climate, and other accidents. Finally, in the inorganic kingdom of nature all individuality disappears. The crystal alone is to be regarded as to a certain extent individual. It is a unity of the tendency in definite directions, fixed by crystallization, which makes the trace of this tendency permanent. It is at the same time a cumulative repetition of its primitive form, bound into unity by an idea, just as the tree is an aggregate of the single germinating fibre which shows itself in every rib of the leaves, in every leaf, in every branch; which repeats itself, and to some extent makes each of these appear as a separate growth, nourishing itself from the greater as a parasite, so that the tree, resembling the crystal, is a systematic aggregate of small plants, although only the whole is the complete expression of an individual Idea, *i. e.,* of this particular grade of the objectification of will. But the individuals of the same species of crystal can have no other difference than such as is produced by external accidents; indeed we can make at pleasure large or small crystals of every species. The individual, however, as such, that is, with traces of an individual character, does not exist further in unorganized nature. All its phenomena are expressions of general forces of nature, *i. e.,* of those grades of the objectification of will which do not objectify themselves (as is the case in organized nature), by means of the difference of the individualities which collectively express the whole of the Idea, but show themselves only in the species, and as a whole, without any variation in each particular example of it. Time, space, multiplicity, and existence conditioned by causes, do not belong to the will or to the Idea (the grade of the objectification of will), but only to their particular phenomena. Therefore such a force of nature as, for example, gravity or electricity, must show itself as such in precisely the same way in all its million phenomena, and only external circumstances can modify these. This unity of its being in all its phenomena, this unchangeable constancy of the appearance of these, whenever, under the guidance of causality, the necessary conditions are present, is called a *law of nature.* If such a law is once learned from experience, then the phenomenon of that force of nature, the character of which is expressed **and** laid down in it, may be accurately forecast and counted upon. But it is just this conformity to law of the phenomena of the lower grades of the objectification of will which gives them such a different aspect from the phenomena of the same will in the higher, *i. e.,* the more distinct, grades of its objectification, in animals, and in men and their actions, where the stronger or weaker influence of the individual character and the susceptibility to motives which often remain hidden from the spectator, because they lie in knowledge, has had the result that the identity of the inner nature of the two kinds of phenomena has hitherto been entirely overlooked.

If we start from the knowledge of the particular, and not from that of the Idea, there is something astonishing, and sometimes even terrible, in the absolute uniformity of the laws of nature. It might astonish us that nature never once forgets her laws; that if, for example, it has once been according to a law of nature that where certain materials are brought together under given conditions, a chemical combination will take place, or gas will be evolved, or they will go on fire; if these conditions are fulfilled, whether by our interposition or entirely by chance (and in this case the accuracy is the more astonishing because unexpected), to-day just as well as a thousand years ago, the determined phenomenon will take place at once and without delay. We are most vividly impressed with the marvellousness of this fact in the case of rare phenomena, which occur only under very complex circumstances, but which we are previously informed will take place if these conditions are fulfilled. For example, when we are told that if certain metals, when arranged alternately in fluid with which an acid has been mixed, are brought into contact, silver leaf brought between the extremities of this combination will suddenly be consumed in a green flame; or that under certain conditions the hard diamond turns into carbonic acid. It is the ghostly omnipresence of natural forces that astonishes us in such cases, and we remark here what in the case of phenomena which happen daily no longer strikes us, how the connection between cause and effect is really as mysterious as that which is imagined between a magic formula and a spirit that must appear when invoked by it. On the other hand, if we have attained to the philosophical knowledge that a force of nature is a definite grade of the objectification of will, that is to say, a definite grade of that which we recognize as our own inmost nature, and that this will, in itself, and distinguished from its phenomena and their forms, lies outside time and space, and that, therefore, the multiplicity, which is conditioned by time and space, does not belong to it, nor directly to the grade of its objectification, *i. e.,* the Idea, but only to the phenomena of the Idea; and if we remember that the law of causality has significance only in relation to time and space, inasmuch as it determines the position of the multitude of phenomena of the different Ideas in which the will reveals itself, governing the order in which they must appear; if, I say, in this knowledge the inner meaning of the great doctrine of Kant has been fully grasped, the doctrine that time, space, and causality do not belong to the thing-in-itself, but merely to the phenomenon, that they are only the forms of our knowledge, not qualities of things in themselves; then we shall understand that this astonishment at the conformity to law and accurate operation of a force of nature, this astonishment at the complete sameness of all its million phenomena and the infallibility of their occurrence, is really like that of a child or a savage who looks for the first time through a glass with many facets at a flower, and marvels at the complete similarity of the innumerable flowers which he sees, and counts the leaves of each of them separately.

Thus every universal, original force of nature is nothing but a low grade of the objectification of will, and we call every such grade an eternal *Idea* in Plato's sense. But a *law of nature* is the relation of the Idea to the form of its manifestation. This form is time, space, and causality, which are necessarily and inseparably connected and related to each other. Through time and space the Idea multiplies itself in innumerable phenomena, but the order according to which it enters these forms of multiplicity is definitely determined by the law of causality; this law is as it were the norm of the limit of these phenomena of different Ideas, in accordance with which time, space, and matter are assigned to them. This norm is therefore necessarily related to the identity of the aggregate of existing matter, which is the common substratum of all those different phenomena. If all these were not directed to that common matter in the possession of which the must be divided, there would be no need for such a law to decide their claims. They might all at once and together fill a boundless space throughout an endless time. Therefore, because all these phenomena of the eternal Ideas are directed to one and the same matter, must there be a rule for their appearance and disappearance; for if there were not, they would not make way for each other. Thus the law of causality is essentially bound up with that of the permanence of substance; they reciprocally derive significance from each other. Time and space, again, are related to them in the same way. For time is merely the possibility of conflicting states of the same matter, and space is merely the possibility of the permanence of the same matter under all sorts of conflicting states. Accordingly, in the preceding book we explained matter as the union of space and time, and this union shows itself as change of the accidents in the permanence of the substance, of which causality or becoming is the universal possibility. And accordingly, we said that matter is through and through causality. We explained the understanding as the subjective correlative of causality, and said matter (and thus the whole world as idea) exists only for the understanding; the understanding is its condition, its supporter as its necessary correlative. I repeat all this in passing, merely to call to mind what was demonstrated in the First Book, for it is necessary for the complete understanding of these two books that their inner agreement should be observed, since what is inseparably united in the actual world as its two sides, will and idea, has, in order that we might understand each of them more clearly in isolation, been dissevered in these two books.

It may not perhaps be superfluous to elucidate further by an example how the law of causality has meaning only in relation to time and space, and the matter which consists in the union of the two. For it determines the limits in accordance with which the phenomena of the forces of nature divide themselves in the possession of matter, while the original forces of nature, as the immediate objectification of will, which, as a thing in itself, is not subordinated to the principle of sufficient reason, lie outside these forms, within which alone all etiological explanation has validity and meaning, and just on that account can never lead us to the inner reality of nature. For this purpose let us think of some kind of machine constructed according to the laws of mechanics. Iron weights begin the motion by their gravity; copper wheels resist by their rigidity, affect and raise each other and the lever by their impenetrability, and so on. Here gravity, rigidity, and impenetrability are original unexplained forces; mechanics only gives us the condition under which, and the manner in which, they manifest themselves, appear, and govern a definite matter, time, and place. If, now, a strong magnet is made to attract the iron of the weight, and overcome its gravity, the movement of the machine stops, and the matter becomes forthwith the scene of quite a different force of nature—magnetism, of which etiology again gives no further explanation than the condition under which it appears. Or let us suppose that the copper discs of such a machine are laid upon zinc plates, and an acid solution introduced between them. At once the same matter of the machine has become subject to another original force, galvanism, which now governs it according to its own laws, and reveals itself in and through its phenomena; and etiology can again tell us nothing about this force except the conditions under which, and the laws in accordance with which, it manifests itself. Let us now raise the temperature and add pure acid; the whole machine burns; that is to say, once more an entirely different force of nature, chemical energy, asserts at this time and in this place irresistible claims to this particular matter, and reveals itself in it as Idea, as a definite grade of the objectification of will. The calcined metal thus produced now unites with an acid, and a salt is obtained which forms itself into crystals. These are the phenomena of another Idea, which in itself is again quite inexplicable, while the appearance of its phenomena is dependent upon certain conditions which etiology can give us. The crystals dissolve, mix with other materials, and vegetation springs up from them—a new phenomenon of will: and so the same permanent matter may be followed *ad infinitum,* to observe how now this and now that natural force obtains a right to it and temporarily takes possession of it, in order to appear and reveal its own nature. The condition of this right, the point of time and space at which it becomes valid, is given by causality, but the explanation founded upon this law only extends thus far. The force itself is a manifestation of will, and as such is not subject to the forms of the principle of sufficient reason, that is, it is groundless. It lies outside all time, is omnipresent, and seems as it were to wait constantly till the circumstances occur under which it can appear and take possession of a definite matter, supplanting the forces which have reigned in it till then. All time exists only for the phenomena of such a force and is without significance for the force itself. Through thousands of years chemical forces slumber in matter till the contact with the reagents sets them free; then they appear; but time exists only for the phenomena, not for the forces themselves. For thousands of years galvanism slumbered in copper and zinc, and they lay quietly beside silver, which must be consumed in flame as soon as all three are brought together under the required conditions. Even in the organic kingdom we see a dry seed preserve the slumbering force through three thousand years, and when at last the favourable circumstances occur, grow up as a plant.[5]

If by this exposition the difference between a force of nature and all its phenomena has been made quite distinct; if we have seen clearly that the former is the will itself at this particular grade of its objectification, but that multiplicity comes to phe-

[5] On the 16th of September, 1840, at a lecture upon Egyptian Archæology delivered by Mr. Pettigrew at the Literary and Scientific Institute of London, he showed some corns of wheat which Sir G. Wilkinson had found in a grave at Thebes, in which they must have lain for three thousand years. They were found in an hermetically sealed vase. Mr. Pettigrew had sowed twelve grains, and obtained a plant which grew five feet high, and the seeds of which were now quite ripe.—*Times*, 21st September, 1840. In the same way in 1830 Mr. Haulton produced in the Medical Botanical Society of London a bulbous root which was found in the hand of an Egyptian mummy, in which it was probably put in observance of some religious rite, and which must have been at least two thousand years old. He had planted it in a flower-pot, in which it grew up and flourished. This is quoted from the Medical Journal of 1830 in the Journal of the Royal Institution of Great Britain, October, 1830, p. 196.— "In the garden of Mr. Grimstone of the Herbarium, Highgate, London, is a pea in full fruit, which has sprung from a pea that Mr. Pettigrew and the officials of the British Museum took out of a vase which had been found in an Egyptian sarcophagus, where it must have lain 2844 years."—*Times*, 16th August, 1844. Indeed, the living toads found in limestone lead to the conclusion that even animal life is capable of such a suspension for thousands of years, if this is begun in the dormant period and maintained by special circumstances.—*S.*

nomena only through time and space, and that the law of causality is nothing but the determination of the position of these phenomena in time and space; then we shall recognize the complete truth and the deep meaning of Malebranche's doctrine of occasional causes (*causes occasionelles*). It is well worth while comparing this doctrine of his, as he explains it in the *"Recherches de la Vérite,"* both in the 3rd Chapter of the second part of the 6th Book, and in the *éclaircissements* appended to this chapter, with this exposition of mine, and observing the complete agreement of the two doctrines in the case of such different systems of thought. Indeed I cannot help admiring how Malebranche, though thoroughly involved in the positive dogmas which his age inevitably forced upon him, yet, in such bonds and under such a burden, hit the truth so happily, so correctly, and even knew how to combine it with these dogmas, at all events verbally.

For the power of truth is incredibly great and of unspeakable endurance. We find constant traces of it in all, even the most eccentric and absurd dogmas, of different times and different lands,—often indeed in strange company, curiously mixed up with other things, but still recognizable.[6] It is like a plant that germinates under a heap of great stones, but still struggles up to the light, working itself through with many deviations and windings, disfigured, worn out, stunted in its growth,—but yet, to the light.

In any case Malebranche is right: every natural cause is only an occasional cause. It only gives opportunity or occasion for the manifestation of the one indivisible will which is the "in-itself" of all things, and whose graduated objectification is the whole visible world. Only the appearance, the becoming visible, in this place, at this time, is brought about by the cause and is so far dependent on it, but not the whole of the phenomenon, nor its inner nature. This is the will itself, to which the principle of sufficient reason has not application, and which is therefore groundless. Nothing in the world has a sufficient cause of its existence generally, but only a cause of existence just here and just now. That a stone exhibits now gravity, now rigidity, now electricity, now chemical qualities, depends upon causes, upon impressions upon it from without, and is to be explained from

[6] Cf. the first sentence of Spencer's *First Principles.*

these. But these qualities themselves, and thus the whole inner nature of the stone which consists in them, and therefore manifests itself in all the ways referred to; thus, in general, that the stone is such as it is, that it exists generally—all this, I say, has no ground, but is the visible appearance of the groundless will. Every cause is thus an occasional cause. We have found it to be so in nature, which is without knowledge, and it is also precisely the same when motives and not causes or stimuli determine the point at which the phenomena are to appear, that is to say, in the actions of animals and human beings. For in both cases it is one and the same will which appears; very different in the grades of its manifestation, multiplied in the phenomena of these grades, and, in respect of these, subordinated to the principle of sufficient reason, but in itself free from all this. Motives do not determine the character of man, but only the phenomena of his character, that is, his actions; the outward fashion of his life, not its inner meaning and content. These proceed from the character which is the immediate manifestation of the will, and is therefore groundless. That one man is bad and another good, does not depend upon motives or outward influences, such as teaching and preaching, and is in this sense quite inexplicable. But whether a bad man shows his badness in petty acts of injustice, cowardly tricks, and low knavery which he practices in the narrow sphere of his circumstances, or whether as a conqueror he oppresses nations, throws a world into lamentation, and sheds the blood of millions; this is the outward form of his manifestation, that which is unessential to it, and depends upon the circumstances in which fate has placed him, upon his surroundings, upon external influences, upon motives; but his decision upon these motives can never be explained from them; it proceeds from the will, of which this man is a manifestation. Of this we shall speak in the Fourth Book. The manner in which the character discloses its qualities is quite analogous to the way in which those of every material body in unconscious nature are disclosed. Water remains water with its intrinsic qualities, whether as a still lake it reflects its banks, or leaps in foam from the cliffs, or, artificially confined, spouts in a long jet into the air. All that depends upon external causes; the one form is as natural to it as the other, but it will always

show the same form in the same circumstances; it is equally ready
for any, but in every case true to its character, and at all times
revealing this alone. So will every human character under all circumstances reveal itself, but the phenomena which proceed from it
will always be in accordance with the circumstances.

§ 27

If, from the foregoing consideration of the forces of nature
and their phenomena, we have come to see clearly how far an
explanation from causes can go, and where it must stop if it is
not to degenerate into the vain attempt to reduce the content of
all phenomena to their mere form, in which case there would
ultimately remain nothing but form, we shall be able to settle in
general terms what is to be demanded of etiology as a whole.
It must seek out the causes of all phenomena in nature, *i. e.,* the
circumstances under which they invariably appear. Then it must
refer the multitude of phenomena which have various forms in
various circumstances to what is active in every phenomenon, and
is presupposed in the cause,—original forces of nature. It must
correctly distinguish between a difference of the phenomenon which
arises from a difference of the force, and one which results merely
from a difference of the circumstances under which the force expresses itself; and with equal care it must guard against taking
the expressions of one and the same force under different circumstances for the manifestations of different forces, and conversely
against taking for manifestations of one and the same force what
originally belongs to different forces. Now this is the direct work
of the faculty of judgment, and that is why so few men are
capable of increasing our insight in physics, while all are able to
enlarge experience. Indolence and ignorance make us disposed to
appeal too soon to original forces. This is exemplified with an
exaggeration that savours of irony in the entities and quiddities of
the schoolmen. Nothing is further from my desire than to favour
their resuscitation. We have just as little right to appeal to the
objectification of will, instead of giving a physical explanation, as
we have to appeal to the creative power of God. For physics demands causes, and the will is never a cause. Its whole relation to

the phenomenon is not in accordance with the principle of sufficient reason. But that which in itself is the will exists in another aspect as idea; that is to say, is phenomenon. As such, it obeys the laws which constitute the form of the phenomenon. Every movement, for example, although it is always a manifestation of will, must yet have a cause from which it is to be explained in relation to a particular time and space; that is, not in general in its inner nature, but as a *particular* phenomenon. In the case of the stone, this is a mechanical cause; in that of the movement of a man, it is a motive; but in no case can it be wanting. On the other hand, the universal common nature of all phenomena of one particular kind, that which must be presupposed if the explanation from causes is to have any sense and meaning, is the general force of nature, which, in physics, must remain a *qualitas occulta,* because with it the etiological explanation ends and the metaphysical begins. But the chain of causes and effects is never broken by an original force to which it has been necessary to appeal. It does not run back to such a force as if it were its first link, but the nearest link, as well as the remotest, presupposes the original force, and could otherwise explain nothing. A series of causes and effects may be the manifestation of the most different kinds of forces, whose successive visible appearances are conducted through it, as I have illustrated above by the example of a metal machine. But the difference of these original forces, which cannot be referred to each other, by no means breaks the unity of that chain of causes, and the connection between all its links. The etiology and the philosophy of nature never do violence to each other, but go hand in hand, regarding the same object from different points of view. Etiology gives an account of the causes which necessarily produce the particular phenomenon to be explained. It exhibits, as the foundation of all its explanations, the universal forces which are active in all these causes and effects. It accurately defines, enumerates, and distinguishes these forces, and then indicates all the different effects in which each force appears, regulated by the difference of the circumstances, always in accordance with its own peculiar character, which it discloses in obedience to an invariable rule, called *a law of nature.* When all this has been thoroughly accomplished by physics in every particular, it will be complete, and its work will be done. There will then remain no unknown force in unorganized nature, nor any effect, which has not been proved to be the manifestation of one of these forces under definite circumstances, in accordance with a law of nature. Yet a law of nature remains merely the observed, rule according to which nature invariably proceeds whenever certain definite circumstances occur. Therefore a law of nature may be defined as a fact expressed generally—*un fait généralisé*—and thus a complete enumeration of all the laws of nature would only be a complete register of facts. The consideration of nature as a whole is thus completed in *morphology,* which enumerates, compares, and arranges all the enduring forms of organized nature. Of the causes of the appearance of the individual creature it has little to say, for in all cases this is procreation (the theory of which is a separate matter), and in rare cases the *generatio æquivoca.* But to this last belongs, strictly speaking, the manner in which all the lower grades of the objectification of will, that is to say, physical and chemical phenomena, appear as individual, and it is precisely the task of etiology to point out the conditions of this appearance. Philosophy, on the other hand, concerns itself only with the universal, in nature as everywhere else. The original forces themselves are here its object, and it recognizes in them the different grades of the objectivity of will, which is the inner nature, the "in-itself" of this world; and when it regards the world apart from will, it explains it as merely the idea of the subject. But if etiology, instead of preparing the way for philosophy, and supplying its doctrines with practical application by means of instances, supposes that its aim is rather to deny the existence of all original forces, except perhaps *one,* the most general, for example, impenetrability, which it imagines it thoroughly understands, and consequently seeks forcibly to refer all the others to it—it forsakes its own province and can only give us error instead of truth. The content of nature is supplanted by its form, everything is ascribed to the circumstances which work from without, and nothing to the inner nature of the thing. Now if it were possible to succeed by this method, a problem in arithmetic would ultimately, as we have already remarked, solve the riddle of the universe. But this is the method adopted by those, referred to above, who think that all physiological effects ought to be reduced to form and combination, this, perhaps, to electricity, and this again to chemism, and chemism to mechanism. The mistake of Descartes, for example, and of all the Atomists, was of this last description. They referred the movements of the globe to the impact of a fluid, and the qualities of matter to the connection and form of the atoms, and hence they laboured to explain all the phenomena of nature as merely manifestations of impenetrability and cohesion. Although this has been given up, precisely the same error is committed in our own day by the electrical, chemical, and mechanical physiologists, who obstinately attempt to explain the whole of life and all the functions of the organism from "form and combination." In Meckel's "Archiv für Physiologie" (1820, vol. v. p. 185) we still find it stated that the aim of physiological explanation is the reduction of organic life to the universal forces with which physics deals. Lamarck also, in his "Philosophie Zoologique," explains life as merely the effect of warmth and electricity: *le calorique et la matière électrique suffisent parfaitement pour composer ensemble cette cause essentielle de la vie* (p. 16).[7] According to this, warmth and electricity would be the "thing-in-itself," and the world of animals and plants its phenomenal appearance. The absurdity of this opinion becomes glaringly apparent at the 306th and following pages of that work. It is well known that all these opinions, that have been so often refuted, have reappeared quite recently with renewed confidence. If we carefully examine the foundation of these views, we shall find that they ultimately involve the presupposition that the organism is merely an aggregate of phenomena of physical, chemical, and mechanical forces, which have come together here by chance, and produced the organism as a freak of nature without further significance. The organism of an animal or of a human being would therefore be, if considered philosophically, not the exhibition of a special Idea, that is, not itself immediate objectivity of the will at a definite higher grade, but in it would appear only those Ideas which objectify the will in electricity, in chemism, and in mechanism. Thus the organism would be as fortuitously con-

---

[7] "Heat and electricity are entirely sufficient to constitute, together, the essential cause of life."

structed by the concurrence of these forces as the forms of men and beasts in clouds and stalactites, and would therefore in itself be no more interesting than they are. However, we shall see immediately how far the application of physical and chemical modes of explanation to the organism may yet, within certain limits, be allowable and useful; for I shall explain that the vital force certainly avails itself of and uses the forces of unorganized nature; yet these forces no more constitute the vital force than a hammer and anvil make a blacksmith. Therefore even the most simple example of plant life can never be explained from these forces by any theory of capillary attraction and endosmosis, much less animal life. The following observations will prepare the way for this somewhat difficult discussion.

It follows from all that has been said that it is certainly an error on the part of natural science to seek to refer the higher grades of the objectification of will to the lower; for the failure to recognize, or the denial of, original and self-existing forces of nature is just as wrong as the groundless assumption of special forces when what occurs is merely a peculiar kind of manifestation of what is already known. Thus Kant rightly says that it would be absurd to hope for a blade of grass from Newton, that is, from one who reduced the blade of grass to the manifestations of physical and chemical forces, of which it was the chance product, and therefore a mere freak of nature, in which no special Idea appeared, *i. e.,* the will did not directly reveal itself in it in a higher and specific grade, but just as in the phenomena of unorganized nature and by chance in this form. The schoolmen, who certainly would not have allowed such a doctrine, would rightly have said that it was a complete denial of the *forma substantialis,* and a degradation of it to the *forma accidentalis.* For the *forma substantialis* of Aristotle denotes exactly what I call the grade of the objectification of will in a thing. On the other hand, it is not to be overlooked that in all Ideas, that is, in all forces of unorganized, and all forms of organized nature, it is *one and the same* will that reveals itself, that is to say, which enters the form of the idea and passes into *objectivity.* Its unity must therefore be also recognizable through an inner relationship between all its phenomena. Now this reveals itself in the higher grades of the objectification of will, where the whole phenomenon is more distinct, thus in the vegetable and animal kingdoms, through the universally prevailing analogy of all forms, the fundamental type which recurs in all phenomena. This has, therefore, become the guiding principle of the admirable zoölogical system which was originated by the French in this century, and it is most completely established in comparative anatomy as *l'unité de plan, l'unformité de l'élément anatomique*. To discover this fundamental type has been the chief concern, or at any rate the praiseworthy endeavour, of the natural philosophers of the school of Schelling, who have in this respect considerable merit, although in many cases their hunt after analogies in nature degenerated into mere conceits. They have, however, rightly shown that that general relationship and family likeness exists also in the Ideas of unorganized nature; for example, between electricity and magnetism, the identity of which was afterwards established; between chemical attraction and gravitation, and so forth. They specially called attention to the fact that *polarity,* that is, the sundering of a force into two qualitatively different and opposed activities striving after reunion, which also shows itself for the most part in space as a dispersion in opposite directions, is a fundamental type of almost all the phenomena of nature, from the magnet and the crystal to man himself. Yet this knowledge has been current in China from the earliest times, in the doctrine of opposition of Yin and Yang. Indeed, since all things in the world are the objectification of one and the same will, and therefore in their inner nature identical, it must not only be the case that there is that unmistakable analogy between them, and that in every phenomenon the trace, intimation, and plan of the higher phenomenon that lies next to it in point of development shows itself, but also because all these forms belong to the world as *ided,* it is indeed conceivable that even in the most universal forms of the idea, in that peculiar framework of the phenomenal world space and time, it may be possible to discern and establish the fundamental type, intimation, and plan of what fills the forms. It seems to have been a dim notion of this that was the origin of the Cabala and all the mathematical philosophy of the Pythagoreans, and also of the Chinese in Y-king. In the school of Schelling also, to which we have already referred, we find, among their efforts to bring to light the similarity among the phenomena of nature, several attempts (though rather unfortunate ones) to deduce laws of nature from the laws of pure space and time. However, one can never tell to what extent a man of genius will realize both endeavours.

Now, although the difference between phenomenon and thing-in-itself is never lost sight of, and therefore the identity of the will which objectifies itself in all Ideas can never (because it has different grades of its objectification) be distorted to mean identity of the particular Ideas themselves in which it appears, so that, for example, chemical or electrical attraction can never be reduced to the attraction of gravitation, although this inner analogy is known, and the former may be regarded as, so to speak, higher powers of the latter, just as little does the similarity of the construction of all animals warrant us in mixing and identifying the species and explaining the more developed as mere variations of the less developed; and although, finally, the physiological functions are never to be reduced to chemical or physical processes, yet, in justification of this procedure, within certain limits, we may accept the following observations as highly probable.

If several of the phenomena of will in the lower grades of its objectification—that is, in unorganized nature—come into conflict because each of them, under the guidance of causality, seeks to possess a given portion of matter, there arises from the conflict the phenomenon of a higher Idea which prevails over all the less developed phenomena previously there, yet in such a way that it allows the essence of these to continue to exist in a subordinate manner, in that it takes up into itself from them something which is analogous to them. This process is only intelligible from the identity of the will which manifests itself in all the Ideas, and which is always striving after higher objectification. We thus see, for example, in the hardening of the bones, an unmistakable analogy to crystallization, as the force which originally had possession of the chalk, although ossification is never to be reduced to crystallization. The analogy shows itself in a weaker degree in the flesh becoming firm. The combination of humours in the animal body and secretion are also analogous to chemical combination and separation. Indeed, the laws of chemistry are still strongly operative in this case, but subordinated, very much modified, and mastered by a higher Idea; therefore mere chemical forces outside the organism will never afford us such humours; but

"Encheiresin naturæ nennt es die Chemie,
Spottet ihrer selbst und weiss nicht wie." [8]

The more developed Idea resulting from this victory over several lower Ideas or objectifications of will, gains an entirely new character by taking up into itself from every Idea over which it has prevailed a strengthened analogy. The will objectifies itself in a new, more distinct way. It originally appears in *generatio æquivoca;* afterwards in assimilation to the given germ, organic moisture, plant, animal, man. Thus from the strife of lower phenomena the higher arise, swallowing them all up, but yet realizing in the higher grade the tendency of all the lower. Here, then, already the law applies—*Serpens nisi serpentem comederit non fit draco.* [9]

I wish it had been possible for me to dispel by clearness of explanation the obscurity which clings to the subject of these thoughts; but I see very well that the reader's own consideration of the matter must materially aid me if I am not to remain uncomprehended or misunderstood. According to the view I have expressed, the traces of chemical and physical modes of operation will indeed be found in the organism, but it can never be explained from them; because it is by no means a phenomenon even accidentally brought about through the united actions of such forces, but a higher Idea which has overcome these lower ideas by *subduing assimilation;* for the *one* will which objectifies itself in all Ideas always seeks the highest possible objectification, and has therefore in this case given up the lower grades of its manifestation after a conflict, in order to appear in a higher grade, and one so much the more powerful. No victory without conflict: since the higher Idea or objectification of will can only appear through the conquest of the lower, it endures the opposition of these lower

[8] "Chemistry calls this nature's 'Eucheiresis,'
And so it stultifies itself, unknowing." (*Faust*)
[9] Unless the serpent eats a serpent he does not become a dragon.

Ideas, which, although brought into subjection, still constantly strive to obtain an independent and complete expression of their being. The magnet that has attracted a piece of iron carries on a perpetual conflict with gravitation, which, as the lower objectification of will, has a prior right to the matter of the iron; and in this constant battle the magnet indeed grows stronger, for the opposition excites it, as it were, to greater effort. In the same way every manifestation of the will, including that which expresses itself in the human organism, wages a constant war against the many physical and chemical forces which, as lower Ideas, have a prior right to that matter. Thus the arm falls, which for a while, overcoming gravity, we have held stretched out; thus the pleasing sensation of health, which proclaims the victory of the Idea of the self-conscious organism over the physical and chemical laws, which originally governed the humours of the body, is so often interrupted, and is indeed always accompanied by greater or less discomfort, which arises from the resistance of these forces, and on account of which the vegetative part of our life is constantly attended by slight pain. Thus also digestion weakens all the animal functions, because it requires the whole vital force to overcome the chemical forces of nature by assimilation. Hence also in general the burden of physical life, the necessity of sleep, and, finally, of death; for at last these subdued forces of nature, assisted by circumstances, win back from the organism, wearied even by the constant victory, the matter it took from them, and attain to an unimpeded expression of their being. We may therefore say that every organism expresses the Idea of which it is the image, only after we have subtracted the part of its force which is expended in subduing the lower Ideas that strive with it for matter. This seems to have been running in the mind of Jacob Böhm when he says somewhere that all the bodies of men and animals, and even all plants, are really half dead. According as the subjection in the organism of these forces of nature, which express the lower grades of the objectification of will, is more or less successful, the more or the less completely does it attain to the expression of its Idea; that is to say, the nearer it is to the *ideal* or the further from it—the *ideal* of beauty in its species.

Thus everywhere in nature we see strife, conflict, and alterna-

tion of victory, and in it we shall come to rocognize more distinctly that variance with itself which is essential to the will.
Every grade of the objectification of will fights for the matter,
the space, and the time of the others. The permanent matter must
constantly change its form; for under the guidance of causality,
mechanical, physical, chemical, and organic phenomena, eagerly
striving to appear, wrest the matter from each other, for each
desires to reveal its own Idea. This strife may be followed through
the whole of nature; indeed nature exists only through it: εἰ γαρ
μη ην το νεικος εν τοις πραγμασιν, ἐν αν ην ἅπαντα, ὡς φησιν Εμπε-
δοκλης· (nam si non inesset in rebus contentio, unum omnia essent,
ut ait Empedocles. Aris. Metaph., B. 5).[10] Yet this strife itself
is only the revelation of that variance with itself which is essential
to the will. This universal conflict becomes most distinctly visible
in the animal kingdom. For animals have the whole of the
vegetable kingdom for their food, and even within the animal
kingdom every beast is the prey and the food of another; that is,
the matter in which its Idea expresses itself must yield itself to
the expression of another Idea, for each animal can only maintain
its existence by the constant destruction of some other. Thus
the will to live everywhere preys upon itself, and in different forms
is its own nourishment, till finally the human race, because it
subdues all the others, regards nature as a manufactory for its
use. Yet even the human race, as we shall see in the Fourth
Book, reveals in itself with most terrible distinctness, this conflict,
this variance with itself of the will, and we find *homo homini
lupus*.[11] Meanwhile we can recognize this strife, this subjugation,
just as well in the lower grades of the objectification of will. Many
insects (especially ichneumon-flies) lay their eggs on the skin, and
even in the body of the larvæ of other insects, whose slow destruction is the first work of the newly hatched brood. The young
hydra, which grows like a bud out of the old one, and afterwards
separates itself from it, fights while it is still joined to the old one
for the prey that offers itself, so that the one snatches it out of
the mouth of the other (Trembley, Polypod., ii., p. 110, and iii.,

[10] If, says Empedocles, strife were not present everywhere, all things
would be one.
[11] Man is a wolf to man.

p. 165). But the bulldog-ant of Australia affords us the most extraordinary example of this kind; for if it is cut in two, a battle begins between the head and the tail. The head seizes the tail with its teeth, and the tail defends itself bravely by stinging the head: the battle may last for half an hour, until they die or are dragged away by other ants. This contest takes place every time the experiment is tried. (From a letter by Howitt in the W. Journal, reprinted in Galignani's Messenger, 17th November, 1855.) On the banks of the Missouri one sometimes sees a mighty oak the stem and branches of which are so encircled, fettered, and interlaced by a gigantic wild vine, that it withers as if choked. The same thing shows itself in the lowest grades; for example, when water and carbon are changed into vegetable sap, or vegetables or bread into blood by organic assimilation; and so also in every case in which animal secretion takes place, along with the restriction of chemical forces to a subordinate mode of activity. This also occurs in unorganized nature, when, for example, crystals in process of formation meet, cross, and mutually disturb each other to such an extent that they are unable to assume the pure crystalline form, so that almost every cluster of crystals is an image of such a conflict of will at this low grade of its objectification; or again, when a magnet forces its magnetism upon iron, in order to express its Idea in it; or when galvanism overcomes chemical affinity, decomposes the closest combinations, and so entirely suspends the laws of chemistry that the acid of a decomposed salt at the negative pole must pass to the positive pole without combining with the alkalies through which it goes on its way, or turning red the litmus paper that touches it. On a large scale it shows itself in the relation between the central body and the planet, for although the planet is in absolute dependence, yet it always resists, just like the chemical forces in the organism; hence arises the constant tension between centripetal and centrifugal force, which keeps the globe in motion, and is itself an example of that universal essential conflict of the manifestation of will which we are considering. For as every body must be regarded as the manifestation of a will, and as will necessarily expresses itself as a struggle, the original condition of every world that is formed into a globe cannot be rest, but motion, a striving forward in boundless space without rest and without end. Neither the law of inertia nor that of causality is opposed to this: for as, according to the former, matter as such is alike indifferent to rest and motion, its original condition may just as well be the one as the other, therefore if we first find it in motion, we have just as little right to assume that this was preceded by a condition of rest, and to inquire into the cause of the origin of the motion, as, conversely, if we found it at rest, we would have to assume a previous motion and inquire into the cause of its suspension. It is, therefore, not needful to seek for a first impulse for centrifugal force, for, according to the hypothesis of Kant and Laplace, it is, in the case of the planets, the residue of the original rotation of the central body, from which the planets have separated themselves as it contracted. But to this central body itself motion is essential; it always continues its rotation, and at the same time rushes forward in endless space, or perhaps circulates round a greater central body invisible to us. This view entirely agrees with the conjecture of astronomers that there is a central sun, and also with the observed advance of our whole solar system, and perhaps of the whole stellar system to which our sun belongs. From this we are finally led to assume a general advance of fixed stars, together with the central sun, and this certainly loses all meaning in boundless space (for motion in absolute space cannot be distinguished from rest), and becomes, as is already the case from its striving and aimless flight, an expression of that nothingness, that failure of all aim, which, at the close of this book, we shall be obliged to recognize in the striving of will in all its phenomena. Thus boundless space and endless time must be the most universal and essential forms of the collective phenomena of will, which exist for the expression of its whole being. Lastly, we can recognize that conflict which we are considering of all phenomena of will against each other in simple matter regarded as such; for the real characteristic of matter is correctly expressed by Kant as repulsive and attractive force; so that even crude matter has its existence only in the strife of conflicting forces. If we abstract from all chemical differences in matter, or go so far back in the chain of causes and effects that as yet there is no chemical difference, there remains mere matter,—the world rounded to a globe, whose life, *i. e.,* objectification of will, is now constituted by the conflict between attractive and repulsive forces, the former as gravitation pressing from all sides towards the centre, the latter as impenetrability always opposing the former either as rigidity or elasticity; and this constant pressure and resistance may be regarded as the objectivity of will in its very lowest grade, and even there it expresses its character.

We should see the will express itself here in the lowest grade as blind striving, an obscure, inarticulate impulse, far from susceptible of being directly known. It is the simplest and the weakest mode of its objectification. But it appears as this blind and unconscious striving in the whole of unorganized nature, in all those original forces which it is the work of physics and chemistry to discover and to study the laws, and each of which manifests itself to us in millions of phenomena which are exactly similar and regular, and show no trace of individual character, but are mere multiplicity through space and time, *i. e.,* through the *principium individuationis,* as a picture is multiplied through the facets of a glass.

From grade to grade objectifying itself more distinctly, yet still completely without consciousness as an obscure striving force, the will acts in the vegetable kingdom also, in which the bond of its phenomena consists no longer properly of causes, but of stimuli; and, finally, also in the vegetative part of the animal phenomenon, in the production and maturing of the animal, and in sustaining its inner economy, in which the manifestation of will is still always necessarily determined by stimuli. The ever-ascending grades of the objectification of will bring us at last to the point at which the individual that expresses the Idea could no longer receive food for its assimilation through mere movement following upon stimuli. For such a stimulus must be waited for, but the food has now come to be of a more special and definite kind, and with the exer-increasing multiplicity of the individual phenomena, the crowd and confusion has become so great that they interfere with each other, and the chance of the individual that is moved merely by stimuli and must wait for its food would be too unfavourable. From the point, therefore, at which the animal has delivered itself from the egg or the womb in which it vegetated without consciousness, its food must be sought out and selected. For this purpose movement following upon motives, and therefore consciousness, becomes necessary, and consequently it appears as an agent, μηχανη,[12] called in at this stage of the objectification of will for the conservation of the individual and the propagation of the species. It appears represented by the brain or a large ganglion, just as every other effort or determination of the will which objectifies itself is represented by an organ, that is to say, manifests itself for the idea as an organ. But with this means of assistance, this μηχανη, the *world as idea* comes into existence at a stroke, with all its forms, object and subject, time, space, multiplicity, and causality. The world now shows its second side. Till now *mere will,* it becomes also *idea,* object of the knowing subject. The will, which up to this point followed its tendency in the dark with unerring certainty, has at this grade kindled for itself a light as a means which became necessary for getting rid of the disadvantage which arose from the throng and the complicated nature of its manifestations, and which would have accrued precisely to the most perfect of them. The hitherto infallible certainty and regularity with which it worked in unorganized and merely vegetative nature, rested upon the fact that it alone was active in its original nature, as blind impulse, will, without assistance, and also without interruption, from a second and entirely different world, the world as idea, which is indeed only the image of its own inner being, but is yet of quite another nature, and now encroaches on the connected whole of its phenomena. Hence its infallible certainty comes to an end. Animals are already exposed to illusion, to deception. They have, however, merely ideas of perception, no conception, no reflection, and they are therefore bound to the present; they cannot have regard for the future. It seems as if this knowledge without reason was not in all cases sufficient for its end, and at times required, as it were, some assistance. For the very remarkable phenomenon presents itself, that the blind working of the will and the activity enlightened by knowledge encroach in a most astonishing manner upon each other's spheres in two kinds of phenomena. In the one case we find in the very midst of those actions of animals which

---

[12] Instrument; *lit.,* machine.

are guided by perceptive knowledge and its motives one kind of action which is accomplished apart from these, and thus through the necessity of the blindly acting will. I refer to those mechanical instincts which are guided by no motive or knowledge, and which yet have the appearance of performing their work from abstract rational motives. The other case, which is opposed to this, is that in which, on the contrary, the light of knowledge penetrates into the workshop of the blindly active will, and illuminates the vegetative functions of the human organism. I mean clairvoyance. Finally, when the will has attained to the highest grade of its objectification, that knowledge of the understanding given to brutes to which the senses supply the data, out of which there arises mere perception confined to what is immediately present, does not suffice. That complicated, many-sided, imaginative being, man, with his many needs, and exposed as he is to innumerable dangers, must, in order to exist, be lighted by a double knowledge; a higher power, as it were, of perceptive knowledge must be given him, and also reason, as the faculty of framing abstract conceptions. With this there has appeared reflection, surveying the future and the past, and, as a consequence, deliberation, care, the power of premeditated action independent of the present, and finally, the full and distinct consciousness of one's own deliberate volition as such. Now if with mere knowledge of perception there arose the possibility of illusion and deception, by which the previous infalli- bility of the blind striving of will was done away with, so that mechanical and other instincts, as expressions of unconscious will, had to lend their help in the midst of those that were con- scious, with the entrance of reason that certainty and infallibility of the expressions of will (which at the other extreme in un- organized nature appeared as strict conformity to law) is almost entirely lost; instinct disappears altogether; deliberation, which is supposed to take the place of everything else, begets (as was shown in the First Book) irresolution and uncertainty; then error be- comes possible, and in many cases obstructs the adequate objectifica- tion of the will in action. For although in the character the will has already taken its definite and unchangeable bent or direction, in accordance with which volition, when occasioned by the presence of a motive, invariably takes place, yet error can falsify its expressions, for it introduces illusive motives that take the place of the real ones which they resemble; as, for example, when superstition forces on a man imaginary motives which impel him to a course of action directly opposed to the way in which the will would otherwise express itself in the given circumstances. Agamemnon slays his daughter; a miser dispenses alms, out of pure egotism, in the hope that he will some day receive an hundredfold; and so on.

Thus knowledge generally, rational as well as merely sensuous, proceeds originally from the will itself, belongs to the inner being of the higher grades of its objectification as a mere μηχανη, a means of supporting the individual and the species, just like any organ of the body. Originally destined for the service of the will for the accomplishment of its aims, it remains almost throughout entirely subjected to its service: it is so in all brutes and in almost all men. Yet we shall see in the Third Book how in certain individual men knowledge can deliver itself from this bondage, throw off its yoke, and, free from all the aims of will, exist purely for itself, simply as a clear mirror of the world, which is the source of art. Finally, in the Fourth Book, we shall see how, if this kind of knowledge reacts on the will, it can bring about self-surrender, i. e., resignation, which is the final goal, and indeed the inmost nature of all virtue and holiness, and is deliverance from the world.

§ 28

We have considered the great multiplicity and diversity of the phenomena in which the will objectifies itself, and we have seen their endless and implacable strife with each other. Yet, according to the whole discussion up to this point, the will itself, as thing-in-itself, is by no means included in that multiplicity and change. The diversity of the (Platonic) Ideas, i. e., grades of objectification, the multitude of individuals in which each of these expresses itself, the struggle of forms for matter,—all this does not concern it, but is only the manner of its objectification, and only through this has an indirect relation to it, by virtue of which it belongs to the expression of the nature of will for the idea. As the magic-lantern shows many different pictures, which are all made visible by one and the same light, so in all the multifarious phenomena which fill the world together or throng after each other as events, only *one will* manifests itself, of which everything is the visibility, the objectivity, and which remains unmoved in the midst of this change; it alone is thing-in-itself; all objects are manifestations, or, to speak the language of Kant, phenomena. Although in man, as (Platonic) Idea, the will finds its clearest and fullest objectification, yet man alone could not express its being. In order to manifest the full significance of the will, the Idea of man would need to appear, not alone and sundered from everything else, but accompanied by the whole series of grades, down through all the forms of animals, through the vegetable kingdom to unorganized nature. All these supplement each other in the complete objectification of will; they are as much presupposed by the Idea of man as the blossoms of a tree presuppose leaves, branches, stem, and root; they form a pyramid, of which man is the apex. If fond of similes, one might also say that their manifestations accompany that of man as necessarily as the full daylight is accompanied by all the gradations of twilight, through which, little by little, it loses itself in darkness; or one might call them the echo of man, and say: Animal and plant are the descending fifth and third of man, the inorganic kingdom is the lower octave. The full truth of this last comparison will only become clear to us when, in the following book, we attempt to fathom the deep significance of music, and see how a connected, progressive melody, made up of high, quick notes, may be regarded as in some sense expressing the life and efforts of man connected by reflection, while the unconnected complemental notes and the slow bass, which make up the harmony necessary to perfect the music, represent the rest of the animal kingdom and the whole of nature that is without knowledge. But of this in its own place, where it will not sound so paradoxical. We find, however, that the *inner necessity* of the gradation of its manifestations, which is inseparable from the adequate objectification of the will, is expressed by an *outer necessity* in the whole of these manifestations themselves, by reason of which man has need of the beasts for his support, the beasts in their grades have need of each other as well as of plants, which in their turn require the ground, water, chemical elements and their combinations, the planet, the sun, rotation and motion round the sun, the curve of the ellipse, &c., &c. At bottom this results from the fact that the will must live on itself, for there exists nothing beside it, and it is a hungry will. Hence arise eager pursuit, anxiety, and suffering.

It is only the knowledge of the unity of will as thing-in-itself, in the endless diversity and multiplicity of the phenomena, that can afford us the true explanation of that wonderful, unmistakable analogy of all the productions of nature, that family likeness on account of which we may regard them as variations on the same ungiven theme. So in like measure, through the distinct and thoroughly comprehended knowledge of that harmony, that essential connection of all the parts of the world, that necessity of their gradation which we have just been considering, we shall obtain a true and sufficient insight into the inner nature and meaning of the undeniable *teleology* [13] of all organized productions of nature, which, indeed, we presupposed *a priori,* when considering and investigating them.

This *teleology* is of a twofold description; sometimes an *inner teleology,* that is, an agreement of all the parts of a particular organism, so ordered that the sustenance of the individual and the species results from it, and therefore presents itself as the end of that disposition or arrangement. Sometimes, however, there is an *outward teleology,* a relation of unorganized to organized nature in general, or of particular parts of organized nature to each other, which makes the maintenance of the whole of organized nature, or of the particular animal species, possible, and therefore presents itself to our judgment as the means to this end.

Inner teleology is connected with the scheme of our work in the following way. If, in accordance with what has been said, all variations of form in nature, and all multiplicity of individuals, belong not to the will itself, but merely to its objectivity and the form of this objectivity, it necessarily follows that the will is indivisible and is present as a whole in every manifestation, although the grades of its objectification, the (Platonic) Ideas, are very different from each other. We may, for the sake of simplicity, regard these different Ideas as in themselves individual and simple

[13] Purposiveness.

acts of the will, in which it expresses its nature more or less. Individuals, however, are again manifestations of the Ideas, thus of these acts, in time, space, and multiplicity. Now, in the lowest grades of objectivity, such an act (or an Idea) retains its unity in the manifestation; while, in order to appear in higher grades, it requires a whole series of conditions and developments in time, which only collectively express its nature completely. Thus, for example the Idea that reveals itself in any general force of nature has always one single expression, although it presents itself differently according to the external relations that are present: otherwise its identity could not be proved, for this is done by abstracting the diversity that arises merely from external relations. In the same way the crystal has only *one* manifestation of life, crystallization, which afterwards has its fully adequate and exhaustive expression in the rigid form, the corpse of that momentary life. The plant, however, does not express the Idea, whose phenomenon it is, at once and through a single manifestation, but in a succession of developments of its organs in time. The animal not only develops its organism in the same manner, in a succession of forms which are often very different (metamorphosis), but this form itself, although it is already objectivity of will at this grade, does not attain to a full expression of its Idea. This expression must be completed through the actions of the animal, in which its empirical character, common to the whole species, manifests itself, and only then does it become the full revelation of the Idea, a revelation which presupposes the particular organism as its first condition. In the case of man, the empirical character is peculiar to every individual (indeed, as we shall see in the Fourth Book, even to the extent of supplanting entirely the character of the species, through the self-surrender of the whole will). That which is known as the empirical character, through the necessary development in time, and the division into particular actions that is conditioned by it, is, when we abstract from this temporal form of the manifestation the *intelligible character,* according to the expression of Kant, who shows his undying merit especially in establishing this distinction and explaining the relation between freedom and necessity, *i. e.,* between the will as thing-in-itself and its manifestations in time. Thus the intelligible character coincides with the Idea, or, more accurately, with the original act of will which reveals itself in it. So far then, not only the empirical character of every man, but also that of every species of animal and plant, and even of every original force of unorganized nature, is to be regarded as the manifestation of an intelligible character, that is, of a timeless, indivisible act of will. I should like here to draw attention in passing to the naïveté with which every plant expresses and lays open its whole character in its mere form, reveals its whole being and will. This is why the physiognomy of plants is so interesting; while in order to know an animal in its Idea, it is necessary to observe the course of its action. As for man, he must be fully investigated and tested, for reason makes him capable of a high degree of dissumulation. The beast is as much more naïve than the man as the plant is more naïve than the beast. In the beast we see the will to live more naked, as it were, than in the man, in whom it is clothed with so much knowledge, and is, moreover, so veiled, through the capacity for dissimulation, that it is almost only by chance, and here and there, that its true nature becomes apparent. In the plant it shows itself quite naked, but also much weaker, as mere blind striving for existence without end or aim. For the plant reveals its whole being at the first glance, and with complete innocence, which does not suffer from the fact that it carries its organs of generation exposed to view on its upper surface, though in all animals they have been assigned to the most hidden part. This innocence of the plant results from its complete want of knowledge. Guilt does not lie in willing, but in willing with knowledge. Every plant speaks to us first of all of its home, of the climate, and the nature of the ground in which it has grown. Therefore, even those who have had little practice easily tell whether an exotic plant belongs to the tropical or the temperate zone, and whether it grows in water, in marshes, on mountain, or on moorland. Besides this, however, every plant expresses the special will of its species, and says something that cannot be uttered in any other tongue. But we must now apply what has been said to the teleological consideration of the organism, so far as it concerns its inner design. If in unorganized nature the Idea, which is everywhere to be regarded as a single act of will, reveals itself also in a single manifestation which is always the same, and thus one may say that here the empirical character directly partakes of the unity of the intelligible, coincides, as it were, with it, so that no inner design can show itself here; if, on the contrary, all organisms express their Ideas through a series of successive developments, conditioned by a multiplicity of co-existing parts, and thus only the sum of the manifestations of the empirical character collectively constitute the expression of the intelligible character; this necessary co-existence of the parts and succession of the stages of development does not destroy the unity of the appearing Idea, the act of will which expresses itself; nay, rather this unity finds its expression in the necessary relation and connection of the parts and stages of development with each other, in accordance with the law of causality. Since it is the will which is one, indivisible, and there-fore entirely in harmony with itself, that reveals itself in the whole Idea as in act, its manifestation, although broken up into a number of different parts and conditions, must yet show this unity again in the thorough agreement of all of these. This is effected by a necessary relation and dependence of all the parts upon each other, by means of which the unity of the Idea is re-established in the manifestation. In accordance with this, we now recognize these different parts and functions of the organism as related to each other reciprocally as means and end, but the organism itself as the final end of all. Consequently, neither the breaking up of the Idea, which in itself is simple, into the multiplicity of the parts and conditions of the organism, on the one hand, nor, on the other hand, the re-establishment of its unity through the neces-sary connection of the parts and functions which arises from the fact that they are the cause and effect; the means and end, of each other, is peculiar and essential to the appearing will as such, to the thing-in-itself, but only to its manifestation in space, time, and causality (mere modes of the principle of sufficient reason, the form of the phenomenon). They belong to the world as idea, not to the world as will; they belong to the way in which the will becomes object, *i. e.,* idea at this grade of its objectivity. Every one who has grasped the meaning of this discussion—a discussion which is perhaps somewhat difficult—will now fully understand the doctrine of Kant, which follows from it, that both the design of organized and the conformity to law of un-organized nature are only introduced by our understanding, and therefore both belong only to the phenomenon, not to the thing-in-itself. The surprise, which was referred to above, at the infallible constancy of the conformity to law of unorganized nature, is essentially the same as the surprise that is excited by design in organized nature; for in both cases what we wonder at is only the sight of the original unity of the Idea, which, for the phenomenon, has assumed the form of multiplicity and diversity.

As regards the second kind of teleology, according to the division made above, the *outer* design, which shows itself, not in the inner economy of the organisms, but in the support and assistance they receive from without, both from unorganized nature and from each other; its general explanation is to be found in the exposition we have just given. For the whole world, with all its phenomena, is the objectivity of the one indivisible will, the Idea, which is related to all other Ideas as harmony is related to the single voice. Therefore that unity of the will must show itself also in the agreement of all its manifestations. But we can very much increase the clearness of this insight if we go somewhat more closely into the manifestations of that outer teleology and agreement of the different parts of nature with each other, an inquiry which will also throw some light on the foregoing exposition. We shall best attain this end by considering the following analogy.

The character of each individual man, so far as it is thoroughly individual, and not entirely included in that of the species, may be regarded as a special Idea, corresponding to a special act of the objectification of will. This act itself would then be his intelligible character, and his empirical character would be the manifestation of it. The empirical character is entirely determined through the intelligible, which is without ground, *i. e.,* as thing-in-itself is not subordinated to the principle of sufficient reason (the form of the phenomenon). The empirical character must in the course of life afford us the express image of the intelligible, and can only become what the nature of the latter demands. But this property extends only to the essential, not to the unessential in the course of life to which it applies. To this unessential belong the detailed events and actions which are the material in which the empirical character shows itself. These are determined by outward circumstances, which present the motives upon which the character reacts according to its nature; and as they may be very different, the outward form of the manifestation of the empirical character, that is, the definite actual or historical form of the course of life, will have to accommodate itself to their influence. Now this form may be very different, although what is essential to the manifestation, its content, remains the same. Thus, for example it is immaterial whether a man plays for nuts or for crowns; but whether a man cheats or plays fairly, that is the real matter; the latter is determined by the intelligible character, the former by outward circumstances. As the same theme may be expressed in a hundred different variations, so the same character may be expressed in a hundred very different lives. But various as the outward influence may be, the empirical character which expresses itself in the course of life must yet, whatever form it takes, accurately objectify the intelligible character, for the latter adapts its objectification to the given material of actual circumstances. We have now to assume something analogous to the influence of outward circumstances upon the life that is determined in essential matters by the character, if we desire to understand how the will, in the original act of its objectification, determines the various Ideas in which it objectifies itself, that is, the different forms of natural existence of every kind, among which it distributes its objectification, and which must therefore necessarily have a relation to each other in the manifestation. We must assume that between all these manifestations of the *one* will there existed a universal and reciprocal adaptation and accommodation of themselves to each other, by which, however, as we shall soon see more clearly, all time-determination is to be excluded, for the Idea lies outside time. In accordance with this, every manifestation must have adapted itself to the surroundings into which it entered, and these again must have adapted themselves to it, although it occupied a much later position in time; and we see this *consensus naturæ* everywhere. Every plant is therefore adapted to its soil and climate, every animal to its element and the prey that will be its food, and is also in some way protected, to a certain extent, against its natural enemy: the eye is adapted to the light and its refrangibility, the lungs and the blood to the air, the air-bladder of fish to water, the eye of the seal to the change of the medium in which it must see, the water-pouch in the stomach of the camel to the drought of the African deserts, the sail of the nautilus to the wind that is to drive its little bark, and so on down to the most special and astonishing outward adaptations. We must abstract however here from all temporal relations, for these can only concern the manifestation of the Idea, not the Idea itself. Accordingly this kind of explanation must also be used retrospectively, and we must not merely admit that every species accommodated itself to the given environment, but also that this environment itself, which preceded it in time, had just as much regard for the being that would some time come into it. For it is one and the same will that objectifies itself in the whole world; it knows no time, for this form of the principle of sufficient reason does not belong to it, nor to its original objectivity, the Ideas, but only to the way in which these are known by the individuals who themselves are transitory, *i. e.,* to the manifestation of the Ideas. Thus, time has no significance for our present examination of the manner in which the objectification of the will distributes itself among the Ideas, and the Ideas whose *manifestations* entered into the course of time earlier, according to the law of causality, to which as phenomena they are subject, have no advantage over those whose manifestation entered later; nay rather, these last are the completest objectifications of the will, to which the earlier manifestations must adapt themselves just as much as they must adapt themselves to the earlier. Thus the course of the planets, the tendency to the ellipse, the rotation of the earth, the division of land and sea, the atmosphere, light, warmth, and all such phenomena, which are in nature what bass is in harmony, adapted themselves in anticipation of the coming species of living creatures of which they were to become the supporter and sustainer. In the same way the ground adapted itself to the nutrition of plants, plants adapted themselves to the nutrition of animals, animals to that of other animals, and conversely they all adapted themselves to the nutrition of the ground. All the parts of nature correspond to each other, for it is *one* will that appears in them all, but the course of time is quite foreign to its original and only *adequate objectification* (this expression will be explained in the following book), the Ideas. Even now, when the species have only to sustain themselves, no longer to come into existence, we see here and there some such forethought of nature extending to the future, and abstracting as it were from the process of time, a self-adaptation of what is to what is yet to come. The bird builds the nest for the young which it does not yet know; the beaver constructs a dam the object of which is unknown to it; ants, marmots, and bees lay in provision for the winter they have never experienced; the spider and the ant-lion make snares, as if with deliberate cunning, for future unknown prey; insects deposit their eggs where the coming brood finds future nourishment. In the spring-time the female flower of the diœcian valisneria unwinds the spirals of its stalk, by which till now it was held at the bottom of the water, and thus rises to the surface. Just then the male flower, which grows on a short stalk from the bottom, breaks away, and so, at the sacrifice of its life, reaches the surface, where it swims about in search of the female. The latter is fructified, and then draws itself down again to the bottom by contracting its spirals, and there the fruit grows. I must again refer here to the larva of the male stag-beetle, which makes the hole in the wood for its metamorphosis as big again as the female does, in order to have room for its future horns. The instinct of animals in general gives us the best illustration of what remains of teleology in nature. For as instinct is an action, like that which is guided by the conception of an end, and yet is entirely without this; so all construction of nature resembles that which is guided by the conception of an end, and yet is entirely without it. For in the outer as in the inner teleology of nature, what we are obliged to think as means and end is, in every case, *the manifestation of the unity of the one will so thoroughly agreeing with itself,* which has assumed multiplicity in space and time for our manner of knowing.

The reciprocal adaptation and self-accommodation of phenomena that springs from this unity cannot, however, annul the inner contradiction which appears in the universal conflict of nature described above, and which is essential to the will. That harmony goes only so far as to render possible the duration of the world and the different kinds of existences in it, which without it would long since have perished. Therefore it only extends to the continuance of the species, and the general conditions of life, but not to that of the individual. If, then, by reason of that harmony and accommodation, the *species* in organized nature and the *universal forces* in unorganized nature continue to exist beside each other, and indeed support each other reciprocally, on the other hand, the inner contradiction of the will which objectifies itself in all these ideas shows itself in the ceaseless internecine war of the *individuals* of these species, and in the constant struggle of the *manifestations* of these natural forces with each other, as we pointed out above. The scene and the object of this conflict is matter, which they try to wrest from each other, and also space and time, the combination of which through the form of causality is, in fact, matter, as was explained in the First Book.

§ 29

I here conclude the second principle division of my exposition, in the hope that, so far as is possible in the case of an entirely new thought, which cannot be quite free from traces of the individuality in which it originated, I have succeeded in conveying to the reader the complete certainty that this world in which we live and have our being is in its whole nature through and through *will,* and at the same time through and through *idea:* that this idea, as such, already presupposes a form, object and subject, is therefore relative; and if we ask what remains if we take away this form, and all those forms which are subordinate to it, and which express the principle of sufficient reason, the answer must be that as something *toto genere* different from idea, this can be nothing but *will,* which is thus properly the *thing-in-itself.* Every one finds that he himself is this will, in which the real nature of the world consists, and he also finds that he is the knowing subject, whose idea the whole world is, the world which exists only in relation to his consciousness, as its necessary supporter. Every one is thus himself in a double aspect the whole world, and microcosm; finds both sides whole and complete in himself. And what he thus recognizes as his own real being also exhausts the being of the whole world—the macrocosm; thus the world, like man, is through and through *will,* and through and through *idea,* and nothing more than this. So we see the philosophy of Thales, which concerned the macrocosm, unite at this point with that of Socrates, which dealt with the microcosm, for the object of both is found to be the same. But all the knowledge that has been communicated in the first two books will gain greater completeness, and consequently greater certainty, from the two following books, in which I hope that several questions that have more or less distinctly arisen in the course of our work will also be sufficiently answered.

In the meantime *one* such question may be more particularly considered, for it can properly arise only so long as one has not fully penetrated the meaning of the foregoing exposition, and may so far serve as an illustration of it. It is this: Every will is a will towards something, has an object, an end of its willing; what then is the final end, or towards what is that will striving that is exhibited to us as the being-in-itself of the world? This question rests, like so many others, upon the confusion of the thing-in-itself with the manifestation. The principle of sufficient reason, of which the law of motivation is also a form, extends only to the latter, not to the former. It is only of phenomena, of individual things, that a ground can be given, never of the will itself, nor of the Idea in which it adequately objectifies itself. So then of every particular movement or change of any kind in nature, a cause is to be sought, that is, a condition that of necessity produced it, but never of the natural force itself which is revealed in this and innumerable similar phenomena; and it is therefore simple misunderstanding, arising from want of consideration, to ask for a cause of gravity, electricity, and so on. Only if one had somehow shown that gravity and electricity were not original special forces of nature, but only the manifestations of a more general force already known, would it be allowable to ask for the cause which made this force produce the phenomena of gravity or of electricity here. All this has been explained at length above. In the same way every particular act of will of a knowing individual (which is itself only a manifestation of will as the thing-in-itself) has necessarily a motive without which that act would never have occurred;

but just as material causes contain merely the determination that at this time, in this place, and in this manner, a manifestation of this or that natural force must take place, so the motive determines only the act of will of a knowing being, at this time, in this place, and under these circumstances, as a particular act, but by no means determines that that being wills in general or wills in this manner; this is the expression of this intelligible character, which, as will itself, the thing-in-itself, is without ground, for it lies outside the province of the principle of sufficient reason. Therefore every man has permanent aims and motives by which he guides his conduct, and he can always give an account of his particular actions; but if he were asked why he wills at all, or why in general he wills to exist, he would have no answer, and the question would indeed seem to him meaningless; and this would be just the expression of his consciousness that he himself is nothing but will, whose willing stands by itself and requires more particular determination by motives only in its individual acts at each point of time.

In fact, freedom from all aim, from all limits, belongs to the nature of the will, which is endless striving. This was already touched on above in the reference to centrifugal force. It also discloses itself in its simplest form in the lowest grade of the objectification of will, in gravitation, which we see constantly exerting itself, though a final goal is obviously impossible for it. For if, according to its will, all existing matter were collected in one mass, yet within this mass gravity, ever striving towards the centre, would still wage war with impenetrability as rigidity or elasticity. The tendency of matter can therefore only be confined, never completed or appeased. But this is precisely the case with all tendencies of all phenomena of will. Every attained end is also the beginning of a new course, and so on *ad infinitum*. The plant raises its manifestation from the seed through the stem and the leaf to the blossom and the fruit, which again is the beginning of a new seed, a new individual, that runs through the old course, and so on through endless time. Such also is the life of the animal; procreation is its highest point, and after attaining to it, the life of the first individual quickly or slowly sinks, while a new life ensures to nature the endurance of the species and repeats the same pheno-

mena. Indeed, the constant renewal of the matter of every organism is also to be regarded as merely the manifestation of this continual pressure and change, and physiologists are now ceasing to
hold that it is the necessary reparation of the matter wasted in
motion, for the possible wearing out of the machine can by no
means be equivalent to the support it is constantly receiving through
nourishment. Eternal becoming, endless flux, characterizes the
revelation of the inner nature of will. Finally, the same thing
shows itself in human endeavours and desires, which always
delude us by presenting their satisfaction as the final end of
will. As soon as we attain to them they no longer appear the
same, and therefore they soon grow stale, are forgotten, and though
not openly disowned, are yet always thrown aside as vanished
illusions. We are fortunate enough if there still remains something to wish for and to strive after, that the game may be
kept up of constant transition from desire to satisfaction, and
from satisfaction to a new desire, the rapid course of which is
called happiness, and the slow course sorrow, and does not sink
into that stagnation that shows itself in fearful ennui that
paralyzes life, vain yearning without a definite object, deadening
languor. According to all this, when the will is enlightened by
knowledge, it always knows what it wills now and here, never
what it wills in general; every particular act of will has its end,
the whole will has none; just as every particular phenomenon of
nature is determined by a sufficient cause so far as concerns its
appearance in this place at this time, but the force which manifests itself in it has no general cause, for it belongs to the thing-in-
itself, to the groundless will. The single example of self-knowledge
of the will as a whole is the idea as a whole, the whole world of
perception. It is the objectification, the revelation, the mirror of
the will. What the will expresses in it will be the subject of our
further consideration.

THIRD BOOK

THE WORLD AS IDEA

SECOND ASPECT

THE IDEA INDEPENDENT OF THE PRINCIPLE OF SUFFICIENT
REASON: THE PLATONIC IDEA: THE OBJECT OF ART

Τί τὸ ὂν μὲν ἀεί, γένεσιν δὲ οὐκ ἔχον; καὶ τί τὸ γιγνόμενον μὲν καὶ
ἀπολλύμενον, ὄντως δε οὐδέποτε ὄν.—ΠΛΑΤΩΝ.

"That which really is, always is, and has no beginning; that which has
a beginning will also be destroyed, and never really is."—*PLATO.*

III

§ 31

. . . I hope that in the preceding book I have succeeded in producing the conviction that what is called in the Kantian philosophy the *thing-in-itself,* and appears there as so significant, and yet so obscure and paradoxical a doctrine, and especially on account of the manner in which Kant introduced it as an inference from the caused to the cause, was considered a stumbling-stone, and, in fact, the weak side of his philosophy,—that this, I say, if it is reached by the entirely different way by which we have arrived at it, is nothing but the *will* when the sphere of that conception is extended and defined in the way I have shown. I hope, further, that after what has been said there will be no hesitation in recognizing the definite grades of the objectification of the will, which is the inner reality of the world, to be what Plato called the *eternal Ideas* or unchangeable forms (εἰδῆ) ; a doctrine which is regarded as the principal, but at the same time the most obscure and paradoxical dogma of his system, and has been the subject of reflection and controversy, of ridicule and of reverence to so many and such differently endowed minds in the course of many centuries.

If now the will is for us the *thing-in-itself,* and the Idea is the immediate objectivity of that will at a definite grade, we find that Kant's thing-in-itself, and Plato's Idea, which to him is the only οντως ον,[1] these two great obscure paradoxes of the two greatest philosophers of the West are not indeed identical, but yet very closely related, and only distinguished by a single circumstance. The purport of these two great paradoxes, with all inner harmony and relationship, is yet so very different on account of the remarkable diversity of the individuality of their authors, that they

[1] Real being.

are the best commentary on each other, for they are like two entirely different roads that conduct us to the same goal. This is
easily made clear. What Kant says is in substance this:—"Time,
space, and causality are not determinations of the thing-in-itself,
but belong only to its phenomenal existence, for they are nothing
but the forms of our knowledge. Since, however, all multiplicity,
and all coming into being and passing away, are only possible
through time, space, and causality, it follows that they also belong
only to the phenomenon, not to the thing-in-itself. But as our
knowledge is conditioned by these forms, the whole of experience
is only knowledge of the phenomenon, not of the thing-in-itself;
therefore its laws cannot be made valid for the thing-in-itself.
This extends even to our own *ego,* and we know it only as phenomenon, and not according to what it may be in itself." This is the
meaning and content of the doctrine of Kant in the important
respect we are considering.

What Plato says is this:—"The things of this world which our
senses perceive have no true being; *they always become, they never
are:* they have only a relative being; they all exist merely in and
through their relations to each other; their whole being may,
therefore, quite as well be called a non-being. They are consequently not objects of a true knowledge (επιστημη), for such a
knowledge can only be of what exists for itself, and always in
the same way; they, on the contrary, are only the objects of an
opinion based on sensation (δοξα μετ' αισθηεως αλογον). So long as
we are confined to the perception of these, we are like men who
sit in a dark cave, bound so fast that they cannot turn their heads,
and who see nothing but the shadows of real things which pass
between them and a fire burning behind them, the light of which
casts the shadows on the wall opposite them; and even of themselves and of each other they see only the shadows on the wall.
Their wisdom would thus consist in predicting the order of the
shadows learned from experience. The real archetypes, on the
other hand, to which these shadows correspond, the eternal Ideas,
the original forms of all things, can alone be said to have true
being (οντως ον), because they *always are, but never become nor
pass away.* To them belongs no *multiplicity;* for each of them is
according to its nature only one, for it is the archetype itself, of

which all particular transitory things of the same kind which are named after it are copies or shadows. They have also *no coming into being nor passing away,* for they are truly being, never becoming nor vanishing, like their fleeting shadows. (It is necessarily presupposed, however, in these two negative definitions, that time, space, and casuality have no significance or validity for these Ideas, and that they do not exist in them.) Of these only can there be true knowledge, for the object of such knowledge can only be that which *always* and in *every* respect (thus in-itself) is; not that which is and again is not, according as we look at it." This is Plato's doctrine.

It is clear, and requires no further proof that the inner meaning of both doctrines is entirely the same; that both explain the visible world as a manifestation, which in itself is nothing, and which only has meaning and a borrowed reality through that which expresses itself in it (in the one case the thing-in-itself, in the other the Idea). To this last, which has true being, all the forms of that phenomenal existence, even the most universal and essential, are, according to both doctrines, entirely foreign. In order to disown these forms Kant has directly expressed them even in abstract terms, and distinctly refused time, space, and casuality as mere forms of the phenomenon to the thing-in-itself. Plato, on the other hand, did not attain to the fullest expression, and has only distinctly refused these forms to his Ideas in that he denies of the Ideas what is only possible through these forms, multiplicity of similar things, coming into being and passing away. Though it is perhaps superfluous, I should like to illustrate this remarkable and important agreement by an example. There stands before us, let us suppose, an animal in the full activity of life. Plato would say, "This animal has no true existence, but merely an apparent existence, a constant becoming, a relative existence which may just as well be called non-being as being. Only the Idea which expresses itself in that animal is truly 'being,' or the animal-in-itself (αυτο το θηριον), which is dependent upon nothing, but is in and for itself (καθ' έτο, αει ώς ἀύτως) ; it has not become, it will not end, but always is in the same way (αει ον, και μηδεποτε ουτε γιγνομενον ουτε απολλυμενόυ). If now we recognize its Idea in this animal, it is all one and of no importance whether we have this animal now before us or its progenitor of a thousand years ago, whether it is here or in a distant land, whether it presents itself in this or that manner, position, or action; whether, lastly, it is this or any other individual of the same species; all this is nothing, and only concerns the phenomenon; the Idea of the animal alone has true being, and is the object of real knowledge." So Plato; Kant would say something of this kind, "This animal is a phenomenon in time, space, and casuality, which are collectively the conditions *a priori* of the possibility of experience, lying in our faculty of knowledge, not determinations of the thing-in-itself. Therefore this animal as we perceive it at this definite point of time, in this particular place, as an individual in the connection of experience (*i. e.,* in the chain of causes and effects), which has come into being, and will just as necessarily pass away, is not a thing-in-itself, but a phenomenon which only exists in relation to our knowledge. To know it as what it may be in itself, that is to say, independent of all the determinations which lie in time, space, and casuality, would demand another kind of knowledge than that which is possible for us through the senses and the understanding. . . ."

§ 34

The transition which we have referred to as possible, but yet to be regarded as only exceptional, from the common knowledge of particular things to the knowledge of the Idea, take place suddenly; for knowledge breaks free from the service of the will, by the subject ceasing to be merely individual, and thus becoming the pure will-less subject of knowledge, which no longer traces relations in accordance with the principle of sufficient reason, but rests in fixed contemplation of the object presented to it, out of its connection with all others, and rises into it.

A full explanation is necessary to make this clear, and the reader must suspend his surprise for awhile, till he has grasped the whole thought expressed in this work, and then it will vanish of itself.

If, raised by the power of the mind, a man relinquishes the common way of looking at things, gives up tracing, under the guidance of the forms of the principle of sufficient reason, their relations to each other, the final goal of which is always a relation to his own will; if he thus ceases to consider the where, the when, the why, and the whither of things, and looks simply and solely at the *what;* if, further, he does not allow abstract thought, the concepts of the reason, to take possession of his consciousness, but, instead of all this, gives the whole power of his mind to perception, sinks himself entirely in this, and lets his whole consciousness be filled with the quiet contemplation of the natural object actually present, whether a landscape, a tree, a mountain, a building, or whatever it may be; inasmuch as he *loses* himself in this object (to use a pregnant German idiom), *i. e.,* forgets even his individuality, his will, and continues to exist only as the pure subject, the clear mirror of the object, so that it is as if the object alone were there, without any one to perceive it, and he can no longer separate the perceiver from the perception, but both have become one, because the whole consciousness is filled and occupied with one single sensuous picture; if thus the object has to such an extent passed out of all relation to something outside it, and the subject out of all relation to the will, then that which is so known is no longer the particular thing as such; but it is the *Idea,* the eternal form, the immediate objectivity of the will at this grade; and, therefore, he who is sunk in this perception is no longer individual, for in such perception the individual has lost himself; but he is *pure,* will-less, painless, timeless *subject of knowledge.* This, which in itself is so remarkable (which I well know confirms the saying that originated with Thomas Paine, *Du sublime au ridicule il n'y a qu'un pas*) [2] will by degrees become clearer and less surprising from what follows. It was this that was running in Spinoza's mind when he wrote: *"Mens æterna est, quatenus res sub æternitatis specie concipit* (Eth. V., pr. 31, Schol.) [3] In such contemplation the particular thing becomes at once the *Idea* of its species, and the perceiving individual becomes *pure subject of knowledge.* The individual, as such, knows only particular things; the pure subject of knowledge knows only Ideas. For the individual is the subject of knowledge in its relation to a definite particu-

---

[2] From the sublime to the ridiculous is but a step.
[3] The mind is eternal in proportion as it sees things in their eternal aspects.

lar manifestation of will, and in subjection to this. This particular manifestation of will is, as such, subordinated to the principle of sufficient reason in all its forms; therefore, all knowledge which relates itself to it also follows the principle of sufficient reason, and no other kind of knowledge is fitted to be of use to the will but this, which always consists merely of relations to the object. The knowing individual as such, and the particular things known by him, are always in some place, at some time, and are links in the chain of causes and effects. The pure subject of knowledge and his correlative, the Idea, have passed out of all these forms of the principle of sufficient reason: time, place, the individual that knows, and the individual that is known, have for them no meaning. When an individual knower has raised himself in the manner described to be pure subject of knowledge, and at the same time has raised the observed object to the Platonic Idea, the *world as idea* appears complete and pure, and the full objectification of the will takes place, for the Platonic Idea alone is its *adequate objectivity*. The Idea includes object and subject in like manner in itself, for they are its one form; but in it they are absolutely of equal importance; for as the object is here, as elsewhere, simply the idea of the subject, the subject, which passes entirely into the perceived object has thus become this object itself, for the whole consciousness is nothing but its perfectly distinct picture. Now this consciousness constitutes the whole *world as idea,* for one imagines the whole of the Platonic Ideas, or grades of the objectivity of will, in their series passing through it. The particular things of all time and space are nothing but Ideas multiplied through the principle of sufficient reason (the form of the knowledge of the individual as such), and thus obscured as regards their pure objectivity. When the Platonic Idea appears, in it subject and object are no longer to be distinguished, for the Platonic Idea, the adequate objectivity of will, the true world as idea, arises only when the subject and object reciprocally fill and penetrate each other completely; and in the same way the knowing and the known individuals, as things in themselves, are not to be distinguished. For if we look entirely away from the true *world as idea,* there remains nothing but *the world as will*. The will is the "in-itself" of the Platonic Idea, which fully objectifies it; it is also the "in-itself" of the particular thing and of the individual that knows it, which objectify it completely. As will, outside the idea and all its forms, it is one and the same in the object contemplated and in the individual, who soars aloft in this contemplation, and becomes conscious of himself as pure subject. These two are, therefore, in themselves not different, for in themselves they are will, which here knows itself; and multiplicity and difference exist only as the way in which this knowledge comes to the will, *i. e.,* only in the phenomenon, on account of its form, the principle of sufficient reason.

Now the known thing, without me as the subject of knowledge, is just as little an object, and not mere will, blind effort, as without the object, without the idea, I am a knowing subject and not mere blind will. This will is in itself, *i. e.,* outside the idea, one and the same with mine: only in the world as idea, whose form is always at least that of subject and object, we are separated as the known and the knowing individual. As soon as knowledge, the world as idea, is abolished, there remains nothing but mere will, blind effort. That it should receive objectivity, become idea, supposes at once both subject and object; but that this should be pure, complete, and adequate objectivity of the will, supposes the object as Platonic Idea, free from the forms of the principle of sufficient reason, and the subject as the pure subject of knowledge, free from individuality and subjection to the will.

Whoever now, has, after the manner referred to, become so absorbed and lost in the perception of nature that he continues to exist only as the pure knowing subject, becomes in this way directly conscious that, as such, he is the condition, that is, the supporter, of the world and all objective existence; for this now shows itself as dependent upon his existence. Thus he draws nature into himself, so that he sees it to be merely an accident of his own being. In this sense Byron says—

> "Are not the mountains, waves, and skies, a part
> Of me and of my soul, as I of them?"

But how shall he who feels this, regard himself as absolutely transitory, in contrast to imperishable nature? Such a man will rather be filled with the consciousness, which the Upanishad of the Veda expresses: *Hæ omnes creaturæ in totum ego sum, et præter me aliud ens non est* (Oupnekhat, i., 122.) [4]

§ 35

In order to gain a deeper insight into the nature of the world, it is absolutely necessary that we should learn to distinguish the will as thing-in-itself from its adequate objectivity, and also the different grades in which this appears more and more distinctly and fully, *i. e.,* the Ideas themselves, from the merely phenomenal existence of these Ideas in the forms of the principle of sufficient reason, the restricted method of knowledge of the individual. We shall then agree with Plato when he attributes actual being only to the Ideas, and allows only an illusive, dream-like existence to things in space and time, the real world for the individual. Then we shall understand how one and the same Idea reveals itself in so many phenomena, and presents its nature only bit by bit to the individual, one side after another. Then we shall also distinguish the Idea itself from the way in which its manifestation appears in the observation of the individual, and recognize the former as essential and the latter as unessential. Let us consider this with the help of examples taken from the most insignificant things, and also from the greatest. When the clouds move, the figures which they form are not essential, but indifferent to them; but that as elastic vapour they are pressed together, drifting along, spread out, or torn asunder by the force of the wind: this is their nature, the essence of the forces which objectify themselves in them, the Idea; their actual forms are only for the individual observer. To the brook that flows over stones, the eddies, the waves, the foam-flakes which it forms are indifferent and unessential; but that it follows the attraction of gravity, and behaves as inelastic, perfectly mobile, formless, transparent fluid: this is its nature; this, *if known through perception,* is its Idea; these accidental forms are only for us so long as we know as individuals. The ice on the window-pane forms itself into crystals according to the laws of crystallization, which reveal the essence of the force of nature

[4] All these creatures are totally myself, and besides myself there is nothing.

that appears here, exhibit the Idea; but the trees and flowers which it traces on the pane are unessential, and are only there for us. What appears in the clouds, the brook, and the crystal is the weakest echo of that will which appears more fully in the plant, more fully still in the beast, and most fully in man. But only the essential in all these grades of its objectification constitutes the Idea; on the other hand, its unfolding or development, because broken up in the forms of the principle of sufficient reason into a multiplicity of many-sided phenomena, is unessential to the Idea, lies merely in the kind of knowledge that belongs to the individual and has reality only for this. The same thing necessarily holds good of the unfolding of that Idea which is the completest objectivity of will. Therefore, the history of the human race, the throng of events, the change of times, the multifarious forms of human life in different lands and countries, all this is only the accidental form of the manifestation of the Idea, does not belong to the Idea itself, in which alone lies the adequate objectivity of the will, but only to the phenomenon which appears in the knowledge of the individual, and is just as foreign, unessential, and indifferent to the Idea itself as the figures which they assume are to the clouds, the form of its eddies and foam-flakes to the brook, or its trees and flowers to the ice.

To him who has thoroughly grasped this, and can distinguish between the will and the Idea, and between the Idea and its manifestation, the events of the world will have significance only so far as they are the letters out of which we may read the Idea of man, but not in and for themselves. He will not believe with the vulgar that time may produce something actually new and significant; that through it, or in it, something absolutely real may attain to existence, or indeed that it itself as a whole has beginning and end, plan and development, and in some way has for its final aim the highest perfection (according to their conception) of the last generation of man, whose life is a brief thirty years. Therefore he will just as little, with Homer, people a whole Olympus with gods to guide the events of time, as, with Ossian, he will take the forms of the clouds for individual beings; for, as we have said, both have just as much meaning as regards the Idea which appears in them. In the manifold forms of human life and in the unceasing change of events, he will regard the Idea only as the abiding and essential, in which the will to live has its fullest objectivity, and which shows its different sides in the capacities, the passions, the errors and the excellences of the human race; in self-interest, hatred, love, fear, boldness, frivolity, stupidity, slyness, wit, genius, and so forth, all of which crowding together and combining in thousands of forms (individuals), continually create the history of the great and the little world, in which it is all the same whether they are set in motion by nuts or by crowns. Finally, he will find that in the world it is the same as in the dramas of Gozzi, in all of which the same persons appear, with like intention, and with a like fate; the motives and incidents are certainly different in each piece, but the spirit of the incidents is the same; the actors in one piece know nothing of the incidents of another, although they performed in it themselves; therefore, after all experience of former pieces, Pantaloon has become no more agile or generous, Tartaglia no more conscientious, Brighella no more courageous, and Columbine no more modest.

Suppose we were allowed for once a clearer glance into the kingdom of the possible, and over the whole chain of causes and effects; if the earth-spirit appeared and showed us in a picture all the greatest men, enlighteners of the world, and heroes that chance destroyed before they were ripe for their work; then the great events that would have changed the history of the world and brought in periods of the highest culture and enlightenment, but which the blindest chance, the most insignificant accident, hindered at the outset; lastly, the splendid powers of great men, that would have enriched whole ages of the world, but which, either misled by error or passion, or compelled by necessity, they squandered uselessly on unworthy or unfruitful objects, or even wasted in play. If we saw all this, we would shudder and lament at the thought of the lost treasures of whole periods of the world. But the earth-spirit would smile and say: "The source from which the individuals and their powers proceed is inexhaustible and unending as time and space; for, like these forms of all phenomena, they also are only phenomena, visibility of the will. No finite measure can exhaust that infinite source; therefore an undiminished eternity is always open for the return of any event or work that was nipped in the bud. In this world of phenomena true loss is just as little possible as true gain. The will alone is; it is the thing in-itself, and the source of all these phenomena. Its self-knowledge and its assertion or denial, which is then decided upon, is the only event in-itself." [5]

§ 36

History follows the thread of events; it is pragmatic so far as it deduces them in accordance with the law of motivation, a law that determines the self-manifesting will wherever it is enlightened by knowledge. At the lowest grades of its objectivity, where it still acts without knowledge, natural science, in the form of etiology, treats of the laws of the changes of its phenomena, and, in the form of morphology, of what is permanent in them. This almost endless task is lightened by the aid of concepts, which comprehend what is general in order that we may deduce what is particular from it. Lastly, mathematics treats of the mere forms, time and space, in which the Ideas, broken up into multiplicity, appear for the knowledge of the subject as individual. All these, of which the common name is science, proceed according to the principle of sufficient reason in its different forms, and their theme is always the phenomenon, its laws, connections, and the relations which result from them. But what kind of knowledge is concerned with that which is outside and independent of all relations, that which alone is really essential to the world, the true content of its phenomena, that which is subject to no change, and therefore is known with equal truth for all time, in a word, the *Ideas,* which are the direct and adequate objectivity of the thing-in-itself, the will? We answer, *Art,* the work of genius. It repeats or reproduces the eternal Ideas grasped through pure contemplation, the essential and abiding in all the phenomena of the world; and according to what the material is in which it reproduces, it is sculpture or painting, poetry or music. Its one source is the knowledge of Ideas; its one aim the communication of this knowledge. While science, following the unresting and inconstant stream of

[5] This last sentence cannot be understood without some acquaintance with the next book.—*S.*

the fourfold forms of reason and consequent, with each end attained sees further, and can never reach a final goal nor attain full satisfaction any more than by running we can reach the place where clouds touch the horizon; art, on the contrary, is everywhere at its goal. For it plucks the object of its contemplation out of the stream of the world's course, and has it isolated before it. And this particular thing, which in that stream was a small perishing part, becomes to art the representative of the whole, an equivalent of the endless multitude in space and time. It therefore pauses at this particular thing; the course of time stops; the relations vanish for it; only the essential, the Idea, is its object. We may, therefore, accurately define it as the *way of viewing things independent of the principle of sufficient reason,* in opposition to the way of viewing them which proceeds in accordance with that principle, and which is the method of experience and of science. This last method of considering things may be compared to a line infinitely extended in a horizontal direction, and the former to a vertical line which cuts it at any point. The method of viewing things which proceeds in accordance with the principle of sufficient reason is the rational method, and it alone is valid and of use in practical life and in science. The method which looks away from the content of this principle is the method of genius, which is only valid and of use in art. The first is the method of Aristotle; the second is, on the whole, that of Plato. The first is like the mighty storm, that rushes along without beginning and without aim, bending, agitating, and carrying away everything before it; the second is like the silent sun-beam, that pierces through the storm quite unaffected by it. The first is like the innumerable showering drops of the waterfall, which, constantly changing, never rest for an instant; the second is like the rainbow, quietly resting on this raging torrent. Only through the pure contemplation described above, which ends entirely in the object, can Ideas be comprehended; and the nature of *genius* consists in pre-eminent capacity for such contemplation. Now, as this requires that a man should entirely forget himself and the relations in which he stands, *genius* is simply the completest *objectivity, i. e.,* the objective tendency of the mind, as opposed to the subjective, which is directed to one's own self—in other words, to the will. Thus genius is the faculty of continuing in the state of pure perception, of losing oneself in perception, and of enlisting in this service the knowledge which originally existed only for the service of the will; that is to say, genius is the power of leaving one's own interests, wishes, and aims entirely out of sight, thus of entirely renouncing one's own personality for a time, so as to remain *pure knowing subject,* clear vision of the world; and this not merely at moments, but for a sufficient length of time, and with sufficient consciousness, to enable one to reproduce by deliberate art what has thus been apprehended, and "to fix in lasting thoughts the wavering images that float before the mind." It is as if, when genius appears in an individual, a far larger measure of the power of knowledge falls to his lot than is necessary for the service of an individual will; and this superfluity of knowledge, being free, now becomes subject purified from will, a clear mirror of the inner nature of the world. This explains the activity, amounting even to disquietude, of men of genius, for the present can seldom satisfy them, because it does not fill their consciousness. This gives them that restless aspiration, that unceasing desire for new things, and for the contemplation of lofty things, and also that longing that is hardly ever satisfied, for men of similar nature and of like stature, to whom they might communicate themselves; whilst the common mortal, entirely filled and satisfied by the common present, ends in it, and finding everywhere his like, enjoys that peculiar satisfaction in daily life that is denied to genius.

Imagination has rightly been recognized as an essential element of genius; it has sometimes even been regarded as identical with it; but this is a mistake. As the objects of genius are the eternal Ideas, the permanent, essential forms of the world and all its phenomena, and as the knowledge of the Idea is necessarily knowledge through perception (is not abstract), the knowledge of the genius would be limited to the Ideas of the objects actually present to his person, and dependent upon the chain of circumstances that brought these objects to him, if his imagination did not extend his horizon far beyond the limits of his actual personal existence, and thus enable him to construct the whole out of the little that comes into his own actual apperception, and so to let almost all possible scenes of life pass before him in his own consciousness.

Further, the actual objects are almost always very imperfect copies of the Ideas expressed in them; therefore the man of genius requires imagination in order to see in things, not that which Nature has actually made, but that which she endeavoured to make, yet could not because of that conflict of her forms among themselves which we referred to in the last book. We shall return to this farther on in treating of sculpture. The imagination then extends the intellectual horizon of the man of genius beyond the objects which actually present themselves to him, both as regards quality and quantity. Therefore extraordinary strength of imagination accompanies, and is indeed a necessary condition of genius. But the converse does not hold, for strength of imagination does not indicate genius; on the contrary, men who have no touch of genius may have much imagination. For as it is possible to consider a real object in two opposite ways, purely objectively, the way of genius grasping its Idea, or in the common way, merely in the relations in which it stands to other objects and to one's own will, in accordance with the principle of sufficient reason, it is also possible to perceive an imaginary object in both of these ways. Regarded in the first way, it is a means to the knowledge of the Idea, the communication of which is the work of art; in the second case, the imaginary object is used to build castles in the air congenial to egotism and the individual humour, and which for the moment delude and gratify; thus only the relations of the phantasies so linked together are known. The man who indulges in such an amusement is a dreamer; he will easily mingle those fancies that delight his solitude with reality, and so unfit himself for real life: perhaps he will write them down, and then we shall have the ordinary novel of every description, which entertains those who are like him and the public at large, for the readers imagine themselves in the place of the hero, and then find the story very agreeable.

The common mortal, that manufacture of Nature which she produces by the thousand every day, is, as we have said, not capable, at least not continuously so, of observation that in every sense is wholly disinterested, as sensuous contemplation, strictly so called, is. He can turn his attention to things only so far as they have some relation to his will, however indirect it may be. Since in this respect, which never demands anything but the knowledge of relations, the abstract conception of the thing is sufficient, and for the most part even better adapted for use; the ordinary man does not linger long over the mere perception, does not fix his attention long on one object, but in all that is presented to him hastily seeks merely the concept under which it is to be brought, as the lazy man seeks a chair, and then it interests him no further. This is why he is so soon done with everything, with works of art, objects of natural beauty, and indeed everywhere with the truly significant contemplation of all the scenes of life. He does not linger; only seeks to know his own way in life, together with all that might at any time become his way. Thus he makes topographical notes in the widest sense; over the consideration of life itself as such he wastes no time. The man of genius, on the other hand, whose excessive power of knowledge frees it at times from the service of will, dwells on the consideration of life itself, strives to comprehend the Idea of each thing, not its relations to other things; and in doing this he often forgets to consider his own path in life, and therefore for the most part pursues it awkwardly enough. While to the ordinary man his faculty of knowledge is a lamp to light his path, to the man of genius it is the sun which reveals the world. This great diversity in their way of looking at life soon becomes visible in the outward appearance both of the man of genius and of the ordinary mortal. The man in whom genius lives and works is easily distinguished by his glance, which is both keen and steady, and bears the stamp of perception, of contemplation. This is easily seen from the likenesses of the few men of genius whom Nature has produced here and there among countless millions. On the other hand, in the case of an ordinary man, the true object of his contemplation, what he is prying into, can be easily seen from his glance, if indeed it is not quite stupid and vacant, as is generally the case. Therefore the expression of genius in a face consists in this, that in it a decided predominance of knowledge over will is visible, and consequently there also shows itself in it a knowledge that is entirely devoid of relation to will, *i. e., pure knowing.* On the contrary, in ordinary countenances there is a predominant expression of will; and we see that knowledge comes into activity only under the impulse of will, and thus is directed merely by motives.

Since the knowledge that pertains to genius, or the knowledge of Ideas, is that knowledge which does not follow the principle of sufficient reason, so, on the other hand, the knowledge which does follow that principle is that which gives us prudence and rationality in life, and which creates the sciences. Thus men of genius are affected with the deficiences entailed in the neglect of this latter kind of knowledge. Yet what I say in this regard is subject to the limitation that it concerns them only in so far as and while they are actually engaged in that kind of knowledge which is peculiar to genius; and this is by no means at every moment of their lives, for the great though spontaneous exertion which is demanded for the comprehension of Ideas free from will must necessarily relax, and there are long intervals during which men of genius are placed in very much the same position as ordinary mortals, both as regards advantages and deficiencies. On this account the action of genius has always been regarded as an inspiration, as indeed the name indicates, as the action of a superhuman being distinct from the individual himself, and which takes possession of him only periodically. The disinclination of men of genius to direct their attention to the content of the principle of sufficient reason will first show itself, with regard to the ground of being, as dislike of mathematics; for its procedure is based upon the most universal forms of the phenomena space and time, which are themselves merely modes of the principle of sufficient reason, and is consequently precisely the opposite of that method of thought which seeks merely the content of the phenomenon, the Idea which expresses itself in it apart from all relations. The logical method of mathematics is also antagonistic to genius, for it does not satisfy but obstructs true insight, and presents merely a chain of conclusions in accordance with the principle of the ground of knowing. The mental faculty upon which it makes the greatest claim is memory, for it is necessary to recollect all the earlier propositions which are referred to. Experience has also proved that men of great artistic genius have no faculty for mathematics; no man was ever very distinguished for both. Alfieri relates that he was never able to understand the fourth proposition of Euclid. Goethe was constantly reproached with his want of mathematical knowledge by the ignorant opponents of his theory of colours. Here certainly, where it was not a question of calculation and measurement upon hypothetical data, but of direct knowledge by the understanding of causes and effects, this reproach was so utterly absurd and inappropriate, that by making it they have exposed their entire want of judgment, just as much as by the rest of their ridiculous arguments. The fact that up to the present day, nearly half a century after the appearance of Goethe's theory of colours, even in Germany the Newtonian fallacies still have undisturbed possession of the professorial chair, and men continue to speak quite seriously of the seven homogeneous rays of light and their different refrangibility, will some day be numbered among the great intellectual peculiarities of men generally, and especially of Germans. From the same cause as we have referred to above, may be explained the equally well-known fact that, conversely, admirable mathematicians have very little susceptibility for works of fine art. This is very naïvely expressed in the well-known anecdote of the French mathematician, who, after having read Racine's "Iphigenia," shrugged his shoulders and asked, *"Qu'est ce que cela prouve?"* [6] Further, as quick comprehension of relations in accordance with the laws of causality and motivation is what specially constitutes prudence or sagacity, a prudent man, so far as and while he is so, will not be a genius, and a man of genius, so far as and while he is so, will not be a prudent man. Lastly, perceptive knowledge generally, in the province of which the Idea always lies, is directly opposed to rational or abstract knowledge, which is guided by the principle of the ground of knowing. It is also well known that we seldom find great genius united with preeminent reasonableness; on the contrary, persons of genius are often subject to violent emotions and irrational passions. But the ground of this is not weakness of reason, but partly unwonted energy of that whole phenomenon of will—the man of genius—which expresses itself through the violence of all his acts of will, and partly preponderance of the knowledge of perception through the senses and understanding over abstract knowledge, producing

[6] "What does that prove?"

a decided tendency to the perceptible, the exceedingly lively impressions of which so far outshine colourless concepts, that they take their place in the guidance of action, which consequently becomes irrational. Accordingly the impression of the present moment is very strong with such persons, and carries them away into unconsidered action, violent emotions and passions. Moreover, since, in general, the knowledge of persons of genius has to some extent freed itself from the service of will, they will not in conversation think so much of the person they are addressing as of the thing they are speaking about, which is vividly present to them; and therefore they are likely to judge or narrate things too objectively for their own interests; they will not pass over in silence what would more prudently be concealed, and so forth. Finally, they are given to soliloquizing, and in general may exhibit certain weaknesses which are actually akin to madness. It has often been remarked that there is a side at which genius and madness touch, and even pass over into each other, and indeed poetical inspiration has been called a kind of madness: *amabilis insania,* Horace calls it (Od., iii., 4),[7] and Wieland in the introduction to "Oberon" speaks of it as "amiable madness." Even Aristotle, as quoted by Seneca (De Tranq. Animi, 15, 16), is reported to have said: *Nullum magnum ingenium sine mixtura dementiæ fuit.*[8] Plato expresses it in the figure of the dark cave, referred to above (De Rep., 7), when he says: "Those who, outside the cave, have seen the true sunlight and the things that have true being (Ideas), cannot afterwards see properly down in the cave, because their eyes are not accustomed to the darkness; they cannot distinguish the shadows, and are jeered at for their mistakes by those who have never left the cave and its shadows." In the "Phædrus" also (p. 317), he distinctly says that there can be no true poet without a certain madness; in fact, (p. 327), that every one appears mad who recognizes the eternal Ideas in fleeting things. Cicero also quotes: *Negatenim sine furore, Democritus, quemquam poetam magnum esse posse; quod idem dicit Plato* (De Divin., i., 37).[9] And, lastly, Pope says—

[7] An amiable insanity.

[8] No great genius has ever existed without a mixture of madness.

[9] Democritus denies that any poet can be great without frenzy; which is likewise the opinion of Plato.

"Great wits to madness sure are near allied,
And thin partitions do their bounds divide."

Especially instructive in this respect in Goethe's "Torquato Tasso," in which he shows us not only the suffering, the martyrdom of genius as such, but also how it constantly passes into madness. Finally, the fact of the direct connection of genius and madness is established by the biographies of great men of genius, such as Rousseau, Byron, and Alfieri, and by anecdotes from the lives of others. On the other hand, I must mention that, by a diligent search in lunatic asylums, I have found individual cases of patients who were unquestionably endowed with great talents, and whose genius distinctly appeared through their madness, which, however, had completely gained the upper hand. Now this cannot be ascribed to chance, for on the one hand the number of mad persons is relatively very small, and on the other hand a person of genius is a phenomenon which is rare beyond all ordinary estimation, and only appears in nature as the greatest exception. It will be sufficient to convince us of this if we compare the number of really great men of genius that the whole of civilized Europe has produced, both in ancient and modern times, with the two hundred and fifty millions who are always living in Europe, and who change entirely every thirty years. In estimating the number of men of outstanding genius, we must of course only count those who have produced works which have retained through all time an enduring value for mankind. I shall not refrain from mentioning, that I have known some persons of decided, though not remarkable, mental superiority, who also showed a slight trace of insanity. It might seem from this that every advance of intellect beyond the ordinary measure, as an abnormal development, disposes to madness. In the meantime, however, I will explain as briefly as possible my view of the purely intellectual ground of the relation between genius and madness, for this will certainly assist the explanation of the real nature of genius, that is to say, of that mental endowment which alone can produce genuine works of art. But this necessitates a brief explanation of madness itself.

A clear and complete insight into the nature of madness, a correct and distinct conception of what constitutes the difference between the sane and the insane, has, as far as I know, not yet been

found. Neither reason nor understanding can be denied to madmen, for they talk and understand, and often draw very accurate
conclusions; they also, as a rule, perceive what is present quite
correctly, and apprehend the connection between cause and effect.
Visions, like the phantasies of delirium, are no ordinary symptom
of madness: delirium falsifies perception, madness the thoughts.
For the most part, madmen do not err in the knowledge of what
is immediately *present;* their raving always relates to what is *absent* and *past*, and only through these to their connection with
what is present. Therefore it seems to me that their malady specially concerns the memory; not indeed that memory fails them
entirely, for many of them know a great deal by heart, and sometimes recognize persons whom they have not seen for a long time;
but rather that the thread of memory is broken, the continuity of
its connection destroyed, and no uniformly connected recollection
of the past is possible. Particular scenes of the past are known correctly, just like the particular present; but there are gaps in their
recollection which they fill up with fictions, and these are either
always the same, in which case they become fixed ideas, and the
madness that results is called monomania or melancholy; or they
are always different, momentary fancies, and then it is called
folly, *fatuitas.* This is why it is so difficult to find out their former
life from lunatics when they enter an asylum. The true and the
false are always mixed up in their memory. Although the immediate present is correctly known, it becomes falsified through its
fictitious connection with an imaginary past; they therefore regard themselves and others as identical with persons who exist
only in their imaginary past; they do not recognize some of their
acquaintances at all, and thus while they perceive correctly what
is actually present, they have only false conceptions of its relations
to what is absent. If the madness reaches a high degree, there is
complete absence of memory, so that the madman is quite incapable
of any reference to what is absent or past, and is only determined
by the caprice of the moment in connection with the fictions which,
in his mind, fill the past. In such a case, we are never for a
moment safe from violence or murder, unless we constantly make
the madman aware of the presence of superior force. The knowledge of the madman has this in common with that of the brute,

both are confined to the present. What distinguishes them is that the brute has really no idea of the past as such, though the past acts upon it through the medium of custom, so that, for example, the dog recognizes its former master even after years, that is to say, it receives the wonted impression at the sight of him; but of the time that has passed since it saw him it has no recollection. The madman, on the other hand, always carries about in his reason an abstract past, but it is a false past, which exists only for him, and that either constantly, or only for the moment. The influence of this false past prevents the use of the true knowledge of the present which the brute is able to make. The fact that violent mental suffering or unexpected and terrible calamities should often produce madness, I explain in the following manner. All such suffering is as an actual event confined to the present. It is thus merely transitory, and is consequently never excessively heavy; it only becomes unendurably great when it is lasting pain; but as such it exists only in thought, and therefore lies in the *memory*. If now such a sorrow, such painful knowledge or reflection, is so bitter that it becomes altogether unbearable, and the individual is prostrated under it, then, terrified Nature seizes upon *madness* as the last resource of life; the mind so fearfully tortured at once destroys the thread of its memory, fills up the gaps with fictions, and thus seeks refuge in madness from the mental suffering that exceeds its strength, just as we cut off a mortified limb and replace it with a wooden one. The distracted Ajax, King Lear, and Ophelia may be taken as examples; for the creations of true genius, to which alone we can refer here, as universally known, are equal in truth to real persons; besides, in this case, frequent actual experience shows the same thing. A faint analogy of this kind of transition from pain to madness is to be found in the way in which all of us often seek, as it were mechanically, to drive away a painful thought that suddenly occurs to us by some loud exclamation or quick movement—to turn ourselves from it, to distract our minds by force.

We see, from what has been said, that the madman has a true knowledge of what is actually present, and also of certain particulars of the past, but that he mistakes the connection, the relation, and therefore falls into error and talks nonsense. Now this is exactly the point at which he comes into contact with the man of genius; for he also leaves out of sight the knowledge of the connection of things, since he neglects that knowledge of relations which conforms to the principle of sufficient reason, in order to see in things only their Ideas, and to seek to comprehend their true nature, which manifests itself to perception, and in regard to which *one thing* represents its whole species, in which way, as Goethe says, one case is valid for a thousand. The particular object of his contemplation, or the present which is perceived by him with extraordinary vividness, appear in so strong a light that the other links of the chain to which they belong are at once thrown into the shade, and thus gives rise to phenomena which have long been recognized as resembling those of madness. That which in particular given things exists only incompletely and weakened by modifications, is raised by the man of genius, through his way of contemplating it, to the Idea of the thing, to completeness: he therefore sees everywhere extremes, and therefore his own action tends to extremes; he cannot hit the mean, he lacks soberness, and the result is what we have said. He knows the Ideas completely but not the individuals. Therefore it has been said that a poet may know mankind deeply and thoroughly, and may yet have a very imperfect knowledge of men. He is easily deceived, and is a tool in the hands of the crafty.

§ 37

Genius, then, consists, according to our explanation, in the capacity for knowing, independently of the principle of sufficient reason, not individual things, which have their existence only in their relations, but the Ideas of such things, and of being oneself the correlative of the Idea, and thus no longer an individual, but the pure subject of knowledge. Yet this faculty must exist in all men in a smaller and different degree; for if not, they would be just as incapable of enjoying works of art as of producing them; they would have no susceptibility for the beautiful or the sublime; indeed, these words could have no meaning for them. We must therefore assume that there exists in all men this power of knowing the Idea in things, and consequently of transcending their personality for the moment, unless indeed there are some men who are capable of no æsthetic pleasure at all. The man of genius excels ordinary men only by possessing this kind of knowledge in a far higher degree and more continuously. Thus, while under its influence he retains the presence of mind which is necessary to enable him to repeat in a voluntary and intentional work what he has learned in this manner; and this repetition is the work of art. Through this he communicates to others the Idea he has grasped. This Idea remains unchanged and the same, so that æsthetic pleasure is one and the same whether it is called forth by a work of art or directly by the contemplation of nature and life. The work of art is only a means of facilitating the knowledge in which this pleasure consists. That the Idea comes to us more easily from the work of art than directly from nature and the real world, arises from the fact that the artist, who knew only the Idea, no longer the actual, has reproduced in his work the pure Idea, has abstracted it from the actual, omitting all disturbing accidents. The artist lets us see the world through his eyes. That he has these eyes, that he knows the inner nature of things apart from all their relations, is the gift of genius, is inborn; but that he is able to lend us this gift, to let us see with his eyes, is acquired, and is the technical side of art. Therefore, after the account which I have given in the preceding pages of the inner nature of æsthetical knowledge in its most general outlines, the following more exact philosophical treatment of the beautiful and the sublime will explain them both, in nature and in art, without separating them further. First of all we shall consider what takes place in a man when he is affected by the beautiful and the sublime; whether he derives this emotion directly from nature, from life, or partakes of it only through the medium of art, does not make any essential, but merely an external, difference.

§ 38

In the æsthetical mode of contemplation we have found *two inseparable constituent parts*—the knowledge of the object, not as individual thing but as Platonic Idea, that is, as the enduring form of this whole species of things; and the self-consciousness of the knowing person, not as individual, but as *pure will-less subject of knowledge.* The condition under which both these constituent parts appear always united was found to be the abandonment of the method of knowing which is bound to the principle of sufficient reason, and which, on the other hand, is the only kind of knowledge that is of value for the service of the will and also for science. Moreover, we shall see that the pleasure which is produced by the contemplation of the beautiful arises from these two constituent parts, sometimes more from the one, sometimes more from the other, according to what the object of the æsthetical contemplation may be.

All *willing* arises from want, therefore from deficiency, and therefore from suffering. The satisfaction of a wish ends it; yet for one wish that is satisfied there remain at least ten which are denied. Further, the desire lasts long, the demands are infinite; the satisfaction is short and scantily measured out. But even the final satisfaction is itself only apparent; every satisfied wish at once makes room for a new one; both are illusions; the one is known to be so, the other not yet. No attained object of desire can give lasting satisfaction, but merely a fleeting gratification; it is like the alms thrown to the beggar, that keeps him alive to-day that his misery may be prolonged till the morrow. Therefore, so long as our consciousness is filled by our will, so long as we are given up to the throng of desires with their constant hopes and fears, so long as we are the subject of willing, we can never have lasting happiness nor peace. It is essentially all the same whether we pursue or flee, fear injury or seek enjoyment; the care for the constant demands of the will, in whatever form it may be, continually occupies and sways the consciousness; but without peace no true well-being is possible. The subject of willing is thus constantly stretched on the revolving wheel of Ixion, pours water into the sieve of the Danaids, is the ever-longing Tantalus.

But when some external cause or inward disposition lifts us suddenly out of the endless stream of willing, delivers knowledge from the slavery of the will, the attention is no longer directed to the motives of willing, but comprehends things free from their relation to the will, and thus observes them without personal interest, without subjectivity, purely objectively, gives itself entirely up to them so far as they are ideas, but not in so far as they are motives. Then all at once the peace which we were always seeking, but which always fled from us on the former path of the desires, comes to us of its own accord, and it is well with us. It is the painless state which Epicurus prized as the highest good and as the state of the gods; for we are for the moment set free from the miserable striving of the will; we keep the Sabbath of the penal servitude of willing; the wheel of Ixion stands still.

But this is just the state which I described above as necessary for the knowledge of the Idea, as pure contemplation, as sinking oneself in perception, losing oneself in the object, forgetting all individuality, surrendering that kind of knowledge which follows the principle of sufficient reason, and comprehends only relations; the state by means of which at once and inseparably the perceived particular thing is raised to the Idea of its whole species, and the knowing individual to the pure subject of will-less knowledge, and as such they are both taken out of the stream of time and all other relations. It is then all one whether we see the sun set from the prison or from the palace.

Inward disposition, the predominance of knowing over willing, can produce this state under any circumstances. This is shown by those admirable Dutch artists who directed this purely objective perception to the most insignificant objects, and established a lasting monument of their objectivity and spiritual peace in their pictures of *still life,* which the æsthetic beholder does not look on without emotion; for they present to him the peaceful, still, frame of mind of the artist, free from will, which was needed to contemplate such insignificant things so objectively, to observe them so attentively, and to repeat this perception so intelligently; and as the picture enables the onlooker to participate in this state, his emotion is often increased by the contrast between it and the unquiet frame of mind, disturbed by vehement willing, in which he finds himself. In the same spirit, landscape-painters, and particularly Ruisdael, have often painted very insignificant country scenes, which produce the same effect even more agreeably.

All this is accomplished by the inner power of an artistic nature alone; but that purely objective disposition is facilitated and assisted from without by suitable objects, by the abundance of

natural beauty which invites contemplation, and even presses itself upon us. Whenever it discloses itself suddenly to our view,
it almost always succeeds in delivering us, though it may be only
for a moment, from subjectivity, from the slavery of the will,
and in raising us to the state of pure knowing. This is why the
man who is tormented by passion, or want, or care, is so suddenly
revived, cheered, and restored by a single free glance into nature:
the storm of passion, the pressure of desire and fear, and all the
miseries of willing are then at once, and in a marvellous manner,
calmed and appeased. For at the moment at which, freed from the
will, we give ourselves up to pure will-less knowing, we pass into
a world from which everything is absent that influenced our
will and moved us so violently through it. This freeing of knowledge lifts us as wholly and entirely away from all that, as do
sleep and dreams; happiness and unhappiness have disappeared;
we are no longer individual; the individual is forgotten; we are
only pure subject of knowledge; we are only that *one* eye of the
world which looks out from all knowing creatures, but which can
become perfectly free from service of will in man alone. Thus
all difference of individuality so entirely disappears, that it is all
the same whether the perceiving eye belongs to a mighty king or
to a wretched beggar; for neither joy nor complaining can pass
that boundary with us. So near us always lies a sphere in which
we escape from all our misery; but who has the strength to continue long in it? As soon as any single relation to our will, to
our person, even of these objects of our pure contemplation,
comes again into consciousness, the magic is at an end; we fall
back into the knowledge which is governed by the principle of
sufficient reason; we know no longer the Idea, but the particular
thing, the link of a chain to which we also belong, and we are
again abandoned to all our woe. Most men remain almost always
at this standpoint because they entirely lack objectivity, *i. e.*,
genius. Therefore they have no pleasure in being alone with
nature; they need company, or at least a book. For their knowledge remains subject to their will; they seek, therefore, in objects, only some relation to their will, and whenever they see
anything that has no such relation, there sounds within them,
like a ground bass in music, the constant inconsolable cry, "It is

of no use to me"; thus in solitude the most beautiful surroundings have for them a desolate, dark, strange, and hostile appearance.

Lastly, it is this blessedness of will-less perception which casts an enchanting glamour over the past and distant, and presents them to us in so fair a light by means of self-deception. For as we think of days long gone by, days in which we lived in a distant place, it is only the objects which our fancy recalls, not the subject of will, which bore about with it then its incurable sorrows just as it bears them now; but they are forgotten, because since then they have often given place to others. Now, objective perception acts with regard to what is remembered just as it would in what is present, if we let it have influence over us, if we surrendered ourselves to it free from will. Hence it arises that, especially when we are more than ordinarily disturbed by some want, the remembrance of past and distant scenes suddenly flits across our minds like a lost paradise. The fancy recalls only what was objective, not what was individually subjective, and we imagine that that objective stood before us then just as pure and undisturbed by any relation to the will as its image stands in our fancy now; while in reality the relation of the objects to our will gave us pain then just as it does now. We can deliver ourselves from all suffering just as well through present objects as through distant ones whenever we raise ourselves to a purely objective contemplation of them, and so are able to bring about the illusion that only the objects are present and not we ourselves. Then, as the pure subject of knowledge, freed from the miserable self, we become entirely one with these objects, and, for the moment, our wants are as foreign to us as they are to them. The world as idea alone remains, and the world as will has disappeared.

In all these reflections it has been my object to bring out clearly the nature and the scope of the subjective element in æsthetic pleasure; the deliverance of knowledge from the service of the will, the forgetting of self as an individual, and the raising of the consciousness to the pure will-less, timeless, subject of knowledge, independent of all relations. With this subjective side of æsthetic contemplation, there must always appear as its necessary correlative the objective side, the intuitive comprehension of the Platonic Idea. But before we turn to the closer consideration of this, and to the achievements of art in relation to it, it is better that we should pause for a little at the subjective side of æsthetic pleasure, in order to complete our treatment of this by explaining the impression of the *sublime* which depends altogether upon it, and arises from a modification of it. After that we shall complete our investigation of æsthetic pleasure by considering its objective side.

But we must first add the following remarks to what has been said. Light is the pleasantest and most gladdening of things; it has become the symbol of all that is good and salutary. In all religions it symbolizes salvation, while darkness symbolizes damnation. Ormuzd dwells in the purest light, Ahrimines in eternal night. Dante's Paradise would look very much like Vauxhall in London, for all the blessed spirits appear as points of light and arrange themselves in regular figures. The very absence of light makes us sad; its return cheers us. Colours excite directly a keen delight, which reaches its highest degree when they are transparent. All this depends entirely upon the fact that light is the correlative and condition of the most perfect kind of knowledge of perception, the only knowledge which does not in any way affect the will. For sight, unlike the affections of the other senses, cannot, in itself, directly and through its sensuous effect, make the *sensation* of the special organ agreeable or disagreeable; that is, it has no immediate connection with the will. Such a quality can only belong to the perception which arises in the understanding, and then it lies in the relation of the object to the will. In the case of hearing this is to some extent otherwise; sounds can give pain directly, and they may also be sensuously agreeable, directly and without regard to harmony and melody. Touch, as one with the feeling of the whole body, is still more subordinated to this direct influence upon the will; and yet there is such a thing as a sensation of touch which is neither painful nor pleasant. But smells are always either agreeable or disagreeable, and tastes still more so. Thus the last two senses are most closely related to the will, and therefore they are always the most ignoble, and have been called by Kant the subjective senses. The pleasure which we experience from light is in fact only the pleasure which arises from the objective possibility of the purest and fullest perceptive knowledge, and as such it may be traced to the fact that pure knowledge, freed and delivered from all will, is in the highest degree pleasant, and of itself constitutes a large part of æsthetic enjoyment. Again, we must refer to this view of light the incredible beauty which we associate with the reflection of objects in water. That lightest, quickest, finest species of the action of bodies upon each other, that to which we owe by far the completest and purest of our perceptions, the action of reflected rays of light, is here brought clearly before our eyes, distinct and perfect, in cause and in effect, and indeed in its entirety, hence the æsthetic delight it gives us, which, in the most important aspect, is entirely based on the subjective ground of æsthetic pleasure, and is delight in pure knowing and its method.

§ 39

All these reflections are intended to bring out the subjective part of æsthetic pleasure; that is to say, that pleasure so far as it consists simply of delight in perceptive knowledge as such, in opposition to will. And as directly connected with this, there naturally follows the explanation of that disposition or frame of mind which has been called the sense of the *sublime*.

We have already remarked above that the transition to the state of pure perception takes place most easily when the objects bend themselves to it, that is, when by their manifold and yet definite and distinct form they easily become representatives of their Ideas, in which beauty, in the objective sense, consists. This quality belongs pre-eminently to natural beauty, which thus affords even to the most insensible at least a fleeting æsthetic satisfaction: indeed it is so remarkable how especially the vegetable world invites æsthetic observation, and, as it were, presses itself upon it, that one might say, that these advances are connected with the fact that these organisms, unlike the bodies of animals, are not for themselves immediate objects of knowledge, and therefore require the assistance of a foreign intelligent individual in order to rise out of the world of blind will and enter the world of idea, and that thus they long, as it were, for this entrance, that they may attain at least indirectly what is denied them directly. But I leave this suggestion which I have hazarded, and which borders perhaps upon extravagance, entirely undecided, for only a very intimate and devoted consideration of nature can raise or justify it. As long as that which raises us from the knowledge of mere relations subject to the will, to æsthetic contemplation, and thereby exalts us to the position of the subject of knowledge free from will, is this fittingness of nature, this significance and distinctness of its forms, on account of which the Ideas individualized in them readily present themselves to us; so long is it merely *beauty* that affects us and the sense of the *beautiful* that is excited. But if these very objects whose significant forms invite us to pure contemplation, have a hostile relation to the human will in general, as it exhibits itself in its objectivity, the human body, if they are opposed to it, so that it is menaced by the irresistible predominance of their power, or sinks into insignificance before their immeasurable greatness; if, nevertheless, the beholder does not direct his attention to this eminently hostile relation to his will, but, although perceiving and recognizing it, turns consciously away from it, forcibly detaches himself from his will and its relations, and, giving himself up entirely to knowledge, quietly contemplates those very objects that are so terrible to the will, comprehends only their Idea, which is foreign to all relation, so that he lingers gladly over its contemplation, and is thereby raised above himself, his person, his will, and all will:—in that case he is filled with the sense of the *sublime,* he is in the state of spiritual exultation, and therefore the object producing such a state is called *sublime.* Thus what distinguishes the sense of the sublime from that of the beautiful is this: in the case of the beautiful, pure knowledge has gained the upper hand without a struggle, for the beauty of the object, *i. e.,* that property which facilitates the knowledge of its Idea, has removed from consciousness without resistance, and therefore imperceptibly, the will and the knowledge of relations which is subject to it, so that what is left is the pure subject of knowledge without even a remembrance of will. On the other hand, in the case of the sublime that state of pure knowledge is only attained by a conscious and forcible breaking away from the relations of the same subject to the will, which are recognized as unfavourable, by a free and conscious transcending of the will and the knowledge related to it.

This exaltation must not only be consciously won, but also consciously retained, and it is therefore accompanied by a constant remembrance of will; yet not of a single particular volition, such as fear or desire, but of human volition in general, so far as it is universally expressed in its objectivity the human body. If a single real act of will were to come into consciousness, through actual personal pressure and danger from the object, then the individual will thus actually influenced would at once gain the upper hand, the peace of contemplation would become impossible, the impression of the sublime would be lost, because it yields to the anxiety, in which the effort of the individual to right itself has sunk every other thought. A few examples will help very much to elucidate this theory of the æsthetic sublime and remove all doubt with regard to it; at the same time they will bring out the different degrees of this sense of the sublime. It is in the main identical with that of the beautiful, with pure will-less knowing, and the knowledge, that necessarily accompanies it of Ideas out of all relation determined by the principle of sufficient reason, and it is distinguished from the sense of the beautiful only by the additional quality that it rises above the known hostile relation of the object contemplated to the will in general. Thus there come to be various degrees of the sublime, and transitions from the beautiful to the sublime, according as this additional quality is strong, bold, urgent, near, or weak, distant, and merely indicated. I think it is more in keeping with the plan of my treatise, first to give examples of these transitions, and of the weaker degrees of the impression of the sublime, although persons whose æsthetical susceptibility in general is not very great, and whose imagination is not very lively, will only understand the examples given later of the higher and more distinct grades of that impression; and they should therefore confine themselves to these, and pass over the examples of the very weak degrees of the sublime that are to be given first.

As man is at once impetuous and blind striving of will (whose pole or focus lies in the genital organs), and eternal, free, serene

subject of pure knowing (whose pole is the brain) ; so, corresponding to this antithesis, the sun is both the source of *light,* the condition of the most perfect kind of knowledge, and therefore of the
most delightful of things—and the source of *warmth,* the first
condition of life, *i. e.,* of all phenomena of will in its higher
grades. Therefore, what warmth is for the will, light is for knowledge. Light is the largest gem in the crown of beauty, and has the
most marked influence on the knowledge of every beautiful object.
Its presence is an indispensable condition of beauty; its favourable
disposition increases the beauty of the most beautiful. Architectural
beauty more than any other object is enhanced by favourable light,
though even the most insignificant things become through its influence most beautiful. If, in the dead of winter, when all nature
is frozen and stiff, we see the rays of the setting sun reflected by
masses of stone, illuminating without warning, and thus favourable only to the purest kind of knowledge, not to the will; the
contemplation of the beautiful effect of the light upon these
masses lifts us, as does all beauty, into a state of pure knowing.
But, in this case, a certain transcending of the interests of the
will is needed to enable us to rise into the state of pure knowing,
because there is a faint recollection of the lack of warmth from
these rays, that is, an absence of the principle of life; there is a
slight challenge to persist in pure knowing, and to refrain from
all willing, and therefore it is an example of a transition from the
sense of the beautiful to that of the sublime. It is the faintest
trace of the sublime in the beautiful; and beauty itself is indeed
present only in a slight degree. The following is almost as weak
an example.

Let us imagine ourselves transported to a very lonely place,
with unbroken horizon, under a cloudless sky, trees and plants in
the perfectly motionless air, no animals, no men, no running
water, the deepest silence. Such surroundings are, as it were, a
call to seriousness and contemplation, apart from all will and
its cravings; but this is just what imparts to such a scene of desolate stillness a touch of the sublime. For, because it affords no
object, either favourable or unfavourable, for the will which is
constantly in need of striving and attaining, there only remains
the state of pure contemplation, and whoever is incapable of this,

is ignominiously abandoned to the vacancy of unoccupied will, and the misery of ennui. So far it is a test of our intellectual worth, of which, generally speaking, the degree of our power of enduring solitude, or our love of it, is a good criterion. The scene we have sketched affords us, then, an example of the sublime in a low degree, for in it, with the state of pure knowing in its peace and all-sufficiency, there is mingled, by way of contrast, the recollection of the dependence and poverty of the will which stands in need of constant action. This is the species of the sublime for which the sight of the boundless prairies of the interior of North America is celebrated.

But let us suppose such a scene, stripped also of vegetation, and showing only naked rocks; then from the entire absence of that organic life which is necessary for existence, the will at once becomes uneasy, the desert assumes a terrible aspect, our mood becomes more tragic; the elevation to the sphere of pure knowing takes place with a more decided tearing of ourselves away from the interests of the will; and because we persist in continuing in the state of pure knowing, the sense of the sublime distinctly appears.

The following situation may occasion this feeling in a still higher degree: Nature convulsed by a storm; the sky darkened by black threatening thunder-clouds; stupendous, naked, overhanging cliffs, completely shutting out the view; rushing, foaming torrents; absolute desert; the wail of the wind sweeping through the clefts of the rocks. Our dependence, our strife with hostile nature, our will broken in the conflict, now appears visibly before our eyes. Yet, so long as the personal pressure does not gain the upper hand, but we continue in æsthetic contemplation, the pure subject of knowing gazes unshaken and unconcerned through that strife of nature, through that picture of the broken will, and quietly comprehends the Ideas even of those objects which are threatening and terrible to the will. In this contrast lies the sense of the sublime.

But the impression becomes still stronger, if, when we have before our eyes, on a large scale, the battle of the raging elements, in such a scene we are prevented from hearing the sound of our own voice by the noise of a falling stream; or, if we are abroad in the storm of tempestuous seas, where the mountainous waves rise and fall, dash themselves furiously against steep cliffs, and toss their spray high into the air; the storm howls, the sea boils, the lightning flashes from black clouds, and the peals of thunder drown the voice of storm and sea. Then, in the undismayed beholder, the two-fold nature of his consciousness reaches the highest degree of distinctness. He perceives himself, on the one hand, as an individual, as the frail phenomenon of will, which the slightest touch of these forces can utterly destroy, helpless against powerful nature, dependent, the victim of chance, a vanishing nothing in the presence of stupendous might; and, on the other hand, as the eternal, peaceful, knowing subject, the condition of the object, and, therefore, the supporter of this whole world; the terrific strife of nature only his idea; the subject itself free and apart from all desires and necessities, in the quiet comprehension of the Ideas. This is the complete impression of the sublime. Here he obtains a glimpse of a power beyond all comparison superior to the individual, threatening it with annihilation.

The impression of the sublime may be produced in quite another way, by presenting a mere immensity in space and time; its immeasurable greatness dwindles the individual to nothing. Adhering to Kant's nomenclature and his accurate division, we may call the first kind the dynamical, and the second the mathematical sublime, although we entirely dissent from his explanation of the inner nature of the impression, and can allow no share in it either to moral reflections, or to hypostases from scholastic philosophy.

If we lose ourselves in the contemplation of the infinite greatness of the universe in space and time, meditate on the thousands of years that are past or to come, or if the heavens at night actually bring before our eyes innumerable worlds and so force upon our consciousness the immensity of the universe, we feel ourselves dwindle to nothing; as individuals, as living bodies, as transient phenomena of will, we feel ourselves pass away and vanish into nothing like drops in the ocean. But at once there arises against this ghost of our own nothingness, against such lying impossibility, the immediate consciousness that all these worlds exist only as our idea, only as modifications of the eternal subject of pure knowing, which we find ourselves to be as soon as we forget our individuality, and which is the necessary supporter of all worlds and all times the condition of their possibility. The vastness of the world which disquieted us before, rests now in us; our dependence upon it is annulled by its dependence upon us. All this, however, does not come at once into reflection, but shows itself merely as the felt consciousness that in some sense or other (which philosophy alone can explain) we are one with the world, and therefore not oppressed, but exalted by its immensity. It is the felt consciousness of this that the Upanishads of the Vedas repeatedly express in such a multitude of different ways; very admirably in the saying already quoted: *Hæ omnes creaturæ in totum ego sum, et præter me aliud ens non est* (Oupnek'hat, vol. i., p. 122). It is the transcending of our own individuality, the sense of the sublime.

We receive this impression of the mathematical-sublime, quite directly, by means of a space which is small indeed as compared with the world, but which has become directly perceptible to us, and affects us with its whole extent in all its three dimensions, so as to make our own body seem almost infinitely small. An empty space can never be thus perceived, and therefore never an open space, but only space that is directly perceptible in all its dimensions by means of the limits which enclose it; thus for example a very high, vast dome, like that of St. Peter's at Rome, or St. Paul's in London. The sense of the sublime here arises through the consciousness of the vanishing nothingness of our own body in the presence of a vastness which, from another point of view, itself exists only in our idea, and of which we are as knowing subject, the supporter. Thus here as everywhere it arises from the contrast between the insignificance and dependence of ourselves as individuals, as phenomena of will, and the consciousness of ourselves as pure subject of knowing. Even the vault of the starry heaven produces this if it is contemplated without reflection; but just in the same way as the vault of stone, and only by its apparent, not its real extent. Some objects of our perception excite in us the feeling of the sublime because, not only on account of their spatial vastness, but also of their great age, that is, their temporal duration, we feel ourselves dwarfed to insignificance in their presence, and yet revel in the pleasure of contemplating them: of this kind are very high mountains, the Egyptian pyramids, and colossal ruins of great antiquity.

Our explanation of the sublime applies also to the ethical, to what is called the sublime character. Such a character arises from this, that the will is not excited by objects which are well calculated to excite it, but that knowledge retains the upper hand in their presence. A man of sublime character will accordingly consider men in a purely objective way, and not with reference to the relations which they might have to his will; he will, for example, observe their faults, even their hatred and injustice to himself, without being himself excited to hatred; he will behold their happiness without envy; he will recognize their good qualities without desiring any closer relations with them; he will perceive the beauty of women, but he will not desire them. His personal happiness or unhappiness will not greatly affect him, he will rather be as Hamlet describes Horatio:—

> ". . . for thou hast been,
> As one, in suffering all, that suffers nothing;
> A man that fortune's buffets and rewards
> Hast ta'en with equal thanks," &c. (A. 3., Sc. 2.)

For in the course of his own life and its misfortunes, he will consider less his individual lot than that of humanity in general, and will therefore conduct himself in its regard, rather as knowing than as suffering.

§ 43

Matter as such cannot be the expression of an Idea. For, as we found in the first book, it is throughout nothing but casuality: its being consists in its casual action. But casuality is a form of the principle of sufficient reason; knowledge of the Idea, on the other hand, absolutely excludes the content of that principle. We also found, in the second book, that matter is the common substratum of all particular phenomena of the Ideas, and consequently is the connecting link between the Idea and the phenomenon, or the particular thing. Accordingly for both of these reasons it is impossible that matter can for itself express any Idea. This is confirmed *a posteriori* by the fact 'that it is impossible to have a perceptible idea of matter as such, but only an abstract conception; in the former, *i. e.,* in perceptible ideas are exhibited only the forms and qualities of which matter is the supporter, and in all of which Ideas reveal themselves. This corresponds also with the fact, that casuality (the whole essence of matter) cannot for itself be presented perceptibly, but is merely a definite casual connection. On the other hand, *every phenomenon* of an Idea, because as such it has entered the form of the principle of sufficient reason, or the *principium individuationis,* must exhibit itself in matter, as one of its qualities. So far then matter is, as we have said, the connecting link between the Idea and the *principium individuationis,* which is the form of knowledge of the individual, or the principle of sufficient reason. Plato is therefore perfectly right in his enumeration, for after the Idea and the phenomenon, which include all other things in the world, he gives matter only, as a third thing which is different from both (Timaus, p. 345). The individual, as a phenomenon of the Idea, is always matter. Every quality of matter is also the phenomenon of an Idea, and as such it may always be an object of æsthetic contemplation, *i. e.,* the Idea expressed in it may always be recognized. This holds good of even the most universal qualities of matter, without which it never appears, and which are the weakest objectivity of will. Such are gravity, cohesion, rigidity, fluidity, sensitiveness to light, and so forth.

If now we consider *architecture* simply as a fine art and apart from its application to useful ends, in which it serves the will and not pure knowledge, and therefore ceases to be art in our sense; we can assign to it no other aim than that of bringing to greater distinctness some of those ideas, which are the lowest grades of the objectivity of will; such as gravity, cohesion, rigidity, hardness, those universal qualities of stone, those first, simplest, most inarticulate manifestations of will; the bass notes of nature; and after these light, which in many respects is their opposite. Even at these low grades of the objectivity of will we see its nature revealing itself in discord; for properly speaking the conflict between gravity and rigidity is the sole æsthetic material of architecture; its problem is to make this conflict appear with perfect distinctness in a multitude of different ways. It solves it by depriving these indestructible forces of the shortest way to their satisfaction, and conducting them to it by a circuitous route, so that the conflict is lengthened and the inexhaustible efforts of both forces become visible in many different ways. The whole mass of the building, if left to its original tendency, would exhibit a mere heap or clump, bound as closely as possible to the earth, to which gravity, the form in which the will appears here, continually presses, while rigidity, also objectivity of will, resists. But this very tendency, this effort, is hindered by architecture from obtaining direct satisfaction, and only allowed to reach it indirectly and by roundabout ways. The roof, for example, can only press the earth through columns, the arch must support itself, and can only satisfy its tendency towards the earth through the medium of the pillars, and so forth. But just by these enforced digressions, just by these restrictions, the forces which reside in the crude mass of stone unfold themselves in the most distinct and multifarious ways; and the purely æsthetic aim of architecture can go no further than this. Therefore the beauty, at any rate, of a building lies in the obvious adaptation of every part, not to the outward arbitrary end of man (so far the work belongs to practical architecture), but directly to the stability of the whole, to which the position, dimensions, and form of every part must have so necessary a relation that, where it is possible, if any one part were taken away, the whole would fall to pieces. For just because each part bears just as much as it conveniently can, and each is supported just where it requires to be and just to the necessary extent, this opposition unfolds itself, this conflict between rigidity and gravity, which constitutes the life, the manifestation of will, in the stone, becomes completely visible, and these lowest grades of the objectivity of will reveal themselves distinctly. In the same way the form of each part must not be determined arbitrarily, but by its end, and its relation to the whole. The column is the simplest form of support, determined simply by its end: the twisted column is tasteless; the four-cornered pillar is in fact not so simple as the round column, though it happens that it is easier to make it. The forms also of frieze, rafter, roof, and dome are entirely determined by their immediate end, and explain them-

selves from it. The decoration of capitals, &c., belongs to sculpture, not to architecture, which admits it merely as extraneous
ornament, and could dispense with it. According to what has been
said, it is absolutely necessary, in order to understand the æsthetic
satisfaction afforded by a work of architecture, to have immediate
knowledge through perception of its matter as regards its weight,
rigidity, and cohesion, and our pleasure in such a work would
suddenly be very much diminished by the discovery that the
material used was pumice-stone; for then it would appear to us
as a kind of sham building. We would be affected in almost the
same way if we were told that it was made of wood, when we
had supposed it to be made of stone, just because this alters and
destroys the relation between rigidity and gravity, and consequently the significance and necessity of all the parts, for these
natural forces reveal themselves in a far weaker degree in a
wooden building. Therefore no real work of architecture as a fine
art can be made of wood, although it assumes all forms so easily;
this can only be explained by our theory. If we were distinctly
told that a building, the sight of which gave us pleasure, was made
of different kinds of material of very unequal weight and consistency, but not distinguishable to the eye, the whole building
would become as utterly incapable of affording us pleasure as a
poem in an unknown language. All this proves that architecture
does not affect us mathematically, but also dynamically, and that
what speaks to us through it is not mere form and symmetry, but
rather those fundamental forces of nature, those first Ideas, those
lowest grades of the objectivity of will. The regularity of the
building and its parts is partly produced by the direct adaptation
of each member to the stability of the whole, partly it serves to
facilitate the survey and comprehension of the whole, and finally,
regular figures to some extent enhance the beauty because they reveal the constitution of space as such. But all this is of subordinate
value and necessity, and by no means the chief concern; indeed
symmetry is not invariably demanded, as ruins are still beautiful. . . .

§ 45

The great problem of historical painting and sculpture is to express directly and for perception the Idea in which the will reaches the highest grade of its objectification. The objective side of the pleasure afforded by the beautiful is here always predominant, and the subjective side has retired into the background. It is further to be observed that at the next grade below this, animal painting, the characteristic is entirely one with the beautiful; the most characteristic lion, wolf, horse, sheep, or ox, was always the most beautiful also. The reason of this is that animals have only the character of their species, no individual character. In the representation of men the character of the species is separated from that of the individual; the former is now called beauty (entirely in the objective sense), but the latter retains the name, character, or expression, and the new difficulty arises of representing both, at once and completely, in the same individual.

Human beauty is an objective expression, which means the fullest objectification of will at the highest grade at which it is knowable, the Idea of man in general, completely expressed in the sensible form. But however much the objective side of the beautiful appears here, the subjective side still always accompanies it. And just because no object transports us so quickly into pure æsthetic contemplation, as the most beautiful human countenance and form, at the sight of which we are instantly filled with unspeakable satisfaction, and raised above ourselves and all that troubles us; this is only possible because this most distinct and purest knowledge of will raises us most easily and quickly to the state of pure knowing, in which our personality, our will with its constant pain, disappears, so long as the pure æsthetic pleasure lasts. Therefore it is as Goethe says: "No evil can touch him who looks upon human beauty; he feels himself at one with himself and with the world." That a beautiful human form is produced by nature must be explained in this way. At this its highest grade the will objectifies itself in an individual; and therefore through circumstances and its own power it completely overcomes all the hindrances and opposition which the phenomena of the lower grades present to it. Such are the forces of nature, from which the will must always first extort and win back the matter that belongs to all its manifestations. Further, the phenomenon of will at its higher grades always has multiplicity in its form. Even the tree is only a systematic aggregate of innumerably repeated sprouting fibres. This combination assumes greater complexity in higher forms, and the human body is an exceedingly complex system of different parts, each of which has a peculiar life of its own, *vita propria,* subordinate to the whole. Now that all these parts are in the proper fashion subordinate to the whole, and co-ordinate to each other, that they all work together harmoniously for the expression of the whole, nothing superfluous, nothing re-stricted; all these are the rare conditions, whose result is beauty, the completely expressed character of the species. So is it in nature. But how in art? One would suppose that art achieved the beautiful by imitating nature. But how is the artist to rec-ognize the perfect work which is to be imitated, and distinguish it from the failures, if he does not anticipate the beautiful *before experience?* And besides this, has nature ever produced a human being perfectly beautiful in all his parts? It has accordingly been thought that the artist must seek out the beautiful parts, dis-tributed among a number of different human beings, and out of them construct a beautiful whole; a perverse and foolish opinion. For it will be asked, how is he to know that just these forms and not others are beautiful? We also see what kind of success at-tended the efforts of the old German painters to achieve the beau-tiful by imitating nature. Observe their naked figures. No knowl-edge of the beautiful is possible purely *a posteriori,* and from mere experience; it is always, at least in part, *a priori,* although quite different in kind, from the forms of the principle of sufficient reason, of which we are conscious *a priori.* These concern the uni-versal form of phenomena as such, as it constitutes the possibility of knowledge in general, the universal *how* of all phenomena, and from this knowledge proceed mathematics and pure natural science. But this other kind of knowledge *a priori,* which makes it possible to express the beautiful, concerns, not the form but the content of phenomena, not the *how* but the *what* of the phenome-non. That we all recognize human beauty when we see it, but that in the true artist this takes place with such clearness that he shows it as he has never seen it, and surpasses nature in his rep-resentation; this is only possible because *we ourselves are* the will whose adequate objectification at its highest grade is here to be judged and discovered. Thus alone have we in fact an anticipation of that which nature (which is just the will that constitutes our own being) strives to express. And in the true genius this anticipation is accompanied by so great a degree of intelligence that he recognizes the Idea in the particular thing, and thus, as it were, *understands the half-uttered speech of nature,* and articulates clearly what she only stammered forth. He expresses in the hard marble that beauty of form which in a thousand attempts she failed to produce, he presents it to nature, saying, as it were, to her, "That is what you wanted to say!" And whoever is able to judge replies, "Yes, that is it." Only in this way was it possible for the genius of the Greeks to find the type of human beauty and establish it as a canon for the school of sculpture; and only by virtue of such an anticipation is it possible for all of us to recognize beauty, when it has actually been achieved by nature in the particular case. This anticipation is the *Ideal.* It is the *Idea* so far as it is known *a priori,* at least half, and it becomes practical for art, because it corresponds to and completes what is given *a posteriori* through nature. The possibility of such an anticipation of the beautiful *a priori* in the artist, and of its recognition *a posteriori* by the critic, lies in the fact that the artist and the critic are themselves the "in-itself" of nature, the will which objectifies itself. For, as Empedocles said, like can only be known by like: only nature can understand itself: only nature can fathom itself: but only spirit also can understand spirit.

The opinion, which is absurd, although expressed by the Socrates of Xenophon (Stobæi Floril, vol. ii., p. 384) that the Greeks discovered the established ideal of human beauty empirically, by collecting particularly beautiful parts, uncovering and noting here a knee, there an arm, has an exact parallel in the art of poetry. The view is entertained, that Shakespeare, for example, observed, and then gave forth from his own experience of life, the innumerable variety of the characters in his dramas, so true, so sustained, so profoundly worked out. The impossiblity and absurdity of such an assumption need not be dwelt upon. It is obvious that the man of genius produces the works of poetic art by means of an anticipation of what is characteristic, just as he produces the works of plastic and pictorial art by means of a prophetic anticipation of the beautiful; yet both require experience as a pattern or model, for thus alone can that which is dimly known *a priori* be called into clear consciousness, and an intelligent representation of it becomes possible.

Human beauty was explained above as the fullest objectification of will at the highest grade at which it is knowable. It expresses itself throvgh the form; and this lies in space alone, and has no necessary connection with time, as, for example, motion has. Thus far then we may say; the adequate objectification of will through a merely spatial phenomenon is beauty, in the objective sense. A plant is nothing but such a merely spatial phenomenon of will; for no motion, and consequently no relation to time (regarded apart from its development), belongs to the expression of its nature; its mere form expresses its whole being and displays it openly. But brutes and men require, further, for the full revelation of the will which is manifested in them, a series of actions, and thus the manifestation in them takes on a direct relation to time. All this has already been explained in the preceding book; it is related to what we are considering at present in the following way. As the merely spatial manifestation of will can objectify it fully or defectively at each definite grade,—and it is this which constitutes beauty or ugliness,—so the temporal objectification of will, *i. e.,* the action, and indeed the direct action, the movement, may correspond to the will, which objectifies itself in it, purely and fully without foreign admixture, without superfluity, without defect, only expressing exactly the act of will determined in each case;—or the converse of all this may occur. In the first case the movement is made with *grace,* in the second case without it. Thus as beauty is the adequate representation of will generally, through its merely spatial manifestation; *grace* is the adequate representation of will through its temporal manifestation, that is to say, the perfectly accurate and fitting expression of each act of will, through the movement and position which objectify it. Since movement and position presuppose the body, Winckelmann's expression is very true and suitable, when he says, "Grace is the proper relation of the acting person to the action" (Works, vol. i., p. 258). It is thus evident that beauty may be attributed to a plant, but no grace, unless in a figurative sense; but to brutes and men, both beauty and grace. Grace consists, according to what has been said, in every movement being performed, and every position assumed, in the easiest, most appropriate and convenient way, and therefore being the pure, adequate expression of its intention, or of the act of will, without any superfluity, which exhibits itself as aimless, meaningless bustle, or as a wooden stiffness. Grace presupposes as its condition a true proportion of all the limbs, and a symmetrical, harmonious figure; for complete ease and evident appropriateness of all positions and movements are only possible by means of these. Grace is therefore never without a certain degree of beauty of person. The two complete and united are the most distinct manifestation of will at the highest grade of its objectification. . . .

§ 51

If now we turn from plastic and pictorial art to poetry, we shall have no doubt that its aim also is the revelation of the Ideas, the grades of the objectification of will, and the communication of them to the hearer with the distinctness and vividness with which the poetical sense comprehends them. Ideas are essentially perceptible; if, therefore, in poetry only abstract conceptions are directly communicated through words, it is yet clearly the intention to make the hearer perceive the Ideas of life in the representatives of these conceptions, and this can only take place through the assistance of his own imagination. But in order to set the imagination to work for the accomplishment of this end, the abstract conceptions, which are the immediate material of poetry as of dry prose, must be so arranged that their spheres intersect each other in such a way that none of them can remain in its abstract universality; but, instead of it, a perceptible representative appears to the imagination; and this is always further modified by the words of the poet according to what his intention may be. As the chemist obtains solid precipitates by combining perfectly clear and transparent fluids, the poet understands how to precipitate, as it were, the concrete, the individual, the perceptible idea, out of the abstract and transparent universality of the concepts by the manner in which he combines them. For the Idea can only be known by perception; and knowledge of the Idea is the end of art. The skill of a master, in poetry as in chemistry, enables us always to obtain the precise precipitate we intended. This end is assisted by the numerous epithets in poetry, by means of which the universality of every concept is narrowed more and more till we reach the perceptible. Homer attaches to almost every substantive an adjective, whose concept intersects and considerably diminishes the sphere of the concept of the substantive, which is thus brought so much the nearer to perception; for example—

> "Εν δ' επεσ' Ωκεανῳ λαμπρον φαος ἠελιοιο,
> 'Ελλκον νυκτα μελαιναν επι ζειδωρον αρουραν." [10]

And—

> "Where gentle winds from the blue heavens sigh,
> There stand the myrtles still, the laurel high,"—

calls up before the imagination by means of a few concepts the whole delight of a southern clime.

Rhythm and rhyme are quite peculiar aids to poetry. I can give no other explanation of their incredibly powerful effect than that our faculties of perception have received from time, to which they are essentially bound, some quality on account of which we inwardly follow, and, as it were, consent to each regularly recurring sound. In this way rhythm and rhyme are partly a means of holding our attention, because we willingly follow the poem read, and partly they produce in us a blind consent to what is read prior to any judgment, and this gives the poem a certain emphatic power of convincing independent of all reasons.

From the general nature of the material, that is, the concepts, which poetry uses to communicate the Ideas, the extent of its province is very great. The whole of nature, the Ideas of all grades, can be represented by means of it, for it proceeds according to the Idea it has to impart, so that its representations are sometimes descriptive, sometimes narrative, and sometimes directly dramatic. If, in the representation of the lower grades of the objectivity of will, plastic and pictorial art generally surpass it, because lifeless nature, and even brute nature, reveals almost its whole being in a

[10] "The splendid light of the sun falls into the ocean, dragging black night down upon the kindly earth."

single well-chosen moment; man, on the contrary, so far as he does not express himself by the mere form and expression of his person, but through a series of actions and the accompanying thoughts and emotions, is the principal object of poetry, in which no other art can compete with it, for here the progress or movement which cannot be represented in plastic or pictorial art just suits its purpose.

The revelation of the Idea, which is the highest grade of the objectivity of will, the representation of man in the connected series of his efforts and actions, is thus the great problem of poetry. It is true that both experience and history teach us to know man; yet oftener men than man, *i. e.*, they give us empirical notes of the behaviour of men to each other, from which we may frame rules for our own conduct, oftener than they afford us deep glimpses of the inner nature of man. The latter function, however, is by no means entirely denied them; but as often as it is the nature of mankind itself that discloses itself to us in history or in our own experience, we have comprehended our experience, and the historian has comprehended history, with artistic eyes, poetically, *i. e.*, according to the Idea, not the phenomenon, in its inner nature, not in its relations. Our own experience is the indispensable condition of understanding poetry as of understanding history; for it is, so to speak, the dictionary of the language that both speak. But history is related to poetry as portrait-painting is related to historical painting; the one gives us the true in the individual, the other the true in the universal; the one has the truth of the phenomenon, and can therefore verify it from the phenomenal, the other has the truth of the Idea, which can be found in no particular phenomenon, but yet speaks to us from them all. The poet from deliberate choice represents significant characters in significant situations; the historian takes both as they come. Indeed, he must regard and select the circumstances and the persons, not with reference to their inward and true significance, which expresses the Idea, but according to the outward, apparent, and relatively important significance with regard to the connection and the consequences. He must consider nothing in and for itself in its essential character and expression, but must look at everything in its relation, in its connection, in its influence upon what follows, and especially upon its own age. Therefore he will not overlook an action of a king, though of little significance, and in itself quite common, because it has results and influence. And, on the other hand, actions of the highest significance of particular and very eminent individuals are not to be recorded by him if they have no consequences. For his treatment follows the principle of sufficient reason, and apprehends the phenomenon, of which this principle is the form. But the poet comprehends the Idea, the inner nature of man apart from all relations, outside all time, the adequate objectivity of the thing-in-itself, at its highest grade. Even in that method of treatment which is necessary for the historian, the inner nature and significance of the phenomena, the kernel of all these shells, can never be entirely lost. He who seeks for it, at any rate, may find it and recognize it. Yet that which is significant in itself, not in its relations, the real unfolding of the Idea, will be found far more accurately and distinctly in poetry than in history, and, therefore, however paradoxical it may sound, far more really genuine inner truth is to be attributed to poetry than to history. For the historian must accurately follow the particular event according to life, as it develops itself in time in the manifold tangled chains of causes and effects. It is, however, impossible that he can have all the data for this; he cannot have seen all and discovered all. He is forsaken at every moment by the original of his picture, or a false one substitutes itself for it, and this so constantly that I think I may assume that in all history the false outweighs the true. The poet, on the contrary, has comprehended the Idea of man from some definite side which is to be represented; thus it is the nature of his own self that objectifies itself in it for him. His knowledge, as we explained above when speaking of sculpture, is half *a priori;* his ideal stands before his mind firm, distinct, brightly illuminated, and cannot forsake him; therefore he shows us, in the mirror of his mind, the Idea pure and distinct, and his delineation of it down to the minutest particular is true as life itself. The great ancient historians are, therefore, in those particulars in which their data fail them, for example, in the speeches of their heroes—poets; indeed their whole manner of handling their material approaches the epic. But this gives their representations unity, and enables them to retain inner truth, even when outward truth was not accessible, or indeed was falsified. And as we compared history to portrait-painting, in contradistinction to poetry, which corresponds to historical painting, we find that Winckelmann's maxim, that the portrait ought to be the ideal of the individual, was followed by the ancient historians, for they represent the individual in such a way as to bring out that side of the Idea of man which is expressed in it. Modern historians, on the contrary, with few exceptions, give us in general only "a dust-bin and a lumber-room, and at the most a chronicle of the principle political events." Therefore, whoever desires to know man in his inner nature, identical in all its phenomena and developments, to know him according to the Idea, will find that the works of the great, immortal poet present a far truer, more distinct picture, than the historians can ever give. For even the best of the historians are, as poets, far from the first; and moreover their hands are tied. In this aspect the relation between the historian and the poet may be illustrated by the following comparison. The mere, pure historian, who works only according to data, is like a man, who without any knowledge of mathematics, has investigated the relations of certain figures, which he has accidentally found, by measuring them; and the problem thus empirically solved is affected of course by all the errors of the drawn figure. The poet, on the other hand, is like the mathematician, who constructs these relations *a priori* in pure perception, and expresses them not as they actually are in the drawn figure, but as they are in the Idea, which the drawing is intended to render for the senses. Therefore Schiller says:—

> "What has never anywhere come to pass,
> That alone never grows old."

Indeed I must attribute greater value to biographies, and especially to autobiographies, in relation to the knowledge of the nature of man, than to history proper, at least as it is commonly handled. Partly because in the former the data can be collected more accurately and completely than in the latter; partly, because in history proper, it is not so much men as nations and heroes that act, and the individuals who do appear, seem so far off, surrounded with such pomp and circumstance, clothed in the stiff robes of state, or heavy, inflexible armour, that it is really hard through all this to recognize the human movements. On the other hand, the life of the individual when described with truth, in a narrow sphere, shows the conduct of men in all its forms and subtleties, the excellence, the virtue, and even holiness of a few, the perversity, meanness, and knavery of most, the dissolute profligacy of some. Besides, in the only aspect we are considering here, that of the inner significance of the phenomenal, it is quite the same whether the objects with which the action is concerned, are, relatively considered, trifling or important, farm-houses or kingdoms: for all these things in themselves are without significance, and obtain it only in so far as the will is moved by them. The motive has significance only through its relation to the will, while the relation which it has as a thing to other things like itself, does not concern us here. As a circle of one inch in diameter, and a circle of forty million miles in diameter, have precisely the same geometrical properties, so are the events and the history of a village and a kingdom essentially the same; and we may study and learn to know mankind as well in the one as in the other. It is also a mistake to suppose that autobiographies are full of deceit and dissimulation. On the contrary, lying (though always possible) is perhaps more difficult there than elsewhere. Dissimulation is easiest in mere conversation; indeed, though it may sound paradoxical, it is really more difficult even in a letter. For in the case of a letter the writer is alone, and looks into himself, and not out on the world, so that what is strange and distant does not easily approach him; and he has not the test of the impression made upon another before his eyes. But the receiver of the letter peruses it quietly in a mood unknown to the writer, reads it repeatedly and at different times, and thus easily finds out the concealed intention. We also get to know an author as a man most easily from his books, because all these circumstances act here still more strongly and permanently. And in an autobiography it is so difficult to dissimulate, that perhaps there does not exist a single one that is not, as a whole, more true, than any history that ever was written. The man who writes his own life surveys it as a whole, the particular becomes small, the near becomes distant, the distant becomes near again, the motives that influenced him shrink; he seats himself at the confessional, and has done so of his own free will; the spirit of lying does not so easily take hold of him here, for there is also in every man an inclination to truth which has first to be overcome whenever he lies, and which here has taken up a specially strong position. The relation between biography and the history of nations may be made clear for perception by means of the following comparison: History shows us mankind as a view from a high mountain shows us nature; we see much at a time, wide stretches, great masses, but nothing is distinct nor recognizable in all the details of its own peculiar nature. On the other hand, the representation of the life of the individual shows us the man, as we see nature if we go about among her trees, plants, rocks, and waters. But in landscape-painting, in which the artist lets us look at nature with his eyes, the knowledge of the Ideas, and the condition of pure will-less knowing, which is demanded by these, is made much easier for us; and, in the same way, poetry is far superior both to history and biography, in the representation of the Ideas which may be looked for in all three. For here also genius holds up to us the magic glass, in which all that is essential and significant appears before us collected and placed in the clearest light, and what is accidental and foreign is left out. . . .

Tragedy is to be regarded, and is recognized as the summit of poetical art, both on account of the greatness of its effect and the difficulty of its achievement. It is very significant for our whole system, and well worthy of observation, that the end of this highest poetical achievement is the representation of the terrible side of life. The unspeakable pain, the wail of humanity, the triumph of evil, the scornful mastery of chance, and the irretrievable fall of the just and innocent, is here presented to us; and in this lies a significant hint of the nature of the world and of existence. It is the strife of will with itself, which here, completely unfolded at the highest grade of its objectivity, comes into fearful prominence. It becomes visible in the suffering of men, which is now introduced, partly through chance and error, which appear as the rulers of the world, personified as fate, on account of their insidiousness, which even reaches the appearance of design; partly it proceeds from man himself, through the self-mortifying efforts of a few, through the wickedness and perversity of most. It is one and the same will that lives and appears in them all, but whose phenomena fight against each other and destroy each other. In one individual it appears powerfully, in another more weakly; in one more subject to reason, and softened by the light of knowledge, in another less so, till at last, in some single case, this knowledge, purified and heightened by suffering itself, reaches the point at which the phenomenon, the veil of Maya, no longer deceives it. It sees through the form of the phenomenon, the *principium individuationis*. The egoism which rests on this perishes with it, so that now the *motives* that were so powerful before have lost their might, and instead of them the complete knowledge of the nature of the world, which has a *quieting* effect on the will, produces resignation, the surrender not merely of life, but of the very will to live. Thus we see in tragedies the noblest men, after long conflict and suffering, at last renounce the ends they have so keenly followed, and all the pleasures of life for ever, or else freely and joyfully surrender life itself. So is it with the steadfast prince of Calderon; with Gretchen in "Faust"; with Hamlet, whom his friend Horatio would willingly follow, but is bade remain a while, and in this harsh world draw his breath in pain, to tell the story of Hamlet, and clear his memory; so also is it with the Maid of Orleans, the Bride of Messina; they all die purified by suffering, *i. e.,* after the will to live which was formerly in them is dead. In the "Mohammed" of Voltaire this is actually expressed in the concluding words which the dying Palmira addresses to Mohammed: "The world is for tyrants: live!" On the other hand, the demand for so-called poetical justice rests on entire misconception of the nature of tragedy, and, indeed, of the nature of the world itself. It boldly appears in all its dullness in the criticisms which Dr. Samuel Johnson made on particular plays of Shakespeare, for he very naïvely laments its entire absence. And its absence is certainly obvious, for in what has Ophelia, Desdemona, or Cordelia offended? But only the dull, optimistic, Protestant-rationalistic, or peculiarly Jewish view of life will make the demand for poetical justice, and find satisfaction in it. The true sense of tragedy is the deeper insight, that it is not his own individual sins that the hero atones for, but original sin, *i. e.,* the crime of existence itself:

> "Pues el delito mayor
> Del hombre es haber nacido";

> ("For the greatest crime of man
> Is that he was born";)

as Calderon exactly expresses it.

I shall allow myself only one remark, more closely concerning the treatment of tragedy. The representation of a great misfortune is alone essential to tragedy. But the many different ways in which this is introduced by the poet may be brought under three specific conceptions. It may happen by means of a character of extraordinary wickedness, touching the utmost limits of possibility, who becomes the author of the misfortune; examples of this kind are Richard III., Iago in "Othello," Shylock in "The Merchant of Venice," Franz Moor, Phædra of Euripides, Creon in the "Antigone," &c., &c. Secondly, it may happen through blind fate, *i. e.,* chance and error; a true pattern of this kind is the Œdipus Rex of Sophocles, the "Trachiniæ" also; and in general most of the tragedies of the ancients belong to this class. Among modern tragedies, "Romeo and Juliet," "Tancred" by Voltaire, and "The Bride of Messina," are examples. Lastly, the misfortune may be brought about by the mere position of the *dramatis personæ* with regard to each other, through their relations; so that there is no need either for a tremendous error or an unheard-of accident, nor yet for a character whose wickedness reaches the limits of human possibility; but characters of ordinary morality, under circumstances such as often occur, are so situated with regard to each other that their position compels them, knowingly and with their eyes open, to do each other the greatest injury, without any one of them being entirely in the wrong. This last kind of tragedy seems to me far to surpass the other two, for it shows us the greatest misfortune, not as an exception, not as something occasioned by rare circumstances or monstrous characters, but as arising easily and of itself out of the actions and characters of men, indeed almost as essential to them, and thus brings it terribly near to us. In the other two kinds we may look on the prodigious fate and the horrible wickedness as terrible powers which certainly threaten us, but only from afar, which we may very well escape without taking refuge in renunciation. But in the last kind of tragedy we see that those powers which destroy happiness and life are such that their path to us also is open at every moment; we see the greatest sufferings brought about by entanglements that our fate might also partake of, and through actions that perhaps we also are capable of performing, and so could not complain of injustice; then shuddering we feel ourselves already in the midst of hell. This last kind of tragedy is also the most difficult of achievement; for the greatest effect has to be produced in it with the least use of means and causes of movement, merely through the position and distribution of the characters; therefore even in many of the best tragedies this difficulty is evaded. Yet one tragedy may be referred to as a perfect model of this kind, a tragedy which in other respects is far surpassed by more than one work of the same great master; it is "Clavigo." "Hamlet" belongs to a certain extent to this class, as far as the relation of Hamlet to Laertes and Ophelia is concerned. "Wallenstein" has also this excellence. "Faust" belongs entirely to this class, if we regard the events connected with Gretchen and her brother as the principal action; also the "Cid" of Corneille, only that it lacks the tragic conclusion, while on the contrary the analogous relation of Max to Thecla has it.[11]

§ 52

Now that we have considered all the fine arts in the general way that is suitable to our point of view, beginning with architecture, the peculiar end of which is to elucidate the objectification of will at the lowest grades of its visibility, in which it shows itself as the dumb unconscious tendency of the mass in accordance with laws, and yet already reveals a breach of the unity of will with itself in a conflict between gravity and rigidity—and ending with the consideration of tragedy, which presents to us at the highest grades of the objectification of will this very conflict with

[11] Cf. Ch. xxxvii. of the Supplement.

itself in terrible magnitude and distinctness; we find that there is still another fine art which has been excluded from our consideration, and had to be excluded, for in the systematic connection of our exposition there was no fitting place for it—I mean *music*. It stands alone, quite cut off from all the other arts. In it we do not recognize the copy or repetition of any Idea of existence in the world. Yet it is such a great and exceedingly noble art, its effect on the inmost nature of man is so powerful, and it is so entirely and deeply understood by him in his inmost consciousness as a perfectly universal language, the distinctness of which surpasses even that of the perceptible world itself, that we certainly have more to look for in it than an *exercitum arithmeticæ occultum nescientis se numerare animi,*[12] which Leibnitz called it. Yet he was perfectly right, as he considered only its immediate external significance, its form. But if it were nothing more, the satisfaction which it affords would be like that which we feel when a sum in arithmetic comes out right, and could not be that intense pleasure with which we see the deepest recesses of our nature find utterance. From our standpoint, therefore, at which the æsthetic effect is the criterion, we must attribute to music a far more serious and deep significance, connected with the inmost nature of the world and our own self, and in reference to which the arithmetical proportions, to which it may be reduced, are related, not as the thing signified, but merely as the sign. That in some sense music must be related to the world as the representation to the thing represented, as the copy to the original, we may conclude from the analogy of the other arts, all of which possess this character, and affect us on the whole in the same way as it does, only that the effect of music is stronger, quicker, more necessary and infallible. Further, its representative relation to the world must be very deep, absolutely true, and strikingly accurate, because it is instantly understood by every one, and has the appearance of a certain infallibility, because its form may be reduced to perfectly definite rules expressed in numbers, from which it cannot free itself without entirely ceasing to be music. Yet the point of comparison between music and the world, the respect in which it stands to the world in the

[12] "A secret arithmetical exercise by a mind which does not know that it is numbering."

relation of a copy or repetition, is very obscure. Men have practiced music in all ages without being able to account for this; content to understand it directly, they renounce all claim to an abstract conception of this direct understanding itself.

I gave my mind entirely up to the impression of music in all its forms, and then returned to reflection and the system of thought expressed in the present work, and thus I arrived at an explanation of the inner nature of music and of the nature of its imitative relation to the world—which from analogy had necessarily to be presupposed—an explanation which is quite sufficient for myself, and satisfactory to my investigation, and which will doubtless be equally evident to any one who has followed me thus far and has agreed with my view of the world. Yet I recognize the fact that it is essentially impossible to prove this explanation, for it assumes and establishes a relation of music, as idea, to that which from its nature can never be idea, and music will have to be regarded as the copy of an original which can never itself be directly presented as idea. I can therefore do no more than state here, at the conclusion of this third book, which has been principally devoted to the consideration of the arts, the explanation of the marvellous art of music which satisfies myself, and I must leave the acceptance or denial of my view to the effect produced upon each of my readers both by music itself and by the whole system of thought communicated in this work. Moreover, I regard it as necessary, in order to be able to assent with full conviction to the exposition of the significance of music I am about to give, that one should often listen to music with constant reflection upon my theory concerning it, and for this again it is necessary to be very familiar with the whole of my system of thought.

The (Platonic) Ideas are the adequate objectification of will. To excite or suggest the knowledge of these by means of the representation of particular things (for works of art themselves are always representations of particular things) is the end of all the other arts, which can only be attained by a corresponding change in the knowing subject. Thus all these arts objectify the will indirectly only by means of the Ideas; and since our world is nothing but the manifestation of the Ideas in multiplicity, though their entrance into the *principium individuationis* (the form of the knowledge possible for the individual as such), music also, since it passes over the Ideas, is entirely independent of the phenomenal world, ignores it altogether, could to a certain extent exist if there was no world at all, which cannot be said of the other arts. Music is as *direct* an objectification and copy of the whole *will* as the world itself, nay, even as the Ideas, whose multiplied manifestation constitutes the world of individual things. Music is thus by no means like the other arts, the copy of the Ideas, but the *copy of the will itself,* whose objectivity the Ideas are. This is why the effect of music is so much more powerful and penetrating than that of the other arts, for they speak only of shadows, but it speaks of the thing itself. Since, however, it is the same will which objectifies itself both in the Ideas and in music, though in quite different ways, there must be, not indeed a direct likeness, but yet a parallel, an analogy, between music and the Ideas whose manifestation in multiplicity and incompleteness is the visible world. The establishing of this analogy will facilitate, as an illustration, the understanding of this exposition, which is so difficult on account of the obscurity of the subject.

I recognize in the deepest tones of harmony, in the bass, the lowest grades of the objectification of will, unorganized nature, the mass of the planet. It is well known that all the high notes which are easily sounded, and die away more quickly, are produced by the vibration in their vicinity of the deep bass-notes. When, also, the low notes sound, the high notes always sound faintly, and it is a law of harmony that only those high notes may accompany a bass-note which actually already sound along with it of themselves (its *sons harmoniques*) on account of its vibration. This is analogous to the fact that the whole of the bodies and organizations of nature must be regarded as having come into existence through gradual development out of the mass of the planet; this is both their supporter and their source, and the same relation subsists between the high notes and the bass. There is a limit of depth, below which no sound is audible. This corresponds to the fact that no matter can be perceived without form and quality, *i. e.,* without the manifestation of a force which cannot be further explained, in which an Idea expresses itself, and, more generally, that no matter can be entirely without will. Thus, as

a certain pitch is inseparable from the note as such, so a certain
grade of the manifestation of will is inseparable from matter. Bass
is thus, for us, in harmony what unorganized nature, the crudest
mass, upon which all rests, and from which everything originates
and develops, is in the world. Now, further, in the whole of the
complemental parts which make up the harmony between the
bass and the leading voice singing the melody. I recognize the
whole gradation of the Ideas in which the will objectifies itself.
Those nearer to the bass are the lower of these grades, the still
unorganized, but yet manifold phenomenal things; the higher
represent to me the world of plants and beasts. The definite intervals of the scale are parallel to the definite grades of the objectification of will, the definite species in nature. The departure from the
arithmetical correctness of the intervals, through some temperament, or produced by the key selected, is analogous to the departure
of the individual from the type of the species. Indeed, even the
impure discords, which give no definite interval, may be compared
to the monstrous abortions produced by beasts of two species, or
by man and beast. But to all these bass and complemental parts
which make up the *harmony* there is wanting that connected progress which belongs only to the high voice singing the melody,
and it alone moves quickly and lightly in modulations and runs,
while all these others have only a slower movement without a
connection in each part for itself. The deep bass moves most
slowly, the representative of the crudest mass. Its rising and falling
occurs only by large intervals, in thirds, fourths, fifths, never by
one tone, unless it is a base inverted by double counterpoint. This
slow movement is also physically essential to it; a quick run or
shake in the low notes cannot even be imagined. The higher complemental parts, which are parallel to animal life, move more
quickly, but yet without melodious connection and significant
progress. The disconnected course of all the complemental parts,
and their regulation by definite laws, is analogous to the fact that
in the whole irrational world, from the crystal to the most perfect
animal, no being has a connected consciousness of its own which
would make its life into a significant whole, and none experiences
a succession of mental developments, none perfects itself by culture,
but everything exists always in the same way according to its

kind, determined by fixed law. Lastly, in the *melody,* in the high, singing, principal voice leading the whole and progressing with unrestrained freedom, in the unbroken significant connection of *one* thought from beginning to end representing a whole, I recognize the highest grade of the objectification of will, the intellectual life and effort of man. As he alone, because endowed with reason, constantly looks before and after on the path of his actual life and its innumerable possibilities, and so achieves a course of life which is intellectual, and therefore connected as a whole; corresponding to this, I say, the *melody* has significant intentional connection from beginning to end. It records, therefore, the history of the intellectually enlightened will. This will expresses itself in the actual world as the series of its deeds; but melody says more, it records the most secret history of this intellectually-enlightened will, pictures every excitement, every effort, every movement of it, all that which the reason collects under the wide and negative concept of feeling, and which it cannot apprehend further through its abstract concepts. Therefore it has always been said that music is the language of feeling and of passion, as words are the language of reason. . . .

Now the nature of man consists in this, that his will strives, is satisfied and strives anew, and so on for ever. Indeed, his happiness and well-being consist simply in the quick transition from wish to satisfaction, and from satisfaction to a new wish. For the absence of satisfaction is suffering, the empty longing for a new wish, languor, *ennui.* And corresponding to this the nature of melody is a constant digression and deviation from the key-note in a thousand ways, not only to the harmonious intervals to the third and dominant, but to every tone, to the dissonant sevenths and to the superfluous degrees; yet there always follows a constant return to the key-note. In all these deviations melody expresses the multifarious efforts of will, but always its satisfaction also by the final return to an harmonious interval, and still more, to the key-note. The composition of melody, the disclosure in it of all the deepest secrets of human willing and feeling, is the work of genius, whose action, which is more apparent here than anywhere else, lies far from all reflection and conscious intention, and may be called an inspiration. The conception is here, as everywhere in art, unfruitful. The composer reveals the inner nature of the world, and expresses the deepest wisdom in a language which his reason does not understand; as a person under the influence of mesmerism tells things of which he has no conception when he awakes. Therefore in the composer, more than in any other artist, the man is entirely separated and distinct from the artist. Even in the explanation of this wonderful art, the concept shows its poverty and limitation. I shall try, however, to complete our analogy. As quick transition from wish to satisfaction, and from satisfaction to a new wish, is happiness and well-being, so quick melodies without great deviations are cheerful; slow melodies, striking painful discords, and only winding back through many bars to the keynote are, as analogous to the delayed and hardly won satisfaction, sad. The delay of the new excitement of will, languor, could have no other expression than the sustained keynote, the effect of which would soon be unbearable; very monotonous and unmeaning melodies approach this effect. The short intelligible subjects of quick dance-music seem to speak only of easily attained common pleasure. On the other hand, the *Allegro maestoso,* in elaborate movements, long passages, and wide deviations, signifies a greater, nobler effort towards a more distant end, and its final attainment. The *Adagio* speaks of the pain of a great and noble effort which despises all trifling happiness. But how wonderful is the effect of the *minor* and *major!* How astounding that the change of half a tone, the entrance of a minor third instead of a major, at once and inevitably forces upon us an anxious painful feeling, from which again we are just as instantaneously delivered by the major. The *Adagio* lengthens in the minor the expression of the keenest pain, and becomes even a convulsive wail. Dance-music in the minor seems to indicate the failure of that trifling happiness which we ought rather to despise, seems to speak of the attainment of a lower end with toil and trouble. The inexhaustibleness of possible melodies corresponds to the inexhaustibleness of Nature in difference of individuals, physiognomies, and courses of life. The transition from one key to an entirely different one, since it altogether breaks the connection with what went before, is like death, for the individual ends in it; but the will which appeared in this individual lives after him as before him, appearing in other individuals, whose consciousness, however, has no connection with his.

But it must never be forgotten, in the investigation of all these analogies I have pointed out, that music has no direct, but merely an indirect relation to them, for it never expresses the phenomenon, but only the inner nature, the in-itself of all phenomena, the will itself. It does not therefore express this or that particular and definite joy, this or that sorrow, or pain, or horror, or delight, or merriment, or peace of mind; but joy, sorrow, pain, horror, delight, merriment, peace of mind *themselves,* to a certain extent in the abstract, their essential nature, without accessories, and therefore without their motives. Yet we completely understand them in this extracted quintessence. Hence it arises that our imagination is so easily excited by music, and now seeks to give form to that invisible yet actively moved spirit-world which speaks to us directly, and clothe it with flesh and blood, *i. e.,* to embody it in an analogous example. This is the origin of the song with words, and finally of the opera, the text of which should therefore never forsake that subordinate position in order to make itself the chief thing and the music a mere means of expressing it, which is a great misconception and a piece of utter perversity; for music always expresses only the quintessence of life and its events, never these themselves, and therefore their differences do not always affect it. It is precisely this universality, which belongs exclusively to it, together with the greatest determinateness, that gives music the high worth which it has as the panacea for all our woes. Thus, if music is too closely united to the words, and tries to form itself according to the events, it is striving to speak a language which is not its own. No one has kept so free from this mistake as Rossini; therefore his music speaks *its own language* so distinctly and purely that it requires no words, and produces its full effect when rendered by instruments alone.

According to all this, we may regard the phenomenal world, or nature, and music as two different expressions of the same thing, which is therefore itself the only medium of their analogy, so that a knowledge of it is demanded in order to understand that analogy. Music, therefore, if regarded as an expression of the world, is in the highest degree a universal language, which is related indeed to the universality of concepts, much as they are related to the particular things. Its universality, however, is by no means that empty universality of abstraction, but quite of a different kind, and is united with thorough and distinct definiteness. In this respect it resembles geometrical figures and numbers, which are the universal forms of all possible objects of experience and applicable to them all *a priori,* and yet are not abstract but perceptible and thoroughly determined. All possible efforts, excitements, and manifestations of will, all that goes on in the heart of man and that reason includes in the wide, negative concept of feeling, may be expressed by the infinite number of possible melodies, but always in the universal, in the mere form, without the material, always according to the thing-in-itself, not the phenomenon, the inmost soul, as it were, of the phenomenon, without the body. This deep relation which music has to the true nature of all things also explains the fact that suitable music played to any scene, action, event, or surrounding seems to disclose to us its most secret meaning, and appears as the most accurate and distinct commentary upon it. This is so truly the case, that whoever gives himself up entirely to the impression of a symphony, seems to see all the possible events of life and the world take place in himself, yet if he reflects, he can find no likeness between the music and the things that passed before his mind. For, as we have said, music is distinguished from all the other arts by the fact that it is not a copy of the phenomenon, or, more accurately, the adequate objectivity of will, but is the direct copy of the will itself, and therefore exhibits itself as the metaphysical to everything physical in the world, and as the thing-in-itself to every phenomenon. We might, therefore, just as well call the world embodied music as embodied will; and this is the reason why music makes every picture, and indeed every scene of real life and of the world, at once appear with higher significance, certainly all the more in proportion as its melody is analogous to the inner spirit of the given phenomenon. It rests upon this that we are able to set a poem to music as a song, or a perceptible representation as a pantomime, or both as an opera. Such particular pictures of human life, set to the universal language of music, are never bound to it or correspond to it with stringent necessity; but they stand to it only in the relation of an example chosen at will to a general concept. In the determinateness of the real, they represent that which music expresses in the universality of mere form. For melodies are to a certain extent, like general concepts, an abstraction from the actual. This actual world, then, the world of particular things, affords the object of perception, the special and individual, the particular case, both to the universality of the concepts and to the universality of the melodies. But these two universalities are in a certain respect opposed to each other; for the concepts contain particulars only as the first forms abstracted from perception, as it were, the separated shell of things; thus they are, strictly speaking, *abstracta;* music, on the other hand, gives the inmost kernel which precedes all forms, or the heart of things. This relation may be very well expressed in the language of the schoolmen by saying the concepts are the *universalia post rem,* but music gives the *universalia ante rem,* and the real world the *universalia in re.* To the universal significance of a melody to which a poem has been set, it is quite possible to set other equally arbitrarily selected examples of the universal expressed in this poem corresponding to the significance of the melody in the same degree. This is why the same composition is suitable to many verses; and this is also what makes the *vaudeville* possible. But that in general a relation is possible between a composition and a perceptible representation rests, as we have said, upon the fact that both are simply different expressions of the same inner being of the world. When now, in the particular case, such a relation is actually given, that is to say, when the composer has been able to express in the universal language of music the emotions of will which constitute the heart of an event, then the melody of the song, the music of the opera, is expressive. But the analogy discovered by the composer between the two must have proceeded from the direct knowledge of the nature of the world unknown to his reason, and must not be an imitation produced with conscious intention by means of conceptions, otherwise the music does not express the inner nature of the will itself, but merely gives an inadequate imitation of its phenomenon. All specially imitative music does this; for example, "The Seasons," by Haydn; also many passages of his "Creation," in which phenomena of the external world are directly imitated; also all battle-pieces. Such music is entirely to be rejected.

The unutterable depth of all music by virtue of which it floats through our consciousness as the vision of a paradise firmly believed in yet ever distant from us, and by which also it is so fully understood and yet so inexplicable, rests on the fact that it restores to us all the emotions of our inmost nature, but entirely without reality and far removed from their pain. So also the seriousness which is essential to it, which excludes the absurd from its direct and peculiar province, is to be explained by the fact that its object is not the idea, with reference to which alone deception and absurdity are possible; but its object is directly the will, and this is essentially the most serious of all things, for it is that on which all depends. How rich in content and full of significance the language of music is, we see from the repetitions, as well as the *Da capo,* the like of which would be unbearable in works composed in a language of words, but in music are very appropriate and beneficial, for, in order to comprehend it fully, we must hear it twice. . . .

The pleasure we receive from all beauty, the consolation which art affords, the enthusiasm of the artist, which enables him to forget the cares of life,—the latter an advantage of the man of genius over other men, which alone repays him for the suffering that increases in proportion to the clearness of consciousness, and for the desert loneliness among men of a different race,—all this rests on the fact that the in-itself of life, the will, existing itself, is, as we shall see farther on, a constant sorrow, partly miserable, partly terrible; while, on the contrary, as idea alone, purely contemplated, or copied by art, free from pain, it presents to us a drama full of significance. This purely knowable side of the world, and the copy of it in any art, is the element of the artist. He is chained to the contemplation of the play, the objectification of will; he remains beside it, does not get tired of contemplating it and representing it in copies; and meanwhile he bears himself the cost of the production of that play, *i. e.,* he himself is the will which objectifies itself, and remains in constant suffering. That pure, true, and deep knowledge of the inner nature of the world becomes now for him an end in itself: he stops there. Therefore it does not become to him a quieter of the will, as, we shall see in the next book, it does in the case of the saint who has attained to resignation; it does not deliver him for ever from life, but only at moments, and is therefore not for him a path out of life, but only an occasional consolation in it, till his power, increased by this contemplation and at last tired of the play, lays hold on the real. The St. Cecilia of Raphael may be regarded as a representation of this transition. To the real, then, we now turn in the following book.

FOURTH BOOK

THE WORLD AS WILL

———

SECOND ASPECT

THE ASSERTION AND DENIAL OF THE WILL TO LIVE, WHEN
SELF-CONSCIOUSNESS HAS BEEN ATTAINED

IV

§ 53

THE last part of our work presents itself as the most serious, for it relates to the action of men, the matter which concerns every one directly and can be foreign or indifferent to none. It is indeed so characteristic of the nature of man to relate everything else to action, that in every systematic investigation he will always treat the part that has to do with action as the result or outcome of the whole work, so far, at least, as it interests him, and will therefore give his most serious attention to this part, even if to no other. In this respect the following part of our work would, in ordinary language, be called practical philosophy, in opposition to the theoretical, which has occupied us hitherto. But, in my opinion, all philosophy is theoretical, because it is essential to it that it should retain a purely contemplative attitude, and should investigate, not prescribe. To become, on the contrary, practical, to guide conduct, to transform character, are old claims, which with fuller insight it ought finally to give up. For here, where the worth or worthlessness of an existence, where salvation or damnation are in question, the dead conceptions of philosophy do not decide the matter, but the inmost nature of man himself, the dæmon that guides him and that has not chosen him, but been chosen by him, as Plato would say; his intelligible character, as Kant expresses himself. Virtue cannot be taught any more than genius; indeed, for it the concept is just as unfruitful as it is in art, and in both cases can only be used as an instrument. It would, therefore, be just as absurd to expect that our moral systems and ethics will produce virtuous, noble, and holy men, as that our æsthetics will produce poets, painters, and musicians.

Philosophy can never do more than interpret and explain what is given. It can only bring to distinct abstract knowledge of the reason the nature of the world which in the concrete, that is, as feeling, expresses itself comprehensibly to every one. This, however, it does in every possible reference and from every point of view. Now, as this attempt has been made from other points of view in the three preceding books with the generality that is proper to philosophy, in this book the action of men will be considered in the same way; and this side of the world might, indeed, be considered the most important of all, not only subjectively, as I remarked above, but also objectively. In considering it I shall faithfully adhere to the method I have hitherto followed, and shall support myself by presupposing all that has already been advanced. There is, indeed, just one thought which forms the content of this whole work. I have endeavoured to work it out in all other spheres, and I shall now do so with regard to human action. I shall then have done all that is in my power to communicate it as fully as possible. . . .

§ 54

The first three books will, it is hoped, have conveyed the distinct and certain knowledge that the world as idea is the complete mirror of the will, in which it knows itself in ascending grades of distinctness and completeness, the highest of which is man, whose nature, however, receives its complete expression only through the whole connected series of his actions. The self-conscious connection of these actions is made possible by reason, which enables a man constantly to survey the whole in the abstract.

The will, which, considered purely in itself, is without knowledge, and is merely a blind incessant impulse, as we see it appear in unorganized and vegetable nature and their laws, and also in the vegetative part of our own life, receives through the addition of the world as idea, which is developed in subjection to it, the knowledge of its own willing and of what it is that it wills. And this is nothing else than the world as idea, life, precisely as it exists. Therefore we called the phenomenal world the mirror of the will, its objectivity. And since what the will wills is always life, just because life is nothing but the representation of that willing for the idea, it is all one and a mere pleonasm if, instead of simply saying "the will," we say "the will to live."

Will is the thing-in-itself, the inner content, the essence of the world. Life, the visible world, the phenomenon, is only the mirror of the will. Therefore life accompanies the will as inseparably as the shadow accompanies the body; and if will exists, so will life, the world, exist. Life is, therefore, assured to the will to live; and so long as we are filled with the will to live we need have no fear for our existence, even in the presence of death. It is true we see the individual come into being and pass away; but the individual is only phenomenal, exists only for the knowledge which is bound to the principle of sufficient reason, to the *principio individuationis*. Certainly, for this kind of knowledge, the individual receives his life as a gift, rises out of nothing, then suffers the loss of this gift through death, and returns again to nothing. But we desire to consider life philosophically, *i. e.,* according to its Ideas, and in this sphere we shall find that neither the will, the thing-in-itself in all phenomena, nor the subject of knowing, that which perceives all phenomena, is affected at all by birth or by death. Birth and death belong merely to the phenomenon of will, thus to life; and it is essential to this to exhibit itself in individuals which come into being and pass away, as fleeting phenomena appearing in the form of time—phenomena of that which in itself knows no time, but must exhibit itself precisely in the way we have said, in order to objectify its peculiar nature. Birth and death belong in like manner to life, and hold the balance as reciprocal conditions of each other, or, if one likes the expression, as poles of the whole phenomenon of life. The wisest of all mythologies, the Indian, expresses this by giving to the very god that symbolizes destruction, death (as Brahma, the most sinful and the lowest god of the Trimurti, symbolizes generation, coming into being, and Vishnu maintaining or preserving), by giving, I say, to Siva as an attribute not only the necklace of skulls, but also the lingam, the symbol of generation, which appears here as the counterpart of death, thus signifying that generation and death are essentially correlatives, which reciprocally neutralize and annul each other. It was precisely the same sentiment that led the Greeks and Romans to adorn their costly sarcophagi, just as we see them now, with feasts, dances, marriages, the chase, fights of wild beasts, bacchanalians, &c.; thus with representations of the full ardour of life, which they place before us not only in such revels and sports, but also in sensual groups, and even go so far as to represent the sexual intercourse of satyrs and goats. Clearly the aim was to point in the most impressive manner away from the death of the mourned individual to the immortal life of nature, and thus to indicate, though without abstract knowledge, that the whole of nature is the phenomenon and also the fulfilment of the will to live. The form of this phenomenon is time, space, and causality, and by means of these individuation, which carries with it that the individual must come into being and pass away. But this no more affects the will to live, of whose manifestation the individual is, as it were, only a particular example or specimen, than the death of an individual injures the whole of nature. For it is not the individual, but only the species that Nature cares for, and for the preservation of which she so earnestly strives, providing for it with the utmost prodigality through the vast surplus of the seed and the great strength of the fructifying impulse. The individual, on the contrary, neither has nor can have any value for Nature, for her kingdom is infinite time and infinite space, and in these infinite multiplicity of possible individuals. Therefore she is always ready to let the individual fall, and hence it is not only exposed to destruction in a thousand ways by the most insignificant accident, but originally destined for it, and conducted towards it by Nature herself from the moment it has served its end of maintaining the species. Thus Nature naïvely expresses the great truth that only the Ideas, not the individuals, have, properly speaking, reality, *i. e.,* are complete objectivity of the will. Now, since man is Nature itself, and indeed Nature at the highest grade of its self-consciousness, but Nature is only the objectified will to live, the man who has comprehended and retained this point of view may well console himself, when contemplating his own death and that of his friends, by turning his eyes to the immortal life of Nature, which he himself is. This is the significance of Siva with the lingam, and of those ancient sarcophagi with their pictures of glowing life, which say to the mourning beholder, *Natura non contristatur.*[1]

That generation and death are to be regarded as something belonging to life, and essential to this phenomenon of the will, arises also from the fact that they both exhibit themselves merely as higher powers of the expression of that in which all the rest of life consists. This is through and through nothing else than the constant change of matter in the fixed permanence of form; and this is what constitutes the transitoriness of the individual and the permanence of the species. Constant nourishment and renewal differ from generation only in degree, and constant excretion differs only in degree from death. The first shows itself most simply and distinctly in the plant. The plant is throughout a constant recurrence of the same impulse of its simplest fibre, which groups itself into leaf and branch. It is a systematic aggregate of similar plants supporting each other, whose constant reproduction is its single impulse. It ascends to the full satisfaction of this tendency through the grades of its metamorphosis, finally to the blossom and fruit, that compendium of its existence and effort in which it now attains, by a short way, to that which is its single aim, and at a stroke produces a thousand-fold what, up till then, it affected only in the particular case—the repetition of itself. Its earlier growth and development stands in the same relation to its fruit as writing stands to printing. With the animal it is clearly quite the same. The process of nourishing is a constant reproduction; the process of reproduction is a higher power of nourishing. The pleasure which accompanies the act of procreation is a higher power of the agreeableness of the sense of life. On the other hand, excretion, the constant exhalation and throwing off of matter, is the same as that which, at a higher power, death, is the contrary of generation. And if here we are always content to retain the form without lamenting the discarded matter, we ought to bear ourselves in the same way if in death the same thing happens, in a higher degree and to the whole, as takes place daily and hourly in a partial manner in excretion: if we are indifferent to the one, we ought not to shrink from the other. Therefore, from this point of view,

[1] Nature is not sad.

it appears just as perverse to desire the continuance of an individuality which will be replaced by other individuals as to desire the permanence of matter which will be replaced by other matter. It appears just as foolish to embalm the body as it would be carefully to preserve its excrement. As to the individual consciousness which is bound to the individual body, it is absolutely interrupted every day by sleep. Deep sleep is, while it lasts, in no way different from death, into which, in fact, it often passes continuously, as in the case of freezing to death. It differs only with regard to the future, the waking. Death is a sleep in which individuality is forgotten; everything else wakes again, or rather never slept.

Above all things, we must distinctly recognize that the form of the phenomenon of will, the form of life or reality, is really only the *present,* not the future nor the past. The latter are only in the conception, exist only in the connection of knowledge, so far as it follows the principle of sufficient reason. No man has ever lived in the past, and none will live in the future; the *present* alone is the form of all life, and is its sure possession which can never be taken from it. The present always exists, together with its content. Both remain fixed without wavering, like the rainbow on the waterfall. For life is firm and certain in the will, and the present is firm and certain in life. Certainly, if we reflect on the thousands of years that are past, of the millions of men who lived in them, we ask, What were they? What has become of them? But, on the other hand, we need only recall our own past life and renew its scenes vividly in our imagination, and then ask again, What was all this? What has become of it? As it is with it, so is it with the life of those millions. Or should we suppose that the past could receive a new existence because it has been sealed by death? Our own past, the most recent part of it, and even yesterday, is now no more than an empty dream of the fancy, and such is the past of all those millions. What was? What is? The will, of which life is the mirror, and knowledge free from will, which beholds it clearly in that mirror. Whoever has not yet recognized this, or will not recognize it, must add to the question asked above as to the fate of past generations of men this question also: Why he, the questioner, is so fortunate as to be conscious of this costly, fleeting, and only real present, while those hundreds of generations of men, even the heroes and philosophers of those ages, have sunk into the night of the past, and have thus become nothing; but he, his insignificant ego, actually exists? or more shortly, though somewhat strangely: Why this now, his now, *is* just now and *was* not long ago? Since he asks such strange questions, he regards his existence and his time as independent of each other, and the former as projected into the latter. He assumes indeed two nows—one which belongs to the object, the other which belongs to the subject, and marvels at the happy accident of their coincidence. But in truth, only the point of contact of the object, the form of which is time, with the subject, which has no mode of the principle of sufficient reason as its form, constitutes the present, as is shown in the essay on the principle of sufficient reason. Now all object is the will so far as it has become idea, and the subject is the necessary correlative of the object. But real objects are only in the present; the past and the future contain only conceptions and fancies, therefore the present is the essential form of the phenomenon of the will, and inseparable from it. The present alone is that which always exists and remains immovable. That which, empirically apprehended, is the most transitory of all, presents itself to the metaphysical vision, which sees beyond the forms of empirical perception, as that which alone endures, the *nunc stans* of the schoolmen. The source and the supporter of its content is the will to live or the thing-in-itself,—which we are. That which constantly becomes and passes away, in that it has either already been or is still to be, belongs to the phenomenon as such on account of its forms, which make coming into being and passing away possible. Accordingly, we must think:—*Quid fuit?—Quod est. Quid erit?—Quod fuit;* [2] and take it in the strict meaning of the words; thus understand not *simile* but *idem*. For life is certain to the will, and the present is certain to life. Thus it is that every one can say: "I am once for all lord of the present, and through all eternity it will accompany me as my shadow: therefore I do not wonder where it has come from, and how it happens that it is exactly now." We might compare time to a constantly revolving sphere; the half that was always sinking would be the past, that which was always rising would be the future; but the indivisible point at the

---

[2] "What has been?—What is. What shall be?—What has been."

top, where the tangent touches, would be the extensionless present. As the tangent does not revolve with the sphere, neither does the present, the point of contact of the object, the form of which is time, with the subject, which has no form, because it does not belong to the knowable, but is the condition of all that is knowable. Or, time is like an unceasing stream, and the present a rock on which the stream breaks itself, but does not carry away with it. The will, as thing-in-itself, is just as little subordinate to the principle of sufficient reason as the subject of knowledge, which, finally, in a certain regard is the will itself or its expression. And as life, its own phenomenon, is assured to the will, so is the present, the single form of real life. Therefore we have not to investigate the past before life, nor the future after death: we have rather to know the *present,* the one form in which the will manifests itself. It will not escape from the will, but neither will the will escape from it. If, therefore, life as it is satisfies, whoever affirms it in every way may regard it with confidences as endless, and banish the fear of death as an illusion that inspires him with the foolish dread that he can ever be robbed of the present, and foreshadows a time in which there is no present; an illusion with regard to time analogous to the illusion with regard to space through which every one imagines the position on the globe he happens to occupy as above, and all other places as below. In the same way every one links the present to his own individuality, and imagines that all present is extinguished with it; that then past and future might be without a present. But as on the surface of the globe every place is above, so the form of all life is the *present,* and to fear death because it robs us of the present, is just as foolish as to fear that we may slip down from the round globe upon which we have now the good fortune to occupy the upper surface. The present is the form essential to the objectification of the will. It cuts time, which extends infinitely in both directions, as a mathematical point, and stands immovably fixed, like an everlasting mid-day with no cool evening, as the actual sun burns without intermission, while it only seems to sink into the bosom of night. Therefore, if a man fears death as his annihilation, it is just as if he were to think that the sun cries out at evening, "Woe is me! for I go down into eternal night." [3] And conversely, whoever is oppressed with the burden of life, whoever desires life and affirms it, but abhors its torments, and especially can no longer endure the hard lot that has fallen to himself, such a man has no deliverance to hope for from death, and cannot right himself by suicide. The cool shades of Orcus allure him only with the false appearance of a haven of rest. The earth rolls from day into night, the individual dies, but the sun itself shines without intermission, an eternal noon. Life is assured to the will to live; the form of life is an endless present, no matter how the individuals, the phenomena of the Idea, arise and pass away in time, like fleeting dreams. Thus even already suicide appears to us as a vain and therefore a foolish action; when we have carried our investigation further it will appear to us in a still less favourable light.

Dogmas change and our knowledge is deceptive; but Nature never errs, her procedure is sure, and she never conceals it. Everything is entirely in Nature, and Nature is entire in everything. She has her centre in every brute. It has surely found its way into existence, and it will surely find its way out of it. In the meantime it lives, fearless and without care, in the presence of annihilation, supported by the consciousness that it is Nature herself, and imperishable as she is. Man alone carries about with him, in abstract conceptions, the certainty of his death; yet this can only trouble him very rarely, when for a single moment some occasion calls it up to his imagination. Against the mighty voice of Nature reflection can do little. In man, as in the brute which does not think, the certainty that springs from his inmost consciousness that he himself is Nature, the world, predominates as a lasting frame of mind; and on account of this no man is observably disturbed by the thought of certain and never-distant death, but lives as if he would live for ever. Indeed this is carried so far that we may say that no one has really a lively conviction of the certainty of his death, otherwise there would be no great difference

---

[3] In Eckermann's "Conversations of Goethe" (vol. i., p. 161), Goethe says: "Our spirit is a being of a nature quite indestructible, and its activity continues from eternity to eternity. It is like the sun, which seems to set only to our earthly eyes, but which, in reality, never sets, but shines on unceasingly." Goethe has taken the simile from me; not I from him.—S.

between his frame of mind and that of a condemned criminal. Every one recognizes that certainty in the abstract and theoretically, but lays it aside like other theoretical truths which are not applicable to practice, without really receiving it into his living consciousness. Whoever carefully considers this peculiarity of human character will see that the psychological explanations of it, from habit and acquiescence in the inevitable, are by no means sufficient, and that its true explanation lies in the deeper ground we have given. The same fact explains the circumstance that at all times and among all peoples dogmas of some kind or other relating to the continued existence of the individual after death arise, and are believed in, although the evidence in support of them must always be very insufficient, and the evidence against them forcible and varied. But, in truth, this really requires no proof, but is recognized by the healthy understanding as a fact, and confirmed by the confidence that Nature never lies any more than she errs, but openly exhibits and naïvely expresses her action and her nature, while only we ourselves obscure it by our folly, in order to establish what is agreeable to our limited point of view.

But this that we have brought to clearest consciousness, that although the particular phenomenon of the will has a temporal beginning and end, the will itself as thing-in-itself is not affected by it, nor yet the correlative of all object, the knowing but never known subject, and that life is always assured to the will to live— this is not to be numbered with the doctrines of immortality. For permanence has no more to do with the will or with the pure subject of knowing, the eternal eye of the world, than transitoriness, for both are predicates that are only valid in time, and the will and the pure subject of knowing lie outside time. Therefore the egoism of the individual (this particular phenomenon of will enlightened by the subject of knowing) can extract as little nourishment and consolation for his wish to endure through endless time from the view we have expressed, as he could from the knowledge that after his death the rest of the eternal world would continue to exist, which is just the expression of the same view considered objectively, and therefore temporally. For every individual is transitory only as phenomenon, but as thing-in-itself is timeless, and therefore endless. But it is also only as phenomenon that an individual is distinguished from the other things of the world; as thing-in-itself he is the will which appears in all, and death destroys the illusion which separates his consciousness from that of the rest: this is immortality. His exemption from death, which belongs to him only as thing-in-itself, is for the phenomenon one with the immortality of the rest of the external world. Hence also, it arises that although the inward and merely felt consciousness of that which we have raised to distinct knowledge is indeed, as we have said, sufficient to prevent the thought of death from poisoning the life of the rational being, because this consciousness is the basis of that love of life which maintains everything living, and enables it to live on at ease as if there were no such thing as death, so long as it is face to face with life, and turns its attention to it, yet it will not prevent the individual from being seized with the fear of death, and trying in every way to escape from it, when it presents itself to him in some particular real case, or even only in his imagination, and he is compelled to contemplate it. For just as, so long as his knowledge was directed to life as such, he was obliged to recognize immortality in it, so when death is brought before his eyes, he is obliged to recognize it as that which it is, the temporal end of the particular temporal phenomenon. What we fear in death is by no means the pain, for it lies clearly on this side of death, and, moreover, we often take refuge in death from pain, just as, on the contrary, we sometimes endure the most fearful suffering merely to escape death for a while, although it would be quick and easy. Thus we distinguish pain and death as two entirely different evils. What we fear in death is the end of the individual, which it openly professes itself to be, and since the individual is a particular objectification of the will to live itself, its whole nature struggles against death. Now when feeling thus exposes us helpless, reason can yet step in and for the most part overcome its adverse influence, for it places us upon a higher standpoint, from which we no longer contemplate the particular but the whole. Therefore a philosophical knowledge of the nature of the world, which extended to the point we have now reached in this work but went no farther, could even at this point of view overcome the terror of death in the measure in which reflection had power over direct feeling in the given individual. A man who had thoroughly assimilated the truths we have already advanced, but had not come to know, either from his own experience or from a deeper insight, that constant suffering is essential to life, who found satisfaction and all that he wished in life, and could calmly and deliberately desire that his life, as he had hitherto known it, should endure for ever or repeat itself ever anew, and whose love of life was so great that he willingly and gladly accepted all the hardships and miseries to which it is exposed for the sake of its pleasures,—such a man would stand "with firm-knit bones on the well-rounded, enduring earth," and would have nothing to fear. Armed with the knowledge we have given him, he would await with indifference the death that hastens towards him on the wings of time. He would regard it as a false illusion, an impotent spectre, which frightens the weak but has no power over him who knows that he is himself the will of which the whole world is the objectification or copy, and that therefore he is always certain of life, and also of the present, the peculiar and only form of the phenomenon of the will. He could not be terrified by an endless past or future in which he would not be, for this he would regard as the empty delusion of the web of Mâyâ. Thus he would no more fear death than the sun fears the night. In the "Bhagavad-Gita" Krishna thus raises the mind of his young pupil Arjuna, when, seized with compunction at the sight of the arrayed hosts (somewhat as Xerxes was), he loses heart and desires to give up the battle in order to avert the death of so many thousands. Krishna leads him to this point of view, and the death of those thousands can no longer restrain him; he gives the sign for battle. This point of view is also expressed by Goethe's Prometheus, especially when he says—

> "Here sit I, form mankind
> In my own image,
> A race like to myself,
> To suffer and to weep,
> Rejoice, enjoy,
> And heed thee not,
> As I."

The philosophy of Bruno and that of Spinoza might also lead any one to this point of view whose conviction was not shaken and weakened by their errors and imperfections. That of Bruno has properly no ethical theory at all, and the theory contained in the philosophy of Spinoza does not really proceed from the inner nature of his doctrine, but is merely tacked on to it by means of weak and palpable sophisms, though in itself it is praiseworthy and beautiful. Finally, there are many men who would occupy this point of view if their knowledge kept pace with their will, i. e., if, free from all illusion, they were in a position to become clearly and distinctly themselves. For this is, for knowledge, the point of view of the complete *assertion of the will to live.*

That the will asserts itself means, that while in its objectivity, i. e., in the world and life, its own nature is completely and distinctly given it as idea, this knowledge does not by any means check its volition; but this very life, so known, is willed as such by the will with knowledge, consciously and deliberately, just as up to this point it willed it as blind effort without knowledge. The opposite of this, the *denial of the will to live,* shows itself if, when that knowledge is attained, volition ends, because the particular known phenomena no longer act as *motives* for willing, but the whole knowledge of the nature of the world, the mirror of the will, which has grown up through the comprehension of the *Ideas,* becomes a *quieter* of the will; and thus free, the will suppresses itself. These quite unfamiliar conceptions are difficult to understand when expressed in this general way, but it is hoped they will become clear through the exposition we shall give presently, with special reference to action, of the phenomena in which, on the other hand, the assertion in its different grades, and, on the other hand, the denial, expresses itself. For both proceed from knowledge, yet not from abstract knowledge, which is expressed in words, but from living knowledge, which is expressed in action and behaviour alone, and is independent of the dogmas which at the same time occupy the reason as abstract knowledge. To exhibit them both, and bring them to distinct knowledge of the reason, can alone be my aim, and not to prescribe or recommend the one or the other, which would be as foolish as it would be useless; for the will in itself is absolutely free and entirely self-determining, and for it there is no law. But before we go on to the exposition referred to, we must first explain and more exactly define this *free-*

dom and its relation to necessity. And also, with regard to the life, the assertion and denial of which is our problem, we must insert a few general remarks connected with the will and its objects. Through all this we shall facilitate the apprehension of the inmost nature of the knowledge we are aiming at, of the ethical significance of methods of action.

Since, as has been said, this whole work is only the unfolding of a single thought, it follows that all its parts have the most intimate connection with each other. Not merely that each part stands in a necessary relation to what immediately precedes it, and only presupposes a recollection of that by the reader, as is the case with all philosophies which consist merely of a series of inferences, but that every part of the whole work is related to every other part and presupposes it. It is, therefore, necessary that the reader should remember not only what has just been said, but all the earlier parts of the work, so that he may be able to connect them with what he is reading, however much may have intervened. Plato also makes this demand upon his readers through the intricate digressions of his dialogues, in which he only returns to the leading thought after long episodes, which illustrate and explain it. In our case this demand is necessary; for the breaking up of our one single thought into its many aspects is indeed the only means of imparting it, though not essential to the thought itself, but merely an artificial form. The division of four principal points of view into four books, and the most careful bringing together of all that is related and homogeneous, assists the exposition and its comprehension; yet the material absolutely does not admit of an advance in a straight line, such as the progress of history, but necessitates a more complicated exposition. This again makes a repeated study of the book necessary, for thus alone does the connection of all the parts with each other become distinct, and only then do they all mutually throw light upon each other and become quite clear.

§ 55

That the will as such is *free,* follows from the fact that, according to our view, it is the thing-in-itself, the content of all phenomena. The phenomena, on the other hand, we recognize as absolutely subordinate to the principle of sufficient reason in its four forms. And since we know that necessity is throughout identical with following from given grounds, and that these are convertible conceptions, all that belongs to the phenomenon, *i. e.,* all that is object for the knowing subject as individual, is in one aspect reason, and in another aspect consequent; and in this last capacity is determined with absolute necessity, and can, therefore, in no respect be other than it is. The whole content of Nature, the collective sum of its phenomena, is thus throughout necessary, and the necessity of every part, of every phenomenon, of every event, can always be proved, because it must be possible to find the reason from which it follows as a consequent. This admits of no exception: it follows from the unrestricted validity of the principle of sufficient reason. In another aspect, however, the same world is for us, in all its phenomena, objectivity of will. And the will, since it is not phenomenon, is not idea or object, but thing-in-itself, and is not subordinate to the principle of sufficient reason, the form of all object; thus is not determined as a consequent through any reason, knows no necessity, *i. e.,* is *free.* The concept of freedom is thus properly a negative concept, for its content is merely the denial of necessity, *i. e.,* the relation of consequent to its reason, according to the principle of sufficient reason. Now here lies before us in its most distinct form the solution of that great contradiction, the union of freedom with necessity, which has so often been discussed in recent times, yet, for far as I know, never clearly and adequately. Everything is as phenomenon, as object, absolutely necessary: *in itself* it is will, which is perfectly free to all eternity. The phenomenon, the object, is necessarily and unalterably determined in that chain of causes and effects which admits of no interruption. But the existence in general of this object, and its specific nature, *i. e.,* the Idea which reveals itself in it, or, in other words, its character, is a direct manifestation of will. Thus, in conformity with the freedom of this will, the object might not be at all, or it might be originally and essentially something quite different from what it is, in which case, however, the whole chain of which it is a link, and which is itself a manifestation of the same will, would be quite different also. But once there and existing, it has entered

the chain of causes and effects, is always necessarily determined
in it, and can, therefore, neither become something else, *i. e.,* change
itself, nor yet escape from the chain, *i. e.,* vanish. Man, like every
other part of Nature, is objectivity of the will; therefore all that
has been said holds good of him. As everything in Nature has its
forces and qualities, which react in a definite way when definitely
affected, and constitute its character, man also has his *character,*
from which the motives call forth his actions with necessity. In this
manner of conduct his empirical character reveals itself, but in this
again his intelligible character, the will in itself, whose determined
phenomenon he is. But man is the most complete phenomenon
of will, and, as we explained in the Second Book, he had to be enlightened with so high a degree of knowledge in order to maintain
himself in existence, that in it a perfectly adequate copy or repetition of the nature of the world under the form of the idea became possible: this is the comprehension of the Ideas, the pure
mirror of the world, as we learnt in the Third Book. Thus in
man the will can attain to full self-consciousness, to distinct and
exhaustive knowledge of its own nature, as it mirrors itself in the
whole world. We saw in the preceding book that art springs from
the actual presence of this degree of knowledge; and at the end of
our whole work it will further appear that, through the same
knowledge, in that the will relates it to itself, a suppression and
self-denial of the will in its most perfect manifestation is possible. So that the freedom which otherwise, as belonging to the
thing-in-itself, can never show itself in the phenomenon, in such
a case does also appear in it, and, by abolishing the nature which
lies at the foundation of the phenomenon, while the latter itself
still continues to exist in time, it brings about a contradiction of
the phenomenon with itself, and in this way exhibits the phenomena
of holiness and self-renunciation. But all this can only be fully
understood at the end of this book. What has just been said
merely affords a preliminary and general indication of how man
is distinguished from all the other phenomena of will by the fact
that freedom, *i. e.,* independence of the principle of sufficient
reason, which only belongs to the will as thing-in-itself, and contradicts the phenomenon, may yet possibly, in his case, appear in
the phenomenon also, where, however, it necessarily exhibits

itself as a contradiction of the phenomenon with itself. In this sense, not only the will in itself, but man also may certainly be called free, and thus distinguished from all other beings. But how this is to be understood can only become clear through all that is to follow, and for the present we must turn away from it altogether. For, in the first place, we must beware of the error that the action of the individual definite man is subject to no necessity, *i. e.,* that the power of the motive is less certain than the power of the cause, or the following of the conclusion from the premises. The freedom of the will as thing-in-itself, if, as has been said, we abstract from the entirely exceptional case mentioned above, by no means extends directly to its phenomenon, not even in the case in which this reaches the highest grade of its visibility, and thus does not extend to the rational animal endowed with individual character, *i. e.,* the person. The person is never free although he is the phenomenon of a free will; for he is already the determined phenomenon of the free volition of this will, and, because he enters the form of every object, the principle of sufficient reason, he develops indeed the unity of that will in a multiplicity of actions, but on account of the timeless unity of that volition in itself, this multiplicity exhibits in itself the regular conformity to law of a force of Nature. Since, however, it is that free volition that becomes visible in the person and the whole of his conduct, relating itself to him as the concept to the definition, every individual action of the person is to be ascribed to the free will, and directly proclaims itself as such in consciousness. Therefore, as was said in the Second Book, every one regards himself *a priori* (*i. e.,* here in this original feeling) as free in his individual actions, in the sense that in every given case every action is possible for him, and he only recognizes *a posteriori* from experience and reflection upon experience that his actions take place with absolute necessity from the coincidence of his character with his motives. Hence it arises that every uncultured man, following his feeling, ardently defends complete freedom in particular actions, while the great thinkers of all ages, and indeed the more profound systems of religion, have denied it. But whoever has come to see clearly that the whole nature of man is will, and he himself only a phenomenon of this will, and that such a phenomenon has, even from the subject itself, the principle of sufficient reason as its necessary form, which here appears as the law of motivation,—such a man will regard it as just as absurd to doubt the inevitable nature of an action when the motive is presented to a given character, as to doubt that the three angles of any triangle are together equal to two right angles. Priestly has very sufficiently proved the necessity of the individual action in his "Doctrine of Philosophical Necessity"; but Kant, whose merit is this respect is specially great, first proved the coexistence of this necessity with the freedom of the will in itself, *i. e.,* apart from the phenomenon, by establishing the distinction between the intelligible and the empirical character. I entirely adhere to this distinction, for the former is the will as thing-in-itself so far as it appears in a definite individual in a definite grade, and the latter is this phenomenon itself as it exhibits itself in time in the mode of action, and in space in the physical structure. In order to make the relation of the two comprehensible, the best expression is that which I have already used in the introductory essay, that the intelligible character of every man is to be regarded as an act of will outside time, and therefore indivisible and unchangeable, and the manifestation of this act of will developed and broken up in time and space and all the forms of the principle of sufficient reason is the empirical character as it exhibits itself for experience in the whole conduct and life of this man. As the whole tree is only the constantly repeated manifestation of one and the same tendency, which exhibits itself in its simplest form in the fibre, and recurs and is easily recognized in the construction of the leaf, shoot, branch, and trunk, so all a man's deeds are merely the constantly repeated expression, somewhat varied in form, of his intelligible character, and the induction based on the sum of all these expressions gives us his empirical character. For the rest, I shall not at this point repeat in my own words Kant's masterly exposition, but presuppose it as known. . . .

The motives which determine the manifestation of the character or conduct influence it through the medium of knowledge. But knowledge is changeable, and often vacillates between truth and error, yet, as a rule, is rectified more and more in the course of life, though certainly in very different degrees. Therefore the conduct of a man may be observably altered without justifying us in concluding that his character has been changed. What the man really and in general wills, the striving of his inmost nature, and the end he pursues in accordance with it, this we can never change by influence upon him from without by instruction, otherwise we could transform him. Seneca says admirably, *velle non discitur;* [4] whereby he preferred truth to his Stoic philosophers, who taught διδακτην ειναι την αρετην (*doceri posse virtutem*).[5] From without the will can only be affected by motives. But these can never change the will itself; for they have power over it only under the presupposition that it is precisely such as it is. All that they can do is thus to alter the direction of its effort, *i. e.,* bring it about that it shall seek in another way than it has hitherto done that which it invariably seeks. Therefore instruction, improved knowledge, in other words, influence from without, may indeed teach the will that it erred in the means it employed, and can therefore bring it about that the end after which it strives once for all according to its inner nature shall be pursued on an entirely different path and in an entirely different object from what has hitherto been the case. But it can never bring about that the will shall will something actually different from what it has hitherto willed; this remains unchangeable, for the will is simply this willing itself, which would have to be abolished. The former, however, the possible modification of knowledge, and through knowledge of conduct, extends so far that the will seeks to attain its unalterable end, for example, Mohammed's paradise, at one time in the real world, at another time in a world of imagination, adapting the means to each, and thus in the first case applying prudence, might, and fraud, and in the second case, abstinence, justice, alms, and pilgrimages to Mecca. But its effort itself has not therefore changed, still less the will itself. Thus, although its action certainly shows itself very different at different times, its willing has yet remained precisely the same. *Velle non discitur.*

For motives to act, it is necessary not only that they should be present, but that they should be known; for, according to a very good expression of the schoolmen, which we referred to once be-

---

[4] "To wish cannot be learned."
[5] "Virtue can be taught."

fore, *causa finalis movet non secundum suum esse reale; sed secundum esse cognitum.* For example, in order that the relation may appear that exists in a given man between egoism and sympathy, it is not sufficient that he should possess wealth and see others in want, but he must also know what he can do with his wealth, both for himself and for others: not only must the suffering of others be presented to him, but he must know both what suffering and also what pleasure is. Perhaps, on a first occasion, he did not know all this so well as on a second; and if, on a similar occasion, he acts differently, this arises simply from the fact that the circumstances were really different, as regards the part of them that depends on his knowing them, although they seem to be the same. As ignorance of actually existing circumstances robs them of their influence, so, on the other hand, entirely imaginary circumstances may act as if they were real, not only in the case of a particular deception, but also in general and continuously. For example, if a man is firmly persuaded that every good action will be repaid him a hundredfold in a future life, such a conviction affects him in precisely the same way as a good bill of exchange at a very long date, and he can give from mere egoism, as from another point of view he would take from egoism. He has not changed himself: *velle non discitur.* It is on account of this great influence of knowledge upon action, while the will remains unchangeable, that the character develops and its different features appear only little by little. Therefore it shows itself different at every period of life, and an impetuous, wild youth may be succeeded by a staid, sober, manly age. Especially what is bad in the character will always come out more strongly with time, yet sometimes it occurs that passions which a man gave way to in his youth are afterwards voluntarily restrained, simply because the motives opposed to them have only then come into knowledge. Hence, also, we are all innocent to begin with, and this merely means that neither we nor others know the evil of our own nature; it only appears with the motives, and only in time do the motives appear in knowledge. Finally we come to know ourselves as quite different from what *a priori* we supposed ourselves to be, and then we are often terrified at ourselves.

Repentance never proceeds from a change of the will (which

is impossible), but from a change of knowledge. The essential and peculiar in what I have always willed I must still continue to will; for I myself am this will which lies outside time and change. I can therefore never repent of what I have willed, though I can repent of what I have done; because, led by false conceptions, I did something that was not in conformity with my will. The discovery of this through fuller knowledge is *repentance.* This extends not merely to worldly wisdom, to the choice of the means, and the judgment of the appropriateness of the end to my own will, but also to what is properly ethical. For example, I may have acted more egotistically than is in accordance with my character, led astray by exaggerated ideas of the need in which I myself stood, or of the craft, falseness, and wickedness of others, or because I hurried too much, *i. e.,* acted without deliberation, determined not by motives distinctly known *in abstracto,* but by merely perceived motives, by the present and the emotion which it excited, and which was so strong that I had not properly the use of my reason; but the return of reflection is thus here also merely corrected knowledge, and from this repentance may proceed, which always proclaims itself by making amends for the past, as far as is possible. Yet it must be observed that, in order to deceive themselves, men prearrange what seem to be hasty errors, but are really secretly considered actions. For we deceive and flatter no one through such fine devices as ourselves. The converse of the case we have given may also occur. I may be misled by too good an opinion of others, or want of knowledge of the relative value of the good things of life, or some abstract dogma in which I have since lost faith, and thus I may act less egotistically than is in keeping with my character, and lay up for myself repentance of another kind. Thus repentance is always corrected knowledge of the relation of an act to its special intention. When the will reveals its Ideas in space alone, *i. e.,* through mere form, the matter in which other Ideas—in this case natural forces—already reign, resists the will, and seldom allows the form that is striving after visibility to appear in perfect purity and distinctness, *i. e.,* in perfect beauty. And there is an analogous hindrance to the will as it reveals itself in time alone, *i. e.,* through actions, in the knowledge which seldom gives it the data quite correctly, so that the action which takes places does not accurately correspond to the will, and leads to repentance. Repentance thus always proceeds from corrected knowledge, not from the change of the will, which is impossible. Anguish of conscience for past deeds is anything but repentance. It is pain at the knowledge of oneself in one's inmost nature, *i. e.,* as will. It rests precisely on the certainty that we have still the same will. If the will were changed, and therefore the anguish of conscience mere repentance, it would cease to exist. The past could then no longer give us pain, for it exhibited the expressions of a will which is no longer that of him who has repented. We shall explain the significance of anguish of conscience in detail farther on.

The influence which knowledge, as the medium of motives, exerts, not indeed upon the will itself, but upon its appearance in actions, is also the source of the principal distinction between the action of men and that of brutes, for their methods of knowledge are different. The brute has only knowledge of perception, the man, through reason, has also abstract ideas, conceptions. Now, although man and brute are with equal necessity determined by their motives, yet man, as distinguished from the brute, has a complete *choice,* which has often been regarded as a freedom of the will in particular actions, although it is nothing but the possibility of a thoroughly-fought-out battle between several motives, the strongest of which then determines it with necessity. For this the motives must have assumed the form of abstract thoughts, because it is really only by means of these that deliberation, *i. e.,* a weighing of opposite reasons for action, is possible. In the case of the brute there can only be a choice between perceptible motives presented to it, so that the choice is limited to the narrow sphere of its present sensuous perception. Therefore the necessity of the determination of the will by the motive, which is like that of the effect by the cause, can be exhibited perceptibly and directly only in the case of the brute, because here the spectator has the motives just as directly before his eyes as their effect; while in the case of man the motives are almost always abstract ideas, which are not communicated to the spectator, and even for the actor himself the necessity of their effect is hidden behind their conflict. For only *in abstracto* can several ideas, as judgments and chains of conclusions, lie beside each other in consciousness, and then, free from all determination of time, work against each other till the stronger overcomes the rest and determines the will. This is the complete *choice* or power of deliberation which man has as distinguished from the brute, and on account of which freedom of the will has been attributed to him, in the belief that his willing is a mere result of the operations of his intellect, without a definite tendency which serves as its basis; while, in truth, the motives work only on the foundation and under the presupposition of his definite tendency, which in his case is individual, *i. e.,* a character. . . . For the rest, this power of deliberation which man possesses is one of those things that make his existence so much more miserable than that of the brute. For in general our greatest sufferings do not lie in the present as ideas of perception or as immediate feelings; but in the reason, as abstract conceptions, painful thoughts, from which the brute, which lives only in the present, and therefore in enviable carelessness, is entirely free.

It seems to have been the dependence, which we have shown, of the human power of deliberation upon the faculty of abstract thinking, and thus also of judging and drawing conclusions also, that led both Descartes and Spinoza to identify the decisions of the will with the faculty of asserting and denying (the faculty of judgment). From this Descartes deduced the doctrine that the will, which, according to him, is indifferently free, is the source of sin, and also of all theoretical error. And Spinoza, on the other hand, concluded that the will is necessarily determined by the motives, as the judgment is by the reasons. The latter doctrine is in a sense true, but it appears as a true conclusion from false premises.

The distinction we have established between the ways in which the brute and man are respectively moved by motives exerts a very wide influence upon the nature of both, and has most to do with the complete and obvious differences of their existence. While an idea of perception is in every case the motive which determines the brute, the man strives to exclude this kind of motivation altogether, and to determine himself entirely by abstract ideas. Thus he uses his prerogative of reason to the greatest possible advantage. Independent of the present, he neither chooses nor avoids the passing pleasure or pain, but reflects on the consequences of both. In most cases, setting aside quite insignificant actions, we are determined by abstract, thought motives, not present impressions. Therefore all particular privation for the moment is for us comparatively light, but all renunciation is terribly hard; for the former concerns only the fleeting present, but the latter concerns the future, and includes in itself innumerable privations, of which it is the equivalent. The causes of our pain, as of our pleasure, lie for the most part, not in the real present, but merely in abstract thoughts. It is these which are often unbearable to us—inflict torments in comparison with which all the sufferings of the animal world are very small; for even our own physical pain is not felt at all when they are present. Indeed, in the case of keen mental suffering, we even inflict physical suffering on ourselves merely to distract our attention from the former to the latter. This is why, in great mental anguish, men tear their hair, beat their breasts, lacerate their faces, or roll on the floor, for all these are in reality only violent means of diverting the mind from an unbearable thought. Just because mental pain, being much greater, makes us insensible to physical pain, suicide is very easy to the person who is in despair, or who is consumed by morbid depression, even though formerly, in comfortable circumstances, he recoiled at the thought of it. In the same way care and passion (thus the play of thought) wear out the body oftener and more than physical hardships. And in accordance with this Epictetus rightly says: Ταρασσει τους ανθρωπους ου τα πραγματα, αλλα τα περι των πραγματων δογματα (*Perturbant homines non res ipsœ, sed de rebus decreta*) (V.);[6] and Seneca: *Plura sunt quœ nos terrent, quam quœ premunt, et sœpius opinione quam re laboramus* (Ep., 5).[7] Eulenspiegel also admirably bantered human nature, for going uphill he laughed, and going down hill he wept. Indeed, children who have hurt themselves often cry, not at the pain, but at the thought of the pain which is awakened when some one condoles with them. Such great differences in conduct and in life arise from the diversity between

[6] "Men are disturbed not by things themselves, but by what they think of them."

[7] "More things terrify us than those that are at hand; and we suffer more often from opinion than from reality."

the methods of knowledge of the brute and man. Further, the appearance of the distinct and decided individual character, the principal distinction between man and the brute, which has scarcely more than the character of the species, is conditioned by the choice between several motives, which is possible only through abstract conceptions. For only after a choice has been made are the resolutions, which vary in different individuals, an indication of the individual character which is different in each; while the action of the brute depends only upon the presence or absence of the impression, supposing this impression to be in general a motive for its species. And, finally, in the case of man, only the resolve, and not the mere wish, is a valid indication of his character both for himself and for others; but the resolve becomes for himself, as for others, a certain fact only through the deed. The wish is merely the necessary consequence of the present impression, whether of the outward stimulus, or the inward passing mood; and is therefore as immediately necessary and devoid of consideration as the action of the brute. Therefore, like the action of the brute, it merely expresses the character of the species, not that of the individual, *i. e.,* it indicates merely what *man in general,* not what the individual who experiences the wish, is capable of doing. The deed alone,—because as human action it always requires a certain deliberation, and because as a rule a man has command of his reason, is considerate, *i. e.,* decides in accordance with considered and abstract motives,—is the expression of the intelligible maxims of his conduct, the result of his inmost willing, and is related as a letter to the word that stands for his empirical character, itself merely the temporal expression of his intelligible character. In a healthy mind, therefore, only deeds oppress the conscience, not wishes and thoughts; for it is only our deeds that hold up to us the mirror of our will. The deed referred to above, that is entirely unconsidered and is really committed in blind passion, is to a certain extent an intermediate thing between the mere wish and the resolve. Therefore, by true repentance, which, however, shows itself as action also, it can be obliterated, as a falsely drawn line, from that picture of our will which our course of life is. I may insert the remark here, as a very good comparison, that the relation between wish and deed has a purely accidental but accurate analogy with that between the accumulation and discharge of electricity.

As the result of the whole of this discussion of the freedom of the will and what relates to it, we find that although the will may, in itself and apart from the phenomenon, be called free and even omnipotent, yet in its particular phenomena enlightened by knowledge, as in men and brutes, it is determined by motives to which the special character regularly and necessarily responds, and always in the same way. We see that because of the possession on his part of abstract or rational knowledge, man, as distinguished from the brutes, has a *choice,* which makes him only the scene of the conflict of his motives, without withdrawing him from their control. This choice is therefore certainly the condition of the possibility of the complete expression of the individual character, but is by no means to be regarded as freedom of the particular volition, *i. e.,* independence of the law of causality, the necessity of which extends to man as to every other phenomenon. Thus the difference between human volition and that of the brutes, which is introduced by reason or knowledge through concepts, extends to the point we have indicated, and no farther. But, what is quite a different thing, there may arise a phenomenon of the human will which is quite impossible in the brute creation, if man altogether lays aside the knowledge of particular things as such which is subordinate to the principle of sufficient reason, and by means of his knowledge of the Ideas sees through the *principium individuationis.* Then an actual appearance of the real freedom of the will as a thing-in-itself is possible, by which the phenomenon comes into a sort of contradiction with itself, as is indicated by the word self-renunciation; and, finally, the "in-itself" of its nature suppresses itself. But this, the one, real, and direct expression of the freedom of the will in itself in the phenomenon, cannot be distinctly explained here, but will form the subject of the concluding part of our work.

Now that we have shown clearly in these pages the unalterable nature of the empirical character, which is just the unfolding of the intelligible character that lies outside time, together with the necessity with which actions follow upon its contact with motives, we hasten to anticipate an argument which may very easily be drawn from this in the interest of bad dispositions. Our character is to be regarded as the temporal unfolding of an extra-temporal, and therefore indivisible and unalterable, act of will, or an intelligible character. This necessarily determines all that is essential in our conduct in life, *i. e.,* its ethical content, which must express itself in accordance with it in its phenomenal appearance, the empirical character; while only what is unessential in this, the outward form of our course of life, depends upon the forms in which the motives present themselves. It might, therefore, be inferred that it is a waste of trouble to endeavour to improve one's character, and that it is wiser to submit to the inevitable, and gratify every inclination at once, even if it is bad. But this is precisely the same thing as the theory of an inevitable fate which is called in recent times Turkish faith. Its true refutation, as it is supposed to have been given by Chrysippus, is explained by Cicero in his book *De Fato,* ch. 12, 13.

Though everything may be regarded as irrevocably predetermined by fate, yet it is so only through the medium of the chain of causes; therefore in no case can it be determined that an effect shall appear without its cause. Thus it is not simply the event that is predetermined, but the event as the consequence of preceding causes; so that fate does not decide the consequence alone, but also the means as the consequence of which it is destined to appear. Accordingly, if some means is not present, it is certain that the consequence also will not be present: each is always present in accordance with the determination of fate, but this is never known to us till afterwards.

As events always take place according to fate, *i. e.,* according to the infinite concatenation of causes, so our actions always take place according to our intelligible character. But just as we do not know the former beforehand, so no *a priori* insight is given us into the latter, but we come to know ourselves only as we come to know other persons *a posteriori* through experience. If the intelligible character involved that we could form a good resolution only after a long conflict with a bad disposition, this conflict would have to come first and be waited for. Reflection on the unalterable nature of the character, on the unity of the source from which all our actions flow, must not mislead us into claiming the decision of the character in favour of one side or the other; it is in the resolve that follows that we shall see what manner of men we are, and mirror ourselves in our actions. This is the explanation of the satisfaction or the anguish of soul with which we look back on the course of our past life. Both are experienced, not because these past deeds have still an existence; they are past, they have been, and now are no more; but their great importance for us lies in their significance, lies in the fact that these deeds are the expression of the character, the mirror of the will, in which we look and recognize our inmost self, the kernel of our will. Because we experience this not before, but only after, it behooves us to strive and fight in time, in order that the picture we produce by our deeds may be such that the contemplation of it may calm us as much as possible, instead of harass us. The significance of this consolation or anguish of soul will, as we have said, be inquired into farther on; but to this place there belongs the inquiry which follows, and which stands by itself.

Besides the intelligible and the empirical character, we must mention a third which is different from them both, the *acquired character,* which one receives in life only through contact with the world, and which is referred to when one is praised as a man of character or censured as being without character. Certainly one might suppose that, since the empirical character, as the phenomenon of the intelligible, is unalterable, and, like every natural phenomenon, is consistent with itself, man would always have to appear like himself and consistent, and would therefore have no need to acquire a character artificially by experience and reflection. But the case is otherwise, and although a man is always the same, yet he does not always understand himself, but often mistakes himself, till he has in some degree acquired real self-knowledge. The empirical character, as a mere natural tendency, is in itself irrational; nay, more, its expressions are disturbed by reason, all the more so the more intellect and power of thought the man has; for these always keep before him what becomes *man in general* as the character of the species, and what is possible for him both in will and in deed. This makes it the more difficult for him to see how much his individuality enables him to will and to accomplish. He finds in himself the germs of all the various human pursuits and powers, but the difference of degree in which they exist in his individuality is not clear to him in the absence of experience; and if he now applies himself to the pursuits which alone correspond to his character, he yet feels, especially at particular moments and in particular moods, the inclination to directly opposite pursuits which cannot be combined with them, but must be entirely suppressed if he desires to follow the former undisturbed. For as our physical path upon earth is always merely a line, not an extended surface, so in life, if we desire to grasp and possess one thing, we must renounce and leave innumerable others on the right hand and on the left. If we cannot make up our minds to this, but, like children at the fair, snatch at everything that attracts us in passing, we are making the perverse endeavour to change the line of our path into an extended surface; we run in a zigzag, skip about like a will o' the wisp, and attain to nothing. Or, to use another comparison, as, according to Hobbes' philosophy of law, every one has an original right to everything but an exclusive right to nothing; yet can obtain an exclusive right to particular things by renouncing his right to all the rest, while others, on their part, do likewise with regard to what he has chosen; so is it in life, in which some definite pursuit, whether it be pleasure, honour, wealth, science, art, or virtue, can only be followed with seriousness and success when all claims that are foreign to it are given up, when everything else is renounced. Accordingly, the mere will and the mere ability are not sufficient, but a man must also *know* what he wills, and *know* what he can do; only then will he show character, and only then can he accomplish something right. Until he attains to that, notwithstanding the natural consistency of the empirical character, he is without character. And although, on the whole, he must remain true to himself, and fulfil his course, led by his dæmon, yet his path will not be a straight line, but wavering and uneven. He will hesitate, deviate, turn back, lay up for himself repentance and pain. And all this is because, in great and small, he sees before him all that is possible and attainable for man in general, but does not know what part of all this is alone suitable for him, can be accomplished by him, and is alone enjoyable by him. He will, therefore, envy many men on account of a position and circumstances which are yet only suitable to their characters and not to his, and in which he would feel unhappy, if indeed he found them endurable at all. For as a fish is at home only in water, a bird in the air, a mole in the earth, so every man is at home only in the atmosphere suitable to him. For example, not all men can breathe the air of court life. From deficiency of proper insight into all this, many a man will make all kinds of abortive attempts, will do violence to his character in particular, and yet, on the whole, will have to yield to it again; and what he thus painfully attains will give him no pleasure; what he thus learns will remain dead; even in an ethical regard, a deed that is too noble for his character, that has not sprung from pure, direct impulse, but from a concept, a dogma, will lose all merit, even in his own eyes, through subsequent egoistical repentance. *Velle non discitur.* We become conscious of the inflexibility of another person's character only through experience, and till then we childishly believe that it is possible, by means of rational ideas, by prayers and entreaties, by example and noblemindedness, ever to persuade any one to leave his own way, to change his course of conduct, to depart from his mode of thinking, or even to extend his capacities: so is it also with ourselves. We must first learn from experience what we desire and what we can do. Till then we know it not, we are without character, and must often be driven back to our own way by hard blows from without. But if we have finally learnt it, then we have attained to what in the world is called character, the *acquired character*. This is accordingly nothing but the most perfect knowledge possible of our own individuality. It is the abstract, and consequently distinct, knowledge of the unalterable qualities of our own empirical character, and of the measure and direction of our mental and physical powers, and thus of the whole strength and weakness of our own individuality. This places us in a position to carry out deliberately and methodically the rôle which belongs to our own person, and to fill up the gaps which caprices or weaknesses produce in it, under the guidance of fixed conceptions. This rôle is in itself unchangeably determined once for all, but hitherto we have allowed it to follow its natural course without any rule. We have now brought to distinct consciousness maxims which are always present to us the form of conduct which is necessarily determined by our own individual nature, and now we conduct it in accordance with them as deliberately as if we had learned it; without ever falling into error through the passing influence of the mood or the impression of the present, without being checked by the bitterness or sweetness of some particular thing we meet with on our path, without delay, without hesitation, without inconsistency. We shall now no longer, as novices, wait, attempt, and grope about in order to see what we really desire and are able to do, but we know this once for all, and in every choice we have only to apply general principles to particular cases, and arrive at once at a decision. We know our will in general, and do not allow ourselves to be led by the passing mood or by solicitations from without to resolve in particular cases what is contrary to it as a whole. We know in the same way the nature and the measure of our strength and our weakness, and thereby are spared much suffering. For we experience no real pleasure except in the use and feeling of our own powers, and the greatest pain is the conscious deficiency of our powers where we need them. If, now, we have discovered where our strength and our weakness lie, we will endeavour to cultivate, employ, and in every way make use of those talents which are naturally prominent in us. We will always turn to those occupations in which they are valuable and to the purpose, and entirely avoid, even with self-renunciation, those pursuits for which we have naturally little aptitude; we will beware of attempting that in which we have no chance of succeeding. Only he who has attained to this will constantly and with full consciousness is completely himself, and will never fail himself at the critical moment, because he will always have known what he could expect from himself. He will often enjoy the satisfaction of feeling his strength, and seldom experience the pain of being reminded of his weakness. The latter is mortification, which causes perhaps the greatest of mental sufferings; therefore it is far more endurable to have our misfortune brought clearly before us than our incapacity. And, further, if we are thus fully acquainted with our strength and our weakness, we will not attempt to make a show of powers which we do not possess; we will not play with base coin, for all such dissimulation misses the mark in the end. For since the whole man is only the phenomenon of his will, nothing can be more perverse than to try, by means of reflection, to become something else than one is, for this is a direct contradiction of the will with itself. The imitation of the qualities and idiosyncrasies of others is much more shameful than to dress in other people's clothes; for it is the judgment of our own worthlessness pronounced by ourselves. Knowledge of our own mind and its capacities of every kind, and their unalterable limits, is in this respect the surest way to the attainment of the greatest possible contentment with ourselves. For it holds good of inward as of outward circumstances that there is for us no consolation so effective as the complete certainty of unalterable necessity. No evil that befalls us pains us so much as the thought of the circumstances by which it might have been warded off. Therefore nothing comforts us so effectually as the consideration of what has happened from the standpoint of necessity, from which all accidents appear as tools in the hand of an overruling fate, and we therefore recognize the evil that has come to us as inevitably produced by the conflict of inner and outer circumstances; in other words, fatalism. We really only complain and storm so long as we hope either to affect others or to excite ourselves to unheard-of efforts. But children and grown-up people know very well to yield contentedly as soon as they clearly see that it absolutely cannot be otherwise. We are like the entrapped elephants, that rage and struggle for many days, till they see that it is useless, and then suddenly offer their necks quietly to the yoke, tamed for ever. We are like King David, who, as long as his son still lived, unceasingly importuned Jehovah with prayers, and behaved himself as if in despair; but as soon as his son was dead, thought no longer about it. Hence it arises that innumerable permanent ills, such as lameness, poverty, low estate, ugliness, a disagreeable dwelling-place, are borne with indifference by innumerable persons, and are no longer felt, like healed wounds, just because these persons know that inward or outward necessity renders it impossible that any change can take place in these things; while those who are more fortunate cannot understand how such misfortunes can be borne. Now as with outward necessity, so also with inward; nothing reconciles so thoroughly as a distinct knowledge of it. If we have once for all distinctly recognized not only our good qualities and our strength, but also our defects and weaknesses, established our aim accordingly, and rest satisfied concerning what cannot be attained, we thus escape in the surest way, as far as our individuality permits, the bitterest of all sorrows, discontentment with ourselves, which is the inevitable result of ignorance of our own individuality, of false conceit and the audacity that proceeds from it.

So much with regard to the *acquired character,* which, indeed, is not of so much importance for ethics proper as for life in the world. But its investigation was related as that of a third species to the investigation of the intelligible and the empirical character, in regard to which we were obliged to enter upon a somewhat detailed inquiry in order to bring out clearly how in all its phenomena the will is subject to necessity, while yet in itself it may be called free and even omnipotent.

§ 56

This freedom, this omnipotence, as the expression of which the whole visible world exists and progressively develops in accordance with the laws which belong to the form of knowledge, can now, at the point at which in its most perfect manifestation it has attained to the completely adequate knowledge of its own nature, express itself anew in two ways. Either it wills here, at the summit of mental endowment and self-consciousness, simply what it willed before blindly and unconsciously, and if so, knowledge always remains its *motive* in the whole as in the particular case. Or, conversely, this knowledge becomes for it a *quieter,* which appeases and suppresses all willing. This is that assertion and denial of the will to live which was stated above in general terms. As, in the reference of individual conduct, a general, not a particular manifestation of will, it does not disturb and modify the development of the character, nor does it find its expression in particular actions; but, neither by an ever more marked appearance of the whole method of action it has followed hitherto, or conversely by the entire suppression of it, it expresses in a living form the maxims which the will has freely adopted in accordance with the knowledge it has now attained to. By the explanations we have just given of freedom, necessity, and character, we have somewhat facilitated and prepared the way for the clearer development of all this, which is the principal subject of this last book. But we shall have done so still more when we have turned our attention to life itself, the willing or not willing of which is the great question, and have endeavoured to find out generally what the will itself, which is everywhere the inmost nature of this life, will really attain by its assertion—in what way and to what extent this assertion satisfies or can satisfy the will; in short, what is generally and mainly to be regarded as its position in this its own world, which in every relation belongs to it.

First of all, I wish the reader to recall the passage with which we closed the Second Book,—a passage occasioned by the question, which met us then, as to the end and aim of the will. Instead of the answer to this question, it appeared clearly before us how, in all the grades of its manifestations, from the lowest to the highest, the will dispenses altogether with a final goal and aim. It always strives, for striving is its sole nature, which no attained goal can put an end to. Therefore it is not susceptible of any final satisfaction, but can only be restrained by hindrances, while in itself it goes on for ever. We see this in the simplest of all natural phenomena, gravity, which does not cease to strive and press towards a mathematical centre to reach which would be the annihilation both of itself and matter, and would not cease even if the whole universe were already rolled into one ball. We see it in the other simple natural phenomena. A solid tends towards fluidity either by melting or dissolving, for only so will its chemical forces be free; rigidity is the imprisonment in which it is held by cold. The fluid tends towards the gaseous state, into which it passes at once as soon as all pressure is removed from it. No body is without relationship, *i. e.,* without tendency or without desire and longing, as Jacob Böhme would say. Electricity transmits its inner self-repulsion to infinity, though the mass of the earth absorbs the effect. Galvanism is certainly, so long as the pile is working, an aimless, unceasingly repeated act of repulsion and attraction. The existence of the plant is just such a restless, never satisfied striving, a ceaseless tendency through ever-ascending forms, till the end, the seed, becomes a new starting-point; and this repeated *ad infinitum*—nowhere an end, nowhere a final satisfaction, nowhere a resting-place. It will also be remembered, from the Second Book, that the multitude of natural forces and organized forms everywhere strive with each other for the matter in which they desire to appear, for each of them possesses only what it has wrested from the others; and thus a constant internecine war is waged, from which, for the most part, arises the resistance through which that striving, which constitutes the inner nature of everything, is at all points hindered; struggles in vain, yet, from its nature, cannot leave off; toils on laboriously till this phenomenon dies, when others eagerly seize its place and its matter.

We have long since recognized this striving, which constitutes the kernel and in-itself of everything, as identical with that which in us, where it manifests itself most distinctly in the light of the fullest consciousness, is called *will*. Its hindrance through an obstacle which places itself between it and its temporary aim we call *suffering*, and, on the other hand, its attainment of the end satisfaction, well-being, happiness. We may also transfer this terminology to the phenomena of the unconscious world, for though weaker in degree, they are identical in nature. Then we see them involved in constant suffering, and without any continuing happiness. For all effort springs from defect—from discontent with one's estate—is thus suffering so long as it is not satisfied; but no satisfaction is lasting, rather it is always merely the starting-point of a new effort. The striving we see everywhere hindered in many ways, everywhere in conflict, and therefore always under the form of suffering. Thus, if there is no final end of striving, there is no measure and end of suffering.

But what we only discover in unconscious Nature by sharpened observation, and with an effort, presents itself distinctly to us in the intelligent world in the life of animals, whose constant suffering is easily proved. But without lingering over these intermediate grades, we shall turn to the life of man, in which all this appears with the greatest distinctness, illuminated by the clearest knowledge; for as the phenomenon of will becomes more complete, the suffering also becomes more and more apparent. In the plant there is as yet no sensibility, and therefore no pain. A certain very small degree of suffering is experienced by the lowest species of animal life—infusoria and radiata; even in insects the capacity to feel and suffer is still limited. It first appears in a high degree with the complete nervous system of vertebrate animals, and always in a higher degree the more intelligence develops. Thus, in proportion as knowledge attains to distinctness, as consciousness ascends, pain also increases, and therefore reaches its highest degree in man. And then, again, the more distinctly a man knows, the more intelligent he is, the more pain he has; the man who is gifted with genius suffers most of all. In this sense, that is, with reference to the degree of knowledge in general, not mere abstract rational knowledge, I understand and use here that saying of the Preacher: *Qui auget scientiam, auget et dolorem.*[8] That philosophical painter or painting philosopher, Tischbein, has very beautifully expressed the accurate relation between the degree of consciousness and that of suffering by exhibiting it in a visible and clear form in a drawing. The upper half of his drawing represents women whose children have been stolen, and who in different groups and attitudes, express in many ways deep maternal pain, anguish, and despair. The lower half of the drawing represents sheep whose lambs have been taken away. They are arranged and grouped in precisely the same way; so that every human head, every human attitude of the upper half, has below a brute head and attitude corresponding to it. Thus we see distinctly how the pain which is possible in the dull brute consciousness is related to the violent grief, which becomes possible only through distinctness of knowledge and clearness of consciousness.

We desire to consider in this way, in *human existence*, the inner and essential destiny of will. Every one will easily recognize that same destiny expressed in various degrees in the life of the brutes, only more weakly, and may also convince himself to his own satisfaction, from the suffering animal world, *how essential to all life is suffering.*

[8] "He that increaseth knowledge increaseth sorrow."

§ 57

At every grade that is enlightened by knowledge, the will appears as an individual. The human individual finds himself as finite in infinite space and time, and consequently as a vanishing quantity compared with them. He is projected into them, and, on account of their unlimited nature, he has always a merely relative, never absolute *when* and *where* of his existence; for his place and duration are finite parts of what is infinite and boundless. His real existence is only in the present, whose unchecked flight into the past is a constant transition into death, a constant dying. For his past life, apart from its possible consequences for the present, and the testimony regarding the will that is expressed in it, is now entirely done with, dead, and no longer anything; and, therefore, it must be, as a matter of reason, indifferent to him whether the content of that past was pain or pleasure. But the present is always passing through his hands into the past; the future is quite uncertain and always short. Thus his existence, even when we consider only its formal side, is a constant hurrying of the present into the dead past, a constant dying. But if we look at it from the physical side; it is clear that, as our walking is admittedly merely a constantly prevented falling, the life of our body is only a constantly prevented dying, an ever-postponed death: finally, in the same way, the activity of our mind is a constantly deferred ennui. Every breath we draw wards off the death that is constantly intruding upon us. In this way we fight with it every moment, and again, at longer intervals, through every meal we eat, every sleep we take, every time we warm ourselves, &c. In the end, Death must conquer, for we became subject to him through birth, and he only plays for a little while with his prey before he swallows it up. We pursue our life, however, with great interest and much solicitude as long as possible, as we blow out a soap-bubble as long and as large as possible, although we know perfectly well that it will burst.

We saw that the inner being of unconscious nature is a constant striving without end and without rest. And this appears to us much more distinctly when we consider the nature of brutes and man. Willing and striving is its whole being, which may be very well compared to an unquenchable thirst. But the basis of all willing is need, deficiency, and thus pain. Consequently, the nature of brutes and man is subject to pain originally and through its very being. If, on the other hand, it lacks objects of desire, because it is at once deprived of them by a too easy satisfaction, a terrible void and ennui comes over it, *i e.,* its being and existence itself becomes an unbearable burden to it. Thus its life swings like a pendulum backwards and forwards between .pain and ennui. This has also had to express itself very oddly in this way; after man had transferred all pain and torments to hell, there then remained nothing over for heaven but ennui.

But the constant striving which constitutes the inner nature of every manifestation of will obtains its primary and most general foundation at the higher grades of objectification, from the fact that here the will manifests itself as a living body, with the iron command to nourish it; and what gives strength to this command is just that this body is nothing but the objectified will to live itself. Man, as the most complete objectification of that will, is in like measure also the most necessitous of all beings: he is through and through concrete willing and needing; he is a concretion of a thousand necessities. With these he stands upon the earth, left to himself, uncertain about everything except his own need and misery. Consequently the care for the maintenance of that existence under exacting demands, which are renewed every day, occupies, as a rule, the whole of human life. To this is directly related the second claim, that of the propagation of the species. At the same time he is threatened from all sides by the most different kinds of dangers, from which it requires constant watchfulness to escape. With cautious steps and casting anxious glances round him he pursues his path, for a thousand accidents and a thousand enemies lie in wait for him. Thus he went while yet a savage, thus he goes in civilized life; there is no security for him.

> "Qualibus in tenebris vitæ, quantisque periclis
>   Degitur hocc' ævi, quodcunque est!"—LUCR. ii., 15.[9]

[9] "In what darkness and in what perils our life is led, such as it is!"

The life of the great majority is only a constant struggle for this existence itself, with the certainty of losing it at last. But what enables them to endure this wearisome battle is not so much the love of life as the fear of death, which yet stands in the background as inevitable, and may come upon them at any moment. Life itself is a sea, full of rocks and whirlpools, which man avoids with the greatest care and solicitude, although he knows that even if he succeeds in getting through with all his efforts and skill, he yet by doing so comes nearer at every step to the greatest, the total, inevitable, and irremediable shipwreck, death; nay, even steers right upon it; this is the final goal of the laborious voyage, and worse for him than all the rocks from which he has escaped.

Now it is well worth observing that, on the one hand, the suffering and misery of life may easily increase to such an extent that death itself, in the flight from which the whole of life consists, becomes desirable, and we hasten towards it voluntarily; and again, on the other hand, that as soon as want and suffering permit rest to a man, ennui is at once so near that he necessarily requires diversion. The striving after existence is what occupies all living things and maintains them in motion. But when existence is assured, then they know not what to do with it; thus the second thing that sets them in motion is the effort to get free from the burden of existence, to make it cease to be felt, "to kill time," *i. e.,* to escape from ennui. Accordingly we see that almost all men who are secure from want and care, now that at last they have thrown off all other burdens, become a burden to themselves, and regard as a gain every hour they succeed in getting through, and thus every diminution of the very life which, till then, they have employed all their powers to maintain as long as possible. Ennui is by no means an evil to be lightly esteemed; in the end it depicts on the countenance real despair. It makes beings who love each other so little as men do, seek each other eagerly, and thus becomes the source of social intercourse. Moreover, even from motives of policy, public precautions are everywhere taken against it, as against other universal calamities. For this evil may drive men to the greatest excesses, just as much as its opposite extreme, famine: the people require *panem et circenses*.[10] The strict penitentiary system of Philadelphia makes use of ennui alone as a means of punishment, through solitary confinement and idleness, and it is found so terrible that it has even led prisoners to commit suicide. As want is the constant scourge of the people, so ennui is that of the fashionable world. In middle-class life ennui is represented by the Sunday, and want by the six week-days.

Thus between desiring and attaining all human life flows on throughout. The wish is, in its nature, pain; the attainment soon begets satiety: the end was only apparent; possession takes away the charm; the wish, the need, presents itself under a new form; when it does not, then follows desolateness, emptiness, ennui, against which the conflict is just as painful as against want. That wish and satisfaction should follow each other neither too quickly nor too slowly reduces the suffering, which both occasion to the smallest amount, and constitutes the happiest life. For that which we might otherwise call the most beautiful part of life, its purest joy, if it were only because it lifts us out of real existence and transforms us into disinterested spectators of it—that is, pure knowledge, which is foreign to all willing, the pleasure of the beautiful, the true delight in art—this is granted only to a very few, because it demands rare talents, and to these few only as a passing dream. And then, even these few, on account of their higher intellectual power, are made susceptible of far greater suffering than duller minds can ever feel, and are also placed in lonely isolation by a nature which is obviously different from that of others; thus here also accounts are squared. But to the great majority of men purely intellectual pleasures are not accessible. They are almost quite incapable of the joys which lie in pure knowledge. They are entirely given up to willing. If, therefore, anything is to win their sympathy, to be *interesting* to them, it must (as is implied in the meaning of the word) in some way excite their *will,* even if it is only through a distant and merely problematical relation to it; the will must not be left altogether out of the question, for their existence lies far more in willing than in knowing,—action and reaction is their one element. We may find in trifles and everyday occurrences the naïve expressions

10 "Bread and circuses."

of this quality. Thus, for example, at any place worth seeing they may visit, they write their names, in order thus to react, to affect the place since it does not affect them. Again, when they see a strange rare animal, they cannot easily confine themselves merely to observing it; they must rouse it, tease it, play with it, merely to experience action and reaction; but this need for excitement of the will manifests itself very specially in the discovery and support of card-playing, which is quite peculiarly the expression of the miserable side of humanity.

But whatever nature and fortune may have done, whoever a man be and whatever he may possess, the pain which is essential to life cannot be thrown off. The ceaseless efforts to banish suffering accomplish no more than to make it change its form. It is essentially deficiency, want, care for the maintenance of life. If we succeed, which is very difficult, in removing pain in this form, it immediately assumes a thousand others, varying according to age and circumstances, such as lust, passionate love, jealousy, envy, hatred, anxiety, ambition, covetousness, sickness, &c., &c. If at last it can find entrance in no other form, it comes in the sad, grey garments of tediousness and ennui, against which we then strive in various ways. If finally we succeed in driving this away, we shall hardly do so without letting pain enter in one of its earlier forms, and the dance begin again from the beginning; for all human life is tossed backwards and forwards between pain and ennui. Depressing as this view of life is, I will draw attention, by the way, to an aspect of it from which consolation may be drawn, and perhaps even a stoical indifference to one's own present ills may be attained. For our impatience at these arises for the most part from the fact that we regard them as brought about by a chain of causes which might easily be different. We do not generally grieve over ills which are directly necessary and quite universal; for example, the necessity of age and of death, and many daily inconveniences. It is rather the consideration of the accidental nature of the circumstances that brought some sorrow just to us, that gives it its sting. But if we have recognized that pain, as such, is inevitable and essential to life, and that nothing depends upon chance but its mere fashion, the form under which it presents itself, that thus our present sorrow fills a place that, without it, would at once be occupied by another which now is excluded by it, and that therefore fate can affect us little in what is essential; such a reflection, if it were to become a living conviction, might produce a considerable degree of stoical equanimity, and very much lessen the anxious care for our own well-being. But, in fact, such a powerful control of reason over directly felt suffering seldom or never occurs.

Besides, through this view of the inevitableness of pain, of the supplanting of one pain by another, and the introduction of a new pain through the passing away of that which preceded it, one might be led to the paradoxical but not absurd hypothesis, that in every individual the measure of the pain essential to him was determined once for all by his nature, a measure which could neither remain empty, nor be more than filled, however much the form of the suffering might change. Thus his suffering and well-being would by no means be determined from without, but only through that measure, that natural disposition, which indeed might experience certain additions and diminutions from the physical condition at different times, but yet, on the whole, would remain the same, and would just be what is called the temperament, or, more accurately, the degree in which he might be εὐκολος or δυσκολος, as Plato expresses it in the First Book of the Republic, *i. e.,* in an easy or difficult mood. This hypothesis is supported not only by the well-known experience that great suffering makes all lesser ills cease to be felt, and conversely that freedom from great suffering makes even the most trifling inconveniences torment us and put us out of humour; but experience also teaches that if a great misfortune, at the mere thought of which we shuddered, actually befalls us, as soon as we have overcome the first pain of it, our disposition remains for the most part unchanged; and, conversely, that after the attainment of some happiness we have long desired, we do not feel ourselves on the whole and permanently very much better off and agreeably situated than before. Only the moment at which these changes occur affects us with unusual strength, as deep sorrow or exulting joy, but both soon pass away, for they are based upon illusion. For they do not spring from the immediately present pleasure or pain, but only from the opening up of a new future which is anticipated in them. Only by borrowing from the future could pain or pleasure be heightened so abnormally, and consequently not enduringly. It would follow, from the hypothesis advanced, that a large part of the feeling of suffering and of well-being would be subjective and determined *a priori*, as is the case with knowing; and we may add the following remarks as evidence in favour of it. Human cheerfulness or dejection are manifestly not determined by external circumstances, such as wealth and position, for we see at least as many glad faces among the poor as among the rich. Further, the motives which induce suicide are so very different, that we can assign no motive that is so great as to bring it about, even with great probability, in every character, and few that would be so small that the like of them had never caused it. Now although the degree of our serenity of sadness is not at all times the same, yet, in consequence of this view, we shall not attribute it to the change of outward circumstances, but to that of the inner condition, the physical state. For when an actual, though only temporary, increase of our serenity, even to the extent of joyfulness, takes place, it usually appears without any external occasion. It is true that we often see our pain arise only from some definite external relation, and are visibly oppressed and saddened by this only. Then we believe that if only this were taken away, the greatest contentment would necessarily ensue. But this is illusion. The measure of our pain and our happiness is on the whole, according to our hypothesis, subjectively determined for each point of time, and the motive for sadness is related to that, just as a blister which draws to a head all the bad humours otherwise distributed is related to the body. The pain which is at that period of time essential to our nature, and therefore cannot be shaken off, would, without the definite external cause of our suffering, be divided at a hundred points, and appear in the form of a hundred little annoyances and cares about things which we now entirely overlook, because our capacity for pain is already filled by that chief evil which has concentrated in a point all the suffering otherwise dispersed. This corresponds also to the observation that if a great and pressing care is lifted from our breast by its fortunate issue, another immediately takes its place, the whole material of which was already there before, yet could not come into consciousness as care because there was no capacity left for it, and therefore this material of care remained indistinct and unobserved in a cloudy form on the farthest horizon of consciousness. But now that there is room, this prepared material at once comes forward and occupies the throne of the reigning care of the day. And if it is very much lighter in its matter than the material of the care which has vanished, it knows how to blow itself out so as apparently to equal it in size, and thus, as the chief care of the day, completely fills the throne.

Excessive joy and very keen suffering always occur in the same person, for they condition each other reciprocally, and are also in common conditioned by great activity of the mind. Both are produced, as we have just seen, not by what is really present, but by the anticipation of the future. But since pain is essential to life, and its degree is also determined by the nature of the subject, sudden changes, because they are always external, cannot really alter its degree. Thus an error and delusion always lies at the foundation of immoderate joy or grief, and consequently both these excessive strainings of the mind can be avoided by knowledge. Every immoderate joy always rests on the delusion that one has found in life what can never be found there—lasting satisfaction of the harassing desires and cares, which are constantly breeding new ones. From every particular delusion of this kind one must inevitably be brought back later, and then when it vanishes must pay for it with pain as bitter as the joy its entrance caused was keen. So far, then, it is precisely like a height from which one can come down only by a fall. Therefore one ought to avoid them; and every sudden excessive grief is just a fall from some such height, the vanishing of such a delusion, and so conditioned by it. Consequently we might avoid them both if we had sufficient control over ourselves to survey things always with perfect clearness as a whole and in their connection, and steadfastly to guard against really lending them the colours which we wish they had. The principal effort of the Stoical ethics was to free the mind from all such delusion and its consequences, and to give it instead an equanimity that could not be disturbed.

For the most part, however, we close our minds against the

knowledge, which may be compared to a bitter medicine, that suffering is essential to life, and therefore does not flow in upon us from without, but that every one carries about with him its perennial source in his own heart. We rather seek constantly for an external particular cause, as it were, a pretext for the pain which never leaves us, just as the free man makes himself an idol, in order to have a master. For we unweariedly strive from wish to wish; and although every satisfaction, however much it promised, when attained fails to satisfy us, but for the most part comes presently to be an error of which we are ashamed, yet we do not see that we draw water with the sieve of the Danaides, but ever hasten to new desires. Thus it either goes on for ever, or, what is more rare and presupposes a certain strength of character, till we reach a wish which is not satisfied and yet cannot be given up. In that case we have, as it were, found what we sought, something that we can always blame, instead of our own nature, as the source of our suffering. And thus, although we are now at variance with our fate, we are reconciled to our existence, for the knowledge is again put far from us that suffering is essential to this existence itself, and true satisfaction impossible. The result of this form of development is a somewhat melancholy disposition, the constant endurance of a single great pain, and the contempt for all lesser sorrows or joys that proceeds from it; consequently an already nobler phenomenon than that constant seizing upon ever-new forms of illusion, which is much more common.

§ 58

All satisfaction, or what is commonly called happiness, is always really and essentially only *negative,* and never positive. It is not an original gratification coming to us of itself, but must always be the satisfaction of a wish. The wish, *i. e.,* some want, is the condition which precedes every pleasure. But with the satisfaction the wish and therefore the pleasure cease. Thus the satisfaction or the pleasing can never be more than the deliverance from a pain, from a want; for such is not only every actual, open sorrow, but every desire, the importunity of which disturbs our peace, and, indeed, the deadening ennui also that makes life a burden to us. It is, however, so hard to attain or achieve anything; difficulties and troubles without end are opposed to every purpose, and at every step hindrances accumulate. But when finally everything is overcome and attained, nothing can ever be gained but deliverance from some sorrow or desire, so that we find ourselves just in the same position as we occupied before this sorrow or desire appeared. All that is even directly given us is merely the want, i. e., the pain. The satisfaction and the pleasure we can only know indirectly through the remembrance of the preceding suffering and want, which ceases with its appearance. Hence it arises that we are not properly conscious of the blessings and advantages we actually possess, nor do we prize them, but think of them merely as a matter of course, for they gratify us only negatively by restraining suffering. Only when we have lost them do we become sensible of their value; for the want, the privation, the sorrow, is the positive, communicating itself directly to us. Thus also we are pleased by the remembrance of past need, sickness, want, and such like, because this is the only means of enjoying the present blessings. And, further, it cannot be denied that in this respect, and from this standpoint of egoism, which is the form of the will to live, the sight or the description of the sufferings of others affords us satisfaction and pleasure in precisely the way Lucretius beautifully and frankly expresses it in the beginning of the Second Book—

> "Suave, mari magno, turbantibus æquora ventis,
> E terra magnum alterius spectare laborem:
> Non, quia vexari quemquam est jucunda voluptas;
> Sed, quibus ipse malis careas, quia cernere suave est." [11]

Yet we shall see farther on that that kind of pleasure, through knowledge of our own well-being obtained in this way, lies very near the source of real, positive wickedness.

That all happiness is only of a negative not a positive nature, that just on this account it cannot be lasting satisfaction and gratification, but merely delivers us from some pain or want

---

[11] "How sweet it is, when the sea is heavy, and the winds rouse the waves, to see, from land, another's suffering! Not because it is a lovely delight that a man should be so troubled, but because it is pleasant to perceive from what evils we ourselves are free."

which must be followed either by a new pain, or by languor, empty longing, and ennui; this finds support in art, that true mirror of the world and life, and especially in poetry. Every epic and dramatic poem can only represent a struggle, an effort, and fight for happiness, never enduring and complete happiness itself. It conducts its heroes through a thousand difficulties and dangers to the goal; as soon as this is reached, it hastens to let the curtain fall; for now there would remain nothing for it to do but to show that the glittering goal in which the hero expected to find happiness had only disappointed him, and that after its attainment he was no better off than before. Because a genuine enduring happiness is not possible, it cannot be the subject of art. Certainly the aim of the idyll is the description of such a happiness, but one also sees that the idyll as such cannot continue. The poet always finds that it becomes either epical in his hands, and in this case it is a very insignificant epic, made up of trifling sorrows, trifling delight, and trifling efforts—this is the commonest case—or else it becomes a merely descriptive poem, describing the beauty of nature, *i. e.,* pure knowing free from will, which certainly, as a matter of fact, is the only pure happiness, which is neither preceded by suffering or want, nor necessarily followed by repentance, sorrow, emptiness, or satiety; but this happiness cannot fill the whole life, but is only possible at moments. What we see in poetry we find again in music; in the melodies of which we have recognized the universal expression of the inmost history of the self-conscious will, the most secret life, longing, suffering, and delight; the ebb and flow of the human heart. Melody is always a deviation from the keynote through a thousand capricious wanderings, even to the most painful discord, and then a final return to the keynote which expresses the satisfaction and appeasing of the will, but with which nothing more can then be done, and the continuance of which any longer would be only a wearisome and unmeaning monotony correspond-ing to ennui.

All that we intend to bring out clearly through these investiga-tions, the impossibility of attaining lasting satisfaction and the negative nature of all happiness, finds its explanation in what is shown at the conclusion of the Second Book: that the will, of which human life, like every phenomenon, is the objectification,

is a striving without aim or end. We find the stamp of this endlessness imprinted upon all the parts of its whole manifestation,
from its most universal form, endless time and space, up to the
most perfect of all phenomena, the life and efforts of man. We
may theoretically assume three extremes of human life, and treat
them as elements of actual human life. First, the powerful will,
the strong passions (Radscha-Guna). It appears in great historical
characters; it is described in the epic and the drama. But it can
also show itself in the little world, for the size of the objects is
measured here by the degree in which they influence the will, not
according to their external relations. Secondly, pure knowing, the
comprehension of the Ideas, conditioned by the freeing of knowledge from the service of will: the life of genius (Satwa-Guna).
Thirdly and lastly, the greatest lethargy of the will, and also of
the knowledge attaching to it, empty longing, life-benumbing
languor (Tama-Guna). The life of the individual, far from
becoming permanently fixed in one of these extremes, seldom
touches any of them, and is for the most part only a weak and
wavering approach to one or the other side, a needy desiring
of trifling objects, constantly recurring, and so escaping ennui. It
is really incredible how meaningless and void of significance when
looked at from without, how dull and unenlightened by intellect
when felt from within, is the course of the life of the great
majority of men. It is a weary longing and complaining, a dream-
like staggering through the four ages of life to death, accompanied
by a series of trivial thoughts. Such men are like clockwork,
which is wound up, and goes it knows not why; and every time
a man is begotten and born, the clock of human life is wound up
anew, to repeat the same old piece it has played innumerable times
before, passage after passage, measure after measure, with insignificant variations. Every individual, every human being and
his course of life, is but another short dream of the endless spirit
of nature, of the persistent will to live; is only another fleeting
form, which it carelessly sketches on its infinite page, space and
time; allows to remain for a time so short that it vanishes into
nothing in comparison with these, and then obliterates to make
new room. And yet, and here lies the serious side of life, every one
of these fleeting forms, these empty fancies, must be paid for

by the whole will to live, in all its activity, with many and deep sufferings, and finally with a bitter death, long feared and coming at last. This is why the sight of a corpse makes us suddenly so serious.

The life of every individual, if we survey it as a whole and in general, and lay stress only upon its most significant features, is really always a tragedy, but gone through in detail, it has the character of a comedy. For the deeds and vexations of the day, the restless irritation of the moment, the desires and fears of the week, the mishaps of every hour, are all through chance, which is ever bent upon some jest, scenes of a comedy. But the never-satisfied wishes, the frustrated efforts, the hopes unmercifully crushed by fate, the unfortunate errors of the whole life, with increasing suffering and death at the end, are always a tragedy. Thus, as if fate would add derision to the miseries of our existence, our life must contain all the woes of tragedy, and yet we cannot even assert the dignity of tragic characters, but in the broad detail of life must inevitably be the foolish characters of a comedy.

But however much great and small trials may fill human life, they are not able to conceal its insufficiency to satisfy the spirit; they cannot hide the emptiness and superficiality of existence, nor exclude ennui, which is always ready to fill up every pause that care may allow. Hence it arises that the human mind, not content with the cares, anxieties, and occupations which the actual world lays upon it, creates for itself an imaginary world also in the form of a thousand different superstitions, then finds all manner of employment with this, and wastes time and strength upon it, as soon as the real world is willing to grant it the rest which it is quite incapable of enjoying. This is accordingly most markedly the case with nations for which life is made easy by the congenial nature of the climate and the soil, most of all with the Hindus, then with the Greeks, the Romans, and later with the Italians, the Spaniards, &c. Demons, gods, and saints man creates in his own image; and to them he must then unceasingly bring offerings, prayers, temple decorations, vows and their fulfilment, pilgrimages, salutations, ornaments for their images, &c. Their service mingles everywhere with the real, and, indeed, obscures it. Every event of life is regarded as the work of these beings; the intercourse with them occupies half the time of life, constantly sustains hope, and by the charm of illusion often becomes more interesting than intercourse with real beings. It is the expression and symptom of the actual need of mankind, partly for help and support, partly for occupation and diversion; and if it often works in direct opposition to the first need, because when accidents and dangers arise valuable time and strength, instead of being directed to warding them off, are uselessly wasted on prayers and offerings; it serves the second end all the better by this imaginary converse with a visionary spirit world; and this is the by no means contemptible gain of all superstitions.

§ 59

If we have so far convinced ourselves *a priori,* by the most general consideration, by investigation of the primary and elemental features of human life, that in its whole plan it is capable of no true blessedness, but is in its very nature suffering in various forms, and throughout a state of misery, we might now awaken this conviction much more vividly within us if, proceeding more *a posteriori,* we were to turn to more definite instances, call up pictures to the fancy, and illustrate by examples the unspeakable misery which experience and history present, wherever one may look and in whatever direction one may seek. But the chapter would have no end, and would carry us far from the standpoint of the universal, which is essential to philosophy; and, moreover, such a description might easily be taken for a mere declamation on human misery, such as has often been given, and, as such, might be charged with one-sidedness, because it started from particular facts. From such a reproach and suspicion our perfectly cold and philosophical investigation of the inevitable suffering which is founded in the nature of life is free, for it starts from the universal and is conducted *a priori.* But confirmation *a posteriori* is everywhere easily obtained. Every one who has awakened from the first dream of youth, who has considered his own experience and that of others, who has studied himself in life, in the history of the past and of his own time, and finally in the works of the

great poets, will, if his judgment is not paralysed by some indelibly imprinted prejudice, certainly arrive at the conclusion
that this human world is the kingdom of chance and error, which
rule without mercy in great things and in small, and along with
which folly and wickedness also wield the scourge. Hence it arises
that everything better only struggles through with difficulty; what
is noble and wise seldom attains to expression, becomes effective
and claims attention, but the absurd and the perverse in the sphere
of thought, the dull and tasteless in the sphere of art, the wicked
and deceitful in the sphere of action, really assert a supremacy,
only disturbed by short interruptions. On the other hand, everything that is excellent is always a mere exception, one case in millions, and therefore, if it presents itself in a lasting work, this,
when it has outlived the enmity of its contemporaries, exists in
isolation, is preserved like a meteoric stone, sprung from an order
of things different from that which prevails here. But as far as the
life of the individual is concerned, every biography is the history
of suffering, for every life is, as a rule, a continual series of great
and small misfortunes, which each one conceals as much as possible, because he knows that others can seldom feel sympathy or
compassion, but almost always satisfaction at the sight of the woes
from which they are themselves for the moment exempt. But
perhaps at the end of life, if a man is sincere and in full possession of his faculties, he will never wish to have it to live over
again, but rather than this, he will much prefer absolute annihilation. The essential content of the famous soliloquy in "Hamlet" is briefly this: Our state is so wretched that absolute annihilation would be decidedly preferable. If suicide really offered
us this, so that the alternative "to be or not to be," in the full
sense of the word, was placed before us, then it would unconditionally be chosen as "a consummation devoutly to be wished."
But there is something in us which tells us that this is not the
case: suicide is not the end; death is not absolute annihilation. In
like manner, what was said by the father of history has not
since been contradicted, that no man has ever lived who has not
wished more than once that he had not to live the following day.
According to this, the brevity of life, which is so constantly lamented, may be the best quality it possesses. If, finally, we should

bring clearly to a man's sight the terrible sufferings and miseries to which his life is constantly exposed, he would be seized with horror; and if we were to conduct the confirmed optimist through the hospitals, infirmaries, and surgical operating-rooms, through prisons, torture-chambers, and slave-kennels, over battle-fields and places of execution; if we were to open to him all the dark abodes of misery, where it hides itself from the glance of cold curiosity, and, finally, allow him to glance into the starving dungeon of Ugolino, he, too, would understand at last the nature of this "best of possible worlds." For whence did Dante take the materials for his hell but from this our actual world? And yet he made a very proper hell of it. And when, on the other hand, he came to the task of describing heaven and its delights, he had an insurmountable difficulty before him, for our world affords no materials at all for this. Therefore there remained nothing for him to do but, instead of describing the joys of paradise, to repeat to us the instruction given him there by his ancestor, by Beatrice, and by various saints. But from this it is sufficiently clear what manner of world it is. Certainly human life, like all bad ware, is covered over with a false lustre: what suffers always conceals itself; on the other hand, whatever pomp or splendour any one can get, he makes a show of openly, and the more inner contentment deserts him, the more he desires to exist as fortunate in the opinion of others: to such an extent does folly go, and the opinion of others is a chief aim of the efforts of every one, although the utter nothingness of it is expressed in the fact that in almost all languages vanity, *vanitas,* originally signifies emptiness and nothingness. But under all this false show, the miseries of life can so increase —and this happens every day—that the death which hitherto has been feared above all things is eagerly seized upon. Indeed, if fate will show its whole malice, even this refuge is denied to the sufferer, and, in the hands of enraged enemies, he may remain exposed to terrible and slow tortures without remedy. In vain the sufferer then calls on his gods for help; he remains exposed to his fate without grace. But this irremediableness is only the mirror of the invincible nature of his will, of which his person is the objectivity. As little as an external power can change or suppress this will, so little can a foreign power deliver it from the miseries which proceed from the life which is the phenomenal appearance of that will. In the principal matter, as in everything else, a man is always thrown back upon himself. In vain does he make to himself gods in order to get from them by prayers and flattery what can only be accomplished by his own will-power. The Old Testament made the world and man the work of a god, but the New Testament saw that, in order to teach that holiness and salvation from the sorrows of this world can only come from the world itself, it was necessary that this god should become man. It is and remains the will of man upon which everything depends for him. Fanatics, martyrs, saints of every faith and name, have voluntarily and gladly endured every torture, because in them the will to live had suppressed itself; and then even the slow destruction of its phenomenon was welcome to them. But I do not wish to anticipate the later exposition. For the rest, I cannot here avoid the statement that, to me, *optimism,* when it is not merely the thoughtless talk of such as harbour nothing but words under their low foreheads, appears not merely as an absurd, but also as a really *wicked* way of thinking, as a bitter mockery of the unspeakable suffering of humanity. Let no one think that Christianity is favourable to optimism; for, on the contrary, in the Gospels world and evil are used as almost synonymous.

§ 60

We have now completed the two expositions it was necessary to insert; the exposition of the freedom of the will itself together with the necessity of its phenomenon, and the exposition of its lot in the world which reflects its own nature, and upon the knowledge of which it has to assert or deny itself. Therefore we can now proceed to bring out more clearly the nature of this assertion and denial itself, which was referred to and explained in a merely general way above. This we shall do by exhibiting the conduct in which alone it finds its expression, and considering it in its inner significance.

The *assertion of the will* is the continuous willing itself, undisturbed by any knowledge, as it fills the life of man in general. For even the body of a man is the objectivity of the will, as it appears at this grade and in this individual. And thus his willing which develops itself in time is, as it were, a paraphrase of his body, an elucidation of the significance of the whole and its parts; it is another way of exhibiting the same thing-in-itself, of which the body is already the phenomenon. Therefore, instead of saying assertion of the will, we may say assertion of the body. The fundamental theme or subject of all the multifarious acts of will is the satisfaction of the wants which are inseparable from the existence of the body in health, they already have their expression in it, and may be referred to the maintenance of the individual and the propagation of the species. But indirectly the most different kinds of motives obtain in this way power over the will, and bring about the most multifarious acts of will. Each of these is only an example, an instance, of the will which here manifests itself generally. Of what nature this example may be, what form the motive may have and impart to it, is not essential; the important point here is that something is willed in general and the degree of intensity with which it is so willed. The will can only become visible in the motives, as the eye only manifests its power of seeing in the light. The motive in general stands before the will in protean forms. It constantly promises complete satisfaction, the quenching of the thirst of will. But whenever it is attained it at once appears in another form, and thus influences the will anew, always according to the degree of the intensity of this will, and its relation to knowledge which are revealed as empirical character, in these very examples and instances.

From the first appearance of consciousness, a man finds himself a willing being, and as a rule, his knowledge remains in constant relation to his will. He first seeks to know thoroughly the objects of his desire, and then the means of attaining them. Now he knows what he has to do, and, as a rule, he does not strive after other knowledge. He moves and acts; his consciousness keeps him always working directly and actively towards the aims of his will; his thought is concerned with the choice of motives. Such is life for almost all men; they wish, they know what they wish, and they strive after it, with sufficient success to keep them from despair, and sufficient failure to keep them from ennui and its consequences. From this proceeds a certain serenity, or at least indifference, which cannot be affected by wealth or poverty; for the rich and the poor do not enjoy what they have, for this, as we have shown, acts in a purely negative way, but what they hope to attain to by their efforts. They press forward with much earnestness, and indeed with an air of importance; thus children also pursue their play. It is always an exception if such a life suffers interruption from the fact that either the æsthetic demand for contemplation or the ethical demand for renunciation proceed from a knowledge which is independent of the service of the will, and directed to the nature of the world in general. Most men are pursued by want all through life, without ever being allowed to come to their senses. On the other hand, the will is often inflamed to a degree that far transcends the assertion of the body, and then violent emotions and powerful passions show themselves, in which the individual not only asserts his own existence, but denies and seeks to suppress that of others when it stands in his way.

The maintenance of the body through its own powers is so small a degree of the assertion of will, that if it voluntarily remains at this degree, we might assume that, with the death of this body, the will also which appeared in it would be extinguished. But even the satisfaction of the sexual passions goes beyond the assertion of one's own existence, which fills so short a time, and asserts life for an indefinite time after the death of the individual. Nature, always true and consistent, here even naïve, exhibits to us openly the inner significance of the act of generation. Our own consciousness, the intensity of the impulse, teaches us that in this act the most decided *assertion of the will to live* expresses itself, pure and without further addition (any denial of other individuals); and now, as the consequence of this act, a new life appears in time and the causal series, *i. e.,* in nature; the begotten appears before the begetter, different as regards the phenomenon, but in himself, *i. e.,* according to the Idea, identical with him. Therefore it is this act through which every species of living creature binds itself to a whole and is perpetuated. Generation is, with reference to the begetter, only the expression, the symptom, of his decided assertion of the will to live: with reference to the begotten, it is not the cause of the will which appears in him, for the will in itself knows neither cause nor effect, but, like all causes, it is merely the occasional cause of the phenomenal appearance of this will at this time in this place. As thing-in-itself, the will of the begetter and that of the begotten are not different, for only the phenomenon, not the thing-in-itself, is subordinate to the *principium individuationis*. With that assertion beyond our own body and extending to the production of a new body, suffering and death, as belonging to the phenomenon of life, have also been asserted anew, and the possibility of salvation, introduced by the completest capability of knowledge, has for this time been shown to be fruitless. Here lies the profound reason of the shame connected with the process of generation. This view is mythically expressed in the dogma of Christian theology that we are all partakers in Adam's first transgression (which is clearly just the satisfaction of sexual passion), and through it are guilty of suffering and death. In this theology goes beyond the consideration of things according to the principle of sufficient reason, and recognizes the Idea of man, the unity of which is re-established out of its dispersion into innumerable individuals through the bond of generation which holds them all together. Accordingly it regards every individual as on one side identical with Adam, the representative of the assertion of life, and, so far, as subject to sin (original sin), suffering, and death; on the other side, the knowledge of the Idea of man enables it to regard every individual as identical with the Saviour, the representative of the denial of the will to live, and, so far as a partaker of his sacrifice of himself, saved through his merits, and delivered from the bands of sin and death, *i. e.,* the world (Rom. v., 12–21). . . . .

The sexual impulse also proves itself the decided and strongest assertion of life by the fact that to man in a state of nature, as to the brutes, it is the final end, the highest goal of life. Self-maintenance is his first effort, and as soon as he has made provision for that, he strives only after the propagation of the species: as a merely natural being he can attempt no more. Nature also, the inner being of which is the will to live itself, impels with all her power both man and the brute towards propagation. Then it has attained its end with the individual, and is quite indifferent to its death, for, as the will to live, it cares only for the preservation of the species, the individual is nothing to it. Because the will to live expresses itself most strongly in the sexual impulse, the inner being of nature, the old poets and philosophers—Hesiod and Parmenides—said very significantly that Eros is the first, the creator, the principle from which all things proceed. (Cf. Arist. Metaph., i., 4). . . .

The genital organs are, far more than any other external member of the body, subject merely to the will, and not at all to knowledge. Indeed, the will shows itself here almost as independent of knowledge, as in those parts which, acting merely in consequence of stimuli, are subservient to vegetative life and reproduction, in which the will works blindly as in unconscious Nature. For generation is only reproduction passing over to a new individual, as it were reproduction at the second power, as death is only excretion at the second power. According to all this, the genitals are properly the *focus* of will, and consequently the opposite pole of the brain, the representative of knowledge, *i. e.,* the other side of the world, the world as idea. The former are the life-sustaining principle ensuring endless life to time. In this respect they were worshipped by the Greeks in the *phallus,* and by the Hindus in the *lingam,* which are thus the symbol of the assertion of the will. Knowledge, on the other hand, affords the possibility of the suppression of willing, of salvation through freedom, of conquest and annihilation of the world.

We already considered fully at the beginning of this Fourth Book how the will to live in its assertion must regard its relation to death. We saw that death does not trouble it, because it exists as something included in life itself and belonging to it. Its opposite, generation, completely counterbalances it; and, in spite of the death of the individual, ensures and guarantees life to the will to live through all time. To express this the Hindus made the *lingam* an attribute of Siva, the god of death. We also fully explained there how he who with full consciousness occupies the standpoint of the decided assertion of life awaits death without fear. We shall therefore say nothing more about this here. Without clear consciousness most men occupy this standpoint and continually assert life. The world exists as the mirror of this assertion, with innumerable individuals in infinite time and space, in infinite suffering, between generation and death without end. Yet from no side is a complaint to be further raised about this; for the will conducts the great tragedy and comedy at its own expense, and is also its own spectator. The world is just what it is because the will, whose manifestation it is, is what it is, because it so wills. The justification of suffering is, that in this phenomenon also the will asserts itself; and this assertion is justified and balanced by the fact that the will bears the suffering. Here we get a glimpse of *eternal justice* in the whole: we shall recognize it later more definitely and distinctly, and also in the particular. But first we must consider temporal or human justice.

§ 61

It may be remembered from the Second Book that in the whole of nature, at all the grades of the objectification of will, there was a necessary and constant conflict between the individuals of all species; and in this way was expressed the inner contradiction of the will to live with itself. At the highest grade of the objectification, this phenomenon, like all others, will exhibit itself with greater distinctness, and will therefore be more easily explained. With this aim we shall next attempt to trace the source of *egoism* as the starting-point of all conflict.

We have called time and space the *principium individuationis,* because only through them and in them is multiplicity of the homogeneous possible. They are the essential forms of natural knowledge, *i. e.,* knowledge springing from the will. Therefore the will everywhere manifests itself in the multiplicity of individuals. But this multiplicity does not concern the will as thing-in-itself, but only its phenomena. The will itself is present, whole and undivided, in every one of these, and beholds around it the innumerably repeated image of its own nature; but this nature itself, the actually real, it finds directly only in its inner self. Therefore every one desires everything for himself, desires to possess, or at least to control, everything, and whatever opposes it it would like to destroy. To this is added, in the case of such beings as have knowledge, that the individual is the supporter of the knowing subject, and the knowing subject is the supporter of the world, *i. e.,* that the whole of Nature outside the knowing subject, and thus

also all other individuals, exist only in its idea; it is only conscious
of them as its idea, thus merely indirectly as something which is
dependent on its own nature and existence; for which its consciousness the world necessarily disappears for it, *i. e.,* its being and
non-being become synonymous and indistinguishable. Every knowing individual is thus in truth, and finds itself as the whole will to
live, or the inner being of the world itself, and also as the complemental condition of the world as idea, consequently as a microcosm which is of equal value with macrocosm. Nature itself, which
is everywhere and always truthful, gives him this knowledge,
originally and independently of all reflection, with simple and
direct certainty. Now from these two necessary properties we
have given the fact may be explained that every individual, though
vanishing altogether and diminished to nothing in the boundless
world, yet makes itself the centre of the world, has regard for its
own existence and well-being before everything else; indeed, from
the natural standpoint, is ready to sacrifice everything else for
this—is ready to annihilate the world in order to maintain its
own self, this drop in the ocean, a little longer. This disposition
is *egoism,* which is essential to everything in Nature. Yet it is
just through egoism that the inner conflict of the will with itself
attains to such a terrible revelation; for this egoism has its continuance and being in that opposition of the microcosm and macrocosm, or in the fact that the objectification of will has the *principium individuationis* for its form, through which the will manifests
itself in the same way in innumerable individuals, and indeed entire
and completely in both aspects (will and idea) in each. Thus,
while each individual is given to itself directly as the whole will
and the whole subject of ideas, other individuals are only given it
as ideas. Therefore its own being, and the maintenance of it, is of
more importance to it than that of all others together. Every one
looks upon his own death as upon the end of the world, while
he accepts the death of his acquaintances as a matter of comparative indifference, if he is not in some way affected by it. In
the consciousness that has reached the highest grade, that of man,
egoism, as well as knowledge, pain and pleasure, must have reached
its highest grade also, and the conflict of individuals which is
conditioned by it must appear in its most terrible form. And

indeed we see this everywhere before our eyes, in small things as in great. Now we see its terrible side in the lives of great tyrants and miscreants, and in world-desolating wars; now its absurd side, in which it is the theme of comedy, and very specially appears as self-conceit and vanity. Rochefoucault understood this better than any one else, and presented it in the abstract. We see it both in the history of the world and in our own experience. But it appears most distinctly of all when any mob of men is set free from all law and order; then there shows itself at once in the distinctest form the *bellum omnium contra omnes*,[12] which Hobbes has so admirably described in the first chapter *De Cive*. We see not only how every one tries to seize from the other what he wants himself, but how often one will destroy the whole happiness or life of another for the sake of an insignificant addition to his own happiness. This is the highest expression of egoism, the manifestations of which in this regard are only surpassed by those of actual wickedness, which seeks, quite disinterestedly the hurt and suffering of others, without any advantage to itself. . . .

§ 68

If we compare life to a course or path through which we must unceasingly run—a path of red-hot coals, with a few cool places here and there; then he who is entangled in delusion is consoled by the cool places, on which he now stands, or which he sees near him, and sets out to run through the course. But he who sees through the *principium individuationis,* and recognises the real nature of the thing-in-itself, and thus the whole, is no longer susceptible of such consolation; he sees himself in all places at once, and withdraws. His will turns round, no longer asserts its own nature, which is reflected in the phenomenon, but denies it. The phenomenon by which this change is marked, is the transition from virtue to asceticism. That is to say, it no longer suffices for such a man to love others as himself, and to do as much for them as for himself; but there arises within him a horror of the nature of which his own phenomenal existence is an expression, the will to live, the kernel and inner nature of that world which is recog-

---

[12] "War of each against all."

nized as full of misery. He therefore disowns this nature which appears in him, and is already expressed through his body, and his action gives the lie to his phenomenal existence, and appears in open contradiction to it. Essentially nothing else but a manifestation of will, he ceases to will anything, guards against attaching his will to anything, and seeks to confirm in himself the greatest indifference to everything. His body, healthy and strong, expresses through the genitals, the sexual impulse; but he denies the will and gives the lie to the body; he desires no sensual gratification under any condition. Voluntary and complete chastity is the first step in asceticism or the denial of the will to live. It thereby denies the assertion of the will which extends beyond the individual life, and gives the assurance that with the life of this body, the will, whose manifestation it is, ceases. Nature, always true and naïve, declares that if this maxim became universal, the human race would die out; and I think I may assume, in accordance with what was said in the Second Book about the connection of all manifestations of will, that with its highest manifestation, the weaker reflection of it would also pass away, as the twilight vanishes along with the full light. With the entire abolition of knowledge, the rest of the world would of itself vanish into nothing; for without a subject there is no object. I should like here to refer to a passage in the Vedas, where it is said: "As in this world hungry infants press round their mother; so do all beings await the holy oblation." Sacrifice means resignation generally, and the rest of nature must look for its salvation to man who is at once the priest and the sacrifice. Indeed it deserves to be noticed as very remarkable, that this thought has also been expressed by the admirable and unfathomably profound Angelus Silesius, in the little poem entitled, "Man brings all to God"; it runs, "Man! all loves thee; around thee great is the throng. All things flee to thee that they may attain to God." But a yet greater mystic, Meister Eckhard, whose wonderful writings are at last accessible (1857) through the edition of Franz Pfeiffer, says the same thing (p. 459) quite in the sense explained here: "I bear witness to the saying of Christ, I, if I be lifted up from the earth, will draw all men unto me (John xii., 32). So shall the good man draw all things up to God, to the source whence they first came. The Masters certify to us that all creatures are made for the sake of man. This is proved in all created things, by the fact that the one makes the use of the other; the ox makes use of the grass, the fish of the water, the bird of the air, the wild beast of the forest. Thus, all created things become of use to the good man. A good man brings to God the one created thing in the other." He means to say, that man makes use of the brutes in this life because, in and with himself, he saves them also. It also seems to me that that difficult passage in the Bible, Rom. viii., 21–24, must be interpreted in this sense.

In Buddhism also, there is no lack of expressions of this truth. For example, when Buddha, still as Bodisatwa, has his horse saddled for the last time, for his flight into the wilderness from his father's house, he says these lines to the horse: "Long hast thou existed in life and in death, but now thou shalt cease from carrying and drawing. Bear me but this once more, O Kantakana, away from here, and when I have attained to the Law (have become Buddha) I will not forget thee" (Foe Koue Ki, trad. p. Abel Rémusat, p. 233).

Asceticism then shows itself further in voluntary and intentional poverty, which not only arises *per accidens,* because the possessions are given away to mitigate the sufferings of others, but is here an end in itself, is meant to serve as a constant mortification of will, so that the satisfaction of the wishes, the sweet of life, shall not again arouse the will, against which self-knowledge has conceived a horror. He who has attained to this point, still always feels, as a living body, as concrete manifestation of will, the natural disposition for every kind of volition; but he intentionally suppresses it, for he compels himself to refrain from doing all that he would like to do, and to do all that he would like not to do, even if this has no further end than that of serving as a mortification of will. Since he himself denies the will which appears in his own person, he will not resist if another does the same, *i. e.,* inflicts wrongs upon him. Therefore every suffering coming to him from without, through chance or the wickedness of others, is welcome to him, every injury, ignominy, and insult; he receives them gladly as the opportunity of learning with certainty that he no longer asserts the will, but gladly sides with every enemy of the manifestation of will which is his own person. Therefore he bears such ignominy and suffering with inexhaustible patience and meekness, returns good for evil without ostentation, and allows the fire of anger to rise within him just as little as that of the desires. And he mortifies not only the will itself, but also its visible form, its objectivity, the body. He nourishes it sparingly, lest its excessive vigour and prosperity should animate and excite more strongly the will, of which it is merely the expression and the mirror. So he practices fasting, and even resorts to chastisement and self-inflicted torture, in order that, by constant privation and suffering, he may more and more break down and destroy the will, which he recognizes and abhors as the source of his own suffering existence and that of the world. If at last death comes, which puts an end to this manifestation of that will, whose existence here has long since perished through free-denial of itself, with the exception of the weak residue of it which appears as the life of this body; it is most welcome, and is gladly received as a longed-for deliverance. Here it is not, as in the case of others, merely the manifestation which ends with death; but the inner nature itself is abolished, which here existed only in the manifestation, and that in a very weak degree; [13] this last slight bond is now broken. For him who thus ends, the world has ended also.

And what I have here described with feeble tongue and only in general terms, is no philosophical fable, invented by myself, and only of to-day; no, it was the enviable life of so many saints and beautiful souls among Christians, and still more among Hindus and Buddhists, and also among the believers of other religions. However different were the dogmas impressed on their reason, the same inward, direct, intuitive knowledge, from which alone all virtue and holiness proceed, expressed itself in precisely the same way in the conduct of life. For here also the great distinction

---

[13] This thought is expressed by a beautiful simile in the ancient philosophical Sanscrit writing, "Sankhya Karica": "Yet the soul remains a while invested with body; as the potter's wheel continues whirling after the pot has been fashioned, by force of the impulse previously given to it. When separation of the informed soul from its corporeal frame at length takes place and nature in respect of it ceases, then is absolute and final deliverance accomplished." Colebrooke, "On the Philosophy of the Hindus: Miscellaneous Essays," vol. i., p. 271. Also in the "Sankhya Karica" by Horace Wilson, § 67, p. 184.—S.

between intuitive and abstract knowledge shows itself; a distinction which is of such importance and universal application in our whole investigation, and which has hitherto been too little attended to. There is a wide gulf between the two, which can be crossed only by the aid of philosophy, as regards the knowledge of the nature of the world. Intuitively or *in concreto,* every man is really conscious of all philosophical truths, but to bring them to abstract knowledge, to reflection, is the work of philosophy, which neither ought nor is able to do more than this.

Thus it may be that the inner nature of holiness, self-renunciation, mortification of our own will, asceticism, is here for the first time expressed abstractly, and free from all mythical elements, as *denial of the will to live,* appearing after the complete knowledge of its own nature has become a quieter of all volition. On the other hand, it has been known directly and realized in practice by saints and ascetics, who had all the same inward knowledge, though they used very different language with regard to it, according to the dogmas which their reason had accepted, and in consequence of which an Indian, a Christian, or a Lama saint must each give a very different account of his conduct, which is, however, of no importance as regards the fact. A saint may be full of the absurdest superstition, or, on the contrary, he may be a philosopher, it is all the same. His conduct alone certifies that he is a saint, for, in a moral regard, it proceeds from knowledge of the world and its nature, which is not abstractly but intuitively and directly apprehended, and is only expressed by him in any dogma for the satisfaction of his reason. It is therefore just as little needful that a saint should be a philosopher as that a philosopher should be a saint; just as it is not necessary that a perfectly beautiful man should be a great sculptor, or that a great sculptor should himself be a beautiful man. In general, it is a strange demand upon a moralist that he should teach no other virtue than that which he himself possesses. To repeat the whole nature of the world abstractly, universally, and distinctly in concepts, and thus to store up, as it were, a reflected image of it in permanent concepts always at the command of the reason; this and nothing else is philosophy. I refer the reader to the passage quoted from Bacon in the First Book.

But the description I have given above of the denial of the will to live, of the conduct of a beautiful soul, of a resigned and voluntarily expiating saint, is merely abstract and general, and therefore cold. As the knowledge from which the denial of the will proceeds is intuitive and not abstract, it finds its most perfect expression, not in abstract conceptions, but in deeds and conduct. Therefore, in order to understand fully what we philosophically express as denial of the will to live, one must come to know examples of it in experience and actual life. Certainly they are not to be met with in daily experience: *Nam omnia præclara tam difficilia quam rara sunt*,[14] Spinoza admirably says. Therefore, unless by a specially happy fate we are made eye-witnesses, we have to content ourselves with descriptions of the lives of such men. Indian literature, as we see from the little that we as yet know through translations, is very rich in descriptions of the lives of saints, penitents, Samanas or ascetics, Sannyâsis or mendicants, and whatever else they may be called. . . . Among Christians also there is no lack of examples which afford us the illustrations we desire. . . . We also see what a matter of indifference it is whether it proceeds from a theistical or an atheistical religion. But as a special and exceedingly full example and practical illustration of the conceptions I have established, I can thoroughly recommend the "Autobiography of Madame de Guion." To become acquainted with this great and beautiful soul, the very thought of whom always fills me with reverence, and to do justice to the excellence of her disposition while making allowance for the superstition of her reason, must be just as delightful to every man of the better sort, as with vulgar thinkers, *i. e.,* the majority, that book will always stand in bad repute. For it is the case with regard to everything, that each man can only prize that which to a certain extent is analogous to him and for which he has at least a slight inclination. This holds good of ethical concerns as well as of intellectual. We might to a certain extent regard the well-known French biography of Spinoza as a case in point, if we used as a key to it that noble introduction to his very insufficient essay, "De Emendatione Intellectus," a passage which I can also recommend as the most effectual means I know of stilling the storm of the passions.

[14] "For all things excellent are as difficult as they are rare."

Finally, even the great Goethe, Greek as he is, did not think it below his dignity to show us this most beautiful side of humanity in the magic mirror of poetic art, for he represented the life of Fräulein Klettenberg in an idealized form in his "Confessions of a Beautiful Soul," and later, in his own biography, gave us also an historical account of it. Besides this, he twice told the story of the life of St. Philippo Neri. The history of the world will, and indeed must, keep silence about the men whose conduct is the best and only adequate illustration of this important point of our investigation, for the material of the history of the world is quite different, and indeed opposed to this. It is not the denial of the will to live, but its assertion and its manifestation in innumerable individuals in which its conflict with itself at the highest grade of its objectification appears with perfect distinctness, and brings before our eyes, now the ascendancy of the individual through prudence, now the might of the many through their mass, now the might of chance personified as fate, always the vanity and emptiness of the whole effort. We, however, do not follow here the course of phenomena in time, but, as philosophers, we seek to investigate the ethical significance of action, and take this as the only criterion of what for us is significant and important. Thus we will not be withheld by any fear of the constant numerical superiority of vulgarity and dullness from acknowledging that the greatest, most important, and most significant phenomenon that the world can show is not the conqueror of the world, but the subduer of it; is nothing but the quiet, unobserved life of a man who has attained to the knowledge in consequence of which he surrenders and denies that will to live which fills everything and strives and strains in all, and which first gains freedom here in him alone, so that his conduct becomes the exact opposite of that of other men. In this respect, therefore, for the philosopher, these accounts of the lives of holy, self-denying men, badly as they are generally written, and mixed as they are with superstition and nonsense, are, because of the significance of the material, immeasurably more instructive and important than even Plutarch and Livy.

It will further assist us much in obtaining a more definite and full knowledge of what we have expressed abstractly and generally, according to our method of exposition, as the denial of the will to live, if we consider the moral teaching that has been imparted with this intention, and by men who were full of this spirit; and this will also show how old our view is, though the pure philosophical expression of it may be quite new. The teaching of this kind which lies nearest to hand is Christianity, the ethics of which are entirely in the spirit indicated, and lead not only to the highest degrees of human love, but also to renunciation. The germ of this last side of it is certainly distinctly present in the writings of the Apostles, but it was only fully developed and expressed later. We find the Apostles enjoining the love of our neighbour as ourselves, benevolence, the requital of hatred with love and well-doing, patience, meekness, the endurance of all possible injuries without resistance, abstemiousness in nourishment to keep down lust, resistance to sensual desire, if possible, altogether. We already see here the first degrees of asceticism, or denial of the will proper. This last expression denotes that which in the Gospels is called denying ourselves and taking up the cross (Matt. xvi., 24, 25; Mark viii., 34, 35; Luke ix., 23, 24; xiv., 26, 27, 33). This tendency soon developed itself more and more, and was the origin of hermits, anchorites, and monasticism—an origin which in itself was pure and holy, but for that very reason unsuitable for the great majority of men; therefore what developed out of it could only be hypocrisy and wickedness, for *abusus optimi pessimus*.[15] In more developed Christianity, we see that seed of asceticism unfold into the full flower in the writings of the Christian saints and mystics. These preach, besides the purest love, complete resignation, voluntary and absolute poverty, genuine calmness, perfect indifference to all worldly things, dying to our own will and being born again in God, entire forgetting of our own person, and sinking ourselves in the contemplation of God. A full exposition of this will be found in Fénélon's "Explication des Maximes des Saints sur la Vie Intérieure." But the spirit of this development of Christianity is certainly nowhere so fully and powerfully expressed as in the writings of the German mystics, in the works of Meister Eckhard, and in that justly famous book "Die Deutsche Theologie," of which Luther says in the introduction to it which he

[15] "The worst abuse is of that which is best."

wrote, that with the exception of the Bible and St. Augustine, he had learnt more from it of what God, Christ, and man are than from any other book. Yet we only got the genuine and correct text of it in the year 1851, in the Stuttgart edition by Pfeiffer. The precepts and doctrines which are laid down there are the most perfect exposition, sprung from deep inward conviction of what I have presented as the denial of the will. It should therefore be studied more closely in that form before it is dogmatized about with Jewish-Protestant assurance. Tauler's "Nachfolgung des armen Leben Christi," and also his "Medulla Animæ," are written in the same admirable spirit, though not quite equal in value to that work. In my opinion the teaching of these genuine Christian mystics, when compared with the teaching of the New Testament, is as alcohol to wine, or what becomes visible in the New Testament as through a veil and mist appears to us in the works of the mystics without cloak or disguise, in full clearness and distinctness. Finally, the New Testament might be regarded as the first initiation, the mystics as the second,—σμικρα και μεγαλα μυστηρια.[16]

We find, however, that which we have called the denial of the will to live more fully developed, more variously expressed, and more vividly represented in the ancient Sanskrit writings than could be the case in the Christian Church and the Western world. That this important ethical view of life could here attain to a fuller development and a more distinct expression is perhaps principally to be ascribed to the fact that it was not confined by an element quite foreign to it, as Christianity is by the Jewish theology, to which its sublime author had necessarily to adapt and accommodate it, partly consciously, partly, it may be, unconsciously. Thus Christianity is made up of two very different constituent parts, and I should like to call the purely ethical part especially and indeed exclusively Christian, and distinguish it from the Jewish dogmatism with which it is combined. If, as has often been feared, and especially at the present time, that excellent and salutary religion should altogether decline, I should look for the reason of this simply in the fact that it does not consist of one single element, but of two originally different elements, which have only

16 "The minor and major mysteries."

been combined through the accident of history. In such a case dissolution had to follow through the separation of these elements, arising from their different relationship to and reaction against the progressive spirit of the age. But even after this dissolution the purely ethical part must always remain uninjured, because it is indestructible. Our knowledge of Hindu literature is still very imperfect. Yet, as we find their ethical teaching variously and powerfully expressed in the Vedas, Puranas, poems, myths, legends of their saints, maxims and precepts, we see that it inculcates love of our neighbour with complete renunciation of self-love; love generally, not confined to mankind, but including all living creatures; benevolence, even to the giving away of the hard-won wages of daily toil; unlimited patience towards all who injure us; the requital of all wickedness, however base, with goodness and love; voluntary and glad endurance of all ignominy; abstinence from all animal food; perfect chastity and renunciation of all sensual pleasure for him who strives after true holiness; the surrender of all possessions, the forsaking of every dwelling-place and of all relatives; deep unbroken solitude, spent in silent contemplation, with voluntary penance and terrible slow self-torture for the absolute mortification of the will, torture which extends to voluntary death by starvation, or by men giving themselves up to crocodiles, or flinging themselves over the sacred precipice in the Himalayas, or being buried alive, or, finally, by flinging themselves under the wheels of the huge car of an idol drawn along amid the singing, shouting, and dancing of bayaderes. And even yet these precepts, whose origin reaches back more than four thousand years, are carried out in practice, in some cases even to the utmost extreme,[17] and this notwithstanding the fact that the Hindu nation has been broken up into so many parts. A religion which demands the greatest sacrifices, and which has yet remained so long in practice in a nation that embraces so many millions of persons, cannot be an arbitrarily invented superstition, but must have its foundation in the nature of man. But besides this, if we read the life of a Christian penitent or saint, and also

[17] At the procession of Jagganath in June, 1840, eleven Hindus threw themselves under the wheels, and were instantly killed. (Letter of an East Indian proprietor in the *Times* of 30th December, 1840.)—*S.*

that of a Hindu saint, we cannot sufficiently wonder at the harmony we find between them. In the case of such radically different dogmas, customs, and circumstances, the inward life and effort of both is the same. And the same harmony prevails in the maxims prescribed for both of them. For example, Tauler speaks of the absolute poverty which one ought to seek, and which consists in giving away and divesting oneself completely of everything from which one might draw comfort or worldly pleasure, clearly because all this constantly affords new nourishment to the will, which it is intended to destroy entirely. And as an Indian counterpart of this, we find in the precepts of Fo that the Saniassi, who ought to be without a dwelling and entirely without property, is further finally enjoined not to lay himself down often under the same tree, lest he should acquire a preference or inclination for it above other trees. The Christian mystic and the teacher of the Vedanta philosophy agree in this respect also, they both regard all outward works and religious exercises as superfluous for him who has attained to perfection. So much agreement in the case of such different ages and nations is a practical proof that what is expressed here is not, as optimistic dullness likes to assert, an eccentricity and perversity of the mind, but an essential side of human nature, which only appears so rarely because of its excellence.

I have now indicated the sources from which there may be obtained a direct knowledge, drawn from life itself, of the phenomena in which the denial of the will to live exhibits itself. In some respects this is the most important point of our whole work; yet I have explained it only quite generally, for it is better to refer to those who speak from direct experience, than to increase the size of this book unduly by weak repetitions of what is said by them.

I wish to add only a little to the general indication of the nature of this state. We saw above that the wicked man, by the vehemence of his volition, suffers constant, consuming, inward pain, and finally, if all objects of volition are exhausted, quenches the fiery thirst of his self-will by the sight of the suffering of others. He, on the contrary, who has attained to the denial of the will to live, however poor, joyless, and full of privation his condition may appear when looked at externally, is yet filled with inward joy and the true peace of heaven. It is not the restless strain of life, the jubilant delight which has been suffering as its preceding or succeeding condition, in the experience of the man who loves life; but it is a peace that cannot be shaken, a deep rest and inward serenity, a state which we cannot behold without the greatest longing when it is brought before our eyes or our imagination, because we at once recognize it as that which alone is right, infinitely surpassing everything else, upon which our better self cries within us the great *sapere aude*.[18] Then we feel that every gratification of our wishes won from the world is merely like the alms which the beggar receives from life to-day that he may hunger again on the morrow; resignation, on the contrary, is like an inherited estate, it frees the owner for ever from all care.

It will be remembered from the Third Book that the æsthetic pleasure in the beautiful consists in great measure in the fact that in entering the state of pure contemplation we are lifted for the moment above all willing, *i. e.,* all wishes and cares; we become, as it were, freed from ourselves. We are no longer the individual whose knowledge is subordinated to the service of its constant willing, the correlative of the particular thing to which objects are motives, but the eternal subject of knowing purified from will, the correlative of the Platonic Idea. And we know that these moments in which, delivered from the ardent strain of will, we seem to rise out of the heavy atmosphere of earth, are the happiest which we experience. From this we can understand how blessed the life of a man must be whose will is silenced, not merely for a moment, as in the enjoyment of the beautiful, but for ever, indeed altogether extinguished, except as regards the last glimmering spark that retains the body in life, and will be extinguished with its death. Such a man, who, after many bitter struggles with his own nature, has finally conquered entirely, continues to exist only as a pure, knowing being, the undimmed mirror of the world. Nothing can trouble him more, nothing can move him, for he has cut all the thousand cords of will which hold us bound to the world, and, as desire, fear, envy, anger, drag us hither and thither in constant pain. He now looks back

18 "Dare to know."

smiling and at rest on the delusions of this world, which once were able to move and agonize his spirit also, but which now stand before him as utterly indifferent to him, as the chess-men when the game is ended, or as, in the morning, the cast-off masquerading dress which worried and disquieted us in a night in Carnival. Life and its forms now pass before him as a fleeting illusion, as a light morning dream before half-waking eyes, the real world already shining through it so that it can no longer deceive; and like this morning dream, they finally vanish altogether without any violent transition. From this we can understand the meaning of Madame Guion when toward the end of her autobiography she often expresses herself thus: "Everything is alike to me; I *cannot* will anything more: often I know not whether I exist or not." . . .

We must not, however, suppose that when, by means of the knowledge which acts as a quieter of will, the denial of the will to live has once appeared, it never wavers or vacillates, and that we can rest upon it as on an assured possession. Rather, it must ever anew be attained by a constant battle. For since the body is the will itself only in the form of objectivity or as manifestation in the world as idea, so long as the body lives, the whole will to live exists potentially, and constantly strives to become actual, and to burn again with all its ardour. Therefore that peace and blessedness in the life of holy men which we have described is only found as the flower which proceeds from the constant victory over the will, and the ground in which it grows is the constant battle with the will to live, for no one can have lasting peace upon earth. We therefore see the histories of the inner life of saints full of spiritual conflicts, temptations, and absence of grace, *i. e.,* the kind of knowledge which makes all motives ineffectual, and as a universal quieter silences all volition, gives the deepest peace and opens the door of freedom. Therefore also we see those who have once attained to the denial of the will to live strive with all their might to keep upon this path, by enforced renunciation of every kind, by penance and severity of life, and by selecting whatever is disagreeable to them, all in order to suppress the will, which is constantly springing up anew. Hence, finally, because they already know the value of salvation, their anxious carefulness to retain the hard-won blessing, their scruples of conscience about every innocent pleasure, or about every little excitement of their vanity, which here also dies last, the most immovable, the most active, and the most foolish of all the inclinations of man. By the term *asceticism,* which I have used so often, I mean in its narrower sense this *intentional* breaking of the will by the refusal of what is agreeable and the selection of what is disagreeable, the voluntarily chosen life of penance and self-chastisement for the continual mortification of the will.

We see this practiced by him who has attained to the denial of the will in order to enable him to persist in it; but suffering in general, as it is inflicted by fate, is a second way of attaining to that denial. Indeed, we may assume that most men only attain to it in this way, and that it is the suffering which is personally experienced, not that which is merely known, which most frequently produces complete resignation, often only at the approach of death. For only in the case of a few is the mere knowledge which, seeing through the *principium individuationis,* first produces perfect goodness of disposition and universal love of humanity, and finally enables them to regard all the suffering of the world as their own; only in the case of a few, I say, is this knowledge sufficient to bring about the denial of the will. Even with him who approaches this point, it is almost invariably the case that the tolerable condition of his own body, the flattery of the moment, the delusion of hope, and the satisfaction of the will, which is ever presenting itself anew, *i. e.,* lust, is a constant hindrance to the denial of the will, and a constant temptation to the renewed assertion of it. Therefore in this respect all these illusions have been personified as the devil. Thus in most cases the will must be broken by great personal suffering before its self-conquest appears. Then we see the man who has passed through all the increasing degrees of affliction with the most vehement resistance, and is finally brought to the verge of despair, suddenly retire into himself, know himself and the world, change his whole nature, rise above himself and all suffering, as if purified and sanctified by it, in inviolable peace, blessedness, and sublimity, willingly renounce everything he previously desired with all his might, and joyfuly embrace death. It is the refined silver of the denial of the will to live that suddenly comes forth from the purifying flame of suffering. It is salvation. Sometimes we see even those who were very wicked purified to this degree by great grief; they have become new beings and are completely changed. Therefore their former misdeeds trouble their consciences no more, yet they willingly atone for them by death, and gladly see the end of the manifestation of that will which is now foreign to them and abhorred by them. The great Goethe has given us a distinct and visible representation of this denial of the will, brought about by great misfortunes and despair of all deliverance, in his immortal masterpiece "Faust," in the story of the sufferings of Gretchen. I know no parallel to this in poetry. It is a perfect example of the second path that leads to the denial of the will, not, as the first, through the mere knowledge of the sufferings of a whole world which one has voluntarily acquired, but through excessive suffering experienced in one's own person. Many tragedies certainly end by conducting their strong-willed heroes to the point of entire resignation, and then generally the will to live and its manifestation end together, but no representation that is known to me brings what is essential to that change so distinctly before us, free from all that is extraneous, as the part of "Faust" I have referred to.

In actual life we see that those unfortunate persons who have to drink to the dregs the greatest cup of suffering, since when all hope is taken from them they have to face with full consciousness a shameful, violent, and often painful death on the scaffold, are very frequently changed in this way. We must not indeed assume that there is so great a difference between their character and that of most men as their fate would seem to indicate, but must attribute the latter for the most part to circumstances; yet they are guilty and to a considerable degree bad. We see, however, many of them, when they have entirely lost hope, changed in the way referred to. They now show actual goodness and purity of disposition, true abhorrence of doing any act in the least degree bad or unkind. They forgive their enemies, even if it is through them that they innocently suffer; and not with words merely and a sort of hypocritical fear of the judges of the lower world, but in reality and with inward earnestness and no desire for revenge. Indeed, their sufferings and death at last become dear to them, for the denial of the will to live has appeared; they often decline the deliverance when it is offered, and die gladly, peacefully, and happily. To them the last secret of life has revealed itself in their excessive pain; the secret that misery and wickedness, sorrow and hate, the sufferer and the inflicter of suffering, however different they may appear to the knowledge which follows the principle of sufficient reason, are in themselves one, the manifestation of that one will to live which objectifies its conflict with itself by means of the *principium individuationis*. They have learned to know both sides in full measure, the badness and the misery; and since at last they see the identity of the two, they reject them both at once; they deny the will to live. In what myths and dogmas they account to their reason for this intuitive and direct knowledge and for their own change is, as has been said, a matter of no importance. . . .

The approach of death and hopelessness are in other respects not absolutely necessary for such a purification through suffering. Even without them the knowledge of the contradiction of the will to live with itself can, through great misfortune and pain, force an entrance, and the vanity of all striving become recognized. Hence it has often happened that men who have led a very restless life in the full strain of the passions, kings, heroes, and adventurers, suddenly change, betake themselves to resignation and penance, become hermits or monks. To this class belong all true accounts of conversions; for example, that of Raymond Lully, who had long wooed a fair lady, and was at last admitted to her chamber, anticipating the fulfilment of all his wishes, when she, opening her bodice, showed him her bosom frightfully eaten with cancer. From that moment, as if he had looked into hell, he was changed; he forsook the court of the king of Majorca, and went into the desert to do penance. If we consider how in both cases the transition from the pleasure to the horror of life was the occasion of it, this throws some light upon the remarkable fact that it is among the French, the most cheerful, gay, sensuous, and frivolous nation in Europe, that by far the strictest of all monastic orders, the Trappists, arose, was re-established by Rancé after its fall, and has maintained itself to the present day in all its purity and strictness, in spite of revolutions, Church reformations, and encroachments of infidelity.

But a knowledge such as that referred to above of the nature of this existence may leave us again along with the occasion of it and the will to live, and with it the previous character may reappear. Thus we see that the passionate Benvenuto Cellini was changed in this way, once when he was in prison, and again when very ill; but when the suffering passed over, he fell back again into his old state. In general, the denial of the will to live by no means proceeds from suffering with the necessity of an effect from its cause, but the will remains free; for this is indeed the one point at which its freedom appears directly in the phenomenon; hence the astonishment which Asmus expresses so strongly at the "transcendental change." In the case of every suffering, it is always possible to conceive a will which exceeds it in intensity and is therefore unconquered by it. Thus Plato speaks in the "Phædon" of men who up to the moment of their execution feast, drink, and indulge in sensuous pleasure, asserting life even to the death. Shakespeare shows us in Cardinal Beaufort the fearful end of a profligate, who dies full of despair, for no suffering or death can break his will, which is vehement to the extreme of wickedness.

The more intense the will is, the more glaring is the conflict of its manifestation, and thus the greater is the suffering. A world which was the manifestation of a far more intense will to live than this world manifests would produce so much the greater suffering; would thus be a hell.

All suffering, since it is a mortification and a call to resignation, has potentially a sanctifying power. This is the explanation of the fact that every great misfortune or deep pain inspires a certain awe. But the sufferer really becomes an object of reverence only when surveying the course of his life as a chain of sorrows, or, mourning some great and incurable misfortune, he does not really look at the special combination of circumstances which has plunged his own life into suffering, nor stops at the single great misfortune that has befallen him; for in so doing his knowledge still follows the principle of sufficient reason, and clings to the particular phenomenon; he still wills life only not under the conditions which have happened to him; but only then, I say, he is truly worthy of reverence when he raises his glance from the particular to the universal, when he regards his suffering as merely an example of the whole, and for him, since in a moral regard he partakes of genius, one case stands for a thousand, so that the whole of life conceived as essentially suffering brings him to resignation. Therefore it inspires reverence when in Goethe's "Torquato Tasso" the princess speaks of how her own life and that of her relations has always been sad and joyless, and yet regards the matter from an entirely universal point of view.

A very noble character we always imagine with a certain trace of quiet sadness, which is anything but a constant fretfulness at daily annoyances (this would be an ignoble trait, and lead us to fear a bad disposition), but is a consciousness derived from knowledge of the vanity of all possessions, of the suffering of all life, not merely of his own. But such knowledge may primarily be awakened by the personal experience of suffering, especially some one great sorrow, as a single unfulfilled wish brought Petrarch to that state of resigned sadness concerning the whole of life which appeals to us so pathetically in his works; for the Daphne he pursued had to flee from his hands in order to leave him, instead of herself, the immortal laurel. When through some such great and irrevocable denial of fate the will is to some extent broken, almost nothing else is desired, and the character shows itself mild, just, noble, and resigned. When, finally, grief has no definite object, but extends itself over the whole of life, then it is to a certain extent a going into itself, a withdrawal, a gradual disappearance of the will, whose visible manifestation, the body, it imperceptibly but surely undermines, so that a man feels a certain loosening of his bonds, a mild foretaste of that death which promises to be the abolition at once of the body and of the will. Therefore a secret pleasure accompanies this grief, and it is this, as I believe, which the most melancholy of all nations has called "the joy of grief." But here also lies the danger of *sentimentality*, both in life itself and in the representation of it in poetry; when a man is always mourning and lamenting without courageously rising to resignation. In this way we lose both earth and heaven, and retain merely a watery sentimentality. Only if suffering assumes the form of pure knowledge, and this, acting as a *quieter of the will*, brings about resignation, is it worthy of reverence. In this regard, however, we feel a certain respect at the sight of every great sufferer which is akin to the feeling excited by virtue and nobility of character, and also seems like a reproach of our own happy condition. We cannot help regarding every sorrow, both our own and those of others, as at least a potential advance towards virtue and holiness, and, on the contrary, pleasures and worldly satisfactions as a retrogression from them. This goes so far, that every man who endures a great bodily or mental suffering, indeed every one who merely performs some physical labour which demands the greatest exertion, in the sweat of his brow and with evident exhaustion, yet with patience and without murmuring, every such man, I say, if we consider him with close attention, appears to us like a sick man who tries a painful cure, and who willingly, and even with satisfaction, endures the suffering it causes him, because he knows that the more he suffers the more the cause of his disease is affected, and that therefore the present suffering is the measure of his cure.

According to what has been said, the denial of the will to live, which is just what is called absolute, entire resignation, or holiness, always proceeds from that quieter of the will which the knowledge of its inner conflict and essential vanity, expressing themselves in the suffering of all living things, becomes. The difference, which we have represented as two paths, consists in whether that knowledge is called up by suffering which is merely and purely *known*, and is freely appropriated by means of the penetration of the *principium individuationis,* or by suffering which is directly *felt* by a man himself. True salvation, deliverance from life and suffering, cannot even be imagined without complete denial of the will. Till then, every one is simply this will itself, whose manifestation is an ephemeral existence, a constantly vain and empty striving, and the world full of suffering we have represented, to which all irrevocably and in like manner belong. For we found above that life is always assured to the will to live, and its one real form is the present, from which they can never escape, since birth and death reign in the phenomenal world. The Indian mythus expresses this by saying "they are born again." The great ethical difference of character means this, that the bad man is infinitely far from the attainment of the knowledge from which the denial of the will proceeds, and therefore he is in truth *actually* exposed to all the miseries which appear in life as *possible;* for even the present fortunate condition of his personality is merely a phenomenon produced by the *principium individuationis,* and a delusion of Mâyâ, the happy dream of a beggar. The sufferings which in the vehemence and ardour of his will he inflicts upon others are the measure of the suffering, the experience of which in his own person cannot break his will, and plainly lead it to the denial of itself. All true and pure love, on the other hand, and even all free justice, proceed from the penetration of the *principium individuationis,* which, if it appears with its full power, results in perfect sanctification and salvation, the phenomenon of which is the state of resignation described above, the unbroken peace which accompanies it, and the greatest delights in death.

§ 69

Suicide, the actual doing away with the individual manifestation of will, differs most widely from the denial of the will to live, which is the single outstanding act of free-will in the manifestation, and is therefore, as Asmus calls it, the transcendental change. This last has been fully considered in the course of our work. Far from being denial of the will, suicide is a phenomenon of strong assertion of will; for the essence of negation lies in this, that the joys of life are shunned, not its sorrows. The suicide wills life, and is only dissatisfied with the conditions under which it has presented itself to him. He therefore by no means surrenders the will to live, but only life, in that he destroys the individual manifestation. He wills life—wills the unrestricted existence and assertion of the body; but the complication of circumstances does not allow this, and there results for him great suffering. The very will to live finds itself so much hampered in this particular manifestation that it cannot put forth its energies. It therefore comes to such a determination as is in conformity with its own nature, which lies outside the conditions of the principle of sufficient reason, and to which, therefore, all particular manifestations are alike indifferent, inasmuch as it itself remains unaffected by all appearing and passing away, and is the inner life of all things; for that firm inward assurance by reason of which we all live free from the constant dread of death, the assurance that a phenomenal existence can never be wanting to the will, supports our action even in the case of suicide. Thus the will to live appears just as much in suicide (Siva) as in the satisfaction of self-preservation (Vishnu) and in the sensual pleasure of procreation (Brahma). This is the inner meaning of the unity of the Trimurtis, which is embodied in its entirety in every human being, though in time it raises now one, now another, of its three heads. Suicide stands in the same relation to the denial of the will as the individual thing does to the Idea. The suicide denies only the individual, not the species. We have already seen that as life is always assured to the will to live, and as sorrow is inseparable from life, suicide, the wilful destruction of the single phenomenal existence, is a vain and foolish act; for the thing-in-itself remains unaffected by it, even as the rainbow endures however fast the drops which support it for the moment may change. But, more than this, it is also the masterpiece of Mâyâ, as the most flagrant example of the contradiction of the will to live with itself. As we found this contradiction in the case of the lowest manifestations of will, in the permanent struggle of all the forces of nature, and of all organic individuals for matter and time and space; and as we saw this antagonism come ever more to the front with terrible distinctness in the ascending grades of the objectification of the will, so at last in the highest grade, the Idea of man, it reaches the point at which, not only the individuals which express the same Idea extirpate each other, but even the same individual declares war against itself. The vehemence with which it wills life, and revolts against what hinders it, namely, suffering, brings it to the point of destroying itself; so that the individual will, by its own act, puts an end to that body which is merely its particular visible expression, rather than permit suffering to break the will. Just because the suicide cannot give up willing, he gives up living. The will asserts itself here even in putting an end to its own manifestation, because it can no longer assert itself otherwise. As, however, it was just the suffering which it so shuns that was able, as mortification of the will, to bring it to the denial of itself, and hence to freedom, so in this respect the suicide is like a sick man, who, after a painful operation which would entirely cure him has been begun, will not allow it to be completed, but prefers to retain his disease. Suffering approaches and reveals itself as the possibility of the denial of will; but the will rejects it, in that it destroys the body, the manifestation of itself, in order that it may remain unbroken. This is the reason why almost all ethical teachers, whether philosophical or religious, condemn suicide, although they themselves can only give far-fetched sophistical reasons for their opinion. But if a human being was ever restrained from committing suicide by purely moral motives, the inmost meaning of this self-conquest (in whatever ideas his reason may have clothed it) was this: "I will not shun suffering, in order that it may help to put an end to the will to live, whose manifestation is so wretched, by so strengthening the knowledge of the real nature of the world which is already beginning to dawn upon me, that it may become the final quieter of my will, and may free me for ever."

It is well known that from time to time cases occur in which the act of suicide extends to the children. The father first kills the children he loves, and then himself. Now, if we consider that conscience, religion, and all influencing ideas teach him to look upon murder as the greatest of crimes, and that, in spite of this, he yet commits it, in the hour of his own death, and when he is altogether uninfluenced by any egotistical motive, such a deed can only be explained in the following manner: in this case, the will of the individual, the father, recognizes itself immediately in the children, though involved in the delusion of mistaking the appearance for the true nature; and as he is at the same time deeply impressed with the knowledge of the misery of all life, he now thinks to put an end to the inner nature itself, along with the appearance, and thus seeks to deliver from existence and its misery both himself and his children, in whom he discerns himself as living again. It would be an error precisely analogous to this to suppose that one may reach the same end as is attained through voluntary chastity by frustrating the aim of nature in fecundation; or indeed if, in consideration of the unendurable suffering of life, parents were to use means for the destruction of their new-born children, instead of doing everything possible to ensure life to that which is struggling into it. For if the will to live is there, as it is the only metaphysical reality, or the thing-in-itself, no physical force can break it, but can only destroy its manifestation at this place and time. It itself can never be transcended except through knowledge. Thus the only way of salvation is, that the will shall manifest itself unrestrictedly, in order that in this individual manifestation it may come to apprehend its own nature. Only as the result of this knowledge can the will transcend itself, and thereby end the suffering which is inseparable from its manifestation. It is quite impossible to accomplish this end by physical force, as by destroying the germ, or by killing the new-born child, or by committing suicide. Nature guides the will to the light, just because it is only in the light that it can work out its salvation. Therefore the aims of Nature are to be promoted in every way as soon as the will to live, which is its inner being, has determined itself.

There is a species of suicide which seems to be quite distinct from the common kind, though its occurrence has perhaps not yet been fully established. It is starvation, voluntarily chosen on the ground of extreme asceticism. All instances of it, however, have been accompanied and obscured by much religious fanaticism, and even superstition. Yet it seems that the absolute denial of will may reach the point at which the will shall be wanting to take the necessary nourishment for the support of the natural life. This kind of suicide is so far from being the result of the will to live, that such a completely resigned ascetic only ceases to live because he has already altogether ceased to will. No other death than that by starvation is in this case conceivable (unless it were the result of some special superstition); for the intention to cut short the torment would itself be a stage in the assertion of will. The dogmas which satisfy the reason of such a penitent delude him with the idea that a being of a higher nature has inculcated the fasting to which his own inner tendency drives him. In the year 1833 all the papers announced that the English historian, Dr. Lingard, had died in January at Dover of voluntary starvation; according to later accounts, it was not he himself, but a relation of his who died. Still in these accounts the persons were

generally ascribed as insane, and it is no longer possible to find out how far this was the case. But I will give here a more recent case of this kind, if it were only to ensure the preservation of one of the rare instances of this striking and extraordinary phenomenon of human nature, which, to all appearance at any rate, belongs to the category to which I wish to assign it and could hardly be explained in any other way. This case is reported in the "Nürnberger Correspondenten" of the 29th July, 1813, in these words:—
"We hear from Bern that in a thick wood near Thurnen a hut has been discovered in which was lying the body of a man who had been dead about a month. His clothes gave little or no clue to his social position. Two very fine shirts lay beside him. The most important article, however, was a Bible interleaved with white paper, part of which had been written upon by the deceased. In this writing he gives the date of his departure from home (but does not mention where his home was). He then says that he was driven by the Spirit of God into the wilderness to pray and fast. During his journey he had fasted seven days and then he had again taken food. After this he had begun again to fast, and continued to do so for the same number of days as before. From this point we find each day marked with a stroke, and of these there are five, at the expiration of which the pilgrim presumably died. There was further found a letter to a clergyman about a sermon which the deceased heard him preach, but the letter was not addressed." Between this voluntary death arising from extreme asceticism and the common suicide resulting from despair there may be various intermediate species and combinations, though this is hard to find out. But human nature has depths, obscurities, and perplexities, the analysis and elucidation of which is a matter of the very greatest difficulty.

§ 70

It might be supposed that the entire exposition (now terminated) of that which I call the denial of the will is irreconcilable with the earlier explanation of necessity, which belongs just as much to motivation as to every other form of the principle of sufficient reason, and according to which, motives, like all causes, are only occasional causes, upon which the character unfolds its nature and reveals it with the necessity of a natural law, on account of which we absolutely denied freedom as *liberum arbitrium indifferentiæ*.[10] But far from suppressing this here I would call it to mind. In truth, real freedom, *i. e.,* independence of the principle of sufficient reason, belongs to the will only as a thing-in-itself, not to its manifestation, whose essential form is everywhere the principle of sufficient reason, the element or sphere of necessity. But the one case in which that freedom can become directly visible in the manifestation is that in which it makes an end of what manifests itself, and because the mere manifestation tion, as a link in the chain of causes, the living body in time, which contains only phenomena, still continues to exist, the will which manifests itself through this phenomenon then stands in contradiction to it, for it denies what the phenomenon expresses. In such a case the organs of generation, for example, as the visible form of the sexual impulse, are there and in health; but yet, in the inmost consciousness, no sensual gratification is desired; and although the whole body is only the visible expression of the will to live, yet the motives which correspond to this will no longer act; indeed, the dissolution of the body, the end of the individual, and in this way the greatest check to the natural will, is welcome and desired. Now, the contradiction between our assertions of the necessity of the determination of the will by motives, in accordance with the character, on the one hand, and of the possibility of the entire suppression of the will whereby the motives become powerless, on the other hand, is only the repetition in the reflection of philosophy of this *real* contradiction which arises from the direct encroachment of the freedom of the will-in-itself, which knows no necessity, into the sphere of the necessity of its manifestation. But the key to the solution of these contradictions lies in the fact that the state in which the character is withdrawn from the power of motives does not proceed directly from the will, but from a changed form of knowledge. So long as the knowledge is merely that which is involved in the *principium individuationis* and exclusively follows the principle of sufficient

---

[19] "Equal freedom of choice."

reason, the strength of the motives is irresistible. But when the *principium individuationis* is seen through, when the Ideas, and indeed the inner nature of the thing-in-itself, as the same will in all, are directly recognized, and from this knowledge a universal quieter of volition arises, then the particular motives become ineffective, because the kind of knowledge which corresponds to them is obscured and thrown into the background by quite another kind. Therefore the character can never partially change, but must, with the consistency of a law of Nature, carry out in the particular the will which it manifests as a whole. But this whole, the character itself, may be completely suppressed or abolished through the change of knowledge referred to above. It is this suppression or abolition which Asmus, as quoted above, marvels at and denotes the "catholic, transcendental change"; and in the Christian Church it has very aptly been called th*e new birth,* and the knowledge from which it springs, the *work of grace.* Therefore it is not a question of a change, but of an entire suppression of the character; and hence it arises that, however different the characters which experience the suppression may have been before it, after it they show a great similarity in their conduct, though every one still speaks very differently according to his conceptions and dogmas.

In this sense, then, the old philosophical doctrine of the freedom of the will, which has constantly been contested and constantly maintained, is not without ground, and the dogma of the Church of the work of grace and the new birth is not without meaning and significance. But we now unexpectedly see both united in one, and we can also now understand in what sense the excellent Malebranche could say, *"La liberté est un mystère,"* [20] and was right. For precisely what the Christian mystics call *the work of grace* and *the new birth,* is for us the single direct expression of *the freedom of the will*. It appears only if the will, having attained to a knowledge of its own real nature, receives from this a *quieter,* by means of which the motives are deprived of their effect, which belongs to the province of another kind of knowledge, the objects of which are merely phenomena. The possibility of the freedom

[20] "Freedom is a mystery."

which thus expresses itself is the greatest prerogative of man, which is for ever wanting to the brute, because the condition of it is the deliberation of reason, which enables him to survey the whole of life independent of the impression of the present. The brute is entirely without the possibility of freedom, as, indeed, it is without the possibility of a proper or deliberate choice following upon a completed conflict of motives, which for this purpose would have to be abstract ideas. Therefore with the same necessity with which the stone falls to the earth, the hungry wolf buries its fangs in the flesh of its prey, without the possibility of the knowledge that it is itself the destroyed as well as the destroyer. *Necessity is the kingdom of nature; freedom is the kingdom of grace.*

Now, because, as we have seen, that *self-suppression of the will* proceeds from knowledge, and all knowledge is involuntary, that denial of will also, that entrance into freedom, cannot be forcibly attained to by intention or design, but proceeds from the inmost relation of knowing and volition in the man, and therefore comes suddenly, as if spontaneously from without. This is why the Church has called it *the work of grace;* and that it still regards it as independent of the acceptance of grace corresponds to the fact that the effect of the quieter is finally a free act of will. And because, in consequence of such a work of grace, the whole nature of man is changed and reversed from its foundation, so that he no longer wills anything of all that he previously willed so intensely, so that it is as if a new man actually took the place of the old, the Church has called this consequence of the work of grace the *new birth.* For what it calls the *natural man,* to which it denies all capacity for good, is just the will to live, which must be denied if deliverance from an existence such as ours is to be attained. Behind our existence lies something else, which is accessible to us only if we have shaken off this world. . . .

THE WORLD AS WILL AND IDEA

Volume II

CHAPTER XIX

THE will, as the thing in itself, constitutes the inner, true, and indestructible nature of man; in itself, however, it is unconscious. For consciousness is conditioned by the intellect, and the intellect is a mere accident of our being; for it is a function of the brain, which, together with the nerves and spinal cord connected with it, is a mere fruit, a product, nay, so far, a parasite of the rest of the organism; for it does not directly enter into its inner constitution, but merely serves the end of self-preservation by regulating the relations of the organism to the external world. The organism itself, on the other hand, is the visibility, the objectivity, of the individual will, the image of it as it presents itself in that very brain (which in the first book we learned to recognize as the condition of the objective world in general), therefore also brought about by its forms of knowledge, space, time, and causality, and consequently presenting itself as extended, successively acting, and material, *i. e.,* as something operative or efficient. The members are both directly felt and also perceived by means of the senses only in the brain. According to this one may say: The intellect is the secondary phenomenon; the organism the primary phenomenon, that is, the immediate manifestation of the will; the will is metaphysical, the intellect physical;—the intellect, like its objects, is merely phenomenal appearance; the will alone is the thing in itself. Then, in a more and more *figurative sense,* thus by way of simile: The will is the substance of man, the intellect the accident; the will is the matter, the intellect is the form; the will is warmth, the intellect is light.

We shall now first of all verify and also elucidate this thesis by the following facts connected with the inner life of man; and on this opportunity perhaps more will be done for the knowledge of the inner man than is to be found in many systematic psychologies.

1. Not only the consciousness of other things, *i. e.,* the apprehension of the external world, but also *self-consciousness,* contains, as was mentioned already above, a knower and a known; otherwise it would not be *consciousness.* For *consciousness* consists in knowing; but knowing requires a knower and a known; therefore there could be no self-consciousness if there were not in it also a known opposed to the knower and different from it. As there can be no object without a subject, so also there can be no subject without an object, *i. e.,* no knower without something different from it which is known. Therefore a consciousness which is through and through pure intelligence is impossible. The intelligence is like the sun, which does not illuminate space if there is no object from which its rays are reflected. The knower himself, as such, cannot be known; otherwise he would be the known of another knower. But now, as the *known* in self-consciousness we find exclusively the *will.* For not merely willing and purposing in the narrowest sense, but also all striving, wishing, shunning, hoping, fearing, loving, hating, in short, all that directly constitutes our own weal and woe, desire and aversion, is clearly only affection of the will, is a moving, a modification of willing and not-willing, is just that which, if it takes outward effect, exhibits itself as an act of will proper. In all knowledge, however, the known is first and essential, not the knower. Therefore in self-consciousness also the known, thus the will, must be what is first and original; the knower, on the other hand, only what is secondary, that which has been added, the mirror. They are related very much as the luminous to the reflecting body; or, again, as the vibrating strings to the resounding-board, in which case the note produced would be consciousness.

2. But in order not merely to describe consciousness figuratively, but to know it thoroughly, we have first of all to find out what appears in the same way in every consciousness, and therefore, as the common and constant element, will also be the essential. Then we shall consider what distinguishes *one* consciousness from an-

other, which accordingly will be the adventitious and secondary element.

Consciousness is positively only known to us as a property of animal nature; therefore we must not, and indeed cannot, think of it otherwise than as *animal consciousness,* so that this expression is tautological. Now, that which in *every* animal consciousness, even the most imperfect and the weakest, is always present, nay, lies at its foundation, is an immediate sense of *longing,* and of the alternate satisfaction and non-satisfaction of it, in very different degrees. This we know to a certain extent *a priori.* For marvellously different as the innumerable species of animals are, and strange as some new form, never seen before, appears to us, we yet assume beforehand its inmost nature, with perfect certainty, as well known, and indeed fully confided to us. We know that the animal *wills,* indeed also *what* it wills, existence, well-being, life, and propagation; and since in this we presuppose with perfect certainty identity with us, we do not hesitate to attribute to it unchanged all the affections of will which we know in ourselves, and speak at once of its desire, aversion, fear, anger, hatred, love, joy, sorrow, longing, &c. On the other hand, whenever phenomena of mere knowledge come to be spoken of we fall at once into uncertainty. We do not venture to say that the animal conceives, thinks, judges, knows: we only attribute to it with certainty ideas in general; because without them its *will* could not have those emotions referred to above. But with regard to the definite manner of knowing of the brutes and the precise limits of it in a given species, we have only indefinite conceptions, and make conjectures. Hence our understanding with them is also often difficult, and is only brought about by skill, in consequence of experience and practice. Here then lie distinctions of consciousness. On the other hand, a longing, desiring, wishing, or a detesting, shunning, and not wishing, is proper to every consciousness: man has it in common with the polyp. This is accordingly the essential element in and the basis of every consciousness. The difference of the manifestations of this in the different species of animal beings depends upon the various extension of their sphere of knowledge, in which the motives of those manifestations lie.

We understand directly from our own nature all actions and behaviour of the brutes which express movements of the will; therefore, so far, we sympathize with them in various ways. On the other hand, the gulf between us and them results simply and solely from the difference of intellect. The gulf which lies between a very sagacious brute and a man of very limited capacity is perhaps not much greater than that which exists between a blockhead and a man of genius; therefore here also the resemblance between them in another aspect, which springs from the likeness of their inclinations and emotions, and assimilates them again to each other, sometimes appears with surprising prominence, and excites astonishment. This consideration makes it clear that in all animal natures the *will* is what is primary and substantial, the *intellect* again is secondary, adventitious, indeed a mere tool for the service of the former, and is more or less complete and complicated, according to the demands of this service. As a species of animals is furnished with hoofs, claws, hands, wings, horns, or teeth according to the aims of its will, so also is it furnished with a more or less developed brain, whose function is the intelligence necessary for its endurance. The more complicated the organization becomes, in the ascending series of animals, the more numerous also are its wants, and the more varied and specially determined the objects which are capable of satisfying them; hence the more complicated and distant the paths by which these are to be obtained, which must now be all known and found: therefore in the same proportion the ideas of the animal must be more versatile, accurate, definite, and connected, and also its attention must be more highly strung, more sustained, and more easily roused, consequently its intellect must be more developed and perfected. Accordingly we see the organ of intelligence, the cerebral system, together with all the organs of sense, keep pace with the increasing wants and the complication of the organism; and the increase of the part of consciousness that has to do with ideas (as opposed to the willing part) exhibits itself in a bodily form in the ever-increasing proportion of the brain in general to the rest of the nervous system, and of the cerebrum to the cerebellum; for (according to Flourens) the former is the workshop of ideas, while the latter is the disposer and orderer of movements. The last step which nature has taken in this respect is, however, disproportionately great. For in man not only does the faculty of ideas of *perception,* which alone existed hitherto, reach the highest degree of perfection, but the *abstract* idea, thought, *i. e., reason,* and with it reflection, is added. Through this important advance of the intellect, thus of the secondary part of consciousness, it now gains a preponderance over the primary part, in so far as it becomes henceforward the predominantly active part. While in the brute the immediate sense of its satisfied or unsatisfied desire constitutes by far the most important part of its consciousness, and the more so indeed the lower the grade of the animal, so that the lowest animals are distinguished from plants only by the addition of a dull idea, in man the opposite is the case. Vehement as are his desires, even more vehement than those of any brute, rising to the level of passions, yet his consciousness remains continuously and predominantly occupied and filled with ideas and thoughts. Without doubt this has been the principal occasion of that fundamental error of all philosophers on account of which they make thought that which is essential and primary in the so-called soul, *i. e.,* in the inner or spiritual life of man, always placing it first, but will, as a mere product of thought, they regard as only a subordinate addition and consequence of it. But if willing merely proceeded from knowing, how could the brutes, even the lower grades of them, with so very little knowledge, often show such an unconquerable and vehement will? Accordingly, since that fundamental error of the philosophers makes, as it were, the accident the substance, it leads them into mistaken paths, which there is afterwards no way of getting out of. Now this relative predominance of the *knowing* consciousness over the *desiring,* consequently of the secondary part over the primary, which appears in man, may, in particular exceptionally favoured individuals, go so far that at the moments of its highest ascendancy, the secondary or knowing part of consciousness detaches itself altogether from the willing part, and passes into free activity for itself, *i. e.,* untouched by the will, and consequently no longer serving it. Thus it becomes purely objective, and the clear mirror of the world, and from it the conceptions of genius then arise, which are the subject of our third book.

3. If we run through the series of grades of animals downwards, we see the intellect always becoming weaker and less perfect, but we by no means observe a corresponding degradation of the will. Rather it retains everywhere its identical nature and shows itself in the form of great attachment to life, care for the individual and the species, egoism and regardlessness of all others, together with the emotions that spring from these. Even in the smallest insect the will is present, complete and entire; it wills what it wills as decidedly and completely as the man. The difference lies merely in *what* it wills, *i. e.,* in the motives, which, however, are the affair of the intellect. It indeed, as the secondary part of consciousness, and bound to the bodily organism, has innumerable degrees of completeness, and is in general essentially limited and imperfect. The *will,* on the contrary, as original and the thing in itself, can never be imperfect, but every act of will is all that it can be. On account of the simplicity which belongs to the will as the thing in itself, the metaphysical in the phenomenon, its nature admits of no degrees, but is always completely itself. Only its *excitement* has degrees, from the weakest inclination to the passion, and also its susceptibility to excitement, thus its vehemence from the phlegmatic to the choleric temperament. The *intellect,* on the other hand, has not merely degrees of *excitement,* from sleepiness to being in the vein, and inspiration, but also degrees of its nature, of the completeness of this, which accordingly rises gradually from the lowest animals, which can only obscurely apprehend, up to man, and here again from the fool to the genius. The *will* alone is everywhere completely itself. For its function is of the utmost simplicity; it consists in willing and not willing, which goes on with the greatest ease, without effort, and requires no practice. Knowing, on the contrary, has multifarious functions, and never takes place entirely without effort, which is required to fix the attention and to make clear the object, and at a higher stage is certainly needed for thinking and deliberation; therefore it is also capable of great improvement through exercise and education. If the intellect presents a simple, perceptible object to the will, the latter expresses at once its approval or disapproval of it, and this even if the intellect has laboriously inquired and pondered, in order from numerous data, by means of difficult combi-

nations, ultimately to arrive at the conclusion as to which of the two seems to be most in conformity with the interests of the will. The latter has meanwhile been idly resting, and when the conclusion is arrived at it enters, as the Sultan enters the Divan, merely to express again its monotonous approval or disapproval, which certainly may vary in degree, but in its nature remains always the same.

This fundamentally different nature of the will and the intellect, the essential simplicity and originality of the former, in contrast to the complicated and secondary character of the latter, becomes still more clear to us if we observe their remarkable interaction within us, and now consider in the particular case, how the images and thoughts which arise in the intellect move the will, and how entirely separated and different are the parts which the two play. We can indeed perceive this even in actual events which excite the will in a lively manner, while primarily and in themselves they are merely objects of the intellect. But, on the one hand, it is here not so evident that this reality primarily existed only in the intellect; and, on the other hand, the change does not generally take place so rapidly as is necessary if the thing is to be easily surveyed, and thereby becomes thoroughly comprehensible. Both of these conditions, however, are fulfilled if it is merely thoughts and phantasies which we allow to act on the will. If, for example, alone with ourselves, we think over our personal circumstances, and now perhaps vividly present to ourselves the menace of an actually present danger and the possibility of an unfortunate issue, anxiety at once compresses the heart, and the blood ceases to circulate in the veins. But if then the intellect passes to the possibility of an opposite issue, and lets the imagination picture the long-hoped-for happiness thereby attained, all the pulses quicken at once with joy and the heart feels light as a feather, till the intellect awakes from its dream. Thereupon, suppose that an occasion should lead the memory to an insult or injury once suffered long ago, at once anger and bitterness pour into the breast that was but now at peace. But then arises, called up by accident, the image of a long-lost love, with which the whole romance and its magic scenes is connected; then that anger will at once give place to profound longing and sadness. Finally, if there occurs to us some former humiliating incident, we shrink together, would like to sink out of sight, blush with shame, and often try forcibly to distract and divert our thoughts by some loud exclamation, as if to scare some evil spirit. One sees, the intellect plays, and the will must dance to it. Indeed the intellect makes the will play the part of a child which is alternately thrown at pleasure into joyful or sad moods by the chatter and tales of its nurse. This depends upon the fact that the will is itself without knowledge, and the understanding which is given to it is without will. Therefore the former is like a body which is moved, the latter like the causes which set it in motion, for it is the medium of motives. Yet in all this the primacy of the will becomes clear again, if this will, which, as we have shown, becomes the sport of the intellect as soon as it allows the latter to control it, once makes its supremacy in the last instance felt by prohibiting the intellect from entertaining certain ideas, absolutely preventing certain trains of thought from arising, because it knows, *i. e.,* learns from that very intellect, that they would awaken in it some one of the emotions set forth above. It now bridles the intellect, and compels it to turn to other things. Hard as this often may be, it must yet be accomplished as soon as the will is in earnest about it, for the resisting in this case does not proceed from the intellect, which always remains indifferent, but from the will itself, which in one respect has an inclination towards an idea that in another respect it abhors. It is in itself interesting to the will simply because it excites it, but at the same time abstract knowledge tells it that this idea will aimlessly cause it a shock of painful or unworthy emotion: it now decides in conformity with this abstract knowledge, and compels the obedience of the intellect. This is called "being master of oneself." Clearly the master here is the will, the servant the intellect, for in the last instance the will always keeps the upper hand, and therefore constitutes the true core, the inner being of man. In this respect the title Ηγεμονικον [1] would belong to the *will;* yet it seems, on the other hand, to apply to the *intellect,* because it is the leader and guide, like the *valet de place* who conducts a stranger. In truth, however,

---

[1] Leader.

the happiest figure of the relation of the two is the strong blind man who carries on his shoulders the lame man who can see.

The relation of the will to the intellect here explained may also be further recognized in the fact that the intellect is originally entirely a stranger to the purposes of the will. It supplies the motives to the will, but it only learns afterwards, completely *a posteriori,* how they have affected it, as one who makes a chemical experiment applies the reagents and awaits the result. Indeed the intellect remains so completely excluded from the real decisions and secret purposes of its own will that sometimes it can only learn them like those of a stranger, by spying upon them and surprising them, and must catch the will in the act of expressing itself in order to get at its real intentions. For example, I have conceived a plan, about which, however, I have still some scruple, but the feasibleness of which, as regards its possibility, is completely uncertain, for it depends upon external and still undecided circumstances. It would therefore certainly be unnecessary to come to a decision about it at present, and so for the time I leave the matter as it is. Now in such a case I often do not know how firmly I am already attached to that plan in secret, and how much, in spite of the scruple, I wish to carry it out: that is, my intellect does not know. But now only let me receive news that it is practicable, at once there rises within me a jubilant, irresistible gladness, that passes through my whole being and takes permanent possession of it, to my own astonishment. For now my intellect learns for the first time how firmly my will had laid hold of that plan, and how thoroughly the plan suited it, while the intellect had regarded it as entirely problematical, and had with difficulty been able to overcome that scruple. Or in another case, I have entered eagerly into a contract which I believed to be very much in accordance with my wishes. But as the matter progresses the disadvantages and burdens of it are felt, and I begin to suspect that I even repent of what I so eagerly pursued; yet I rid myself of this feeling by assuring myself that even if I were not bound I would follow the same course. Now, however, the contract is unexpectedly broken by the other side, and I perceive with astonishment that this happens to my great satisfaction and relief.

Often we don't know what we wish or what we fear. We may entertain a wish for years without even confessing it to ourselves, or even allowing it to come to clear consciousness; for the intellect must know nothing about it, because the good opinion which we have of ourselves might thereby suffer. But if it is fulfilled we learn from our joy, not without shame, that we have wished this. For example, the death of a near relation whose heir we are. And sometimes we do not know what we really fear, because we lack the courage to bring it to distinct consciousness. Indeed we are often in error as to the real motive from which we have done something or left it undone, till at last perhaps an accident discovers to us the secret, and we know that what we have held to be the motive was not the true one, but another which we had not wished to confess to ourselves, because it by no means accorded with the good opinion we entertained of ourselves. For example, we refrain from doing something on purely moral grounds, as we believe, but afterwards we discover that we were only restrained by fear, for as soon as all danger is removed we do it. In particular cases this may go so far that a man does not even guess the true motive of his action, nay, does not believe himself capable of being influenced by such a motive; and yet it is the true motive of his action. We may remark in passing that in all this we have a confirmation and explanation of the rule of La Rochefoucauld: *"L'amour-propre est plus habile que le plus habile homme du monde"*; [2] nay, even a commentary on the Delphic γνωθι σεαυτον [3] and its difficulty. If now, on the contrary, as all philosophers imagine, the intellect constituted our true nature and the purposes of the will were a mere result of knowledge, then only the motive from which we imagined that we acted would be decisive of our moral worth; in analogy with the fact that the intention, not the result, is in this respect decisive. But really then the distinction between imagined and true motive would be impossible. Thus all cases here set forth, to which every one who pays attention may observe analogous cases in himself, show us how the intellect is so strange to the will that it is sometimes even mystified by it: for it indeed supplies it with motives, but does not penetrate

[2] "Self-love is cleverer than the cleverest man in the world."
[3] "Know thyself."

into the secret workshop of its purposes. It is indeed a confidant of the will, but a confidant that is not told everything. This is also further confirmed by the fact, which almost every one will some time have the opportunity of observing in himself, that sometimes the intellect does not thoroughly trust the will. If we have formed some great and bold purpose, which as such is yet really only a promise made by the will to the intellect, there often remains within us a slight unconfessed doubt whether we are quite in earnest about it, whether in carrying it out we will not waver or draw back, but will have sufficient firmness and persistency to fulfil it. It therefore requires the deed to convince us ourselves of the sincerity of the purpose.

All these facts prove the absolute difference of the will and the intellect, the primacy of the former and the subordinate position of the latter.

4. The *intellect* becomes tired; the *will* is never tired. After sustained work with the head we feel the tiredness of the brain, just like that of the arm after sustained bodily work. All *knowing* is accompanied with effort; *willing,* on the contrary, is our very nature, whose manifestations take place without any weariness and entirely of their own accord. Therefore, if our will is strongly excited, as in all emotions, thus in anger, fear, desire, grief, &c., and we are now called upon to know, perhaps with the view of correcting the motives of that emotion, the violence which we must do ourselves for this purpose is evidence of the transition from the original natural activity proper to ourselves to the derived, indirect, and formed activity. For the will alone is . . . is active without being called upon, and therefore often too early and too much, and it knows no weariness. Infants who scarcely show the first weak trace of intelligence are already full of self-will: through unlimited, aimless roaring and shrieking they show the pressure of will with which they swell, while their willing has yet no object, *i. e.,* they will without knowing what they will. What Cabanis has observed is also in point here: *"Toutes ces passions, qui se succèdent d'une manière si rapide, se peignent avec tant de naïveté, sur le visage mobile des enfants. Tandis que les faibles muscles de leurs bras et de leurs jambes savent encore a peine former quelque mouvements indécis, les muscles de la face*

expriment déja par des mouvements, distincts presque toute la suite des affections générales propres à la nature humaine: et l'observateur attentif reconnait facilement dans ce tableau les traits caractéristiques de l'homme futur" (*Rapports du Physique et Moral,* vol. i., p. 123).[4] The intellect, on the contrary, develops slowly, following the completion of the brain and the maturity of the whole organism, which are its conditions, just because it is merely a somatic function. It is because the brain attains its full size in the seventh year that from that time forward children become so remarkably intelligent, inquisitive, and reasonable. But then comes puberty; to a certain extent it affords a support to the brain, or a resounding-board, and raises the intellect at once by a large step, as it were by an octave, corresponding to the lowering of the voice by that amount. But at once the animal desires and passions that now appear resist the reasonableness that has hitherto prevailed and to which they have been added. Further evidence is given of the indefatigable nature of the will by the fault which is, more or less, peculiar to all men by nature, and is only overcome by education—*precipitation.* It consists in this, that the will hurries to its work before the time. This work is the purely active and executive part, which ought only to begin when the explorative and deliberative part, thus the work of knowing, has been completely and thoroughly carried out. But this time is seldom waited for. Scarcely are a few data concerning the circumstances before us, or the event that has occurred, or the opinion of others conveyed to us, superficially comprehended and hastily gathered together by knowledge, than from the depths of our being the will, always ready and never weary, comes forth unasked, and shows itself as terror, fear, hope, joy, desire, envy, grief, zeal, anger, or courage, and leads to rash words and deeds, which are generally followed by repentance when time has taught us that the hegemonicon, the intellect, has not been able to finish half its work of comprehending the circumstances, reflecting on

---

[4] "All these passions, which follow one another so quickly, picture themselves naïvely on the mobile faces of infants. While their feeble muscles, arms, and legs hardly know yet how to make the vaguest movements, the muscles of the face already express, by distinct movements, all the principal emotions proper to human nature; and the attentive observer easily recognizes in this picture the characteristic traits of the future man."

their connection, and deciding what is prudent, because the will did not wait for it, but sprang forward long before its time with "Now it is my turn!" and at once began the active work, without the intellect being able to resist, as it is a mere slave and bond-man of the will, and not, like it, αυτοματος, nor active from its own power and its own impulse; therefore it is easily pushed aside and silenced by a nod of the will, while on its part it is scarcely able, with the greatest efforts, to bring the will even to a brief pause, in order to speak. This is why the people are so rare, and are found almost only among Spaniards, Turks, and perhaps Englishmen, who even under circumstances of provocation *keep the head uppermost,* imperturbably proceed to comprehend and investigate the state of affairs, and when others would already be beside themselves, still ask further questions, which is something quite different from the indifference founded upon apathy and stupidity of many Germans and Dutchmen. Iffland used to give an excellent representation of this admirable quality, as Hetmann of the Cossacks, in Benjowski, when the conspirators have enticed him into their tent and hold a rifle to his head, with the warning that they will fire it if he utters a cry, Iffland blew into the mouth of the rifle to try whether it was loaded. Of ten things that annoy us, nine would not be able to do so if we understood them thoroughly in their causes, and therefore knew their necessity and true nature; but we would do this much oftener if we made them the object of reflection before making them the object of wrath and indignation. For what bridle and bit are to an un-manageable horse the intellect is for the will in man; by this bridle it must be controlled by means of instruction, exhortation, culture, &c., for in itself it is as wild and impetuous an impulse as the force that appears in the descending waterfall, nay, as we know, it is at bottom identical with this. In the height of anger, in intoxication, in despair, it has taken the bit between its teeth, has run away, and follows its original nature. In the *Mania sine delirio* it has lost bridle and bit altogether, and shows now most distinctly its original nature, and that the intellect is as different from it as the bridle from the horse. In this condition it may also be compared to a clock which, when a certain screw is taken away, runs down without stopping.

Thus this consideration also shows us the will as that which is original, and therefore metaphysical; the intellect, on the other hand, as something subordinate and physical. For as such the latter is, like everything physical, subject to *vis inertiæ,* consequently only active if it is set agoing by something else, the will, which rules it, manages it, rouses it to effort, in short, imparts to it the activity which does not originally reside in it. Therefore it willingly rests whenever it is permitted to do so, often declares itself lazy and disinclined to activity; through continued effort it becomes weary to the point of complete stupefaction, is exhausted, like the voltaic pile, through repeated shocks. Hence all continuous mental work demands pauses and rest, otherwise stupidity and incapacity ensue, at first of course only temporarily; but if this rest is persistently denied to the intellect it will become excessively and continuously fatigued, and the consequence is a permanent deterioration of it, which in an old man may pass into complete incapacity, into childishness, imbecility, and madness. It is not to be attributed to age in and for itself, but to long-continued tyrannical over-exertion of the intellect or brain, if this misfortune appears in the last years of life. This is the explanation of the fact that Swift became mad, Kant became childish, Walter Scott, and also Wordsworth, Southey, and many *minorum gentium,*[5] became dull and incapable. Goethe remained to the end clear, strong, and active-minded, because he, who was always a man of the world and a courtier, never carried on his mental occupations with self-compulsion. The same holds good of Wieland and of Knebel, who lived to the age of ninety-one, and also of Voltaire. Now all this proves how very subordinate and physical and what a mere tool the intellect is. Just on this account it requires, during almost a third part of its lifetime, the entire suspension of its activity in sleep, *i. e.,* the rest of the brain, of which it is the mere function, and which therefore just as truly precedes it as the stomach precedes digestion, or as a body precedes its impulsion, and with which in old age it flags and decays. The will, on the contrary, as the thing in itself, is never lazy, is absolutely untiring, its activity is its essence, it never ceases willing, and when, during deep sleep, it is forsaken of the intellect, and therefore cannot act outwardly

[5] "Lesser gentry."

in accordance with motives, it is active as the vital force, cares the more uninterruptedly for the inner economy of the organism, and as *vis naturæ medicatrix* [6] sets in order again the irregularities that have crept into it. For it is not, like the intellect, a function of the body; *but the body is its function;* therefore it is, *ordine rerum,*[7] prior to the body, as its metaphysical substratum, as the in-itself of its phenomenal appearance. It shares its unwearying nature, for the time that life lasts, with the heart, that *primum mobile* of the organism, which has therefore become its symbol and synonym. Moreover, it does not disappear in the old man, but still continues to will what it has willed, and indeed becomes firmer, more inflexible, than it was in youth, more implacable, self-willed, and unmanageable, because the intellect has become less susceptible: therefore in old age the man can perhaps only be matched by taking advantage of the weakness of his intellect.

Moreover, the prevailing *weakness* and *imperfection* of the intellect, as it is shown in the want of judgment, narrow-mindedness, perversity, and folly of the great majority of men, would be quite inexplicable if the intellect were not subordinate, adventitious, and merely instrumental, but the immediate and original nature of the so-called soul, or in general of the inner man: as all philosophers have hitherto assumed it to be. For how could the original nature in its immediate and peculiar function so constantly err and fail? The *truly* original in human consciousness, the *willing,* always goes on with perfect success; every being wills unceasingly, capably, and decidedly. To regard the immorality in the will as an imperfection of it would be a fundamentally false point of view. For morality has rather a source which really lies above nature, and therefore its utterances are in contradiction with it. Therefore morality is in direct opposition to the natural will, which in itself is completely egoistic; indeed the pursuit of the path of morality leads to the abolition of the will.

5. That the *will* is what is real and essential in man, and the *intellect* only subordinate, conditioned, and produced, is also to be seen in the fact that the latter can carry on its function with perfect purity and correctness only so long as the will is silent and

---

[6] "The healing power of nature."
[7] "In the order of things."

pauses. On the other hand, the function of the intellect is disturbed by every observable excitement of the will, and its result is falsified by the intermixture of the latter; but the converse does not hold, that the intellect should in the same way be a hindrance to the will. Thus the moon cannot shine when the sun is in the heavens, but when the moon is in the heavens it does not prevent the sun from shining.

A great *fright* often deprives us of our senses to such an extent that we are petrified, or else do the most absurd things; for example, when fire has broken out run right into the flames. *Anger* makes us no longer know what we do, still less what we say. *Zeal,* therefore called blind, makes us incapable of weighing the arguments of others, or even of seeking out and setting in order our own. *Joy* makes us inconsiderate, reckless, and foolhardy, and *desire* acts almost in the same way. *Fear* prevents us from seeing and laying hold of the resources that are still present, and often lie close beside us. Therefore for overcoming sudden dangers, and also for fighting with opponents and enemies, the most essential qualifications are *coolness and presence of mind.* The former consists in the silence of the will so that the intellect can act; the latter in the undisturbed activity of the intellect under the pressure of events acting on the will; therefore the former is the condition of the latter, and the two are nearly related; they are seldom to be found, and always only in a limited degree. But they are of inestimable advantage, because they permit the use of the intellect just at those times when we stand most in need of it, and therefore confer decided superiority. He who is without them knows only what he should have done or said when the opportunity has passed. It is very appropriately said of him who is violently moved, *i. e.,* whose will is so strongly excited that it destroys the purity of the function of the intellect, he is *disarmed;* for the correct knowledge of the circumstances and relations is our defense and weapon in the conflict with things and with men. In this sense Balthazar Gracian says: *"Es la passion enemiga declarada de la cordura"* (Passion is the declared enemy of prudence). If now the intellect were not something completely different from the will, but, as has been hitherto supposed, knowing and willing had the same root, and were equally original functions of an absolutely simple nature, then with the rousing and heightening of the will, in which the emotion consists, the intellect would necessarily also be heightened; but, as we have seen, it is rather hindered and depressed by this; whence the ancients called emotion *animi perturbatio.* The intellect is really like the reflecting surface of water, but the water itself is like the will, whose disturbance therefore at once destroys the clearness of that mirror and the distinctness of its images. The *organism* is the will itself, is embodied will, *i. e.,* will objectively perceived in the brain. Therefore many of its functions, such as respiration, circulation, secretion of bile, and muscular power, are heightened and accelerated by the pleasurable, and in general the healthy, emotions. The *intellect,* on the other hand, is the mere function of the brain, which is only nourished and supported by the organism as a parasite. Therefore every perturbation of the *will,* and with it of the *organism,* must disturb and paralyse the function of the brain, which exists for itself and for no other wants than its own, which are simply rest and nourishment.

But this disturbing influence of the activity of the will upon the intellect can be shown, not only in the perturbations brought about by emotions, but also in many other, more gradual, and therefore more lasting falsifications of thought by our inclinations. *Hope* makes us regard what we wish, and *fear* what we are apprehensive of, as probable and near, and both exaggerate their object. Plato (according to Ælian, V. H., 13, 28) very beautifully called hope the dream of the waking. Its nature lies in this, that the will, when its servant the intellect is not able to produce what it wishes, obliges it at least to picture it before it, in general to undertake the rôle of comforter, to appease its lord with fables, as a nurse a child, and so to dress these out that they gain an appearance of likelihood. Now in this the intellect must do violence to its own nature, which aims at the truth, for it compels it, contrary to its own laws, to regard as true things which are neither true nor probable, and often scarcely possible, only in order to appease, quiet, and send to sleep for a while the restless and unmanageable *will.* Here we see clearly who is master and who is servant. Many may well have observed that if a matter which is of importance to them may turn out in several different ways, and they have brought all of these into one disjunctive judgment which in their opinion is complete, the actual result is yet quite another, and one wholly unexpected by them: but perhaps they will not have considered this, that this result was then almost always the one which was unfavourable to them. The explanation of this is, that while their *intellect* intended to survey the possibilities completely, the worst of all remained quite invisible to it; because the *will,* as it were, covered it with its hand, that is, it so mastered the intellect that it was quite incapable of glancing at the worst case of all, although, since it actually came to pass, this was also the most probable case. Yet in very melancholy dispositions, or in those that have become prudent through experience like this, the process is reversed, for here apprehension plays the part which was formerly played by hope. The first appearance of danger throws them into groundless anxiety. If the intellect begins to investigate the matter it is rejected as incompetent, nay, as a deceitful sophist, because the heart is to be believed, whose fears are now actually allowed to pass for arguments as to the reality and greatness of the danger. So then the intellect dare make no search for good reasons on the other side, which, if left to itself, it would soon recognize, but is obliged at once to picture to them the most unfortunate issue, even if it itself can scarcely think this issue possible:

> "Such as we know is false, yet dread in sooth,
> Because the worst is ever nearest truth."
> —BYRON (*Lara,* c. 1).

Love and *hate* falsify our judgment entirely. In our enemies we see nothing but faults—in our loved ones nothing but excellences, and even their faults appear to us amiable. Our *interest,* of whatever kind it may be, exercises a like secret power over our judgment; what is in conformity with it at once seems to us fair, just, and reasonable; what runs contrary to it presents itself to us, in perfect seriousness, as unjust and outrageous, or injudicious and absurd. Hence so many prejudices of position, profession, nationality, sect, and religion. A conceived hypothesis gives us lynx-eyes for all that confirms it, and makes us blind to all that contradicts it. What is opposed to our party, our plan, our wish, our hope, we often cannot comprehend and grasp at all, while it is clear to every one else; but what is favourable to these, on the other hand, strikes our eye from afar. What the heart opposes the head will not admit. We firmly retain many errors all through life, and take care never to examine their ground, merely from a fear, of which we ourselves are conscious, that we might make the discovery that we had so long believed and so often asserted what is false. Thus then is the intellect daily befooled and corrupted by the impositions of inclination. This has been very beautifully expressed by Bacon of Verulam in the words: *Intellectus* LUMINIS SICCI *non est; sed recipit infusionem a voluntate et affectibus: id quod generat ad quod vult scientias: quod enim mavult homo, id potius credit.* (*Org. Nov.,* i., 14).[8] Clearly it is also this that opposes all new fundamental opinions in the sciences and all refutations of sanctioned errors, for one will not easily see the truth of that which convicts one of incredible want of thought. It is explicable, on this ground alone, that the truths of Goethe's doctrine of colours, which are so clear and simple, are still denied by the physicists; and thus Goethe himself has had to learn what a much harder position one has if one promises men instruction than if one promises them amusement. Hence it is much more fortunate to be born a poet than a philosopher. But the more obstinately an error was held by the other side, the more shameful does the conviction afterwards become. In the case of an overthrown system, as in the case of a conquered army, the most prudent is he who first runs away from it.

A trifling and absurd, but striking, example of that mysterious and immediate power which the will exercises over the intellect, is the fact that in doing accounts we make mistakes much oftener in our own favour than to our disadvantage, and this without the slightest dishonest intention, merely from the unconscious tendency to diminish our *Debit* and increase our *Credit.*

Lastly, the fact is also in point here, that when advice is given the slightest aim or purpose of the adviser generally outweighs his insight, however great it may be; therefore we dare not assume that he speaks from the latter when we suspect the exist-

---

[8] "The intellect is not a dry light, but receives an infusion from the will and the emotions; which results in sciences-as-we-wish; for what a man prefers he will rather believe."

ence of the former. How little perfect sincerity is to be expected even from otherwise honest persons whenever their interests are in any way concerned we can gather from the fact that we so often deceive ourselves when hope bribes us, or fear befools us, or suspicion torments us, or vanity flatters us, or any hypothesis blinds us, or a small aim which is close at hand injures a greater but more distant one; for in this we see the direct and unconscious disadvantageous influence of the will upon knowledge. Accordingly it ought not to surprise us if in asking advice the will of the person asked directly dictates the answer even before the question could penetrate to the forum of his judgment.

I wish in a single word to point out here what will be fully explained in the following book, that the most perfect knowledge, thus the purely objective comprehension of the world, *i. e.,* the comprehension of genius, is conditioned by a silence of the will so profound that while it lasts even the individuality vanishes from consciousness and the man remains *as the pure subject of knowing,* which is the correlative of the *Idea.*

The disturbing influence of the will upon the intellect, which is proved by all these phenomena, and, on the other hand, the weakness and frailty of the latter, on account of which it is incapable of working rightly whenever the will is in any way moved, gives us then another proof that the will is the radical part of our nature, and acts with original power, while the intellect, as adventitious and in many ways conditioned, can only act in a subordinate and conditional manner.

There is no direct disturbance of the will by the intellect corresponding to the disturbance and clouding of knowledge by the will that has been shown. Indeed we cannot well conceive such a thing. No one will wish to construe as such the fact that motives wrongly taken up lead the will astray, for this is a fault of the intellect in its own function, which is committed quite within its own province, and the influence of which upon the will is entirely indirect. It would be plausible to attribute *irresolution* to this, for in its case, through the conflict of the motives which the intellect presents to the will, the latter is brought to a standstill, thus is hindered. But when we consider it more closely, it becomes very clear that the cause of this hindrance does not lie in the activity of the *intellect* as such, but entirely in *external objects* which are brought about by it, for in this case they stand in precisely such a relation to the will, which is here interested, that they draw it with nearly equal strength in different directions. This real cause merely acts *through* the intellect as the medium of motives, though certainly under the assumption that it is keen enough to comprehend the objects in their manifold relations. Irresolution, as a trait of character, is just as much conditioned by qualities of the will as of the intellect. It is certainly not peculiar to exceedingly limited minds, for their weak understanding does not allow them to discover such manifold qualities and relations in things, and moreover is so little fitted for the exertion of reflection and pondering these, and then the probable consequences of each step, that they rather decide at once according to the first impression, or according to some simple rule of conduct. The converse of this occurs in the case of persons of considerable understanding. Therefore, whenever such persons also possess a tender care for their own well-being, *i. e.,* a very sensitive egoism, which constantly desires to come off well and always to be safe, this introduces a certain anxiety at every step, and thereby irresolution. This quality therefore indicates throughout not a want of understanding but a want of courage. Yet very eminent minds survey the relations and their probable developments with such rapidity and certainty, that if they are only supported by some courage they thereby acquire that quick decision and resolution that fits them to play an important part in the affairs of the world, if time and circumstances afford them the opportunity.

The only decided, direct restriction and disturbance which the will can suffer from the intellect as such may indeed be the quite exceptional one, which is the consequence of an abnormally preponderating development of the intellect, thus of that high endowment which has been defined as genius. This is decidedly a hindrance to the energy of the character, and consequently to the power of action. Hence it is not the really great minds that make historical characters, because they are capable of bridling and ruling the mass of men and carrying out the affairs of the world; but for this persons of much less capacity of mind are qualified when they have great firmness, decision, and persistency of will, such as is quite inconsistent with very high intelligence. Accordingly, where this very high intelligence exists we actually have a case in which the intellect directly restricts the will.

6. In opposition to the hindrances and restrictions which it has been shown the intellect suffers from the will, I wish now to show, in a few examples, how, conversely, the functions of the intellect are sometimes aided and heightened by the incitement and spur of the will; so that in this also we may recognize the primary nature of the one and the secondary nature of the other, and it may become clear that the intellect stands to the will in the relation of a tool.

A motive which affects us strongly, such as a yearning desire or a pressing need, sometimes raises the intellect to a degree of which we had not previously believed it capable. Difficult circumstances, which impose upon us the necessity of certain achievements, develop entirely new talents in us, the germs of which were hidden from us, and for which we did not credit ourselves with any capacity. The understanding of the stupidest man becomes keen when objects are in question that closely concern his wishes; he now observes, weighs, and distinguishes with the greatest delicacy even the smallest circumstances that have reference to his wishes or fears. This has much to do with the cunning of half-witted persons, which is often remarked with surprise. On this account Isaiah rightly says, *vexatio dat intellectum,* which is therefore also used as a proverb. Akin to it is the German proverb, *"Die Noth ist die Mutter der Künste"* ("Necessity is the mother of the arts") ; when, however, the fine arts are to be excepted, because the heart of every one of their works, that is, the conception, must proceed from a perfectly will-less, and only thereby purely objective, perception, if they are to be genuine. Even the understanding of the brutes is increased considerably by necessity, so that in cases of difficulty they accomplish things at which we are astonished. For example, they almost all calculate that it is safer not to run away when they believe they are not seen; therefore the hare lies still in the furrow of the field and lets the sportsman pass close to it; insects, when they cannot escape, pretend to be dead, &c. We may obtain a fuller knowledge of this influence from the special history of the self-education of the wolf, under the spur of the great difficulty of its position in civilized Europe; it is to be found in the second letter of Leroy's excellent book, *"Lettres sur l'intelligence et la perfectibilité des animaux."* Immediately afterwards, in the third letter, there follows the high school of the fox, which in an equally difficult position has far less physical strength. In its case, however, this is made up for by great understanding; yet only through the constant struggle with want on the one hand and danger on the other, thus under the spur of the will, does it attain that high degree of cunning which distinguishes it especially in old age. In all these enhancements of the intellect the will plays the part of a rider who with the spur urges the horse beyond the natural measure of its strength.

In the same way the memory is enhanced through the pressure of the will. Even if it is otherwise weak, it preserves perfectly what has value for the ruling passion. The lover forgets no opportunity favourable to him, the ambitious man forgets no circumstance that can forward his plans, the avaricious man never forgets the loss he has suffered, the proud man never forgets an injury to his honour, the vain man remembers every word of praise and the most trifling distinction that falls to his lot. And this also extends to the brutes: the horse stops at the inn where once long ago it was fed; dogs have an excellent memory for all occasions, times, and places that have afforded them choice morsels; and foxes for the different hiding-places in which they have stored their plunder.

Self-consideration affords opportunity for finer observations in this regard. Sometimes, through an interruption, it has entirely escaped me what I have just been thinking about, or even what news I have just heard. Now if the matter had in any way even the most distant personal interest, the after-feeling of the impression which it made upon the *will* has remained. I am still quite conscious how far it affected me agreeably or disagreeably, and also of the special manner in which this happened, whether, even in the slightest degree, it vexed me, or made me anxious, or irritated me, or depressed me, or produced the opposite of these affections. Thus the mere relation of the thing to my will is retained in the memory after the thing itself has vanished, and this often becomes the clue to lead us back to the thing itself. The sight of a man sometimes affects us in an analogous manner, for we remember merely in general that we have had something to do with him, yet without knowing where, when, or what it was, or who he is. But the sight of him still recalls pretty accurately the feeling which our dealings with him excited in us, whether it was agreeable or disagreeable, and also in what degree and in what way. Thus our memory has preserved only the response of the will, and not that which called it forth. We might call what lies at the foundation of this process the memory of the heart; it is much more intimate than that of the head. Yet at bottom the connection of the two is so far-reaching that if we reflect deeply upon the matter we will arrive at the conclusion that memory in general requires the support of a will as a connecting point, or rather as a thread upon which the memories can range themselves, and which holds them firmly together, or that the will is, as it were, the ground to which the individual memories cleave, and without which they could not last; and that therefore in a pure intelligence, *i. e.,* in a merely knowing and absolutely will-less being, a memory cannot well be conceived. Accordingly the improvement of the memory under the spur of the ruling passion, which has been shown above, is only the higher degree of that which takes place in all retention and recollection; for its basis and condition is always the will. Thus in all this also it becomes clear how very much more essential to us the will is than the intellect. The following facts may also serve to confirm this.

The intellect often obeys the will; for example, if we wish to remember something, and after some effort succeed; so also if we wish now to ponder something carefully and deliberately, and in many such cases. Sometimes, again, the intellect refuses to obey the will; for example, if we try in vain to fix our minds upon something, or if we call in vain upon the memory for something that was intrusted to it. The anger of the will against the intellect on such occasions makes its relation to it and the difference of the two very plain. Indeed the intellect, vexed by this anger, sometimes officiously brings what was asked of it hours afterwards, or even the following morning, quite unexpectedly and unseasonably. On the other hand, the will never really obeys the intellect; but the latter is only the ministerial council of that sovereign; it presents all kinds of things to the will, which then selects what is in conformity with its nature, though in doing so it determines itself with necessity, because this nature is unchangeable and the motives now lie before it. Hence no system of ethics is possible which moulds and improves the will itself. For all teaching only affects *knowledge,* and knowledge never determines the will itself, *i. e.,* the *fundamental character* of willing, not only its application to the circumstances present. Rectified knowledge can only modify conduct so far as it proves more exactly and judges more correctly what objects of the will's choice are within its reach; so that the will now measures its relation to things more correctly, sees more clearly what it desires, and consequently is less subject to error in its choice. But over the will itself, over the main tendency or fundamental maxim of it, the intellect has no power. To believe that knowledge really and fundamentally determines the will is like believing that the lantern which a man carries by night is the *primum mobile* of his steps. Whoever, taught by experience or the admonitions of others, knows and laments a fundamental fault of his character, firmly and honestly forms the intention to reform and give it up; but in spite of this, on the first opportunity, the fault receives free course. New repentance, new intentions, new transgressions. When this has been gone through several times he becomes conscious that he cannot improve himself, that the fault lies in his nature and personality, indeed is one with this. Now he will blame and curse his nature and personality, will have a painful feeling, which may rise to anguish of consciousness, but to change these he is not able. Here we see that which condemns and that which is condemned distinctly separate: we see the former as a merely theoretical faculty, picturing and presenting the praiseworthy, and therefore desirable, course of life, but the other as something real and unchangeably present, going quite a different way in spite of the former: and then again the first remaining behind with impotent lamentations over the nature of the other, with which, through this very distress, it again identifies itself. Will and intellect here separate very distinctly. But here the will shows itself as the stronger, the invincible, unchangeable, primitive, and at the same time as the essential thing in question, for the intellect deplores its errors, and finds no comfort in the correctness of the *knowledge,* as its own function. Thus the intellect shows itself entirely secondary, as the spectator of the deeds of another, which it accompanies with impotent praise and blame, and also as determinable from without, because it learns from experience, weighs and alters its precepts. Accordingly, a comparison of our manner of thinking at different periods of our life will present a strange mixture of permanence and changeableness. On the one hand, the moral tendency of the man in his prime and the old man is still the same as was that of the boy; on the other hand, much has become so strange to him that he no longer knows himself, and wonders how he ever could have done or said this and that. In the first half of life to-day for the most part laughs at yesterday, indeed looks down on it with contempt; in the second half, on the contrary, it more and more looks back at it with envy. But on closer examination it will be found that the changeable element was the *intellect,* with its functions of insight and knowledge, which, daily appropriating new material from without, presents a constantly changing system of thought, while, besides this, it itself rises and sinks with the growth and decay of the organism. The will on the contrary, the basis of this, thus the inclinations, passions, and emotions, the character, shows itself as what is unalterable in consciousness. Yet we have to take account of the modifications that depend upon physical capacities for enjoyment, and hence upon age. Thus, for example, the eagerness for sensuous pleasure will show itself in childhood as a love of dainties, in youth and manhood as the tendency to sensuality, and in old age again as a love of dainties.

7. If, as is generally assumed, the will proceeded from knowledge, as its result or product, then where there is much will there would necessarily also be much knowledge, insight, and understanding. This, however, is absolutely not the case; rather, we find in many men a strong, *i. e.,* decided, resolute, persistent, unbending, wayward, and vehement will, combined with a very weak and incapable understanding, so that every one who has to do with them is thrown into despair, for their will remains inaccessible to all reasons and ideas, and is not to be got at, so that it is hidden, as it were, in a sack, out of which it wills blindly. Brutes have

often violent, often stubborn wills, but yet very little understanding. Finally, plants will only without any knowledge at all.

If willing sprang merely from knowledge, our *anger* would necessarily be in every case exactly proportionate to the occasion, or at least to our relation to it, for it would be nothing more than the result of the present knowledge. This, however, is rarely the case; rather, anger generally goes far beyond the occasion. Our fury and rage, the *furor brevis,* often upon small occasions, and without error regarding them, is like the raging of an evil spirit which, having been shut up, only waits its opportunity to dare to break loose, and now rejoices that it has found it. This could not be the case if the foundation of our nature were a *knower,* and willing were merely a result of *knowledge;* for how came there into the result what did not lie in the elements? The conclusion cannot contain more than the premises. Thus here also the will shows itself as of a nature quite different from knowledge, which only serves it for communication with the external world, but then the will follows the laws of its own nature without taking from the intellect anything but the occasion.

The intellect, as the mere tool of the will, is as different from it as the hammer from the smith. So long as in a conversation the intellect alone is active it remains *cold.* It is almost as if the man himself were not present. Moreover, he cannot then, properly speaking, compromise himself, but at the most can make himself ridiculous. Only when the will comes into play is the man really present: now he becomes *warm,* nay, it often happens, *hot.* It is always the will to which we ascribe the warmth of life; on the other hand, we say the *cold* understanding, or to investigate a thing *coolly, i. e.,* to think without being influenced by the will. If we attempt to reverse the relation, and to regard the will as the tool of the intellect, it is as if we made the smith the tool of the hammer.

Nothing is more provoking, when we are arguing against a man with reasons and explanation, and taking all pains to convince him, under the impression that we have only to do with his *understanding,* than to discover at last that he *will* not understand; that thus we had to do with his *will,* which shuts itself up against the truth and brings into the field wilful misunderstandings, chicaneries, and sophisms in order to intrench itself behind its understanding and its pretended want of insight. Then he is certainly not to be got at, for reasons and proofs applied against the will are like the blows of a phantom produced by mirrors against a solid body. Hence the saying so often repeated, *"Stat pro ratione voluntas."* [9] Sufficient evidence of what has been said is afforded by ordinary life. But unfortunately proofs of it are also to be found on the path of the sciences. The recognition of the most important truths, of the rarest achievements, will be looked for in vain from those who have an interest in preventing them from being accepted, an interest which either springs from the fact that such truths contradict what they themselves daily teach, or else from this, that they dare not make use of them and teach them; or if all this be not the case they will not accept them, because the watchword of mediocrity will always be, *Si quelqu'un excelle parmi nous, qu'il aille exceller ailleurs,* as Helvetius has admirably rendered the saying of the Ephesian in the fifth book of Cicero's *"Tusculanæ"* (c. 36),[10] or as a saying of the Abyssinian Fit Arari puts it, "Among quartzes adamant is outlawed." Thus whoever expects from this always numerous band a just estimation of what he has done will find himself very much deceived, and perhaps for a while he will not be able to understand their behaviour, till at last he finds out that while he applied himself to *knowledge* he had to do with the *will,* thus is precisely in the position described above, nay, is really like a man who brings his case before a court the judges of which have all been bribed. Yet in particular cases he will receive the fullest proof that their will and not their insight opposed him, when one or other of them makes up his mind to plagiarism. Then he will see with astonishment what good judges they are, what correct perception of the merit of others they have, and how well they know how to find out the best, like the sparrows, who never miss the ripest cherries.

The counterpart of the victorious resistance of the will to knowledge here set forth appears if in expounding our reasons and proofs we have the will of those addressed with us. Then all

[9] "The will takes the place of reason."
[10] "If anyone excels among us, let him go and excel elsewhere."

are at once convinced, all arguments are telling, and the matter is
at once clear as the day. This is well known to popular speakers.
In the one case, as in the other, the will shows itself as that which
has original power, against which the intellect can do nothing.

8. But now we shall take into consideration the individual
qualities, thus excellences and faults of the will and character
on the one hand, and of the intellect on the other, in order to
make clear, in their relation to each other, and their relative worth,
the complete difference of the two fundamental faculties. History
and experience teach that the two appear quite independent of
each other. That the greatest excellence of mind will not easily
be found combined with equal excellence of character is sufficiently
explained by the extraordinary rarity of both, while their opposites
are everywhere the order of the day; hence we also daily find the
latter in union. However, we never infer a good will from a superior mind, nor the latter from the former, nor the opposite from the
opposite, but every unprejudiced person accepts them as perfectly
distinct qualities, the presence of which each for itself has to be
learned from experience. Great narrowness of mind may coexist
with great goodness of heart, and I do not believe Balthazar
Gracian was right in saying (*Discreto,* p. 406), *"No ay simple,
que no sea malicioso"* ("There is no simpleton who would not be
malicious"), though he has the Spanish proverb in his favour,
"Nunca la necedad anduvo sin malicia" ("Stupidity is never without malice"). Yet it may be that many stupid persons become
malicious for the same reason as many hunchbacks, from bitterness
on account of the neglect they have suffered from nature, and because they think they can occasionally make up for what they
lack in understanding through malicious cunning, seeking in this
a brief triumph. From this, by the way, it is also comprehensible
why almost every one easily becomes malicious in the presence of
a very superior mind. On the other hand, again, stupid people
have very often the reputation of special good-heartedness, which
yet so seldom proves to be the case that I could not help wondering
how they had gained it, till I was able to flatter myself that I
had found the key to it in what follows. Moved by a secret inclination, every one likes best to choose for his more intimate
intercourse some one to whom he is a little superior in understand-

ing, for only in this case does he find himself at his ease, because, according to Hobbes, *"Omnis animi voluptas, omnisque alacritas in eo sita est, quod quis habeat quibuscum conferens se, possit magnifice sentire de se ipso"* (*De Cive*, i., 5).[11] For the same reason every one avoids him who is superior to himself; wherefore Lichtenberg quite rightly observes: "To certain men a man of mind is a more odious production than the most pronounced rogue." And similarly Helvetius says: *"Les gens médiocres ont un instinct sür et prompt, pour connâître et fuir les gens d'esprit."* [12] And Dr. Johnson assures us that "there is nothing by which a man exasperates most people more than by displaying a superior ability of brilliancy in conversation. They seem pleased at the time, but their envy makes them curse him in their hearts" (Boswell; aet. anno 74). In order to bring this truth, so universal and so carefully concealed, more relentlessly to light, I add the expression of it by Merck, the celebrated friend of Goethe's youth, from his story *"Lindor"*: "He possessed talents which were given him by nature and acquired by himself through learning; and thus it happened that in most society he left the worthy members of it far behind." If, in the moment of delight at the sight of an extraordinary man, the public swallows these superiorities also, without actually at once putting a bad construction upon them, yet a certain impression of this phenomenon remains behind, which, if it is often repeated, may on serious occasions have disagreeable future consequences for him who is guilty of it. Without any one consciously noting that on this occasion he was insulted, no one is sorry to place himself tacitly in the way of the advancement of this man. Thus on this account great mental superiority isolates more than anything else, and makes one, at least silently, hated. Now it is the opposite of this that makes stupid people so generally liked; especially since many can only find in them what, according to the law of their nature referred to above, they must seek. Yet this the true reason of such an inclination no one will confess to himself, still less to others; and therefore, as a plausible pretext

[11] "Every pleasure and vivacity of the mind lies in this, that one has something wherein, comparing himself with others, he can think himself magnificent."

[12] "Mediocre people have a sure and ready instinct to know and fly from men of genius."

for it, will impute to those he has selected a special goodness of heart, which, as we have said, is in reality only very rarely and accidentally found in combination with mental incapacity. Want of understanding is accordingly by no means favourable or akin to goodness of character. But, on the other hand, it cannot be asserted that great understanding is so; nay, rather, no scoundrel has in general been without it. Indeed even the highest intellectual eminence can coexist with the worst moral depravity.

If now it is said of one man, "He has a good heart, though a bad head," but of another, "He has a very good head, yet a bad heart," every one feels that in the first case the praise far outweighs the blame—in the other case the reverse. Answering to this, we see that if some one has done a bad deed his friends and he himself try to remove the guilt from the *will* to the *intellect,* and to give out that faults of the heart were faults of the head; roguish tricks they will call *errors,* will say they were merely want of understanding, want of reflection, light-mindedness, folly; nay, if need be, they will plead a paroxysm, momentary mental aberration, and if a heavy crime is in question, even madness, only in order to free the *will* from the guilt. And in the same way, we ourselves, if we have caused a misfortune or injury, will before others and ourselves willingly impeach our *stultitia,* simply in order to escape the reproach of *malitia.* In the same way, in the case of the equally unjust decision of the judge, the difference, whether he has erred or been bribed, is so infinitely great. All this sufficiently proves that the *will* alone is the real and essential, the kernel of the man, and the *intellect* is merely its tool, which may be constantly faulty without the will being concerned. The accusation of want of understanding is, at the moral judgment-seat, no accusation at all; on the contrary, it even gives privileges. And so also, before the courts of the world, it is everywhere sufficient to deliver a criminal from all punishment that his guilt should be transferred from his will to his intellect, by proving either unavoidable error or mental derangement, for then it is of no more consequence than if hand or foot had slipped against the will.

Everywhere those who are responsible for any piece of work appeal, in the event of its turning out unsatisfactorily, to their good intentions, of which there was no lack. Hereby they believe that they secure the essential, that for which they are properly answerable, and their true self; the inadequacy of their faculties, on the other hand, they regard as the want of a suitable tool.

If a man is *stupid,* we excuse him by saying that he cannot help it; but if we were to excuse a *bad* man on the same grounds we would be laughed at. And yet the one, like the other, is innate. This proves that the will is the man proper, the intellect merely its tool.

Thus it is always only our *willing* that is regarded as depending upon ourselves, *i. e.,* as the expression of our true nature, and for which we are therefore made responsible. Therefore it is absurd and unjust if we are taken to task for our beliefs, thus for our knowledge: for we are obliged to regard this as something which, although it changes in us, is as little in our power as the events of the external world. And here, also, it is clear that the *will* alone is the inner and true nature of man; the *intellect,* on the contrary, with its operations, which go on as regularly as the external world, stands to the will in the relation of something external to it, a mere tool.

9. High mental capacities have always been regarded as the gift of nature or the gods; and on that account they have been called *Gaben, Begabung, ingenii dotes,* gifts (a man highly gifted), regarding them as something different from the man himself, something that has fallen to his lot through favour. No one, on the contrary, has even taken this view of moral excellences, although they also are innate; they have rather always been regarded as something proceeding from the man himself, essentially belonging to him, nay, constituting his very self. But it follows now from this that the will is the true nature of man; the intellect, on the other hand, is secondary, a tool, a gift.

Answering to this, all religious promise a reward beyond life, in eternity, for excellences of the *will* or heart, but none for excellences of the head or understanding. Virtue expects its reward in that world; prudence hopes for it in this; genius, again, neither in this world nor in that; it is its own reward. Accordingly the will is the eternal part, the intellect the temporal.

Connection, communion, intercourse among men is based, as a rule, upon relations which concern the *will,* not upon such as concern the *intellect*. The first kind of communion may be called the *material*, the other the *formal*. Of the former kind are the bonds of family and relationship, and further, all connections that rest upon any common aim or interest, such as that of trade or profession, of the corporation, the party, the faction, &c. In these it merely amounts to a question of views, of aims; along with which there may be the greatest diversity of intellectual capacity and culture. Therefore not only can any one live in peace and unity with any one else, but can act with him and be allied to him for the common good of both. Marriage also is a bond of the heart, not of the head. It is different, however, with merely formal communion, which aims only at an exchange of thought; this demands a certain equality of intellectual capacity and culture. Great differences in this respect place between man and man an impassable gulf: such lies, for example, between a man of great mind and a fool, between a scholar and a peasant, between a courtier and a sailor. Natures as heterogeneous as this have therefore trouble in making themselves intelligible so long as it is a question of exchanging thoughts, ideas, and views. Nevertheless close *material* friendship may exist between them, and they may be faithful allies, conspirators, or men under mutual pledges. For in all that concerns the will alone, which includes friendship, enmity, honesty, fidelity, falseness, and treachery, they are perfectly homogeneous, formed of the same clay, and neither mind nor culture make any difference here; indeed here the ignorant man often shames the scholar, the sailor the courtier. For at the different grades of culture there are the same virtues and vices, emotions and passions; and although somewhat modified in their expression, they very soon mutually recognize each other even in the most heterogeneous ididuals, upon which the similarly disposed agree and the opposed are at enmity.

Brilliant qualities of mind win admiration, but never affection; this is reserved for the moral, the qualities of the character. Every one will choose as his friend the honest, the good-natured, and even the agreeable, complaisant man, who easily concurs, rather than the merely able man. Indeed many will be preferred to the latter, on account of insignificant, accidental, outward qualities which just suit the inclination of another. Only the man who has much mind himself will wish able men for his society; his friendship, on the other hand, he will bestow with reference to moral qualities; for upon this depends his really high appreciation of a man in whom a single good trait of character conceals and expiates great want of understanding. The known goodness of a character makes us patient and yielding towards weaknesses of understanding, as also towards the dullness and childishness of age. A distinctly noble character along with the entire absence of intellectual excellence and culture presents itself as lacking nothing; while, on the contrary, even the greatest mind, if affected with important moral faults, will always appear blamable. For as torches and fireworks become pale and insignificant in the presence of the sun, so intellect, nay, genius, and also beauty, are outshone and eclipsed by the goodness of the heart. When this appears in a high degree it can make up for the want of those qualities to such an extent that one is ashamed of having missed them. Even the most limited understanding, and also grotesque ugliness, whenever extraordinary goodness of heart declares itself as accompanying them, become as it were transfigured, outshone by a beauty of a higher kind, for now a wisdom speaks out of them before which all other wisdom must be dumb. For goodness of heart is a transcendent quality; it belongs to an order of things that reaches beyond this life, and is incommensurable with any other perfection. When it is present in a high degree it makes the heart so large that it embraces the world, so that now everything lies within it, no longer without; for it identifies all natures with its own. It then extends to others also that boundless indulgence which otherwise each one only bestows on himself. Such a man is incapable of becoming angry; even if the malicious mockery and sneers of others have drawn attention to his own intellectual or physical faults, he only reproaches himself in his heart for having been the occasion of such expressions, and therefore, without doing violence to his own feelings, proceeds to treat those persons in the kindest manner, confidently hoping that they will turn from their error with regard to him, and recognize themselves in him also. What is wit and genius against this?—what is Bacon of Verulam?

Our estimation of our own selves leads to the same result as we have here obtained by considering our estimation of others. How different is the self-satisfaction which we experience in a moral regard from that which we experience in an intellectual regard! The former arises when, looking back on our conduct, we see that with great sacrifices we have practiced fidelity and honesty, that we have helped many, forgiven many, have behaved better to others than they have behaved to us; so that we can say with King Lear, "I am a man more sinned against than sinning"; and to its fullest extent if perhaps some noble deed shines in our memory. A deep seriousness will accompany the still peace which such a review affords us; and if we see that others are inferior to us here, this will not cause us any joy, but we will rather deplore it, and sincerely wish that they were as we are. How entirely differently does the knowledge of our intellectual superiority affect us! Its ground bass is really the saying of Hobbes quoted above: *Omnis animi voluptas, omnisque alacritas in eo sita est, quod quis habeat, quibuscum conferens se, possit magnifice sentire de se ipso.* Arrogant, triumphant vanity, proud, contemptuous looking down on others, inordinate delight in the consciousness of decided and considerable superiority, akin to pride of physical advantages,—that is the result here. This opposition between the two kinds of self-satisfaction shows that the one concerns our true inner and eternal nature, the other a more external, merely temporal, and indeed scarcely more than a mere physical excellence. The *intellect* is in fact simply the function of the brain; the *will,* on the contrary, is that whose function is the whole man, according to his being and nature.

10. Upon what depends the *identity of the person?* Not upon the matter of the body; it is different after a few years. Not upon its form, which changes as a whole and in all its parts; all but the expression of the glance, by which, therefore, we still know a man even after many years; which proves that in spite of all changes time produces in him something in him remains quite untouched by it. It is just this by which we recognize him even after the longest intervals of time, and find the former man entire. It is the same with ourselves, for, however old we become, we yet feel within that we are entirely the same as we were when we were young, nay, when we were still children. This, which unaltered

always remains quite the same, and does not grow old along with us, is really the kernel of our nature, which does not lie in time. It is assumed that the identity of the person rests upon that of consciousness. But by this is understood merely the connected recollection of the course of life; hence it is not sufficient. We certainly know something more of our life than of a novel we have formerly read, yet only very little. The principal events, the interesting scenes, have impressed themselves upon us; in the remainder a thousand events are forgotten for one has been retained. The older we become the more do things pass by us without leaving any trace. Great age, illness, injury of the brain, madness, may deprive us of memory altogether, but the identity of the person is not thereby lost. It rests upon the identical *will* and the unalterable character of the person. It is it also which makes the expression of the glance unchangeable. In the *heart* is the man, not in the head. It is true that, in consequence of our relation to the external world, we are accustomed to regard as our real self the subject of knowledge, the knowing I, which wearies in the evening, vanishes in sleep, and in the morning shines brighter with renewed strength. This is, however, the mere function of the brain, and not our own self. Our true self, the kernel of our nature, is what is behind that, and really knows nothing but willing and not willing, being content and not content, with all the modifications of this, which are called feelings, emotions, and passions. This is that which produces the other, does not sleep with it when it sleeps, and in the same way when it sinks in death remains uninjured. Everything, on the contrary, that belongs to *knowledge* is exposed to oblivion; even actions of moral significance can sometimes, after years, be only imperfectly recalled, and we no longer know accurately and in detail how we acted on a critical occasion. But the *character itself,* to which the actions only testify, cannot be forgotten by us; it is now still quite the same as then. The will itself, alone and for itself, is permanent, for it alone is unchangeable, indestructible, not growing old, not physical, but metaphysical, not belonging to the phenomenal appearance, but to that itself which so appears. How the identity of consciousness also, so far as it goes, depends upon it I have shown above, so I need not dwell upon it further here.

11. Aristotle says in passing, in his book on the comparison of the desirable, "To live well is better than to live" (βελτιον του ζην το ευ ζην, Top. iii., 2). From this we might infer, by double contraposition, not to live is better than to live badly. This is also evident to the intellect; yet the great majority live very badly rather than not at all. This clinging to life cannot therefore have its ground in the *object* of life, since life, as was shown in the fourth book, is really a constant suffering, or at the least, as will be shown further on, a business which does not cover its expenses; thus that clinging to life can only be founded in the *subject* of it. But it is not founded in the *intellect,* it is no result of reflection, and in general is not a matter of choice; but this willing of life is something that is taken for granted: it is a *prius* of the intellect itself. We ourselves are the will to live, and therefore we must live, well or ill. Only from the fact that this clinging to a life which is so little worth to them is entirely *a priori* and not *a posteriori* can we explain the excessive fear of death that dwells in every living thing, which Rochefoucauld has expressed in his last reflection, with rare frankness and naïveté, and upon which the effect of all tragedies and heroic actions ultimately rests, for it would be lost if we prized life only according to its objective worth. Upon this inexpressible *horror mortis* [13] is also founded the favourite principle of all ordinary minds, that whosoever takes his own life must be mad; yet not less the astonishment, mingled with a certain admiration, which this action always excites even in thinking minds, because it is so opposed to the nature of all living beings that in a certain sense we are forced to admire him who is able to perform it. For suicide proceeds from a purpose of the intellect, but our will to live is a *prius* of the intellect. Thus this consideration also confirms the primacy of the will in self-consciousness.

12. On the other hand, nothing proves more clearly the secondary, dependent, conditioned nature of the *intellect* than its periodical intermittence. In deep sleep all knowing and forming of ideas ceases. But the kernel of our nature, the metaphysical part of it which the organic functions necessarily presuppose as their *primum mobile,* must never pause if life is not to cease, and, moreover,

---

[13] "Horror of death."

as something metaphysical and therefore incorporeal, it requires no rest. Therefore the philosophers who set up a *soul* as this metaphysical kernel, *i. e.,* an originally and essentially *knowing* being, see themselves forced to the assertion that this soul is quite untiring in its perceiving and knowing, therefore continues these even in deep sleep; only that we have no recollection of this when we awake. The falseness of this assertion, however, was easy to see whenever one had rejected that *soul* in consequence of Kant's teaching. For sleep and waking prove to the unprejudiced mind in the clearest manner that knowing is a secondary function and conditioned by the organism, just like any other. Only the *heart* is untiring, because its beating and the circulation of the blood are not directly conditioned by nerves, but are just the original manifestation of the will. Also all other physiological functions governed merely by ganglionic nerves, which have only a very indirect and distant connection with the brain, are carried on during sleep, although the secretions take place more slowly; the beating of the heart itself, on account of its dependence upon respiration, which is conditioned by the cerebral system (*medulla oblongata*), becomes with it a little slower. The stomach is perhaps most active in sleep, which is to be attributed to its special consensus with the now resting brain, which occasions mutual disturbances. The *brain* alone, and with it knowing, pauses entirely in deep sleep. For it is merely the minister of foreign affairs, as the ganglion system is the minister of the interior. The brain, with its function of knowing, is only a *vedette* established by the will for its external ends, which, up in the watch-tower of the head, looks round through the windows of the senses and marks where mischief threatens and where advantages are to be looked for, and in accordance with whose report the will decides. This *vedette,* like every one engaged on active service, is then in a condition of strain and effort, and therefore it is glad when, after its watch is completed, it is again withdrawn, as every watch gladly retires from its post. This withdrawal is going to sleep, which is therefore so sweet and agreeable, and to which we are so glad to yield; on the other hand, being roused from sleep is unwelcome, because it recalls the *vedette* suddenly to its post. One generally feels also after the beneficent systole the reappearance of the difficult diastole, the reseparation of the intellect from the will. A so-called *soul,* which was originally and radically a *knowing* being, would, on the contrary, necessarily feel on awaking like a fish put back into water. In sleep, when merely the vegetative life is carried on, the will works only according to its original and essential nature, undisturbed from without, with no diminution of its power through the activity of the brain and the exertion of knowing, which is the heaviest organic function, yet for the organism merely a means, not an end; therefore, in sleep the whole power of the will is directed to the maintenance and, where it is necessary, the improvement of the organism. Hence all healing, all favourable crises, take place in sleep; for the *vis naturæ medicatrix* has free play only when it is delivered from the burden of the function of knowledge. The embryo which has still to form the body therefore sleeps continuously, and the new-born child the greater part of its time. In this sense Burdach (*Physiologie,* vol. iii., p. 484) quite rightly declares sleep to be the *original state.*

With reference to the brain itself, I account to myself for the necessity of sleep more fully through an hypothesis which appears to have been first set up in Neumann's book, *"Von den Krankheiten des Menschen,"* 1834, vol. 4, § 216. It is this, that the nutrition of the brain, thus the renewal of its substance from the blood, cannot go on while we are awake, because the very eminent organic function of knowing and thinking would be disturbed or put an end to by the low and material function of nutrition. This explains the fact that sleep is not a purely negative condition, a merely pausing of the activity of the brain, but also shows a positive character. This makes itself known through the circumstance that between sleep and waking there is no mere difference of degree, but a fixed boundary, which, as soon as sleep intervenes, declares itself in dreams which are completely different from our immediately preceding thoughts. A further proof of this is that when we have dreams which frighten us we try in vain to cry out, or to ward off attacks, or to shake off sleep; so that it is as if the connecting-link between the brain and the motor nerves, or between the cerebrum and the cerebullum (as the regulator of movements) were abolished; for the brain remains in its isolation and sleep holds us fast as with brazen claws.

Finally, the positive character of sleep can be seen in the fact that a certain degree of strength is required for sleeping. Therefore too great fatigue or natural weakness prevents us from seizing it, *capere somnum*. This may be explained from the fact that the *process of nutrition* must be introduced if sleep is to ensue: the brain must, as it were, begin to feed. Moreover, the increased flow of blood into the brain during sleep is explicable from the nutritive process; and also the position of the arms laid together above the head, which is instinctively assumed because it furthers this process: also why children, so long as their brain is still growing, require a great deal of sleep, while in old age, on the other hand, when a certain atrophy of the brain, as of all the parts, takes place, sleep is short; and finally why excessive sleep produces a certain dullness of consciousness, the consequence of a certain hypertrophy of the brain, which in the case of habitual excess of sleep may become permanent and produce imbecility: ανιη και πολυς ὑπνος (*noxœ est etiam multus somnus*), Od. 15, 394.[14] The need of sleep is therefore directly proportionate to the intensity of the brain-life, thus to the clearness of the consciousness. Those animals whose brain-life is weak and dull sleep little and lightly; for example, reptiles and fishes: and here I must remind the reader that the winter sleep is sleep only in name, for it is not an inaction of the brain alone, but of the whole organism, thus a kind of apparent death. Animals of considerable intelligence sleep deeply and long. Men also require more sleep the more developed, both as regards quantity and quality, and the more active their brain is. Montaigne relates of himself that he had always been a long sleeper, that he had passed a large part of his life sleeping, and at an advanced age still slept from eight to nine hours at a time (Liv. iii., chap. 13). Descartes also is reported to have slept a great deal (Baillet, *Vie de Descartes,* 1693, p. 288). Kant allowed himself seven hours for sleep, but it was so hard for him to do with this that he ordered his servant to force him against his will, and without listening to his remonstrances, to get up at the set time (Jachmann, *Immanuel Kant,* p. 162). For the more completely awake a man is, *i. e.,* the clearer and more lively his consciousness, the greater for him is the necessity of sleep, thus the deeper and longer he

[14] "Much sleep is injurious."

sleeps. Accordingly much thinking or hard brain-work increases the need of sleep. That sustained muscular exertion also makes us sleepy is to be explained from the fact that in this the brain continuously, by means of the *medulla oblongata,* the spinal marrow, and the motor nerves, imparts the stimulus to the muscles which affects their irritability, and in this way it exhausts its strength. The fatigue which we observe in the arms and legs has accordingly its real seat in the brain; just as the pain which these parts feel is really experienced in the brain; for it is connected with the motor nerves, as with the nerves of sense. The muscles which are not actuated from the brain—for example, those of the heart—accordingly never tire. The same grounds explain the fact that both during and after great muscular exertion we cannot think acutely. That one has far less energy in mind in summer than in winter is partly explicable from the fact that in summer one sleeps less; for the deeper one has slept, the more completely awake, the more lively, is one afterwards. This, however, must not mislead us into extending sleep unduly, for then it loses in intension, *i. e.,* in deepness and soundness, what it gains in extension; whereby it becomes mere loss of time. This is what Goethe means when he says (in the second part of "Faust") of morning slumber: "Sleep is husk: throw it off." Thus in general the phenomenon of sleep most specially confirms the assertion that consciousness, apprehension, knowing, thinking, is nothing original in us, but a conditioned and secondary state. It is a luxury of nature, and indeed its highest, which it can therefore the less afford to pursue without interruption the higher the pitch to which it has been brought. It is the product, the efflorescence of the cerebral nerve-system, which is itself nourished like a parasite by the rest of the organism. This also agrees with what is shown in our third book, that knowing is so much the purer and more perfect the more it has freed and severed itself from the will, whereby the purely objective, the æsthetic comprehension, appears. Just as an extract is so much the purer the more it has been separated from that out of which it is extracted and been cleared of all sediment. The opposite is shown by the *will,* whose most immediate manifestation is the whole organic life, and primarily the untiring heart.

This last consideration is related to the theme of the following chapter, to which it therefore makes the transition: yet the following observation belongs to it: In magnetic somnambulism the consciousness is doubled: two trains of knowledge, each connected in itself, but quite different from each other, arise; the waking consciousness knows nothing of the somnambulent. But the will retains in both the same character, and remains throughout identical; it expresses in both the same inclinations and aversions. For the function may be doubled, but not the true nature.

THE WORLD AS WILL AND IDEA

VOLUME III

CHAPTER XXXI

ON GENIUS

WHAT is properly denoted by the name genius is the predominating capacity for that kind of knowledge which has been described in the two preceding chapters, the knowledge from which all genuine works of art and poetry, and even of philosophy, proceed. Accordingly, since this has for its objects the Platonic Ideas, and these are not comprehended in the abstract, but *only perceptibly,* the essence of genius must lie in the perfection and energy of the knowledge of *perception.* Corresponding to this, the works which we hear most decidedly designated works of genius are those which start immediately from perception and devote themselves to perception; thus those of plastic and pictorial art, and then those of poetry, which gets its perceptions by the assistance of the imagination. The difference between genius and mere talent makes itself noticeable even here. For talent is an excellence which lies rather in the greater versatility and acuteness of discursive than of intuitive knowledge. He who is endowed with talent thinks more quickly and more correctly than others; but the genius beholds another world from them all, although only because he has a more profound perception of the world which lies before them also, in that it presents itself in his mind more objectively, and consequently in greater purity and distinctness.

The intellect is, according to its destination, merely the medium of motives; and in accordance with this it originally comprehends nothing in things but their relations to the will, the direct, the indirect, and the possible. In the case of the brutes, where it is almost entirely confined to the direct relations, the matter is just on that account most apparent: what has no relation to their will does not exist for them. Therefore we sometimes see with surprise that even clever animals do not observe at all something conspicuous to them; for example, they show no surprise at obvious alterations in our person and surroundings. In the case of normal men the indirect, and even the possible, relations to the will are added, the sum of which make up the total of useful knowledge; but here also knowledge remains confined to the relations. Therefore the normal mind does not attain to an absolutely pure, objective picture of things, because its power of perception, whenever it is not spurred on by the will and set in motion, at once becomes tired and inactive, because it has not enough energy of its own elasticity and without an *end* in view to apprehend the world in a purely objective manner. Where, on the other hand, this takes place—where the brain has such a surplus of the power of ideation that a pure, distinct, objective image of the external world exhibits itself *without any aim;* an image which is useless for the intentions of the will, indeed, in the higher degrees, disturbing, and even injurious to them—there, the natural disposition, at least, is already present for that abnormity which the name genius denotes, which signifies that here a *genius* foreign to the will, *i. e.,* to the I proper, as it were coming from without, seems to be active. But to speak without a figure: genius consists in this, that the knowing faculty has received a considerably greater development than the *service of the will,* for which alone it originally appeared, demands. Therefore, strictly speaking, physiology might to a certain extent class such a superfluity of brain activity, and with it of brain itself, among the *monstra per excessum,* which, it is well known, it co-ordinates with *monstra per defectum* and those *per situm mutatum.*[1] Thus genius consists in an abnormally large measure of intellect, which can only find its use by being applied to the universal of existence, whereby it then devotes itself to the service of the whole human race, as the normal intellect to that of the individual. In order to make this perfectly comprehensible one might say: If the normal man consists of two-thirds will and one-third intellect, the genius, on the contrary, has two-thirds intellect and one-third will. This might, then, be further illustrated by a chemical simile: the base and the acid of a neutral salt are distinguished by the fact that in each of the two the radical has the

---

[1] "Monsters by excess, defect, or abnormal position."

converse relation to oxygen to that which it has in the other. The base or the alkali is so because in it the radical predominates with reference to oxygen, and the acid is so because in it oxygen predominates. In the same way now the normal man and the genius are related in respect of will and intellect. From this arises a thorough distinction between them, which is visible even in their whole nature and behaviour, but comes out most clearly in their achievements. One might add the difference that while that total opposition between the chemical materials forms the strongest affinity and attraction between them, in the human race the opposite is rather wont to be found.

The first manifestation which such a superfluity of the power of knowledge calls forth shows itself for the most part in the most original and fundamental knowledge, *i. e.,* in knowledge of *perception,* and occasions the repetition of it in an image; hence arise the painter and the sculptor. In their case, then, the path between the apprehension of genius and the artistic production is the shortest; therefore the form in which genius and its activity here exhibits itself is the simplest and its description the easiest. Yet here also the source is shown from which all genuine productions in every art, in poetry, and indeed in philosophy, have their origin, although in the case of these the process is not so simple.

Let the result arrived at in the first book be here borne in mind, that all perception is intellectual and not merely sensuous. If one now adds the exposition given here, and, at the same time, in justice considers that the philosophy of the last century denoted the perceptive faculty of knowledge by the name "lower powers of the soul," we will not think it so utterly absurd nor so deserving of the bitter scorn with which Jean Paul quotes it in his *"Vorschule der Æsthetik,"* that Adelung, who had to speak the language of his age, placed genius in "a remarkable strength of the lower powers of the soul." The work just referred to of this author, who is so worthy of our admiration, has great excellences, but yet I must remark that all through, whenever a theoretical explanation and, in general, instruction is the end in view, a style of exposition which is constantly indulging in displays of wit and hurrying along in mere similes cannot be well adapted to the purpose.

It is, then, *perception* to which primarily the peculiar and true nature of things, although still in a conditioned manner, discloses and reveals itself. All conceptions and everything thought are mere abstractions, consequently partial ideas taken from perception, and have only arisen by thinking away. All profound knowledge, even wisdom properly so called, is rooted in the *perceptive* apprehension of things, as we have fully considered in the supplements to the first book. A *perceptive* apprehension has always been generative process in which every genuine work of art, every immortal thought, received the spark of life. All primary thought takes place in pictures. From conceptions, on the other hand, arise the works of mere talent, the merely rational thoughts, imitations, and indeed all that is calculated merely with reference to the present need and contemporary conditions.

But if now our perception were constantly bound to the real present of things, its material would be entirely under the dominion of chance, which seldom produces things at the right time, seldom arranges them for an end and for the most part presents them to us in very defective examples. Therefore the *imagination* is required in order to complete, arrange, give the finishing touches to, retain, and repeat at pleasure all those significant pictures of life, according as the aims of a profoundly penetrating knowledge and of the significant work whereby they are to be communicated may demand. Upon this rests the high value of imagination, which is an indispensable tool of genius. For only by virtue of imagination can genius ever, according to the requirements of the connection of its painting or poetry or thinking, call up to itself each object or event in a lively image, and thus constantly draw fresh nourishment from the primary source of all knowledge, perception. The man who is endowed with imagination is able, as it were, to call up spirits, who at the right time reveal to him the truths which the naked reality of things exhibits only weakly, rarely, and then for the most part at the wrong time. Therefore the man without imagination is related to him, as the mussel fastened to its rock, which must wait for what chance may bring it, is related to the freely moving or even winged animal. For such a man knows nothing but the actual perception of the senses: till it comes he gnaws at conceptions and abstractions which are yet mere shells and husks, not the kernel of knowledge. He will never achieve anything great, unless it be in calculating and mathematics. The works of plastic and pictorial art of poetry, as also the achievements of mimicry, may also be regarded as means by which those who have no imagination may make up for this defect as far as possible, and those who are gifted with it may facilitate the use of it.

Thus, although the kind of knowledge which is peculiar and essential to genius is knowledge of *perception,* yet the special object of this knowledge by no means consists of the particular things, but of the Platonic Ideas which manifest themselves in these, as their apprehension was analyzed above. Always to see the universal in the particular is just the fundamental characteristic of genius, while the normal man knows in the particular only the particular as such, for only as such does it belong to the actual which alone has interests for him, *i. e.,* relations to the *will.* The degree in which every one not merely thinks, but actually perceives, in the particular thing, only the particular, or a more or less universal up to the most universal of the species, is the measure of his approach to genius. And corresponding to this, only the nature of things generally, the universal in them, the whole, is the special object of genius. The investigation of the particular phenomena is the field of the talents, in the real sciences, whose special object is always only the relations of things to each other.

What was fully shown in the preceding chapter, that the apprehension of the Ideas is conditioned by the fact that the knower is the *pure subject* of knowledge, *i. e.,* that the will entirely vanishes from consciousness, must be borne in mind here. The pleasure which we have in many of Goethe's songs which bring the landscape before our eyes, or in Jean Paul's sketches of nature, depends upon the fact that we thereby participate in the objectivity of those minds, *i. e.,* the purity with which in them the world as idea separated from the world as will, and, as it were, entirely emancipated itself from it. It also follows from the fact that the kind of knowledge peculiar to genius is essentially that which is purified from all will and its relations, that the works of genius do not proceed from intention or choice, but it is guided in them by a kind of instinctive necessity. What is called the awaking of genius, the hour of initiation, the moment of inspiration, is nothing but the attainment of freedom by the intellect, when, delivered for a while from its service under the will, it does not now sink into inactivity or lassitude, but is active for a short time entirely alone and spontaneously. Then it is of the greatest purity, and becomes the clear mirror of the world; for, completely severed from its origin, the will, it is now the world as idea itself, concentrated in *one* consciousness. In such moments, as it were, the souls of immortal works are begotten. On the other hand, in all intentional reflection the intellect is not free, for indeed the will guides it and prescribes it its theme.

The stamp of commonness, the expression of vulgarity, which is impressed on the great majority of countenances consists really in this, that in them becomes visible the strict subordination of their knowledge to their will, the firm chain which binds these two together, and the impossibility following from this of apprehending things otherwise than in their relation to the will and its aims. On the other hand, the expression of genius which constitutes the evident family likeness of all highly gifted men consists in this, that in it we distinctly read the liberation, the manumission of the intellect from the service of the will, the predominance of knowledge over volition; and because all anxiety proceeds from the will, and knowledge, on the contrary, is in and for itself painless and serene, this gives to their lofty brow and clear, perceiving glance, which are not subject to the service of the will and its wants, that look of great, almost supernatural serenity which at times breaks through, and consists very well with the melancholy of their other features, especially the mouth, and which in this relation may be aptly described by the motto of Giordano Bruno: *In tristitia hilaris, in hilaritate tristis.*[2]

The will, which is the root of the intellect, opposes itself to any activity of the latter which is directed to anything else but its own aims. Therefore the intellect is only capable of a purely objective and profound comprehension of the external world when it had freed itself at least for a while from this its root. So long as it remains bound to the will, it is of its own means capable of no activity, but sleeps in a stupor, whenever the will (the in-

---

[2] "Hilarious in sadness, sad in hilarity."

terests) does not awake it, and set it in motion. If, however, this
happens, it is indeed very well fitted to recognize the relations
of things according to the interest of the will, as the prudent
mind does, which, however, must always be an awakened mind,
i. e., a mind actively aroused by volition; but just on this account
it is not capable of comprehending the purely objective nature of
things. For the willing and the aims make it so one-sided that it
sees in things only that which relates to these, and the rest either
disappears or enters consciousness in a falsified form. For example,
the traveller in anxiety and haste will see the Rhine and its banks
only as a line, and the bridges over it only as lines cutting it. In
the mind of the man who is filled with his own aims the world appears as a beautiful landscape appears on the plan of a battlefield.
Certainly these are extremes, taken for the sake of distinctness;
but every excitement of the will, however slight, will have as its
consequence a slight but constantly proportionate falsification of
knowledge. The world can only appear in its true colour and
form, in its whole and correct significance, when the intellect,
devoid of willing, moves freely over the objects, and without being
driven on by the will is yet energetically active. This is certainly
opposed to the nature and determination of the intellect, thus to a
certain extent unnatural, and just on this account exceedingly rare;
but it is just in this that the essential nature of genius lies, in
which alone that condition takes place in a high degree and is of
some duration, while in others it only appears approximately and
exceptionally. I take it to be in the sense expounded here that
Jean Paul (*Vorschule der Æsthetik,* § 12) places the essence of
genius in *reflectiveness.* The normal man is sunk in the whirl and
tumult of life, to which he belongs through his will; his intellect
is filled with the things and events of life; but he does not know
these things nor life itself in their objective significance; as the
merchant on 'Change in Amsterdam apprehends perfectly what
his neighbour says, but does not hear the hum of the whole Exchange, like the sound of the sea, which astonishes the distant
observer. From the genius, on the contrary, whose intellect is
delivered from the will, and thus from the person, what concerns
these does not conceal the world and things themselves; but he
becomes distinctly conscious of them, he apprehends them in and

for themselves in objective perception; in this sense he is *reflective*.

It is *reflectiveness* which enables the painter to repeat the natural objects which he contemplates faithfully upon the canvas, and the poet accurately to call up again the concrete present, by means of abstract conceptions, by giving it utterance and so bringing it to distinct consciousness, and also to express everything in words which others only feel. The brute lives entirely without reflection. It has consciousness, *i. e.,* it knows itself and its good and ill, also the objects which occasion these. But its knowledge remains always subjective, never becomes objective; everything that enters it seems a matter of course, and therefore can never become for it a theme (an object of exposition) nor a problem (an object of meditation). Its consciousness is thus entirely *immanent.* Not certainly the same, but yet of kindred nature, is the consciousness of the common type of man, for his apprehension also of things and the world is predominantly subjective and remains prevalently immanent. It apprehends the things in the world, but not the world; its own action and suffering, but not itself. As now in innumerable gradations the distinctness of consciousness rises, reflectiveness appears more and more; and thus it is brought about little by little that sometimes, though rarely, and then again in very different degrees of distinctness, the question passes through the mind like a flash, "What is all this?" or again, "How is it really fashioned?" The first question, if it attains great distinctness and continued presence, will make the philosopher, and the other, under the same conditions, the artist or the poet. Therefore, then, the high calling of both of these has its root in the reflectiveness which primarily springs from the distinctness with which they are conscious of the world and their own selves, and thereby come to reflect upon them. But the whole process springs from the fact that the intellect through its preponderance frees itself for a time from the will, to which it is originally subject.

The considerations concerning genius here set forth are connected by way of supplement with the exposition of the *ever wider separation of the will and the intellect,* which can be traced in the whole series of existences. This reaches its highest grade in genius, where it extends to the entire liberation of the intellect from its root the will, so that here the intellect becomes perfectly free, whereby the *world as idea* first attains to complete objectification.

A few remarks now concerning the individuality of genius. Aristotle has already said, according to Cicero (*Tusc.*, i., 33), *"Omnes ingeniosos melancholicos esse";* [3] which without doubt is connected with the passage of Aristotle's *"Problemata"* (xxx.) 1. Goethe also says: "My poetic rapture was very small, so long as I only encountered good; but it burnt with a bright flame when I fled from threatening evil. The tender poem, like the rainbow, is only drawn on a dark ground; hence the genius of the poet loves the element of melancholy."

This is to be explained from the fact that since the will constantly re-establishes its original sway over the intellect, the latter more easily withdraws from this under unfavourable personal relations; because it gladly turns from adverse circumstances, in order to a certain extent to divert itself, and now directs itself with so much the greater energy to the foreign external world, thus more easily becomes purely objective. Favourable personal relations act conversely. Yet as a whole and in general the melancholy which accompanies genius depends upon the fact that the brighter the intellect which enlightens the will to live, the more distinctly does it perceive the misery of its condition. The melancholy disposition of highly gifted minds which has so often been observed has its emblem in Mont Blanc, the summit of which is for the most part lost in clouds; but when sometimes, especially in the early morning, the veil of clouds is rent and now the mountain looks down on Chamounix from its height in the heavens above the clouds, then it is a sight at which the heart of each of us swells from its profoundest depths. So also the genius, for the most part melancholy, shows at times that peculiar serenity already described above, which is possible only for it, and springs from the most perfect objectivity of the mind. It floats like a ray of light upon his lofty brow: *In tristitia hilaris, in hilaritate tristis.*

All bunglers are so ultimately because their intellect, still too firmly bound to the will, only becomes active when spurred on by it, and therefore remains entirely in its service. They are ac-

[3] "All men of genius are melancholy."

cordingly only capable of personal aims. In conformity with these they produce bad pictures, insipid poems, shallow, absurd, and very often dishonest philosophemes, when it is to their interest to recommend themselves to high authorities by a pious disingenuousness. Thus all their action and thought is personal. Therefore they succeed at most in appropriating what is external, accidental, and arbitrary in the genuine works of others as mannerisms, in doing which they take the shell instead of the kernel, and yet imagine they have attained to everything, nay, have surpassed those works. If, however, the failure is patent, yet many hope to attain success in the end through their good intentions. But it is just this good will which makes success impossible; because this only pursues personal ends, and with these neither art nor poetry nor philosophy can ever be taken seriously. Therefore the saying is peculiarly applicable to such persons: "They stand in their own light." They have no idea that it is only the intellect delivered from the government of the will and all its projects, and therefore freely active, that makes one capable of genuine productions, because it alone imparts true seriousness; and it is well for them that they have not, otherwise they would leap into the water. The *good will* is in *morality* everything; but in art it is nothing. In art, as the word itself indicates (*Kunst*), what alone is of consequence is ability (*Können*). It all amounts ultimately to this, where the true *seriousness* of the man lies. In almost all it lies exclusively in their own well-being and that of their families; therefore they are in a position to promote this and nothing else; for no purpose, no voluntary and intentional effort, imparts the true, profound, and proper seriousness, or makes up for it, or more correctly, takes its place. For it always remains where nature has placed it; and without it everything is only half performed. Therefore, for the same reason, persons of genius often manage so badly for their own welfare. As a leaden weight always brings a body back to the position which its centre of gravity thereby determines demands, so the true seriousness of the man always draws the strength and attention of the intellect back to that in which it lies; everything else the man does *without true seriousness*. Therefore only the exceedingly rare and abnormal men whose true seriousness does not lie in the personal and practical, but in the objective and theoretical, are in a position to apprehend what is essential in the things of the world, thus the highest truths, and reproduce them in any way. For such a seriousness of the individual, falling outside himself in the objective, is something foreign to the nature of man, something unnatural, or really supernatural: yet on account of this alone is the man *great;* and therefore what he achieves is then ascribed to a *genius* different from himself, which takes possession of him. To such a man his painting, poetry, or thinking is an *end;* to others it is a *means.* The latter thereby seek their own things, and, as a rule, they know how to further them, for they flatter their contemporaries, ready to serve their wants and humours; therefore for the most part they live in happy circumstances; the former often in very miserable circumstances. For he sacrifices his personal welfare to his *objective end;* he cannot indeed do otherwise, because his seriousness lies there. They act conversely; therefore they are *small,* but he is *great.* Accordingly his work is for all time, but the recognition of it generally only begins with posterity: they live and die with their time. In general he only is great who in his work, whether it is practical or theoretical, seeks *not his own concerns,* but pursues an *objective end* alone; he is so, however, even when in the practical sphere this end is a misunderstood one, and even if in consequence of this it should be a crime. *That he seeks not himself and his own concerns,* this makes him under all circumstances *great. Small,* on the other hand, is all action which is directed to personal ends; for whoever is thereby set in activity knows and finds himself only in his own transient and insignificant person. He who is great, again, finds himself in all, and therefore in the whole: he lives not, like others, only in the microcosm, but still more in the macrocosm. Hence the whole interests him, and he seeks to comprehend it in order to represent it, or to explain it, or to act practically upon it. For it is not strange to him; he feels that it concerns him. On account of this extension of his sphere he is called *great.* Therefore that lofty predicate belongs only to the true hero, in some sense, and to genius: it signifies that they, contrary to human nature, have not sought their own things, have not lived for themselves, but for all. As now clearly the great majority must *constantly* be small, and can *never* become great, the converse of this, that one should be great throughout, that is, constantly and every moment, is yet not possible—

"For man is made of common clay,
And custom is his nurse."

Every great man must often be only the individual, have only himself in view, and that means he must be small. Upon this depends the very true remark, that no man is a hero to his valet, and not upon the fact that the valet cannot appreciate the hero; which Goethe, in the *"Wahlverwandhschaften"* (vol. ii., chap. 5), serves up as an idea of Ottilie's.

Genius is its own reward: for the best that one is, one must necessarily be for oneself. "Whoever is born with a talent, to a talent, finds in this his fairest existence," says Goethe. When we look back at a great man of former times, we do not think, "How happy is he to be still admired by all of us!" but, "How happy must he have been in the immediate enjoyment of a mind at the surviving traces of which centuries revive themselves!" Not in the fame, but in that whereby it is attained, lies the value, and in the production of immortal children the pleasure. Therefore those who seek to show the vanity of posthumous fame from the fact that he who obtains it knows nothing of it, may be compared to the wiseacre who very learnedly tried to demonstrate to the man who cast envious glances at a heap of oyster-shells in his neighbour's yard the absolute uselessness of them.

According to the exposition of the nature of genius which has been given, it is so far contrary to nature, inasmuch as it consists in this, that the intellect, whose real destination is the service of the will, emancipates itself from this service in order to be active on its own account. Accordingly genius is an intellect which has become untrue to its destination. Upon this depend the *disadvantages* connected with it, for the consideration of which we shall now prepare the way by comparing genius with the less decided predominance of the intellect.

The intellect of the normal man, strictly bound to the service of the will, and therefore really only occupied with the apprehension of motives, may be regarded as a complex system of wires, by means of which each of these puppets is set in motion in the theatre of the world. From this arises the dry, grave seriousness of most people, which is only surpassed by that of the brutes, who never laugh. On the other hand, we might compare the genius, with his unfettered intellect, to a living man playing along with the large puppets of the famous puppet-show at Milan, who would be the only one among them who would understand everything, and would therefore gladly leave the stage for a while to enjoy the play from the boxes;—that is the reflectiveness of genius. But even the man of great understanding and reason, whom one might almost call wise, is very different from the genius, and in this way, that his intellect retains a *practical* tendency, is concerned with the choice of the best ends and means, therefore remains in the service of the will, and accordingly is occupied in a manner that is thoroughly in keeping with nature. The firm, practical seriousness of life which the Romans denoted *gravitas* presupposes that the intellect does not forsake the service of the will in order to wander away after that which does not concern the will; therefore it does not admit of that separation of the will and the intellect which is the condition of genius. The able, nay, eminent man, who is fitted for great achievements in the practical sphere, is so precisely because objects rouse his will in a lively manner, and spur him on to the ceaseless investigation of their relations and connections. Thus his intellect has grown up closely connected with his will. Before the man of genius, on the contrary, there floats in his objective comprehension the phenomenon of the world, as something foreign to him, an object of contemplation, which expels his will from consciousness. Round this point turns the distinction between the capacity for *deeds* and for *works*. The latter demand objectivity and depth of knowledge, which presupposes entire separation of the intellect from the will; the former, on the other hand, demands the application of knowledge, presence of mind, and decision, which required that the intellect should uninterruptedly attend to the service of the will. Where the bond between the intellect and the will is loosened, the intellect, turned away from its natural destination, will neglect the service of the will; it will, for example, even in the need of the moment, preserve its emancipation, and perhaps be unable to avoid taking in the picturesque impression of the surroundings, from which danger threatens the individual. The intellect of the reasonable and understanding man, on the other hand, is constantly at its post, is directed to the circumstances and their requirements. Such a man will therefore in all cases determine and carry out what is suitable to the case, and consequently will by no means fall into those eccentricities, personal slips, nay, follies, to which the genius is exposed, because his intellect does not remain exclusively the guide and guardian of his will, but sometimes more, sometimes less, is laid claim to by the purely objective. In the contrast of Tasso and Antonio, Goethe has illustrated the opposition, here explained in the abstract, in which these two entirely different kinds of capacity stand to each other. The kinship of genius and madness, so often observed, depends chiefly upon that separation of the intellect from the will which is essential to genius, but is yet contrary to nature. But this separation itself is by no means to be attributed to the fact that genius is accompanied by less intensity of will; for it is rather distinguished by a vehement and passionate character; but it is to be explained from this, that the practically excellent person, the man of deeds, has merely the whole, full measure of intellect required for an energetic will while most men lack even this; but genius consists in a completely abnormal, actual superfluity of intellect, such as is required for the service of no will. On this account the men of genuine works are a thousand times rarer than the men of deeds. It is just that abnormal superfluity of intellect by virtue of which it obtains the decided preponderance, sets itself free from the will, and now, forgetting its origin, is freely active from its own strength and elasticity; and from this the creations of genius proceed.

Now further, just this, that genius in working consists of the free intellect, *i. e.,* of the intellect emancipated from the service of the will, has as a consequence that its productions serve no useful ends. The work of genius is music, or philosophy, or paintings, or poetry; it is nothing to use. To be of no use belongs to the character of the works of genius; it is their patent of nobility. All other works of men are for the maintenance or easing of our existence; only those we are speaking of are not; they alone exist for their own sake, and are in this sense to be regarded as the flower or the net profit of existence. Therefore our heart swells at the enjoyment of them, for we rise out of the heavy earthly atmosphere of want. Analogous to this, we see the beautiful, even apart from these, rarely combined with the useful. Lofty and beautiful trees bear no fruit; the fruit-trees are small, ugly cripples. The full garden rose is not fruitful, but the small, wild, almost scentless roses are. The most beautiful buildings are not the useful ones; a temple is no dwelling-house. A man of high, rare mental endowments compelled to apply himself to a merely useful business, for which the most ordinary man would be fitted, is like a costly vase decorated with the most beautiful painting which is used as a kitchen pot; and to compare useful people with men of genius is like comparing building-stone with diamonds.

Thus the merely practical man uses his intellect that for which nature destined it, the comprehension of the relations of things, partly to each other, partly to the will of the knowing individual. The genius, on the other hand, uses it, contrary to its destination, for the comprehension of the objective nature of things. His mind, therefore, belongs not to himself, but to the world, to the illumination of which, in some sense, it will contribute. From this must spring manifold *disadvantages* to the individual favoured with genius. For his intellect will in general show those faults which are rarely wanting in any tool which is used for that for which it has not been made. First of all, it will be, as it were, the servant of two masters, for on every opportunity it frees itself from the service to which it was destined in order to follow its own ends, whereby it often leaves the will very inopportunely in a fix, and thus the individual so gifted becomes more or less useless for life, nay, in his conduct sometimes reminds us of madness. Then, on account of its highly developed power of knowledge, it will see in things more the universal than the particular; while the service of the will principally requires the knowledge of the particular. But, again, when, as opportunity offers, that whole abnormally heightened power of knowledge directs itself with all its energy to the circumstances and miseries of the will, it will be apt to apprehend these too vividly, to behold all in too glaring colours, in too bright a light, and in a fearfully exaggerated form, whereby the individual falls into mere extremes. The following may serve to explain this more accurately. All great theoretical achievements, in whatever sphere they may be, are brought about in this way: Their author directs all the forces of his mind upon one point, in which he lets them unite and concentrate so strongly, firmly, and exclusively that now the whole of the rest of the world vanishes for him, and his object fills all reality. Now this great and powerful concentration which belongs to the privileges of genius sometimes appears for it also in the case of objects of the real world and the events of daily life, which then, brought under such a focus, are magnified to such a monstrous extent that they appear like the flea, which under the solar miscroscope assumes the stature of an elephant. Hence it arises that highly gifted individuals sometimes are thrown by trifles into violent emotions of the most various kinds, which are incomprehensible to others, who see them transported with grief, joy, care, fear, anger, &c., by things which leave the everyday man quite composed. Thus, then, the genius lacks *soberness,* which simply consists in this, that one sees in things nothing more than actually belongs to them, especially with reference to our possible ends; therefore no sober-minded man can be a genius. With the disadvantages which have been enumerated there is also associated hyper-sensibility, which an abnormally developed nervous and cerebral system brings with it, and indeed in union with the vehemence and passionateness of will which is certainly characteristic of genius, and which exhibits itself physically as energy of the pulsation of the heart. From all this very easily arises that extravagance of disposition, that vehemence of the emotions, that quick change of mood under prevailing melancholy, which Goethe has presented to us in Tasso. What reasonableness, quiet composure, finished surveyal, certainty and proportionateness of behaviour is shown by the well-endowed normal man in comparison with the now dreamy absentness, and now passionate excitement of the man of genius, whose inward pain is the mother's lap of immortal works! To all this must still be added that genius lives essentially alone. It is too rare to find its like with ease, and too different from the rest of men to be their companion. With them it is the will, with him it is knowledge, that predominates; therefore their pleasures are not his, and his are not theirs. They are merely moral beings, and have merely personal relations; he is at the same time a pure intellect, and as such belongs to the whole of humanity. The course of thought of the intellect which is detached from its mother soil, the will, and only returns to it periodically, will soon show itself entirely different from that of the normal intellect, still cleaving to its stem. For this reason, and also on account of the dissimilarity of the pace, the former is not adapted for thinking in common, *i. e.,* for conversation with the others: they will have as little pleasure in him and his oppressive superiority as he will in them. They will therefore feel more comfortable with their equals, and he will prefer the entertainment of his equals, although, as a rule, this is only possible through the works they have left behind them. Therefore Chamfort says very rightly: *"Il y a peu de vices qui empêchent un homme d'avoir beaucoup d'amis, autant que peuvent le faire de trop grandes qualités."* [4] The happiest lot that can fall to the genius is release from action, which is not his element, and leisure for production. From all this it results that although genius may highly bless him who is gifted with it, in the hours in which, abandoned to it, he revels unhindered in its delight, yet it is by no means fitted to procure for him a happy course of life; rather the contrary. This is also confirmed by the experience recorded in biographies. Besides this there is also an external incongruity, for the genius, in his efforts and achievements themselves, is for the most part in contradiction and conflict with his age. Mere men of talent come always at the right time; for as they are roused by the spirit of their age, and called forth by its needs, they are also capable only of satisfying these. They therefore go hand in hand with the advancing culture of their contemporaries or with the gradual progress of a special science: for this they reap reward and approval. But to the next generation their works are no longer enjoyable; they must be replaced by others, which again are not permanent. The genius, on the contrary, comes into his age like a comet into the paths of the planets, to whose well-regulated and comprehensible order his entirely eccentric course is foreign. Accordingly he cannot go hand in hand with the existing, regular progress of the culture of the age,

[4] "There are few vices that can so hinder a man from having many friends, as can the possession of superior qualities."

but flings his works far out on to the way in front (as the dying emperor flung his spear among the enemy), upon which time has first to overtake them. The man of talent can achieve what is beyond the power of achievement of other men, but not what is beyond their power of apprehension: therefore he at once finds those who prize him. But the achievement of the man of genius, on the contrary, transcends not only the power of achievement, but also the power of apprehension of others; therefore they do not become directly conscious of him. The man of talent is like the marksman who hits a mark the others cannot hit; the man of genius is like the marksman who hits a mark they cannot even see to; therefore they get news of him only indirectly, and thus late; and even this they accept only upon trust and faith. Accordingly Goethe says in one of his letters, "Imitation is inborn in us; what to imitate is not easily recognized. Rarely is what is excellent found; still more rarely is it prized." And Chamfort says: *"Il en est de la valeur des hommes comme de celle des diamans, qui à une certaine mesure de grosseur, de pureté, de perfection, ont un prix fixe et marqué, mais qui, par-delà cette mesure, restent sans prix, et ne trouvent point d'acheteurs."* [5] And Bacon of Verulam has also expressed it: *"Infirmarum virtutum, apud vulgus, laus est, mediarum admiratio, supremarum sensus nullus"* (*De augm. sc.*, L. vi., c. 3).[6] Indeed, one might perhaps reply, *Apud vulgus!* But I must then come to his assistance with Machiavelli's assurance: *"Nel monde non è se non volgo";* [7] as also Thilo (*Ueber den Ruhm*) remarks, that to the vulgar herd there generally belongs one more than each of us believes. It is a consequence of this late recognition of the works of the man of genius that they are rarely enjoyed by their contemporaries, and accordingly in the freshness of colour which synchronism and presence imparts, but, like figs and dates, much more in a dry than in a fresh state.

If, finally, we consider genius from the somatic side, we find it conditioned by several anatomical and physiological qualities,

---

[5] "It is with the value of men as with that of diamonds, which, up to a certain degree of size, purity, and perfection, have a fixed and marked price, but which, beyond that degree, remain without price and find no buyers."

[6] "Among the people there is praise for the smaller virtues, administration for the middling ones, but no sense of the greatest."

[7] "There is nothing else in the world but the vulgar."

which individually are seldom present in perfection, and still more seldom perfect together, but which are yet all indispensably required; so that this explains why genius only appears as a perfectly isolated and almost portentous exception. The fundamental condition is an abnormal predominance of sensibility over irritability and reproductive power; and what makes the matter more difficult, this must take place in a male body. (Women may have great talent, but no genius, for they always remain subjective.) Similarly the cerebral system must be perfectly separated from the ganglion system by complete isolation, so that it stands in complete opposition to the latter; and thus the brain pursues its parasitic life on the organism in a very decided, isolated, powerful, and independent manner. Certainly it will thereby very easily affect the rest of the organism injuriously, and through its heightened life and ceaseless activity wear it out prematurely, unless it is itself possessed of energetic vital force and a good constitution: thus the latter belong to the conditions of genius. Indeed even a good stomach is a condition on account of the special and close agreement of this part with the brain. But chiefly the brain must be of unusual development and magnitude, especially broad and high. On the other hand, its depth will be inferior, and the cerebrum will abnormally preponderate in proportion to the cerebellum. Without doubt much depends upon the configuration of the brain as a whole and in its parts; but our knowledge is not yet sufficient to determine this accurately, although we easily recognize the form of skull that indicates a noble and lofty intelligence. The texture of the mass of the brain must be of extreme fineness and perfection, and consist of the purest, most concentrated, tenderest, and most excitable nerve-substance; certainly the quantitative proportion of the white to the grey matter has a decided influence, which, however, we are also unable as yet to specify. However, the report of the *post-mortem* on the body of Byron [8] shows that in his case the white matter was in unusually large proportion to the grey, and also that his brain weighed six pounds. Cuvier's brain weighed five pounds; the normal weight is three pounds. In contrast to the superior size of the brain, the spinal cord and nerves must be

[8] In Medwin's "Conversations of Lord Byron," p. 333.

unusually thin. A beautifully arched, high and broad skull of thin bone must protect the brain without in any way cramping it. This whole quality of the brain and nervous system is the inheritance from the mother, to which we shall return in the following book. But it is quite insufficient to produce the phenomenon of genius if the inheritance from the father is not added, a lively, passionate temperament, which exhibits itself somatically as unusual energy of the heart, and consequently of the circulation of the blood, especially towards the head. For, in the first place, that turgescence peculiar to the brain on account of which it presses against its walls is increased by this; therefore it forces itself out of any opening in these which has been occasioned by some injury; and secondly, from the requisite strength of the heart the brain receives that internal movement different from its constant rising and sinking at every breath, which consists in a shaking of its whole mass at every pulsation of the four cerebral arteries, and the energy of which must correspond to the here increased quantity of the brain, as this movement in general is an indispensable condition of its activity. To this, therefore, small stature and especially a short neck is favourable, because by the shorter path the blood reaches the brain with more energy; and on this account great minds have seldom large bodies. Yet that shortness of the distance is not indispensable; for example, Goethe was of more than middle height. If, however, the whole condition connected with the circulation of the blood, and therefore coming from the father is wanting, the good quality of the brain coming from the mother, will at most produce a man of talent, a fine understanding, which the phlegmatic temperament thus introduces supports; but a phlegmatic genius is impossible. This condition coming from the father explains many faults of temperament described above. But, on the other hand, if this condition exists without the former, thus with an ordinarily or even badly constructed brain, it gives vivacity without mind, heat without light, hot-headed persons, men of unsupportable restlessness and petulance. That of two brothers only one has genius, and that one generally the elder, as, for example, in Kant's case, is primarily to be explained from the fact that the father was at the age of strength and passion only when he was begotten;

although also the other condition originating with the mother may be spoiled by unfavourable circumstances.

I have further to add here a special remark on the *childlike* character of the genius, *i. e.,* on a certain resemblance which exists between genius and the age of childhood. In childhood, as in the case of genius, the cerebral and nervous system decidedly preponderates, for its development hurries far in advance of that of the rest of the organism; so that already at the seventh year the brain has attained its full extension and mass. On the other hand, the development of the genital system begins latest, and irritability, reproduction, and genital function are in full force only at the age of manhood, and then, as a rule, they predominate over the brain function. Hence it is explicable that children, in general, are so sensible, reasonable, desirous of information, and teachable, nay, on the whole, are more disposed and fitted for all theoretical occupation than grown-up people. They have, in consequence of that course of development, more intellect than will, *i. e.,* than inclinations, desire, and passion. For intellect and brain are one, and so also is the genital system one with the most vehement of all desires: therefore I have called the latter the focus of the will. Just because the fearful activity of this system still slumbers, while that of the brain has already full play, childhood is the time of innocence and happiness, the paradise of life, the lost Eden on which we look longingly back through the whole remaining course of our life. But the basis of that happiness is that in childhood our whole existence lies much more in knowing than in willing—a condition which is also supported from without by the novelty of all objects. Hence in the morning sunshine of life the world lies before us so fresh, so magically gleaming, so attractive. The small desires, the weak inclinations, and trifling cares of childhood are only a weak counterpoise to that predominance of intellectual activity. The innocent and clear glance of children, at which we revive ourselves, and which sometimes in particular cases reaches the sublime contemplative expression with which Raphael has glorified his cherubs, is to be explained from what has been said. Accordingly the mental powers develop much earlier than the needs they are destined to serve; and here, as everywhere, nature proceeds very designedly. For in this time of predominating intelligence the man collects a great store of knowledge for future wants which at the time are foreign to him. Therefore his intellect, now unceasingly active, eagerly apprehends all phenomena, broods over them and stores them up carefully for the coming time,—like the bees, who gather a great deal more honey than they can consume, in anticipation of future need. Certainly what a man acquires of insight and knowledge up to the age of puberty is, taken as a whole, more than all that he afterwards learns, however learned he may become; for it is the foundation of all human knowledge. Up till the same time plasticity predominates in the child's body, and later, by a metastasis, its forces throw themselves into the system of generation; and thus with puberty the sexual passion appears, and now, little by little, the will gains the upper hand. Then childhood, which is prevailingly theoretical and desirous of learning, is followed by the restless, now stormy, now melancholy, period of youth, which afterwards passes into the vigorous and earnest age of manhood. Just because that impulse pregnant with evil is wanting in the child is its volition so adapted and subordinated to knowledge, whence arises that character of innocence, intelligence, and reasonableness which is peculiar to the age of childhood. On what, then, the likeness between childhood and genius depends I scarcely need to express further: upon the surplus of the powers of knowledge over the needs of the will, and the predominance of the purely intellectual activity which springs from this. Really every child is to a certain extent a genius, and the genius is to a certain extent a child. The relationship of the two shows itself primarily in the naïveté and sublime simplicity which is characteristic of true genius; and besides this it appears in several traits, so that a certain childishness certainly belongs to the character of the genius. In Riemer's *"Mittheilungen über Goethe"* (vol. i., p. 184) it is related that Herder and others found fault with Goethe, saying he was always a big child. Certainly they were right in what they said, but they were not right in finding fault with it. It has also been said of Mozart that all his life he remained a child (Nissen's Biography of Mozart, pp. 2 and 529). Schlichtegrolls *"Nekrology"* (for 1791, vol. ii., p. 109) says of him: "In his art he early became a man, but in all other relations he always remained a child." Every genius is even for this reason a big child; he looks out into the world as into something strange, a play, and therefore with purely objective interest. Accordingly he has just as little as the child that dull gravity of ordinary men, who, since they are capable only of subjective interests, always see in things mere motives for their action. Whoever does not to a certain extent remain all his life a big child, but becomes a grave, sober, thoroughly composed, and reasonable man, may be a very useful and capable citizen of this world; but never a genius. In fact, the genius is so because that predominance of the sensible system and of intellectual activity which is natural to childhood maintains itself in him in an abnormal manner through his whole life, thus here becomes perennial. A trace of this certainly shows itself in many ordinary men up to the period of their youth; therefore, for example, in many students a purely intellectual tendency and an eccentricity suggestive of genius is unmistakable. But nature returns to her track; they assume the chrysalis form and reappear at the age of manhood, as incarnate Philistines, at whom we are startled when we meet them again in later years. Upon all this that has been expounded here depends Goethe's beautiful remark: "Children do not perform what they promise; young people very seldom; and if they do keep their word, the world does not keep its word with them" (*Wahlverwandtschaften,* Pt. i., ch. 10)—the world which afterwards bestows the crowns which it holds aloft for merit on those who are the tools of its low aims or know how to deceive it. In accordance with what has been said, as there is a mere beauty of youth, which almost every one at some time possesses (*beauté du diable*), so there is a mere intellectuality of youth, a certain mental nature disposed and adapted for apprehending, understanding, and learning, which every one has in childhood, and some have still in youth, but which is afterwards lost, just like that beauty. Only in the case of a very few, the chosen, the one, like the other, lasts through the whole life; so that even in old age a trace of it still remains visible; these are the truly beautiful and the men of true genius.

CHAPTER XXXII

ON MADNESS

THE health of the mind properly consists in perfect recollection. Of course this is not to be understood as meaning that our memory preserves everything. For the past course of our life shrinks up in time, as the path of the wanderer looking back shrinks up in space: sometimes it is difficult for us to distinguish the particular years; the days have for the most part become unrecognizable. Really, however, only the exactly similar events, recurring an innumerable number of times, so that their images, as it were, conceal each other, ought so to run together in the memory that they are individually unrecognizable; on the other hand, every event in any way peculiar or significant we must be able to find again in memory, if the intellect is normal, vigorous, and quite healthy. In the text I have explained *madness* as the *broken thread* of this memory, which still runs on regularly, although in constantly decreasing fullness and distinctness. The following considerations may serve to confirm this.

The memory of a healthy man affords a certainty as to an event he has witnessed, which is regarded as just as firm and sure as his present apprehension of things; therefore, if sworn to by him, this event is thereby established in a court of law. On the other hand, the mere suspicion of madness will at once weaken the testimony of a witness. Here, then, lies the criterion between the healthy mind and insanity. Whenever I doubt whether an event which I remember really took place, I throw upon myself the suspicion of madness: unless it is that I am uncertain whether it was not a mere dream. If another doubts the reality of an event, related by me as an eye-witness, without mistrusting my honesty, then he regards me as insane. Whoever comes at last, through constantly recounting an event which originally was fabricated by him, to believe in it himself is, in this one point, really insane. We may ascribe to an insane person flashes of wit, single clever thoughts, even correct judgments, but his testimony as to past events no man will consider valid. In the Lalitavistara, well known to be the history of Buddha Sakya-Muni, it is related that at the moment of his birth all the sick became well, all the blind saw, all the deaf heard, and all mad people "recovered their memory." This last is mentioned in two passages.[1]

My own experience of many years has led me to the opinion that madness occurs proportionally most frequently among actors. But what a misuse they make of their memory! Daily they have to learn a new part or refresh an old one; but these parts are entirely without connection, nay, are in contradiction and contrast with each other, and every evening the actor strives to forget himself entirely and be some quite different person. This kind of thing paves the way for madness.

The exposition of the origin of madness given in the text will become more comprehensible if it is remembered how unwillingly we think of things which powerfully injure our interests, wound our pride, or interfere with our wishes; with what difficulty do we determine to lay such things before our own intellect for careful and serious investigation; how easily, on the other hand, we unconsciously break away or sneak off from them again; how, on the contrary, agreeable events come into our minds of their own accord, and, if driven away, constantly creep in again, so that we dwell on them for hours together. In that resistance of the will to allowing what is contrary to it to come under the examination of the intellect lies the place at which madness can break in upon the mind. Each new adverse event must be assimilated by the intellect, i. e., it must receive a place in the system of the truths connected with our will and its interests, whatever it may have to displace that is more satisfactory. Whenever this has taken place, it already pains us much less; but this operation itself is often very painful, and also, in general, only takes

[1] *Rgya Tcher Rol Pa, Hist. de Bouddha Chakya Mouni, trad. du Tibétain, p. Foucaux,* 1848, *pp.* 91 *et* 99.

place slowly and with resistance. However, the health of the mind can only continue so long as this is in each case properly carried out. If, on the contrary, in some particular case, the resistance and struggles of the will against the apprehension of some knowledge reaches such a degree that that operation is not performed in its integrity, then certain events or circumstances become for the intellect completely suppressed, because the will cannot endure the sight of them, and then, for the sake of the necessary connection, the gaps that thus arise are filled up at pleasure; thus madness appears. For the intellect has given up its nature to please the will: the man now imagines what does not exist. Yet the madness which has thus arisen is now the lethe of unendurable suffering; it was the last remedy of harassed nature, *i. e.,* of the will.

Let me mention here in passing a proof of my view which is worth noticing. Carlo Gozzi, in the *"Monstro turchino,"* act i., scene 2, presents to us a person who has drunk a magic potion which produces forgetfulness, and this person appears exactly like a madman.

In accordance with the above exposition one may thus regard the origin of madness as a violent "casting out of the mind" of anything, which, however, is only possible by "taking into the head" something else. The converse process is more rare, that the "taking into the head" comes first, and the "casting out of the mind" second. It takes place, however, in those cases in which the occasion of insanity is kept constantly present to the mind and cannot be escaped from; thus, for example, in the case of many who have gone mad from love, erotomaniacs, where the occasion of their madness is constantly longed after; also in the case of madness which has resulted from the fright of some sudden horrible occurrence. Such patients cling, as it were, convulsively to the thought they have grasped, so that no other, or at least none opposed to it, can arise. In both processes, however, what is essential to madness remains the same, the impossibility of a uniformly connected recollection, such as is the basis of our healthy and rational reflection. Perhaps the contrast of the ways in which they arise, set forth here, might, if applied with judgment, afford a sharp and profound principle of division of delusions proper.

For the rest, I have considered only the physical origin of madness, thus what is introduced by external, objective occasions. More frequently, however, it depends upon purely physical causes, upon malformations or partial disorganization of the brain or its membranes, also upon the influence which other parts affected with disease exercise upon the brain. Principally in the latter kind of madness false sense-perceptions, hallucinations, may arise. Yet the two causes of madness will generally partake of each other, particularly the psychical of the physical. It is the same as with suicide, which is rarely brought about by an external occasion alone, but a certain physical discomfort lies at its foundation; and according to the degree which this attains to a greater or less external occasion is required; only in the case of the very highest degree is no external occasion at all required. Therefore there is no misfortune so great that it would influence every one to suicide, and none so small that one like it has not already led to it. I have shown the psychical origin of madness as, at least according to all appearance, it is brought about in the healthy mind by a great misfortune. In the case of those who are already strongly disposed to madness physically a very small disappointment will be sufficient to induce it. For example, I remember a man in a madhouse who had been a soldier, and had gone out of his mind because his officer had addressed him as *Er*.[2] In the case of decided physical disposition no occasion at all is required when this has come to maturity. The madness which has sprung from purely psychical causes may, perhaps, by the violent perversion of the course of thought which has produced it, also introduce a kind of paralysis or other depravity of some part of the brain, which, if not soon done away with, becomes permanent. Therefore madness is only curable at first, and not after a longer time.

Pinel taught that there is a *mania sine delirio,* frenzy without insanity. This was controverted by Esquirol, and since then much has been said for and against it. The question can only be decided empirically. But if such a state really does occur, then it is to be explained from the fact that here the will periodically

[2] In German inferiors are sometimes addressed as *Er* instead of *Sie.*
—*Trs.*

entirely withdraws itself from the government and guidance of the intellect, and consequently of motives, and thus it then appears as a blind, impetuous, destructive force of nature, and accordingly manifests itself as the desire to annihilate everything that comes in its way. The will thus let loose is like the stream which has broken through the dam, the horse that has thrown his rider, or a clock out of which the regulating screws have been taken. Yet only the reason, thus *reflective* knowledge, is included in that suspension, not *intuitive* knowledge also; otherwise the will would remain entirely without guidance, and consequently the man would be immovable. But, on the contrary, the man in a frenzy apprehends objects, for he breaks out upon them; thus he has also consciousness of his present action, and afterwards remembrance of it. But he is entirely without reflection, thus without any guidance of the reason, consequently quite incapable of any consideration or regard for the absent, the past, or the future. When the attack is over, and the reason has regained its command, its function is correct, because here its proper activity has not been perverted or destroyed, but only the will has found the means to withdraw itself from it entirely for a while.

CHAPTER XXXVIII

ON HISTORY

IN the passage of the first volume referred to below I have fully shown that more is achieved for our knowledge of mankind by poetry than by history, and why this is so; inasmuch as more real instruction was to be expected from the former than the latter. Aristotle has also confessed this, for he says: "καὶ φιλοσοφώτερον καὶ σπουδαιότερον ποίησις ἱστορίας εστιν" *De poët.,* c. 9.[1] Yet, in order to cause no misunderstanding as to the value of history, I wish here to express my thoughts about it.

In every class and species of things the facts are innumerable, the individuals infinite in number, the variety of their differences unapproachable. At the first glance at them the curious mind becomes giddy; however much it investigates, it sees itself condemned to ignorance. But then comes science: it separates the innumerable multitude, arranges it under generic conceptions, these again under conceptions of species, whereby it opens the path to a knowledge of the general and the particular, which also comprehends the innumerable individuals, for it holds good of all without one being obliged to consider each particular for itself. Thus it promises satisfaction to the investigating mind. Then all sciences place themselves together, and above the real world of individual things, as that which they have divided among them. Over them all, however, moves philosophy, as the most general, and therefore important, rational knowledge, which promises the conclusions for which the others have only prepared the way. History alone cannot properly enter into that series, since it cannot boast of the same advantage as the others, for it lacks the fundamental characteristic of science, the subordination of what is known, instead of which it can only present its co-

[1] "Poetry is superior to history, and more philosophical."

ordination. Therefore there is no system of history, as there is of every other science. It is therefore certainly rational knowledge, but it is not a science. For it never knows the particular by means of the general, but must comprehend the particular directly, and so, as it were, creeps along the ground of experience; while the true sciences move above it, because they have obtained comprehensive conceptions by means of which they command the particular, and, at least within certain limits, anticipate the possibility of things within their sphere, so that they can be at ease even about what may yet have to come. The sciences, since they are systems of conceptions, speak always of species; history speaks of individuals. It would accordingly be a science of individuals, which is a contradiction. It also follows that the sciences all speak of that which always is: history, on the other hand, of that which is once, and then no more. Since, further, history has to do with the absolutely particular and individuals, which from its nature is inexhaustible, it knows everything only imperfectly and half. Besides, it must also let itself be taught by every new day in its trivial commonplaceness what as yet it did not know at all. If it should be objected that in history also there is subordination of the particular under the general, because the periods, the governments, and other general changes, or political revolutions, in short, all that is given in historical tables, is the general, to which the special subordinates itself, this would rest upon a false comprehension of the conception of the general. For the general in history here referred to is merely *subjective, i. e.,* its generality springs merely from the inadequacy of the individual knowledge of the things, but not *objective, i. e.,* a conception in which the things would actually already be thought together. Even the most general in history is in itself only a particular and individual, a long period of time, or an important event; therefore the special is related to this as the part to the whole, but not as the case to the rule; which, on the contrary, takes place in all the sciences proper because they afford conceptions and not mere facts. On this account in these sciences by a correct knowledge of the general we can determine with certainty the particular that arises. If, for example, I know the laws of the triangle in general, I can then also tell what must be the properties of the triangle laid before me; and what holds good of all mammals, for example, that they have double ventricles of the heart, exactly seven cervical vertebræ, lungs, diaphragm, bladder, five senses, &c., I can also assert of the strange bat which has just been caught, before dissecting it. But not so in history, where the general is no objective general of the conception, but merely a subjective general of my knowledge, which can only be called general inasmuch as it is superficial. Therefore I may always know in general of the Thirty Years' War that it was a religious war, waged in the seventeenth century; but this general knowledge does not make me capable of telling anything more definite about its course. The same opposition is also confirmed by the fact that in the real sciences the special and individual is that which is most certain, because it rests upon immediate apprehension; the general truths, again, are only abstracted from it; therefore something false may be more easily assumed in the latter. But in history, conversely, the most general is the most certain; for example, the periods, the succession of the kings, the revolutions, wars, and treaties of peace; the particulars, again, of the events and their connection is uncertain, and becomes always more so the further one goes into details. Therefore history is the more interesting the more special it is, but the less to be trusted, and approaches then in every respect to the romance. For the rest, what importance is to be attached to the boasted pragmatic teaching of history he will best be able to judge who remembers that sometimes it was only after twenty years that he understood the events of his own life in their true connection, although the data for this were fully before him, so difficult is the combination of the action of the motives under the constant interferences of chance and the concealment of the intentions. Since now history really always has for its object only the particular, the individual fact, and regards this as the exclusively real, it is the direct opposite and counterpart of philosophy, which considers things from the most general point of view, and has intentionally the general as its object, which remains identical in every particular; therefore in the particular philosophy sees only the general, and recognizes the change in its manifestation as unessential: φιλοκαθολου γαρ ὁ φιλοσοφος.[2] While history teaches us that at every time something else has been, philosophy tries to assist us to the insight that at all times exactly the same was, is, and shall be. In truth, the essence of human life, as of nature in general, is given complete in every present time, and therefore only requires depth of comprehension in order to be exhaustively known. But history hopes to make up for depth by length and breadth; for it every present time is only a fragment which must be supplemented by the past, the length of which is, however, infinite, and to which again an infinite future is joined. Upon this rests the opposition between philosophical and historical minds; the former want to go to the bottom, the latter want to go through the whole series. History shows on every side only the same under different forms; but whoever does not come to know this in one or a few will hardly attain to a knowledge of it by going through all the forms. The chapters of the history of nations are at bottom only distinguished by the names and dates; the really essential content is everywhere the same.

Now since the material of art is the *Idea,* and the material of science the *concept,* we see both occupied with that which always exists and constantly in the same manner, not something which now is and now is not, now is thus and now otherwise; therefore both have to do with that which Plato set up as the exclusive object of real rational knowledge. The material of history, on the other hand, is the particular in its particularity and contingency, which at one time is, and then for ever is no more, the transient complexities of a human world moved like clouds in the wind, a world which is often entirely transformed by the most trifling accident. From this point of view the material of history appears to us as scarcely a worthy object of the serious and painful consideration of the human mind, the human mind which, just because it is so transitory, ought to choose for its consideration that which passes not away.

Finally, as regards the endeavour —specially introduced by the Hegelian pseudo-philosophy, everywhere so pernicious and stupefying to the mind—to comprehend the history of the world as

2 "A philosopher is a lover of generalizations."

a planned whole, or as they call it, "to construe it organically," a crude and positive realism lies at its foundation, which takes the phenomenon for the inner being of the world, and imagines that this phenomenon, its forms and events, are the chief concern; in which it is secretly supported by certain mythological notions which it tacitly assumes: otherwise one might ask for what spectators such a comedy was really produced. For, since only the individual, and not the human race, has actual, immediate unity of consciousness, the unity of the course of life of the race is a mere fiction. Besides, as in nature only the species are real, and the genera are mere abstractions, so in the human race only the individuals and their course of life are real, the peoples and their lives mere abstractions. Finally, constructive histories, guided by a positive optimism, always ultimately end in a comfortable, rich, fat State, with a well-regulated constitution, good justice and police, useful arts and industries, and, at the most, in intellectual perfection; for this, in fact, is alone possible, since what is moral remains essentially unaltered. But it is the moral element which, according to the testimony of our inmost consciousness, is the whole concern: and this lies only in the individual as the tendency of his will. In truth, only the life of each individual has unity, connection, and true significance: it is to be regarded as an instruction, and the meaning of it is moral. Only the incidents of our *inner* life, since they concern the will, have true reality, and are actual events; because the will alone is the thing in itself. In every microcosm lies the whole macrocosm, and the latter contains nothing more than the former. Multiplicity is phenomenal, and external events are mere configurations of the phenomenal world, and have therefore directly neither reality nor significance, but only indirectly through their relation to the wills of the individuals. The endeavour to explain and interpret them directly is accordingly like the endeavour to see in the forms of the clouds groups of men and animals. What history narrates is in fact only the long, heavy, and confused dream of humanity.

The Hegelians, who regard the philosophy of history as indeed the chief end of all philosophy, are to be referred to Plato, who unweariedly repeats that the object of philosophy is that which is unchangeable and always remains, not that which now is thus and now otherwise. All those who set up such constructions of the course of the world, or, as they call it, of history, have failed to grasp the principal truth of all philosophy, that what is is at all times the same, all becoming and arising are only seeming; the Ideas alone are permanent; time ideal. This is what Plato holds, this is what Kant holds. One ought therefore to seek to understand what exists, what really *is,* to-day and always, *i. e.,* to know the Ideas (in Plato's sense). Fools, on the contrary, imagine that something must first become and happen. Therefore they concede to history the chief place in their philosophy, and construct it according to a preconceived plan of the world, according to which everything is ordered for the best, which is then supposed *finaliter* to appear, and will be a glorious thing. Accordingly they take the world as perfectly real, and place the end of it in the poor earthly happiness, which, however much it may be fostered by men and favoured by fate, is a hollow, deceptive, decaying, and sad thing, out of which neither constitutions and legal systems nor steam-engines and telegraphs can ever make anything that is essentially better. The said philosophers and glorifiers of history are accordingly simple realists, and also optimists and eudæmonists, consequently dull fellows and incarnate philistines; and besides are really bad Christians, for the true spirit and kernel of Christianity, as also of Brahmanism and Buddhism, is the knowledge of the vanity of earthly happiness, the complete contempt for it, and the turning away from it to an existence of another, nay, an opposite, kind. This, I say, is the spirit and end of Christianity, the true "humour of the matter"; and not, as they imagine, monotheism; therefore even atheistic Buddhism is far more closely related to Christianity than optimistic Judaism or its variety Islamism.

A true philosophy of history ought not therefore to consider, as all these do, what (to use Plato's language) always *becomes* and never *is,* and hold this to be the true nature of things; but it ought to fix its attention upon that which always is and never becomes nor passes away. Thus it does not consist in raising the temporal ends of men to eternal and absolute ends, and then with art and imagination constructing their progress through all complications; but in the insight that not only in its development, but in its very nature, history is mendacious; for, speaking of mere individuals and particular events, it pretends always to relate something different, while from beginning to end it repeats always the same thing under different names and in a different dress. The true philosophy of history consists in the insight that in all these endless changes and their confusion we have always before us only the same, even, unchanging nature, which to-day acts in the same way as yesterday and always; thus it ought to recognize the identical in all events, of ancient as of modern times, of the East as of the West; and, in spite of all difference of the special circumstances, of the costume and the customs, to see everywhere the same humanity. This identical element which is permanent through all change consists in the fundamental qualities of the human heart and head—many bad, few good. The motto of history in general should run: *Eadem, sed aliter.*[3] If one has read Herodotus, then in a philosophical regard one has already studied history enough. For everything is already there that makes up the subsequent history of the world: the efforts, action, sufferings, and fate of the human race as it proceeds from the qualities we have referred to, and the physical earthly lot.

If in what has been said we have recognized that history, regarded as a means for the knowledge of the nature of man, is inferior to poetry; then, that it is not in the proper sense a science; finally, that the endeavour to construct it as a whole with beginning, middle, and end, together with a significant connection, is vain, and based upon misunderstanding: it would look as if we wished to deny it all value if we did not show in what its value consists. Really, however, there remains for it, after this conquest by art and rejection by science, a quite special province, different from both, in which it exists most honourably.

What reason is to the individual that is history to the human race. By virtue of reason, man is not, like the brute, limited to the narrow, perceptible present, but also knows the incomparably more extended past, with which it is linked, and out of which it has proceeded; and only thus has he a proper understanding of the present itself, and can even draw inferences as to the future. The brute, on the other hand, whose knowledge, devoid of re-

[3] "The same things, but differently."

flection, is on this account limited to the present, even when it is tamed, moves about among men ignorant, dull, stupid, helpless, and dependent. Analogous to this is the nation that does not know its own history, is limited to the present of the now living generation, and therefore does not understand itself and its own present, because it cannot connect it with a past, and explain it from this; still less can it anticipate the future. Only through history does a nation become completely conscious of itself. Accordingly history is to be regarded as the rational consciousness of the human race, and is to the race what the reflected and connected consciousness is to the individual who is conditioned by reason, a consciousness through the want of which the brute is confined to the narrow, perceptible present. Therefore every gap in history is like a gap in the recollective self-consciousness of a man; and in the presence of a monument of ancient times which has outlived the knowledge of itself, as, for example, the Pyramids, or temples and palaces in Yucatan, we stand as senseless and stupid as the brute in the presence of the action of man, in which it is implicated in his service; or as a man before something written in an old cipher of his own, the key to which he has forgotten; nay, like a somnambulist who finds before him in the morning what he has done in his sleep. In this sense, then, history is to be regarded as the reason, or the reflected consciousness, of the human race, and takes the place of an immediate self-consciousness common to the whole race, so that only by virtue of it does the human race come to be a whole, come to be a humanity. This is the true value of history, and accordingly the universal and predominating interest in it depends principally upon the fact that it is a personal concern of the human race. Now, what language is for the reason of individuals, as an indispensable condition of its use, writing is for the reason of the whole race here pointed out; for only with this does its real existence begin, as that of the individual reason begins first with language. Writing serves to restore unity to the consciousness of the human race, which is constantly interrupted by death, and therefore fragmentary; so that the thought which has arisen in the ancestor is thought out by his remote descendant; it finds a remedy for the breaking up of the human race and its consciousness into an in-

numerable number of ephemeral individuals, and so bids defiance
to the ever hurrying time, in whose hand goes forgetfulness. As
an attempt to accomplish this we must regard not only written,
but also *stone* monuments, which in part are older than the
former. For who will believe that those who, at incalculable
cost, set in action the human powers of many thousands for
many years in order to construct the pyramids, monoliths, rock
tombs, obelisks, temples, and palaces which have already existed
for thousands of years, could have had in view the short span of
their own life, too short to let them see the finishing of the construction, or even the ostensible end which the ignorance of the
many required them to allege? Clearly their real end was to
speak to their latest descendants, to put themselves in connection
with these, and so to establish the unity of the consciousness of
humanity. The buildings of the Hindus, the Egyptians, even the
Greeks and Romans, were calculated to last several thousand
years, because through higher culture their horizon was a wider
one; while the buildings of the Middle Ages and of modern times
have been intended, at the most, to last only a few centuries;
which, however, is also due to the fact that men trusted more
to writing after its use had become general, and still more since
from its womb was born the art of printing. Yet even in the
buildings of more recent times we see the desire to speak to
posterity; and, therefore, it is shameful if they are destroyed
or disfigured in order to serve low utilitarian ends. Written monuments have less to fear from the elements, but more to fear from
barbarians, than stone ones; they accomplish far more. The
Egyptians wished to combine the two, for they covered their
stone monuments with hieroglyphics, nay, they added paintings
in case the hieroglyphics should no longer be understood.

CHAPTER XLIV

THE METAPHYSICS OF THE LOVE OF THE SEXES

"Ye wise men, highly, deeply learned,
Who think it out and know,
How, when, and where do all things pair?
Why do they kiss and love?
Ye men of lofty wisdom, say
What happened to me then;
Search out and tell me where, how, when,
And why it happened thus."
—BÜRGER.

THIS chapter is the last of four whose various reciprocal relations, by virtue of which, to a certain extent, they constitute a subordinate whole, the attentive reader will recognize without its being needful for me to interrupt my exposition by recalling them or referring to them.

We are accustomed to see poets principally occupied with describing the love of the sexes. This is as a rule the chief theme of all dramatic works, tragical as well as comical, romantic as well as classical, Indian as well as European. Not less is it the material of by far the largest part of lyrical and also of epic poetry, especially if we class with the latter the enormous piles of romances which for centuries every year has produced in all the civilized countries of Europe as regularly as the fruits of the earth. As regards their main contents, all these works are nothing else than many-sided brief or lengthy descriptions of the passion we are speaking of. Moreover, the most successful pictures of it—such, for example, as *Romeo and Juliet, La Nouvelle Hélöise,* and *Werther*—have gained immortal fame. Yet, when Rochefoucauld imagines that it is the same with passionate love as with ghosts, of which every one speaks, but which no one has seen; and Lichtenberg also in his essay, *"Ueber die Macht*

330

der Liebe," disputes and denies the reality and naturalness of that passion, they are greatly in error. For it is impossible that something which is foreign and contrary to human nature, thus a mere imaginary caricature, could be unweariedly represented by poetic genius in all ages, and received by mankind with unaltered interest; for nothing that is artistically beautiful can be without truth:—

> *"Rien n'est beau que le vrai; le vrai seul est aimable."* [1]
>
> BOILEAU.

Certainly, however, it is also confirmed by experience, although not by the experience of every day, that that which as a rule only appears as a strong yet still controllable inclination may rise under certain circumstances to a passion which exceeds all others in vehemence, and which then sets aside all considerations, overcomes all obstacles with incredible strength and perseverance, so that for its satisfaction life is risked without hesitation, nay, if that satisfaction is still withheld, is given as the price of it. Werthers and Jacopo Ortis exist not only in romance, but every year can show at least half a dozen of them in Europe: *Sed ignotis perierunt mortibus illi;*[2] for their sorrows find no other chroniclers than the writers of official registers or the reporters of the newspapers. Yet the readers of the police news in English and French journals will attest the correctness of my assertion. Still greater, however, is the number of those whom the same passion brings to the madhouse. Finally, every year can show cases of the double suicide of a pair of lovers who are opposed by outward circumstances. In such cases, however, it is inexplicable to me how those who, certain of mutual love, expect to find the supremest bliss in the enjoyment of this, do not withdraw themselves from all connections by taking the extremest steps, and endure all hardships, rather than give up with life a pleasure which is greater than any other they can conceive. As regards the lower grades of that passion, and the mere approaches to it, every one has them daily before his eyes, and, as long as he is not old, for the most part also in his heart.

[1] "Nothing is beautiful but the true; and only the true is lovable."
[2] "They died with unknown deaths."

So then, after what has here been called to mind, no one can doubt either the reality or the importance of the matter; and therefore, instead of wondering that a philosophy should also for once make its own this constant theme of all poets, one ought rather to be surprised that a thing which plays throughout so important a part in human life has hitherto practically been disregarded by philosophers altogether, and lies before us as raw material. The one who has most concerned himself with it is Plato, especially in the "Symposium" and the "Phædrus." Yet what he says on the subject is confined to the sphere of myths, fables, and jokes, and also for the most part concerns only the Greek love of youths. The little that Rousseau says upon our theme in the *"Discours sur l'inégalité"* (p. 96, ed. Bip.) is false and insufficient. Kant's explanation of the subject in the third part of the essay, *"Ueber das Gefühl des Schönen und Erhabenen"* (pp. 435 *seq.* of Rosenkranz's edition), is very superficial and without practical knowledge, therefore it is also partly incorrect. Lastly, Platner's treatment of the matter in his "Anthropology" (§§ 1347 *seq.*) every one will find dull and shallow. On the other hand, Spinoza's definition, on account of its excessive naïveté, deserves to be quoted for the sake of amusement: *"Amor est titillatio, concomitante idea causæ externæ* (*Eth.* iv., prop. 44, *dem.*)* [3] Accordingly I have no predecessors either to make use of or to refute. The subject has pressed itself upon me objectively, and has entered of its own accord into the connection of my consideration of the world. Moreover, least of all can I hope for approbation from those who are themselves under the power of this passion, and who accordingly seek to express the excess of their feelings in the sublimest and most ethereal images. To them my view will appear too physical, too material, however metaphysical and even transcendent it may be at bottom. Meanwhile let them reflect that if the object which to-day inspires them to write madrigals and sonnets had been born eighteen years earlier it would scarcely have won a glance from them.

For all love, however, ethereally it may bear itself, is rooted in the sexual impulse alone, nay, it absolutely is only a more definitely determined, specialized, and indeed in the strictest sense

---

[3] "Love is a titillation, accompanied by the idea of its external cause."

individualized sexual impulse. If now, keeping this in view, one considers the important part which the sexual impulse in all its degrees and nuances plays not only on the stage and in novels, but also in the real world, where, next to the love of life, it shows itself the strongest and most powerful of motives, constantly lays claim to half the powers and thoughts of the younger portion of mankind, is the ultimate goal of almost all human effort, exerts an adverse influence on the most important events, interrupts the most serious occupations every hour, sometimes embarrasses for a while even the greatest minds, does not hesitate to intrude with its trash interfering with the negotiations of statesmen and the investigations of men of learning, knows how to slip its love letters and locks of hair even into ministerial portfolios and philosophical manuscripts, and no less devises daily the most entangled and the worst actions, destroys the most valuable relationships, breaks the firmest bonds, demands the sacrifice sometimes of life or health, sometimes of wealth, rank, and happiness, nay, robs those who are otherwise honest of all conscience, makes those who have hitherto been faithful, traitors; accordingly, on the whole, appears as a malevolent demon that strives to pervert, confuse, and overthrow everything;—then one will be forced to cry, Wherefore all this noise? Wherefore the straining and storming, the anxiety and want? It is merely a question of every Hans finding his Grethe.[4] Why should such a trifle play so important a part, and constantly introduce disturbance and confusion into the well-regulated life of man? But to the earnest investigator the spirit of truth gradually reveals the answer. It is no trifle that is in question here; on the contrary, the importance of the matter is quite proportionate to the seriousness and ardour of the effort. The ultimate end of all love affairs, whether they are played in sock or cothurnus, is really more important than all other ends of human life, and is therefore quite worthy of the profound seriousness with which every one pursues it. That which is decided by it is nothing less than *the composition of the next generation*. The *dramatis personæ* who shall appear when we are withdrawn are here determined, both as regards their ex-

[4] I have not ventured to express myself distinctly here: the courteous reader must therefore translate the phrase into Aristophanic language.—*S.*

istence and their nature, by these frivolous love affairs. As the being, the *existentia,* of these future persons is absolutely conditioned by our sexual impulse generally, so their nature, *essentia,* is determined by the individual selection in its satisfaction *i. e.,* by sexual love, and is in every respect irrevocably fixed by this. This is the key of the problem: we shall arrive at a more accurate knowledge of it in its application if we go through the degrees of love, from the passing inclination to the vehement passion, when we shall also recognize that the difference of these grades arises from the degree of the individualization of the choice.

The collective love affairs of the present generation taken together are accordingly, of the whole human race, the serious *meditatio compositionis generationis futuræ, e qua iterum pendent innumeræ generationes.*[5] This high importance of the matter, in which it is not a question of individual weal or woe, as in all other matters, but of the existence and special nature of the human race in future times, and therefore the will of the individual appears at a higher power as the will of the species;— this it is on which the pathetic and sublime elements in affairs of love depend, which for thousands of years poets have never wearied of representing in innumerable examples; because no theme can equal in interest this one, which stands to all others which only concern the welfare of individuals as the solid body to the surface, because it concerns the weal and woe of the species. Just on this account, then, is it so difficult to impart interest to a drama without the element of love, and, on the other hand, this theme is never worn out even by daily use.

That which presents itself in the individual consciousness as sexual impulse in general, without being directed towards a definite individual of the other sex, is in itself, and apart from the phenomenon, simply the will to live. But what appears in consciousness as a sexual impulse directed to a definite individual is in itself the will to live as a definitely determined individual. Now in this case the sexual impulse, although in itself a subjective need, knows how to assume very skilfully the mask of an objective admiration, and thus to deceive our consciousness; for

---

[5] A meditation on the composition of the future generation, on which innumerable generations depend.

nature requires this stratagem to attain its ends. But yet that in every case of falling in love, however objective and sublime this admiration may appear, what alone is looked to is the production of an individual of a definite nature is primarily confirmed by the fact that the essential matter is not the reciprocation of love, but possession, *i. e.,* the physical enjoyment. The certainty of the former can therefore by no means console us for the want of the latter; on the contrary, in such a situation many a man has shot himself. On the other hand, persons who are deeply in love, and can obtain no return of it, are contented with possession, *i. e.,* with the physical enjoyment. This is proved by all forced marriages, and also by the frequent purchase of the favour of a woman, in spite of her dislike, by large presents or other sacrifices, nay, even by cases of rape. That this particular child shall be begotten is, although unknown to the parties concerned, the true end of the whole love story; the manner in which it is attained is a secondary consideration. Now, however loudly persons of lofty and sentimental soul, and especially those who are in love, may cry out here about the gross realism of my view, they are yet in error. For is not the definite determination of the individualities of the next generation a much higher and more worthy end than those exuberant feelings and supersensible soap bubbles of theirs? Nay, among earthly aims, can there be one which is greater or more important? It alone corresponds to the profoundness with which passionate love is felt, to the seriousness with which it appears, and the importance which it attributes even to the trifling details of its sphere and occasion. Only so far as this end is assumed as the true one do the difficulties encountered, the infinite exertions and annoyances made and endured for the attainment of the loved object, appear proportionate to the matter. For it is the future generation, in its whole indivdual determinateness, that presses into existence by means of those efforts and toils. Nay, it is itself already active in that careful, definite, and arbitrary choice for the satisfaction of the sexual impulse which we call love. The growing inclination of two lovers is really already the will to live of the new individual which they can and desire to produce; nay, even in the meeting of their longing glances its new life breaks out, and announces itself as a future individuality harmoniously and well composed. They feel the longing for an actual union and fusing together into a single being, in order to live on only as this; and this longing receives its fulfilment in the child which is produced by them, as that in which the qualities transmitted by them both, fused and united in one being, live on. Conversely, the mutual, decided and persistent aversion between a man and a maid is a sign that what they could produce would only be a badly organized, in itself inharmonious and unhappy being. Hence there lies a deeper meaning in the fact that Calderon, though he calls the atrocious Semiramis the daughter of the air, yet introduces her as the daughter of rape followed by the murder of the husband.

But, finally, what draws two individuals of different sex exclusively to each other with such power is the will to live, which exhibits itself in the whole species, and which here anticipates in the individual which these two can produce an objectification of its nature answering to its aims. This individual will have the will, or character, from the father, the intellect from the mother, and the corporization from both; yet, for the most part, the figure will take more after the father, the size after the mother,—according to the law which comes out in the breeding of hybrids among the brutes, and principally depends upon the fact that the size of the fœtus must conform to the size of the uterus. Just as inexplicable as the quite special individuality of any man, which is exclusively peculiar to him, is also the quite special and individual passion of two lovers; indeed at bottom the two are one and the same: the former is *explicite* what the latter was *implicite*. The moment at which the parents begin to love each other—to fancy each other, as the very happy English expression has it—is really to be regarded as the first appearance of a new individual and the true *punctum saliens* [6] of its life, and, as has been said, in the meeting and fixing of their longing glances there appears the first germ of the new being, which certainly, like all germs, is generally crushed out. This new individual is to a certain extent a new (Platonic) Idea; and now, as all Ideas strive with the greatest vehemence to enter the phenomenal world, eagerly seizing for this end upon the matter which the law of casualty divides among

[6] "Salient feature."

them all, so also does this particualr Idea of a human individuality strive with the greatest eagerness and vehemence towards its
realization in the phenomenon. This eagerness and vehemence is
just the passion of the two future parents for each other. It has
innumerable degrees, the two extremes of which may at any rate
be described as Αφροδιτη πανδημος and ουρανια; in its nature, however, it is everywhere the same. On the other hand, it will be in
degree so much the more powerful the more *individualized* it is;
that is, the more the loved individual is exclusively suited, by
virtue of all his or her parts and qualities, to satisfy the desire of
the lover and the need established by his or her own individuality.
What is really in question here will become clear in the further
course of our exposition. Primarily and essentially the inclination
of love is directed to health, strength, and beauty, consequently
also to youth; because the will first of all seeks to exhibit the specific
character of the human species as the basis of all individuality:
ordinary amorousness (Αφροδιτη πανδημος) does not go much further. To these, then, more special claims link themselves on,
which we shall investigate in detail further on, and with which,
when they see satisfaction before them, the passion increases. But
the highest degrees of this passion spring from that suitableness of
two individualities to each other on account of which the will,
i. e., the character, of the father and the intellect of the mother,
in their connection, make up precisely that individual towards
which the will to live in general which exhibits itself in the whole
species feels a longing proportionate to this its magnitude, and
which therefore exceeds the measure of a mortal heart, and the
motives of which, in the same way, lie beyond the sphere of the
individual intellect. This is thus the soul of the true and great
passion. Now the more perfect is the mutual adaptation of two individuals to each other in each of the many respects which have
further to be considered, the stronger will be their mutual passion.
Since there do not exist two individuals exactly alike, there must
be for each particular man a particular woman—always with
reference to what is to be produced—who corresponds most perfectly. A really passionate love is as rare as the accident of these
two meeting. Since, however, the possibility of such a love is
present in every one, the representations of it in the works of the

poets are comprehensible to us. Just because the passion of love really turns about that which is to be produced, and its qualities, and because its kernel lies here, a friendship without any admixture of sexual love can exist between two young and good-looking persons of different sex, on account of the agreement of their disposition, character, and mental tendencies; nay, as regards sexual love there may even be a certain aversion between them. The reason of this is to be sought in the fact that a child produced by them would have physical or mental qualities which were inharmonious; in short, its existence and nature would not answer the ends of the will to live as it exhibits itself in the species. On the other hand, in the case of difference of disposition, character, and mental tendency, and the dislike, nay, enmity, proceeding from this, sexual love may yet arise and exist; when it then blinds us to all that; and if it here leads to marriage it will be a very unhappy one.

Let us now set about the more thorough investigation of the matter. Egoism is so deeply rooted a quality of all individuals in general, that in order to rouse the activity of an individual being egoistical ends are the only ones upon which we can count with certainty. Certainly the species has an earlier, closer, and greater claim upon the individual than the perishable individuality itself. Yet when the individual has to act, and even make sacrifices for the continuance and quality of the species, the importance of the matter cannot be made so comprehensible to his intellect, which is calculated merely with regard to individual ends, as to have its proportionate effect. Therefore in such a case nature can only attain its ends by implanting a certain illusion in the individual, on account of which that which is only a good for the species appears to him as a good for himself, so that when he serves the species he imagines he is serving himself; in which process a mere chimera, which vanishes immediately afterwards, floats before him, and takes the place of a real thing as a motive. This illusion is instinct. In the great majority of cases this is to be regarded as the sense of the species, which presents what is of benefit to *it* to the will. Since, however, the will has here become individual, it must be so deluded that it apprehends through the sense of the individual what the sense of the species presents to it, thus imagines it is fol-

lowing individual ends while in truth it is pursuing ends which
are merely general (taking this word in its strictest sense). The
external phenomenon of instinct we can best observe in the brutes
where its rôle is most important; but it is in ourselves alone that
we arrive at a knowledge of its internal process, as of everything
internal. Now it is certainly supposed that man has almost no
instinct; at any rate only this, that the new-born babe seeks for
and seizes the breast of its mother. But, in fact, we have a very
definite, distinct, and complicated instinct, that of the selection of
another individual for the satisfaction of the sexual impulse, a
selection which is so fine, so serious, and so arbitrary. With this
satisfaction in itself, *i. e.,* so far as it is a sensual pleasure resting
upon a pressing want of the individual, the beauty or ugliness of
the other individual has nothing to do. Thus the regard for this
which is yet pursued with such ardour, together with the careful
selection which springs from it, is evidently connected, not with
the chooser himself—although he imagines it is so—but with the
true end, that which is to be produced, which is to receive
the type of the species as purely and correctly as possible. Through a thousand physical accidents and moral aberrations there arise a great variety of deteriorations of the human
form; yet its true type, in all its parts, is always again established: and this takes place under the guidance of the sense
of beauty, which always directs the sexual impulse, and without
which this sinks to the level of a disgusting necessity. Accordingly,
in the first place, every one will decidedly prefer and eagerly desire
the most beautiful individuals, *i. e.,* those in whom the character
of the species is mostly purely impressed; but, secondly, each one
will specially regard as beautiful in another individual those per-
fections which he himself lacks, nay, even those imperfections
which are the opposite of his own. Hence, for example, little men
love big women, fair persons like dark, &c. &c. The delusive
ecstasy which seizes a man at the sight of a woman whose beauty
is suited to him, and pictures to him a union with her as the highest good, is just the *sense of the species,* which, recognizing the
distinctly expressed stamp of the same, desires to perpetuate it with
this individual. Upon this decided inclination to beauty depends the
maintenance of the type of the species: hence it acts with such

great power. We shall examine specially further on the considerations which it follows. Thus what guides man here is really an instinct which is directed to doing the best for the species, while the man himself imagines that he only seeks the heightening of his own pleasure. In fact, we have in this an instructive lesson concerning the inner nature of all instinct, which, as here, almost always sets the individual in motion for the good of the species. For clearly the pains with which an insect seeks out a particular flower, or fruit, or dung, or flesh, or, as in the case of the ichneumonidæ, the larva of another insect, in order to deposit its eggs there only, and to attain this end shrinks neither from trouble nor danger, is thoroughly analogous to the pains with which for his sexual satisfaction a man carefully chooses a woman with definite qualities which appeal to him individually, and strives so eagerly after her that in order to attain this end he often sacrifices his own happiness in life, contrary to all reason, by a foolish marriage, by love affairs which cost him wealth, honour, and life, even by crimes such as adultery or rape, all merely in order to serve the species in the most efficient way, although at the cost of the individual, in accordance with the will of nature which is everywhere sovereign. Instinct, in fact, is always an act which seems to be in accordance with the conception of an end, and yet is entirely without such a conception. Nature implants it wherever the acting individual is incapable of understanding the end, or would be unwilling to pursue it. Therefore, as a rule, it is given only to the brutes, and indeed especially to the lowest of them which have least understanding; but almost only in the case we are here considering it is also given to man, who certainly could understand the end, but would not pursue it with the necessary ardour, that is, even at the expense of his individual welfare. Thus here, as in the case of all instinct, the truth assumes the form of an illusion, in order to act upon the will. It is a voluptuous illusion which leads the man to believe he will find a greater pleasure in the arms of a woman whose beauty appeals to him than in those of any other; or which indeed, exclusively directed to a single individual, firmly convinces him that the possession of her will ensure him excessive happiness. Therefore he imagines he is taking trouble and making sacrifices for his own pleasure, while he does so merely for the maintenance of the regular type of the species, or else a quite special individuality, which can only come from these parents, is to attain to existence. The character of instinct is here so perfectly present, thus an action which seems to be in accordance with the conception of an end, and yet is entirely without such a conception, that he who is drawn by that illusion often abhors the end which alone guides it, procreation, and would like to hinder it; thus it is in the case of almost all illicit love affairs. In accordance with the character of the matter which has been explained, every lover will experience a marvellous disillusion after the pleasure he has at last attained, and will wonder that what was so longingly desired accomplishes nothing more than every other sexual satisfaction; so that he does not see himself much benefited by it. That wish was related to all his other wishes as the species is related to the individual, thus as the infinite to the finite. The satisfaction, on the other hand, is really only for the benefit of the species, and thus does not come within the consciousness of the individual, who, inspired by the will of the species, here served an end with every kind of sacrifice, which was not his own end at all. Hence, then, every lover, after the ultimate consummation of the great work, finds himself cheated; for the illusion has vanished by means of which the individual was here the dupe of the species. Accordingly Plato very happily says: "ἡδονη ἁπαντων αγαζονεστατον." (Phileb. 319.) [7]

But all this reflects light on the instincts and mechanical tendencies of the brutes. They also are, without doubt, involved in a kind of illusion, which deceives them with the prospect of their own pleasure, while they work so laboriously and with so much self-denial for the species, the bird builds its nest, the insect seeks the only suitable place for its eggs, or even hunts for prey which, unsuited for its own enjoyment, must be laid beside the eggs as food for the future larvæ, the bees, the wasps, the ants apply themselves to their skilful dwellings and highly complicated economy. They are all guided with certainty by an illusion, which conceals the service of the species under the mask of an egotistical end. This is probably the only way to comprehend the inner or subjective process that lies at the foundation of the manifestations

---

[7] "The pleasure of all men is the emptiest."

of instinct. Outwardly, however, or objectively, we find in those creatures which are to a large extent governed by instinct, especially in insects, a preponderance of the ganglion system, *i. e.,* the *subjective* nervous system, over the objective or cerebral system; from which we must conclude that they are moved, not so much by objective, proper apprehension as by subjective ideas exciting desire, which arise from the influence of the ganglion system upon the brain, and accordingly by a kind of illusion; and this will be the *physiological* process in the case of all instinct. For the sake of illustration I will mention as another example of instinct in the human species, although a weak one, the capricious appetite of women who are pregnant. It seems to arise from the fact that the nourishment of the embryo sometimes requires a special or definite modification of the blood which flows to it, upon which the food which produces such a modification at once presents itself to the pregnant woman as an object of ardent longing, thus here also an illusion arises. Accordingly woman has one instinct more than man; and the ganglion system is also much more developed in the woman. That man has fewer instincts than the brutes and that even these few can be easily led astray, may be explained from the great preponderance of the brain in his case. The sense of beauty which instinctively guides the selection for the satisfaction of sexual passion is led astray when it degenerates into the tendency to pederasty; analogous to the fact that the blue-bottle (*Musca vomitoria*), instead of depositing its eggs, according to instinct, in putrefying flesh, lays them in the blossom of the *Arum dracunculus,* deceived by the cadaverous smell of this plant.

Now that an instinct entirely directed to that which is to be produced lies at the foundation of all sexual love will receive complete confirmation from the fuller analysis of it, which we cannot therefore avoid. First of all we have to remark here that by nature man is inclined to inconstancy in love, woman to constancy. The love of the man sinks perceptibly from the moment it has obtained satisfaction; almost every other woman charms him more than the one he already possesses; he longs for variety. The love of the woman, on the other hand, increases just from that moment. This is a consequence of the aim of nature which is directed to the maintenance, and therefore to the greatest possible increase, of the species. The man can easily beget over a hundred children a year; the woman, on the contrary, with however many men, can yet only bring one child a year into the world (leaving twin births out of account). Therefore the man always looks about after other women; the woman, again, sticks firmly to the one man; for nature moves her, instinctively and without reflection, to retain the nourisher and protector of the future offspring. Accordingly faithfulness in marriage is with the man artificial, with the woman it is natural, and thus adultery on the part of the woman is much less pardonable than on the part of the man, both objectively on account of the consequences and also subjectively on account of its unnaturalness.

But in order to be thorough and gain full conviction that the pleasure in the other sex, however objective it may seem to us, is yet merely disguised instinct, *i. e.,* sense of the species, which strives to maintain its type, we must investigate more fully the considerations which guide us in this pleasure, and enter into the details of this, rarely as these details which will have to be mentioned here may have figured in a philosophical work before. These considerations divide themselves into those which directly concern the type of the species, *i. e.,* beauty, those which are concerned with physical qualities, and lastly, those which are merely relative, which arise from the requisite correction or neutralization of the one-sided qualities and abnormities of the two individuals by each other. We shall go through them one by one.

The first consideration which guides our choice and inclination is age. In general we accept the age from the years when menstruation begins to those when it ceases, yet we give the decided preference to the period from the eighteenth to the twenty-eighth year. Outside of those years, on the other hand, no woman can attract us: an old woman, *i. e.,* one who no longer menstruates, excites our aversion. Youth without beauty has still always attraction; beauty without youth has none. Clearly the unconscious end which guides us here is the possibility of reproduction in general: therefore every individual loses attraction for the opposite sex in proportion as he or she is removed from the fittest period for begetting or conceiving. The second consideration is that of health. Acute diseases only temporarily disturb us, chronic diseases or cachexia repel us, because they are transmitted to the child. The third consideration is the skeleton, because it is the basis of the type of the species. Next to age and disease nothing repels us so much as a deformed figure; even the most beautiful face cannot atone for it; on the contrary, even the ugliest face when accompanied by a straight figure is unquestionably preferred. Further, we feel every disproportion of the skeleton most strongly; for example, a stunted, dumpy, short-boned figure, and many such; also a halting gait, where it is not the result of an extraneous accident. On the other hand, a strikingly beautiful figure can make up for all defects: it enchants us. Here also comes in the great value which all attach to the smallness of the feet: it depends upon the fact that they are an essential characteristic of the species, for no animal has the tarsus and the metatarsus taken together so small as man, which accords with his upright walk; he is a plantigrade. Accordingly Jesus Sirach also says (xxvi. 23, according to the revised translation by Kraus): "A woman with a straight figure and beautiful feet is like columns of gold in sockets of silver." The teeth also are important; because they are essential for nourishment and quite specially hereditary. The fourth consideration is a certain fulness of flesh; thus a predominance of the vegetative function, of plasticity; because this promises abundant nourishment for the fœtus; hence great leanness repels us in a striking degree. A full female bosom exerts an exceptional charm upon the male sex; because, standing in direct connection with the female functions of propagation, it promises abundant nourishment to the new-born child. On the other hand, excessively fat women excite our disgust: the cause is that this indicates atrophy of the uterus, thus barrenness; which is not known by the head, but by instinct. The last consideration of all is the beauty of the face. Here also before everything else the bones are considered; therefore we look principally for a beautiful nose, and a short turned-up nose spoils everything. A slight inclination of the nose downwards or upwards has decided the happiness in life of innumerable maidens, and rightly so, for it concerns the type of the species. A small mouth, by means of small maxillæ, is very essential as specifically characteristic of the human countenance, as distinguished from the muzzle of the brutes. A receding or, as it were, cut-away chin is especially disagreeable, because *mentum prominulum* is an exclusive characteristic of our species. Finally comes the regard for beautiful eyes and forehead; it is connected with the psychical qualities, especially the intellectual which are inherited from the mother.

The unconscious considerations which, on the other hand, the inclination of women follows naturally cannot be so exactly assigned. In general the following may be asserted: They give the preference to the age from thirty to thirty-five years, especially over that of youths who yet really present the height of human beauty. The reason is that they are not guided by taste but by instinct, which recognizes in the age named the acme of reproductive power. In general they look less to beauty, especially of the face. It is as if they took it upon themselves alone to impart this to the child. They are won principally by the strength of the man, and the courage which is connected with this; for these promise the production of stronger children, and also a brave protector for them. Every physical defect of the man, every divergence from the type, may with regard to the child be removed by the woman in reproduction, through the fact that she herself is blameless in these respects, or even exceeds in the opposite direction. Only those qualities of the man have to be excepted which are peculiar to his sex, and which therefore the mother cannot give to the child: such are the manly structure of the skeleton, broad shoulders, slender hips, straight bones, muscular power, courage, beard, &c. Hence it arises that women often love ugly men, but never an unmanly man, because they cannot neutralize his defects.

The second class of the considerations which lie at the foundation of sexual love are those which regard psychical qualities. Here we shall find that the woman is throughout attracted by the qualities of the heart or character in the man, as those which are inherited from the father. The woman is won especially by firmness of will, decision, and courage, and perhaps also by honesty and good-heartedness. On the other hand, intellectual gifts exercise no direct and instinctive power over her, just because they are not inherited from the father. Want of understanding does a man no harm with women; indeed extraordinary mental endowment, or even genius, might sooner influence them unfavourably as an abnormity. Hence one often sees an ugly, stupid, and coarse fellow get the better of a cultured, able, and amiable man with women. Also marriages from love are sometimes consummated between natures which are mentally very different: for example, the man is rough, powerful, and stupid; the woman tenderly sensitive, delicately thoughtful, cultured, æsthetic, &c.; or the man is a genius and learned, the woman a goose:

> *"Sic visum Veneri; cui placet impares*
> *Formas atque animos sub juga aënea*
> *Sævo mittere cum joco."* [8]

The reason is, that here quite other considerations than the intellectual predominate,—those of instinct. In marriage what is looked to is not intellectual entertainment, but the production of children: it is a bond of the heart, not in the head. It is a vain and absurd pretense when women assert that they have fallen in love with the mind of a man, or else it is the over-straining of a degenerate nature. Men, on the other hand, are not determined in their instinctive love by the qualities of character of the woman; hence so many Socrateses have found their Xantippes; for example, Shakespeare, Albrecht Dürer, Byron, &c. The intellectual qualities, however, certainly influence here, because they are inherited from the mother. Yet their influence is easily outweighed by that of physical beauty, which acts directly, as concerning a more essential point. However, it happens, either from the feeling or the experience of that influence, that mothers have their daughters taught the fine arts, languages, and so forth in order to make them attractive to men, whereby they wish to assist the intellect by artificial means, just as, in case of need, they assist the hips and the bosom. Observe that here we are speaking throughout only of that entirely immediate instinctive attraction from which alone love properly so called grows. That a woman of culture and understanding prizes understanding and intellect in a man, that a man from rational reflection should test and have regard to the character of his bride, has nothing to do with the matter with

---

[8] "So it is decreed by Venus, whom it pleases, with bitter jest, to put unequal bodies and minds under the iron yoke."

which we are dealing here. Such things lie at the bottom of a rational choice in marriage, but not of the passionate love, which is our theme.

Hitherto I have only taken account of the *absolute* considerations, *i. e.,* those which hold good for every one: I come now to the *relative* considerations, which are individual, because in their case what is looked to is the rectification of the type of the species, which is already defectively presented, the correction of the divergences from it which the chooser's own person already bears in itself, and thus the return to the pure presentation of the type. Here, then, each one loves what he lacks. Starting from the individual constitution, and directed to the individual constitution, the choice which rests upon such relative considerations is much more definite, decided, and exclusive than that which proceeds merely from the absolute considerations; therefore the source of really passionate love will lie, as a rule, in these relative considerations, and only that of the ordinary and slighter inclination in the absolute considerations. Accordingly it is not generally precisely correct and perfect beauties that kindle great passions. For such a truly passionate inclination to arise something is required which can only be expressed by a chemical metaphor: two persons must neutralize each other, like acid and alkali, to a neutral salt. The essential conditions demanded for this are the following. First: all sex is one-sided. This one-sidedness is more distinctly expressed in one individual than in another; therefore in every individual it can be better supplemented and neutralized by one than by another individual of the opposite sex, for each one requires a one-sidedness which is the opposite of his own to complete the type of humanity in the new individual that is to be produced, the constitution of which is always the goal towards which all tends. Physiologists know that manhood and womanhood admit of innumerable degrees, through which the former sinks to the repulsive gynander and hypospadæus, and the latter rises to the graceful androgyne; from both sides complete hermaphroditism can be reached, at which point stand those individuals who, holding the exact mean between the two sexes, can be attributed to neither, and consequently are unfit to propagate the species. Accordingly, the neutralization of two individualities by each other, of which we are speaking, demands that the definite degree of *his* manhood shall exactly correspond to the definite degree of *her* womanhood; so that the one-sidedness of each exactly annuls that of the other. Accordingly, the most manly man will seek the most womanly woman, and *vice versa,* and in the same way every individual will seek another corresponding to him or her in degree of sex. Now how far the required relation exists between two individuals is instinctively felt by them, and, together with the other relative considerations, lies at the foundation of the higher degrees of love. While, therefore, the lovers speak pathetically of the harmony of their souls, the heart of the matter is for the most part the agreement or suitableness pointed out here with reference to the being which is to be produced and its perfection, and which is also clearly of much more importance than the harmony of their souls, which often, not long after the marriage, resolves itself into a howling discord. Now, here come in the further relative considerations, which depend upon the fact that every one endeavours to neutralize by means of the other his weaknesses, defects, and deviations from the type, so that they will not perpetuate themselves, or even develop into complete abnormalities in the child which is to be produced. The weaker a man is as regards muscular power the more will he seek for strong women; and the woman on her side will do the same. But since now a less degree of muscular power is natural and regular in the woman, woman as a rule will give the preference to strong men. Further, the size is an important consideration. Little men have a decided inclination for big women, and *vice versa;* and indeed in a little man the preference for big women will be so much the more passionate if he himself was begotten by a big father, and only remains little through the influence of his mother; because he has inherited from his father the vascular system and its energy, which was able to supply a large body with blood. If, on the other hand, his father and grandfather were both little, that inclination will make itself less felt. At the foundation of the aversion of a big woman to big men lies the intention of nature to avoid too big a race, if with the strength which *this* woman could impart to them they would be too weak to live long. If, however, such a woman selects a big husband, perhaps for the sake of being more presentable in society, then, as a rule, her offspring will have to atone for her folly. Further, the consideration as to the complexion is very decided. Blondes prefer dark persons, or brunettes; but the latter seldom prefer the former. The reason is, that fair hair and blue eyes are in themselves a variation from the type, almost an abnormality, analogous to white mice, or at least to grey horses. In no part of the world, not even in the vicinity of the pole, are they indigenous, except in Europe, and are clearly of Scandinavian origin. I may here express my opinion in passing that the white colour of the skin is not natural to man, but that by nature he has a black or brown skin, like our forefathers the Hindus; that consequently a white man has never originally sprung from the womb of nature, and that thus there is no such thing as a white race, much as this is talked of, but every white man is a faded or bleached one. Forced into the strange world, where he exists only like an exotic plant, and like this requires in winter the hothouse, in the course of thousands of years man became white. The gipsies, an Indian race which immigrated only about four centuries ago, show the transition from the complexion of the Hindu to our own. Therefore in sexual love nature strives to return to dark hair and brown eyes as the primitive type; but the white colour of the skin has become a second nature, though not so that the brown of the Hindu repels us. Finally, each one also seeks in the particular parts of the body the corrective of his own defects and aberrations, and does so the more decidedly the more important the part is. Therefore snub-nosed individuals have an inexpressible liking for hook-noses, parrot-faces; and it is the same with regard to all other parts. Men with excessively slim, long bodies and limbs can find beauty in a body which is even beyond measure stumpy and short. The considerations with regard to temperament act in an analogous manner. Each will prefer the temperament opposed to his own; yet only in proportion as his own is decided. Whoever is himself in some respect very perfect does not indeed seek and love imperfection in this respect, but is yet more easily reconciled to it than others; because he himself insures the children against great imperfection of this part. For example, whoever is himself very white will not object to a yellow complexion; but whoever has the latter will find dazzling whiteness divinely beautiful. The rare case in which a man falls in love with a decidedly ugly woman occurs when, besides the exact harmony of the degree of sex explained above, the whole of her abnormalities are precisely the opposite, and thus the corrective, of his. The love is then wont to reach a high degree.

The profound seriousness with which we consider and ponder each bodily part of the woman, and she on her part does the same, the critical scrupulosity with which we inspect a woman who begins to please us, the capriciousness of our choice, the keen attention with which the bridegroom observes his betrothed, his carefulness not to be deceived in any part, and the great value which he attaches to every excess or defect in the essential parts, all this is quite in keeping with the importance of the end. For the new being to be produced will have to bear through its whole life a similar part. For example, if the woman is only a little crooked, this may easily impart to her son a hump, and so in all the rest. Consciousness of all this certainly does not exist. On the contrary, every one imagines that he makes that careful selection in the interest of his own pleasure (which at bottom cannot be interested in it at all) ; but he makes it precisely as, under the presupposition of his own corporization, is most in keeping with the interest of the species, to maintain the type of which as pure as possible is the secret task. The individual acts here, without knowing it, by order of something higher than itself, the species; hence the importance which it attaches to things which may and indeed must be, indifferent to itself as such. There is something quite peculiar in the profound unconscious seriousness with which two young persons of opposite sex who see each other for the first time regard each other, in the searching and penetrating glance they cast at one another, in the careful review which all the features and parts of their respective persons have to endure. This investigating and examining is the *meditation of the genius of the species* on the individual which is possible through these two and the combination of its qualities. According to the results of this meditation is the degree of their pleasure in each other and their yearning for each other. This yearning, even after it has attained a considerable degree, may be suddenly extinguished again by the discovery of something that had previously remained unobserved. In this way, then, the genius of the species meditates concerning the coming race in all who are capable of reproduction. The nature of this race is the great work with which Cupid is occupied, unceasingly active, speculating, and pondering. In comparison with the importance of his great affair, which concerns the species and all coming races, the affairs of individuals in their whole ephemeral totality are very trifling; therefore he is always ready to sacrifice these regardlessly. For he is related to them as an immortal to mortals, and his interests to theirs as infinite to finite. Thus, in the consciousness of managing affairs of a higher kind than all those which only concern individual weal or woe, he carries them on sublimely, undisturbed in the midst of the tumult of war, or in the bustle of business life, or during the raging of a plague, and pursues them even into the seclusion of the cloister.

We have seen in the above that the intensity of love increases with its individualization, because we have shown that the physical qualities of two individuals can be such that, for the purpose of restoring as far as possible the type of the species, the one is quite specially and perfectly the completion or supplement of the other, which therefore desires it exclusively. Already in this case a considerable passion arises, which at once gains a nobler and more sublime appearance from the fact that it is directed to an individual object, and to it alone; thus, as it were, arises at the special order of the species. For the opposite reason, the mere sexual impulse is ignoble, because without individualization it is directed to all, and strives to maintain the species only as regards quantity, with little respect to quality. But the individualizing, and with it the intensity of the love, can reach so high a degree that without its satisfaction all the good things in the world, and even life itself, lose their value. It is then a wish which attains a vehemence that no other wish ever reaches, and therefore makes one ready for any sacrifice, and in case its fulfilment remains unalterably denied, may lead to madness or suicide. At the foundation of such an excessive passion there must lie, besides the considerations we have shown above, still others which we have not thus before our eyes. We must therefore assume that here not only the corporization, but the *will* of the man and the *intellect* of the woman are specially suitable to each other, in consequence of which a perfectly definite individual can be produced by them alone, whose existence the genius of the species has here in view, for reasons which are inaccessible to us, since they lie in the nature of the thing in itself. Or, to speak more exactly, the will to live desires here to objectify itself in a perfectly definite individual, which can only be produced by this father with this mother. This metaphysical desire of the will in itself has primarily no other sphere of action in the series of existences than the hearts of the future parents, which accordingly are seized with this ardent longing, and now imagine themselves to desire on their own account what really for the present has only a purely metaphysical end, *i. e.,* an end which lies outside the series of actually existing things. Thus it is the ardent longing to enter existence of the future individual which has first become possible here, a longing which proceeds from the primary source of all being, and exhibits itself in the phenomenal world as the lofty passion of the future parents for each other, paying little regard to all that is outside itself; in fact, as an unparalleled illusion, on account of which such a lover would give up all the good things of this world to enjoy the possession of this woman, who yet can really give him nothing more than any other. That yet it is this possession that is kept in view here is seen from the fact that even this lofty passion, like all others, is extinguished in its enjoyment—to the great astonishment of those who are possessed by it. It also becomes extinct when, through the woman turning out barren (which, according to Hufeland, may arise from nineteen accidental constitutional defects), the real metaphysical end is frustrated; just as daily happens in millions of germs trampled under foot, in which yet the same metaphysical life principle strives for existence; for which there is no other consolation than that an infinity of space, time, and matter, and consequently inexhaustible opportunity for return, stands open to the will to live.

The longing of love, the ἵμερος, which the poets of all ages are unceasingly occupied with expressing in innumerable forms, and do not exhaust the subject, nay, cannot do it justice, this longing, which attaches the idea of endless happiness to the possession of a particular woman, and unutterable pain to the thought that this possession cannot be attained,—this longing and this pain cannot obtain their material from the wants of an ephemeral individual; but they are the sighs of the spirit of the species, which sees here,

to be won or lost, a means for the attainment of its ends which
cannot be replaced, and therefore groans deeply. The species alone
has infinite life, and therefore is capable of infinite desires, infinite
satisfaction, and infinite pain. But these are here imprisoned in the
narrow breast of a mortal. No wonder, then, if such a breast seems
like to burst, and can find no expression for the intimations of
infinite rapture or infinite misery with which it is filled. This, then,
affords the materials for all erotic poetry of a sublime kind, which
accordingly rises into transcendent metaphors, soaring above all
that is earthly. This is the theme of Petrarch, the material for the
St. Preuxs, Werthers, and Jacopo Ortis, who apart from it could
not be understood nor explained. For that infinite esteem for the
loved one cannot rest upon some spiritual excellences, or in general
upon any objective, real qualities of hers; for one thing, because
she is often not sufficiently well known to the lover, as was the
case with Petrarch. The spirit of the species alone can see at
one glance what *worth* she has for *it,* for its ends. And great passions also arise, as a rule, at the first glance:

> "Who ever loved that loved not at first sight?"
> —SHAKESPEARE, *As You Like It,* Act iii., Sc. 5.

In this regard a passage in the romance of *"Guzman de Alfar-
ache,"* by Mateo Aleman, which has been famous for 250 years,
is remarkable: *"No es necessario, para que uno ame, que pase
distancia de tiempo, que siga discurso, ni haga eleccion, sino que
con aquella primera y sola vista, concurran juntamente cierta
correspondencia ó consonancia, ó lo que acó solemos vulgarmente
decir, una confrontacion de sangre, ó que por particular influxo
suelen mover las estrellas."* (For one to love it is not necessary
that much time should pass, that he should set about reflecting
and make a choice; but only that at that first and only glance
a certain correspondence and consonance should be encountered
on both sides, or that which in common life we are wont to call
a *sympathy of the blood,* and to which a special influence of the
stars generally impels. P. ii., lib. iii., c. 5.) Accordingly the loss
of the loved one, through a rival, or through death, is also for
the passionate lover a pain that surpasses all others, just because
it is of a transcendental kind, since it affects him not merely as

an individual, but attacks him in his *essentia æterna,* in the life of the species into whose special will and service he was here called. Hence jealousy is such torment and so grim, and the surrender of the loved one is the greatest of all sacrifices. A hero is ashamed of all lamentations except the lamentation of love, because in this it is not he but the species that laments. In Calderon's "Zenobia the Great" there is in the first act a scene between Zenobia and Decius in which the latter says:

> *"Cielos, luego tu me quieres?*
> *Perdiera cien mil victorias,*
> *Volviérame,"* &c.

(Heaven, then thou lovest me? For this I would lose a thousand victories, would turn about, &c.)

Here, honour, which hitherto outweighed every interest, is beaten out of the field as soon as sexual love, *i. e.,* the interest of the species, comes into play, and sees before it a decided advantage; for this is infinitely superior to every interest of mere individuals, however important it may be. Therefore to this alone honour, duty, and fidelity yield after they have withstood every other temptation, including the threat of death. In the same way we find in private life that conscientiousness is in no point so rare as in this: it is here sometimes set aside even by persons who are otherwise honest and just, and adultery is recklessly committed when passionate love, *i. e.,* the interest of the species, has mastered them. It even seems as if in this they believed themselves to be conscious of a higher right than the interests of individuals can ever confer; just because they act in the interest of the species. In this reference Chamfort's remark is worth noticing: *"Quand un homme et une femme ont l'un pour l'autre une passion violente, il me semble toujours que quelque soient les obstacles qui les séparent, un mari, des parens, etc., les deux amans sont l'un à l'autre, de par la Nature, qu'ils s'appartiennent de droit divin, malgré les lois et les conventions humaines."* [9] Whoever is inclined to be incensed at this should be referred to the remarkable in-

[9] "When a man and a woman have a violent passion for one another, it always seems to me that whatever the obstacles that separate them, whether husband or parents, etc., the two lovers belong to each other by Nature and divine right, despite human conventions and laws."

dulgence which the Saviour shows in the Gospel to the woman taken in adultery, in that He also assumes the same guilt in the case of all present. From this point of view the greater part of the "Decameron" appears as mere mocking and jeering of the genius of the species at the rights and interests of individuals which it tramples under foot. Differences of rank and all similar circumstances, when they oppose the union of passionate lovers, are set aside with the same ease and treated as nothing by the genius of the species, which, pursuing its ends that concern innumerable generations, blows off as spray such human laws and scruples. From the same deep-lying grounds, when the ends of passionate love are concerned, every danger is willingly encountered, and those who are otherwise timorous here become courageous. In plays and novels also we see, with ready sympathy, the young persons who are fighting the battle of their love, *i. e.,* the interest of the species, gain the victory over their elders, who are thinking only of the welfare of the individuals. For the efforts of the lovers appear to us as much more important, sublime, and therefore right, than anything that can be opposed to them, as the species is more important than the individual. Accordingly the fundamental theme of almost all comedies is the appearance of the genius of the species with its aims, which are opposed to the personal interest of the individuals presented, and therefore threaten to undermine their happiness. As a rule it attains its end, which, as in accordance with poetical justice, satisfies the spectator, because he feels that the aims of the species are much to be preferred to those of the individual. Therefore at the conclusion he leaves the victorious lovers quite confidently, because he shares with them the illusion that they have founded their own happiness, while they have rather sacrificed it to the choice of the species, against the will and foresight of their elders. It has been attempted in single, abnormal comedies to reverse the matter and bring about the happiness of the individuals at the cost of the aims of the species; but then the spectator feels the pain which the genius of the species suffers, and is not consoled by the advantages which are thereby assured to the individuals. As examples of this kind two very well-known little pieces occur to me: *"La reine de 16 ans,"* and *"Le mariage de raison."* In tragedies containing love affairs, since the aims of the species are frustrated, the lovers who were its tools, generally perish also; for example, in "Romeo and Juliet," "Tancred," "Don Carlos," "Wallenstein," "The Bride of Messina," and many others.

The love of a man often affords comical, and sometimes also tragical phenomena; both because, taken possession of by the spirit of the species, he is now ruled by this, and no longer belongs to himself: his conduct thereby becomes unsuited to the individual. That which in the higher grades of love imparts such a tinge of poetry and sublimeness to his thoughts, which gives them even a transcendental and hyperphysical tendency, on account of which he seems to lose sight altogether of his real, very physical aim, is at bottom this, that he is now inspired by the spirit of the species whose affairs are infinitely more important than all those which concern mere individuals, in order to found under the special directions of this spirit the whole existence of an indefinitely long posterity with this individual and exactly determined nature, which it can receive only from him as father and the woman he loves as mother, and which otherwise could never, *as such,* attain to existence, while the objectification of the will to live expressly demands this existence. It is the feeling that he is acting in affairs of such transcendent importance which raises the lover so high above everything earthly, nay, even above himself, and gives such a hyperphysical clothing to his very physical desires, that love becomes a poetical episode even in the life of the most prosaic man; in which last case the matter sometimes assumes a comical aspect. That mandate of the will which objectifies itself in the species exhibits itself in the consciousness of the lover under the mask of the anticipation of an infinite blessedness which is to be found for him in the union with this female individual. Now, in the highest grades of love this chimera becomes so radiant that if it cannot be attained life itself loses all charm, and now appears so joyless, hollow, and insupportable that the disgust at it even overcomes the fear of death, so that it is then sometimes voluntarily. cut short. The will of such a man has been caught in the vortex of the will of the species, or this has obtained such a great predominance over the individual will that if such a man cannot be effective in the first capacity,

he disdains to be so in the last. The individual is here too weak
a vessel to be capable of enduring the infinite longing of the
will of the species concentrated upon a definite object. In this
case, therefore, the issue is suicide, sometimes the double suicide
of the two lovers; unless, to save life, nature allows madness to
intervene, which then covers with its veil the consciousness of
that hopeless state. No year passes without proving the reality
of what has been expounded by several cases of all these kinds.

Not only, however, has the unsatisfied passion of love sometimes a tragic issue, but the satisfied passion also leads oftener
to unhappiness than to happiness. For its demands often conflict
so much with the personal welfare of him who is concerned that
they undermine it, because they are incompatible with his other
circumstances, and disturb the plan of life built upon them. Nay,
not only with external circumstances is love often in contradiction, but even with the lover's own individuality, for it flings
itself upon persons who, apart from the sexual relation, would
be hateful, contemptible, and even abhorrent to the lover. But
so much more powerful is the will of the species than that of
the individual that the lover shuts his eyes to all those qualities
which are repellent to him, overlooks all, ignores all, and binds
himself for ever to the object of his passion—so entirely is he
blinded by that illusion, which vanishes as soon as the will of the
species is satisfied, and leaves behind a detested companion for
life. Only from this can it be explained that we often see very
reasonable and excellent men bound to termagants and she-devils,
and cannot conceive how they could have made such a choice.
On this account the ancients represented love as blind. Indeed, a
lover may even know distinctly and feel bitterly the faults of
temperament and character of his bride, which promise him a
miserable life, and yet not be frightened away:—

> "I ask not, I care not,
>   If guilt's in thy heart,
> I know that I love thee
>   Whatever thou art."

For ultimately he seeks not his own things, but those of a third
person, who has yet to come into being, although he is involved

in the illusion that what he seeks is his own affair. But it is just this not seeking of one's own things which is everywhere the stamp of greatness, that gives to passionate love also a touch of sublimity, and makes it a worthy subject of poetry. Finally, sexual love is compatible even with the extremest hatred towards its object: therefore Plato has compared it to the love of the wolf for the sheep. This case appears when a passionate lover, in spite of all efforts and entreaties, cannot obtain a favourable hearing on any condition:—

> "I love and hate her."
> —SHAKESPEARE, *Cymbeline*, Act iii., Sc. 5.

The hatred of the loved one which then is kindled sometimes goes so far that the lover murders her, and then himself. One or two examples of this happen generally every year; they will be found in the newspapers. Therefore Goethe's lines are quite correct:—

> "By all despised love! By hellish element!
> Would that I knew a worse, that I might swear by!"

It is really no hyperbole if a lover describes the coldness of his beloved and the delight of her vanity, which feeds on his sufferings, as cruelty; for he is under the influence of an impulse which, akin to the instinct of insects, compels him, in spite of all grounds of reason, to pursue his end unconditionally, and to undervalue everything else: he cannot give it up. Not one but many a Petrarch has there been who was compelled to drag through life the unsatisfied ardour of love, like a fetter, an iron weight at his foot, and breathe his sighs in lonely woods; but only in the one Petrarch dwelt also the gift of poetry; so that Goethe's beautiful lines hold good of him:—

> "And when in misery the man was dumb
> A god gave me the power to tell my sorrow."

In fact, the genius of the species wages war throughout with the guardian geniuses of individuals, is their pursuer and enemy, always ready relentlessly to destroy personal happiness in order to carry out its ends; nay, the welfare of whole nations has sometimes been sacrified to its humours. An example of this is given us by Shakespeare in *Henry VI., Pt. III.,* Act iii, Sc. 2 and 3. All this depends upon the fact that the species, as that in which the root of our being lies, has a closer and earlier right to us than the individual; hence its affairs take precedence. From the feeling of this the ancients personified the genius of the species in Cupid, a malevolent, cruel, and therefore ill-reputed god, in spite of his childish appearance; a capricious, despotic demon, but yet lord of gods and men:

"Συ δ'ω θεων τυραννε κ'ανθρωπων, Ερως!" [10]

A deadly shot, blindness, and wings are his attributes. The latter signify inconstancy; and this appears, as a rule, only with the disillusion which is the consequence of satisfaction.

Because the passion depended upon an illusion, which represented that which has only value for the species as valuable for the individual, the deception must vanish after the attainment of the end of the species. The spirit of the species which took possession of the individual sets it free again. Forsaken by this spirit, the individual falls back into its original limitation and narrowness, and sees with wonder that after such a high, heroic, and infinite effort nothing has resulted for its pleasure but what every sexual gratification affords. Contrary to expectation, it finds itself no happier than before. It observes that it has been the dupe of the will of the species. Therefore, as a rule, a Theseus who has been made happy will forsake his Ariadne. If Petrarch's passion has been satisfied, his song would have been silenced from that time forth, like that of the bird as soon as the eggs are laid.

Here let me remark in passing that however much my metaphysics of love will displease the very persons who are entangled in this passion, yet if rational considerations in general could avail anything against it, the fundamental truth disclosed by me would necessarily fit one more than anything else to subdue it. But the saying of the old comedian will, no doubt, remain true: *"Quæ res in se neque consilium, neque modum habet ullum, eam consilio regere non potes."* [11]

[10] "Thou, O love, tyrant over gods and men!"
[11] "You cannot rule with counsel that which has no sense or measure in it."

Marriages from love are made in the interest of the species, not of the individuals. Certainly the persons concerned imagine they are advancing their own happiness; but their real end is one which is foreign to themselves, for it lies in the production of an individual which is possible only through them. Brought together by this aim, they ought henceforth to try to get on together as well as possible. But very often the pair brought together by that instinctive illusion, which is the essence of passionate love, will, in other respects, be of very different natures. This comes to light when the illusion vanishes, as it necessarily must. Accordingly love marriages, as a rule, turn out unhappy; for through them the coming generation is cared for at the expense of the present. *"Quien se casa por amores, ha de vivir con dolores"* (Who marries from love must live in sorrow), says the Spanish proverb. The opposite is the case with marriages contracted for purposes of convenience, generally in accordance with the choice of the parents. The considerations prevailing here, of whatever kind they may be, are at least real, and cannot vanish of themselves. Through them, however, the happiness of the present generation is certainly cared for, to the disadvantage of the coming generation, and notwithstanding this it remains problematical. The man who in his marriage looks to money more than to the satisfaction of his inclination lives more in the individual than in the species; which is directly opposed to the truth; hence it appears unnatural, and excites a certain contempt. A girl who, against the advice of her parents, rejects the offer of a rich and not yet old man, in order, setting aside all consideration of convenience, to choose according to her instinctive inclination alone, sacrifices her individual welfare to the species. But just on this account one cannot withhold from her a certain approbation; for she has preferred what is of most importance, and has acted in the spirit of nature (more exactly, of the species), while the parents advised in the spirit of individual egoism. In accordance with all this, it appears as if in making a marriage either the individual or the interests of the species must come off a loser. And this is generally the case; for that convenience and passionate love should go hand in hand is the rarest of lucky accidents. The physical, moral, or intellectual deficiency of the nature of most men may to some extent have its ground in the fact that marriages are ordinarily entered into not from pure choice and inclination, but from all kinds of external considerations, and on account of accidental circumstances. If, however, besides convenience, inclination is also to a certain extent regarded, this is, as it were, an agreement with the genius of the species. Happy marriages are well known to be rare; just because it lies in the nature of marriage that its chief end is not the present but the coming generation. However, let me add, for the consolation of tender, loving natures, that sometimes passionate sexual love associates itself with a feeling of an entirely different origin—real friendship based upon agreement of disposition, which yet for the most part only appears when sexual love proper is extinguished in its satisfaction. This friendship will then generally spring from the fact that the supplementing and corresponding physical, moral, and intellectual qualities of the two individuals, from which sexual love arose, with reference to the child to be produced, are, with reference also to the individuals themselves, related to each other in a supplementary manner as opposite qualities of temperament and mental gifts, and thereby form the basis of a harmony of disposition.

The whole metaphysics of love here dealt with stands in close connection with my metaphysics in general, and the light which it throws upon this may be summed up as follows:

We have seen that the careful selection for the satisfaction of the sexual impulse, a selection which rises through innumerable degrees up to that of passionate love, depends upon the highly serious interest which man takes in the special personal constitution of the next generation. Now this exceedingly remarkable interest confirms two truths which have been set forth in the preceding chapters. (1.) The indestructibility of the true nature of man, which lives on in that coming generation. For that interest which is so lively and eager, and does not spring from reflection and intention, but from the inmost characteristics and tendencies of our nature, could not be so indelibly present and exercise such great power over man if he were absolutely perishable, and were merely followed in time by a race actually and entirely different from him. (2.) That his true nature lies more in the species than in the individual. For that interest in the special nature of the species, which is the root of all love, from the passing inclination to the serious passion, is for every one really the highest concern, the success or failure of which touches him most sensibly; therefore it is called *par excellence* the affair of the heart. Moreover, when this interest has expressed itself strongly and decidedly, everything which merely concerns one's own person is postponed and necessarily sacrificed to it. Through this, then, man shows that the species lies closer to him than the individual, and he lives more immediately in the former than in the latter. Why does the lover hang with complete abandonment on the eyes of his chosen one, and is ready to make every sacrifice for her? Because it is his immortal part that longs after her; while it is only his mortal part that desires everything else. That vehement or intense longing directed to a particular woman is accordingly an immediate pledge of the indestructibility of the kernel of our being, and of its continued existence in the species. But to regard this continued existence as something trifling and insufficient is an error which arises from the fact that under the conception of the continued life of the species one thinks of nothing more than the future existence of beings similar to us, but in no regard identical with us; and this again because, starting from knowledge directed towards without, one takes into consideration only the external form of the species as we apprehend it in perception, and not its inner nature. But it is just this inner nature which lies at the foundation of our own consciousness as its kernel, and hence indeed is more immediate than this itself, and, as thing in itself, free from the *principium individuationis,* is really the same and identical in all individuals, whether they exist together or after each other. Now this is the will to live, thus just that which desires life and continuance so vehemently. This accordingly is spared and unaffected by death. It can attain to no better state than its present one; and consequently for it, with life, the constant suffering and striving of the individuals is certain. To free it from this is reserved for the denial of the will to live, as the means by which the individual will breaks away from the stem of the species, and surrenders that existence in it. We lack conceptions for that which it now is; indeed all data for such conceptions are wanting. We can only describe it as that which is free to be will to live or not. Buddhism denotes the latter case by the word Nirvana. It is the point which remains forever unattainable to all human knowledge, just as such.

If now, from the standpoint of this last consideration, we contemplate the turmoil of life, we behold all occupied with its want and misery, straining all their powers to satisfy its infinite needs and to ward off its multifarious sorrows, yet without daring to hope anything else than simply the preservation of this tormented existence for a short span of time. In between, however, in the midst of the tumult, we see the glances of two lovers meet longingly: yet why so secretly, fearfully, and stealthily? Because these lovers are the traitors who seek to perpetuate the whole want and drudgery, which would otherwise speedily reach an end; this they wish to frustrate, as others like them have frustrated it before.

ESSAYS

I. THE WISDOM OF LIFE

I. PERSONALITY, OR WHAT A MAN IS

WHAT a man *is* contributes much more to his happiness than what he *has,* or how he is regarded by others. What a man is, and so what he has in his own person, is always the chief thing to consider; for his individuality accompanies him always and everywhere, and gives its color to all his experiences. In every kind of enjoyment, for instance, the pleasure depends principally upon the man himself. Every one admits this in regard to physical, and how much truer it is of intellectual, pleasure. When we use that English expression, "to enjoy one's self," we are employing a very striking and appropriate phrase; for observe—one says, not "he enjoys Paris," but "he enjoys himself in Paris." To a man possessed of an ill-conditioned individuality, all pleasure is like delicate wine in a mouth made bitter with gall. Therefore, in the blessings as well as in the ills of life, less depends upon what befalls us than upon the way in which it is met, that is, upon the kind and degree of our general susceptibility. What a man is and has in himself, —in a word, personality, with all its entails, is the only immediate and direct factor in his happiness and welfare. All else is mediate and indirect, and its influence can be neutralized and frustrated; but the influence of personality never. This is why the envy which personal qualities excite is the most implacable of all,— as it is also the most carefully dissembled.

Further, the constitution of our consciousness is the ever-present and lasting element in all we do or suffer; our individuality is persistently at work, more or less, at every moment of our life: all other influences are temporal, incidental, fleeting, and subject to every kind of chance and change. This is why Aristotle says: *It is not wealth but character that lasts.*[1] And just for the same

[1] Eth. Eud., vii. 2. 37.

reason we can more easily bear a misfortune which comes to us
entirely from without, than one which we have drawn upon ourselves; for fortune may always change, but not character. Therefore, subjective blessings,—a noble nature, a capable head, a joyful temperament, bright spirits, a well-constituted, perfectly sound
physique, in a word, *mens sana in corpore sano,* are the first and
most important elements in happiness; so that we should be more
intent on promoting and preserving such qualities than on the
possession of external wealth and external honor.

And of all these, the one which makes us the most directly
happy is a genial flow of good spirits; for this excellent quality
is its own immediate reward. The man who is cheerful and merry
has always a good reason for being so,—the fact, namely, that
he is so. There is nothing which, like this quality, can so completely replace the loss of every other blessing. If you know anyone who is young, handsome, rich and esteemed, and you want
to know, further, if he is happy, ask, Is he cheerful and genial?
—and if he is, what does it matter whether he is young or old,
straight or hump-backed, poor or rich?—he is happy. In my early
days I once opened an old book and found these words: *"If you
laugh a great deal, you are happy; if you cry a great deal, you are
unhappy"*;—a very simple remark, no doubt; but just because it is
so simple I have never been able to forget it, even though it is
in the last degree a truism. So if cheerfulness knocks at our door,
we should throw it wide open, for it never comes inopportunely;
instead of that, we often make scruples about letting it in. We
want to be quite sure that we have every reason to be contented;
then we are afraid that cheerfulness of spirits may interfere with
serious reflections or weighty cares. Cheerfulness is a direct and
immediate gain,—the very coin, as it were, of happiness, and not,
like all else, merely a cheque upon the bank; for it alone makes
us immediately happy in the present moment, and that is the
highest blessing for beings like us, whose existence is but an in-
finitesimal moment between two eternities. To secure and promote this feeling of cheerfulness should be the supreme aim of
all our endeavours after happiness.

Now it is certain that nothing contributes so little to cheerfulness as riches, or so much, as health. Is it not in the lower classes,

the so-called working classes, more especially those of them who live in the country, that we see cheerful and contented faces? and is it not amongst the rich, the upper classes, that we find faces full of ill-humor and vexation? Consequently we should try as much as possible to maintain a high degree of health; for cheerfulness is the very flower of it. I need hardly say what one must do to be healthy—avoid every kind of excess, all violent and unpleasant emotion, all mental overstrain, take daily exercise in the open air, cold baths and such like hygienic measures. For without a proper amount of daily exercise no one can remain healthy; all the processes of life demand exercise for the due performance of their functions, exercise not only of the parts more immediately concerned, but also of the whole body. For, as Aristotle rightly says, *Life is movement;* it is its very essence. Ceaseless and rapid motion goes on in every part of the organism. The heart, with its complicated double systole and diastole, beats strongly and untiringly; with twenty-eight beats it has to drive the whole of the blood through arteries, veins and capillaries; the lungs pump like a steam-engine, without intermission; the intestines are always in peristaltic action; the glands are all constantly absorbing and secreting; even the brain has a double motion of its own, with every beat of the pulse and every breath we draw. When people can get no exercise at all, as is the case with the countless numbers who are condemned to a sedentary life, there is a glaring and fatal disproportion between outward inactivity and inner tumult. For this ceaseless internal motion requires some external counterpart, and the want of it produces effects like those of emotion which we are obliged to suppress. Even trees must be shaken by the wind, if they are to thrive.

How much our happiness depends upon our spirits, and these again upon our state of health, may be seen by comparing the influence which the same external circumstances or events have upon us when we are well and strong with the effects which they have when we are depressed and troubled with ill-health. It is not what things are objectively and in themselves, but what they are for us, in our way of looking at them, that makes us happy or the reverse. As Epictetus says, *Men are not influenced by things, but by their thoughts about things.* And, in general, nine-tenths of our happiness depends upon health alone. With health, everything is a source of pleasure; without it, nothing else, whatever it may be, is enjoyable; even the other personal blessings,—a great mind, a happy temperament—are degraded and dwarfed for want of it. So it is really with good reason that, when two people meet, the first thing they do is to inquire after each other's health, and to express the hope that it is good; for good health is by far the most important element in human happiness. It follows from all this that the greatest of follies is to sacrifice health for any other kind of happiness, whatever it may be, for gain, advancement, learning or fame, let alone, then, for fleeting sensual pleasures. Everything else should rather be postponed to it.

But however much health may contribute to that flow of good spirits which is so essential to our happiness, good spirits do not entirely depend upon health; for a man may be perfectly sound in his physique and still possess a melancholy temperament and be generally given up to sad thoughts. The ultimate cause of this is undoubtedly to be found in innate, and therefore unalterable, physical constitution, especially in the more or less normal relation of a man's sensitiveness to his muscular and vital energy. Abnormal sensitiveness produces inequality of spirits, a predominating melancholy, with periodical fits of unrestrained liveliness. A genius is one whose nervous power or sensitiveness is largely in excess; as Aristotle [2] has very correctly observed, *Men distinguished in philosophy, politics, poetry or art appear to be all of a melancholy temperament.* Shakespeare has very neatly expressed this radical and innate diversity of temperament in those lines in *The Merchant of Venice:*

> *Nature has framed strange fellows in her time;*
> *Some that will evermore peep through their eyes,*
> *And laugh, like parrots at a bag-piper;*
> *And others of such vinegar aspect,*
> *That they'll not show their teeth in way of smile,*
> *Though Nestor swear the jest be laughable.*

This is the difference which Plato draws between εὔκολος and δύσκολος—the man of *easy,* and the man of difficult disposition —in proof of which he refers to the varying degrees of suscepti-

[2] Probl. xxx., ep. 1.

bility which different people show to pleasurable and painful impressions; so that one man will laugh at what makes another despair. As a rule, the stronger the susceptibility to unpleasant impressions, the weaker is the susceptibility to pleasant ones, and *vice versa*. If it is equally possible for an event to turn out well or ill, the δύσκολος will be annoyed or grieved if the issue is unfavourable, and will not rejoice, should it be happy. On the other hand, the εὔκολος will neither worry nor fret over an unfavorable issue, but rejoice if it turns out well. If the one is successful in nine out of ten undertakings, he will not be pleased, but rather annoyed that one has miscarried; whilst the other, if only a single one succeeds, will manage to find consolation in the fact and remain cheerful. But here is another instance of the truth, that hardly any evil is entirely without its compensation; for the misfortunes and sufferings which the δύσκολοι, that is, people of gloomy and anxious character, have to overcome, are, on the whole, more imaginary and therefore less real than those which befall the gay and careless; for a man who paints everything black, who constantly fears the worst and takes measures accordingly, will not be disappointed so often in this world, as one who always looks upon the bright side of things. And when a morbid affection of the nerves, or a derangement of the digestive organs, plays into the hands of an innate tendency to gloom, this tendency may reach such a height that permanent discomfort produces a weariness of life. So arises an inclination to suicide, which even the most trivial unpleasantness may actually bring about; nay, when the tendency attains its worst form, it may be occasioned by nothing in particular, but a man may resolve to put an end to his existence, simply because he is permanently unhappy, and then coolly and firmly carry out his determination; as may be seen by the way in which the sufferer, when placed under supervision, as he usually is, eagerly waits to seize the first unguarded moment, when, without a shudder, without a struggle or recoil, he may use the now natural and welcome means of effecting his release.[3] Even the healthiest, perhaps even the most cheerful man,

[3] For a detailed description of this condition of mind *Cf.* Esquirol, *Des maladies mentales.* (This and all subsequent notes are Schopenhauer's, unless otherwise indicated.)

may resolve upon death under certain circumstances; when, for instance, his sufferings, or his fears of some inevitable misfortune, reach such a pitch as to outweigh the terrors of death. The only difference lies in the degree of suffering necessary to bring about the fatal act, a degree which will be high in the case of a cheerful, and low in that of a gloomy man. The greater the melancholy, the lower need the degree be; in the end, it may even sink to zero. But if a man is cheerful, and his spirits are supported by good health, it requires a high degree of suffering to make him lay hands upon himself. There are countless steps in the scale between the two extremes of suicide, the suicide which springs merely from a morbid intensification of innate gloom, and the suicide of the healthy and cheerful man, who has entirely objective grounds for putting an end to his existence.

Beauty is partly an affair of health. It may be reckoned as a personal advantage; though it does not, properly speaking, contribute directly to our happiness. It does so indirectly, by impressing other people; and it is no unimportant advantage, even in man. Beauty is an open letter of recommendation, predisposing the heart to favor the person who presents it. As is well said in Homer, the gift of beauty is not lightly to be thrown away, that glorious gift which none can bestow save the gods alone.

The most general survey shows us that the two foes of human happiness are pain and boredom. We may go further, and say that in the degree in which we are fortunate enough to get away from the one, we approach the other. Life presents, in fact, a more or less violent oscillation between the two. The reason of this is that each of these two poles stands in a double antagonism to the other, external or objective, and inner or subjective. Needy surroundings and poverty produce pain; while, if a man is more than well off, he is bored. Accordingly, while the lower classes are engaged in a ceaseless struggle with need, in other words, with pain, the upper carry on a constant and often desperate battle with boredom.[4] The inner or subjective antagonism arises

---

[4] And the extremes meet; for the lowest state of civilization, a nomad or wandering life, finds its counterpart in the highest, where everyone is at times a tourist. The earlier stage was a case of necessity; the latter is a remedy for boredom.

from the fact that, in the individual, susceptibility to pain varies inversely with susceptibility to boredom, because susceptibility is directly proportionate to mental power. Let me explain. A dull mind is, as a rule, associated with dull sensibilities, nerves which no stimulus can affect, a temperament, in short, which does not feel pain or anxiety very much, however great or terrible it may be. Now, intellectual dullness is at the bottom of that *vacuity of soul* which is stamped on so many faces, a state of mind which betrays itself by a constant and lively attention to all the trivial circumstances in the external world. This is the true source of boredom—a continual panting after excitement, in order to have a pretext for giving the mind and spirits something to occupy them. The kind of things people choose for this purpose shows that they are not very particular, as witness the miserable pastimes they have recourse to, and their ideas of social pleasure and con-versation: or again, the number of people who gossip on the doorstep or gape out of the window. It is mainly because of this inner vacuity of soul that people go in quest of society, diversion, amusement, luxury of every sort, which lead many to extravagance and misery. Nothing is so good a protection against such misery as inward wealth, the wealth of the mind, because the greater it grows, the less room it leaves for boredom. The inexhaustible activity of thought! finding ever new material to work upon in the multifarious phenomena of self and nature, and able and ready to form new combinations of them,—there you have some-thing that invigorates the mind, and apart from moments of relaxa-tion, sets it far above the reach of boredom.

But, on the other hand, this high degree of intelligence is rooted in a high degree of susceptibility, greater strength of will, greater passionateness; and from the union of these qualities comes an increased capacity for emotion, an enhanced sensibility to all mental and even bodily pain, greater impatience of obstacles, greater resentment of interruption;—all of which tendencies are augmented by the power of the imagination, the vivid character of the whole range of thought, including what is disagreeable. This applies, in various degrees, to every step in the long scale of mental power, from the veriest dunce to the greatest genius that ever lived. Therefore the nearer anyone is, either from a subjective or from an objective point of view, to one of those sources of suffering in human life, the farther he is from the other. And so a man's natural bent will lead him to make his objective world conform to his subjective as much as possible; that is to say, he will take the greatest measures against that form of suffering to which he is most liable. The wise man will, above all, strive after freedom from pain and annoyance, quiet and leisure, consequently a tranquil, modest life, with as few encounters as may be; and so, after a little experience of his so-called fellowmen, he will elect to live in retirement, or even, if he is a man of great intellect, in solitude. For the more a man has in himself, the less he will want from other people,—the less, indeed, other people can be to him. This is why a high degree of intellect tends to make a man unsocial. True, if *quality* of intellect could be made up for by quantity, it might be worth while to live even in the great world; but unfortunately, a hundred fools together will not make one wise man.

But the individual who stands at the other end of the scale is no sooner free from the pangs of need than he endeavours to get pastime and society at any cost, taking up with the first person he meets, and avoiding nothing so much as himself. For in solitude, where every one is thrown upon his own resources, what a man has in himself comes to light; the fool in fine raiment groans under the burden of his miserable personality, a burden which he can never throw off, whilst the man of talent peoples the waste places with his animating thoughts. Seneca declares that folly is its own burden,—*omnis stultitia laborat fastidio sui,*—a very true saying, with which may be compared the words of Jesus, the son of Sirach, *The life of a fool is worse than death.*[5] And, as a rule, it will be found that a man is sociable just in the degree in which he is intellectually poor and generally vulgar. For one's choice in this world does not go much beyond solitude on one side and vulgarity on the other. It is said that the most sociable of all people are the negroes; and they are at the bottom of the scale in intellect. I remember reading once in a French paper[6] that the blacks in North America, whether free or en-

[5] Ecclesiasticus, xxii. 11.
[6] *Le Commerce,* Oct. 19th, 1837.

slaved, are fond of shutting themselves up in large numbers in the smallest space, because they cannot have too much of one another's snubnosed company.

The brain may be regarded as a kind of parasite of the organism, a pensioner, as it were, who dwells with the body: and leisure, that is, the time one has for the free enjoyment of one's consciousness or individuality, is the fruit or produce of the rest of existence, which is in general only labor and effort. But what does most people's leisure yield?—boredom and dullness; except, of course, when it is occupied with sensual pleasure or folly. How little such leisure is worth may be seen in the way in which it is spent: and, as Ariosto observes, how miserable are the idle hours of ignorant men!—*ozio lungo d'uomini ignoranti.* Ordinarily people think merely how they shall *spend* their time; a man of any talent tries to *use* it. The reason why people of limited intellect are apt to be bored is that their intellect is absolutely nothing more than the means by which the motive power of the will is put into force: and whenever there is nothing particular to set the will in motion, it rests, and their intellect takes a holiday, because, equally with the will, it requires something external to bring it into play. The result is an awful stagnation of whatever power a man has—in a word, boredom. To counteract this miserable feeling, men run to trivialities which please for the moment they are taken up, hoping thus to engage the will in order to rouse it to action, and so set the intellect in motion; for it is the latter which has to give effect to these motives of the will. Compared with real and natural motives, these are but as paper money to coin; for their value is only arbitrary—card games and the like, which have been invented for this very purpose. And if there is nothing else to be done, a man will twirl his thumbs or beat the devil's tattoo; or a cigar may be a welcome substitute for exercising his brains. Hence, in all countries the chief occupation of society is card-playing,[7] and it is the gauge of its value, and an outward sign that it is bankrupt in thought. Because people

[7] *Translator's Note.*—Card-playing to this extent is now, no doubt, a thing of the past, at any rate amongst the nations of northern Europe. The present fashion is rather in favor of a dilettante interest in art or literature. (I wonder.—W. D.)

have no thoughts to deal in, they deal cards, and try to win one another's money. Idiots! But I do not wish to be unjust; so let me remark that it may certainly be said in defense of card-playing that it is a preparation for the world and for business life, because one learns thereby how to make a clever use of fortuitous but unalterable circumstances (cards, in this case), and to get as much out of them as one can: and to do this a man must learn a little dissimulation, and how to put a good face upon a bad business. But, on the other hand, it is exactly for this reason that card-playing is so demoralizing, since the whole object of it is to employ every kind of trick and machination in order to win what belongs to another. And a habit of this sort, learnt at the card-table, strikes root and pushes its way into practical life: and in the affairs of every day a man gradually comes to regard *meum* and *tuum* in much the same light as cards, and to consider that he may use to the utmost whatever advantages he possesses, so long as he does not come within the arm of the law. Examples of what I mean are of daily occurrence in mercantile life. Since, then, leisure is the flower, or rather the fruit, of existence, as it puts a man into possession of himself, those are happy indeed who possess something real in themselves. But what do you get from most people's leisure?—only a good-for-nothing fellow, who is terribly bored and a burden to himself. Let us, therefore, rejoice, dear brethren, for *we are not children of the bondwoman, but of the free.*

Further, as no land is so well off as that which requires few imports, or none at all, so the happiest man is one who has enough in his own inner wealth, and requires little or nothing from outside for his maintenance, for imports are expensive things, reveal dependence, entail danger, occasion trouble, and when all is said and done, are a poor substitute for home produce. No man ought to expect much from others, or, in general, from the external world. What one human being can be to another is not a very great deal: in the end every one stands alone, and the important thing is *who* it is that stands alone. Here, then, is another application of the general truth which Goethe recognizes in *Dichtung* and *Wahrheit* (Bk. III.), that in everything a man has ultimately to appeal to himself; or, as Goldsmith puts it in *The Traveller:*

> *Still to ourselves in every place consign'd*
> *Our own felicity we make or find.*

Himself is the source of the best and most a man can be or achieve. The more this is so—the more a man finds his sources of pleasure in himself—the happier he will be. Therefore, it is with great truth that Aristotle [8] says, *To be happy means to be self-sufficient.* For all other sources of happiness are in their nature most uncertain, precarious, fleeting, the sport of chance; and so even under the most favorable circumstances they can easily be exhausted; nay, this is unavoidable, because they are not always within reach. And in old age these sources of happiness must necessarily dry up:—love leaves us then, and wit, desire to travel, delight in horses, aptitude for social intercourse; friends and relations, too, are taken from us by death. Then more than ever, it depends upon what a man has in himself; for this will stick to him longest; and at any period of life it is the only genuine and lasting source of happiness. There is not much to be got anywhere in the world. It is filled with misery and pain; and if a man escapes these, boredom lies in wait for him at every corner. Nay more; it is evil which generally has the upper hand, and folly makes the most noise. Fate is cruel, and mankind is pitiable. In such a world as this, a man who is rich in himself is like a bright, warm, happy room at Christmastide, while without are the frost and snow of a December night. Therefore, without doubt, the happiest destiny on earth is to have the rare gift of a rich individuality, and, more especially to be possessed of a good endowment of intellect; this is the happiest destiny, though it may not be, after all, a very brilliant one.

There was a great wisdom in that remark which Queen Christina of Sweden made, in her nineteenth year, about Descartes, who had then lived for twenty years in the deepest solitude in Holland, and, apart from report, was known to her only by a single essay: *M. Descartes,* she said, *is the happiest of men, and his condition*

[8] Eth. Eud., vii. 2.

seems to me much to be envied.[9] Of course, as was the case with Descartes, external circumstances must be favorable enough to allow a man to be master of his life and happiness; or, as we read in *Ecclesiastes,* [10]—*Wisdom is good together with an inheritance, and profitable unto them that see the sun.* The man to whom nature and fate have granted the blessing of wisdom, will be most anxious and careful to keep open the fountains of happiness which he has in himself; and for this, independence and leisure are necessary. To obtain them, he will be willing to moderate his desires and harbor his resources, all the more because he is not, like others, restricted to the external world for his pleasures. So he will not be misled by expectations of office, or money, or the favor and applause of his fellowmen, into surrendering himself in order to conform to low desires and vulgar tastes. It is a great piece of folly to sacrifice the inner for the outer man, to give the whole or the greater part of one's quiet, leisure and independence for splendor, rank, pomp, titles and honor. This is what Goethe did. My good luck drew me quite in the other direction.

The truth which I am insisting upon here, the truth, namely, that the chief source of human happiness is internal, is confirmed by that most accurate observation of Aristotle in the *Nichomachean Ethics,*[11] that every pleasure presupposes some sort of activity, the application of some sort of power, without which it cannot exist. The doctrine of Aristotle's, that a man's happiness consists in the free exercise of his highest faculties, is also enunciated by Stobæus in his exposition of the Peripatetic philosophy: [12] *Happiness,* he says, *means vigorous and successful activity in all your undertakings;* and he explains that by *vigor* (ἀρέτη) he means *mastery* in any thing, whatever it be. Now, the original purpose of those forces with which nature has endowed man is to enable him to struggle against the difficulties which beset him on all sides. But if this struggle comes to an end, his unemployed forces become a burden to him; and he has to set to work and play

---

[9] *Vie de Descartes,* par Baillet. Liv. vii., ch. 10.
[10] vii. 12.
[11] i., 7 and vii., 13, 14.
[12] Ecl. eth. ii., ch. 7.

with them,—to use them, I mean, for no purpose at all, beyond
avoiding the other source of human suffering, boredom, to which
he is at once exposed. It is the upper classes, people of wealth,
who are the greatest victims of boredom. Lucretius long ago
described their miserable state, and the truth of his description
may be still recognized today, in the life of every great capital—
where the rich man is seldom in his own halls, because it bores
him to be there, and still he returns thither, because he is no
better off outside;—or else he is away in post-haste to his house
in the country, as if it were on fire; and he is no sooner arrived
there, than he is bored again, and seeks to forget everything in
sleep, or else hurries back to town once more.[13] In their youth,
such people must have had a superfluity of muscular and vital
energy,—powers which, unlike those of the mind, cannot maintain their full degree of vigor very long; and in later years they
either have no mental powers at all, or cannot develop any for
want of employment which would bring them into play; so that
they are in a wretched plight. *Will,* however, they still possess,
for this is the only power that is inexhaustible; and they try to
stimulate their will by passionate excitement, such as games of
chance for high stakes—undoubtedly a most degrading form of
vice. And one may say generally that if a man finds himself with
nothing to do, he is sure to choose some amusement suited to
the kind of power in which he excels,—bows, it may be, or chess;
hunting or painting; horse-racing or music; cards, or poetry,
heraldry, philosophy, or some other dilettante interest. We might
classify these interests methodically, by reducing them to expressions of the three fundamental powers, the factors, that is to
say, which go to make up the physiological constitution of man;
and further, by considering these powers by themselves, and apart
from any of the definite aims which they may subserve, and simply
as affording three sources of possible pleasure, out of which every
man will choose what suits him, according as he excels in one
direction or another.

First of all come the pleasures of *vital energy,* of food, drink,
digestion, rest and sleep; and there are parts of the world where
it can be said that these are characteristic and national pleasures,

[13] III., 1073.

Secondly, there are the pleasures of *muscular energy,* such as walking, running, wrestling, dancing, fencing, riding and similar athletic pursuits, which sometimes take the form of sport, and sometimes of a military life and real warfare. Thirdly, there are the pleasures of sensibility, such as observation, thought, feeling, or a taste for poetry or culture, music, learning, reading, meditation, invention, philosophy and the like. As regards the value, relative worth and duration of each of these kinds of pleasure, a great deal might be said, which, however, I leave the reader to supply. But every one will see that the nobler the power which is brought into play, the greater will be the pleasure which it gives; for pleasure always involves the use of one's own powers, and happiness consists in a frequent repetition of pleasure. No one will deny that in this respect the pleasures of sensibility occupy a higher place than either of the other two fundamental kinds; which exist in an equal, nay, in a greater degree in brutes; it is this preponderating amount of sensibility which distinguishes man from other animals. Now, our mental powers are forms of sensibility, and therefore a preponderating amount of it makes us capable of that kind of pleasure which has to do with mind, so-called intellectual pleasure; and the more sensibility predominates, the greater the pleasure will be.

The normal, ordinary man takes a vivid interest in anything only in so far as it excites his will, that is to say, is a matter of personal interest to him. But constant excitement of the will is never an unmixed good, to say the least; in other words, it involves pain. Card-playing, that universal occupation of "good society" everywhere, is a device for providing this kind of excitement, and that, too, by means of interests so small as to produce slight and momentary, instead of real and permanent, pain. Card-playing is, in fact, a mere tickling of the will.

On the other hand, a man of powerful intellect is capable of taking a vivid interest in things in the way of mere *knowledge,* with no admixture of *will;* nay, such an interest is a necessity to him. It places him in a sphere where pain is an alien,—a diviner air, where the gods live serene. Look on these two pictures—the life of the masses, one long, dull record of struggle

and effort entirely devoted to the petty interests of personal
welfare, to misery in all its forms, a life beset by intolerable boredom as soon as ever those aims are satisfied and the man is thrown
back upon himself, whence he can be roused again to some sort
of movement only by the wild fire of passion. On the other side
you have a man endowed with a high degree of mental power,
leading an existence rich in thought and full of life and meaning, occupied by worthy and interesting objects as soon as ever
he is free to give himself to them, bearing in himself a source
of the noblest pleasure. What external promptings he wants come
from the works of nature, and from the contemplation of human
affairs and the achievements of the great of all ages and countries, which are thoroughly appreciated by a man of this type
alone, as being the only one who can quite understand and feel
with them. And so it is for him alone that those great ones have
really lived; it is to him that they make their appeal; the rest
are but casual hearers who only half understand either them
or their followers. Of course, this characteristic of the intellectual man implies that he has one more need than the others,
the need of reading, observing, studying, meditating, practicing,
the need, in short, of undisturbed leisure. For, as Voltaire has
very rightly said, *there are no real pleasures without real needs;*
and the need of them is why to such a man pleasures are accessible which are denied to others,—the varied beauties of nature
and art and literature. To heap these pleasures round people who
do not want them and cannot appreciate them, is like expecting
gray hairs to fall in love. A man who is privileged in this respect
leads two lives, a personal and an intellectual life; and the latter
gradually comes to be looked upon as the true one, and the
former as merely a means to it. Other people make this shallow,
empty and troubled existence an end in itself. To the life of
the intellect such a man will give the preference over all his other
occupations: by the constant growth of insight and knowledge,
this intellectual life, like a slowly-forming work of art, will acquire a consistency, a permanent intensity, a unity which becomes
ever more and more complete; compared with which, a life devoted to the attainment of personal comfort, a life that may

broaden indeed, but can never be deepened, makes but a poor show: and yet, as I have said, people make this baser sort of existence an end in itself.

The ordinary life of every day, so far as it is not moved by passion, is tedious and insipid; and if it is so moved, it soon becomes painful. Those alone are happy whom nature has favored with some superfluity of intellect, something beyond what is just necessary to carry out the behests of their will; for it enables them to lead an intellectual life as well, a life unattended by pain and full of vivid interests. Mere leisure, that is to say, intellect unoccupied in the service of the will, is not of itself sufficient: there must be a real superfluity of power, set free from the service of the will and devoted to that of the intellect; for, as Seneca says, *otium sine litteris mors est et vivi hominis sepultura* —illiterate leisure is a form of death, a living tomb. Varying with the amount of the superfluity, there will be countless developments in this second life, the life of the mind; it may be the mere collection and labelling of insects, birds, minerals, coins, or the highest achievements of poetry and philosophy. The life of the mind is not only a protection against boredom; it also wards off the pernicious effects of boredom; it keeps us from bad company, from the many dangers, misfortunes, losses and extravagances which the man who places his happiness entirely in the objective world is sure to encounter. My philosophy, for instance, has never brought me in a six-pence; but it has spared me many an expense.

The ordinary man places his life's happiness in things external to him, in property, rank, wife and children, friends, society, and the like, so that when he loses them or finds them disappointing, the foundation of his happiness is destroyed. In other words, his centre of gravity is not in himself; it is constantly changing its place, with every wish and whim. If he is a man of means, one day it will be his house in the country, another buying horses, or entertaining friends, or traveling,—a life, in short, of general luxury, the reason being that he seeks his pleasure in things outside him. Like one whose health and strength are gone, he tries to regain by the use of jellies and drugs, instead of by developing his own vital power, the true source of what he has lost. Before proceeding to the opposite, let us compare with this common type the man who comes midway between the two, endowed, it may be, not exactly with distinguished powers of mind, but with somewhat more than the ordinary amount of intellect. He will take a dilettante interest in art, or devote his attention to some branch of science —botany, for example, or physics, astronomy, history, and find a great deal of pleasure in such studies, and amuse himself with them when external forces of happiness are exhausted or fail to satisfy him any more. Of a man like this it may be said that his centre of gravity is partly in himself. But a dilettante interest in art is a very different thing from creative activity; and an amateur pursuit of science is apt to be superficial and not to penetrate to the heart of the matter. A man cannot entirely identify himself with such pursuits, or have his whole existence so completely filled and permeated with them that he loses all interest in everything else. It is only the highest intellectual power, what we call *genius,* that attains to this degree of intensity, making all time and existence its theme, and striving to express its peculiar conception of the world, whether it contemplates life as the subject of poetry or of philosophy. Hence, undisturbed occupation with himself, his own thoughts and works, is a matter of urgent necessity to such a man; solitude is welcome, leisure is the highest good, and everything else is unnecessary, nay, even burdensome.

This is the only type of man of whom it can be said that his centre of gravity is entirely in himself; which explains why it is that people of this sort—and they are very rare—no matter how excellent their character may be, do not show that warm and unlimited interest in friends, family, and the community in general, of which others are so often capable; for if they have only themselves they are not inconsolable for the loss of everything else. This gives an isolation to their character, which is all the more effective since other people never really quite satisfy them, as being, on the whole, of a different nature: nay more, since this difference is constantly forcing itself upon their notice they get accustomed to move about amongst mankind as alien beings, and in thinking of humanity in general, to say *they* instead of *we.*

So the conclusion we come to is that the man whom nature

has endowed with intellectual wealth is the happiest; so true
it is that the subjective concerns us more than the objective;
for whatever the latter may be, it can work only indirectly,
secondly, and through the medium of the former—a truth finely
expressed by Lucian:—

$$\Pi\lambda o\hat{v}\tau os\ \dot{o}\ \tau\hat{\eta}s\ \psi v\chi\hat{\eta}s\ \pi\lambda o\hat{v}\tau os\ \mu\acute{o}\nu os\ \dot{\epsilon}\sigma\tau\grave{\iota}\nu\ \dot{a}\lambda\eta\theta\acute{\eta}s$$
$$T\check{a}\lambda\lambda a\ \delta'\acute{\epsilon}\chi\epsilon\iota\ \check{a}\tau\eta\nu\ \pi\lambda\epsilon\acute{\iota}o\nu a\ \cdot\tau\omega\nu\ \kappa\tau\epsilon\acute{a}\nu\omega\nu\mathrm{—}^{[14]}$$

the wealth of the soul is the only true wealth, for with all other
riches comes a bane even greater than they. The man of inner
wealth wants nothing from outside but the negative gift of undisturbed leisure; to develop and mature his intellectual faculties, that is, to enjoy his wealth; in short, he wants permission to
be himself, his whole life long, every day and every hour. If he
is destined to impress the character of his mind upon a whole
race, he has only one measure of happiness or unhappiness—to
succeed or fail in perfecting his powers and completing his work.
All else is of small consequence. Accordingly, the greatest minds
of all ages have set the highest value upon undisturbed leisure,
as worth exactly as much as the man himself. *Happiness appears
to consist in leisure,* says Aristotle;[15] and Diogenes Laertius reports that *Socrates praised leisure as the fairest of all possessions.*
So, in the *Nichomachean Ethics,* Aristotle concludes that a life
devoted to philosophy is the happiest; or, as he says in the *Politics,*[16] *the free exercise of any power, whatever it may be, is happiness.* This again, tallies with what Goethe says in *Wilhelm
Meister: The man who is born with a talent which he is meant
to use, finds his greatest happiness in using it.*

But to be in possession of undisturbed leisure, is far from being
the common lot; nay, it is something alien to human nature, for
the ordinary man's destiny is to spend life in procuring what is
necessary for the subsistence of himself and his family; he is a
son of struggle and need, not a free intelligence. So people as
a rule soon get tired of undisturbed leisure, and it becomes burdensome if there are no fictitious and forced aims to occupy it, play,

[14] Epigrammata, 12.
[15] Eth. Nichom. x., 7.
[16] iv., 11.

pastime and hobbies of every kind. For this very reason it is full
of possible danger, and *difficilis in otio quies* is a true saying,—
it is difficult to keep quiet if you have nothing to do. On the
other hand, a measure of intellect far surpassing the ordinary,
is as unnatural as it is abnormal. But if it exists, and the man endowed with it is to be happy, he will want precisely that undisturbed leisure which the others find burdensome or pernicious;
for without it he is a Pegasus in harness, and consequently unhappy. If these two unnatural circumstances, external, and internal, undisturbed leisure and great intellect, happen to coincide
in the same person, it is a great piece of fortune; and if the
fate is so far favorable, a man can lead the higher life, the life
protected from the two opposite sources of human suffering, pain
and boredom, from the painful struggle for existence, and the incapacity for enduring leisure which is free existence itself)—
evils which may be escaped only by being mutually neutralized.

But there is something to be said in opposition to this view.
Great intellectual gifts mean an activity pre-eminently nervous
in its character, and consequently a very high degree of susceptibility to pain in every form. Further, such gifts imply an
intense temperament, larger and more vivid ideas, which, as the
inseparable accompaniment of great intellectual power, entail on
its possessor a corresponding intensity of the emotions, making
them incomparably more violent than those to which the ordinary
man is a prey. Now, there are more things in the world pro-
ductive of pain than of pleasure. Again, a large endowment of
intellect tends to estrange the man who has it from other people
and their doings; for the more a man has in himself, the less he
will be able to find in them; and the hundred things in which
they take delight, he will think shallow and insipid. Here, then,
perhaps, is another instance of that law of compensation which
makes itself felt everywhere. How often one hears it said, and
said, too, with some plausibility, that the narrow-minded man
is at bottom the happiest, even though his fortune is unenviable.
I shall make no attempt to forestall the reader's own judgment
on this point; more especially as Sophocles himself has given
utterance to two diametrically opposite opinions:—

Πολλῷ τὸ φρονεῖν εὐδαιμονίας
πρῶτον ὑπάρχει.[17]

he says in one place—wisdom is the greatest part of happiness;
and again, in another passage, he declares that the life of the
thoughtless is the most pleasant of all—

Ἐν τᾷ φρονεῖν γὰρ μηδὲν ἥδιστος βίος.[18]

The philosophers of the *Old Testament* find themselves in a like
contradiction.

The life of a fool is worse than death [19]

and—

In much wisdom is much grief;
and he that increaseth knowledge increaseth sorrow.[20]

I may remark, however, that a man who has no mental needs,
because his intellect is of the narrow and normal amount, is,
in the strict sense of the word, what is called a *philistine*—an
expression at first peculiar to the German language, a kind of slang
term at the Universities, afterwards used, by analogy, in a higher
sense, though still in its original meaning, as denoting one who is
not *a Son of the Muses*. A philistine is and remains ἀμούσος ἀνήρ.
I should prefer to take a higher point of view, and apply the
term *philistine* to people who are always seriously occupied with
realities which are no realities; but as such a definition would be
a transcendental one, and therefore not generally intelligible, it
would hardly be in place in the present treatise, which aims at
being popular. The other definition can be more easily elucidated,
indicating, as it does, satisfactorily enough, the essential nature
of all those qualities which distinguish the philistine. He is defined to be *a man without mental needs*. From this it follows,
firstly, *in relation to himself,* that he has *no intellectual pleasures;*
for, as was remarked before, there are no real pleasures without
real needs. The philistine's life is animated by no desire to gain
knowledge and insight for their own sake, or to experience that

[17] Antigone, 1347–8.
[18] Ajax, 554.
[19] Ecclesiasticus, xxii., 11.
[20] Ecclesiastes, i., 18.

true æsthetic pleasure which is so nearly akin to them. If pleasures of this kind are fashionable, and the philistine finds himself compelled to pay attention to them, he will force himself to do so, but he will take as little interest in them as possible. His only real pleasures are of a sensual kind, and he thinks that these indemnify him for the loss of the others. To him oysters and champagne are the height of existence; the aim of his life is to procure what will contribute to his bodily welfare, and he is indeed in a happy way if this causes him some trouble. If the luxuries of life are heaped upon him, he will inevitably be bored, and against boredom he has a great many fancied remedies, balls, theatres, parties, cards, gambling, horses, women, drinking, traveling and so on; all of which can not protect a man from being bored, for where there are no intellectual needs, no intellectual pleasures are possible. The peculiar characteristic of the philistine is a dull, dry kind of gravity, akin to that of animals. Nothing really pleases, or excites, or interests him, for sensual pleasure is quickly exhausted, and the society of philistines soon becomes burdensome, and one may even get tired of playing cards. True, the pleasures of vanity are left, pleasures which he enjoys in his own way, either by feeling himself superior in point of wealth, or rank, or influence and power to other people, who thereupon pay him honor; or, at any rate, by going about with those who have a superfluity of these blessings, sunning himself in the reflection of their splendor—what the English call a *snob*.

From the essential nature of the philistine it follows, secondly, *in regard to others,* that, as he possesses no intellectual, but only physical need, he will seek the society of those who can satisfy the latter, but not the former. The last thing he will expect from his friends is the possession of any sort of intellectual capacity; nay, if he chances to meet with it, it will rouse his antipathy and even hatred; simply because in addition to an unpleasant sense of inferiority, he experiences, in his heart, a dull kind of envy, which has to be carefully concealed even from himself. Nevertheless, it sometimes grows into a secret feeling of rancor. But for all that, it will never occur to him to make his own ideas of worth or value conform to the standard of such qualities; he will continue to give the preference to rank and riches, power and influence, which in his eyes seem to be the only genuine advantages in the world; and his wish will be to excel in them himself. All this is the consequence of his being a man *without intellectual needs*. The great affliction of all philistines is that they have no interest in *ideas,* and that, to escape being bored, they are in constant need of *realities*. But realities are either unsatisfactory or dangerous; when they lose their interest, they become fatiguing. But the ideal world is illimitable and calm,

> *something afar*
> *From the sphere of our sorrow.*

2. PROPERTY, OR WHAT A MAN HAS

EPICURUS divides the needs of mankind into three classes, and the division made by this great professor of happiness is a true and a fine one. First come natural and necessary needs, such as, when not satisfied, produce pain,—food and clothing, *victus et amictus,* needs which can easily be satisfied. Secondly, there are those needs which, though natural, are not necessary, such as the gratification of certain of the senses. I may add, however, that in the report given by Diogenes Laertius, Epicurus does not mention which of the senses he means; so that on this point my account of his doctrine is somewhat more definite and exact than the original. These are needs rather more difficult to satisfy. The third class consists of needs which are neither natural nor necessary, the needs of luxury and prodigality, show and splendor, which never come to an end, and are very hard to satisfy.[21]

It is difficult, if not impossible, to define the limits which reason should impose on the desire for wealth; for there is no absolute or definite amount of wealth which will satisfy a man. The amount is always relative, that is to say, just so much as will maintain the proportion between what he wants and what he gets; for to measure a man's happiness only by what he gets, and not also by what he expects to get, is as futile as to try to express a fraction which shall have a numerator but no denominator. A man never feels the loss of things which it never occurs to him to ask for; he is just as happy without them; whilst another, who may have a hundred times as much, feels miserable because he has not got the one thing he wants. In fact, here too, every man has an horizon of his own, and he will expect as much as he thinks it is possible for him to get. If an object within his horizon looks as though he could confidently reckon on getting

---

[21] Cf. Diogenes Laertius, Bk. x., ch. xxvii., pp. 127 and 149; also Cicero *de finibus,* i., 13.

it, he is happy; but if difficulties come in the way, he is miserable.
What lies beyond his horizon has no effect at all upon him. So it
is that the vast possessions of the rich do not agitate the poor,
and conversely, that a wealthy man is not consoled by all his
wealth for the failure of his hopes. Riches, one may say, are like
sea-water; the more you drink the thirstier you become; and the
same is true of fame. The loss of wealth and prosperity leaves
a man, as soon as the first pangs of grief are over, in very much
the same habitual temper as before; and the reason of this is,
that as soon as fate diminishes the amount of his possessions, he
himself immediately reduces the amount of his claims. But when
misfortune comes upon us, to reduce the amount of our claims is
just what is most painful; once that we have done so, the pain
becomes less and less, and is felt no more; like an old wound
which has healed. Conversely, when a piece of good fortune befalls us, our claims mount higher and higher, as there is nothing
to regulate them; it is in this feeling of expansion that the delight of it lies. But it lasts no longer than the process itself, and
when the expansion is complete, the delight ceases; we have become accustomed to the increase in our claims, and consequently
indifferent to the amount of wealth which satisfies them. There
is a passage in the *Odyssey* [22] illustrating this truth, of which I
may quote the last two lines:

$$\text{Τοῖος γὰρ νόος ἐστὶν ἐπιχθονίων ἀνθρώπων}$$
$$\text{Οἶον ἐφ ημαρ ἄγει πατὴρ ἀνδρῶν τε θεῶν τε.}$$

—the thoughts of man that dwells on the earth are as the day
granted him by the father of gods and men. Discontent springs
from a constant endeavor to increase the amount of our claims,
when we are powerless to increase the amount which will satisfy
them.

When we consider how full of needs the human race is, how
its whole existence is based upon them, it is not a matter for
surprise that *wealth* is held in more sincere esteem, nay, in greater
honor, than anything else in the world; nor ought we to wonder
that gain is made the only good of life, and everything that does
not lead to it pushed aside or thrown overboard—philosophy, for

[22] xviii., 130–7.

instance, by those who profess it. People are often reproached for wishing for money above all things, and for loving it more than anything else; but it is natural and even inevitable for people to love that which, like an unwearied Proteus, is always ready to turn itself into whatever object their wandering wishes or manifold desires may for the moment fix upon: Everything else can satisfy only *one* wish, *one* need: food is good only if you are hungry; wine, if you are able to enjoy it; drugs, if you are sick; fur for the winter; love for youth, and so on. These are all only relatively good, ἀγαθα πρός τι. Money alone is absolutely good, because it is not only a concrete satisfaction of one need in particular; it is an abstract satisfaction of all.

If a man has an independent fortune, he should regard it as a bulwark against the many evils and misfortunes which he may encounter; he should not look upon it as giving him leave to get what pleasure he can out of the world, or as rendering it incumbent upon him to spend it in this way. People who are not born with a fortune, but end by making a large one through the exercise of whatever talents they possess, almost always come to think that their talents are their capital, and that the money they have gained is merely the interest upon it; they do not lay by a part of their earnings to form a permanent capital, but spend their money much as they have earned it. Accordingly, they often fall into poverty; their earnings decreased, or come to an end altogether, either because their talent is exhausted by becoming antiquated,—as, for instance, very often happens in the case of fine art; or else it was valid only under a special conjunction of circumstances which has now passed away. There is nothing to prevent those who live on the common labor of their hands from treating their earnings in that way if they like; because their kind of skill is not likely to disappear, or, if it does, it can be replaced by that of their fellow-workmen; moreover, the kind of work they do is always in demand; so that what the proverb says is quite true, *a useful trade is a mine of gold*. But with artists and professionals of every kind the case is quite different, and that is the reason why they are well paid. They ought to build up a capital out of their earnings; but they recklessly look upon them as merely interest, and end in ruin. On the other hand, people who inherit money know, at least, how to distinguish between capital and interest, and most of them try to make their capital secure and not encroach upon it; nay, if they can, they put by at least an eighth of their interests in order to meet future contingencies. So most of them maintain their position. These few remarks about capital and interest are not applicable to commercial life, for merchants look upon money only as a means of further gain, just as a workman regards his tools; so even if their capital has been entirely the result of their own efforts, they try to preserve and increase it by using it. Accordingly, wealth is nowhere so much at home as in the merchant class.

It will generally be found that those who know what it is to have been in need and destitution are very much less afraid of it, and consequently more inclined to extravagance, than those who know poverty only by hearsay. People who have been born and bred in good circumstances are as a rule much more careful about the future, more economical, in fact, than those who, by a piece of good luck, have suddenly passed from poverty to wealth. This looks as if poverty were not really such a very wretched thing as it appears from a distance. The true reason, however, is rather the fact that the man who has been born into a position of wealth comes to look upon it as something without which he could no more live than he could live without air; he guards it as he does his very life; and so he is generally a lover of order, prudent and economical. But the man who has been born into a poor position looks upon it as the natural one, and if by any chance he comes in for a fortune, he regards it as a superfluity, something to be enjoyed or wasted, because, if it comes to an end, he can get on just as well as before, with one anxiety the less; or, as Shakespeare says in Henry VI.: [23]

> .... *the adage must be verified,*
> *That beggars mounted run their horse to death.*

But it should be said that people of this kind have a firm and excessive trust, partly in fate, partly in the peculiar means which have already raised them out of need and poverty,—a trust not only of the head, but of the heart also; and so they

[23] Part III., Act 1., Sc. 4.

do not, like the man born rich, look upon the shallows of poverty as bottomless, but console themselves with the thought that once they have touched ground again, they can take another upward flight. It is this trait in human character which explains the fact that women who were poor before their marriage often make greater claims, and are more extravagant, than those who have brought their husbands a rich dowry; because, as a rule, rich girls bring with them, not only a fortune, but also more eagerness, nay, more of the inherited instinct, to preserve it, than poor girls do. If anyone doubts the truth of this, and thinks that it is just the opposite, he will find authority for his view in Ariosto's first Satire; but, on the other hand, Dr. Johnson agrees with my opinion. *A woman of fortune,* he says, *being used to the handling of money, spends it judiciously; but a woman who gets the command of money for the first time upon her marriage, has such a gusto in spending it, that she throws it away with great profusion.*[24] And in any case let me advise anyone who marries a poor girl not to leave her the capital but only the interest, and to take especial care that she has not the management of the children's fortune.

I do not by any means think that I am touching upon a subject which is not worth my while to mention when I recommend people to be careful to preserve what they have earned or inherited. For to start life with just as much as will make one independent, that is, allow one to live comfortably without having to work—even if one has only just enough for oneself, not to speak of a family—is an advantage which cannot be overestimated; for it means exemption and immunity from that chronic disease of penury, which fastens on the life of man like a plague; it is emancipation from that forced labor which is the natural lot of every mortal. Only under a favorable fate like this can a man be said to be born free, to be, in the proper sense of the word, *sui juris,* master of his own time and powers, and able to say every morning, *This day is my own.* And just for the same reason the difference between the man who has a hundred a year and the man who has a thousand, is infinitely smaller than the difference between the former and a man who has nothing at all.

[24] Boswell's Life of Johnson: ann: 1776, ætat: 67.

But inherited wealth reaches its utmost value when it falls to the individual endowed with mental powers of a high order, who is resolved to pursue a line of life not compatible with the making of money; for he is then doubly endowed by fate and can live for his genius; and he will pay his debt to mankind a hundred times, by achieving what no other could achieve, by producing some work which contributes to the general good, and redounds to the honor of humanity at large. Another, again, may use his wealth to further philanthropic schemes, and make himself well-deserving of his fellowmen. But a man who does none of these things, who does not even try to do them, who never attempts to learn the rudiments of any branch of knowledge so that he may at least do what he can towards promoting it—such a one, born as he is into riches, is a mere idler and thief of time, a contemptible fellow. He will not even be happy, because, in his case, exemption from need delivers him up to the other extreme of human suffering, boredom, which is such martyrdom to him, that he would have been better off if poverty had given him something to do. And as he is bored he is apt to be extravagant, and so lose the advantage of which he showed himself unworthy. Countless numbers of people find themselves in want, simply because, when they had money, they spent it only to get momentary relief from the feeling of boredom which oppressed them.

It is quite another matter if one's object is success in political life, where favor, friends and connections are all-important, in order to mount by their aid step by step on the ladder of promotion, and perhaps gain the topmost rung. In this kind of life, it is much better to be cast upon the world without a penny; and if the aspirant is not of noble family, but is a man of some talent, it will redound to his advantage to be an absolute pauper. For what every one most aims at in ordinary contact with his fellows is to prove them inferior to himself; and how much more is this the case in politics. Now, it is only an absolute pauper who has such a thorough conviction of his own complete, profound and positive inferiority from every point of view, of his own utter insignificance and worthlessness, that he can take his place quietly

in the political machine.[25] He is the only one who can keep on
bowing low enough, and even go right down upon his face if
necessary; he alone can submit to everything and laugh at it;
he alone knows the entire worthlessness of merit; he alone uses
his loudest voice and his boldest type whenever he has to speak
or write of those who are placed over his head, or occupy any
position of influence; and if they do a little scribbling, he is ready
to applaud it as a masterwork. He alone understands how to beg,
and so betimes, when he is hardly out of his boyhood, he becomes
a high priest of that hidden mystery which Goethe brings to light.

> *Uber's Niederträchtige*
> *Niemand sich beklage:*
> *Denn es ist das Machtige*
> *Was man dir auch sage:*

—it is no use to complain of low aims; for, whatever people may
say, they rule the world.

On the other hand, the man who is born with enough to live
upon is generally of a somewhat independent turn of mind; he
is accustomed to keep his head up; he has not learned all the arts
of the beggar; perhaps he even presumes a little upon the possession of talents which, as he ought to know, can never compete
with cringing mediocrity; in the long run he comes to recognize
the inferiority of those who are placed over his head, and when
they try to put insults upon him, he becomes refractory and shy.
This is not the way to get on in the world. Nay, such a man may
at least incline to the opinion freely expressed by Voltaire: *We
have only two days to live; it is not worth our while to spend
them* in cringing to contemptible rascals. But alas! let me observe
by the way, that *contemptible rascal* is an attribute which may
be predicated of an abominable number of people. What Juvenal
says—it is difficult to rise if your poverty is greater than your
talent—

[25] *Translator's Note.*—Schopenhauer is probably here making one of
his most virulent attacks upon Hegel; in this case on account of what he
thought to be the philosopher's abject servility to the government of his
day. Though the Hegelian system has been the fruitful mother of many
liberal ideas, there can be no doubt that Hegel's influence, in his own
lifetime, was an effective support of Prussian bureaucracy.

Haud facile emregunt quorum virtutibus obstat
Res angusta domi—

is more applicable to a career of art and literature than to a
political and social ambition.

Wife and children I have not reckoned amongst a man's possessions: he is rather in their possession. It would be easier to
include friends under that head; but a man's friends belong to
him not a whit more than he belongs to them.

II. COUNSELS AND MAXIMS

I. GENERAL RULES

THE first and foremost rule for the wise conduct of life seems to me to be contained in a view to which Aristotle parenthetically refers in the *Nichomachean Ethics*:[1] ὁ φρόνιμος τὸ ἄλυπον διώκει οὐ τὸ ἡδύ, or, as it may be rendered, *not pleasure, but freedom from pain, is what the wise man will aim at.* The truth cɪ this remark turns upon the negative character of happiness,—the fact that pleasure is only the negation of pain, and that pain is the positive element in life. Though I have given a detailed proof of this proposition in my chief work, I may supply one more illustration of it here, drawn from a circumstance of daily occurrence. Suppose that, with the exception of some sore oɪ painful spot, we are physically in a sound and healthy condition: the sore of this one spot will completely absorb our attention, causing us to lose the sense of general well-being, and destroying all our comfort in life. In the same way, when all our affairs but one turn out as we wish, the single instance in which our aims are frustrated is a constant trouble to us, even though it be something quite trivial. We think a great deal about it, and very little about those other and more important matters in which we have been successful. In both these cases what has met with resistance is *the will;* in the one case, as it is objectified in the organism, in the other, as it presents itself in the struggle of life; and in both, it is plain that the satisfaction of the will consists in nothing else than that it meets with no resistance. It is, therefore, a satisfaction which is not directly felt; at most, we can become conscious of it only when we reflect upon our condition. But that which checks or arrests the will is something positive; it proclaims its own presence. All pleasure consists in merely removing this check—

[1] vii., (12) 12.

in other words, in freeing us from its action; and hence pleasure
is a state which can never last very long.

This is the true basis of the above excellent rule quoted from
Aristotle, which bids us direct our aim, not toward securing what
is pleasurable and agreeable in life, but toward avoiding, as far as
possible, its innumerable evils. If this were not the right course to
take, that saying of Voltaire's, *Happiness is but a dream and sorrow is real,* would be as false as it is, in fact, true. A man who
desires to make up the book of his life and determine where the
balance of happiness lies, must put down in his accounts, not the
pleasures which he has enjoyed, but the evils which he has escaped.
That is the true method of eudæmonology; for all eudæmonology
must begin by recognizing that its very name is a euphemism, and
that *to live happily* only means *to live less unhappily*—to live a
tolerable life. There is no doubt that life is given us, not to be
enjoyed, but to be overcome—to be got over. There are numerous
expressions illustrating this—such as *degere vitam, vita defungi;*
or in Italian, *si scampa così;* or in German, *man muss suchen
durchzukommen; er wird schon durch die Welt kommen,* and
so on. In old age it is indeed a consolation to think that the work
of life is over and done with. The happiest lot is not to have experienced the keenest delights or the greatest pleasures, but to have
brought life to a close without any very great pain, bodily or
mental. To measure the happiness of a life by its delights or
pleasures is to apply a false standard. For pleasures are and remain something negative; that they produce happiness is a delusion, cherished by envy to its own punishment. Pain is felt to be
something positive, and hence its absence is the true standard of
happiness. And if, over and above freedom from pain, there is also
an absence of boredom, the essential conditions of earthly happiness are attained; for all else is chimerical.

It follows from this that a man should never try to purchase
pleasure at the cost of pain, or even at the risk of incurring it; to
do so is to pay what is positive and real, for what is negative and
illusory; while there is a net profit in sacrificing pleasure for the
sake of avoiding pain. In either case it is a matter of indifference
whether the pain follows the pleasure or precedes it. While it is a
complete inversion of the natural order to try to turn this scene

of misery into a garden of pleasure, to aim at joy and pleasure rather than at the greatest possible freedom from pain—and yet how many do it!—there is some wisdom in taking a gloomy view, in looking upon the world as a kind of hell, and in confining one's efforts to securing a little room that shall not be exposed to the fire. The fool rushes after the pleasures of life and finds himself their dupe; the wise man avoids its evils; and even if, notwithstanding his precautions, he falls into misfortunes, that is the fault of fate, not of his own folly. As far as he is successful in his endeavors, he cannot be said to have lived a life of illusion; for the evils which he shuns are very real. Even if he goes too far out of his way to avoid evils, and makes an unnecessary sacrifice of pleasure, he is, in reality, not the worse off for that; for all pleasures are chimerical, and to mourn for having lost any of them is a frivolous, and even ridiculous proceeding.

The failure to recognize this truth—a failure promoted by optimistic ideas—is the source of much unhappiness. In moments free from pain, our restless wishes present, as it were in a mirror, the image of a happiness that has no counterpart in reality, seducing us to follow it; in doing so we bring pain upon ourselves, and that is something undeniably real. Afterwards, we come to look with regret upon the lost state of painlessness; it is a paradise which we have gambled away; it is no longer with us, and we long in vain to undo what has been done.

One might well fancy that these visions of wishes fulfilled were the work of some evil spirit, conjured up in order to entice us away from that painless state which forms our highest happiness.

A careless youth may think that the world is meant to be enjoyed, as though it were the abode of some real or positive happiness, which only those fail to attain who are not clever enough to overcome the difficulties that lie in the way. This false notion takes a stronger hold on him when he comes to read poetry and romance, and to be deceived by outward show—the hypocrisy that characterizes the world from beginning to end; on which I shall have something to say presently. The result is that his life is the more or less deliberate pursuit of positive happiness; and happiness he takes to be equivalent to a series of definite pleasures. In seeking for these pleasures he encounters danger—a fact which should not be forgotten. He hunts for game that does not exist; and so he ends by suffering some very real and positive misfortune —pain, distress, sickness, loss, care, poverty, shame, and all the thousand ills of life. Too late he discovers the trick that has been played upon him.

But if the rule I have mentioned is observed, and a plan of life is adopted which proceeds by avoiding pain—in other words, by taking measures of precaution against want, sickness, and distress in all its forms, the aim is a real one, and something may be achieved which will be great in proportion as the plan is not disturbed by striving after the chimera of positive happiness. This agrees with the opinion expressed by Goethe in the *Elective Affinities,* and there put into the mouth of Mittler—the man who is always trying to make other people happy: *To desire to get rid of an evil is a definite object, but to desire a better fortune than one has is blind folly.* The same truth is contained in that fine French proverb: *le mieux est l'ennemi du bien*—leave well alone. And, as I have remarked in my chief work, this is the leading thought underlying the philosophical system of the Cynics. For what was it led the Cynics to repudiate pleasure in every form, if it was not the fact that pain is, in a greater or less degree, always bound up with pleasure? To go out of the way of pain seemed to them so much easier than to secure pleasure. Deeply impressed as they were by the negative nature of pleasure and the positive nature of pain, they consistently devoted all their efforts to the avoidance of pain. The first step to that end was, in their opinion, a complete and deliberate repudiation of pleasure, as something which served only to entrap the victim in order that he might be delivered over to pain.

We are all born, as Schiller says, in Arcadia. In other words, we come into the world full of claims to happiness and pleasure, and we cherish the fond hope of making them good. But, as a rule, Fate soon teaches us, in a rough and ready way that we really possess nothing at all, but that everything in the world is at its command, in virtue of an unassailable right, not only to all we have or acquire, to wife or child, but even to our very limbs, our arms, legs, eyes and ears, nay, even to the nose in the middle of our face. And in any case, after some little time, we learn by experience that happiness and pleasure are a *fata morgana,* which, visible from afar, vanish as we approach; that, on the other hand, suffering and pain are a reality which makes its presence felt without any intermediary, and for its effect, stand in no need of illusion or the play of false hope.

If the teaching of experience bears fruit in us, we soon give up the pursuit of pleasure and happiness, and think much more about making ourselves secure against the attacks of pain and suffering. We see that the best the world has to offer is an existence free from pain—a quiet, tolerable life; and we confine our claims to this, as to something we can more surely hope to achieve. For the safest way of not being very miserable is not to expect to be very happy. Merck, the friend of Goethe's youth, was conscious of this truth when he wrote: *It is the wretched way people have of setting up a claim to happiness—and, that too, in a measure corresponding with their desires—that ruins everything in this world. A man will make progress if he can get rid of this claim,*[2] *and desire nothing but what he sees before him.* Accordingly it is advisable to put very moderate limits upon our expectations of pleasure, possessions, rank, honor, and so on; because it is just this striving and struggling to be happy, to dazzle the world, to lead a life full of pleasure, which entails great misfortune. It is prudent and wise, I say, to reduce one's claims, if only for the reason that it is extremely easy to be very unhappy; while to be very happy is not indeed difficult, but quite impossible. With justice sings the poet of life's wisdom:

> *Auream quisquis mediocritatem*
> *Diligit, tutus caret obsoleti*
> *Sordibus tecti, caret invidenda*
> > *Sobrius aula.*
> *Sævius ventis agitatur ingens*
> *Pinus: et celsæ graviori casu*
> *Decidunt turres; feriuntque summos*
> > *Fulgura montes.*[3]

—the golden mean is best—to live free from the squalor of a mean abode, and yet not be a mark for envy. It is the tall pine which is

---

[2] Letters to and from Merck.
[3] Horace. Odes, II., x.

cruelly shaken by the wind, the highest summits that are struck
in the storm, and the lofty towers that fall so heavily.

He who has taken to heart the teaching of my philosophy—
who knows, therefore, that our whole existence is something which
had better not have been, and that to disown and disclaim it is
the highest wisdom—he will have no great expectations from anything or any condition in life: he will spend passion upon nothing
in the world, nor lament over-much if he fails in any of his undertakings. He will feel the deep truth of what Plato [4] says: οὔτε
τι τῶν ἀνθρωπίνων ἄξιον ὅν μεγάλης σπονδῆς—nothing in human
affairs is worth any great anxiety; or, as the Persian poet has it,

> *Though from thy grasp all worldly things should flee,*
> *Grieve not for them, for they are nothing worth:*
> *And though a world in thy possession be,*
> *Joy not, for worthless are the things of earth.*
> *Since to that better world 'tis given to thee*
> *To pass, speed on, for this is nothing worth.*[5]

The chief obstacle to our arriving at these salutary views is
that hypocrisy of the world to which I have already alluded—an
hypocrisy which should be early revealed to the young. Most of
the glories of the world are mere outward show, like the scenes
on a stage: there is nothing real about them. Ships festooned and
hung with pennants, firing of cannon, illuminations, beating of
drums and blowing of trumpets, shouting and applauding—these
are all the outward sign, the pretense and suggestion,—as it were
the hieroglyphic,—of *joy:* but just there, joy is, as a rule, not to
be found; it is the only guest who has declined to be present at
the festival. Where this guest may really be found, he comes
generally without invitation; he is not formally announced, but
slips in quietly by himself *sans façon;* often making his appearance
under the most unimportant and trivial circumstances, and in the
commonest company; anywhere, in short, but where the society is
brilliant and distinguished. Joy is like the gold in the Australian
mines—found only now and then, as it were, by the caprice of

---

[4] *Republic,* x., 604.
[5] *Translator's Note.* From the Anvár-i Suhailí—*The Lights of Canopus*
being the Persian version of the *Table of Bidpai.* Translated by E. B.
Eastwick, ch. iii. Story vi., p. 289.

chance, and according to no rule or law; oftenest in very little grains, and very seldom in heaps. All that outward show which I have described, is only an attempt to make people believe that it is really joy which has come to the festival; and to produce this impression upon the spectators is, in fact, the whole object of it.

With *mourning* it is just the same. That long funeral procession, moving up so slowly; how melancholy it looks! what an endless row of carriages! But look into them—they are all empty; the coachmen of the whole town are the sole escort the dead man has to his grave. Eloquent picture of the friendship and esteem of the world! This is the falsehood, the hollowness, the hypocrisy of human affairs!

Take another example—a roomful of guests in full dress, being received with great ceremony. You could almost believe that this is a noble and distinguished company; but, as a matter of fact, it is compulsion, pain and boredom who are the real guests. For where many are invited, it is a rabble—even if they all wear stars. Really good society is everywhere of necessity very small. In brilliant festivals and noisy entertainments, there is always, at bottom, a sense of emptiness prevalent. A false tone is there: such gatherings are in strange contrast with the misery and barrenness of our existence. The contrast brings the true condition into relief. Still, these gatherings are effective from the outside; and that is just their purpose. Chamfort [6] makes the excellent remark that *society—les cercles, les salons, ce qu'on appelle le monde*—is like a miserable play, or a bad opera, without any interest in itself, but supported for a time by mechanical aid, costumes and scenery.

And so, too, with academies and chairs of philosophy. You have a kind of sign-board hung out to show the apparent abode of *wisdom:* but wisdom is another guest who declines the invitation; she is to be found elsewhere. The chiming of bells, ecclesiastical millinery, attitudes of devotion, insane antics—these are the pretense, the false show of *piety.* And so on. Everything in the world

[6] *Translator's Note.* Nicholas "Chamfort" (1741–94), a French miscellaneous writer, whose brilliant conversation, power of sarcasm, and epigrammatic force, coupled with an extraordinary career, render him one of the most interesting and remarkable men of his time. Schopenhauer undoubtedly owed much to this writer, to whom he constantly refers.

is like a hollow nut; there is little kernel anywhere, and when it does exist, it is still more rare to find it in the shell. You may look for it elsewhere, and find it, as a rule, only by chance.

To estimate a man's condition in regard to happiness, it is necessary to ask, not what things please him, but what things trouble him; and the more trivial these things are in themselves, the happier the man will be. To be irritated by trifles, a man must be well off; for in misfortunes trifles are unfelt.

Care should be taken not to build the happiness of life upon a *broad foundation*—not to require a great many things in order to be happy. For happiness on such a foundation is the most easily undermined; it offers many more opportunities for accidents; and accidents are always happening. The architecture of happiness follows a plan in this respect just the opposite of that adopted in every other case, where the broadest foundation offers the greatest security. Accordingly, to reduce your claims to the lowest possible degree, in comparison with your means,—of whatever kind these may be—is the surest way of avoiding extreme misfortune.

To make extensive preparations for life—no matter what form they may take—is one of the greatest and commonest of follies. Such preparations presuppose, in the first place, a long life, the full and complete term of years appointed to man—and how few reach it! and even if it be reached, it is still too short for all the plans that have been made; for to carry them out requires more time than was thought necessary at the beginning. And then how many mischances and obstacles stand in the way! how seldom the goal is ever reached in human affairs!

And lastly, even though the goal should be reached, the changes which Time works in us have been left out of the reckoning: we forget that the capacity whether for achievement or for enjoyment does not last a whole lifetime. So we often toil for things which are no longer suited to us when we attain them; and again, the years we spend in preparing for some work, unconsciously rob us of the power for carrying it out.

How often it happens that a man is unable to enjoy the wealth which he acquired at so much trouble and risk, and that the fruits of his labor are reserved for others; or that he is incapable of filling the position which he has won after so many years of toil and struggle. Fortune has come too late for him; or, contrarily, he has come too late for fortune,—when, for instance, he wants to achieve great things, say, in art or literature: the popular taste has changed, it may be; a new generation has grown up, which takes no interest in his work; others have gone a shorter way and got the start of him. These are the facts of life which Horace must have had in view, when he lamented the uselessness of all advice:—

> *quid eternis minorem*
> *Consiliis animum fatigas?* [9]

The cause of this commonest of all follies is that optical illusion of the mind from which everyone suffers, making life, at its beginning, seem of long duration; and at its end, when one looks back over the course of it, how short a time it seems! There is some advantage in the illusion; but for it, no great work would ever be done.

Our life is like a journey on which, as we advance, the landscape takes a different view from that which it presented at first, and changes again, as we come nearer. This is just what happens—especially with our wishes. We often find something else, nay, something better than what we are looking for; and what we look for, we often find on a very different path from that on which we began a vain search. Instead of finding, as we expected, pleasure, happiness, joy, we get experience, insight, knowledge—a real and permanent blessing, instead of a fleeting and illusory one.

This is the thought that runs through *Wilhelm Meister,* like the bass in a piece of music. In this work of Goethe's, we have a novel of the *intellectual* kind, and, therefore, superior to all others, even to Sir Walter Scott's, which are, one and all, *ethical;* in other words, they treat of human nature only from the side of the will. So, too, in the *Zauberflöte*—that grotesque, but still significant, and even hieroglyphic—the same thought is symbolized, but in great, coarse lines, much in the way in which scenery is painted. Here the symbol would be complete if Tamino were in the end to be cured of his desire to possess Tamina, and received, in her

[9] Odes, II., xi.

stead, initiation into the mysteries of the Temple of Wisdom. It is quite right for Papageno, his necessary contrast, to succeed in getting his Papagena.

Men of any worth or value soon come to see that they are in the hands of Fate, and gratefully submit to be moulded by its teachings. They recognize that the fruit of life is experience, and not happiness; they become accustomed and content to exchange hope for insight; and, in the end, they can say, with Petrarch, that all they care for is to learn:—

Altro diletto che 'mparar, non provo.

It may even be that they to some extent still follow their old wishes and aims, trifling with them, as it were, for the sake of appearances; all the while really and seriously looking for nothing but instruction; a process which lends them an air of genius, a trait of something contemplative and sublime.

In their search for gold, the alchemists discovered other things— gunpowder, china, medicines, the laws of nature. There is a sense in which we are all alchemists.

2. THE AGES OF LIFE

THERE is a very fine saying of Voltaire's to the effect that every age of life has its own peculiar mental character, and that a man will feel completely unhappy if his mind is not in accordance with his years:—

> Qui n'a pas l'esprit de son âge,
> De son âge atout le malheur.

It will, therefore, be a fitting close to our speculations upon the nature of happiness, if we glance at the changes which the various periods of life produce in us.

Our whole life long it is *the present,* and the present alone, that we actually possess: the only difference is that at the beginning of life we look forward to a long future, and that towards the end we look back upon a long past; also that our temperament, but not our character, undergoes certain well-known changes, which make *the present* wear a different color at each period of life.

I have elsewhere stated that in childhood we are more given to using our *intellect* than our *will;* and I have explained why this is so.[10] It is just for this reason that the first quarter of life is so happy: as we look back upon it in after years, it seems a sort of lost paradise. In childhood our relations with others are limited, our wants are few,—in a word, there is little stimulus for the will; and so our chief concern is the extension of our knowledge. The intellect—like the brain, which attains its full size in the seventh year,[11] is developed early, though it takes time to mature; and

[10] *Translator's Note.*—Schopenhauer refers to *Die Welt als Wille und Vorstellung,* Bk. II., c. 31, p. 451 (4th edit.), where he explains that this is due to the fact that at that period of life the brain and nervous system are much more developed than any other part of the organism.

[11] *Translator's Note.*—This statement is not quite correct. The weight of the brain increases rapidly up to the seventh year, more slowly between the sixteenth and the twentieth years, still more slowly till between thirty and forty years of age, when it attains its maximum. At each decennial period after this, it is supposed to decrease in weight on the average, an ounce for every ten years.

it explores the whole world of its surroundings in its constant search for nutriment: it is then that existence is in itself an ever fresh delight, and all things sparkle with the charm of novelty.

This is why the years of childhood are like a long poem. For the function of poetry, as of all art, is to grasp the *Idea*—in the Platonic sense; in other words, to apprehend a particular object in such a way as to perceive its essential nature, the characteristics it has in common with all other objects of the same kind; so that a single object appears as the representative of a class, and the results of one experience hold good for a thousand.

It may be thought that my remarks are opposed to fact, and that the child is never occupied with anything beyond the individual object or events which are presented to it from time to time, and then only in so far as they interest and excite its will for the moment; but this is not really the case. In those early years, life—in the full meaning of the word, is something so new and fresh, and its sensations are so keen and unblunted by repetition, that, in the midst of all its pursuits and without any clear consciousness of what it is doing, the child is always silently occupied in grasping the nature of life itself,—in arriving at its fundamental character and general outline by means of separate scenes and experiences; or, to use Spinoza's phraseology, the child is learning to see the things and persons about it *sub specie aeternitatis,*—as particular manifestations of universal law.

The younger we are, then, the more does every individual object represent for us the whole class to which it belongs; but as the years increase, this becomes less and less the case. That is the reason why youthful impressions are so different from those of old age. And that is also why the slight knowledge and experience gained in childhood and youth afterwards come to stand as the permanent rubric, or heading, for all the knowledge acquired in later life,—those early forms of knowledge passing into categories, as it were, under which the results of subsequent experience are classified; though a clear consciousness of what is being done, does not always attend upon the process.

In this way the earliest years of a man's life lay the foundation of his view of the world, whether it be shallow or deep; and although this view may be extended and perfected later on, it is not materially altered. It is an effect of this purely objective and therefore poetical view of the world,—essential to the period of childhood and promoted by the as yet undeveloped state of the volitional energy—that, as children, we are concerned much more with the acquisition of pure knowledge than with exercising the power of will. Hence that grave, fixed look observable in so many children, of which Raphael makes such a happy use in his depiction of cherubs, especially in the picture of the *Sistine Madonna*. The years of childhood are thus rendered so full of bliss that the memory of them is always coupled with longing and regret.

While we thus eagerly apply ourselves to learning the outward aspect of things, as the primitive method of understanding the objects about us, education aims at instilling into us *ideas*. But ideas furnish no information as to the real and essential nature of objects, which, as the foundation and true content of all knowledge, can be reached only by the process called *intuition*. This is a kind of knowledge which can in no wise be instilled into us from without; we must arrive at it by and for ourselves.

Hence a man's intellectual as well as his moral qualities proceed from the depths of his own nature, and are not the result of external influences; and no educational scheme—of Pestalozzi, or of any one else—can turn a born simpleton into a man of sense. The thing is impossible! He was born a simpleton, and a simpleton he will die.

It is the depth and intensity of this early intuitive knowledge of the external world that explain why the experiences of childhood take such a firm hold on the memory. When we were young, we were completely absorbed in our immediate surroundings; there was nothing to distract our attention from them; we looked upon the objects about us as though they were the only ones of their kind, as though, indeed, nothing else existed at all. Later on, when we come to find out how many things there are in the world, this primitive state of mind vanishes, and with it our patience.

I have said elsewhere [12] that the world, considered as *object,*—in other words, as it is *presented* to us objectively,—wears in general a pleasing aspect; but that in the world, considered as

[12] *Die Welt als Wille und Vorstellung*, Bk. II., c. 31, p. 426–7 (4th Edit.), to which the reader is referred for a detailed explanation of my meaning.

subject,—that is, in regard to its inner nature, which is *will,*—pain and trouble predominate. I may be allowed to express the matter, briefly, thus: *the world is glorious to look at, but dreadful in reality.*

Accordingly, we find that, in the years of childhood, the world is much better known to us on its outer or objective side, namely, as the presentation of will, than on the side of its inner nature, namely, as the will itself. Since the objective side wears a pleasing aspect, and the inner or subjective side, with its tale of horror, remains as yet unknown, the youth, as his intelligence develops, takes all the forms of beauty that he sees, in nature and in art, for so many objects of blissful existence; they are so beautiful to the outward eye that, on their inner side, they must, he thinks, be much more beautiful still. So the world lies before him like another Eden; and this is the Arcadia in which we are all born.

A little later, this state of mind gives birth to a thirst for real life—the impulse to do and suffer—which drives a man forth into the hurly-burly of the world. There he learns the other side of existence, the inner side, the will, which is thwarted at every step. Then comes the great period of disillusion, a period of very gradual growth; but once it has fairly begun, a man will tell you that he has got over all his false notions—*l'âge des illusions est passé;* and yet the process is only beginning, and it goes on extending its sway and applying more and more to the whole of life.

So it may be said that in childhood, life looks like the scenery in a theatre, as you view it from a distance; and that in old age it is like the same scenery when you come up quite close to it.

And, lastly, there is another circumstance that contributes to the happiness of childhood. As spring commences, the young leaves on the trees are similar in color and much the same in shape; and in the first years of life we all resemble one another and harmonize very well. But with puberty divergence begins; and, like the radii of a circle, we go further and further apart.

The period of youth, which forms the remainder of this earlier half of our existence—and how many advantages it has over the later half!—is troubled and made miserable by the pursuit of happiness, as though there were no doubt that it can be met with somewhere in life,—a hope that always ends in failure and leads to

discontent. An illusory image of some vague future bliss—born of
a dream and shaped by fancy—floats before our eyes; and we
search for the reality in vain. So it is that the young man is
generally dissatisfied with the position in which he finds himself,
whatever it may be; he ascribes his disappointment solely to the
state of things that meets him on his first introduction to life,
when he had expected something very different; whereas it is only
the vanity and wretchedness of human life everywhere that he is
now for the first time experiencing.

It would be a great advantage to a young man if his early training could eradicate the idea that the world has a great deal to
offer him. But the usual result of education is to strengthen this
delusion; and our first ideas of life are generally taken from
fiction rather than from fact.

In the bright dawn of our youthful days, the poetry of life
spreads out a gorgeous vision before us, and we torture ourselves
by longing to see it realized. We might as well wish to grasp the
rainbow! The youth expects his career to be like an interesting
romance; and there lies the germ of that disappointment which
I have been describing.[13] What lends a charm to all these visions
is just the fact that they are visionary and not real, and that in
contemplating them we are in the sphere of pure knowledge,
which is sufficient in itself and free from the noise and struggle
of life. To try to realize those visions is to make them an object
of *will*—a process which always involves pain.[14]

If the chief feature of the earlier half of life is a never-satisfied
longing after happiness, the later half is characterized by the dread
of misfortune. For, as we advance in years, it becomes in a greater
or less degree clear that all happiness is chimerical in its nature,
and that pain alone is real. Accordingly, in later years, we, or,
at least, the more prudent amongst us, are more intent upon
eliminating what is painful from our lives and making our position secure, than on the pursuit of positive pleasure. I may observe,
by the way, that in old age, we are better able to prevent misfortunes from coming, and in youth better able to bear them when
they come.

[13] Cf. loc. cit., p. 428.
[14] Let me refer the reader, if he is interested in the subject, to the volume already cited, chapter 37.

In my young days, I was always pleased to hear a ring at my door: ah! thought I, now for something pleasant. But in later life my feelings on such occasions were rather akin to dismay than to pleasure: heaven help me! thought I, what am I to do? A similar revulsion of feeling in regard to the world of men takes place in all persons of any talent or distinction. For that very reason they cannot be said properly to belong to the world; in a greater or less degree, according to the extent of their superiority, they stand alone. In their youth they have a sense of being abandoned by the world; but later on, they feel as though they had escaped it. The earlier feeling is an unpleasant one, and rests upon ignorance; the second is pleasurable—for in the meantime they have come to know what the world is.

The consequence of this is that, as compared with the earlier, the later half of life, like the second part of a musical period, has less of passionate longing and more restfulness about it. And why is this the case? Simply because, in youth, a man fancies that there is a prodigious amount of happiness and pleasure to be had in the world, only that it is difficult to come by it; whereas, when he becomes old, he knows that there is nothing of the kind; he makes his mind completely at ease on the matter, enjoys the present hour as well as he can, and even takes a pleasure in trifles.

The chief result gained by experience of life is *clearness of view*. That is what distinguishes the man of mature age, and makes the world wear such a different aspect from that which is presented in his youth or boyhood. It is only then that he sees things quite plain, and takes them for that which they really are: while in earlier years he saw a phantom-world, put together out of the whims and crotchets of his own mind, inherited prejudice and strange delusion: the real world was hidden from him, or the vision of it distorted. The first thing that experience finds to do is to free us from the phantoms of the brain—those false notions that have been put into us in youth.

To prevent their entrance at all would, of course, be the best form of education, even though it were only negative in aim: but it would be a task full of difficulty. At first the child's horizon would have to be limited as much as possible, and yet within that limited sphere none but clear and correct notions would have to be given; only after the child had properly appreciated everything within it, might the sphere be gradually enlarged; care being always taken that nothing was left obscure, or half or wrongly understood. The consequence of this training would be that the child's notions of men and things would always be limited and simple in their character; but, on the other hand, they would be clear and correct, and only need to be extended, not to be rectified. The same line might be pursued on into the period of youth. This method of education would lay special stress upon the prohibition of novel reading; and the place of novels would be taken by suitable biographical literature—the life of Franklin, for instance, or Moritz' *Anton Reiser*.[15]

In our early days we fancy that the leading events in our life, and the persons who are going to play an important part in it, will make their entrance to the sound of drums and trumpets; but when, in old age, we look back, we find that they all came in quite quietly, slipped in, as it were, by the side door, almost unnoticed.

From the point of view we have been taking up until now, life may be compared to a piece of embroidery, of which, during the first half of his time, a man gets a sight of the right side, and during the second half, of the wrong. The wrong side is not so pretty as the right, but it is more instructive; it shows the way in which the threads have been worked together.

Intellectual superiority, even if it is of the highest kind, will not secure for a man a preponderating place in conversation until after he is forty years of age. For age and experience, though they can never be a substitute for intellecual talent, may far outweigh it; and even in a person of the meanest capacity, they give a certain counterpoise to the power of an extremely intellectual man, so long as the latter is young. Of course I allude here to personal superiority, not to the place a man may gain by his works.

And on passing his fortieth year, any man of the slightest power of mind—any man, that is, who has more than the sorry share of intellect with which Nature has endowed five-sixths of mankind—will hardly fail to show some trace of misanthropy. For, as is natural, he has by that time inferred other people's char-

---

[15] *Translator's Note.*—Moritz was a miscellaneous writer of the last century (1757–93). His *Anton Reiser,* composed in the form of a novel, is practically an autobiography.

acter from an examination of his own; with the result that he has
been gradually disappointed to find that in the qualities of the
head or in those of the heart—and usually in both—he reaches
a level to which they do not attain; so he gladly avoids having
anything more to do with them. For it may be said, in general,
that every man will love or hate solitude—in other words, his
own society—just in proportion as he is worth anything in himself. Kant has some remarks upon this kind of misanthropy in his
Critique of the Faculty of Judgment.[16]

In a young man, it is a bad sign, as well from an intellectual
as from a moral point of view, if he is precocious in understanding
the ways of the world, and in adapting himself to its pursuits; if
he at once knows how to deal with men, and enters upon life, as
it were, fully prepared. It argues a vulgar nature. On the other
hand, to be surprised and astonished at the way people act, and to
be clumsy and cross-grained in having to do with them, indicates
a character of the nobler sort.

The cheerfulness and vivacity of youth are partly due to the fact
that, when we are ascending the hill of life, death is not visible:
it lies down at the bottom of the other side. But once we have
crossed the top of the hill, death comes in view—death, which,
until then, was known to us only by hearsay. This makes our
spirits droop, for at the same time we begin to feel that our vital
powers are on the ebb. A grave seriousness now takes the place of
that early extravagance of spirit; and the change is noticeable
even in the expression of a man's face. As long as we are young,
people may tell us what they please! we look upon life as endless and use our time recklessly; but the older we become, the
more we practice economy. For towards the close of life, every day
we live gives us the same kind of sensation as the criminal experiences at every step on his way to be tried.

From the standpoint of youth, life seems to stretch away into
an endless future; from the standpoint of old age, to go back
but a little way into the past; so that, at the beginning, life presents
us with a picture in which the objects appear a great way off,
as though we had reversed our telescope; while in the end every-

16 *Kritik der Urtheilskraft,* Part I., § 29, Note ad fin.

thing seems so close. To see how short life is, a man must have grown old, that is to say, he must have lived long.

On the other hand, as the years increase, things look smaller, one and all; and Life, which had so firm and stable a base in the days of our youth, now seems nothing but a rapid flight of moments, every one of them illusory: we have come to see that the whole world is vanity!

Time itself seems to go at a much slower pace when we are young; so that not only is the first quarter of life the happiest, it is also the longest of all; it leaves more memories behind it. If a man were put to it, he could tell you more out of the first quarter of his life than out of two of the remaining periods. Nay, in the spring of life, as in the spring of the year, the days reach a length that is positively tiresome; but in the autumn, whether of the year or of life, though they are short, they are more genial and uniform.

But why is it that to an old man his past life appears so short? For this reason: his memory is short; and so he fancies that his life has been short too. He no longer remembers the insignificant parts of it, and much that was unpleasant is now forgotten; how little, then, there is left! For, in general, a man's memory is as imperfect as his intellect; and he must make a practice of reflecting upon the lessons he has learned and the events he has experienced, if he does not want them both to sink gradually into the gulf of oblivion. Now, we are unaccustomed to reflect upon matters of no importance, or, as a rule, upon things that we have found disagreeable, and yet that is necessary if the memory of them is to be preserved. But the class of things that may be called insignificant is continually receiving fresh additions: much that wears an air of importance at first, gradually becomes of no consequence at all from the fact of its frequent repetition; so that in the end we actually lose count of the number of times it happens. Hence we are better able to remember the events of our earlier than of our later years. The longer we live, the fewer are the things that we can call important or significant enough to deserve further consideration, and by this alone can they be fixed in the memory; in other words, they are forgotten as soon as they are past. Thus it is that time runs on, leaving always fewer traces of its passage.

Further, if disagreeable things have happened to us, we do not care to ruminate upon them, least of all when they touch our vanity, as is usually the case; for few misfortunes fall upon us for which we can be held entirely blameless. So people are very ready to forget many things that are disagreeable, as well as many that are unimportant.

It is from this double cause that our memory is so short; and a man's recollection of what has happened always becomes proportionately shorter, the more things that have occupied him in life. The things we did in years gone by, the events that happened long ago, are like those objects on the coast which, to the seafarer on his outward voyage, become smaller every minute, more unrecognizable and harder to distinguish.

Again, it sometimes happens that memory and imagination will call up some long past scene as vividly as if it had occurred only yesterday; so that the event in question seems to stand very near to the present time. The reason of this is that it is impossible to call up all the intervening period in the same vivid way, as there is no one figure pervading it which can be taken in at a glance; and besides, most of the things that happened in that period are forgotten, and all that remains of it is the general knowledge that we have lived through it—a mere notion of abstract existence, not a direct vision of some particular experience. It is this that causes some single event of long ago to appear as though it took place but yesterday: the intervening time vanishes, and the whole of life looks incredibly short. Nay, there are occasional moments in old age when we can scarcely believe that we are so advanced in years, or that the long past lying behind us has had any real existence—a feeling which is mainly due to the circumstance that the present always seems fixed and immovable as we look at it. These and similar mental phenomena are ultimately to be traced to the fact that it is not our nature in itself, but only the outward presentation of it, that lies in time, and that the present is the point of contact between the world as subject and the world as object.[17]

[17] *Translator's Note.*—By this remark Schopenhauer means that *will*, which, as he argues, forms the inner reality underlying all the phenomena

Again, why is it that in youth we can see no end to the years that seem to lie before us? Because we are obliged to find room for all the things we hope to attain in life. We cram the years so full of projects that if we were to try to carry them all out, death would come prematurely though we reached the age of Methuselah.

Another reason why life looks so long when we are young, is that we are apt to measure its length by the few years we have already lived. In those early years things are new to us, and so they appear important; we dwell upon them after they have happened and often call them to mind; and thus in youth life seems replete with incident, and therefore of long duration.

Sometimes we credit ourselves with a longing to be in some distant spot, whereas, in truth, we are only longing to have the time back again which we spent there—days when we were younger and fresher than we are now. In those moments Time mocks us by wearing the mask of space; and if we travel to the spot, we can see how much we have been deceived.

There are two ways of reaching a great age, both of which presuppose a sound constitution as a *conditio sine quâ non*. They may be illustrated by two lamps, one of which burns a long time with very little oil, because it has a very thin wick; and the other just as long, though it has a very thick one, because there is plenty of oil to feed it. Here, the oil is the vital energy, and the difference in the wick is the manifold way in which the vital energy is used.

Up to our thirty-sixth year, we may be compared, in respect of the way in which we use our vital energy, to people who live on the interest of their money: what they spend to-day, they have again to-morrow. But from the age of thirty-six onwards, our position is like that of the investor who begins to entrench upon his capital. At first he hardly notices any difference at all, as the greater part of his expenses is covered by the interest of his securities; and if the deficit is but slight, he pays no attention to it. But the

of life and nature, is not in itself affected by time; but that, on the other hand, time is necessary for the objectification of the will, for the will as presented in the passing phenomena of the world. Time is thus definable as the condition of change, and the present time as the only point of contact between reality and appearance.

deficit goes on increasing, until he awakes to the fact that it is becoming more serious every day: his position becomes less and less secure, and he feels himself growing poorer and poorer, while he has no expectation of this drain upon his resources coming to an end. His fall from wealth to poverty becomes faster every moment—like the fall of a solid body in space, until at last he has absolutely nothing left. A man is truly in a woeful plight if both the terms of this comparison—his vital energy and his wealth —really begin to melt away at one and the same time. It is the dread of this calamity that makes love of possession increase with age.

On the other hand, at the beginning of life, in the years before we attain majority, and for some little time afterwards— the state of our vital energy puts us on a level with those who each year lay by a part of their interest and add it to their capital: in other words, not only does their interest come in regularly, but the capital is constantly receiving additions. This happy condition of affairs is sometimes brought about—with health as with money —under the watchful care of some honest guardian. O happy youth, and sad old age!

Nevertheless, a man should economize his strength even when he is young. Aristotle [18] observes that amongst those who were victors at Olympia only two or three gained a prize at two different periods, once in boyhood and then again when they came to be men; and the reason of this was that the premature efforts which the training involved, so completely exhausted their powers that they failed to last on into manhood. As this is true of muscular, so it is still more true of nervous energy, of which all intellectual achievements are the manifestation. Hence, those infant prodigies—*ingenia praecocia*—the fruit of a hot-house education, who surprise us by their cleverness as children, afterwards turn out very ordinary folk. Nay, the manner in which boys are forced into an early acquaintance with the ancient tongues may, perhaps, be to blame for the dullness and lack of judgment which distinguish so many learned persons.

I have said that almost every man's character seems to be specially suited to some one period of life, so that on reaching

[18] *Politics.*

it the man is at his best. Some people are charming so long as they are young, and afterwards there is nothing attractive about them; others are vigorous and active in manhood, and then lose all the value they possess as they advance in years; many appear to best advantage in old age, when their character assumes a gentler tone, as becomes men who have seen the world and take life easily. This is often the case with the French.

This peculiarity must be due to the fact that the man's character has something in it akin to the qualities of youth or manhood or old age—something which accords with one or another of these periods of life, or perhaps acts as a corrective to its special failings.

The mariner observes the progress he makes only by the way in which objects on the coast fade away into the distance and apparently decrease in size. In the same way a man becomes conscious that he is advancing in years when he finds that people older than himself begin to seem young to him.

It has already been remarked that the older a man becomes, the fewer are the traces left in his mind by all that he sees, does or experiences, and the cause of this has been explained. There is thus a sense in which it may be said that it is only in youth that a man lives with a full degree of consciousness, and that he is only half alive when he is old. As the years advance, his consciousness of what goes on about him dwindles, and the things of life hurry by without making any impression upon him, just as none is made by a work of art seen for the thousandth time. A man does what his hand finds to do, and afterwards he does not know whether he has done it or not.

As life becomes more and more unconscious, the nearer it approaches the point at which all consciousness ceases, the course of time itself seems to increase in rapidity. In childhood all the things and circumstances of life are novel; and that is sufficient to awake us to the full consciousness of existence: hence, at that age, the day seems of such immense length. The same thing happens when we are traveling: one month seems longer then than four spent at home. Still, though time seems to last longer when we are young or on a journey, the sense of novelty does not prevent it from now and then in reality hanging heavily upon our hands under both these circumstances, at any rate more than is the case when we are old or staying at home. But the intellect gradually becomes so rubbed down and blunted by long habituation to such impressions that things have a constant tendency to produce less and less impression upon us as they pass by; and this makes time seem increasingly less important, and therefore shorter in duration: the hours of the boy are longer than the days of the old man. Accordingly, time goes faster and faster the longer we live, like a ball rolling down a hill. Or, to take another example: as in a revolving disc, the further a point lies from the centre, the more rapid is its rate of progression, so it is in the wheel of life; the further you stand from the beginning, the faster time moves for you. Hence it may be said that as far as concerns the immediate sensation that time makes upon our minds, the length of any given year is in direct proportion to the number of times it will divide our whole life: for instance, at the age of fifty the year appears to us only one-tenth as long as it did at the age of five.

This variation in the rate at which time appears to move, exercises a most decided influence upon the whole nature of our existence at every period of it. First of all, it causes childhood—even though it embrace only a span of fifteen years—to seem the longest period of life, and therefore the richest in reminiscences. Next, it brings it about that a man is apt to be bored just in proportion as he is young. Consider, for instance, that constant need of occupation—whether it is work or play—that is shown by children: if they come to an end of both work and play, a terrible feeling of boredom ensues. Even in youth people are by no means free from this tendency, and dread the hours when they have nothing to do. As manhood approaches, boredom disappears; and old men find the time too short when their days fly past them like arrows from a bow. Of course, I must be understood to speak of *men,* not of decrepit *brutes.* With this increased rapidity of time, boredom mostly passes away as we advance in life; and as the passions with all their attendant pain are then laid asleep, the burden of life is, on the whole, appreciably lighter in later years than in youth, provided, of course, that health remains. So it is that the period immediately preceding the weakness and troubles of old age, receives the name of a man's *best years*. That may be a true appellation, in view of the comfortable feeling which those years bring; but for all that the years of youth, when our consciousness is lively and open to every sort of impression, have this privilege—that then the seeds are sown and the buds come forth; it is the springtime of the mind. Deep truths may be perceived, but can never be excogitated—that is to say, the first knowledge of them is immediate, called forth by some momentary impression. This knowledge is of such a kind as to be attainable only when the impressions are strong, lively and deep; and if we are to be acquainted with deep truths, everything depends upon a proper use of our early years. In later life, we may be better able to work upon other people,—upon the world, because our natures are then finished and rounded off, and no more a prey to fresh views; but then the world is less able to work upon us. These are the years of action and achievement; while youth is the time for forming fundamental conceptions, and laying down the ground-work of thought.

In youth it is the outward aspect of things that most engages us; while in age, thought or reflection is the predominating quality of the mind. Hence, youth is the time for poetry, and age is more inclined to philosophy. In practical affairs it is the same: a man shapes his resolutions in youth more by the impression that the outward world makes upon him; whereas, when he is old, it is thought that determines his actions. This is partly to be explained by the fact that it is only when a man is old that the results of outward observation are present in sufficient numbers to allow of their being classified according to the ideas they represent,—a process which in its turn causes those ideas to be more fully understood in all their bearings, and the exact value and amount of trust to be placed in them, fixed and determined; while at the same time he has grown accustomed to the impressions produced by the various phenomena of life, and their effects on him are no longer what they were.

Contrarily, in youth, the impressions that things make, that is to say, the outward aspects of life, are so overpoweringly strong, especially in the case of people of lively and imaginative disposition, that they view the world like a picture; and their chief concern is the figure they cut in it, the appearance they present; nay, they are unaware of the extent to which this is the case. It is a quality of mind that shows itself—if in no other way—in that personal vanity, and that love of fine clothes, which distinguish young people.

There can be no doubt that the intellectual powers are most capable of enduring great and sustained efforts in youth, up to the age of thirty-five at latest; from which period their strength begins to decline, though very gradually. Still, the later years of life, and even old age itself, are not without their intellectual compensation. It is only then that a man can be said to be really rich in experience or in learning; he has then had .time and opportunity enough to enable him to see and think over life from all its sides; he has been able to compare one thing with another, and to discover points of contact and connecting links, so that only then are the true relations of things rightly understood. Further, in old age there comes an increased depth in the knowledge that was acquired in youth; a man has now many more illustrations of any ideas he may have attained; things which he thought he knew when he was young, he now knows in reality. And besides, his range of knowledge is wider; and in whatever direction it extends, it is thorough, and therefore formed into a consistent and connected whole; whereas in youth knowledge is always defective and fragmentary.

A complete and adequate notion of life can never be attained by any one who does not reach old age; for it is only the old man who sees life whole and knows its natural course; it is only he who is acquainted—and this is most important—not only with its entrance, like the rest of mankind, but with its exit too; so that he alone has a full sense of its utter vanity; whilst the others never cease to labor under the false notion that everything will come right in the end.

On the other hand, there is more conceptive power in youth, and at that time of life a man can make more out of the little that he knows. In age, judgment, penetration and thoroughness predominate. Youth is the time for amassing the material for a knowledge of the world that shall be distinctive and peculiar,—for an original view of life, in other words, the legacy that a man of genius leaves to his fellow-men; it is, however, only in later years that he becomes master of his material. Accordingly it will be found that, as a rule, a great writer gives his best work to the world when he is about fifty years of age. But though the tree of knowledge must reach its full height before it can bear fruit, the roots of it lie in youth.

Every generation, no matter how paltry its character, thinks itself much wiser than the one immediately preceding it, let alone those that are more remote. It is just the same with the different periods in a man's life; and yet often, in the one case no less than in the other, it is a mistaken opinion. In the years of physical growth, when our powers of mind and our stores of knowledge are receiving daily additions, it becomes a habit for to-day to look down with contempt upon yesterday. The habit strikes root, and remains even after the intellectual powers have begun to decline,—when to-day should rather look up with respect to yesterday. So it is that we often unduly depreciate the achievements as well as the judgments of our youth.

This seems the place for making the general observation, that, although in its main qualities a man's *intellect* or *head,* as well as his *character* or *heart,* is innate, yet the former is by no means so unalterable in its nature as the latter. The fact is that the intellect is subject to very many transformations, which, as a rule, do not fail to make their actual appearance; and this is so, partly because the intellect has a deep foundation in the physique, and partly because the material with which it deals is given in experience. And so, from a physical point of view, we find that if a man has any peculiar power, it first gradually increases in strength until it reaches its acme, after which it enters upon a path of slow decadence, until it ends in imbecility. But, on the other hand, we must not lose sight of the fact that the material which gives employment to a man's powers and keeps them in activity,—the subject-matter of thought and knowledge, experience, intellectual attainments, the practice of seeing to the bottom of things, and so a perfect mental vision, form in themselves a mass which continues to increase in size, until the time comes when weakness shows itself, and the man's powers suddenly fail. The way in which these two distinguishable elements combine in the same nature,—the one absolutely unalterable, and the other subject to change in two directions opposed to each other—explains the variety of mental attitude and the dissimilarity of value which attach to a man at different periods of life.

The same truth may be more broadly expressed by saying that the first forty years of life furnish the text, while the remaining thirty supply the commentary; and that without the commentary we are unable to understand aright the true sense and coherence of the text, together with the moral it contains and all the subtle application of which it admits.

Towards the close of life, much the same thing happens as at the end of a *bal masqué*—the masks are taken off. Then you can see who the people really are, with whom you have come into contact in your passage through the world. For by the end of life characters have come out in their true light, actions have borne fruit, achievements have been rightly appreciated, and all shams have fallen to pieces. For this, Time was in every case requisite.

But the most curious fact is that it is also only towards the close of life than a man really recognizes and understands his own true self,—the aims and objects he has followed in life, more especially the kind of relation in which he has stood to other people and to the world. It will often happen that as a result of this knowledge, a man will have to assign himself a lower place than he formerly thought was his due. But there are exceptions to this rule; and it will occasionally be the case that he will take a higher position than he had before. This will be owing to the fact that he had no adequate notion of the *baseness* of the world, and that he set up a higher aim for himself than was followed by the rest of mankind.

The progress of life shows a man the stuff of which he is made.

It is customary to call youth the happy, and age the sad part of life. This would be true if it were the passions that made a man happy. Youth is swayed to and fro by them; and they give a great deal of pain and little pleasure. In age the passions cool and leave a man at rest, and then forthwith his mind takes a contemplative tone; the intellect is set free and attains the upper hand. And since, in itself, intellect is beyond the range of pain, man feels happy just in so far as his intellect is the predominating part of him.

It need only be remembered that all pleasure is negative, and that pain is positive in its nature, in order to see that the passions can never be a source of happiness, and that age is not the less to be envied on the ground that many pleasures are denied it. For every sort of pleasure is never anything more than the quietive of some need or longing; and that pleasure should come to an end as soon as the need ceases, is no more a subject of complaint than that a man cannot go on eating after he has had his dinner, or fall asleep again after a good night's rest.

So far from youth being the happiest period of life, there is much more truth in the remark made by Plato, at the beginning of the *Republic,* that the prize should rather be given to old age, because then at last a man is freed from the animal passion which has hitherto never ceased to disquiet him. Nay, it may even be said that the countless and manifold humors which have their source in this passion, and the emotions that spring from it, produce a mild state of madness; and this lasts as long as the man is subject to the spell of the impulse—this evil spirit, as it were, of which there is no riddance—so that he never really becomes a reasonable being until the passion is extinguished.

There is no doubt that, in general, and apart from individual circumstances and particular dispositions, youth is marked by a certain melancholy and sadness, while genial sentiments attach to old age; and the reason for this is nothing but the fact that the young man is still under the service, nay, the forced labor, imposed by that evil spirit, which scarcely ever leaves him a moment to himself. To this source may be traced, directly or indirectly, almost all and every ill that befalls or menaces mankind. The old man is genial and cheerful because, after long lying in the bonds of passion, he can now move about in freedom.

Still, it should not be forgotten that, when this passion is extinguished, the true kernel of life is gone, and nothing remains but the hollow shell; or, from another point of view, life then becomes like a comedy, which, begun by real actors, is continued and brought to an end by automata dressed in their clothes.

However that may be, youth is the period of unrest, and age

of repose; and from that very circumstance, the relative degree of pleasure belonging to each may be inferred. The child stretches out its little hands in the eager desire to seize all the pretty things that meet its sight, charmed by the world because all its senses are still so young and fresh. Much the same thing happens with the youth, and he displays greater energy in his quest. He, too, is charmed by all the pretty things and the many pleasing shapes that surround him; and forthwith his imagination conjures up pleasures which the world can never realize. So he is filled with an ardent desire for he knows not what delights—robbing him of all rest and making happiness impossible. But when old age is reached, all this is over and done with, partly because the blood runs cooler and the senses are no longer so easily allured; partly because experience has shown the true value of things and the futility of pleasure, whereby illusion has been gradually dispelled, and the strange fancies and prejudices which previously concealed or distorted a free and true view of the world, have been dissipated and put to flight; with the result that a man can now get a juster and clearer view, and see things as they are, and also in a measure attain more or less insight into the nullity of all things on this earth.

It is this that gives almost every old man, no matter how ordinary his faculties may be, a certain tincture of wisdom, which distinguishes him from the young. But the chief result of all this change is the peace of mind that ensues—a great element in happiness, and, in fact, the condition and essence of it. While the young man fancies that there is a vast amount of good things in the world, if he could only come at them, the old man is steeped in the truth of the Preacher's words, that *all things are vanity*—knowing that, however gilded the shell, the nut is hollow.

In these later years, and not before, a man comes to a true appreciation of Horace's maxim: *Nil admirari*. He is directly and sincerely convinced of the vanity of everything and that all the glories of the world are as nothing: his illusions are gone. He is no more beset with the idea that there is any particular amount of happiness anywhere, in the palace or in the cottage, any more than he himself enjoys when he is free from bodily or mental pain. The worldly distinctions of great and small, high and low, exist for him no longer; and in this blissful state of mind the old man may look down with a smile upon all false notions. He is completely undeceived, and knows that whatever may be done to adorn human life and deck it out in finery, its paltry character will soon show through the glitter of its surroundings; and that, paint and bejewel it as one may, it remains everywhere much the same,—an existence which has no true value except in freedom from pain, and is never to be estimated by the presence of pleasure, let alone, then, of display.[19]

Disillusion is the chief characteristic of old age; for by that time the fictions are gone which gave life its charm and spurred on the mind to activity; the splendors of the world have been proved null and vain; its pomp, grandeur and magnificence are faded. A man has then found out that behind most of the things he wants, and most of the pleasures he longs for, there is very little after all; and so he comes by degrees to see that our existence is all empty and void. It is only when he is seventy years old that he quite understands the first words of the Preacher; and this again explains why it is that old men are sometimes fretful and morose.

It is often said that the common lot of old age is disease and weariness of life. Disease is by no means essential to old age; especially where a really long span of years is to be attained; for as life goes on, the conditions of health and disorder tend to increase—*crescente vita, crescit sanitas et morbus*. And as far as weariness or boredom is concerned, I have stated above why old age is even less exposed to that form of evil than youth. Nor is boredom by any means to be taken as a necessary accompaniment of that solitude, which, for reasons that do not require to be explained, old age certainly cannot escape; it is rather the fate that awaits those who have never known any other pleasures but the gratification of the senses and the delights of society—who have left their minds unenlightened and their faculties unused. It is quite true that the intellectual faculties decline with the approach of old age; but where they were originally strong, there will always be enough left to combat the onslaught of boredom. And then again, as I have said, experience, knowledge, reflection, and skill in dealing with men, combine to give an old man an

[19] Cf. Horace, *Epist.* I., 12, 1-4.

increasingly accurate insight into the ways of the world; his judgment becomes keen and he attains a coherent view of life: his mental vision embraces a wider range. Constantly finding new uses for his stores of knowledge and adding to them at every opportunity, he maintains uninterrupted that inward process of self-education, which gives employment and satisfaction to the mind, and thus forms the due reward of all its efforts.

All this serves in some measure as a compensation for decreased intellectual power. And besides, Time, as I have remarked, seems to go much more quickly when we are advanced in years; and this is in itself a preventive of boredom. There is no great harm in the fact that a man's bodily strength decreases in old age, unless, indeed, he requires it to make a living. To be poor when one is old, is a great misfortune. If a man is secure from that, and retains his health, old age may be a very passable time of life. Its chief necessity is to be comfortable and well off; and, in consequence, money is then prized more than ever, because it is a substitute for failing strength. Deserted by Venus, the old man likes to turn to Bacchus to make him merry. In the place of wanting to see things, to travel and learn, comes the desire to speak and teach. It is a piece of good fortune if the old man retains some of his love of study or of music or of the theatre,—if, in general, he is still somewhat susceptible to the things about him; as is, indeed, the case with some people to a very late age. At that time of life, *what a man has in himself* is of greater advantage to him than ever it was before.

There can be no doubt that most people who have never been anything but dull and stupid, become more and more of automata as they grow old. They have always thought, said and done the same things as their neighbors; and nothing that happens now can change their disposition, or make them act otherwise. To talk to old people of this kind is like writing on the sand; if you produce any impression at all, it is gone almost immediately; old age is here nothing but the *caput mortuum* of life—all that is essential to manhood is gone. There are cases in which nature supplies a third set of teeth in old age, thereby apparently demonstrating the fact that that period of life is a second childhood.

It is certainly a very melancholy thing that all a man's faculties tend to waste away as he grows old, and at a rate that increases in rapidity: but still, this is a necessary, nay, a beneficial, arrangement, as otherwise death, for which it is a preparation, would be too hard to bear. So the greatest boon that follows the attainment of extreme old age is *euthanasia,*—an easy death, not ushered in by disease, and free from all pain and struggle.[20] For let a man live as long as he may, he is never conscious of any moment but the present, one and indivisible; and in those late years the mind loses more every day by sheer forgetfulness than ever it gains anew.

The main difference between youth and age will always be that youth looks forward to life, and old age to death; and that while the one has a short past and a long future before it, the case is just the opposite with the other. It is quite true that when a man is old, to die is the only thing that awaits him; while if he is young, he may expect to live; and the question arises which of the two fates is the more hazardous, and if life is not a matter which, on the whole, it is better to have behind one than before? Does not the Preacher say: *the day of death* [*is better*] *than the day of one's birth?* [21] It is certainly a rash thing to wish for long life; [22] for as the Spanish proverb has it, it means to see much evil,—*Quien larga vida vive mucho mal vide.*

[20] See *Die Welt als Wille und Vorstellung,* Bk. II., ch. 41, for a further description of this happy end to life.

[21] Ecclesiastes vii., 1.

[22] The life of man cannot, strictly speaking, be called either *long* or *short,* since it is the ultimate standard by which duration of time in regard to all other things is measured.

In one of the Vedic *Upanishads* (*Oupnekhat,* II.) the natural length of human life is put down at one hundred years. And I believe this to be right. I have observed, as a matter of fact that it is only people who exceed the age of ninety who attain *euthanasia,*—who die, that is to say, of no disease, apoplexy or convulsion, and pass away without agony of any sort; nay, who sometimes even show no pallor, but expire generally in a sitting attitude, and often after a meal,—or, I may say, simply cease to live rather than die. To come to one's end before the age of ninety, means to die of disease, in other words, prematurely.

Now the Old Testament (Psalms xc., 10) puts the limit of human life at seventy, and if it is very long, at eighty years; and what is more noticeable still, Herodotus (i., 32 and iii., 22) says the same thing. But this is wrong; and the error is due simply to a rough and superficial estimate of the results of daily experience. For if the natural length of life were from seventy to eighty years, people would die, about that time, of

A man's individual career is not, as Astrology wishes to make out, to be predicted from observation of the planets; but the course of human life in general, as far as the various periods of it are concerned, may be likened to the succession of the planets: so that we may be said to pass under the influence of each one of them in turn.

At ten, *Mercury* is in the ascendant; and at that age, a youth, like this planet, is characterized by extreme mobility within a narrow sphere, where trifles have a great effect upon him; but under the guidance of so crafty and eloquent a god, he easily makes great progress. *Venus* begins her sway during his twentieth year, and then a man is wholly given up to the love of women. At thirty, *Mars* comes to the front, and he is now all energy and strength,—daring, pugnacious and arrogant.

When a man reaches the age of forty, he is under the rule of the four *Asteroids;* that is to say, his life has gained something in extension. He is frugal; in other words, by the help of *Ceres,* he favors what is useful; he has his own hearth, by the influence of *Vesta; Pallas* has taught him that which is necessary for him to know; and his wife—his *Juno*—rules as the mistress of his house.

But at the age of fifty, *Jupiter* is the dominant influence. At that period a man has outlived most of his contemporaries, and he can feel himself superior to the generation about him. He is still in the full enjoyment of his strength, and rich in experience and knowledge; and if he has any power and position of his own, he is endowed with authority over all who stand in his immediate surroundings. He is no more inclined to receive orders from others; he wants to take command himself. The work most suitable to him now is to guide and rule within his own sphere. This is the point

mere old age. Now this is certainly not the case. If they die then, they die, like younger people, *of disease;* and disease is something abnormal. Therefore it is not natural to die at that age. It is only when they are between ninety and a hundred that people die of old age; die, I mean, without suffering from any disease, or showing any special signs of their condition, such as a struggle, death-rattle, convulsion, pallor,—the absence of all which constitutes *euthanasia.* The natural length of human life is a hundred years; and in assigning that limit the Upanishads are right once more.

where Jupiter culminates, and where the man of fifty years is at his best.

Then comes *Saturn,* at about the age of sixty, a weight as of *lead,* dull and slow:—

> *But old folks, many feign as they were dead;*
> *Unwieldy, slow, heavy and pale as lead.*

Last of all, *Uranus;* or, as the saying is, a man goes to heaven.

I cannot find a place for *Neptune,* as this planet has been very thoughtlessly named; because I may not call it as it should be called—*Eros.* Otherwise I should point out how Beginning and End meet together, and how closely and intimately Eros is connected with Death: how Orcus, or Amenthes, as the Egyptians called him, is not only the receiver but the giver of all things— λαμβάνων καὶ διδούς. Death is the great reservoir of Life. Everything comes from Orcus; everything that is alive now was once there. Could we but understand the great trick by which that is done, all would be clear!

III. STUDIES IN PESSIMISM

SO far as I know, none but the votaries of monotheistic, that is to say, Jewish religions, look upon suicide as a crime. This is all the more striking, inasmuch as neither in the Old nor in the New Testament is there to be found any prohibition or positive disapproval of it; so that religious teachers are forced to base their condemnation of suicide on philosophical grounds of their own invention. These are so very bad that writers of this kind endeavor to make up for the weakness of their arguments by the strong terms in which they express their abhorrence of the practice; in other words, they declaim against it. They tell us that suicide is the greatest piece of cowardice; that only a madman could be guilty of it; and other insipidities of the same kind; or else they make the nonsensical remark that suicide is *wrong;* when it is quite obvious that there is nothing in the world to which every man has a more unassailable right than to his own life and person.

Suicide, as I have said, is actually accounted a crime; and a crime which, especially under the vulgar bigotry that prevails in England, is followed by an ignominious burial and the seizure of the man's property; and for that reason, in a case of suicide, the jury almost always brings in a verdict of insanity. Now let the reader's own moral feelings decide as to whether or not suicide is a criminal act. Think of the impression that would be made upon you by the news that some one you know had committed the crime, say, of murder or theft, or been guilty of some act of cruelty or deception; and compare it with your feelings when you hear that he has met a voluntary death. While in the one case a lively sense of indignation and extreme resentment will be aroused, and you will call loudly for punishment or revenge, in the other you will be moved to grief and sympathy; and mingled with your thoughts will be admiration for his courage, rather than the moral disapproval which follows upon a wicked action. Who has not had acquaintances, friends, relations, who of their own free will have left this world; and are these to be thought of with horror as criminals? Most emphatically, No! I am rather of opinion that the clergy should be challenged to explain what right they have to go into the pulpit, or take up their pens, and stamp as a crime an action which many men whom we hold in affection and honor have committed; and to refuse an honorable burial to those who relinquish this world voluntarily. They have no Biblical authority to boast of, as justifying their condemnation of suicide; nay, not even any philosophical arguments that will hold water; and it must be understood that it is arguments we want, and that we will not be put off with mere phrases or words of abuse. If the criminal law forbids suicide, that is not an argument valid in the Church; and besides, the prohibition is ridiculous; for what penalty can frighten a man who is not afraid of death itself? If the law punishes people for trying to commit suicide, it is punishing the want of skill that makes the attempt a failure.

The ancients, moreover, were very far from regarding the matter in that light. Pliny says: *Life is not so desirable a thing as to be protracted at any cost. Whoever you are, you are sure to die, even though your life has been full of abomination and crime. The chief of all remedies for a troubled mind is the feeling that among the blessings which Nature gives to man, there is none greater than an opportune death; and the best of it is that every one can avail himself of it.*[1] And elsewhere the same writer declares: *Not even to God are all things possible; for He could not compass His own death, if He willed to die, and yet in all the miseries of our earthly life, this is the best of His gifts to man.*[2] Nay, in Massilia and on the isle of Ceos, the man who could give valid reasons for relinquishing his life, was handed the cup of hemlock by the magistrate; and that, too, in public.[3] And in

---

[1] Hist. Nat. Lib. xxviii., 1.
[2] Loc. cit. Lib. ii., c. 7.
[3] Valerius Maximus; hist. Lib. ii., c. 6, § 7 et 8. Heraclides Ponticus; fragmenta de rebus publicis, ix. Aeliani variæ historiæ, iii., 37. Strabo; Lib. x., c. 5, 6.

ancient times, how many heroes and wise men died a voluntary
death. Aristotle,[4] it is true, declared suicide to be an offense
against the State, although not against the person; but in Stobæus'
exposition of the Peripatetic philosophy there is the following
remark: *The good man should flee life when his misfortunes become too great; the bad man, also, when he is too prosperous.* And
similarly: *So he will marry and beget children and take part in the
affairs of the State, and, generally, practice virtue and continue to
live; and then, again, if need be, and at any time necessity compels
him, he will depart to his place of refuge in the tomb.*[5] And we
find that the Stoics actually praised suicide as a noble and heroic
action, as hundreds of passages show; above all in the works of
Seneca, who expresses the strongest approval of it. As is well
known, the Hindoos look upon suicide as a religious act, especially
when it takes the form of self-immolation by widows; but also
when it consists in casting oneself under the wheels of the chariot
of the god Juggernaut, or being eaten by crocodiles in the Ganges,
or being drowned in the holy tanks in the temples, and so on.
The same thing occurs on the stage—that mirror of life. For
example, in *L'Orphelin de la Chine,*[6] a celebrated Chinese play,
almost all the noble characters end by suicide; without the
slightest hint anywhere, or any impression being produced on the
spectator, that they are committing a crime. And in our own
theatre it is much the same—Palmira, for instance, in *Mahomet,*
or Mortimer in *Maria Stuart,* Othello, Countess Terzky.[7] Is
Hamlet's monologue the meditation of a criminal? He merely
declares that if we had any certainty of being annihilated by it,
death would be infinitely preferable to the world as it is. But
there lies the rub!

The reasons advanced against suicide by the clergy of monotheistic, that is to say, Jewish religions, and by those philosophers
who adapt themselves thereto, are weak sophisms which can easily

---

[4] *Eth. Nichom.,* v. 15.
[5] Stobæus. *Ecl. Eth.* ii., c. 7, pp. 286, 312.
[6] Traduit par St. Julien, 1834.
[7] *Translator's Note.*—Palmira: a female slave in Goethe's play of
Mahomet. Mortimer: a would-be lover and rescuer of Mary in Schiller's
Maria Stuart. Countess Terzky: a leading character in Schiller's *Wallenstein's Tod.*

be refuted.[8] The most thorough-going refutation of them is given by Hume in his *Essay on Suicide*. This did not appeal until after his death, when it was immediately suppressed, owing to the scandalous bigotry and outrageous ecclesiastical tyranny that prevailed in England; and hence only a very few copies of it were sold under cover of secrecy and at a high price. This and another treatise by that great man have come to us from Basle, and we may be thankful for the reprint.[9] It is a great disgrace to the English nation that a purely philosophical treatise, which, proceeding from one of the first thinkers and writers in England, aimed at refuting the current arguments against suicide by the light of cold reason, should be forced to sneak about in that country, as though it were some rascally production, until at last it found refuge on the Continent. At the same time it shows what a good conscience the Church has in such matters.

In my chief work I have explained the only valid reason existing against suicide on the score of morality. It is this: that suicide thwarts the attainment of the highest moral aim by the fact that, for a real release from this world of misery, it substitutes one that is merely apparent. But from a *mistake* to a *crime* is a far cry; and it is as a crime that the clergy of Christendom wish us to regard suicide.

The inmost kernel of Christianity is the truth that suffering— *the Cross*—is the real end and object of life. Hence Christianity condemns suicide as thwarting this end; whilst the ancient world, taking a lower point of view, held it in approval, nay, in honor.[10] But if that is to be accounted a valid reason against suicide, it in-

[8] See my treatise on the *Foundation of Morals*, § 5.

[9] *Essays on Suicide* and the *Immortality of the Soul*, by the late David Hume, Basle, 1799, sold by James Decker.

[10] *Translator's Note.*—Schopenhauer refers to *Die Welt als Wille und Vorstellung*, vol. i., § 69, where the reader may find the same argument stated at somewhat greater length. According to Schopenhauer, moral freedom—the highest ethical aim—is to be obtained only by a denial of the will to live. Far from being a denial, suicide is an emphatic assertion of this will. For it is in fleeing from the pleasures, not from the sufferings of life, that this denial consists. When a man destroys his existence as an individual, he is not by any means destroying his will to live. On the contrary, he would like to live if he could do so with satisfaction to himself; if he could assert his will against the power of circumstance; but circumstance is too strong for him.

volves the recognition of asceticism; that is to say, it is valid only from a much higher ethical standpoint than has ever been adopted by moral philosophers in Europe. If we abandon that high standpoint, there is no tenable reason left, on the score of morality, for condemning suicide. The extraordinary energy and zeal with which the clergy of monotheistic religions attack suicide is not supported either by any passages in the Bible or by any considerations of weight; so that it looks as though they must have some secret reason for their contention. May it not be this—that the voluntary surrender of life is a bad compliment for him who said that *all things were very good?* If this is so, it offers another instance of the crass optimism of these religions,—denouncing suicide to escape being denounced by it.

It will generally be found that, as soon as the terrors of life reach the point at which they outweigh the terrors of death, a man will put an end to his life. But the terrors of death offer considerable resistance; they stand like a sentinel at the gate leading out of this world. Perhaps there is no man alive who would not have already put an end to his life, if this end had been of a purely negative character, a sudden stoppage of existence. There is something positive about it; it is the destruction of the body; and a man shrinks from that, because his body is the manifestation of the will to live.

However, the struggle with that sentinel is, as a rule, not so hard as it may seem from a long way off, mainly in consequence of the antagonism between the ills of the body and the ills of the mind. If we are in great bodily pain, or the pain lasts a long time, we become indifferent to other troubles; all we think about is to get well. In the same way great mental suffering makes us insensible to bodily pain; we despise it; nay, if it should outweigh the other, it distracts our thoughts, and we welcome it as a pause in mental suffering. It is this feeling that makes suicide easy; for the bodily pain that accompanies it loses all significance in the eyes of one who is tortured by an excess of mental suffering. This is especially evident in the case of those who are driven to suicide by some purely morbid and exaggerated ill-humor. No special effort to overcome their feelings is necessary, nor do such people require to be worked up in order to take the step; but as soon as the keeper into whose charge they are given leaves them for a couple of minutes, they quickly bring their life to an end.

When, in some dreadful and ghastly dream, we reach the moment of greatest horror, it awakes us; thereby banishing all the hideous shapes that were born of the .night. And life is a dream: when the moment of greatest horror compels us to break it off, the same thing happens.

Suicide may also be regarded as an experiment—a question which man puts to Nature, trying to force her to an answer. The question is this: What change will death produce in a man's existence and in his insight into the nature of things? It is a clumsy experiment to make; for it involves the destruction of the very consciousness which puts the question and awaits the answer.

2. ON EDUCATION

THE human intellect is said to be so constituted that *general ideas* arise by abstraction from *particular observations,* and therefore come after them in point of time. If this is what actually occurs, as happens in the case of a man who has to depend solely upon his own experience for what he learns—who has no teacher and no book,—such a man knows quite well which of his particular observations belong to and are represented by each of his general ideas. He has a perfect acquaintance with both sides of his experience, and accordingly, he treats everything that comes in his way from a right standpoint. This might be called the *natural* method of education.

Contrarily, the *artificial* method is to hear what other people say, to learn and to read, and so to get your head crammed full of general ideas before you have any sort of extended acquaintance with the world as it is, and as you may see it for yourself. You will be told that the particular observations which go to make these general ideas will come to you later on in the course of experience; but until that time arrives, you apply your general ideas wrongly, you judge men and things from a wrong standpoint, you see them in a wrong light, and treat them in a wrong way. So it is that education perverts the mind.

This explains why it so frequently happens that, after a long course of learning and reading, we enter upon the world in our youth, partly with an artless ignorance of things, partly with wrong notions about them; so that our demeanor savors at one moment of a nervous anxiety, at another of a mistaken confidence. The reason of this is simply that our head is full of general ideas which we are now trying to turn to some use, but which we hardly ever apply rightly.(This is the result of acting in direct opposition to the natural development of the mind by obtaining general ideas first, and particular observations last: it is putting

438

the cart before the horse.) Instead of developing the child's own faculties of discernment, and teaching it to judge and think for itself, the teacher uses all his energies to stuff its head full of the ready-made thoughts of other people. The mistaken views of life, which spring from a false application of general ideas, have afterwards to be corrected by long years of experience; and it is seldom that they are wholly corrected. This is why so few men of learning are possessed of common-sense, such as is often to be met with in people who have had no instruction at all.

To acquire a knowledge of the world might be defined as the aim of all education; and it follows from what I have said that special stress should be laid upon beginning to acquire this knowledge *at the right end*. As I have shown, this means, in the main, that the particular observation of a thing shall precede the general idea of it; further, that narrow and circumscribed ideas shall come before ideas of a wide range. It means, therefore, that the whole system of education shall follow in the steps that must have been taken by the ideas themselves in the course of their formation. But whenever any of these steps are skipped or left out, the instruction is defective, and the ideas obtained are false; and finally, a distorted view of the world arises, peculiar to the individual himself—a view such as almost everyone entertains for some time, and most men for as long as they live. No one can look into his own mind without seeing that it was only after reaching a very mature age, and in some cases when he least expected it, that he came to a right understanding or a clear view of many matters in his life, that, after all, were not very difficult or complicated. Up till then, they were points in his knowledge of the world which were still obscure, due to his having skipped some particular lesson in those early days of his education, whatever it may have been like—whether artificial and conventional, or of that natural kind which is based upon individual experience.

It follows that an attempt should be made to find out the strictly natural course of knowledge, so that education may proceed methodically by keeping to it; and that children may become acquainted with the ways of the world, without getting wrong ideas into their heads, which very often cannot be got out again. If this plan were adopted, special care would have to be taken to prevent children from using words without clearly understanding their meaning and application. The fatal tendency to be satisfied with words instead of trying to understand things—to learn phrases by heart, so that they may prove a refuge in time of need, exists, as a rule, even in children; and the tendency lasts on into manhood, making the knowledge of many learned persons to consist in mere verbiage.

However, the main endeavor must always be to let particular observations precede general ideas, and not *vice versa,* as is usually and unfortunately the case; as though a child should come feet foremost into the world, or a verse be begun by writing down the rhyme! The ordinary method is to imprint ideas and opinions, in the strict sense of the word, *prejudices,* on the mind of the child, before it has had any but a very few particular observations. It is thus that he afterwards comes to view the world and gather experience through the medium of those ready-made ideas, rather than to let his ideas be formed for him out of his own experience of life, as they ought to be.

A man sees a great many things when he looks at the world for himself, and he sees them from many sides; but this method of learning is not nearly so short or so quick as the method which employs abstract ideas and makes hasty generalizations about everything. Experience, therefore, will be a long time in correcting preconceived ideas, or perhaps never bring its task to an end; for wherever a man finds that the aspect of things seem to contradict the general ideas he has formed, he will begin by rejecting the evidence it offers as partial and one-sided; nay, he will shut his eyes to it altogether and deny that it stands in any contradiction at all with his preconceived notions, in order that he may thus preserve them uninjured. So it is that many a man carries about a burden of wrong notions all his life long—crotchets, whims, fancies, prejudices, which at last become fixed ideas. The fact is that he has never tried to form his fundamental ideas for himself out of his own experience of life, his own way of looking at the world, because he has taken over his ideas ready-made from other people; and this it is that makes him—as it makes how many others!—so shallow and superficial.

Instead of that method of instruction, care should be taken to educate children on the natural lines. No idea should ever be established in a child's mind otherwise than by what the child can see for itself, or at any rate it should be verified by the same means; and the result of this would be that the child's ideas, if few, would be well-grounded and accurate. It would learn how to measure things by its own standard rather than by another's; and so it would escape a thousand strange fancies and prejudices, and not need to have them eradicated by the lessons it will subsequently be taught in the school of life. The child would, in this way, have its mind once for all habituated to clear views and thorough-going knowledge; it would use its own judgment and take an unbiased estimate of things.

And, in general, children should not form their notions of what life is like from the copy before they have learned it from the original, to whatever aspect of it their attention may be directed. Instead, therefore, of hastening to place *books,* and books alone, in their hands, let them be made acquainted, step by step, with *things*—with the actual circumstances of human life. And above all let care be taken to bring them to a clear and objective view of the world as it is, to educate them always to derive their ideas directly from real life, and to shape them in conformity with it—not to fetch them from other sources, such as books, fairy tales, or what people say—then to apply them ready-made to real life. For this will mean that their heads are full of wrong notions, and that they will either see things in a false light or try in vain to *remodel the world* to suit their views, and so enter upon false paths; and that, too, whether they are only constructing theories of life or engaged in the actual business of it. It is incredible how much harm is done when the seeds of wrong notions are laid in the mind in those early years, later on to bear a crop of prejudice; for the subsequent lessons, which are learned from real life in the world, have to be devoted mainly to their extirpation. *To unlearn the evil* was the answer, according to Diogenes Laertius, Anthisthenes gave, when he was asked what branch of knowledge was most necessary; and we can see what he meant.

No child under the age of fifteen should receive instruction in subjects which may possibly be the vehicle of serious error, such as philosophy, religion, or any other branch of knowledge where it is necessary to take large views; because wrong notions imbibed early can seldom be rooted out, and of all the intellectual faculties, judgment is the last to arrive at maturity. The child should give its attention either to subjects where no error is possible at all, such as mathematics, or to those in which there is no particular danger in making a mistake, such as languages, natural science, history, and so on. And in general, the branches of knowledge which are to be studied at any period of life should be such as the mind is equal to at that period and can perfectly understand. Childhood and youth form the time for collecting materials, for getting a special and thorough knowledge of the individual and particular things. In those years it is too early to form views on a large scale; and ultimate explanations must be put off to a later date. The faculty of judgment, which cannot come into play without mature experience, should be left to itself; and care should be taken not to anticipate its action by inculcating prejudice, which will paralyze it for ever.

On the other hand, the memory should be specially taxed in youth, since it is then that it is strongest and most tenacious. But in choosing the things that should be committed to memory the utmost care and forethought must be exercised; as lessons well learnt in youth are never forgotten. This precious soil must therefore be cultivated so as to bear as much fruit as possible. If you think how deeply rooted in your memory are those persons whom you knew in the first twelve years of your life, how indelible the impression made upon you by the events of those years, how clear your recollection of most of the things that happened to you then, most of what was told or taught you, it will seem a natural thing to take the susceptibility and tenacity of the mind at that period as the ground work of education. This may be done by a strict observance of method, and a systematic regulation of the impressions which the mind is to receive.

But the years of youth allotted to a man are short, and memory is, in general, bound within narrow limits; still more so, the memory of any one individual. Since this is the case, it is all-important to fill the memory with what is essential and material in any branch of knowledge, to the exclusion of everything else. The decision as to what is essential and material should rest with the master-minds in every department of thought; their choice should be made after the most mature deliberation, and the outcome of it fixed and determined. Such a choice would have to proceed by sifting the things which it is necessary and important for a man to know in general, and then, necessary and important for him to know in any particular business or calling. Knowledge of the first kind would have to be classified, after an encyclopædic fashion, in graduated courses, adapted to the degree of general culture which a man may be expected to have in the circumstances in which he is placed; beginning with a course limited to the necessary requirements of primary education, and extending upwards to the subjects treated of in all the branches of philosophical thought. The regulation of the second kind of knowledge would be left to those who had shown genuine mastery in the several departments into which it is divided; and the whole system would provide an elaborate rule or canon for intellectual education, which would, of course, have to be revised every ten years. Some such arrangement as this would employ the youthful power of the memory to best advantage, and supply excellent working material to the faculty of judgment, when it made its appearance later on.

A man's knowledge may be said to be mature, in other words, it has reached the most complete state of perfection to which he, as an individual, is capable of bringing it, when an exact correspondence is established between the whole of his abstract ideas and the things he has actually perceived for himself. This will mean that each of his abstract ideas rests, directly or indirectly, upon a basis of observation, which alone endows it with any real value; and also that he is able to place every observation he makes under the right abstract idea which belongs to it. Maturity is the work of experience alone; and therefore it requires time. The knowledge we derive from our own observation is usually distinct from that which we acquire through the medium of abstract ideas; the one coming to us in the natural way, the other by what people tell us, and the course of instruction we receive, whether it is good or bad. The result is, that in youth there is generally very little agreement or correspondence between our abstract ideas, which are merely phases in the mind, and that real knowledge which we have obtained by our own observation. It is only later on that a gradual approach

takes place between these two kinds of knowledge, accompanied
by a mutual correction of error; and knowledge is not mature until this coalition is accomplished. This maturity or perfection of
knowledge is something quite independent of another kind of perfection, which may be of a high or a low order—the perfection, I
mean, to which a man may bring his own individual faculties;
which is measured, not by any correspondence between the two
kinds of knowledge, but by the degree of intensity which each kind
attains.

For the practical man the most needful thing is to acquire an
accurate and profound knowledge of *the ways of the world.* But
this, though the most needful, is also the most wearisome of all
studies, as a man may reach a great age without coming to the
end of his task; whereas, in the domain of the sciences, he masters
the more important facts when he is still young. In acquiring that
knowledge of the world, it is while he is a novice, namely, in boyhood and in youth, that the first and hardest lessons are put before
him; but it often happens that even in later years there is still a
great deal to be learned.

The study is difficult enough in itself; but the difficulty is
doubled by *novels,* which represent a state of things in life and
the world, such as, in fact, does not exist. Youth is credulous, and
accepts these views of life, which then become part and parcel
of the mind; so that, instead of a merely negative condition of
ignorance, you have positive error—a whole tissue of false notions
to start with; and at a later date these actually spoil the schooling
of experience, and put a wrong construction on the lessons it
teaches. If, before this, the youth had no light at all to guide him,
he is now misled by a will-o'-the-wisp; still more often is this the
case with a girl. They have both had a false view of things foisted
on them by reading novels; and expectations have been aroused
which can never be fulfilled. This generally exercises a baneful
influence on their whole life. In this respect those whose youth has
allowed them no time or opportunity for reading novels—those
who work with their hands and the like—are in a position of
decided advantage. There are a few novels to which this reproach
cannot be addressed—nay, which have an effect the contrary
of bad. First and foremost, to give an example, *Gil Blas,* and the

other works of Le Sage (or rather their Spanish originals) ; further, *The Vicar of Wakefield,* and, to some extent Sir Walter Scott's novels. *Don Quixote* may be regarded as a satirical exhibition of the error to which I am referring.

SCHILLER'S poem in honor of women, *Würde der Frauen,* is the result of much careful thought, and it appeals to the reader by its antithetic style and its use of contrast; but as an expression of the true praise which should be accorded to them, it is, I think, inferior to these few words of Jouy's: *Without women, the beginning of our life would be helpless; the middle, devoid of pleasure; and the end, of consolation.* The same thing is more feelingly expressed by Byron in *Sardanapalus:*

> *The very first*
> *Of human life must spring from woman's breast,*
> *Your first small words are taught you from her lips,*
> *Your first tears quench'd by her, and your last sighs*
> *Too often breathed out in a woman's hearing,*
> *When men have shrunk from the ignoble care*
> *Of watching the last hour of him who led them.*
>
> (Act I., Scene 2.)

These two passages indicate the right standpoint for the appreciation of women.

You need only look at the way in which she is formed, to see that woman is not meant to undergo great labor, whether of the mind or of the body. She pays the debt of life not by what she does, but by what she suffers; by the pains of childbearing and care for the child, and by submission to her husband, to whom she should be a patient and cheering companion. The keenest sorrows and joys are not for her, nor is she called upon to display a great deal of strength. The current of her life should be more gentle, peaceful and trivial than man's, without being essentially happier or unhappier.

Women are directly fitted for acting as the nurses and teachers of our early childhood by the fact that they are themselves childish, frivolous and short-sighted; in a word, they are big children all

446

their life long—a kind of intermediate stage between the child and the full-grown man, who is man in the strict sense of the word. See how a girl will fondle a child for days together, dance with it and sing to it; and then think what a man, with the best will in the world, could do if he were put in her place.

With young girls Nature seems to have had in view what, in the language of the drama, is called *a striking effect;* as for a few years she dowers them with a wealth of beauty and is lavish in her gift of charm, at the expense of all the rest of their life; so that during those years they may capture the fantasy of some man to such a degree that he is hurried away into undertaking the honorable care of them, in some form or other, as long as they live—a step for which there would not appear to be any sufficient warranty if reason only directed his thoughts. Accordingly, Nature has equipped woman, as she does all her creatures, with the weapons and implements requisite for the safe-guarding of her existence, and for just as long as it is necessary for her to have them. Here, as elsewhere, Nature proceeds with her usual economy; for just as the female ant, after fecundation, loses her wings, which are then superfluous, nay, actually a danger to the business of breeding; so, after giving birth to one or two children, a woman generally loses her beauty; probably, indeed, for similar reasons.

And so we find that young girls, in their hearts, look upon domestic affairs or work of any kind as of secondary importance, if not actually as a mere jest. The only business that really claims their earnest attention is love, making conquests, and everything connected with this—dress, dancing, and so on.

The nobler and more perfect a thing is, the later and slower it is in arriving at maturity. A man reaches the maturity of his reasoning powers and mental faculties hardly before the age of twenty-eight; a woman at eighteen. And then, too, in the case of woman, it is only reason of a sort—very niggard in its dimensions. That is why women remain children their whole life long; never seeing anything but what is quite close to them, cleaving to the present moment, taking appearance for reality, and preferring trifles to matters of the first importance. For it is by virtue of his reasoning faculty that man does not live in the present only, like the brute, but looks about him and considers the past and the future; and this is the origin of prudence, as well as of that care and anxiety which so many people exhibit. Both the advantages and the disadvantages which this involves, are shared in by the woman to a smaller extent because of her weaker power of reasoning. She may, in fact, be described as intellectually short-sighted, because, while she has an intuitive understanding of what lies quite close to her, her field of vision is narrow and does not reach to what is remote; so that things which are absent, or past, or to come, have much less effect upon women than upon men. This is the reason why women are more often inclined to be extravagant, and sometimes carry their inclination to a length that borders upon madness. In their hearts, women think that it is men's business to earn money and theirs to spend it—if possible during their husband's life, but, at any rate, after his death. The very fact that their husband hands them over his earnings for purposes of housekeeping, strengthens them in this belief.

However many disadvantages all this may involve, there is at least this to be said in its favor; that the woman lives more in the present than the man, and that, if the present is at all tolerable, she enjoys it more eagerly. This is the source of that cheerfulness which is peculiar to women, fitting her to amuse man in his hours of recreation, and, in case of need, to console him when he is borne down by the weight of his cares.

It is by no means a bad plan to consult women in matters of difficulty, as the Germans used to do in ancient times; for their way of looking at things is quite different from ours, chiefly in the fact that they like to take the shortest way to their goal, and, in general, manage to fix their eyes upon what lies before them; while we, as a rule, see far beyond it, just because it is in front of our noses. In cases like this, we need to be brought back to the right standpoint, so as to recover the near and simple view.

Then, again, women are decidedly more sober in their judgment than we are, so that they do not see more in things than is really there; whilst, if our passions are aroused, we are apt to see things in an exaggerated way, or imagine what does not exist.

The weakness of their reasoning faculty also explains why it is that women show more sympathy for the unfortunate than men do, and so treat them with more kindness and interest; and why it is that, on the contrary, they are inferior to men in point of justice, and less honorable and conscientious. For it is just because their reasoning power is weak that present circumstances have such a hold over them, and those concrete things, which lie directly before their eyes, exercise a power which is seldom counteracted to any extent by abstract principles of thought, by fixed rules of conduct, firm resolutions, or, in general, by consideration for the past and the future, or regard for what is absent and remote. Accordingly, they possess the first and main elements that go to make a virtuous character, but they are deficient in those secondary qualities which are often a necessary instrument in the formation of it.[11]

Hence, it will be found that the fundamental fault of the female character is that it has *no sense of justice*. This is mainly due to the fact, already mentioned, that women are defective in the powers of reasoning and deliberation; but it is also traceable to the position which Nature has assigned to them as the weaker sex. They are dependent, not upon strength, but upon craft; and hence their instinctive capacity for cunning, and their ineradicable tendency to say what is not true. For as lions are provided with claws and teeth, and elephants and boars with tusks, bulls with horns, and cuttle fish with its clouds of inky fluid, so Nature has equipped woman, for her defense and protection, with the arts of dissimulation; and all the power which Nature has conferred upon man in the shape of physical strength and reason, has been bestowed upon women in this form. Hence, dissimulation is innate in woman, and almost as much a quality of the stupid as of the clever. It is as natural for them to make use of it on every occasion as it is for those animals to employ their means of defense when they are attacked; they have a feeling that in doing so they are only within their rights. Therefore a woman who is perfectly truthful and not given to dissimulation is perhaps an impossibility, and for this very reason they are so quick at seeing through dissimulation in others that it is not a wise thing to attempt it with them. But this fundamental

[11] In this respect they may be compared to an animal organism which contains a liver but no gall-bladder. Here let me refer to what I have said in my treatise on *The Foundation of Morals*, § 17.

defect which I have stated, with all that it entails, gives rise to falsity, faithlessness, treachery, ingratitude, and so on. Perjury in a court of justice is more often committed by women than by men. It may, indeed, be generally questioned whether women ought to be sworn in at all. From time to time one finds repeated cases everywhere of ladies, who want for nothing, taking things from shop-counters when no one is looking, and making off with them.

Nature has appointed that the propagation of the species shall be the business of men who are young, strong and handsome; so that the race may not degenerate. This is the firm will and purpose of Nature in regard to the species, and it finds its expression in the passions of women. There is no law that is older or more powerful than this. Woe, then, to the man who sets up claims and interests that will conflict with it; whatever he may say and do, they will be unmercifully crushed at the first serious encounter. For the innate rule that governs women's conduct, though it is secret and unformulated, nay, unconscious in its working, is this: *We are justified in deceiving those who think they have acquired rights over the species by paying little attention to the individual, that is, to us. The constitution and, therefore, the welfare of the species have been placed in our hands and committed to our care, through the control we obtain over the next generation, which proceeds from us; let us discharge our duties conscientiously.* But women have no abstract knowledge of this leading principle; they are conscious of it only as a concrete fact; and they have no other method of giving expression to it than the way in which they act when the opportunity arrives. And then their conscience does not trouble them so much as we fancy; for in the darkest recesses of their heart, they are aware that in committing a breach of their duty towards the individual, they have all the better fulfilled their duty towards the species, which is infinitely greater.[12]

And since women exist in the main solely for the propagation of the species, and are not destined for anything else, they live, as a rule, more for the species than for the individual, and in

[12] A more detailed discussion of the matter in question may be found in my chief work, *Die Welt als Wille und Vorstellung,* vol. ii., ch. 44.

their hearts take the affairs of the species more seriously than those of the individual. This gives their whole life and being a certain levity; the general bent of their character is in a direction fundamentally different from that of man; and it is this which produces that discord in married life which is so frequent, and almost the normal state.

The natural feeling between men is mere indifference, but between women it is actual enmity. The reason of this is that trade-jealousy—*odium figulinum*—which, in the case of men does not go beyond the confines of their own particular pursuit; but, with women, embraces the whole sex; since they have only one kind of business. Even when they meet in the street, women look at one another like Guelphs and Ghibellines. And it is a patent fact that when two women make first acquaintance with each other, they behave with more constraint and dissimulation than two men would show in a like case; and hence it is that an exchange of compliments between two women is a much more ridiculous proceeding than between two men. Further, whilst a man will, as a general rule, always preserve a certain amount of consideration and humanity in speaking to others, even to those who are in a very inferior position, it is intolerable to see how proudly and disdainfully a fine lady will generally behave towards one who is in a lower social rank (I do not mean a woman who is in her service), whenever she speaks to her. The reason of this may be that, with women, differences of rank are much more precarious than with us; because, while a hundred considerations carry weight in our case, in theirs there is only one, namely, with which man they have found favor; as also that they stand in much nearer relations with one another than men do, in consequence of the one-sided nature of their calling. This makes them endeavor to lay stress upon differences of rank.

It is only the man whose intellect is clouded by his sexual impulses that could give the name of *the fair sex* to that undersized, narrow-shouldered, broad-hipped, and short-legged race; for the whole beauty of the sex is bound up with this impulse. Instead of calling them beautiful, there would be more warrant for describing women as the unæsthetic sex. Neither for music, nor for poetry, nor for fine art, have they really and truly any

sense or susceptibility; it is a mere mockery if they make a pretense of it in order to assist their endeavour to please. Hence, as
a result of this, they are incapable of taking a *purely objective
interest* in anything; and the reason of it seems to me to be as
follows. A man tries to acquire *direct* mastery over things, either
by understanding them, or by forcing them to do his will. But
a woman is always and everywhere reduced to obtaining this
mastery *indirectly,* namely, through a man; and whatever direct
mastery she may have is entirely confined to him. And so it lies
in woman's nature to look upon everything only as a means for
conquering man; and if she takes an interest in anything else,
it is simulated—a mere roundabout way of gaining her ends by
coquetry, and feigning what she does not feel. Hence, even Rousseau declared: *Women have, in general, no love for any art;
they have no proper knowledge of any; and they have no genius.*[13]

No one who sees at all below the surface can have failed to
remark the same thing. You need only observe the kind of attention women bestow upon a concert, an opera, or a play—the
childish simplicity, for example, with which they keep on chatter-
ing during the finest passages in the greatest masterpieces. If it
is true that the Greeks excluded women from their theatres they
were quite right in what they did; at any rate you would have
been able to hear what was said upon the stage. In our day,
besides, or in lieu of saying, *Let a woman keep silence in the
church,* it would be much to the point to say *Let a woman keep
silence in the theatre.* This might, perhaps, be put up in big letters
on the curtain.

And you cannot expect anything else of women if you consider
that the most distinguished intellects among the whole sex have
never managed to produce a single achievement in the fine arts
that is really great, genuine, and original; or given to the world
any work of permanent value in any sphere. This is most strikingly shown in regard to painting, where mastery of technique
is at least as much within their power as within ours—and hence
they are diligent in cultivating it; but still, they have not a
single great painting to boast of, just because they are deficient
in that objectivity of mind which is so directly indispensable in

[13] Lettre à d'Alembert. Note xx.

painting. They never get beyond a subjective point of view. It is quite in keeping with this that ordinary women have no real susceptibility for art at all; for Nature proceeds in strict sequence —*non facit saltum*. And Huarte [14] in his *Examen de ingenios para las scienzias*—a book which has been famous for three hundred years—denies women the possession of all the higher faculties. The case is not altered by particular and partial exceptions; taken as a whole, women are, and remain, thoroughgoing Philistines, and quite incurable. Hence, with that absurd arrangement which allows them to share the rank and title of their husbands they are a constant stimulus to his ignoble ambitions. And, further, it is just because they are Philistines that modern society, where they take the lead and set the tone, is in such a bad way. Napoleon's saying—that *women have no rank*—should be adopted as the right standpoint in determining their position in society; and as regards their other qualities Chamfort [15] makes the very true remarks: *They are made to trade with our own weaknesses and our follies, but not with our reason. The sympathies that exist between them and men are skin-deep only, and do not touch the mind or the feelings or the character.* They form the *sexus sequior* —the second sex, inferior in every respect to the first; their infirmities should be treated with consideration; but to show them great reverence is extremely ridiculous, and lowers us in their eyes. When Nature made two divisions of the human race, she did not draw the line exactly through the middle. These divisions are polar and opposed to each other, it is true; but the difference between them is not qualitative merely, it is also quantitative.

This is just the view which the ancients took of woman, and the view which people in the East take now; and their judgment as to her proper position is much more correct than ours, with our old French notions of gallantry and our preposterous system of reverence—that highest product of Teutonico-Christian stupidity. These notions have served only to make women more arrogant and overbearing; so that one is occasionally reminded of

[14] *Translator's Note.*— Juan Huarte (1520?–1590) practiced as a physician at Madrid. The work cited by Schopenhauer is well known, and has been translated into many languages.

[15] *Translator's Note.*—See *Counsels and Maxims*, p. 12. Note.

the holy apes in Benares, who in the consciousness of their sanctity and inviolable position, think they can do exactly as they please.

But in the West, the woman, and especially the *lady*, finds herself in a false position; for woman, rightly called by the ancients, *sexus sequior*, is by no means fit to be the object of our honor and veneration, or to hold her head higher than man and be on equal terms with him. The consequences of this false position are sufficiently obvious. Accordingly, it would be a very desirable thing if this Number-Two of the human race were in Europe also relegated to her natural place, and an end put to that lady nuisance, which not only moves all Asia to laughter, but would have been ridiculed by Greece and Rome as well. It is impossible to calculate the good effects which such a change would bring about in our social, civil and political arrangements. There would be no necessity for the Salic law: it would be a superfluous truism. In Europe the *lady*, strictly so-called, is a being who should not exist at all; she should be either a housewife or a girl who hopes to become one; and she should be brought up, not to be arrogant, but to be thrifty and submissive. It is just because there are such people as *ladies* in Europe that the women of the lower classes, that is to say, the great majority of the sex, are much more unhappy than they are in the East. And even Lord Byron says: *Thought of the state of women under the ancient Greeks—convenient enough. Present state, a remnant of the barbarism of the chivalric and the feudal ages—artificial and unnatural. They ought to mind home—and be well fed and clothed —but not mixed in society. Well educated, too, in religion—but to read neither poetry nor politics—nothing but books of piety and cookery. Music—drawing—dancing—also a little gardening and ploughing now and then. I have seen them mending the roads in Epirus with good success. Why not, as well as hay-making and milking?*

The laws of marriage prevailing in Europe consider the woman as the equivalent of the man—start, that is to say, from a wrong position. In our part of the world where monogamy is the rule, to marry means to halve one's rights and double one's duties. Now, when the laws gave woman equal rights with man, they ought also to have endowed her with a masculine intellect. But the fact is, that just in proportion as the honors and privileges which the laws accord to women, exceed the amount which nature gives, is there a diminution in the number of women who really participate in these privileges; and all the remainder are deprived of their natural rights by just so much as is given to the others over and above their share. For the institution of monogamy, and the laws of marriage which it entails, bestow upon the woman an unnatural position of privilege, by considering her throughout as the full equivalent of the man, which is by no means the case; and seeing this, men who are shrewd and prudent very often scruple to make so great a sacrifice and to acquiesce in so unfair an arrangement.

Consequently, whilst among polygamous nations every woman is provided for, where monogamy prevails the number of married women is limited; and there remains over a large number of women without stay or support, who, in the upper classes, vegetate as useless old maids, and in the lower succumb to hard work for which they are not suited; or else become *filles de joie,* whose life is as destitute of joy as it is of honor. But under the circumstances they become a necessity; and their position is openly recognized as serving the special end of warding off temptation from those women favored by fate, who have found, or may hope to find, husbands. In London alone there are 80,000 prostitutes. What are they but the women, who, under the institution of monogamy have come off worse? Theirs is a dreadful fate: they are human sacrifices offered up on the altar of monogamy. The women whose wretched position is here described are the inevitable set-off to the European lady with her arrogance and pretension. Polygamy is therefore a real benefit to the female sex if it is taken as a whole. And, from another point of view, there is no true reason why a man whose wife suffers from chronic illness, or remains barren, or has gradually become too old for him, should not take a second. The motives which induce so many people to become converts to Mormonism [16] appear to be just those which militate against the unnatural institution of monogamy.

Moreover, the bestowal of unnatural rights upon women has

[16] *Translator's Note.*—The Mormons have recently given up polygamy, and received the American franchise in its stead.

imposed upon them unnatural duties, and, nevertheless, a breach of these duties makes them unhappy. Let me explain. A man may often think that his social or financial position will suffer if he marries, unless he makes some brilliant alliance. His desire will then be to win a woman of his own choice under conditions other than those of marriage, such as will secure her position and that of the children. However fair, reasonable, fit and proper these conditions may be, and the woman consents by foregoing that undue amount of privilege which marriage alone can bestow, she to some extent loses her honor, because marriage is the basis of civic society; and she will lead an unhappy life, since human nature is so constituted that we pay an attention to the opinion of other people which is out of all proportion to its value. On the other hand, if she does not consent, she runs the risk either of having to be given in marriage to a man whom she does not like, or of being landed high and dry as an old maid; for the period during which she has a chance of being settled for life is very short. And in view of this aspect of the institution of monogamy, Thomasius' profoundly learned treatise, *de Concubinatu,* is well worth reading; for it shows that, amongst all nations and in all ages, down to the Lutheran Reformation, concubinage was permitted; nay, that it was an institution which was to a certain extent actually recognized by law, and attended with no dishonour. It was only the Lutheran Reformation that degraded it from this position. It was seen to be a further justification for the marriage of the clergy; and then, after that, the Catholic Church did not dare to remain behind-hand in the matter.

There is no use arguing about polygamy; it must be taken as *de facto* existing everywhere, and the only question is as to how it shall be regulated. Where are there, then, any real monogamists? We all live, at any rate, for a time, and most of us, always, in polygamy. And so, since every man needs many women, there is nothing fairer than to allow him, nay, to make it incumbent upon him, to provide for many women. This will reduce woman to her true and natural position as a subordinate being; and the *lady*—that monster of European civilization and Teutonico-Christian stupidity—will disappear from the world, leaving only *women*, but no more *unhappy women*, of whom Europe is now full.

In India, no woman is ever independent, but in accordance with the law of Manu,[17] she stands under the control of her father, her husband, her brother or her son. It is, to be sure, a revolting thing that a widow should immolate herself upon her husband's funeral pyre; but it is also revolting that she should spend her husband's money with her paramours—the money for which he toiled his whole life long, in the consoling belief that he was providing for his children. Happy are those who have kept the middle course—*medium tenuere beati.*

The first love of a mother for her child is, with the lower animals as with men, of a purely *instinctive* character, and so it ceases when the child is no longer in a physically helpless condition. After that, the first love should give way to one that is based on habit and reason; but this often fails to make its appearance, especially where the mother did not love the father. The love of a father for his child is of a different order, and more likely to last; because it has its foundation in the fact that in the child he recognizes his own inner self; that is to say, his love for it is metaphysical in its origin.

In almost all nations, whether of the ancient or the modern world, even amongst the Hottentots,[18] property is inherited by the male descendants alone; it is only in Europe that a departure has taken place; but not amongst the nobility, however. That the property which has cost men long years of toil and effort, and been won with so much difficulty, should afterwards come into the hands of women, who then, in their lack of reason, squander it in a short time, or otherwise fool it away, is a grievance and a wrong as serious as it is common, which should be prevented by limiting the right of women to inherit. In my opinion, the best arrangement would be that by which women, whether widows or daughters, should never receive anything beyond the interest for life on property secured by mortgage, and in no case the property itself, or the capital, except where all male descendants

[17] Ch. V., v. 148.
[18] Leroy, *Lettres philosophiques sur l'intelligence et la perfectibilité des animaux, avec quelques lettres sur l'homme,* p. 298, Paris, 1802.

fail. The people who make money are men, not women; and it follows from this that women are neither justified in having unconditional possession of it, nor fit persons to be entrusted with its administration. When wealth, in any true sense of the word, that is to say, funds, houses or land, is to go to them as an inheritance they should never be allowed the free disposition of it. In their case a guardian should always be appointed; and hence they should never be given the free control of their own children, wherever it can be avoided. The vanity of women, even though it should not prove to be greater than that of men, has this much danger in it, that it takes an entirely material direction. They are vain, I mean, of their personal beauty, and then of finery, show and magnificence. That is just why they are so much in their element in society. It is this, too, which makes them so inclined to be extravagant, all the more as their reasoning power is low. Accordingly we find an ancient writer describing woman as in general of an extravagant nature—Γυνὴ τὸ σύνολον ἔστι δαπανηρὸν Φύσει.[19] But with men vanity often takes the direction of non-material advantages, such as intellect, learning, courage.

In the *Politics* [20] Aristotle explains the great disadvantage which accrued to the Spartans from the fact that they conceded too much to their women, by giving them the right of inheritance and dower, and a great amount of independence; and he shows how much this contributed to Sparta's fall. May it not be the case in France that the influence of women, which went on increasing steadily from the time of Louis XIII., was to blame for that gradual corruption of the Court and the Government, which brought about the Revolution of 1789, of which all subsequent disturbances have been the fruit? However that may be, the false position which women occupy, demonstrated as it is, in the most glaring way, by the institution of the *lady,* is a fundamental defect in our social scheme, and this defect, proceeding from the very heart of it, must spread its baneful influence in all directions.

[19] Brunck's *Gnomici poetae graeci,* v. 115.
[20] Bk. I., ch. 9.

That woman is by nature meant to obey may be seen by the fact that every woman who is placed in the unnatural position of complete independence, immediately attaches herself to some man, by whom she allows herself to be guided and ruled. It is because she needs a lord and master. If she is young, it will be a lover; if she is old, a priest.

KANT wrote a treatise on *The Vital Powers*. I should prefer to
write a dirge for them. The super-abundant display of vitality,
which takes the form of knocking, hammering, and tumbling
things about, has proved a daily torment to me all my life long.
There are people, it is true—nay, a great many people—who
smile at such things, because they are not sensitive to noise; but
they are just the very people who are also not sensitive to argument, or thought, or poetry, or art, in a word, to any kind of
intellectual influence. The reason of it is that the tissue of their
brains is of a very rough and coarse quality. On the other hand,
noise is a torture to intellectual people. In the biographies of
almost all great writers, or wherever else their personal utterances are recorded, I find complaints about it; in the case of Kant,
for instance, Goethe, Lichtenberg, Jean Paul; and if it should
happen that any writer has omitted to express himself on the
matter, it is only for want of an opportunity.

This aversion to noise I should explain as follows: If you cut
up a large diamond into little bits, it will entirely lose the value
it had as a whole; and an army divided up into small bodies of
soldiers, loses all its strength. So a great intellect sinks to the
level of an ordinary one, as soon as it is interrupted and disturbed,
its attention distracted and drawn off from the matter in hand;
for its superiority depends upon its power of concentration—
of bringing all its strength to bear upon one theme, in the same
way as a concave mirror collects into one point all the rays of
light that strike upon it. Noisy interruption is a hindrance to this
concentration. That is why distinguished minds have always shown
such an extreme dislike to disturbance in any form, as something
that breaks in upon and distracts their thoughts. Above all have
they been averse to that violent interruption that comes from
noise. Ordinary people are not much put out by anything of the
sort. The most sensible and intelligent of all nations in Europe

lays down the rule, *Never Interrupt!* as the eleventh command-ment. Noise is the most impertinent of all forms of interruption. It is not only an interruption, but also a disruption of thought. Of course, where there is nothing to interrupt, noise will not be so particularly painful. Occasionally it happens that some slight but constant noise continues to bother and distract me for a time before I become distinctly conscious of it. All I feel is a steady increase in the labor of thinking—just as though I were trying to walk with a weight on my foot. At last I find out what it is.

Let me now, however, pass from genus to species. The most inexcusable and disgraceful of all noises is the cracking of whips —a truly infernal thing when it is done in the narrow resound-ing streets of a town. I denounce it as making a peaceful life im-possible; it puts an end to all quiet thought. That this cracking of whips should be allowed at all seems to me to show in the clear-est way how senseless and thoughtless is the nature of mankind. No one with anything like an idea in his head can avoid a feeling of actual pain at this sudden, sharp crack, which paralyzes the brain, rends the thread of reflection, and murders thought. Every time this noise is made, it must disturb a hundred people who are applying their minds to business of some sort, no matter how trivial it may be; while on the thinker its effect is woeful and disastrous, cutting his thoughts asunder, much as the executioner's axe severs the head from the body. No sound, be it ever so shrill, cuts so sharply into the brain as this cursed cracking of whips; you feel the sting of the lash right inside your head; and it affects the brain in the same way as touch affects a sensitive plant, and for the same length of time.

With all due respect for the most holy doctrine of utility, I really cannot see why a fellow who is taking away a wagon-load of gravel or dung should thereby obtain the right to kill in the bud the thoughts which may happen to be springing up in ten thousand heads—the number he will disturb one after another in half an hour's drive through the town. Hammering, the bark-ing of dogs, and the crying of children are horrible to hear; but your only genuine assassin of thought is the crack of a whip; it exists for the purpose of destroying every pleasant moment of quiet thought that any one may now and then enjoy. If the driver had no other way of urging on his horse than by making this most abominable of all noises, it would be excusable; but quite the contrary is the case. This cursed cracking of whips is not only unnecessary, but even useless. Its aim is to produce an effect upon the intelligence of the horse; but through the constant abuse of it, the animal becomes habituated to the sound, which falls upon blunted feelings and produces no effect at all. The horse does not go any faster for it. You have a remarkable example of this in the ceaseless cracking of his whip on the part of a cab-driver, while he is proceeding at a slow pace on the lookout for a fare. If he were to give his horse the slightest touch with the whip, it would have much more effect. Supposing, however, that it were absolutely necessary to crack the whip in order to keep the horse constantly in mind of its presence, it would be enough to make the hundredth part of the noise. For it is a well-known fact that, in regard to sight and hearing, animals are sensitive to even the faintest indications; they are alive to things that we can scarcely perceive. The most surprising instances of this are furnished by trained dogs and canary birds.

It is obvious, therefore, that here we have to do with an act of pure wantonness; nay, with an impudent defiance offered to those members of the community who work with their heads by those who work with their hands. That such infamy should be tolerated in a town is a piece of barbarity and iniquity, all the more as it could easily be remedied by a police-notice to the effect that every lash shall have a knot at the end of it. There can be no harm in drawing the attention of the mob to the fact that the classes above them work with their heads, for any kind of headwork is mortal anguish to the man in the street. A fellow who rides through the narrow alleys of a populous town with unemployed post-horses or cart-horses, and keeps on cracking a whip several yards long with all his might, deserves there and then to stand down and receive five really good blows with a stick.

All the philanthropists in the world, and all the legislators, meeting to advocate and decree the total abolition of corporal punishment, will never persuade me to the contrary! There is something even more disgraceful than what I have just mentioned. Often enough you may see a carter walking along the street, quite alone, without any horses, and still cracking away incessantly; so accustomed has the wretch become to it in consequence of the unwarrantable toleration of this practice. A man's body and the needs of his body are now everywhere treated with a tender indulgence. Is the thinking mind then, to be the only thing that is never to obtain the slightest measure of consideration or protection, to say nothing of respect? Carters, porters, messengers—these are the beasts of burden amongst mankind; by all means let them be treated justly, fairly, indulgently, and with fore-thought; but they must not be permitted to stand in the way of the higher endeavors of humanity by wantonly making a noise. How many great and splendid thoughts, I should like to know, have been lost to the world by the crack of a whip? If I had the upper hand, I should soon produce in the heads of these people an indissoluble association of ideas between cracking a whip and getting a whipping.

Let us hope that the more intelligent and refined among the nations will make a beginning in this matter, and then that the Germans may take example by it and follow suit.[21] Meanwhile, I may quote what Thomas Hood says of them:[22] *For a musical nation, they are the most noisy I ever met with.* That they are so is due to the fact, not that they are more fond of making a noise than other people—they would deny it if you asked them— but that their senses are obtuse; consequently, when they hear a noise, it does not affect them much. It does not disturb them in reading or thinking, simply because they do not think; they only smoke, which is their substitute for thought. The general toleration of unnecessary noise—the slamming of doors, for instance, a very unmannerly and ill-bred thing—is direct evidence that the prevailing habit of mind is dullness and lack of thought. In Germany it seems as though care were taken that no one should ever think for mere noise—to mention one form of it, the way in which drumming goes on for no purpose at all.

Finally, as regards the literature of the subject treated of in

---

[21] According to a notice issued by the Society for the Protection of Animals in Munich, the superfluous whipping and the cracking of whips were, in December, 1858, positively forbidden in Nuremberg.

[22] In *Up the Rhine*.

this chapter, I have only one work to recommend, but it is a good one. I refer to a poetical epistle in *terzo rimo* by the famous painter Bronzino, entitled *De' Romori: a Messer Luca Martini.* It gives a detailed description of the torture to which people are put by the various noises of a small Italian town. Written in a tragic-comic style, it is very amusing. The epistle may be found in *Opere burlesche del Berni, Aretino ed altri,* Vol. II., p. 258; apparently published in Utrecht in 1771.

IV. RELIGION

A DIALOGUE

*D*EMOPHELES. Between ourselves, my dear fellow, I don't care about the way you sometimes have of exhibiting your talent for philosophy; you make religion a subject for sarcastic remarks, and even for open ridicule. Every one thinks his religion sacred, and therefore you ought to respect it.

Philalethes. That doesn't follow! I don't see why, because other people are simpletons, I should have any regard for a pack of lies. I respect truth everywhere, and so I can't respect what is opposed to it. My maxim is *Vigeat veritas et pereat mundus,* like the lawyers' *Fiat justitia et pereat mundus.* Every profession ought to have an analogous advice.

Demopheles. Then I suppose doctors should say *Fiant pilulae et pereat mundus,*—there wouldn't be much difficulty about that!

Philalethes. Heaven forbid! You must take everything *cum grano salis.*

Demopheles. Exactly; that's why I want you to take religion *cum grano salis.* I want you to see that one must meet the requirements of the people according to the measure of their comprehension. Where you have masses of people of crude susceptibilities and clumsy intelligence, sordid in their pursuits and sunk in drudgery, religion provides the only means of proclaiming and making them feel the high import of life. For the average man takes an interest, primarily, in nothing but what will satisfy his physical needs and hankerings, and beyond this, give him a little amusement and pastime. Founders of religion and philosophers come into the world to rouse him from his stupor and point to the lofty meaning of existence; philosophers for the few, the emancipated, founders of religion for the many, for humanity at large. For, as your friend Plato has said, the multitude can't be philosophers, and you shouldn't forget that. Religion is the metaphysics of the masses; by all means let them keep it: let it therefore command external respect, for to discredit it is to take it away. Just as they have popular poetry, and the popular wisdom of proverbs, so they must have popular metaphysics too: for mankind absolutely needs *an interpretation of life;* and this, again, must be suited to popular comprehension. Consequently, this interpretation is always an allegorical investiture of the truth: and in practical life and in its effects on the feelings, that is to say, as a rule of action and as a comfort and consolation in suffering and death, it accomplishes perhaps just as much as the truth itself could achieve if we possessed it. Don't take offense at its unkempt, grotesque and apparently absurd form; for with your education and learning, you have no idea of the roundabout ways by which people in their crude state have to receive their knowledge of deep truths. The various religions are only various forms in which the truth, which taken by itself is above their comprehension, is grasped and realized by the masses; and truth becomes inseparable from these forms. Therefore, my dear sir, don't take it amiss if I say that to make a mockery of these forms is both shallow and unjust.

Philalethes. But isn't it every bit as shallow and unjust to demand that there shall be no other system of metaphysics but this one, cut out as it is to suit the requirements and comprehension of the masses? that its doctrine shall be the limit of human speculation, the standard of all thought, so that the metaphysics of the few, the emancipated, as you call them, must be devoted only to confirming, strengthening, and explaining the metaphysics of the masses? that the highest powers of human intelligence shall remain unused and undeveloped, even be nipped in the bud, in order that their activity may not thwart the popular metaphysics? And isn't this just the very claim which religion sets up? Isn't it a little too much to have tolerance and delicate forbearance preached by what is intolerance and cruelty itself? Think of the heretical tribunals, inquisitions, religious wars, crusades, Socrates' cup of poison, Bruno's and Vanini's death in the flames! Is all this to-day quite a thing of the past? How can genuine philosophical effort, sincere search after truth, the noblest calling of the noblest men, be let and hindered more completely than by a conventional system of metaphysics enjoying a State monopoly, the principles of which are impressed into every head in earliest youth, so earnestly, so deeply, and so firmly, that, unless the mind is miraculously elastic, they remain indelible? In this way the groundwork of all healthy reason is once for all deranged; that is to say, the capacity for original thought and unbiased judgment, which is weak enough in itself, is, in regard to those subjects to which it might be applied, forever paralyzed and ruined.

Demopheles. Which means, I suppose, that people have arrived at a conviction which they won't give up in order to embrace yours instead.

Philalethes. Ah! if it were only a conviction based on insight. Then one could bring arguments to bear, and the battle would be fought with equal weapons. But religions admittedly appeal, not to conviction as the result of argument, but to belief as demanded by revelation. And as the capacity for believing is strongest in childhood, special care is taken to make sure of this tender age. This has much more to do with the doctrines of belief taking root than threats and reports of miracles. If, in early childhood, certain fundamental views and doctrines are paraded with unusual solemnity, and an air of the greatest earnestness never before visible in anything else; if, at the same time, the possibility of a doubt about them be completely passed over, or touched upon only to indicate that doubt is the first step to eternal perdition, the resulting impression will be so deep that, as a rule, that is, in almost every case, doubt about them will be almost as impossible as doubt about one's own existence. Hardly one in ten thousand will have the strength of mind to ask himself seriously and earnestly—is that true? To call such as can do it strong minds, *esprits forts,* is a description more apt than is generally supposed. But for the ordinary mind there is nothing so absurd or revolting but what, if inculcated in that way, the strongest belief in it will strike root. If, for example, the killing of a heretic or infidel were essential to the future salvation of his soul, almost every one would make it the chief event of his life, and in dying would draw consolation and strength from the remembrance that he had succeeded. As a matter of fact, almost every Spaniard in days gone by used to look upon an *auto da fé* as the most pious of all acts and one most agreeable to God. A parallel to this may be found in the

way in which the Thugs (a religious sect in India, suppressed a
short time ago by the English, who executed numbers of them)
express their sense of religion and their veneration for the goddess
Kali; they take every opportunity of murdering their friends and
traveling companions, with the object of getting possession of
their goods, and in the serious conviction that they are thereby
doing a praiseworthy action, conducive to their eternal welfare.[1]
The power of religious dogma, when inculcated early, is such as
to stifle conscience, compassion, and finally every feeling of humanity. But if you want to see with your own eyes and close at hand
what timely inoculation will accomplish, look at the English.
Here is a nation favored before all others by nature; endowed,
more than all others, with discernment, intelligence, power of
judgment, strength of character; look at them, abased and made
ridiculous, beyond all others, by their stupid ecclesiastical superstition, which appears amongst their other abilities like a fixed idea
or monomania. For this they have to thank the circumstance
that education is in the hands of the clergy, whose endeavor it is
to impress all the articles of belief, at the earliest age, in a way
that amounts to a kind of paralysis of the brain; this in its turn
expresses itself all their life in an idiotic bigotry, which makes
otherwise most sensible and intelligent people amongst them de-
grade themselves so that one can't make head or tail of them. If
you consider how essential to such a masterpiece is inoculation in
the tender age of childhood, the missionary system appears no
longer only as the acme of human importunity, arrogance and im-
pertinence, but also as an absurdity, if it doesn't confine itself to
nations which are still in their infancy, like Caffirs, Hottentots,
South Sea Islanders, etc. Amongst these races it is successful; in
India, the Brahmans treat the discourses of the missionaries with
contemptuous smiles of approbation, or simply shrug their shoulders. And one may say generally that the proselytizing efforts of
the missionaries in India, in spite of the most advantageous facili-
ties, are, as a rule, a failure. An authentic report in the Vol. XXI.
of the Asiatic Journal (1826) states that after so many years
of missionary activity not more than three hundred living converts

[1] Cf. Illustrations of the history and practice of the Thugs, London,
1837; also the *Edinburg Review,* Oct.–Jan., 1836–7.

were to be found in the whole of India, where the population of the English possessions alone comes to one hundred and fifteen millions; and at the same time it is admitted that the Christian converts are distinguished for their extreme immorality. Three hundred venal and bribed souls out of so many millions! There is no evidence that things have gone better with Christianity in India since then, in spite of the fact that the missionaries are now trying, contrary to stipulation and in schools exclusively designed for secular English instruction, to work upon the children's minds as they please, in order to smuggle in Christianity; against which the Hindoos are most jealously on their guard. As I have said, childhood is the time to sow the seeds of belief, and not manhood; more especially where an earlier faith has taken root. An acquired conviction such as is feigned by adults is, as a rule, only the mask for some kind of personal interest. And it is the feeling that this is almost bound to be the case which makes a man who has changed his religion in mature years an object of contempt to most people everywhere; who thus show that they look upon religion, not as a matter of reasoned conviction, but merely as a belief inoculated in childhood, before any test can be applied. And that they are right in their view of religion is also obvious from the way in which not only the masses, who are blindly credulous, but also the clergy of every religion, who, as such, have faithfully and zealously studied its sources, foundations, dogmas and disputed points, cleave as a body to the religion of their particular country; consequently for a minister of one religion or confession to go over to another is the rarest thing in the world. The Catholic clergy, for example, are fully convinced of the truth of all the tenets of their Church, and so are the Protestant clergy of theirs, and both defend the principles of their creeds with like zeal. And yet the conviction is governed merely by the country native to each; to the South German ecclesiastic the truth of the Catholic dogma is quite obvious, to the North German, the Protestant. If then, these convictions are based on objective reasons, the reasons must be climatic, and thrive, like plants, some only here, some only there. The convictions of those who are thus locally convinced are taken on trust and believed by the masses everywhere.

Demopheles. Well, no harm is done, and it doesn't make any real difference. As a fact, Protestantism is more suited to the North, Catholicism to the South.

Philalethes. So it seems. Still I take a higher standpoint, and keep in view a more important object, the progress, namely, of the knowledge of truth among mankind. And from this point of view, it is a terrible thing that, wherever a man is born, certain propositions are inculcated in him in earliest youth, and he is assured that he may never have any doubts about them, under penalty of thereby forfeiting eternal salvation; propositions, I mean, which affect the foundation of all our other knowledge and accordingly determine for ever, and, if they are false, distort for ever, the point of view from which our knowledge starts; and as, further, the corollaries of these propositions touch the entire system of our intellectual attainments at every point, the whole of human knowledge is thoroughly adulterated by them. Evidence of this is afforded by every literature; the most striking by that of the Middle Age, but in a too considerable degree by that of the fifteenth and sixteenth centuries. Look at even the first minds of all those epochs; how paralyzed they are by false fundamental positions like these; how, more especially, all insight into the true constitution and working of nature is, as it were, blocked up. During the whole of the Christian period Theism lies like a mountain on all intellectual, and chiefly on all philosophical efforts, and arrests or stunts all progress. For the scientific men of these ages God, devil, angels, demons hid the whole of nature; no inquiry was followed to the end, nothing ever thoroughly examined; everything which went beyond the most obvious casual nexus was immediately set down to those personalities. *"It was at once explained by a reference to God, angels or demons,"* as Pomponatius expressed himself when the matter was being discussed, *"and philosophers at any rate having nothing analogous."* There is, to be sure, a suspicion of irony in this statement of Pomponatius, as his perfidy in other matters is known; still, he is only giving expression to the general way of thinking of his age. And if, on the other hand, any one possessed the rare quality of an elastic mind, which alone could burst the bonds, his writings and he himself with them were burnt; as happened to Bruno and Vanini. How completely an ordinary mind is paralyzed by that early preparation in metaphysics is seen in the most vivid way and on its most ridiculous side, where such a one undertakes to criticise the doctrines of an alien creed. The efforts of the ordinary man are generally found to be directed to a careful exhibition of the incongruity of its dogmas with those of his own belief: he is at great pains to show that not only do they not say, but certainly do not mean, the same thing; and with that he thinks, in his simplicity, that he has demonstrated the falsehood of the alien creed. He really never dreams of putting the question which of the two may be right; his own articles of belief he looks upon as *a priori* true and certain principles.

Demopheles. So that's your higher point of view? I assure you there is a higher still. *First live, then philosophize* is a maxim of more comprehensive import than appears at first sight. The first thing to do is to control the raw and evil dispositions of the masses, so as to keep them from pushing injustice to extremes, and from committing cruel, violent and disgraceful acts. If you were to wait until they had recognized and grasped the truth, you would undoubtedly come too late; and truth, supposing that it had been found, would surpass their powers of comprehension. In any case an allegorical investiture of it, a parable or myth, is all that would be of any service to them. As Kant said, there must be a public standard of Right and Virtue; it must always flutter high overhead. It is a matter of indifference what heraldic figures are inscribed on it, so long as they signify what is meant. Such an allegorical representation of truth is always and everywhere, for humanity at large, a serviceable substitute for a truth to which it can never attain,—for a philosophy which it can never grasp; let alone the fact that it is daily changing its shape, and has in no form as yet met with general acceptance. Practical aims, then, my good Philalethes, are in every respect superior to theoretical.

Philalethes. What you say is very like the ancient advice of Timæus of Locrus, the Pythagorean, *stop the mind with falsehood if you can't speed it with truth.* I almost suspect that your plan is the one which is so much in vogue just now, that you want to impress upon me that

> The hour is nigh
> When we may feast in quiet.

You recommend us, in fact, to take timely precautions, so that the waves of the discontented raging masses mayn't disturb us at table. But the whole point of view is as false as it is now-a-days popular and commended; and so I make haste to enter a protest against it. It is *false,* that state, justice, law cannot be upheld without the assistance of religion and its dogmas; and that justice and public order need religion as a necessary complement, if legislative enactments are to be carried out. It is *false,* were it repeated a hundred times. An effective and striking argument to the contrary is afforded by the ancients, especially the Greeks. They had nothing at all of what we understand by religion. They had no sacred documents, no dogma to be learned and its acceptance furthered by every one, its principles to be inculcated early on the young. Just as little was moral doctrine preached by the ministers of religion, nor did the priests trouble themselves about morality or about what the people did or left undone. Not at all. The duty of the priests was confined to temple-ceremonial, prayers, hymns, sacrifices, processions, lustrations and the like, the object of which was anything but the moral improvement of the individual. What was called religion consisted, more especially in the cities, in giving temples here and there to some of the gods of the greater tribes, in which the worship described was carried on as a state matter, and was consequently, in fact, an affair of police. No one, except the functionaries performing, was in any way compelled to attend, or even to believe in it. In the whole of antiquity there is no trace of any obligation to believe in any particular dogma. Merely in the case of an open denial of the existence of the gods, or any other reviling of them, a penalty was imposed, and that on account of the insult offered to the state, which served those gods; beyond this it was free to every one to think of them what he pleased. If any one wanted to gain the favor of those gods privately, by prayer or sacrifice, it was open to him to do so at his own expense and at his own risk; if he didn't do it, no one made any objection, least of all the state. In the case of the Romans, every one had his own Lares and Penates at home; they were, however, in reality, only the venerated busts of ancestors. Of the immortality of the soul and a life beyond the grave, the ancients had no firm, clear, or, least of all, dogmatically fixed idea, but very loose, fluctuating, indefinite and problematical notions, every one in his own way: and the ideas about the gods were just as varying, individual and vague. There was, therefore, really no *religion,* in our sense of the word, amongst the ancients. But did anarchy and lawlessness prevail amongst them on that account? Is not law and civil order, rather, so much their work, that it still forms the foundation of our own? Was there not complete protection for property, even though it consisted for the most part of slaves? And did not this state of things last for more than a thousand years? So that I can't recognize, I must even protest against the practical aims and the necessity of religion in the sense indicated by you, and so popular now-a-days, that is, as an indispensable foundation of all legislative arrangements. For, if you take that point of view, the pure and sacred endeavor after truth would, to say the least, appear quixotic, and even criminal, if it ventured, in its feeling of justice, to denounce the authoritative creed as a usurper who had taken possession of the throne of truth and maintained his position by keeping up the deception.

Demopheles. But religion is not opposed to truth; it itself teaches truth. And as the range of its activity is not a narrow lecture room, but the world and humanity at large, religion must conform to the requirements and comprehension of an audience so numerous and so mixed. Religion must not let truth appear in its naked form; or, to use a medical simile, it must not exhibit it pure, but must employ a mythical vehicle, a medium, as it were. You can also compare truth in this respect to certain chemical stuffs which in themselves are gaseous, but which for medicinal uses, as also for preservation or transmission, must be bound to a stable, solid base, because they would otherwise volatilize. Chlorine gas, for example, is for all purposes applied only in the form of chlorides. But if truth, pure, abstract and free from all mythical alloy, is always to remain unattainable, even by philosophers, it might be compared to fluorine, which cannot even be isolated, but must always appear in combination with other elements. Or, to take a less scientific simile, truth, which is inexpressible except by means of myth and allegory, is like water, which can be carried about only in vessels; a philosopher who insists on obtaining it pure is like a man who breaks the jug in order to get the water by itself. This is, perhaps, an exact analogy. At any rate, religion is truth allegorically and mythically expressed, and so rendered attainable and digestible by mankind in general. Mankind couldn't possibly take it pure and unmixed, just as we can't breathe pure oxygen; we require an addition of four times its bulk in nitrogen. In plain language, the profound meaning, the high aim of life, can only be unfolded and presented to the masses symbolically, because they are incapable of grasping it in its true signification. Philosophy, on the other hand, should be like the Eleusinian mysteries, for the few, the *élite*.

Philalethes. I understand. It comes, in short, to truth wearing the garment of falsehood. But in doing so it enters on a fatal alliance. What a dangerous weapon is put into the hands of those who are authorized to employ falsehood as the vehicle of truth! If it is as you say, I fear the damage caused by the falsehood will be greater than any advantage the truth could ever produce. Of course, if the allegory were admitted to be such, I should raise no objection; but with the admission it would rob itself of all respect, and consequently, of all utility. The allegory must, therefore, put in a claim to be true in the proper sense of the word, and maintain the claim; while, at the most, it is true only in an allegorical sense. Here lies the irreparable mischief, the permanent evil; and this is why religion has always been and always will be in conflict with the noble endeavor after pure truth.

Demopheles. Oh no! that danger is guarded against. If religion mayn't exactly confess its allegorical nature, it gives sufficient indication of it.

Philalethes. How so?

Demopheles. In its mysteries. "Mystery," is in reality only a technical theological term for religious allegory. All religions have their mysteries. Properly speaking, a mystery is a dogma which is plainly absurd, but which, nevertheless, conceals in itself a lofty truth, and one which by itself would be completely incomprehensible to the ordinary understanding of the raw multitude. The multitude accepts it in this disguise on trust, and believes it, without being led astray by the absurdity of it, which even to its intelligence is obvious; and in this way it participates in the kernel of the matter so far as it is possible for it to do so. To explain what I mean, I may add that even in philosophy an attempt has been made to make use of a mystery. Pascal, for example, who was at once a pietist, a mathematician, and a philosopher, says in this threefold capacity: *God is everywhere center and nowhere periphery*. Malebranche has also the just remark: *Liberty is a mystery*. One could go a step further and maintain that in religions everything is mystery. For to impart truth, in the proper sense of the word, to the multitude in its raw state is absolutely impossible; all that can fall to its lot is to be enlightened by a mythological reflection of it. Naked truth is out of place before the eyes of the profane vulgar; it can only make its appearance thickly veiled. Hence, it is unreasonable to require of a religion that it shall be true in the proper sense of the word; and this, I may observe in passing, is now-a-days the absurd contention of Rationalists and Supernaturalists alike. Both start from the position that religion must be the real truth; and while the former demonstrate that it is not the truth, the latter obstinately maintain that it is; or rather, the former dress up and arrange the allegorical element in such a way, that, in the proper sense of the word, it could be true, but would be, in that case, a platitude; while the latter wish to maintain that it is true in the proper sense of the word, without any further dressing; a belief, which, as we ought to know is only to be enforced by inquisitions and the stake. As a fact, however, myth and allegory really form the proper element of religion; and under this indispensable condition, which is imposed by the intellectual limitation of the multitude, religion provides a sufficient satisfaction for those metaphysical requirements of mankind which are indestructible. It takes the place of that pure philosophical truth which is infinitely difficult and perhaps never attainable.

Philalethes. Ah! just as a wooden leg takes the place of a natural one; it supplies what is lacking, barely does duty for it, claims to be regarded as a natural leg, and is more or less artfully put together. The only difference is that, whilst a natural leg as a rule preceded the wooden one, religion has everywhere got the start of philosophy.

Demopheles. That may be, but still for a man who hasn't a natural leg, a wooden one is of great service. You must bear in mind that the metaphysical needs of mankind absolutely require satisfaction, because the horizon of men's thoughts must have a background and not remain unbounded. Man has, as a rule, no faculty for weighing reasons and discriminating between what is false and what is true; and besides, the labor which nature and the needs of nature impose upon him, leaves him no time for such enquiries, or for the education which they presuppose. In his case, therefore, it is no use talking of a reasoned conviction; he has to fall back on belief and authority. If a really true philosophy were to take the place of religion, nine-tenths at least of mankind would have to receive it on authority; that is to say, it too would be a matter of faith, for Plato's dictum, that the multitude can't be philosophers, will always remain true. Authority, however, is an affair of time and circumstance alone, and so it can't be bestowed on that which has only reason in its favor, it must accordingly be allowed to nothing but what has acquired it in the course of history, even if it is only an allegorical representation of truth. Truth in this form, supported by authority, appeals first of all to those elements in the human constitution which are strictly metaphysical, that is to say, to the need man feels of a theory in regard to the riddle of existence which forces itself upon his notice, a need arising from the consciousness that behind the physical in the world there is a metaphysical, something permanent as the foundation of constant change. Then it appeals to the will, to the fears and hopes of mortal beings living in constant struggle; for whom, accordingly, religion creates gods and demons whom they can cry to, appease and win over. Finally, it appeals to that moral consciousness which is undeniably present in man, lends to it that corroboration and support without which it would not easily maintain itself in the struggle against so many temptations. It is just from this side that religion affords an inexhaustible source of consolation and comfort in the innumerable trials of life, a comfort which does not leave men in death, but rather then only unfolds its full efficacy. So religion may be compared to one who takes a blind man by the hand and leads him, because he is unable to see for himself, whose concern it is to reach his destination, not to look at everything by the way.

Philalethes. That is certainly the strong point of religion. If it is a fraud, it is a pious fraud; that is undeniable. But this makes priests something between deceivers and teachers of morality; they daren't teach the real truth, as you have quite rightly explained, even if they knew it, which is not the case. A true philosophy, then, can always exist, but not a true religion; true, I mean, in the proper understanding of the word, not merely in that flowery or allegorical sense which you have described; a sense in which all religions would be true, only in various degrees. It is quite in keeping with the inextricable mixture of weal and woe, honesty and deceit, good and evil, nobility and baseness, which is the average characteristic of the world everywhere, that the most important, the most lofty, the most sacred truths can make their appearance only in combination with a lie, can even borrow strength from a lie as from something that works more powerfully on mankind; and, as revelation, must be ushered in by a lie. This might, indeed, be regarded as the *cachet* of the moral world. However, we won't give up the hope that mankind will eventually reach a point of maturity and education at which it can on the one side produce, and on the other receive, the true philosophy. *Simplex sigillum veri:* the naked truth must be so simple and intelligible that it can be imparted to all in its true form, without any admixture of myth and fable, without disguising it in the form of *religion.*

Demopheles. You've no notion how stupid most people are.

Philalethes. I am only expressing a hope which I can't give up. If it were fulfilled, truth in its simple and intelligible form would of course drive religion from the place it has so long occupied as its representative, and by that very means kept open for it. The time would have come when religion would have carried out her object and completed her course: the race she had brought to years of discretion she could dismiss, and herself depart in peace: that would be the *euthanasia* of religion. But as long as she lives, she has two faces, one of truth, one of fraud. According as you look at one or the other, you will bear her favor or ill-will. Religion must be regarded as a necessary evil, its necessity resting on the pitiful imbecility of the great majority of mankind, incapable of grasping the truth, and therefore requiring, in its pressing need, something to take its place.

Demopheles. Really, one would think that you philosophers had truth in a cupboard, and that all you had to do was to go and get it!

Philalethes. Well, if we haven't got it, it is chiefly owing to the pressure put upon philosophy by religion at all times and in all places. People have tried to make the expression and communication of truth, even the contemplation and discovery of it, impossible, by putting children, in their earliest years, into the hands of priests to be manipulated; to have the lines, in which their fundamental thoughts are henceforth to run, laid down with such firmness as, in essential matters, to be fixed and determined for this whole life. When I take up the writings even of the best intellects of the sixteenth and seventeenth centuries, (more especially if I have been engaged in Oriental studies,) I am sometimes shocked to see how they are paralyzed and hemmed in on all sides by Jewish ideas. How can any one think out the true philosophy when he is prepared like this?

Demopheles. Even if the philosophy were to be discovered, religion wouldn't disappear from the world, as you seem to think. There can't be one system of metaphysics for everybody; that's rendered impossible by the natural differences of intellectual power between man and man, and the differences, too, which education makes. It is a necessity for the great majority of mankind to engage in that severe bodily labor which cannot be dispensed with if the ceaseless requirements of the whole race are to be satisfied. Not only does this leave the majority no time for education, for learning, for contemplation; but by virtue of the hard and fast antagonism between muscles and mind, the intelligence is blunted by so much exhausting bodily labor, and becomes heavy, clumsy, awkward, and consequently incapable of grasping any other than quite simple situations. At least nine-tenths of the human race falls under this category. But still the people require a system of metaphysics, that is, an account of the world and our existence, because such an account belongs to the most natural needs of mankind, they require a popular system; and to be popular it must combine many rare qualities. It must be easily understood, and at the same time possess, on the proper points, a certain amount of obscurity, even of impenetrability; then a correct and satisfactory system of morality must be bound up with its dogmas; above all, it must afford inexhaustible consolation in suffering and death; the consequence of all this is, that it can be true only in an allegorical and not in a real sense. Further, it must have the support of an authority which is impressive by its great age, by being universally recognized, by its documents, their tone and utterances; qualities which are so extremely difficult to combine that many a man wouldn't be so ready, if he considered the matter, to help to undermine a religion, but would reflect that what he is attacking is a people's most sacred treasure. If you want to form an opinion on religion, you should always bear in mind the character of the great multitude for which it is destined, and form a picture to yourself of its complete inferiority, moral and intellectual. It is incredible how far this inferiority goes, and how perseveringly a spark of truth will glimmer on even under the crudest covering of monstrous fable or grotesque ceremony, clinging indestructibly, like the odor of musk, to everything that has once come into contact with it. In illustration of this, consider the profound wisdom of the Upanishads, and then look at the mad idolatry in the India of to-day, with its pilgrimages, processions and festivities, or at the insane and ridiculous goings-on of the Saniassi. Still one can't deny that in all this insanity and nonsense there lies some obscure purpose which accords with, or is a reflection of the profound wisdom I mentioned. But for the brute multitude, it had to be dressed up in this form. In such a contrast as this we have the two poles of humanity, the wisdom of the individual and the bestiality of the many, both of which find their point of contact in the moral sphere. That saying from the Kurral must occur to everybody: *Base people look like men, but I have never seen their exact counterpart.* The man of education may, all the same, interpret religion to himself *cum grano salis;* the man of learning, the contemplative spirit may secretly exchange it for a philosophy. But here again one philosophy wouldn't suit everybody; by the laws of affinity every system would draw to itself that public to whose education and capacities it was most suited. So there is always an inferior metaphysical system of the schools for the educated multitude, and a higher one for the *élite*. Kant's lofty doctrine, for instance, had to be degraded to the level of the schools and ruined by such men as Fries, Krug and Salat. In short, here, if anywhere, Goethe's maxim is true, *One does not suit all*. Pure faith in revelation and pure metaphysics are for the two extremes, and for the intermediate steps mutual modifications of both in innumerable combinations and gradations. And this is rendered necessary by the immeasurable differences which nature and education have placed between man and man.

Philalethes. The view you take reminds me seriously of the mysteries of the ancients, which you mentioned just now. Their fundamental purpose seems to have been to remedy the evil arising from the differences of intellectual capacity and education. The plan was, out of the great multitude utterly impervious to unveiled truth, to select certain persons who might have it revealed to them up to a given point; out of these, again, to choose others to whom more would be revealed, as being able to grasp more; and so on up to the Popes. These grades correspond to the little, greater and greatest mysteries. The arrangement was founded on a correct estimate of the intellectual inequality of mankind.

Demopheles. To some extent the education in our lower, middle and high schools corresponds to the varying grades of initiation into the mysteries.

Philalethes. In a very approximate way; and then only in so far as subjects of higher knowledge are written about exclusively in Latin. But since that has ceased to be the case, all the mysteries are profaned.

Demopheles. However that may be, I wanted to remind you that you should look at religion more from the practical than from the theoretical side. *Personified* metaphysics may be the enemy of religion, but all the same *personified* morality will be its friend. Perhaps the metaphysical element in all religions is false; but the moral element in all is true. This might perhaps be presumed from the fact that they all disagree in their metaphysics, but are in accord as regards morality.

Philalethes. Which is an illustration of the rule of logic that false premises may give a true conclusion.

Demopheles. Let me hold you to your conclusion: let me remind you that religion has two sides. If it can't stand when looked at from its theoretical, that is, its intellectual side; on the other hand, from the moral side, it proves itself the only means of guiding, controlling and mollifying those races of 'animals endowed with reason, whose kinship with the ape does not exclude a kinship with the tiger. But at the same time religion is, as a rule, a sufficient satisfaction for their dull metaphysical necessities. You don't seem to me to possess a proper idea of the difference, wide as the heavens asunder, the deep gulf between your man of learning and enlightenment, accustomed to the process of thinking, and the heavy, clumsy, dull and sluggish consciousness of humanity's beasts of burden, whose thoughts have once and for all taken the direction of anxiety about their livelihood, and cannot be put in motion in any other; whose muscular strength is so exclusively brought into play that the nervous power, which makes intelligence, sinks to a very low ebb. People like that must have something tangible which they can lay hold of on the slippery and thorny pathway of their life, some sort of beautiful fable, by means of which things can be imparted to them which their crude intelligence can entertain only in picture and parable. Profound explanations and fine distinctions are thrown away upon them. If you conceive religion in this light, and recollect that its aims are above all practical, and only in a subordinate degree theoretical, it will appear to you as something worthy of the highest respect.

Philalethes. A respect which will finally rest upon the principle that the end sanctifies the means. I don't feel in favor of a compromise on a basis like that. Religion may be an excellent means of training the perverse, obtuse and ill-disposed members of the biped race: in the eyes of the friend of truth every fraud, even though it be a pious one, is to be condemned. A system of deception, a pack of lies, would be a strange means of inculcating virtue. The flag to which I have taken the oath is truth; I shall remain faithful to it everywhere, and whether I succeed or not,

I shall fight for light and truth! If I see religion on the wrong side——

Demopheles. But you won't. Religion isn't a deception: it is true and the most important of all truths. Because its doctrines are, as I have said, of such a lofty kind that the multitude can't grasp them without an intermediary, because, I say, its light would blind the ordinary eye, it comes forward wrapt in the veil of allegory and teaches, not indeed what is exactly true in itself, but what is true in respect of the lofty meaning contained in it; and, understood in this way, religion is the truth.

Philalethes. It would be all right if religion were only at liberty to be true in a merely allegorical sense. But its contention is that it is down-right true in the proper sense of the word. Herein lies the deception, and it is here that the friend of truth must take up a hostile position.

Demopheles. The deception is a *sine quâ non.* If religion were to admit that it was only the allegorical meaning in its doctrine which was true, it would rob itself of all efficacy. Such rigorous treatment as this would destroy its invaluable influence on the hearts and morals of mankind. Instead of insisting on that with pedantic obstinacy, look at its great achievements in the practical sphere, its furtherance of good and kindly feelings, its guidance in conduct, the support and consolation it gives to suffering humanity in life and death. How much you ought to guard against letting theoretical cavils discredit in the eyes of the multitude, and finally wrest from it, something which is an inexhaustible source of consolation and tranquillity, something which, in its hard lot, it needs so much, even more than we do. On that score alone, religion should be free from attack.

Philalethes. With that kind of argument you could have driven Luther from the field, when he attacked the sale of indulgences. How many a one got consolation from the letters of indulgence, a consolation which nothing else could give, a complete tranquillity; so that he joyfully departed with the fullest confidence in the packet of them which he held in his hand at the hour of death, convinced that they were so many cards of admission to all the nine heavens. What is the use of grounds of consolation and tranquillity which are constantly overshadowed by the

Damocles-sword of illusion? The truth, my dear sir, is the only safe thing; the truth alone remains steadfast and trusty; it is the only solid consolation; it is the indestructible diamond.

Demopheles. Yes, if you had truth in your pocket, ready to favor us with it on demand. All you've got are metaphysical systems, in which nothing is certain but the headaches they cost. Before you take anything away, you must have something better to put in its place.

Philalethes. That's what you keep on saying. To free a man from error is to give, not to take away. Knowledge that a thing is false is a truth. Error always does harm; sooner or later it will bring mischief to the man who harbors it. Then give up deceiving people; confess ignorance of what you don't know, and leave every one to from his own articles of faith for himself. Perhaps they won't turn out so bad, especially as they'll rub one another's corners down, and mutually rectify mistakes. The existence of many views will at any rate lay a foundation of tolerance. Those who possess knowledge and capacity may betake themselves to the study of philosophy, or even in their own persons carry the history of philosophy a step further.

Demopheles. That'll be a pretty business! A whole nation of raw metaphysicians, wrangling and eventually coming to blows with one another!

Philalethes. Well, well, a few blows here and there are the sauce of life; or at any rate a very inconsiderable evil compared with such things as priestly dominion, plundering of the laity, persecution of heretics, courts of inquisition, crusades, religious wars, massacres of St. Bartholomew. These have been the result of popular metaphysics imposed from without; so I stick to the old saying that you can't get grapes from thistles, nor expect good to come from a pack of lies.

Demopheles. How often must I repeat that religion is anything but a pack of lies? It is truth itself, only in a mythical, allegorical vesture. But when you spoke of your plan of everyone being his own founder of religion, I wanted to say that a particularism like this is totally opposed to human nature, and would consequently destroy all social order. Man is a metaphysical animal,—that is to say, he has paramount metaphysical necessities; accordingly, he

conceives life above all in its metaphysical signification, and wishes
to bring everything into line with that. Consequently, however
strange it may sound in view of the uncertainty of all dogmas,
agreement in the fundamentals of metaphysics is the chief thing,
because a genuine and lasting bond of union is only possible among
those who are of one opinion on these points. As a result of this,
the main point of likeness and of contrast between nations is
rather religion than government, or even language; and so the
fabric of society, the State, will stand firm only when founded
on a system of metaphysics which is acknowledged by all. This,
of course, can only be a popular system,—that is, a religion: it
becomes part and parcel of the constitution of the State, of all
the public manifestations of the national life, and also of all
solemn acts of individuals. This was the case in ancient India,
among the Persians, Egyptians, Jews, Greeks and Romans; it is
still the case in the Brahman, Buddhist and Mohammedan nations. In China there are three faiths, it is true, of which the most
prevalent—Buddhism—is precisely the one which is not protected
by the State; still, there is a saying in China, universally acknowledged, and of daily application, that "the three faiths are only
one,"—that is to say, they agree in essentials. The Emperor confesses all three together at the same time. And Europe is the union
of Christian States: Christianity is the basis of every one of the
members, and the common bond of all. Hence Turkey, though
geographically in Europe, is not properly to be reckoned as belonging to it. In the same way, the European princes hold their
place "by the grace of God," and the Pope is the vicegerent of
God. Accordingly, as his throne was the highest, he used
to wish all thrones to be regarded as held in fee from
him. In the same way, too, Archbishops and Bishops, as
such, possessed temporal power; and in England they still have
seats and votes in the Upper House. Protestant princes, as such,
are heads of their churches: in England, a few years ago, this
was a girl eighteen years old. By the revolt from the Pope, the
Reformation shattered the European fabric, and in a special degree dissolved the true unity of Germany by destroying its common religious faith. This union, which had practically come to an
end, had, accordingly, to be restored later on by artificial and

purely political means. You see, then, how closely connected a common faith is with the social order and the constitution of every State. Faith is everywhere the support of the laws and the constitution, the foundation, therefore, of the social fabric, which could hardly hold together at all if religion did not lend weight to the authority of government and the dignity of the ruler.

Philalethes. Oh, yes, princes use God as a kind of bogey to frighten grown-up children to bed with, if nothing else avails: that's why they attach so much importance to the Deity. Very well. Let me, in passing, recommend our rulers to give their serious attention, regularly twice every year, to the fifteenth chapter of the First Book of Samuel, that they may be constantly reminded of what it means to prop the throne on the altar. Besides, since the stake, that *ultima ration theologorum,* has gone out of fashion, this method of government has lost its efficacy. For, as you know, religions are like glow-worms; they shine only when it is dark. A certain amount of general ignorance is the condition of all religions, the element in which alone they can exist. And as soon as astronomy, natural science, geology, history, the knowledge of countries and peoples have spread their light broadcast, and philosophy finally is permitted to say a word, every faith founded on miracles and revelation must disappear; and philosophy takes its place. In Europe the day of knowledge and science dawned towards the end of the fifteenth century with the appearance of the Renaissance Platonists: its sun rose higher in the sixteenth and seventeenth centuries so rich in results, and scattered the mists of the Middle Age. Church and Faith were compelled to disappear in the same proportion; and so in the eighteenth century English and French philosophers were able to take up an attitude of direct hostility; until, finally, under Frederick the Great, Kant appeared, and took away from religious belief the support it had previously enjoyed from philosophy: he emancipated the handmaid of theology, and in attacking the question with German thoroughness and patience, gave it an earnest instead of a frivolous tone. The consequence of this is that we see Christianity undermined in the nineteenth century, a serious faith in it almost completely gone; we see it fighting even for bare existence, whilst anxious princes try to set it up a little by artificial means, as a doctor uses a drug on a dying patient. In this connection there is a passage in Condorcet's *"Des Progrès de l'esprit humain,"* which looks as if written as a warning to our age: "the religious zeal shown by philosophers and great men was only a political devotion; and every religion which allows itself to be defended as a belief that may usefully be left to the people, can only hope for an agony more or less prolonged." In the whole course of the events which I have indicated, you may always observe that faith and knowledge are related as the two scales of a balance; when the one goes up, the other goes down. So sensitive is the balance that it indicates momentary influences. When, for instance, at the beginning of this century, those inroads of French robbers under the leadership of Bonaparte, and the enormous efforts necessary for driving them out and punishing them, had brought about a temporary neglect of science and consequently a certain decline in the general increase of knowledge, the Church immediately began to raise her head again and Faith began to show fresh signs of life; which, to be sure, in keeping with the times, was partly poetical in its nature. On the other hand, in the more than thirty years of peace which followed, leisure and prosperity furthered the building up of science and the spread of knowledge in an extraordinary degree: the consequence of which is what I have indicated, the dissolution and threatened fall of religion. Perhaps the time is approaching which has so often been prophesied, when religion will take her departure from European humanity, like a nurse which the child has outgrown: the child will now be given over to the instructions of a tutor. For there is no doubt that religious doctrines which are founded merely on authority, miracles and revelations, are only suited to the childhood of humanity. Everyone will admit that a race, the past duration of which on the earth all accounts, physical and historical, agree in placing at not more than some hundred times the life of a man of sixty, is as yet only in its first childhood.

Demopheles. Instead of taking an undisguised pleasure in prophesying the downfall of Christianity, how I wish you would consider what a measureless debt of gratitude European humanity owes to it, how greatly it has benefited by the religion which, after a long interval, followed it from its old home in the East. Europe received from Christianity ideas which were quite new to it, the knowledge, I mean, of the fundamental truth that life cannot be an end-in-itself, that the true end of our existence lies beyond it. The Greeks and Romans had placed this end altogether in our present life, so that in this sense they may certainly be called blind heathens. And, in keeping with this view of life, all their virtues can be reduced to what is serviceable to the community, to what is useful in fact. Aristotle says quite naïvely, *Those virtues must necessarily be the greatest which are the most useful to others.* So the ancients thought patriotism the highest virtue, although it is really a very doubtful one, since narrowness, prejudice, vanity and an enlightened self-interest are main elements in it. Just before the passage I quoted, Aristotle enumerates all the virtues, in order to discuss them singly. They are *Justice, Courage, Temperance, Magnificence, Magnanimity, Liberality, Gentleness, Good Sense* and *Wisdom.* How different from the Christian virtues! Plato himself, incomparably the most transcendental philosopher of pre-Christian antiquity, knows no higher virtue than *Justice;* and he alone recommends it unconditionally and for its own sake, whereas the rest make a happy life, *vita beata,* the aim of all virtue, and moral conduct the way to attain it. Christianity freed European humanity from this shallow, crude identification of itself with the hollow, uncertain existence of every day,

cœlumque tueri
Jussit, et erectos ad sidera tollere vultus.

Christianity, accordingly, does not preach mere Justice, but *the Love of Mankind, Compassion, Good Works, Forgiveness, Love of your Enemies, Patience, Humility, Resignation, Faith* and *Hope.* It even went a step further, and taught that the world is of evil, and that we need deliverance. It preached despisal of the world, self-denial, chastity, giving up of one's will, that is, turning away from life and its illusory pleasures. It taught the healing power of pain: an instrument of torture is the symbol of Christianity. I am quite ready to admit that this earnest, this only correct view of life was thousands of years previously spread all

over Asia in other forms, as it is still, independently of Christianity; but for European humanity it was a new and great revelation. For it is well known that the population of Europe consists
of Asiatic races driven out as wanderers from their own homes,
and gradually settling down in Europe; on their wanderings these
races lost the original religion of their homes, and with it the
right view of life: so, under a new sky, they formed religions
for themselves, which were rather crude; the worship of Odin,
for instance, the Druidic or the Greek religion, the metaphysical
content of which was little and shallow. In the meantime the
Greeks developed a special, one might almost say, an instinctive
sense of beauty, belonging to them alone of all the nations which
have ever existed on the earth, peculiar, fine and exact: so that
their mythology took, in the mouth of their poets, and in the
hands of their artists, an exceedingly beautiful and pleasing shape.
On the other hand, the true and deep significance of life was lost
to the Greeks and Romans. They lived on like grown-up children, till Christianity came and recalled them to the serious side
of existence.

Philalethes. And to see the effects one need only compare
antiquity with the Middle Age; the time of Pericles, say, with the
fourteenth century. You could scarcely believe you were dealing
with the same kind of beings. There, the finest development of
humanity, excellent institutions, wise laws, shrewdly apportioned
offices, rationally ordered freedom, all the arts, including poetry
and philosophy, at their best; the production of works which,
after thousands of years, are unparalleled, the creations, as it
were, of a higher order of beings, which we can never imitate;
life embellished by the noblest fellowship, as portrayed in Xenophon's *Banquet*. Look on the other picture, if you can; a time at
which the Church had enslaved the minds, and violence the bodies
of men, that knights and priests might lay the whole weight of
life upon the common beast of burden, the third estate. There,
you have might as right, Feudalism and Fanaticism in close alliance, and in their train abominable ignorance and darkness of
mind, a corresponding intolerance, discord of creeds, religious
wars, crusades, inquisitions and persecutions; as the form of fellow-

ship, chivalry, compounded of savagery and folly, with its pedantic system of ridiculous false pretenses carried to an extreme, its degrading superstition and apish veneration for women. Gallantry is the residue of this veneration, deservedly requited as it is by feminine arrogance; it affords continual food for laughter to all Asiatics, and the Greeks would have joined in it. In the golden Middle Ages the practice developed into a regular and methodical service of women; it imposed deeds of heroism, *cours d'amour,* bombastic Troubadour songs, etc.; although it is to be observed that these last buffooneries, which had an intellectual side, were chiefly at home in France; whereas amongst the material sluggish Germans, the knights distinguished themselves rather by drinking and stealing; they were good at boozing and filling their castles with plunder; though in the courts, to be sure, there was no lack of insipid love songs. What caused this utter transformation? Migration and Christianity.

Demopheles. I am glad you reminded me of it. Migration was the source of the evil; Christianity the dam on which it broke. It was chiefly by Christianity that the raw, wild hordes which came flooding in were controlled and tamed. The savage man must first of all learn to kneel, to venerate, to obey; after that he can be civilized. This was done in Ireland by St. Patrick, in Germany, by Winifred the Saxon, who was a genuine Boniface. It was migration of peoples, the last advance of Asiatic races towards Europe, followed only by the fruitless attempts of those under Atilla, Genghis Khan, and Timur, and as a comic afterpiece, by the gypsies,—it was this movement which swept away the humanity of the ancients. Christianity was precisely the principle which set itself to work against this savagery; just as later, through the whole of the Middle Age, the Church and its hierarchy were most necessary to set limits to the savage barbarism of those masters of violence, the princes and knights: it was what broke up the ice-floes in that mighty deluge. Still, the chief aim of Christianity is not so much to make this life pleasant as to render us worthy of a better. It looks away over this span of time, over this fleeting dream, and seeks to lead up to eternal welfare. Its tendency is ethical in the highest sense of the word, a sense unknown in Europe till its advent; as I have shown you, by putting the morality and religion of the ancients side by side with those of Christendom.

Philalethes. You are quite right as regards theory: but look at the practice! In comparison with the ages of Christianity the ancient world was unquestionably less cruel than the Middle Age, with its deaths by exquisite torture, its innumerable burnings at the stake. The ancients, further, were very enduring, laid great stress on justice, frequently sacrificed themselves for their country, showed such traces of every kind of magnanimity, and such genuine manliness, that to this day an acquaintance with their thoughts and actions is called the study of Humanity. The fruits of Christianity were religious wars, butcheries, crusades, inquisitions, extermination of the natives in America, and the introduction of African slaves in their place; and among the ancients there is nothing analogous to this, nothing that can be compared with it; for the slaves of the ancients, the *familia,* the *vernæ,* were a contented race, and faithfully devoted to their masters' service, and as different from the miserable negroes of the sugar plantations, which are a disgrace to humanity, as their two colors are distinct. Those special moral delinquencies for which we reproach the ancients, and which are perhaps less uncommon now-a-days than appears on the surface to be the case, are trifles compared with the Christian enormities I have mentioned. Can you then, all considered, maintain that mankind has been really made morally better by Christianity?

Demopheles. If the results haven't everywhere been in keeping with the purity and truth of the doctrine, it may be because the doctrine has been too noble, too elevated for mankind, that its aim has been placed too high. It was so much easier to come up to the heathen system, or to the Mohammedan. It is precisely what is noble and dignified that is most liable everywhere to misuse and fraud: *abusus optimi pessimus.* Those high doctrines have accordingly now and then served as a pretext for the most abominable proceedings, and for acts of unmitigated wickedness. The downfall of the institutions of the old world, as well as of its arts and sciences, is, as I have said, to be attributed to the inroad of foreign barbarians. The inevitable result of this inroad was that ignorance and savagery got the upper hand; consequently violence and knavery established their dominion, and knights and priests became a burden to mankind. It is partly, however, to be explained by the fact that the new religion made eternal and not temporal welfare the object of desire, taught that simplicity of heart was to be preferred to knowledge, and looked askance at all worldly pleasure. Now the arts and sciences subserve worldly pleasure; but in so far as they could be made serviceable to religion they were promoted, and attained a certain degree of perfection.

Philalethes. In a very narrow sphere. The sciences were suspicious companions, and as such, were placed under restrictions: on the other hand, darling ignorance, that element so necessary to a system of faith, was carefully nourished.

Demopheles. And yet mankind's possessions in the way of knowledge up to that period, which were preserved in the writings of the ancients, were saved from destruction by the clergy, especially by those in the monasteries. How would it have fared if Christianity hadn't come in just before the migration of peoples.

Philalethes. It would really be a most useful inquiry to try to make, with the coldest impartiality, an unprejudiced, careful and accurate comparison of the advantages and disadvantages which may be put down to religion. For that, of course, a much larger knowledge of historical and psychological data than either of us command would be necessary. Academies might make it a subject for a prize essay.

Demopheles. They'll take good care not to do so.

Philalethes. I'm surprised to hear you say that: it's a bad lookout for religion. However, there are academies which, in proposing a subject for competition, make it a secret condition that the prize is to go to the man who best interprets their own view. If we could only begin by getting a statistician to tell us how many crimes are prevented every year by religious, and how many by other motives, there would be very few of the former. If a man feels tempted to commit a crime, you may rely upon it that the first consideration which enters his head is the penalty appointed for it, and the chances that it will fall upon him: then comes, as a second consideration, the risk to his reputation. If I am not mistaken, he will ruminate by the hour on these two impediments, before he ever takes a thought of religious considerations. If he gets safely over those two first bulwarks against crime, I think religion alone will very rarely hold him back from it.

Demopheles. I think that it will very often do so, especially when its influence works through the medium of custom. An atrocious act is at once felt to be repulsive. What is this but the effect of early impressions? Think, for instance, how often a man, especially if of noble birth, will make tremendous sacrifices to perform what he has promised, motived entirely by the fact that his father has often earnestly impressed upon him in his childhood that "a man of honor" or "a gentleman" or a "cavalier" always keeps his word inviolate.

Philalethes. That's no use unless there is a certain inborn honorableness. You mustn't ascribe to religion what results from innate goodness of character, by which compassion for the man who would suffer by his crime keeps a man from committing it. This is the genuine moral motive, and as such it is independent of all religions.

Demopheles. But this is a motive which rarely affects the multitude unless it assumes a religious aspect. The religious aspect at any rate strengthens its power for good. Yet without any such natural foundation, religious motives alone are powerful to prevent crime. We need not be surprised at this in the case of the multitude, when we see that even people of education pass now and then under the influence, not indeed of religious motives, which are founded on something which is at least allegorically true, but of the most absurd superstition, and allow themselves to be guided by it all their life long; as, for instance, undertaking nothing on a Friday, refusing to sit down thirteen at a table, obeying chance omens, and the like. How much more likely is the multitude to be guided by such things? You can't form any adequate idea of the narrow limits of the mind in its raw state; it is a place of absolute darkness, especially when, as often happens, a bad, unjust and malicious heart is at the bottom of it. People in this condition—and they form the great bulk of humanity—must be led and controlled as well as may be, even if it be by really superstitious motives; until such time as they become sus-

ceptible to truer and better ones. As an instance of the direct
working of religion, may be cited the fact, common enough, in
Italy especially, of a thief restoring stolen goods, through the
influence of his confessor, who says he won't absolve him if he
doesn't. Think again of the case of an oath, where religion shows
a most decided influence; whether it be that a man places himself expressly in the position of a purely *moral being,* and as such
looks upon himself as solemnly appealed to, as seems to be the
case in France, where the formula is simply *je le jure,* and also
among the Quakers, whose solemn *yea* and *nay* is regarded as a
substitute for the oath; or whether it be that a man really believes he is pronouncing something which may affect his eternal
happiness,—a belief which is presumably only the investiture
of the former feeling. At any rate, religious considerations are
a means of awakening and calling out a man's moral nature. How
often it happens that a man agrees to take a false oath, and then,
when it comes to the point, suddenly refuses, and truth and right
win the day.

Philalethes. Oftener still false oaths are really taken, and truth
and right trampled under foot, though all witnesses of the oath
know it well! Still you are quite right to quote the oath as an
undeniable example of the practical efficacy of religion. But, in
spite of all you've said, I doubt whether the efficacy of religion
goes much beyond this. Just think; if a public proclamation were
suddenly made announcing the repeal of all the criminal laws,
I fancy neither you nor I would have the courage to go home
from here under the protection of religious motives. If, in the
same way, all religions were declared untrue, we could, under the
protection of the laws alone, go on living as before, without any
special addition to our apprehensions or our measures of precaution. I will go beyond this, and say that religions have very frequently exercised a decidedly demoralizing influence. One may
say generally that duties towards God and duties towards humanity are in inverse ratio. It is easy to let adulation of the Deity
make amends for lack of proper behaviour towards man. And so
we see that in all times and in all countries the great majority
of mankind find it much easier to beg their way to heaven by
prayers than to deserve to go there by their actions. In every

religion it soon comes to be the case that faith, ceremonies, rites and the like, are proclaimed to be more agreeable to the Divine will than moral actions; the former, especially if they are bound up with the emoluments of the clergy, gradually come to be looked upon as a substitute for the latter. Sacrifices in temples, the saying of masses, the founding of chapels, the planting of crosses by the roadside, soon come to be the most meritorious works, so that even great crimes are expiated by them, as also by penance, subjection to priestly authority, confessions, pilgrimages, donations to the temples and the clergy, the building of monasteries and the like. The consequence of all this is that the priests finally appear as middlemen in the corruption of the gods. And if matters don't go quite so far as that, where is the religion whose adherents don't consider prayers, praise and manifold acts of devotion, a substitute, at least in part, for moral conduct? Look at England, where by an audacious piece of priestcraft, the Christian Sunday, introduced by Constantine the Great as a substitute for the Jewish Sabbath, is in a mendacious way identified with it, and takes its name,—and this in order that the commands of Jehovah for the Sabbath (that is, the day on which the Almighty had to rest from His six days' labor, so that it is essentially the last day of the week,) might be applied to the Christian Sunday, the *dies solis,* the first day of the week which the sun opens in glory, the day of devotion and joy. The consequence of this fraud is that "Sabbath-breaking," or "the desecration of the Sabbath," that is, the slightest occupation, whether of business or pleasure, all games, music, sewing, worldly books, are on Sundays looked upon as great sins. Surely the ordinary man must believe that if, as his spiritual guides impress upon him, he is only constant in "a strict observance of the holy Sabbath," and is "a regular attendant at Divine Service," that is, if he only invariably idles away his time on Sundays, and doesn't fail to sit two hours in church to hear the same litany for the thousandth time and mutter it in tune with the others, he may reckon on indulgence in regard to those little peccadilloes which he occasionally allows himself. Those devils in human form, the slave owners and slave traders in the Free States of North America (they should be called the Slave States) are, as a rule, orthodox, pious Anglicans who would consider it a grave sin to work on Sundays; and have confidence in this, and their regular attendance at church, they hope for eternal happiness. The demoralizing tendency of religion is less problematical than its moral influence. How great and how certain that moral influence must be to make amends for the enormities which religions, especially the Christian and Mohammedan religions, have produced and spread over the earth! Think of the fanaticism, the endless persecutions, the religious wars, that sanguinary frenzy of which the ancients had no conception! think of the crusades, a butchery lasting two hundred years and inexcusable, its war cry *"It is the will of God,"* its object to gain possession of the grave of one who preached love and sufferance! think of the cruel expulsion and extermination of the Moors and Jews from Spain! think of the orgies of blood, the inquisitions, the heretical tribunals, the bloody and terrible conquests of the Mohammedans in three continents, or those of Christianity in America, whose inhabitants were for the most part, and in Cuba entirely, exterminated. According to Las Cases, Christianity murdered twelve millions in forty years, of course all *in majorem Dei gloriam,* and for the propagation of the Gospel, and because what wasn't Christian wasn't even looked upon as human! I have, it is true, touched upon these matters before; but when in our day, we hear of *Latest News from the Kingdom of God,*[2] we shall not be weary of bringing old news to mind. And above all, don't let us forget India, the cradle of the human race, or at least of that part of it to which we belong, where first Mohammedans, and then Christians, were most cruelly infuriated against the adherents of the original faith of mankind. The destruction or disfigurement of the ancient temples and idols, a lamentable, mischievous and barbarous act, still bears witness to the monotheistic fury of the Mohammedans, carried on from Mahmud, the Ghaznevid of cursed memory, down to Aurangzeb, the fratricide, whom the Portuguese Christians have zealously imitated by destruction of temples and the *auto de fé* of the inquisition at Goa. Don't let us forget the chosen people of God, who after they had, by Jehovah's express command, stolen

---

[2] A missionary paper, of which the 40th annual number appeared in 1856.

from their old and trusty friends in Egypt the gold and silver
vessels which had been lent to them, made a murderous and
plundering inroad into "the Promised Land," with the murderer
Moses at their head, to tear it from the rightful owners,—again,
by the same Jehovah's express and repeated commands, showing
no mercy, exterminating the inhabitants, women, children and all
(Joshua, ch. ix and x). And all this, simply because they weren't
circumcized and didn't know Jehovah, which was reason enough
to justify every enormity against them; just as for the same reason, in earlier times, the infamous knavery of the patriarch Jacob
and his chosen people against Hamor, King of Shalem, and his
people, is reported to his glory because the people were unbe-
lievers! (Genesis xxxiii., 18.) Truly, it is the worst side of religions
that the believers of one religion have allowed themselves every
sin again those of another, and with the utmost ruffianism and
cruelty persecuted them; the Mohammedans against the Christians
and Hindoos; the Christians against the Hindoos, Mohammedans,
American natives, Negroes, Jews, heretics, and others.

Perhaps I go too far in saying *all* religions. For the sake of
truth, I must add that the fanatical enormities perpetrated in the
name of religion are only to be put down to the adherents of
monotheistic creeds, that is, the Jewish faith and its two branches,
Christianity and Islamism. We hear of nothing of the kind in
the case of Hindoos and Buddhists. Although it is a matter of
common knowledge that about the fifth century of our era Buddhism was driven out by the Brahmans from its ancient home in
the southernmost part of the Indian peninsula, and afterwards
spread over the whole of the rest of Asia, as far as I know, we
have no definite account of any crimes of violence, or wars, or
cruelties, perpetrated in the course of it.

That may, of course, be attributable to the obscurity which
veils the history of those countries; but the exceedingly mild character of their religion, together with their unceasing inculcation
of forbearance towards all living things, and the fact that Brahmanism by its caste system properly admits no proselytes, allows one
to hope that their adherents may be acquitted of shedding blood
on a large scale, and of cruelty in any form. Spence Hardy, in

his excellent book on *Eastern Monachism,* praises the extraordinary tolerance of the Buddhists, and adds his assurance that the annals of Buddhism will furnish fewer instances of religious persecution than those of any other religion.

As a matter of fact, it is only to monotheism that intolerance is essential; an only god is by his nature a jealous god, who can allow no other god to exist. Polytheistic gods, on the other hand, are naturally tolerant; they live and let live; their own colleagues are the chief objects of their sufferance, as being gods of the same religion. This toleration is afterwards extended to foreign gods, who are, accordingly, hospitably received, and later on admitted, in some cases, to an equality of rights; the chief example of which is shown by the fact, that the Romans willingly admitted and venerated Phrygian, Egyptian and other gods. Hence it is that monotheistic religions alone furnish the spectacle of religious wars, religious persecutions, heretical tribunals, that breaking of idols and destuction of images of the gods, that razing of Indian temples, and Egyptian colossi, which had looked on the sun three thousand years, just because a jealous god had said, *Thou shalt make no graven image.*

But to return to the chief point. You are certainly right in insisting on the strong metaphysical needs of mankind; but religion appears to me to be not so much a satisfaction as an abuse of those needs. At any rate we have seen that in regard to the furtherance of morality, its utility is, for the most part, problematical, its disadvantages, and especially the atrocities which have followed in its train, are patent to the light of day. Of course it is quite a different matter if we consider the utility of religion as a prop of thrones; for where these are held "by the grace of God," throne and altar are intimately associated; and every wise prince who loves his throne and his family will appear at the head of his people as an exemplar of true religion. Even Machiavelli, in the eighteenth chapter of his book, most earnestly recommended religion to princes. Beyond this, one may say that revealed religions stand to philosophy exactly in the relation of "sovereigns by the grace of God," to "the sovereignty of the people"; so that the two former terms of the parallel are in natural alliance.

Demopheles. Oh, don't take that tone! You're going hand in hand with ochlocracy and anarchy, the arch enemy of all legislative order, all civilization and all humanity.

Philalethes. You are right. It was only a sophism of mine, what the fencing master calls a feint. I retract it. But see how disputing sometimes makes an honest man unjust and malicious. Let us stop.

Demopheles. I can't help regretting that, after all the trouble I've taken, I haven't altered your disposition in regard to religion. On the other hand, I assure you that everything you have said hasn't shaken my conviction of its high value and necessity.

Philalethes. I fully believe you; for, as we may read in Hudibras—

> A man convinc'd against his will
> Is of the same opinion still.

My consolation is that, alike in controversies and in taking mineral waters, the after effects are the true ones.

Demopheles. Well, I hope it'll be beneficial in your case.

Philalethes. It might be so, if I could digest a certain Spanish proverb:

Demopheles. Which is?

Philalethes. Behind the cross stands the devil.

Demopheles. Come, don't let us part with sarcasms. Let us rather admit that religion, like Janus, or better still, like the Brahman god of death, Yama, has two faces, and like him, one friendly, the other sullen. Each of us has kept his eye fixed on one alone.

Philalethes. You are right, old fellow.

V. THE ART OF LITERATURE

I. ON AUTHORSHIP

THERE are, first of all, two kinds of authors: those who write for the subject's sake, and those who write for writing's sake. While the one have had thoughts or experiences which seem to them worth communicating, the others want money; and so they write, for money. Their thinking is part of the business of writing. They may be recognized by the way in which they spin out their thoughts to the greatest possible length; then, too, by the very nature of their thoughts, which are only half-true, perverse, forced, vacillating; again, by the aversion they generally show to saying anything straight out, so that they may seem other than they are. Hence their writing is deficient in clearness and definiteness, and it is not long before they betray that their only object in writing at all is to cover paper. This sometimes happens with the best authors; now and then, for example, with Lessing in his *Dramaturgie,* and even in many of Jean Paul's romances. As soon as the reader perceives this, let him throw the book away; for time is precious. The truth is that when an author begins to write for the sake of covering paper, he is cheating the reader; because he writes under the pretext that he has something to say.

Writing for money and reservation of copyright are, at bottom, the ruin of literature. No one writes anything that is worth writing, unless he writes entirely for the sake of his subject. What an inestimable boon it would be, if in every branch of literature there were only a few books, but those excellent! This can never happen, as long as money is to be made by writing. It seems as though the money lay under a curse; for every author degenerates as soon as he begins to put pen to paper in any way for the sake of gain. The best works of the greatest men all come from the time when they had to write for nothing or for very little. And here, too, that Spanish proverb holds good, which declares that honor and money are not to be found in the same purse—*honora y provecho no caben en un saco*. The reason why Literature is in such a bad plight now-a-days is simply and solely that people write books to make money. A man who is in want sits down and writes a book, and the public is stupid enough to buy it. The secondary effect of this is the ruin of language.

A great many bad writers make their whole living by that foolish mania of the public for reading nothing but what has just been printed,—journalists, I mean. Truly, a most appropriate name. In plain language it is *journeymen, day-laborers!*

Again, it may be said that there are three kinds of authors. First come those who write without thinking. They write from a full memory, from reminiscences; it may be, even straight out of other people's books. This class is the most numerous. Then come those who do their thinking whilst they are writing. They think in order to write; and there is no lack of them. Last of all come those authors who think before they begin to write. They are rare.

Authors of the second class, who put off their thinking until they come to write, are like a sportsman who goes forth at random and is not likely to bring very much home. On the other hand, when an author of the third or rare class writes, it is like a *battue*. Here the game has been previously captured and shut up within a very small space; from which it is afterwards let out, so many at a time, into another space, also confined. The game cannot possibly escape the sportsman; he has nothing to do but aim and fire—in other words, write down his thoughts. This is a kind of sport from which a man has something to show.

But even though the number of those who really think seriously before they begin to write is small, extremely few of them think about *the subject itself*: the remainder think only about the books that have been written on the subject, and what has been said by others. In order to think at all, such writers need the more direct and powerful stimulus of having other people's thoughts before them. These become their immediate theme; and the result is that they are always under their influence, and so never, in any real sense of the word, are original. But the former are roused to thought by the subject itself, to which their thinking is thus immediately directed. This is the only class that produces writers of abiding fame.

It must, of course, be understood that I am speaking here of writers who treat of great subjects; not of writers on the art of making brandy.

Unless an author takes the material on which he writes out of his own head, that is to say, from his own observation, he is not worth reading. Book-manufacturers, compilers, the common run of history-writers, and many others of the same class, take their material immediately out of books; and the material goes straight to their finger-tips without even paying freight or undergoing examination as it passes through their heads, to say nothing of elaboration or revision. How very learned many a man would be if he knew everything that was in his own books! The consequence of this is that these writers talk in such a loose and vague manner, that the reader puzzles his brain in vain to understand what it is of which they are really thinking. They are thinking of nothing. It may now and then be the case that the book from which they copy has been composed exactly in the same way: so that writing of this sort is like a plaster cast of a cast; and in the end, the bare outline of the face, and that, too, hardly recognizable, is all that is left to your Antinous. Let compilations be read as seldom as possible. It is difficult to avoid them altogether; since compilations also include those text-books which contain in a small space the accumulated knowledge of centuries.

There is no greater mistake than to suppose that the last work is always the more correct; that what is written later on is in every case an improvement on what was written before; and that change always means progress. Real thinkers, men of right judgment, people who are in earnest with their subject,—these are all exceptions only. Vermin is the rule everywhere in the world: it is always on the alert, taking the mature opinions of the thinkers, and industriously seeking to improve upon them (save the mark!) in its own peculiar way.

If the reader wishes to study any subject, let him beware of rushing to the newest books upon it, and confining his attention to them alone, under the notion that science is always advancing, and that the old books have been drawn upon in the writing of the new. They have been drawn upon, it is true; but how? The writer of the new book often does not understand the old books thoroughly, and yet he is unwilling to take their exact words; so he bungles them, and says in his own bad way that which has been said very much better and more clearly by the old writers, who wrote from their own lively knowledge of the subject. The new writer frequently omits the best things they say, their most striking illustrations, their happiest remarks; because he does not see their value or feel how pregnant they are. The only thing that appeals to him is what is shallow and insipid.

It often happens that an old and excellent book is ousted by new and bad ones, which, written for money, appear with an air of great pretension and much puffing on the part of friends. In science a man tries to make his mark by bringing out something fresh. This often means nothing more than that he attacks some received theory which is quite correct, in order to make room for his own false notions. Sometimes the effort is successful for a time; and then a return is made to the old and true theory. These innovators are serious about nothing but their own precious self: it is this that they want to put forward, and the quick way of doing so, as they think, is to start a paradox. Their sterile heads take naturally to the path of negation; so they begin to deny truths that have long been admitted—the vital power, for example, the sympathetic nervous system, *generatio equivoca,* Bichat's distinction between the working of the passions and the working of intelligence; or else they want us to return to crass atomism, and the like. Hence it frequently happens that *the course of science is retrogressive.*

To this class of writers belong those translators who not only translate their author but also correct and revise him; a proceeding which always seems to me impertinent. To such writers I say: Write books yourself which are worth translating, and leave other people's works as they are!

The reader should study, if he can, the real authors, the men who have founded and discovered things; or, at any rate, those who are recognized as the great masters in every branch of knowledge. Let him buy second-hand books rather than read their contents in new ones. To be sure, it is easy to add to any new discovery—*inventis aliquid addere facile est;* and, therefore, the student, after well mastering the rudiments of his subject, will have to make himself acquainted with the more recent additions to the knowledge of it. And, in general, the following rule may be laid down here as elsewhere: if a thing is new, it is seldom good; because if it is good, it is only for a short time new.

What the address is to a letter, the title should be to a book; in other words, its main object should be to bring the book to those amongst the public who will take an interest in its contents. It should, therefore, be expressive; and since by its very nature it must be short, it should be concise, laconic, pregnant, and if possible give the contents in one word. A prolix title is bad; and so is one that says nothing, or is obscure and ambiguous, or even, it may be, false and misleading; this last may possibly involve the book in the same fate as overtakes a wrongly addressed letter. The worst titles of all are those which have been stolen, those, I mean, which have already been borne by other books; for they are in the first place a plagiarism, and secondly the most convincing proof of a total lack of originality in the author. A man who has not enough originality to invent a new title for his book, will be still less able to give it new contents. Akin to these stolen titles are those which have been imitated, that is to say, stolen to the extent of one half; for instances, long after I had produced my treatise *On Will in Nature,* Oersted wrote a book entitled *On Mind in Nature.*

A book can never be anything more than the impress of its author's thoughts; and the value of these will lie either in *the matter about which he has thought,* or in the *form* which his thoughts take, in other words, *what it is that he has thought about it.*

The matter of books is most various; and various also are the several excellences attaching to books on the score of their matter. By matter I mean everything that comes within the domain of actual experience; that is to say, the facts of history and the facts of nature, taken in and by themselves and in their widest sense. Here it is the *thing* treated of, which gives its peculiar character to the book; so that a book can be important, whoever it was that wrote it.

But in regard to the form, the peculiar character of a book depends upon the *person* who wrote it. It may treat of matters which are accessible to everyone and well known; but it is the way in which they are treated, what it is that is thought about them, that gives the book its value; and this comes from its author. If, then, from this point of view a book is excellent and beyond comparison, so is its author. It follows that if a writer is worth reading, his merit rises just in proportion as he owes little to his matter; therefore, the better known and the more hackneyed this is, the greater he will be. The three great tragedians of Greece, for example, all worked at the same subject-matter.

So when a book is celebrated, care should be taken to note whether it is so on account of its matter or its form; and a distinction should be made accordingly.

Books of great importance on account of their matter may proceed from very ordinary and shallow people, by the fact that they alone have had access to this matter; books, for instance, which describe journeys in distant lands, rare natural phenomena, or experiments; or historical occurrences of which the writers were witnesses, or in connection with which they have spent much time and trouble in the research and special study of original documents.

On the other hand, where the matter is accessible to everyone or very well known, everything will depend upon the form; and what it is that is thought about the matter will give the book all the value it possesses. Here only a really distinguished man will be able to produce anything worth reading; for the others will think nothing but what anyone else can think. They will just produce an impress of their own minds; but this is a print of which everyone possesses the original.

However, the public is very much more concerned to have matter than form; and for this very reason it is deficient in any high degree of culture. The public shows its preference in this respect in the most laughable way when it comes to deal with poetry; for there it devotes much trouble to the task of tracking out the actual events or personal circumstances in the life of the poet which served as the occasion of his various works; nay, these events and circumstances come in the end to be of greater importance than the works themselves; and rather than read Goethe himself, people prefer to read what has been written about him, and to study the legend of Faust more industriously than the drama of that name. And when Bürger declared that "people would write learned disquisitions on the question, Who Leonora really was," we find this literally fulfilled in Goethe's case; for we now possess a great many learned disquisitions on Faust and the legend attaching to him. Study of this kind is, and remains, devoted to the material of the drama alone. To give such preference to the matter over the form, is as though a man were to take a fine Etruscan vase, not to admire its shape or coloring, but to make a chemical analysis of the clay and paint of which it is composed.

The attempt to produce an effect by means of the material employed—an attempt which panders to this evil tendency of the public—is most to be condemned in branches of literature where any merit there may be lies expressly in the form; I mean, in poetical work. For all that, it is not rare to find bad dramatists trying to fill the house by means of the matter about which they write. For example, authors of this kind do not shrink from putting on the stage any man who is in any way celebrated, no matter whether his life may have been entirely devoid of dramatic incident; and sometimes, even, they do not wait until the persons immediately connected with him are dead.

The distinction between matter and form to which I am here alluding also holds good of conversation. The chief qualities which enable a man to converse well are intelligence, discernment, wit and vivacity: these supply the form of conversation. But it is not long before attention has to be paid to the matter of which he speaks; in other words, the subjects about which it is possible to converse with him—his knowledge. If this is very small, his conversation will not be worth anything, unless he possesses the above-named formal qualities in a very exceptional degree; for he will have nothing to talk about but those facts of life and nature which everybody knows. It will be just the opposite, however, if a man is deficient in these formal qualities, but has an amount of knowledge which lends value to what he says. This value will then depend entirely upon the matter of his conversation; for, as the Spanish proverb has it, *mas sabe el necio en su casa, que el sabio en la agena*—a fool knows more of his own business than a wise man does of others'.

2. ON STYLE

STYLE is the physiognomy of the mind, and a safer index to character than the face. To imitate another man's style is like wearing a mask, which, be it never so fine, is not long in arousing disgust and abhorrence, because it is lifeless; so that even the ugliest living face is better. Hence those who write in Latin and copy the manner of ancient authors, may be said to speak through a mask; the reader, it is true, hears what they say, but he cannot observe their physiognomy too; he cannot see their *style*. With the Latin works of writers who think for themselves, the case is different, and their style is visible; writers, I mean, who have not condescended to any sort of imitation, such as Scotus Erigena, Petrarch, Bacon, Descartes, Spinoza, and many others. An affectation in style is like making grimaces. Further, the language in which a man writes is the physiognomy of the nation to which he belongs; and here there are many hard-and-fast differences, beginning from the language of the Greeks, down to that of the Caribbean islanders.

To form a provincial estimate of the value of a writer's productions, it is not directly necessary to know the subject on which he has thought, or what it is that he has said about it; that would imply a perusal of all his works. It will be enough, in the main, to know *how* he has thought. This, which means the essential temper or general quality of his mind, may be precisely determined by his style. A man's style shows the *formal* nature of all his thoughts—the formal nature which can never change, be the subject or the character of his thoughts what it may: it is, as it were, the dough out of which all the contents of his mind are kneaded. When Eulenspiegel was asked how long it would take to walk to the next village, he gave the seemingly incongruous answer: *Walk*. He wanted to find out by the man's pace the distance he would cover in a given time. In the same way, when I have read a few pages of an author, I know fairly well how far he can bring me.

Every mediocre writer tries to mask his own natural style, because in his heart he knows the truth of what I am saying. He is thus forced, at the outset, to give up any attempt at being frank or naïve—a privilege which is thereby reserved for superior minds, conscious of their own worth, and therefore sure of themselves. What I mean is that these everyday writers are absolutely unable to resolve upon writing just as they think; because they have a notion that, were they to do so, their work might possibly look very childish and simple. For all that, it would not be without its value. If they would only go honestly to work, and say, quite simply, the things they have really thought, and just as they have thought them, these writers would be readable and, within their own proper sphere, even instructive.

But instead of that, they try to make the reader believe that their thoughts have gone much further and deeper than is really the case. They say what they have to say in long sentences that wind about in a forced and unnatural way; they coin new words and write prolix periods which go round and round the thought and wrap it up in a sort of disguise. They tremble between the two separate aims of communicating what they want to say and of concealing it. Their object is to dress it up so that it may look learned or deep, in order to give people the impression that there is very much more in it than for the moment meets the eye. They either jot down their thoughts bit by bit, in short, ambiguous, and para-doxical sentences, which apparently mean much more than they say,—of this kind of writing Schelling's treatises on natural philosophy are a splendid instance; or else they hold forth with a deluge of words and the most intolerable diffusiveness, as though no end of fuss were necessary to make the reader understand the deep meaning of their sentences, whereas it is some quite simple if not actually trivial idea,—examples of which may be found in plenty in the popular works of Fichte, and the philosophical manuals of a hundred other miserable dunces not worth mention-ing; or, again, they try to write in some particular style which they have been pleased to take up and think very grand, a style, for example, *par excellence* profound and scientific, where the reader is tormented to death by the narcotic effect of long-spun periods without a single idea in them,—such as are furnished in a special measure by those most impudent of all mortals, the Hegelians;[1] or it may be that it is an intellectual style they have striven after, where it seems as though their object were to go crazy altogether; and so on in many other cases. All these endeavors to put off the *nascetur ridiculus mus*—to avoid showing the funny little creature that is born after such mighty throes—often make it difficult to know what it is that they really mean. And then, too, they write down words, nay, even whole sentences, without attaching any meaning to them themselves, but in the hope that some one else will get sense out of them.

And what is at the bottom of all this? Nothing but the untiring effort to sell words for thoughts; a mode of merchandise that is always trying to make fresh openings for itself, and by means of odd expressions, turns of phrase, and combinations of every sort, whether new or used in a new sense, to produce the appearance of intellect in order to make up for the very painfully felt lack of it.

It is amusing to see how writers with this object in view will attempt first one mannerism and then another, as though they were putting on the mask of intellect! This mask may possibly deceive the inexperienced for a while, until it is seen to be a dead thing, with no life in it at all; it is then laughed at and exchanged for another. Such an author will at one moment write in a dithyrambic vein, as though he were tipsy; at another, nay, on the very next page, he will be pompous, severe, profoundly learned and prolix, stumbling on in the most cumbrous way and chopping up everything very small; like the late Christian Wolf, only in a modern dress. Longest of all lasts the mask of unintelligibility; but this is only in Germany, whither it was introduced by Fichte, perfected by Schelling, and carried to its highest pitch in Hegel—always with the best results.

And yet nothing is easier than to write so that no one can understand; just as contrarily, nothing is more difficult than to express deep things in such a way that every one must necessarily grasp them. All the arts and tricks I have been mentioning are rendered superfluous if the author really has any brains; for that

[1] In their Hegel-gazette, commonly known as *Jahrbücher der wissenschaftlichen Literatur.*

allows him to show himself as he is, and confirms to all time Horace's maxim that good sense is the source and origin of good style:

Scribendi recte sapere est et principium et fons.

But those authors I have named are like certain workers in metal, who try a hundred different compounds to take the place of gold—the only metal which can never have any substitute. Rather than do that, there is nothing against which a writer should be more upon his guard than the manifest endeavor to exhibit more intellect than he really has; because this makes the reader suspect that he possesses very little; since it is always the case that if a man affects anything, whatever it may be, it is just there that he is deficient.

That is why it is praise to an author to say that he is *naïve;* it means that he need not shrink from showing himself as he is. Generally speaking, to be naïve is to be attractive; while lack of naturalness is everywhere repulsive. As a matter of fact we find that every really great writer tries to express his thoughts as purely, clearly, definitely and shortly as possible. Simplicity has always been held to be a mark of truth; it is also a mark of genius. Style receives its beauty from the thought it expresses; but with sham-thinkers the thoughts are supposed to be fine because of the style. Style is nothing but the mere silhouette of thought; and an obscure or bad style means a dull or confused brain.

The first rule, then, for a good style is that *the author should have something to say;* nay, this is in itself almost all that is necessary. Ah, how much it means! The neglect of this rule is a fundamental trait in the philosophical writing, and, in fact, in all the reflective literature, of my country, more especially since Fichte. These writers all let it be seen that they want to appear as though they had something to say; whereas they have nothing to say. Writing of this kind was brought in by the pseudo-philosophers at the Universities, and now it is current everywhere, even among the first literary notabilities of the age. It is the mother of that strained and vague style, where there seem to be two or even more meanings in the sentence; also of that prolix and cumbrous manner of expression, called *le stile empesé;* again, of that mere waste of words which consists in pouring them out like a flood; finally, of that trick of concealing the direst poverty of thought under a farrago of never-ending chatter, which clacks away like a windmill and quite stupefies one—stuff which a man may read for hours together without getting hold of a single clearly expressed and definite idea.[2] However, people are easy-going, and they have formed the habit of reading page upon page of all sorts of such verbiage, without having any particular idea of what the author really means. They fancy it is all as it should be, and fail to discover that he is writing simply for writing's sake.

On the other hand, a good author, fertile in ideas, soon wins his reader's confidence that, when he writes, he has really and truly *something to say;* and this gives the intelligent reader patience to follow him with attention. Such an author, just because he really has something to say, will never fail to express himself in the simplest and most straightforward manner; because his object is to awaken the very same thought in the reader that he has in himself, and no other. So he will be able to affirm with Boileau that his thoughts are everywhere open to the light of the day, and that his verse always says something, whether it says it well or ill:

> Ma pensée au grand jour partout s'offre et s'expose,
> Et mon vers, bien ou mal, dit toujours quelque chose:

while of the writers previously described it may be asserted, in the words of the same poet, that they talk much and never say anything at all—*qui parle beaucoup ne disent jamais rien.*

Another characteristic of such writers is that they always avoid a positive assertion wherever they can possibly do so, in order to leave a loophole for escape in case of need. Hence they never fail to choose the more *abstract* way of expressing themselves; whereas intelligent people use the more *concrete;* because the latter brings things more within the range of actual demonstration, which is the source of all evidence.

There are many examples proving this preference for abstract

---

[2] Select examples of the art of writing in this style are to be found almost *passim* in the *Jahrbücher* published at Halle, afterwards called the *Deutschen Jahrbücher.*

expression; and a particularly ridiculous one is afforded by the use of the verb *to condition* in the sense of *to cause* or *to produce*. People say *to condition something* instead of *to cause it,* because being abstract and indefinite it says less; it affirms that *A* cannot happen without *B,* instead of that *A* is caused by *B*. A back door is always left open; and this suits people whose secret knowledge of their own incapacity inspires them with a perpetual terror of all positive assertion; while with other people it is merely the effect of that tendency by which everything that is stupid in literature or bad in life is immediately imitated—a fact proved in either case by the rapid way in which it spreads. The Englishman uses his own judgment in what he writes as well as in what he does; but there is no nation of which this eulogy is less true than of the Germans. The consequence of this state of things is that the word *cause* has of late almost disappeared from the language of literature, and people talk only of *condition*. The fact is worth mentioning because it is so characteristically ridiculous.

The very fact that these commonplace authors are never more than half-conscious when they write, would be enough to account for their dullness of mind and the tedious things they produce. I say they are only half-conscious, because they really do not themselves understand the meaning of the words they use: they take words ready-made and commit them to memory. Hence when they write, it is not so much words as whole phrases that they put together—*phrases banales*. This is the explanation of that palpable lack of clearly-expressed thought in what they say. The fact is that they do not possess the die to give this stamp to their writing; clear thought of their own is just what they have not got. And what do we find in its place?—a vague, enigmatical intermixture of words, current phrases, hackneyed terms, and fashionable expressions. The result is that the foggy stuff they write is like a page printed with very old type.

On the other hand, an intelligent author really speaks to us when he writes, and that is why he is able to rouse our interest and commune with us. It is the intelligent author alone who puts individual words together with a full consciousness of their meaning, and chooses them with deliberate design. Consequently, his discourse stands to that of the writer described above, much as a picture that has been really painted, to one that has been produced by the use of a stencil. In the one case, every word, every touch of the brush, has a special purpose; in the other, all is done mechanically. The same distinction may be observed in music. For just as Lichtenberg says that Garrick's soul seemed to be in every muscle in his body, so it is the omnipresence of intellect that always and everywhere characterizes the work of genius.

I have alluded to the tediousness which marks the works of these writers; and in this connection it is to be observed, generally, that tediousness is of two kinds; objective and subjective. A work is objectively tedious when it contains the defect in question; that is to say, when its author has no perfectly clear thought or knowledge to communicate. For if a man has any clear thought or knowledge in him, his aim will be to communicate it, and he will direct his energies to this end; so that the ideas he furnishes are everywhere clearly expressed. The result is that he is neither diffuse, nor unmeaning, nor confused, and consequently not tedious. In such a case, even though the author is at bottom in error, the error is at any rate clearly worked out and well thought over, so that it is at least formally correct; and thus some value always attaches to the work. But for the same reason a work that is objectively tedious is at all times devoid of any value whatever.

The other kind of tediousness is only relative: a reader may find a work dull because he has no interest in the question treated of in it, and this means that his intellect is restricted. The best work may, therefore, be tedious subjectively, tedious, I mean, to this or that particular person; just as, contrarily, the worst work may be subjectively engrossing to this or that particular person who has an interest in the question treated of, or in the writer of the book.

It would generally serve writers in good stead if they would see that, whilst a man should, if possible, think like a great genius, he should talk the same language as everyone else. Authors should use common words to say uncommon things. But they do just the opposite. We find them trying to wrap up trivial ideas in grand words, and to clothe their very ordinary thoughts in the most extraordinary phrases, the most far-fetched, unnatural, and out-of-the-way expressions. Their sentences perpetually stalk about on stilts. They take so much pleasure in bombast, and write in such a high-flown, bloated, affected, hyperbolical and acrobatic style that their prototype is Ancient Pistol, whom his friend Falstaff once impatiently told to say what he had to say *like a man of this world*.[3]

There is no expression in any other language exactly answering to the French *stile empesé;* but the thing itself exists all the more often. When associated with affectation, it is in literature what assumption of dignity, grand airs and primness are in society; and equally intolerable. Dullness of mind is fond of donning this dress; just as in ordinary life it is stupid people who like being demure and formal.

An author who writes in the prim style resembles a man who dresses himself up in order to avoid being confounded or put on the same level with a mob—a risk never run by the *gentleman,* even in his worst clothes. The plebeian may be known by a certain showiness of attire and a wish to have everything spick and span; and in the same way, the commonplace person is betrayed by his style.

Nevertheless, an author follows a false aim if he tries to write exactly as he speaks. There is no style of writing but should have a certain trace of kinship with the *epigraphic* or *monumental* style, which is, indeed, the ancestor of all styles. For an author to write as he speaks is just as reprehensible as the opposite fault, to speak as he writes; for this gives a pedantic effect to what he says, and at the same time makes him hardly intelligible.

An obscure and vague manner of expression is always and everywhere a very bad sign. In ninety-nine cases out of a hundred it comes from vagueness of thought; and this again almost always means that there is something radically wrong and incongruous about the thought itself—in a word, that it is incorrect. When a right thought springs up in the mind, it strives after expression and is not long in reaching it; for clear thought easily finds words to fit it. If a man is capable of thinking anything at all, he is also always able to express it in clear, intelligible, and unambiguous terms. Those writers who construct difficult, obscure, involved, and equivocal sentences, most certainly do not know aright what

[3] *King Henry IV.,* Part II, Act v., Sc. 3.

it is that they want to say: they have only a dull consciousness of it, which is still in the stage of struggle to shape itself as thought. Often, indeed, their desire is to conceal from themselves and others that they really have nothing at all to say. They wish to appear to know what they do not know, to think what they do not think, to say what they do not say. If a man has some real communication to make, which will he choose—an indistinct or clear way of expressing himself? Even Quintilian remarks that things which are said by a highly educated man are often easier to understand and much clearer; and that the less educated a man is, the more obscurely he will write—*plerumque accidit ut faciliora sint ad intelligendum et lucidiora multo quae a doctissimo quoque dicuntur. . . . Erit ergo etiam obscurior quo quisque deterior.*

An author should avoid enigmatical phrases; he should know whether he wants to say a thing or does not want to say it. It is this indecision of style that makes so many writers insipid. The only case that offers an exception to this rule arises when it is necessary to make a remark that is in some way improper.

As exaggeration generally produces an effect the opposite of that aimed at; so words, it is true, serve to make thought intelligible—but only up to a certain point. If words are heaped up beyond it, the thought becomes more and more obscure again. To find where the point lies is the problem of style, and the business of the critical faculty; for a word too much always defeats its purpose. This is what Voltaire means when he says that *the adjective is the enemy of the substantive.* But, as we have seen, many people try to conceal their poverty of thought under a flood of verbiage.

Accordingly let all redundancy be avoided, all stringing together of remarks which have no meaning and are not worth perusal. A writer must make a sparing use of the reader's time, patience and attention; so as to lead him to believe that his author writes what is worth careful study, and will reward the time spent upon it. It is always better to omit something good than to add that which is not worth saying at all. This is the right application of Hesiod's maxim, πλέον ἥμισυ πάντος [4]—the half is more than the whole. *Le secret pour être ennuyeux, c'est de tout dire.*

---

[4] *Works and Days,* 40.

Therefore, if possible, the quintessence only! mere leading thoughts! nothing that the reader would think for himself. To use many words to communicate few thoughts is everywhere the unmistakable sign of mediocrity. To gather much thought into few words stamps a man of genius.

Truth is most beautiful undraped; and the impression it makes is deep in proportion as its expression has been simple. This is so, partly because it then takes unobstructed possession of the hearer's whole soul, and leaves him no by-thought to distract him; partly, also, because he feels that here he is not being corrupted or cheated by the arts of rhetoric, but that all the effect of what is said comes from the thing itself. For instance, what declamation on the vanity of human existence could ever be more telling than the words of Job? *Man that is born of a woman hath but a short time to live and is full of misery. He cometh up, and is cut down, like a flower; he fleeth as it were a shadow, and never continueth in one stay.*

For the same reason Goethe's naïve poetry is incomparably greater than Schiller's rhetoric. It is this, again, that makes many popular songs so affecting. As in architecture an excess of decoration is to be avoided, so in the art of literature a writer must guard against all rhetorical finery, all useless amplification, and all superfluity of expression in general; in a word, he must strive after *chastity* of style. Every word that can be spared is hurtful if it remains. The law of simplicity and naïveté holds good of all fine art; for it is quite possible to be at once simple and sublime.

True brevity of expression consists in everywhere saying only what is worth saying, and in avoiding tedious detail about things which everyone can supply for himself. This involves correct discrimination between what it necessary and what is superfluous. A writer should never be brief at the expense of being clear, to say nothing of being grammatical. It shows lamentable want of judgment to weaken the expression of a thought, or to stunt the meaning of a period for the sake of using a few words less. But this is the precise endeavor of that false brevity nowadays so much in vogue, which proceeds by leaving out useful words and even by sacrificing grammar and logic. It is not only that such writers spare a word by making a single verb or adjective do duty for several different periods, so that the reader, as it were, has to grope his way through them in the dark; they also practice, in many other respects, an unseeming economy of speech, in the effort to effect what they foolishly take to be brevity of expression and conciseness of style. By omitting something that might have thrown a light over the whole sentence, they turn it into a conundrum, which the reader tries to solve by going over it again and again.[5]

It is wealth and weight of thought, and nothing else, that gives brevity to style, and makes it concise and pregnant. If a writer's ideas are important, luminous, and generally worth communicating, they will necessarily furnish matter and substance enough to fill out the periods which give them expression, and make these in all their parts both grammatically and verbally complete; and so much will this be the case that no one will ever find them hollow, empty or feeble. The diction will everywhere be brief and pregnant, and allow the thought to find intelligible and easy expression, and even unfold and move about with grace.

Therefore instead of contracting his words and forms of speech, let a writer enlarge his thoughts. If a man has been thinned by illness and finds his clothes too big, it is not by cutting them down, but by recovering his usual bodily condition, that he ought to make them fit him again.

Let me here mention an error of style, very prevalent nowadays, and, in the degraded state of literature and the neglect of ancient language, always on the increase; I mean *subjectivity*. A writer commits this error when he thinks it enough if he himself knows what he means and wants to say, and takes no thought for the reader, who is left to get at the bottom of it as best he can. This is as though the author were holding a monologue; whereas, it

[5] *Translator's Note.*—In the original, Schopenhauer here enters upon a lengthy examination of certain common errors in the writing and speaking of German. His remarks are addressed to his own countrymen, and would lose all point, even if they were intelligible, in an English translation. But for those who practice their German by conversing or corresponding with Germans, let me recommend what he there says as a useful corrective to a slipshod style, such as can easily be contracted if it is assumed that the natives of a country always know their own language perfectly.

ought to be a dialogue; and a dialogue, too, in which he must express himself all the more clearly inasmuch as he cannot hear the questions of his interlocutor.

Style should for this very reason never be subjective, but *objective;* and it will not be objective unless the words are so set down that they directly force the reader to think precisely the same thing as the author thought when he wrote them. Nor will this result be obtained unless the author has always been careful to remember that thought so far follows the law of gravity that it travels from head to paper much more easily than from paper to head; so that he must assist the latter passage by every means in his power. If he does this, a writer's words will have a purely objective effect, like that of a finished picture in oils; whilst the subjective style is not much more certain in its working than spots on the wall, which look like figures only to one whose phantasy has been accidentally aroused by them; other people see nothing but spots and blurs. The difference in question applies to literary method as a whole; but it is often established also in particular instances. For example, in a recently published work I found the following sentence: *I have not written in order to increase the number of existing books.* This means just the opposite of what the writer wanted to say, and is nonsense as well.

He who writes carelessly confesses thereby at the very outset that he does not attach much importance to his own thoughts. For it is only where a man is convinced of the truth and importance of his thoughts, that he feels the enthusiasm necessary for an untiring and assiduous effort to find the clearest, finest, and strongest expression for them,—just as for sacred relics or priceless works of art there are provided silvern or golden receptacles. It was this feeling that led ancient authors, whose thoughts, expressed in their own words, have lived thousands of years, and therefore bear the honored title of *classics,* always to write with care. Plato, indeed, is said to have written the introduction to his *Republic* seven times over in different ways.

As neglect of dress betrays want of respect for the company a man meets, so a hasty, careless, bad style shows an outrageous lack of regard for the reader, who then rightly punishes it by refusing to read the book. It is especially amusing to see reviewers

criticising the works of others in their own most careless style—
the style of a hireling. It is as though a judge were to come into
court in dressing-gown and slippers! If I see a man badly and
dirtily dressed, I feel some hesitation, at first, in entering into
conversation with him: and when, on taking up a book, I am
struck at once by the negligence of its style, I put it away.

Good writing should be governed by the rule that a man can
think only one thing clearly at a time; and, therefore, that he
should not be expected to think two or even more things in one
and the same moment. But this is what is done when a writer
breaks up his principal sentence into little pieces, for the purpose
of pushing into the gaps thus made two or three other thoughts
by way of parenthesis; thereby unnecessarily and wantonly confus-
ing the reader. And here it is again my own countrymen who
are chiefly in fault. That German lends itself to this way of
writing, makes the thing possible, but does not justify it. No prose
reads more easily or pleasantly than French, because, as a rule,
it is free from the error in question. The Frenchman strings his
thoughts together, as far as he can, in the most logical and natural
order, and so lays them before his reader one after the other for
convenient deliberation, so that every one of them may receive
undivided attention. The German, on the other hand, weaves them
together into a sentence which he twists and crosses, and crosses
and twists again; because he wants to say six things all at once,
instead of advancing them one by one. His aim should be to attract and hold the reader's attention; but, above and beyond
neglect of this aim, he demands from the reader that he shall set
the above mentioned rule at defiance, and think three or four
different thoughts at one and the same time; or since that is impossible, that his thoughts shall succeed each other as quickly as
the vibrations of a cord. In this way an author lays the foundation of his *stile empesé,* which is then carried to perfection by
the use of high-flown, pompous expressions to communicate the
simplest things, and other artifices of the same kind.

In those long sentences rich in involved parenthesis, like a box
of boxes one within another, and padded out like roast geese
stuffed with apples, it is really the *memory* that is chiefly taxed;
while it is the understanding and the judgment which should be

called into play, instead of having their activity thereby actually hindered and weakened. This kind of sentence furnishes the reader with mere half-phrases, which he is then called upon to collect carefully and store up in his memory, as though they were the pieces of a torn letter, afterwards to be completed and made sense of by the other halves to which they respectively belong. He is expected to go on reading for a little without exercising any thought, nay, exerting only his memory, in the hope that, when he comes to the end of the sentence, he may see its meaning and so receive something to think about; and he is thus given a great deal to learn by heart before obtaining anything to understand. This is manifestly wrong and an abuse of the reader's patience.

The ordinary writer has an unmistakable preference for this style, because it causes the reader to spend time and trouble in understanding that which he would have understood in a moment without it; and this makes it look as though the writer had more depth and intelligence than the reader. This is, indeed, one of those artifices referred to above, by means of which mediocre authors unconsciously, and as it were by instinct, strive to conceal their poverty of thought and give an appearance of the opposite. Their ingenuity in this respect is really astounding.

It is manifestly against all sound reason to put one thought obliquely on top of another, as though both together formed a wooden cross. But this is what is done where a writer interrupts what he has begun to say, for the purpose of inserting some quite alien matter; thus depositing with the reader a meaningless half-sentence, and bidding him keep it until the completion comes. It is much as though a man were to treat his guests by handing them an empty plate, in the hope of something appearing upon it. And commas used for a similar purpose belong to the same family as notes at the foot of the page and parentheses in the middle of the text; nay, all three differ only in degree. If Demosthenes and Cicero occasionally inserted words by ways of parenthesis, they would have done better to have refrained.

But this style of writing becomes the height of absurdity when the parentheses are not even fitted into the frame of the sentence, but wedged in so as directly to shatter it. If, for instance, it is an impertinent thing to interrupt another person when he is speaking, it is no less impertinent to interrupt oneself. But all bad, careless, and hasty authors, who scribble with the bread actually before their eyes, use this style of writing six times on a page, and rejoice in it. It consists in—it is advisable to give rule and example together, wherever it is possible—breaking up one phrase in order to glue in another. Nor is it merely out of laziness that they write thus. They do it out of stupidity; they think there is a charming *légèreté* about it; that it gives life to what they say. No doubt there are a few rare cases where such a form of sentence may be pardonable.

Few write in the way in which an architect builds; who, before he sets to work, sketches out his plan, and thinks it over down to its smallest details. Nay, most people write only as though they were playing dominoes; and, as in this game, the pieces are arranged half by design, half by chance, so it is with the sequence and connection of their sentences. They only have an idea of what the general shape of their work will be, and of the aim they set before themselves. Many are ignorant even of this, and write as the coral-insects build; period joins to period, and the Lord only knows what the author means.

3. ON THINKING FOR ONESELF

A LIBRARY may be very large; but if it is in disorder, it is not so useful as one that is small but well arranged. In the same way, a man may have a great mass of knowledge, but if he has not worked it up by thinking it over for himself, it has much less value than a far smaller amount which he has thoroughly pondered. For it is only when a man looks at his knowledge from all sides, and combines the things he knows by comparing truth with truth, that he obtains a complete hold over it and gets it into his power. A man cannot turn over anything in his mind unless he knows it; he should, therefore, learn something; but it is only when he has turned it over that he can be said to know it.

Reading and learning are things that anyone can do of his own free will; but not so *thinking*. Thinking must be kindled, like a fire by a draught; it must be sustained by some interest in the matter in hand. This interest may be of purely objective kind, or merely subjective. The latter comes into play only in things that concern us personally. Objective interest is confined to heads that think by nature; to whom thinking is as natural as breathing; and they are very rare. This is why most men of learning show so little of it.

It is incredible what a different effect is produced upon the mind by thinking for oneself, as compared with reading. It carries on and intensifies that original difference in the nature of two minds which leads the one to think and the other to read. What I mean is that reading forces alien thoughts upon the mind— thoughts which are as foreign to the drift and temper in which it may be for the moment, as the seal is to the wax on which it stamps its imprint. The mind is thus entirely under compulsion from without; it is driven to think this or that, though for the moment it may not have the slightest impulse or inclination to do so.

But when a man thinks for himself, he follows the impulse of his own mind, which is determined for him at the time, either by his environment or some particular recollection. The visible world of a man's surroundings does not, as reading does, impress a *single* definite thought upon his mind, but merely gives the matter and occasion which lead him to think what is appropriate to his nature and present temper. So it is, that much reading deprives the mind of all elasticity; it is like keeping a spring continually under pressure. The safest way of having no thoughts of one's own is to take up a book every moment one has nothing else to do. It is this practice which explains why erudition makes most men more stupid and silly than they are by nature, and prevents their writings obtaining any measure of success. They remain, in Pope's words:

> *For ever reading, never to be read!* [6]

Men of learning are those who have done their reading in the pages of a book. Thinkers and men of genius are those who have gone straight to the book of Nature; it is they who have enlightened the world and carried humanity further on its way.

If a man's thoughts are to have truth and life in them, they must, after all, be his own fundamental thoughts; for these are the only ones that he can fully and wholly understand. To read another's thoughts is like taking the leavings of a meal to which we have not been invited, or putting on the clothes which some unknown visitor has laid aside. The thought we read is related to the thought which springs up in ourselves, as the fossil-impress of some prehistoric plant to a plant as it buds forth in springtime.

Reading is nothing more than a substitute for thought of one's own. It means putting the mind into leading-strings. The multitude of books serves only to show how many false paths there are, and how widely astray a man may wander if he follows any of them. But he who is guided by his genius, he who thinks for himself, who thinks spontaneously and exactly, possesses the only compass by which he can steer aright. A man should read only when his own thoughts stagnate at their source, which will happen often

---

[6] *Dunciad,* iii., 194.

enough even with the best of minds. On the other hand, to take up a book for the purpose of scaring away one's own original thoughts is sin against the Holy Spirit. It is like running away from Nature to look at a museum of dried plants or gaze at a landscape in copperplate.

A man may have discovered some portion of truth or wisdom, after spending a great deal of time and trouble in thinking it over for himself and adding thought to thought; and it may sometimes happen that he could have found it all ready to hand in a book and spared himself the trouble. But even so, it is a hundred times more valuable if he has acquired it by thinking it out for himself. For it is only when we gain our knowledge in this way that it enters as an integral part, a living member, into the whole system of our thought; that it stands in complete and firm relation with what we know; that it is understood with all that underlies it and follows from it; that it wears the color, the precise shade, the distinguishing mark, of our own way of thinking; that it comes exactly at the right time, just as we felt the necessity for it; that it stands fast and cannot be forgotten. This is the perfect application, nay, the interpretation, of Goethe's advice to earn our inheritance for ourselves so that we may really possess it:

> *Was due ererbt von deinen Vätern hast,*
> *Erwirb es, um es zu besitzen.*[7]

The man who thinks for himself, forms his own opinions and learns the authorities for them only later on, when they serve but to strengthen his belief in them and in himself. But the book-philosopher starts from the authorities. He reads other people's books, collects their opinions, and so forms a whole for himself, which resembles an automaton made up of anything but flesh and blood. Contrarily, he who thinks for himself creates a work like a living man as made by Nature. For the work comes into being as a man does; the thinking mind is impregnated from without, and it then forms and bears its child.

Truth that has been merely learned is like an artificial limb, a false tooth, a waxen nose; at best, like a nose made out of another's flesh; it adheres to us only because it is put on. But truth

[7] *Faust,* I., 329.

acquired by thinking of our own is like a natural limb; it alone really belongs to us. This is the fundamental difference between the thinker and the mere man of learning. The intellectual attainments of a man who thinks for himself resemble a fine painting, where the light and shade are correct, the tone sustained, the color perfectly harmonized; it is true to life. On the other hand, the intellectual attainments of the mere man of learning are like a large palette, full of all sorts of colors, which at most are systematically arranged, but devoid of harmony, connection and meaning.

Reading is thinking with some one else's head instead of one's own. To think with one's own head is always to aim at developing a coherent whole—a system, even though it be not a strictly complete one; and nothing hinders this so much as too strong a current of others' thoughts, such as comes of continual reading. These thoughts, springing every one of them from different minds, belonging to different systems, and tinged with different colors, never of themselves flow together into an intellectual whole; they never form a unity of knowledge, or insight, or conviction; but, rather, fill the head with a Babylonian confusion of tongues. The mind that is over-loaded with alien thought is thus deprived of all clear insight, and is well-nigh disorganized. This is a state of things observable in many men of learning; and it makes them inferior in sound sense, correct judgment and practical tact, to many illiterate persons, who, after obtaining a little knowledge from without, by means of experience, intercourse with others, and a small amount of reading, have always subordinated it to, and embodied it with, their own thought.

The really scientific *thinker* does the same thing as these illiterate persons, but on a larger scale. Although he has need of much knowledge, and so must read a great deal, his mind is nevertheless strong enough to master it all, to assimilate and incorporate it with the system of his thoughts, and so to make it fit in with the organic unity of his insight, which, though vast, is always growing. And in the process, his own thought, like the bass in an organ, always dominates everything and is never drowned by other tones, as happens with minds which are full of mere antiquarian lore; where shreds of music, as it were, in every key, mingle confusedly, and no fundamental note is heard at all.

Those who have spent their lives in reading, and taken their wisdom from books, are like people who have obtained precise information about a country from the descriptions of many travelers. Such people can tell a great deal about it; but after all, they have no connected, clear, and profound knowledge of its real condition. But those who have spent their lives in thinking, resemble the travelers themselves; they alone really know what they are talking about; they are acquainted with the actual state of affairs, and are quite at home in the subject.

The thinker stands in the same relation to the ordinary book-philosopher as an eye-witness does to the historian; he speaks from direct knowledge of his own. That is why all those who think for themselves come, at bottom, to much the same conclusion. The differences they present are due to their different points of view; and when these do not affect the matter, they all speak alike. They merely express the result of their own objective perception of things. There are many passages in my works which I have given to the public only after some hesitation, because of their parodoxical nature; and afterwards I have experienced a pleasant surprise in finding the same opinion recorded in the works of great men who lived long ago.

The book-philosopher merely reports what one person has said and another meant, or the objections raised by a third, and so on. He compares different opinions, ponders, criticises, and tries to get at the truth of the matter; herein on a par with the critical historian. For instance, he will set out to inquire whether Leibnitz was not for some time a follower of Spinoza, and questions of a like nature. The curious student of such matters may find conspicuous examples of what I mean in Herbart's *Analytical Elucidation of Morality and Natural Right,* and in the same author's *Letters on Freedom.* Surprise may be felt that a man of the kind should put himself to so much trouble; for, on the face of it, if he would only examine the matter for himself, he would speedily attain his object by the exercise of a little thought. But there is a small difficulty in the way. It does not depend upon his own will. A man can always sit down and read, but not—think. It is with thoughts as with men; they cannot always be summoned at pleasure; we must wait for them to come. Thought about a subject must appear of itself, by a happy and harmonious combination of external stimulus with mental temper and attention; and it is just that which never seems to come to these people.

This truth may be illustrated by what happens in the case of matters affecting our own personal interest. When it is necessary to come to some resolution in a matter of that kind, we cannot well sit down at any given moment and think over the merits of the case and make up our mind; for, if we try to do so, we often find ourselves unable, at that particular moment, to keep our mind fixed upon the subject; it wanders off to other things. Aversion to the matter in question is sometimes to blame for this. In such a case we should not use force, but wait for the proper frame of mind to come of itself. It often comes unexpectedly and returns again and again; and the variety of temper in which we approach it at different moments puts the matter always in a fresh light. It is this long process which is understood by the term *a ripe resolution*. For the work of coming to a resolution must be distributed; and in the process much that is overlooked at one moment occurs to us at another; and the repugnance vanishes when we find, as we usually do, on a closer inspection, that things are not so bad as they seemed.

This rule applies to the life of the intellect as well as to matters of practice. A man must wait for the right moment. Not even the greatest mind is capable of thinking for itself at all times. Hence a great mind does well to spend its leisure in reading, which, as I have said, is a substitute for thought; it brings stuff to the mind by letting another person do the thinking; although that is always done in a manner not our own. Therefore, a man should not read too much, in order that his mind may not become accustomed to the substitute and thereby forget the reality; that it may not form the habit of walking in well-worn paths; nor by following an alien course of thought grow a stranger to its own. Least of all should a man quite withdraw his gaze from the real world for the mere sake of reading; as the impulse and the temper which prompt to thought of one's own come far oftener from the world of reality than from the world of books. The real life that a man sees before him is the natural subject of thought; and in its strength as the primary element of existence, it can more easily than anything else rouse and influence the thinking mind.

After these considerations, it will not be matter for surprise that a man who thinks for himself can easily be distinguished from the book-philosopher by the very way in which he talks, by his marked earnestness, and the originality, directness, and personal conviction that stamp all his thoughts and expressions. The book-philosopher, on the other hand, lets it be seen that everything he has is second-hand; that his ideas are like the number and trash of an old furniture-shop, collected together from all quarters. Mentally, he is dull and pointless—a copy of a copy. His literary style is made up of conventional, nay, vulgar phrases, and terms that happen to be current; in this respect much like a small State where all the money that circulates is foreign, because it has no coinage of its own.

Mere experience can as little as reading supply the place of thought. It stands to thinking in the same relation in which eating stands to digestion and assimilation. When experience boasts that to its discoveries alone is due the advancement of the human race, it is as though the mouth were to claim the whole credit of maintaining the body in health.

The works of all truly capable minds are distinguished by a character of *decision* and *definiteness,* which means they are clear and free from obscurity. A truly capable mind always knows definitely and clearly what it is that it wants to express, whether its medium is prose, verse, or music. Other minds are not decisive and not definite; and by this they may be known for what they are.

The characteristic sign of a mind of the highest order is that it always judges at first hand. Everything it advances is the result of thinking for itself; and this is everywhere evident by the way in which it gives its thoughts utterance. Such a mind is like a Prince. In the realm of intellect its authority is imperial, whereas the authority of minds of a lower order is only delegated as may be seen in their style, which has no independent stamp of its own.

Every one who really thinks for himself is so far like a monarch. His position is undelegated and supreme. His judgments, like royal decrees, spring from his own sovereign power and proceed directly from himself. He acknowledges authority as little as a monarch admits a command; he subscribes to nothing but what he has himself authorized. The multitude of common minds, laboring under all sorts of current opinions, authorities, prejudices, is like the people, which silently obeys the law and accepts orders from above.

Those who are so zealous and eager to settle debated questions by citing authorities, are really glad when they are able to put the understanding and the insight of others into the field in place of their own, which are wanting. Their number is legion. For, as Seneca says, there is no man but prefers belief to the exercise of judgment—*unusquisque mavult credere quam judicare.* In their controversies such people make a promiscuous use of the weapon of authority, and strike out at one another with it. If any one chances to become involved in such a contest, he will do well not to try reason and argument as a mode of defense; for against a weapon of that kind these people are like Siegfrieds, with a skin of horn, and dipped in the flood of incapacity for thinking and judging. They will meet his attack by bringing up their authorities as a way of abashing him—*argumentum ad vere- cundiam,* and then cry out that they have won the battle.

In the real world, be it never so fair, favorable and pleasant, we always live subject to the law of gravity which we have to be constantly overcoming. But in the world of intellect we are disembodied spirits, held in bondage to no such law, and free from penury and distress. Thus it is that there exists no happiness on earth like that which, at the auspicious moment, a fine and fruitful mind finds in itself.

The presence of a thought is like the presence of a woman we love. We fancy we shall never forget the thought nor become indifferent to the dear one. But out of sight, out of mind! The finest thought runs the risk of being irrevocably forgotten if we do not write it down, and the darling of being deserted if we do not marry her.

There are plenty of thoughts which are valuable to the man who thinks them; but only few of them which have enough strength to produce repercussive or reflect action—I mean, to win the reader's sympathy after they have been put on paper.

But still it must not be forgotten that a true value attaches only to what a man has thought in the first instance *for his own case.* Thinkers may be classed according as they think chiefly for their own case or for that of others. The former are the genuine independent thinkers; they really think and are really independent; they are the true *philosophers;* they alone are in earnest. The pleasure and the happiness of their existence consists in thinking. The others are the *sophists;* they want to seem that which they are not, and seek their happiness in what they hope to get from the world. They are in earnest about nothing else. To which of these two classes a man belongs may be seen by his whole style and manner. Lichtenberg is an example for the former class; Herder, there can be no doubt, belongs to the second.

When one considers how vast and how close to us is *the problem of existence*—this equivocal, tortured, fleeting, dream-like existence of ours—so vast and so close that a man no sooner discovers it than it overshadows and obscures all other problems and aims; and when one sees how all men, with few and rare exceptions, have no clear consciousness of the problem, nay, seem to be quite unaware of its presence, but busy themselves with everything rather than with this, and live on, taking no thought but for the passing day and the hardly longer span of their own personal future, either expressly discarding the problem or else over-ready to come to terms with it by adopting some system of popular metaphysics and letting it satisfy them; when, I say, one takes all this to heart, one may come to the opinion that man may be said to be *a thinking being* only in a very remote sense, and henceforth feel no special surprise at any trait of human thoughtlessness or folly; but know, rather, that the normal man's intellectual range of vision does indeed extend beyond that of the brute, whose whole existence is, as it were, a continual present, with no consciousness of the past or the future, but not such an immeasurable distance as is generally supposed.

This is, in fact, corroborated by the way in which most men converse; where their thoughts are found to be chopped up fine, like chaff, so that for them to spin out a discourse of any length is impossible.

If this world were peopled by really thinking beings, it could not be that noise of every kind would be allowed such generous limits, as is the case with the most horrible and at the same time aimless form of it.[10] If Nature had meant man to think, she would not have given him ears; or, at any rate, she would have furnished them with air-tight flaps, such as are the enviable possession of the bat. But, in truth, man is a poor animal like the rest, and his powers are meant only to maintain him in the struggle for existence; so he must need keep his ears always open, to announce of themselves, by night as by day, the approach of the pursuer.

[8] *Translator's Note.*—Schopenhauer refers to the cracking of whips. See the Essay *On Noise* in *Studies in Pessimism*.

4. ON BOOKS AND READING

IGNORANCE is degrading only when found in company with riches. The poor man is restrained by poverty and need: labor occupies his thoughts, and takes the place of knowledge. But rich men who are ignorant live for their lusts only, and are like the beasts of the field; as may be seen every day: and they can also be reproached for not having used wealth and leisure for that which gives them their greatest value.

When we read, another person thinks for us: we merely repeat his mental process. In learning to write, the pupil goes over with his pen what the teacher has outlined in pencil: so in reading; the greater part of the work of thought is already done for us. This is why it relieves us to take up a book after being occupied with our own thoughts. And in reading, the mind is, in fact, only the playground of another's thoughts. So it comes about that if anyone spends almost the whole day in reading, and by way of relaxation devotes the intervals to some thoughtless pastime, he gradually loses the capacity for thinking; just as the man who always rides, at last forgets how to walk. This is the case with many learned persons: they have read themselves stupid. For to occupy every spare moment in reading, and to do nothing but read, is even more paralyzing to the mind than constant manual labor, which at least allows those engaged in it to follow their own thoughts. A spring never free from the pressure of some foreign body at last loses its elasticity; and so does the mind if other people's thoughts are constantly forced upon it. Just as you can ruin the stomach and impair the whole body by taking too much nourishment, so you can overfill and choke the mind by feeding it too much. The more you read, the fewer are the traces left by what you have read: the mind becomes like a tablet crossed over and over with writing. There is no time for ruminating, and in no other way can you assimilate what you have read. If you read on and on without setting your own thoughts to work, what you have read cannot strike root, and is generally lost. It is, in fact, just the same with mental as with bodily food: hardly the fifth part of what one takes is assimilated. The rest passes off in evaporation, respiration and the like.

The result of all this is that thoughts put on paper are nothing more than footsteps in the sand: you see the way the man has gone, but to know what he saw on his walk, you want his eyes.

There is no quality of style that can be gained by reading writers who possess it; whether it be persuasiveness, imagination, the gift of drawing comparisons, boldness, bitterness, brevity, grace, ease of expression or wit, unexpected contrasts, a laconic or naïve manner, and the like. But if these qualities are already in us, exist, that is to say, potentially, we can call them forth and bring them to consciousness; we can learn the purposes to which they can be put; we can be strengthened in our inclination to use them, or get courage to do so; we can judge by examples the effect of applying them, and so acquire the correct use of them; and of course it is only when we have arrived at that point that we actually possess these qualities. The only way in which reading can form style is by teaching us the use to which we can put our own natural gifts. We must have these gifts before we begin to learn the use of them. Without them, reading teaches us nothing but cold, dead mannerisms and makes us shallow imitators.

The strata of the earth preserve in rows the creatures which lived in former ages; and the array of books on the shelves of a library stores up in like manner the errors of the past and the way in which they have been exposed. Like those creatures, they too were full of life in their time, and made a great deal of noise; but now they are stiff and fossilized, and an object of curiosity to the literary palæontologist alone.

Herodotus relates that Xerxes wept at the sight of his army, which stretched further than the eye could reach, in the thought that of all these, after a hundred years, not one would be alive. And in looking over a huge catalogue of new books, one might weep at thinking that, when ten years have passed, not one of them will be heard of.

It is in literature as in life: wherever you turn, you stumble at once upon the incorrigible mob of humanity, swarming in all directions, crowding and soiling everything, like flies in summer. Hence the number, which no man can count, of bad books, those rank weeds of literature, which draw nourishment from the corn and choke it. The time, money and attention of the public, which rightfully belong to good books and their noble aims, they take for themselves: they are written for the mere purpose of making money or procuring places. So they are not only useless; they do positive mischief. Nine-tenths of the whole of our present literature has no other aim than to get a few shillings out of the pockets of the public; and to this end author, publisher and reviewer are in league.

Let me mention a crafty and wicked trick, albeit a profitable and successful one, practised by littérateurs, hack writers, and voluminous authors. In complete disregard of good taste and the true culture of the period, they have succeeded in getting the whole of the world of fashion into leading strings, so that they are all trained to read in time, and all the same thing, viz., *the newest books;* and that for the purpose of getting food for conversation in the circles in which they move. This is the aim served by bad novels, produced by writers who were once celebrated, as Spindler, Bulwer Lytton, Eugene Sue. What can be more miserable than the lot of a reading public like this, always bound to peruse the latest works of extremely commonplace persons who write for money only, and who are therefore never few in number? and for this advantage they are content to know by name only, the works of the few superior minds of all ages and all countries. Literary newspapers, too, are a singularly cunning device for robbing the reading public of the time which, if culture is to be attained, should be devoted to the genuine productions of literature, instead of being occupied by the daily bungling commonplace persons.

Hence, in regard to reading, it is a very important thing to be able to refrain. Skill in doing so consists in not taking into one's hands any book merely because at the time it happens to be extensively read; such as political or religious pamphlets, novels, poetry, and the like, which make a noise, and may even attain to several editions in the first and last year of their existence. Consider, rather, that the man who writes for fools is always sure of a large audience; be careful to limit your time for reading, and devote it exclusively to the works of those great minds of all times and countries, who o'ertop the rest of humanity, those whom the voice of fame points to as such. These alone really educate and instruct. You can never read bad literature too little, nor good literature too much. Bad books are intellectual poison; they destroy the mind. Because people always read what is new instead of the best of all ages, writers remain in the narrow circle of the ideas which happen to prevail in their time; and so the period sinks deeper and deeper into its own mire.

There are at all times two literatures in progress, running side by side, but little known to each other; the one real, the other only apparent. The former grows into permanent literature; it is pursued by those who live *for* science or poetry; its course is sober and quiet, but extremely slow; and it produces in Europe scarcely a dozen works in a century; these, however, are permanent. The other kind is pursued by persons who live *on* science or poetry; it goes at a gallop with much noise and shouting of partisans; and every twelve-month puts a thousand works on the market. But after a few years one asks, Where are they? where is the glory which came so soon and made so much clamor? This kind may be called fleeting, and the other, permanent literature.

In the history of politics, half a century is always a considerable time; the matter which goes to form them is ever on the move; there is always something going on. But in the history of literature there is often a complete standstill for the same period; nothing has happened, for clumsy attempts don't count. You are just where you were fifty years previously.

To explain what I mean, let me compare the advance of knowledge among mankind to the course taken by a planet. The false paths on which humanity usually enters after every important advance are like the epicycles in the Ptolemaic system, and after passing through one of them, the world is just where it was before it entered it. But the great minds, who really bring the race further on its course do not accompany it on the epicycles it makes from time to time. This explains why posthumous fame is often bought at the expense of contemporary praise, and *vice versa*. An instance of such an epicycle is the philosophy started by Fichte and Schelling, and crowned by Hegel's caricature of it. This epicycle was a deviation from the limit to which philosophy had been ultimately brought by Kant; and at that point I took it up again afterwards, to carry it further. In the intervening period the sham philosophers I have mentioned and some others went through their epicycle, which had just come to an end; so that those who went with them on their course are conscious of the fact that they are exactly at the point from which they started.

This circumstance explains why it is that, every thirty years or so, science, literature, and art, as expressed in the spirit of the time, are declared bankrupt. The errors which appear from time to time mount to such a height in that period that the mere weight of their absurdity makes the fabric fall; whilst the opposition to them has been gathering force at the same time. So an upset takes place, often followed by an error in the opposite direction. To exhibit these movements in their periodical return would be the true practical aim of the history of literature: little attention, however, is paid to it. And besides, the comparatively short duration of these periods makes it difficult to collect the data of epochs long gone by, so that it is most convenient to observe how the matter stands in one's own generation. An instance of this tendency, drawn from physical science, is supplied in the Neptunian geology of Werter.

But let me keep strictly to the example cited above, the nearest we can take. In German philosophy, the brilliant epoch of Kant was immediately followed by a period which aimed rather at being imposing than at convincing. Instead of being thorough and clear, it tried to be dazzling, hyperbolical, and, in a special degree, unintelligible: instead of seeking truth, it intrigued. Philosophy could make no progress in this fashion; and at last the whole school and its method became bankrupt. For the effrontery of Hegel and his fellows came to such a pass,—whether because they talked such sophisticated nonsense, or were so unscrupulously puffed, or because the entire aim of this pretty piece of work was quite obvious,—that in the end there was nothing to prevent charlatanry of the whole business from becoming manifest to everybody: and when, in consequence of certain disclosures, the favor it had enjoyed in high quarters was withdrawn, the system was openly ridiculed. This most miserable of all the meagre philosophies that have ever existed came to grief, and dragged down with it into the abysm of discredit, the systems of Fichte and Schelling which had preceded it. And so, as far as Germany is concerned, the total philosophical incompetence of the first half of the century following upon Kant is quite plain: and still the Germans boast of their talent for philosophy in comparison with foreigners, especially since an English writer has been so maliciously ironical as to call them "a nation of thinkers."

For an example of the general system of epicycles drawn from the history of art, look at the school of sculpture which flourished in the last century and took its name from Bernini, more especially at the development of it which prevailed in France. The ideal of this school was not antique beauty, but commonplace nature: instead of the simplicity and grace of ancient art, it represented the manners of a French minuet.

This tendency became bankrupt when, under Wincklemann's direction, a return was made to the antique school. The history of painting furnishes an illustration in the first quarter of the century, when art was looked upon merely as a means and instrument of mediæval religious sentiment, and its themes consequently drawn from ecclesiastical subjects alone: these, however, were treated by painters who had none of the true earnestness of faith, and in their delusion they followed Francesco Francia, Pietro Perugino, Angelico da Fiesole and others like them, rating them higher even than the really great masters who followed. It was in view of this terror, and because in poetry an analogous aim had at the same time found favor, that Goethe wrote his parable *Pfaffenspiel*. This school, too, got the reputation of being whimsical, became bankrupt, and was followed by a return to nature, which proclaimed itself in *genre* pictures and scenes of life of every kind, even though it now and then strayed into what was vulgar.

The progress of the human mind in literature is similar. The history of literature is for the most part like the catalogue of a museum of deformities; the spirit in which they keep best is pigskin. The few creatures that have been born in goodly shape need not be looked for there. They are still alive, and are everywhere to be met with in the world, immortal, and with their years ever green. They alone form what I have called real literature; the history of which, poor as it is in persons, we learn from our youth up out of the mouths of all educated people, before compilations recount it for us.

As an antidote to the prevailing monomania for reading literary histories, in order to be able to chatter about everything, without having any real knowledge at all, let me refer to a passage in Lichtenberg's works (vol. II., p. 302), which is well worth perusal.

I believe that the over-minute acquaintance with the history of science and learning, which is such a prevalent feature of our day, is very prejudicial to the advance of knowledge itself. There is pleasure in following up this history; but as a matter of fact, it leaves the mind, not empty indeed, but without any power of its own, just because it makes it so full. Whoever has felt the desire, not to fill up his mind, but to strengthen it, to develop his faculties and aptitudes, and generally, to enlarge his powers, will have found that there is nothing so weakening as intercourse with a so-called littérateur, on a matter of knowledge on which he has not thought at all, though he knows a thousand little facts appertaining to its history and literature. It is like reading a cookery-book when you are hungry. I believe that so-called literary history will never thrive amongst thoughtful people, who are conscious of their own worth and the worth of real knowledge. These people are more given to employing their own reason than to troubling themselves to know how others have employed theirs. The worst of it is that, as you will find, the more knowledge takes the direction of literary research, the less the power of promoting knowledge becomes; the only thing that increases is pride in the possession of it. Such persons believe that they possess knowledge in a greater degree than those who really possess it. It is surely a well-founded remark, that knowledge never makes its possessor proud. Those alone let themselves be blown out with pride, who incapable of extending knowledge in their own persons, occupy themselves with clearing up dark points in its history, or are able to recount what others have done. They are proud, because they consider this occupation, which is mostly of a mechanical nature, the practice of knowledge. I could illustrate what I mean by examples, but it would be an odious task.

Still, I wish some one would attempt a *tragical* history of literature, giving the way in which the writers and artists, who form the proudest possession of the various nations which have given them birth, have been treated by them during their lives. Such a history would exhibit the ceaseless warfare, which what was good and genuine in all times and countries has had to wage with what was bad and perverse. It would tell of the martyrdom of almost all those who truly enlightened humanity, of almost all the great masters of every kind of art: it would show us how, with few exceptions, they were tormented to death, without recognition, without sympathy, without followers; how they lived in poverty and misery, whilst fame, honor, and riches, were the lot of the unworthy; how their fate was that of Esau, who, while he was hunting and getting venison for his father, was robbed of the blessing by Jacob, disguised in his brother's clothes, how, in spite of all, they were kept up by the love of their work, until at last the bitter fight of the teacher of humanity is over, until the immortal laurel is held out to him, and the hour strikes when it can be said:

> Der schwere Panzer wird zum Flügelkleid
> Kurz ist der Schmerz, unendlich ist die Freude.

> The heavy armor seems like wings in flight;
> Brief is the pain, unending the delight.

THE END